AF847822

Law, Economics and Evolutionary Theory

Law, Economics and Evolutionary Theory

Edited by

Peer Zumbansen

Canada Research Chair in Transnational Economic Governance and Legal Theory, Osgoode Hall Law School, York University, Canada

and

Gralf-Peter Calliess

Chair of Private Law, Comparative and International Economic Law and Legal Theory, University of Bremen, Germany

Edward Elgar

Cheltenham, UK • Northampton, MA, USA

© The Editors and Contributors Severally 2011

All rights reserved. No part of this publication may be reproduced, stored in a retrieval system or transmitted in any form or by any means, electronic, mechanical or photocopying, recording, or otherwise without the prior permission of the publisher.

Published by
Edward Elgar Publishing Limited
The Lypiatts
15 Lansdown Road
Cheltenham
Glos GL50 2JA
UK

Edward Elgar Publishing, Inc.
William Pratt House
9 Dewey Court
Northampton
Massachusetts 01060
USA

A catalogue record for this book
is available from the British Library

Library of Congress Control Number: 2010925971

MIX
Paper from
responsible sources
FSC® C018575
FSC
www.fsc.org

ISBN 978 1 84844 823 0 (cased)

Typeset by Servis Filmsetting Ltd, Stockport, Cheshire
Printed and bound by MPG Books Group, UK

Contents

Contributors

Marc Amstutz, Prof. Dr. iur, LL.M. (Harv.), holds the Chair for Private Law, Commercial and Legal Theory at the University of Fribourg, Switzerland.

Amitai Aviram is a Professor of Law and the Lynn and Daniel Murray Faculty Scholar at the University of Illinois. He studies mechanisms of norm enforcement in private legal systems and law's role in manipulating perceptions.

Bruce L. Benson, Ph.D. (Texas A&M), is the Economics Department Chair at Florida State University where he also holds a DeVoe Moore Professorship and has been named as a University Distinguished Research Professor as well as a Professor of Law by Courtesy.

Gralf-Peter Calliess, Prof. Dr. jur., holds the Chair in Private Law, Comparative and International Economic Law, and Legal Theory, at the University of Bremen, Germany.

Fabio Carvalho is a Director of Alvarez & Marsal, an international consulting firm, in Sao Paolo, Brazil. He holds an LL.M. degree from the University of Cambridge.

Paul A. David is Emeritus Fellow of All Souls College, Oxford and Professional Fellow at United Nations University–MERIT (Maastricht).

Simon Deakin is a Professor of Law at the University of Cambridge and a Fellow of Peterhouse, Cambridge.

Bart Du Laing, Ph.D. (KULeuven), is a Postdoctoral Fellow of the Research Foundation – Flanders (FWO) at Ghent University's Department of Legal Theory and Legal History.

Martina Eckardt, Prof. Dr., holds the Chair for Public Economics and Finance, at the Andrássy University, Budapest, Hungary.

Thráinn Eggertsson is Professor of Economics at the School of Business, University of Iceland and Global Distinguished Professor of Politics at New York University.

Jörg Freiling holds the LEMEX Chair for Small Business and Entrepreneurship at the University of Bremen.

Wolfgang Kerber is Professor of Economics at the Department of Business Administration and Economics, Philipps-University Marburg, Germany.

Richard H. McAdams is the Bernard D. Meltzer Professor of Law at the University of Chicago.

Joel Mokyr is the Robert H. Strotz Professor of Arts and Sciences and Professor of Economics and History at Northwestern University and Sackler Professor (by special appointment) at the Eitan Berglas School of Economics at the University of Tel Aviv.

Eric A. Posner is Kirkland and Ellis Professor of Law, University of Chicago.

Moritz Renner studied law in Berlin, Padova and Columbia Law School and received his Ph.D. from the University of Bremen in 2010.

Erich Schanze is Professor Emeritus for Civil Law and International Business Law at the University of Marburg, Germany, Professor II at the Universitetet i Bergen, Norway, and Visiting Professor for Law and Economics at the University of St. Gallen, Switzerland.

Jan M. Smits is Professor of European Private Law and Comparative Law in the University of Maastricht and Research Professor of Comparative Legal Studies in the University of Helsinki.

Mauro Zamboni is Research Associate at The Collaborative Research Centre 597 'Transformations of the State' (University of Bremen, Germany) and Associate Professor at the Stockholm University, Faculty of Law, Stockholm Center for Commerical Law (Sweden).

Peer Zumbansen studied law in Frankfurt, Paris and Harvard and is Professor of Law and the Canada Research Chair in Transnational Economic Governance and Legal Theory at Osgoode Hall Law School in Toronto. He is the founding Director of the Critical Research Laboratory in Law & Society (www.criticalresearchlab.org) and served as Associate Dean (Research, Graduate Studies and Institutional Relations) from 2007 to 2009.

Foreword

The self-interested behavior that lies at the heart of economic theories of why firms exist and grow manifests itself in two very different variants, both of which were recognized by the Nobel Committee last year. One is opportunistic behavior of the kind that Oliver Williamson in particular paid attention to, which necessitates the construction of legal and hierarchical safeguards to minimize the costs of opportunism in exchange relations. The other is cooperative or even altruistic behaviour, that has been the focus of Elinor Ostrom's work, which results in the possibility of transactions taking place, even when the prevailing conditions do not provide sufficient formal support.

One way to conceptualize the ways in which firms mitigate the problems arising from both opportunism as well as cooperation is to view them as co-evolutionary processes. The essential feature of these co-evolutionary processes is that firms are not merely subject to selection rules, but through their own agency, they are in a position to influence the content of the rules they are governed by. The outcome of these processes is dependent on the variety of self-interested behaviour in question. If such co-evolutionary processes are driven by self-interested behaviour of the opportunistic kind, the result is likely to be something like destructive lobbying or regulatory capture. If, on the other hand, they represent a cooperative variety, this can result in new solutions to persistent problems of underinvestment and lack of technological capability, such as in the context of public–private partnerships as a tool for economic development.

It is precisely in such negotiated environments where law and economics intersect, and where the co-evolutionary processes between market and non-market participants generate the effective rules of the game. The various contributions in this book illustrate the variety of ways in which the emergence of new ideas and technologies results in the creation of new institutions. Indeed, with the deepening of globalization and economic interdependence, the complexity of how the game is played and the variety of players has increased, making it imperative for scholars from different disciplines to join their forces to enable more robust analyses of the forces shaping the contemporary global economy. It is this ambition that is so exhilarating about this wonderful collection of papers that brings together distinguished contributors from economics, law and sociology. *Law, Economics and Evolutionary Theory* represents an important and admirable effort to encourage more interdisciplinary work on topics that could not be more pertinent or timely.

Sarianna Lundan
Professor, University of Bremen

Acknowledgements

The contributions to this volume have been written by economists, legal scholars, historians, sociologists and political scientists. A collaboration among such a diverse group of scholars, across disciplinary, geographical and time boundaries, demands a considerable amount of ground-work, logistical patience and persistence and – above all – the commitment on the part of the participating scholars to see the project through to the end. We are grateful to our authors to the present volume for their courage and interest to contribute to this ambitious, interdisciplinary collection. We are furthermore grateful to the Collaborative Research Centre 'Transformations of the State' at the University of Bremen, Germany and its Speaker, Professor Stephan Leibfried, for generously supporting an international workshop at which some of the papers in this volume were first presented in October 2007. This workshop was jointly organized between the CRC and the *German Law Journal*, constituting the Journal's Fifth Annual International Conference. Complementing the intermittently substantively revised and expanded papers from this event, are chapters by renowned scholars in the field, most of which have been written expressly for this volume. Where we are including work that draws on scholarship previously published elsewhere, we are grateful to the following institutions for their generous permission to do so: the *German Law Journal*, the *Illinois Law Review* and *Cliometrica*.

We would like to express our gratitude to Petra Schreiber, Monika Sniegs and Mauro Zamboni for helping organize the initial workshop in Bremen. Finally, we wish to express our immense gratefulness to Ruba Ali, Ph.D. candidate at Osgoode Hall Law School in Toronto, for helping to format the manuscript, and to Maria Panezi, Ph.D. candidate at Osgoode Hall and Visiting Researcher at Harvard Law School, for her diligence and care in formatting and compiling the final manuscript.

Law, economics and evolutionary theory: state of the art and interdisciplinary perspectives

Peer Zumbansen and Gralf-Peter Calliess

> The power of law to survive through centuries is equally apparent. As a consequence a great deal, if not most, of law operates in a territory for which it was not originally designed, or in a society which is radically different from that which created the law.[1]

1. BEFORE THE EVOLUTIONARY CHALLENGE: ECONOMICS AND LAW DISCOVER INSTITUTIONS AND 'SOCIAL NORMS'

In 1859 Charles Darwin published his most acclaimed work, *On the Origin of Species*, and after that nothing was the same in the history of human knowledge.[2] Darwin's work did not only radically change our perception of the origin and development of nature. His ideas on the mechanisms of evolution were soon transferred to the social sciences, though often in misconceived forms such as 'social Darwinism'[3] or caught up in highly charged, polemical debates surrounding school curricula and the collision of religion and evolution.[4] As Kurt Dopfer recently noted, '[t]he publication of On the Origin of Species by Charles Darwin in 1859 set off a paradigmatic earthquake in the sciences, and to some degree in society at large.'[5] Since then, evolutionary concepts have been successfully applied, refined and drawn upon to explain long-term developments and change in human relations, societies, culture, and civilization. In jurisprudence, authors such as Henry Sumner Maine[6] and Oliver Wendell Holmes[7] have relied on evolutionary ideas for explaining the structures of change in the common law. Despite differences in opinion

---

[1] Watson (1982).

[2] See Darwin (1859); see further the general overview as to both the roots of and the debate Darwin's ideas created in Bowler (2003).

[3] See Johnson (2008); Haferkamp and Smelser (1992), 4–6; for a particular (post WWI) observation on German scientists' embrace of Darwinism, see Keller (1918); see the response of Keller's discussion of social and legal evolution by Brown (1919), 394–400, in particular 397, 398: 'I think the term "legal evolution" a useful and suggestive way of expressing some of the most fundamental characteristics of the long process involved in the history of law.'

[4] See, e.g., Frazzetto (2004), 662–665; see also: *The Social and Legal Dimensions of the Evolution Debate in the United States*, Pew Forum on Religion and Public Life, 4 February 2009, available at: http://pewforum.org/docs/?DocID=396.

[5] Dopfer (2005), 3–55, 12.

[6] Maine (1861), chapter 2.

[7] Holmes (1881), chapters 1 and 2; Holmes (1899), 443–63.

regarding the analogies between biological and legal evolution, legal scholars writing after Holmes generally acknowledged a degree of purpose in legal interpretation and statutory legislation:

> A novel statute or precedent suggests [. . .] variation (purposeful, perhaps, but still variation) in a general flow of things in which there is a continuing response to the call of circumstance – adjustment to environment. The nature of the process is apt to be observed by that lack of perspective which prevents us from seeing the old and the new in their true relation. The legislator is not, as he may imagine himself, a Columbus. Not infrequently, he is merely making explicit what was really implicit in pre-existing law.[8]

Besides this distinct disrespect of the Legal Realists for the contention that judges were merely engaged in 'finding' the law, legal scholars quickly began to ascertain the relevance not only of comparative[9] but also of historical, detailed studies of different legal cultures, if one wanted to make any more generalizable assertions regarding legal change.[10]

Meanwhile, in economic theory, Schumpeter's[11] emphasis on economic growth as the key to economic analysis helped prepare the ground for evolutionary theory, himself harkening back onto Smith's inquiry into circumstances contributing to the particular dynamics of economic change in his time.[12] Subsequently, in particular Hayek's 1945 knowledge-based account of market processes[13] and Alchian's 1950 essay on 'Uncertainty, Evolution, and Economic Theory'[14] were among the first to pave the way for a promising promotion of evolutionary concepts in economics,[15] with important parallel developments in the natural sciences.[16] As we will discuss below, evolutionary thinking has continued to play a particularly important role in the development of more recent economic theorizing about economic growth and social change, in particular in its challenging the neo-classical economists, again, with Schumpeter sounding the bells of attack early on.[17] It was above all the focus on the dynamics of economic change in contrast to the neoclassicals' focus on mechanics and to a model analysis of economic equilibria that would eventually open doors to the wealth of institutional and interdisciplinary economic thinking that characterizes the work by scholars such as Douglass C. North, Sidney G. Winter and Richard R. Nelson, Oliver E. Williamson and Elinor Ostrom. This economic analysis is importantly complemented and embedded in the

---

[8] Brown (1919) 394–400, 398, 399.

[9] See, for example, Dawson (1968).

[10] Watson (1982) 1121–57, 1122, 1124–25: 'To understand the nature of legal change and the relationship between legal rules and society, I believe it is necessary to look at a number of legal systems and at the changes in them over a long period of time.' The article is of particular interest for Watson's response to critics from within the 'law & society' movement contesting his claim of a 'divergence of law and society'.

[11] Schumpeter (1942 [2008]).

[12] Nelson (2007), 27–41.

[13] Hayek (1945), 519–530; Hayek (2002), 9–23; see also Hayek (1949).

[14] Alchian (1950), 211–21.

[15] For an account of the parallel emergence of evolutionary thinking in social and natural sciences, see Hull (1988). See also Hull (1995), 67–104, and Haken (2005), 70–85.

[16] See previous note. Compare also Prigogine's observation that '[L]aws of nature no longer express certitudes, but "possibilities"', cited in Dopfer (2005), 3–55, 11.

[17] Schumpeter (1934 [1983]), (1942 [2008]).

historical-economic work by scholars such as Joel Mokyr and Paul David[18] and the sociological work by scholars such as Nico Stehr and Volker Meja.[19] The 2009 award of the Nobel Prize in Economics to Williamson and Ostrom constitutes an important milestone in the evolution of economic and institutional thought and invites us to cast a light back onto this theoretical trajectory over the preceding decades, opening up an ample view of the manifold overlappings and reciprocal enrichments that have been occurring between economic and legal theorizing. Such attempts at mutual understanding and enrichment are certain to encounter numerous roadblocks and impasses, not least due to the co-evolutionary nature of the respective fields and their rationalities.[20] While the breathtaking ascendance of 'law and economics'[21] has irreversibly transformed both practice and theory of law, the economist's depiction of this alleged cross-disciplinary dialogue is as legendary[22] as the potential interdisciplinary dialogue between law *and* economics has often been limited.

The project pursued in the present volume hopes to go beyond the 'law and economics' perspective that has been so immensely influential in legal practice and academia by focusing on the dimension of evolution within each of the two disciplines in order to carve out, from that perspective, the possible future possibilities and directions of cross-disciplinary pollination between legal and economic thinking. With both disciplines inherently aspiring to conceptualize models, principles and systems of social order, the discovery of a dynamic dimension in the development of the respective apparatus could not come as a surprise: evidently, in both disciplines, law and economics, different ideas of evolution have long inspired a host of varying usages and assessments.[23]

Our suggested task of identifying instantiations of a meaningful reciprocal engagement between legal and economic thought is likely to bring to the fore particular moments of debate or outstanding publications that had a decisive impact on the development of this disciplinary co-existence. Clearly, Coase's 1960 article on 'The Problem of Social Cost', said to have 'had more policy influence than any other economic text',[24] marks without doubt one such historical moment. The research and teaching agenda it projected for lawyers in the decades to come, were immense, despite Coase's own perhaps tongue-in-cheek assertion that his interest in fact had never been to give rise to any such thing as 'law and economics'.[25] Aptly identified by Coase then and later, was the complexity of adequately bridging the two disciplines in order to make meaningful assertions across the fence. And yet, today, there can be no doubt that in spite of such challenges, lawyers have

---

18 See Mokyr (2002), Ch. 7, and Mokyr (2005a); Mokyr (2005b), 195–218; Mokyr, in this volume. David (2008), 151–194; David, in this volume.

19 Stehr (2002); Stehr (2005), 299–322.

20 Dopfer (2005), 3–55, 18: 'A young discipline, such as evolutionary economics, suffers from a *language deficit*.' Compare with Amstutz, in this volume and with Teubner (2002), 161–82.

21 Branson (1989), 745, likened its proliferation in academic corporate law to a 'prairie fire'. See also, Cheffins (2004).

22 See only the debate between Coase and Simpson: Simpson (1996a), 53–97; Simpson (1996b), 99–101 and Coase (1996), 103–119. See also the recent revisiting of this dispute by Hovenkamp (2009), 633–49.

23 For an excellent assessment, see Elliott (1985), 38–94.

24 Hovenkamp (2009), at 649.

25 Coase (1996), 103–119, 104–105.

anything but grown tired to apply economic thinking to the development of legal frameworks, across a wide range of legal fields. Meanwhile, economists have been persistent in assessing the role and increasingly the 'nature' of legal regulation in relation to alternative forms of social ordering, something that has been both informing and shaping the evolution of theoretical work done on property rights[26] on the basis of which emerged comprehensive concepts of economic governance,[27] the economics of institutions,[28] institutional diversity,[29] and social norms.[30] This work has altogether contributed to the development of fairly robust assessments of the 'environment' of economic development drawing on a host of different disciplinary depictions of formal and informal institutions.[31] As powerfully illustrated by the recently again increased interest in 'informal rules', or social norms, there appears to be a shared perception among economists and lawyers of how customs, social practices, indigenous norms can fit into the description of legal enforcement mechanisms embedding an otherwise far-reaching system of social self-regulation, precisely because the 'legal' nature of these social norms is in question. Particularly in light of the work done by sociologists and lawyers regarding the changing nature of state regulation in the context of privatization of norm-creation and the delegation of law-making authority to private and quasi-public bodies,[32] economic theorizing has become increasingly sensitive to the underlying assumptions relating to the desired stability of property rights enforcement,[33] with the more long-term consequences of this development and the more recent interest in the cognitive basis for individual choice-making[34] still to be assessed. What seems to be clear, however, is that both economists and legal scholars are hard at work at further scrutinizing the dynamics of the evolution of both formal and informal rules, the former being interested to a large degree in the challenges of informal rules to the devising of sound economic models for emerging or transforming economies,[35] while the latter are engaged in a critique of the political nature of social norms.[36]

---

26 Demsetz (1967), 347–59; North (1981), 17–19.

27 Williamson (2000), 595–613; Williamson (2005), 1–18.

28 Eggertsson (1990); Eggertsson (1996), 6–24, 25: '. . . at the frontier of research there is also a need and scope for experimental work with an alternative paradigm.'

29 Ostrom (2007), 239–64.

30 Drobak (2006).

31 Eggertsson (1996), 6–24, 11: 'As the institutional framework consists of formal and informal rules and their enforcement, research at this level intrudes into the domain of political science, sociology, and anthropology, along with law and history.'

32 A good overview is provided by Lobel (2004), 342–469. See also the analysis and critique by Aman Jr. (2007), 802.

33 Ostrom (2007), 239–64; see already Ostrom (2005), 21–22, drawing on the legal pluralist critique on rigid rule categorizations along the lines of 'public' or 'private'.

34 Eggertsson (1996), 6–24, 21; see also Aguilera et al. (2004), 836–863.

35 See e.g. Williamson (1996); and from the point of view of law, see Posner (1998), 1–11.

36 Posner (2000); Hadfield and Talley (2006), 414–41; see the discussion in Calliess and Zumbansen (2010), ch. 2, ch. 5.

2. MEANWHILE: ADVANCES IN SOCIOLOGICAL THEORY, ECONOMICS AND LAW

In many ways, these developments can be said to have their origin in theoretical advances made in sociology, economics and legal theory. As regards the first, in 1983, the German sociologist Niklas Luhmann published what would soon be regarded as a seminal work: *Social Systems*. In this book, Luhmann reconceptualized Talcott Parsons' theory of social systems on the basis of the biological concept of *autopoiesis*.[37] Luhmann thus aimed at developing an all-encompassing theory of society as a self-referential system of communication, explicitly drawing upon evolutionary approaches.[38] Luhmann's concept of evolution, which constituted a crucial element for his general theory of society, played a decisive role for law: by explaining how evolution occurred through an unending process of *variation*, *selection* and *retention*, Luhmann was able to provide an intricably persuasive model for the explanation of legal change – a model which was on the one hand extremely sensitive to the 'embeddedness' of law in social structures – much like the Realists had indeed seen it – but at the same time, emphasizing law's particular mode of change, adaptation and evolution.[39] With view to the fate of evolutionary theory in law, it is important to note, that legal theorists close to systems theory – such as Gunther Teubner[40] and Karl-Heinz Ladeur[41] – have always insisted on a particular, critical distance to social theories of law's embeddedness on the one hand and to theories of the 'unity of law'[42] on the other, while certainly engaging with the same conceptual challenges – concerning the relationship between law and society – that these theories were facing. Over time, these explorations have contributed to a considerably rich landscape of conceptual and theoretical assessments of law's evolutionary trends and prospects – studies that eventually received important impulses from both comparative legal scholarship[43] as well as from a fast emerging scholarship focusing on the conundrical yet intriguing coupling of 'globalization and the law'.[44] The continuing, indeed highly productive tension between normative and systems theoretical accounts of the continuing transformation of state governance within and beyond the confines of the nation state has been informing and shaping an immensely rich debate.[45]

---

37 Luhmann (1996).

38 See also Luhmann (1975), 150–169; Luhmann (1978), 413–440; Luhmann (1989), 176–220.

39 For a concise reconstruction of law's mode of change, see only Teubner (1984), 291–301; but see also the recent, highly interesting development of this theory in Teubner (2009), 1–23.

40 Teubner (1983), 239–85.

41 See the April 2009 German Law Journal Symposium in celebration of Professor Ladeur's work 'The Law of the Network Society' (eds.,L Viellechner et al., http://www.germanlawjournal.com/pdf/Vol10No04/pdf_table_of_contents_Vol_10_No_04.pdf).

42 See, for example, the work by Baldus (1995), and by Felix (1998); for an earlier, decidedly political rejection of a concept of 'unity of law', see Neumann (1964), 22–68, and the excellent study on Carl Schmitt by Maus (1980).

43 See Frankenberg (1985), 411–55; Buxbaum (1996), 201–230; Sacco (2002), 727–36; Reimann (2002), 671–700; Glenn (2005), 863–98; Riles (2005), 973.

44 Teubner (1992), 1443–62; Teubner (1997a), 763–87; Zumbansen (2002), 400–432; Calliess (2001); Berman (2005), 485–556; Scott (2005), 757–73.

45 See, for example, the contributions to Brunkhorst (2009), Schulte and Stichweh (2008) and Zumbansen and Skordas (2009). See already the contributions to Niesen and Herborth (2007).

Around the same time that Luhmann published 'Social Systems', a small revolution occurred in economics that elevated evolutionary theory onto a stage for everyone to see and consolidated its place in the discipline: In 1982, the economists Richard Nelson and Sydney Winter laid out a systematic account of evolutionary elements in the theory of business and economics,[46] by publishing a book that has been depicted as an 'ice-breaker that arguably gave the early process its critical momentum'.[47] At the outset of their programme was the observation that the dramatic dimensions of technological change posed particular challenges to economic theories of growth. From this premise, Nelson and Winter revisited Schumpeter's contribution in search of inspiration and encouragement[48] to think beyond neo-classical frameworks that they found to be at odds with a highly differentiated landscape of economic innovation and production.[49] Building on and expanding further a 'behavioral' approach to firms,[50] Nelson and Winter posited – against the neo-classical assumption of firms' maximization orientation – that 'a firm at any time operates largely according to a set of decision rules that link a domain of environmental stimuli to a range of responses on the part of firms. While neoclassical theory would attempt to deduce these decision rules from maximization on the part of the firm, the behavioral theory simply takes them as given and observable.'[51] At the heart of their concept of the firm as operating within a particular environment was the idea that it would be impossible to describe the dynamics of change of inter-organizational decisions without taking into account the manifold input and output relations between the firm and its – constantly changing[52] – environment. This contention still lies at the base of Nelson's and Winter's theory today: 'At the broadest level, and possibly the deepest, the difference between evolutionary economic theory that is taking shape, and the neoclassical theory that has dominated microeconomic theorizing over the last thirty years, is that evolutionary theory sees the economy as always in the process of change, with economic activity almost always proceeding in a context that is not completely

---

[46] Nelson and Winter (1982); see already their essays leading up to the book: Nelson and Winter (1973), 440–449; Nelson and Winter (1974), 886–905; for a discussion of Nelson's and Winter's proximity to Schumpeter and an ultimately skeptical assessment of Nelson's & Winter's contribution, see Ruttan (1997), 1520–1529, at 1524: 'dead end'.

[47] Dopfer (2005), 3–55, 3.

[48] Nelson (2006), at 4 'strongly inspired by Schumpeter'.

[49] Nelson and Winter (1974), 886–905, 890: 'It seems obvious that research on economic growth within the neoclassical theory is creating new intellectual problems more rapidly than it is solving them. One can continue to search for solutions to these problems guided by the assumptions of neoclassical theory. Or, one can try a new tack.'

[50] See already Alchian (1950), 211–21, 218: '. . . the consequence of this is that modes of behavior replace optimum equilibrium conditions as guiding rules of action.'

[51] Nelson and Winter (1974), at 891.

[52] Alchian (1950), 211–21, 219: 'Comparability of resulting situations is destroyed by the changing environment. As a consequence, the measure of goodness of actions in anything except a tolerable–intolerable sense is lost, and the possibility of an individual's converging to the optimum activity via a trial-and-error process disappears. Trial and error becomes life or death. It cannot serve as a basis of the individual's method of convergence to a "maximum" or optimum position. Success is discovered by the economic system through a blanketing shotgun process, not by the individual through a converging search.'

familiar to the actors, or perfectly understood by them.'[53] In the following, this approach has inspired a true plethora of innovative studies in management[54] and organizational studies,[55] industrial organization,[56] the theory of the firm,[57] in political economy[58] as well as in legal theory.[59] Meanwhile, the originators of this line of thinking have themselves embarked on a very fruitful revisiting and further development of some of their initial starting points,[60] eventually opening up perspectives for a better understanding of evolutionary processes as 'learning processes'.[61]

3. THE ROLE OF INSTITUTIONS IN ECONOMIC THOUGHT

Among these, sociology as well as business and economics seem to have taken the lead in further developing evolutionary theories of institutional change,[62] spurred by the emergence of New Institutional Economics centring around Douglass North[63] and Oliver Williamson[64] – with 'new' evolutionary economics continuing to push for further sophistication of the theoretical apparatus.[65] The importance of this research lies in its untiring – if varied – engagement with the tension between market and non-market regulation, a tension which powerfully unfolds from within the definition of 'institutions'. In Professor North's words, 'Institutions are the humanly devised constraints that structure political, economic and social interaction. They consist of both informal constraints (sanctions, taboos, customs, traditions, and codes of conduct), and formal rules (laws, property rights).'[66] In his important study of 1990, he observed: 'As defined here, they [institutions] therefore are the framework within human interaction takes place.'[67] It is against this relatively flexible definition that North has been arguing for the central role of institutions for long-term economic performance. North's contribution to an increasingly interdisciplinary dialogue concerning market regulation in historical perspective can hardly be overestimated. As academic interest in the nature, culture and trajectory

---

53 Nelson (2006), 1. See also Nelson (1995), 48–90.

54 Mahoney and Pandian (1992), 363–80.

55 Zollo and Winter (2002), 339–51.

56 Dosi and Malerba (2002), 619–22.

57 See, for example, Whittington et al. (1999), 519–551, and the contributions to Dimaggio (2001).

58 Hall and Soskice (2001).

59 See, e.g., G. Teubner (1999a), 7–25 in Ziman (2002), 161–82

60 See, in this context, Nelson (2007), 27–41, 31, highlighting the need to take a more comprehensive look at the institutions shaping technological change, here referring to 'social technologies'.

61 Nelson (2007), preceding note, at 34.

62 Nelson (1995), 48–90.

63 North (1990); North (1991), 97–112; North (1994), 359–68 (Nobel Prize Lecture); North (2005).

64 Williamson (1985); Williamson (1981), 1537–68.

65 Nelson (2006), 6: 'The new evolutionary growth theory that is emerging sees economic growth as the result of the coevolution of technologies, firm and industry structures, and supporting and governing institutions.'

66 North (1991), 97–112, at 97.

67 North (1990), at 4.

of the market[68] among legal scholars, economists, economic historians, geographers and political economists again soared in recent years,[69] Douglass North's insistence on an interdisciplinary, historically grounded analysis of the different institutions that structure market behaviour proved to be a crucial contribution to a more engaged and more challenging exchange between scholars in different disciplines. Building on and eventually substantively expanding his earlier interest in 'institutions' per se, North in his more recent work has adopted a decidedly social-theory perspective, from which he places a central emphasis on the nature and volatility of societal change and on the resulting uncertainty, that characterizes long-term oriented theorizing. Central to this reorientation is the role of intentionality with regard to institutional change.[70] With this, North connects his important institutionalist framework to the increasingly influential[71] work in behavioural finance[72] and behavioural law and economics[73] and makes thus a powerful argument for the necessity to take the complexity of market structures and behaviors seriously – a lesson which will continue to inspire future interdisciplinary research not only in corporate finance and corporate governance,[74] but also in economic sociology, geography and regulatory theory.[75] Next to the field of *economic geography* that has been gaining new attraction for economists and globally oriented policy makers with regard to regional differences in economic growth and development,[76] and *regulatory theory*, which over the past 15 years has become something of an umbrella concept for interdisciplinary governance studies,[77] it is in *economic sociology* that we can see a number of important

---

68 See of course already White (1981), 517–47.

69 See, e.g., Lie (1997), 341–60; Rosenbaum (2000), 455–82; Fligstein (2001); see also the contributions to Nee and Swedberg (2005a), and Nee and Swedberg (2005b), 789–818. Besides the recent renaissance in economic sociology, the contributions by scholars interested in the 'Varieties of Capitalism' are of particular interest in this regard: see, e.g., the landmark volume by Hall and Soskice (2001), and the preceding work by Soskice (1999), 101–134, and Hollingsworth (1997), 133–47, as well as Streeck (2001), 1–38.

70 North (2005).

71 See the hesitant treatment, at the time, by one of the most astute scholars of the Efficient Capital Market Hypothesis (ECMH) himself: Fama (1998), 283–306, 284: 'anomalies'.

72 See the foundational work on the ECMH by Fama (1970), 383–417; Jensen (1970), 95–101; Gilson and Kraakman (1984), 549–644 – see also Gilson and Kraakman (2003), 715, and Stout (2003), 635.

73 See the contributions to Sunstein (2000); for a very informative discussion and overview, see Klöhn (2006), 80–153.

74 See the brilliant example: Aguilera et al. (2004), 836–63.

75 As a representative example of work grown out of long-term analysis of the shortcomings of the ECMH, see the scholarship by Thaler (1987), 197–201; Thaler (1999), 12–17; see now Thaler and Sunstein (2008).

76 See, e.g., the World Bank (2009); see the contributions to Clark et al. (2003); see also the famous launch by Paul Krugman in 1992 of 'new economic geography' (Krugman (1992)), and Krugman (1998), 7-17; see further relatively recent creation of a new academic journal in this area: Journal of Economic Geography (OUP, since 2001), complementing among others the long-standing Economic Geography (Clark University, since 1925).

77 See, e.g., the overview by Burris et al. (2008), 1–66; see also the meanwhile seminal article in legal scholarship by Lobel (2004), 342–469; for a refreshing perspective with regard to the EU, see Möllers (2006), 313–36; with regard to global financial regulation, see the poignant contribution by Black and Rouch (2008), 218–33.

strides in recent years, both with regard to its engagement with institutional economics as well as with law.[78] It is from here that important impulses for a more serious, interdisciplinary study of 'law in context', 'law and society' and 'social norms' in their relation to traditional jurisprudence are likely going to be received still.[79]

Surely, not only at a time such as when The Economist would dedicate an issue to '*Modern Economic Theory. Where it went wrong – and how the crisis is changing it*' with a number of outspoken defamations of financial economics' hubris concerning perfect markets[80] have economists cast models into doubt that had been designed to explain economic growth. As indicated above, after Keynes' 1936 *General Theory* and its eventual interim relativization (and subsequent revival[81]), the theoretical advances by North and other scholars of New Institutional Economics[82] are among the most sophisticated and most promising economist contributions to an integrated analysis of economic developments. It is in fact on the basis of and in engagement with the wealth and the challenging, analytical potential of the institutionalist framework that other disciplines such as political economy, economic sociology, economic geography and, certainly, law have been developing over the past decades. This context makes for an intriguing moment to engage in an interdisciplinary analysis of the evolutionary trajectories of law and economics. The proffered depictions, explanations and assessments as they are voiced with regard to the 2008 financial and economic crisis, not only by those who had always 'known', 'warned' or were 'ignored', feed into and complement what will continue to unfold as a crucially important theoretical engagement with the models and toolkits economists, lawyers and social theorists have been relying on since the early 1980s. While the need for an interdisciplinary and integrated study of the current crisis thus lies in the evident ambiguity of the very starting points of any assessment,[83] the promise of an interdisciplinary study of institutions goes further still: precisely because of the distinct premises and normative orientations in legal and economic thinking, there is a great need for continued translation of methodological approaches in both disciplines.[84] The appearance of one in the

---

78 See only Nee and Swedberg (2005b), 789–818, 795: 'Slowly [. . .] it has been realized by economic sociologists that *law* constitutes a central part of the modern economy . . .'. See, in this context, Swedberg (2003), 1–37.

79 See, e.g., the definition of 'institution' provided by Nee and Swedberg, op. cit., 797–8: 'An institution may be conceptualized as a dominant system of interrelated informal and formal elements – customs, shared beliefs, norms, and rules – which actors orient their actions to when they pursue their interests. In this view, institutions are dominant social structures which provide a conduit for social and collective action by facilitating and structuring the interests of actors and enforcing principal agent relationships. It follows from this interest-related definition that institutional change involves not simply remaking the formal rules, but requires the realignment of interests, norms, and power.'

80 The Economist, 18–24 July 2009, 12, 68–72.

81 Skidelsky (2009); Davidson (2009).

82 For an interim excellent introduction and overview see Voigt (2002); meanwhile, see Williamson (2005), 1–18, and Ostrom (2005), and the contributions to Ostrom (2007), 239–64. A very instructive paper is still Williamson (2000), 595–613.

83 For an intriguing perspective on the correlation of different periodizations, see Mokyr (2005a).

84 Calliess and Renner (2009), 260–80, 262.

other – economics in law[85] and law in economics[86] – has indeed increased rather than limited the need for further dialogue and translation.

As legal scholars and economists continue to demarcate the boundaries of states and markets, we can discern a lot of parallel engagement with evolutionary theory's conceptualizations of institutional lock-in[87] and path-dependency:[88] such studies are particularly relevant with regard to lawyers' and economists' ongoing attempts to gain a better understanding of the meaning and lessons from 'market failure', a term that has frequently been referred to not only for an identification of the *occasion* but also of the *scope* of state intervention.[89] Market failure thus presents a formidable example for the illustration of the urgent need of collaborative and interdisciplinary analysis of the institutions involved in successful or failing regulation. For law, a study of market failure goes to the heart of its own understanding, as the definition of a legal concept of market is intimately tied to the foundational understanding of law as such,[90] because it cannot simply presuppose a market as such.[91] In turn, for economics, and for New Institutional Economics in particular, the question is whether the theoretical framework has a convincing analytical and conceptual grip on contemporary complex regulatory constellations. As has repeatedly been highlighted by Paul David, the general observation that 'history matters'[92] by itself is about as explanatory or illuminating as the claim that market failures challenge the embedding legal enforcement system in a straightforward, causal manner:[93]

> From the foregoing it may be seen that a proper understanding of path-dependence, and of the possibilities of externalities leading to market failure, is not without interesting implications for economic policy. But those are not at all the sorts of glib conclusions that some critics have alleged must follow if one believes that history really matters – namely, that government should try to pick winners rather than let markets make mistakes. Quite the contrary . . . [. . .]. One thing that public policy could do is to try to delay the market from committing to the future inextricably, before enough information has been obtained about the likely technical or organizational and legal implications, of an early, precedent-setting decision.[94]

In another paper, Professor David observed that

> [I]f there are ways thus to represent the coevolution of microeconomic behavior with regard to technology choices (technical standardization), or conformance with social norms (custom and

---

85 Rubin (1977), 51–63; Priest (1977), 65–82; Eidenmüller (1995); Kennedy (1982), 563.

86 Bernstein (1992), 115–157; Hadfield (2001), 40–45; Greif (2006).

87 Arthur (1989), 116–131.

88 Arthur (1989), preceding note; Arthur (1994); David (1985), 332–7; see also Baumol (1986), 1072–85; Roe (1996), 641–68.

89 Zerbe Jr and McCurdy (2000), 10-14, at 10.

90 Hale (1923), 470–94; Wiethölter (1972), 531–9; Campbell (1997), 307–336; Zumbansen (2007a), 191–233; see also Lindblom (1995), 684–8, 685: 'Market rules do not permit one simply to appropriate what one wants. Appropriating another person's labor we call slavery, and appropriating assets we call theft. Nor do market rules provide any social instrument for *collective* reassignment of claims.'

91 See only Hale, previous note; see also the instructive discussion and analysis in Johns (2007), 116–38.

92 David (2000).

93 David (2008), 151–94.

94 David (2000), 14.

convention) and correlated patterns of ideology or beliefs carrying normative force (subjective conformism), the explanatory apparatus available to economists studying long-term trends in technology and social institutions will surely be much more powerful.[95]

As pointed out by Duncan Kennedy, in a comment on Robert Clark, 'costs' are a merely allusive concept, that can hardly carry enough weight on their own to identify or even justify action on the part of a public or private actor.[96] Tightly connected to such an observation is David's own contention that we must apply a much more differentiated toolkit to explore the interaction between different market actors over time in order to get a better understanding of why things go wrong and how we arrive at such an assessment. What emerges from Professor David's observations is a cautionary approach towards a concept of market failure that is not again re-embedded in a comprehensive historical and systematic institutional study. 'History matters', then, is not a sophisticated enough proposal to engage in a layered, interdisciplinary analysis of how which institutions play a crucial role in the organization of today's market economies. While the concept of path dependency has been developed primarily with confined, nationally grown markets in mind, its relevance for transnational markets and transnational regulatory theory follows from the realization of the stickiness of existing (and newly created) regulatory structures, something which – as before in the case of *lex mercatoria*[97] – any globally or transnationally aspiring regulatory concept will necessarily have to take into account.[98]

4. TOWARDS A RENEWED INTERDISCIPLINARY PERSPECTIVE

What follows from the above is that an evolutionary perspective is crucial in the emerging new phase of interdisciplinary inquiry into the relationship between 'public' and 'private' ordering, 'state' vs. 'market' regulation and that there is a continued need to further refine the concept of 'institution'. For such an interdisciplinary dialogue to unfold in an effective way, the continued engagement with each other's methodological starting points and premises is crucial. It is thus necessary to open up respective toolkits and analytical frameworks to comparative and interdisciplinary scrutiny.

It is then against this background, that we can begin to see how reflections, internal to economist and economic-historical theorizing, are in fact mirrored, paralleled and sometimes even anticipated in other disciplines that have been engaging, one way or the other,

---

95 David (2008), 175.

96 Kennedy (1981), 1275–83, at 1281: 'an obstacle because it makes the world as it is look rational and necessary, even just (who can object to "cost reduction"?), as opposed to arbitrary and contingent. This is a misrepresentation that has an effect: it diverts energy from the job of finding the truths we need to know about the world if we are to be effective in transforming it; it diverts energy from the task of figuring out what the world should be like.'

97 Drahos and Braithwaite (2001), 103–128, 110, 111: 'a spectacular example of transnational private ordering'. With regard to the authors' characterization of the bottom-up nature of *lex mercatoria* as an example of transnational norm creation, see also J. Koven Levit (2007), 393–420, and L. Catá Backer (2009).

98 P. Zumbansen (2007b), 467–96, 488; Zumbansen (2008), 246–76; Calliess and Zumbansen (2010).

with the concept or the idea of institutions in the recent past.[99] Within law, and in particular outside of contract law which has attracted a plethora of focused assessments from the part of New Institutional Economics (NIE),[100] there has certainly been an intensive and fruitful engagement with NIE in corporate law theory.[101] More recently still, NIE has been subject to lively exchanges within Public International Law.[102] Another example is the recent revival of lawyers' interest in Hayek's idea of spontaneous evolution.[103] Partly in answer to such developments, partly in building on earlier starting points in Marx, Durkheim and Weber, the recently newly burgeoning field of economic sociology[104] has been making extremely fruitful contributions to an altogether inspiring, interdisciplinary discussion about the nature of markets and institutions.[105] For their part, lawyers have been pressured to respond to this challenge from a particular set of perspectives, partly constituted through the uncertainties connected to increasingly contractualized public services and a fundamental reconsideration of law's role in market regulation,[106] partly through an intricate mix of privatized[107] as well as transnational[108] modes of norm-generation. This development within legal doctrine and legal theory – in the midst of which we find a vividly continuing debate about 'social norms'[109] – is of interest

---

[99] A brilliant historical and conceptual analysis is provided by Joel Mokyr, *The Institutional Origins of the Industrial Revolution*, unpublished Ms., Northwestern University 2007.

[100] Here, the field is vast and polarized: see, e.g., Williamson (2000), 595–613, 599; Scott (2004), 369–90; Campbell (2004), 645–78.

[101] See the early contributions, building on Coase (1937, 1960), by Alchian and Demsetz (1972), 777–95, Fama and Jensen (1983), 327–49, and Williamson (1981), 1537–68; building on these foundations, e.g., Roe (1996), 641–68; Roe (2002), 233–71; Cheffins (2001), 459–84; Cheffins (2004), 456–506; Bratton and McCahery (2001); Gourevitch (2003), 1829–80; Zumbansen (2006), 534–56.

[102] van Aaken (2009), 33–57; Zumbansen (2009), 62–70; Guzman (2008), and the *Symposium* on Guzman's book in **1** International Theory 283–343 (2009).

[103] See Hayek (1960 [2006]), 53: 'For the first time it was shown that an evident order which was not the product of a designing human intelligence need not therefore be ascribed to the design of a higher, supernatural intelligence, but that there was a third possibility – the emergence of order as the result of adaptive evolution'; for the distinction between 'economy' (as 'an organization or an arrangement in which someone consciously uses means in the service of a uniform hierarchy of ends') and 'market' ('spontaneous order'), see Hayek (1968 [2002]), 9–23, at 14; see already F. Hayek (1945), 519–30, reprinted in Hayek (1949 [1996]), 77–91 at 88: 'We make constant use of formulas, symbols, and rules whose meaning we do not understand and through the use of which we avail ourselves of the assistance of knowledge which individually we do not possess. We have developed these practices and institutions by building upon habits and institutions which have proved successful in their own sphere and which have in turn become the foundation of the civilization we have built up.' For a defence against an outsider's critique of the normative implications of spontaneous order, see, e.g., Sugden (1989), 85–97, 97; see also the recent discussion, see Hardos and Rahoc (2008).

[104] For an assessment, see Nee and Swedberg (2005b), 789–818.

[105] Beckert (2007); Beckert and Streeck (2008), Beckert (2009), 245–69. Nee and Swedberg (2005b), 789–818; see already the landmark work by Swedberg (1998), and the collection of essays in Nee and Swedberg (2005b).

[106] Aman Jr (2001), 379–400; Teubner (1999b), 51–82; Zumbansen (2008a), 769–805.

[107] Ellickson (1991).

[108] Teubner (1997b), 3–28.

[109] See Posner (2000); Drobak (ed) (2006); for a critical perspective see the author of 'Order without Law', Ellickson (1998), 537–565; see also the magnificent analysis of the inherent

beyond the unsurprisingly recurring, traditional lawyers' laments concerning the loss of regulatory capability and sovereignty.[110] Even before the recent economic crisis began to unfold, it had become clear to regulatory and legal theoreticians that the transformation of Western welfare states in the context of an IT-driven globalization of markets of goods, production, services and migration posed a new set of conceptual challenges that could henceforth only be approached from within an interconnected interdisciplinary agenda.[111]

And yet, despite these manifold intersections, the different strands of evolutionary theory have not been brought together for a comprehensive analysis of the change of legal and economic institutions. The elephant in the room continues to be the tension between *economic* and *legal* governance, or more precisely the relation between the social order as conceived either from an economic or from a legal perspective. So far unanswered remains the question regarding the reasons for the existence of a legal order beyond its affirmation as an *enforcement* framework for market ordering. As shown by Donald Elliott's astute analysis of evolutionary theories in legal and economic scholarship 25 years ago, 'Economic theories of legal evolution also depend on the assumption that a legal system already exists.'[112] By not, however, being able to answer whether the legal system predates – historically or normatively – the economic system, the economic story of markets and their embeddedness in a legal enforcement mechanism remains on a purely abstract level: it distinguishes between the market and the state by resorting to terms such as market and non-market order mechanisms. This, however, attempts to answer the question as to what constitutes the relation between the two spheres without providing for a definition of or a justification of the distinction in the first place. That the legal system exists to remedy market failures does not explain whether the market failure is in fact something else than a political or regulatory failure.[113] It is here, where the evolutionary strands in law, economics and sociology have much to contribute.

5. CONCLUSION: LEGAL AND ECONOMIC GOVERNANCE OF THE TRANSNATIONAL KNOWLEDGE SOCIETY

It is a certain irony, that not only the politically self-conscious exclamation that 'We are all Realists Now', resounding many years ago,[114] would eventually be succeeded by the

depoliticizing effects of the anti-regulatory efficiency claim advanced by norm proponents, by Charny (1996), 1841–58, one of the many outstanding papers in the excellent Symposium Issue on 'Law, Economics, and Norms', published in 144 University of Pennsylvania Law Review 1643–2339 (1996); with regard to the 'norms vs. regulation' conflict for example in the current debate over a Common Frame of Reference for European Private Law, see, on the one hand: Smits (2006), 85, and, on the other: Hesselink (2008).

110 Zumbansen (2007c), 181–190.

111 See e.g. Levi-Faur (2004), 12–29, and Sassen (2003), 1–22; Ladeur (2000).

112 Elliott (1985), 38–94, at 71.

113 For an early analysis of this connection, see of course Hale (1923), 470–494; Cohen (1927), 8–30.

114 Singer (1988), 465–544, at 467.

realization that, in fact, 'We are all Economists Now',[115] but that we seem to now be experiencing yet another relativization of perspective. A pronouncement of the sort 'We are all Interdisciplinary Governance Scholars Now', would, however, have only a faint ring to it. The underlying conundrum is that of the trajectories of institutional and normative change, which occupy much of economic and legal inquiry, before and in light of the global financial and economic crisis of 2008–2009. Meanwhile, the intellectual competition over the primacy of economic or legal reasoning in the imagination of ('sustainable', 'good', 'just') governance occurs in the shadow of a dramatic transformation of the spaces for economic and legal ordering. Precisely at a moment where legal scholars, political scientists and sociologists have come to accept the transnational challenge to the traditional concepts of law and legal regulation,[116] also the economists' ascription to law, the state and to the correlation between the two as constituting the relevant enforcement framework for economic action needs to be revisited. It is here where we can identify an urgent need and already promising contours of an interdisciplinary inquiry into the nature of 'institutions' of economic and legal governance. Much seems to be at stake: as a utopia of transnational governance continues to linger at the horizon of libertarian imaginations of globally integrated markets, neither discipline appears yet to have an appropriate governance theory at hand. The space of human interaction and of regulation beyond the nation state can be depicted either as the Wild West of unrestrained individual liberty, or as an extremely fragile and contested space of struggles over recognition, politics and community.[117] In the face of this, has 'law lost its lieu?'[118] Is the 'Global Bukowina', which inspired legal sociologists at the respective beginnings and ends of the twentieth century, a realm of law, of social norms or of economic liberties?[119] What are we to make of these distinctions, after all? To be sure, this process does not continue in a quiet state of contentment and wonder, but rather in surprise, happenstance and terror.[120] We understand concurring work on 'global governance' to provide an important contribution to a more adequate analysis of the pressing legitimacy and accountability concerns arising from a fragmented regulatory landscape.[121] In an attempt to complement this research, we posit that an evolutionary perspective on governance offers a further set of insights into the changes in legal and economic governance. It is from this perspective, that we might see emerging 'lessons' from a parallel observation of legal and economic governance. Drawing on the distinction between markets and hierarchies, as developed and expressed in work following Coase[122] and Williamson[123] on the one hand and on the analysis of markets as spaces of discovery, learning and adaptation,[124] on the other, we are in an

---

[115] Regarding the slogan as used with reference to legal realism and for the surrounding debate, see Leiter (1996), 261–79.

[116] Jessup (1956); Keohane and Nye (2000), 1–41; Harvey (2009).

[117] See, for example, Kreide (2009), 18–34; Cotterrell (2008), 1–18.

[118] Amstutz (2008), 476. See also Kaldor (2003) (as to the civil society); Brunkhorst (2005); and Luhmann (1982), 131–8 (describing the fragmentation of world society).

[119] See Teubner (1997), 3–28.

[120] For recent illustrations, see d. Sousa Santos (2008), 247-270, and Marazzi (2010).

[121] Beck (2009); Stone Sweet (2009), 621–45.

[122] R. Coase (1937), 386–405.

[123] Williamson (1975); Williamson (2000), 595–613; Williamson (2005), 1–18.

[124] Hayek (1945), 519–30; Hayek (1968 [2002]), 9–23; Tiebout (1956), 416–24.

increasingly narrow applicatory space for a traditional understanding of legal regulation, as informed by a set of constitutional, normative ideals and embedded in a stable institutional framework. In this situation, however, we are faced with the 'stripping down' of law from a functionalist perspective. This function, in a context of a dramatically changing institutional environment,[125] re-emerges as a stubborn insistence on the distinction between legal and illegal. In concert with 'economic governance', legal governance finds its place and calling in contra-factually upholding a normative aspiration to continue to make the distinction between legal and illegal – despite the absence of its traditional institutional framework. Law, then, can only purport to illustrate the challenges of having to identify, create and constantly re-adapt the context in which it is possible to make this distinction. This is what is meant with the need for contemporary governance theories to look beyond traditional concepts of political order and democratic governance.[126]

As already illustrated by evolutionary theory's noted 'language deficit',[127] the same struggle over semantics marks the interdisciplinary confusion over the terms, basis and contours of 'governance'. While it is true, that '[t]oday's problems are determined by the fact that the fundamental structural change of functional differentiation has destroyed the Old European semantics without residue, and that even the most hectic post-modern *polysémies* can be understood only as a restless search for socially adequate self-descriptions,' catastrophes and the change in social structures lead to a ruining of semantics.[128] Communication, then, from the perspective of systems theory, constituting the semantics of the particular observing systems such as law, politics, economics and others, is, in the context of fiercely competing 'truth' claims brought forward from different social rationalities, inevitably *thrown back onto itself*. The legal system must – and will – process the change in its environment by relying on its very own available operations[129] that now will follow into the depths of societal differentiation to focus on what Mariana Valverde refers to as the small 'T's in comparison to the large 'T' in a search for truthfulness.[130] The same idea applies to other social systems as well, as the recent theorizing over 'institutional diversity' amply illustrates.[131] Taken together, we are left with contradicting impressions of a world falling apart, of reference systems eroding, on the one hand, and of interdisciplinary enrichment, inspiration and emerging understandings on the other.

This volume accepts this apparent contradiction by bringing together research from different fields and with different perspectives on the problem of institutional evolution. The basis for this volume was an interdisciplinary research project on *Law, the State and Evolutionary Theory*, jointly conducted by the Collaborative Research Center *Transformations of the State* at the University of Bremen (Germany)[132] and the *German Law Journal*.[133] In addition to work developed in this context, the present volume

125 Compare Willke (2007), Ch. 1 and Ch. 2.
126 Willke, previous note, 7.
127 Dopfer (2005), 3–55, 18.
128 Teubner (2006), 41–64, with reference to Luhmann (2004).
129 Luhmann (1985); Luhmann (1992), 1419–41.
130 Valverde (2003), ch.1.
131 Ostrom (2005); Ostrom (2007), 239–64.
132 www.sfb597.uni-bremen.de
133 www.germanlawjournal.com

contains a number of chapters by some of the most prominent evolutionary theory scholars working today. The collection thus aims at providing a reference point for scholars from different traditions and different fields for an inquiry into the meaning and promises of evolutionary theory for future theorizing about legal and economic governance. The authors contributing to this volume specifically employ evolutionary theory in order to explore the challenges arising from the fundamental transformation of statehood that has been so powerfully captured by Saskia Sassen as an erosion of state sovereignty both from 'below', brought about by processes of privatization and emerging forms of public-private governance, and from 'above', through processes of transnationalization of collaborative, regulatory governance.[134]

By contributing to an ongoing exploration of evolutionary approaches to economics, law and their respective intersections, its first and foremost goal is to provide an overview of the variety of evolutionary perspectives, and how these have been contributing to the design of theories of institutional change in response to the contemporary complex realities of legal and economic change. In that sense, the following chapters should be understood as providing a necessary first step for putting forward for discussion a number of methodological elements towards an evolutionary theory that can fruitfully be employed in both law and economics in order to address some of the most pressing questions of contemporary social theory.

6. OVERVIEW OF THE VOLUME

Against this background the contributors to this volume reflect on evolutionary approaches to explaining institutional change from different perspectives and, according to the latter, the volume has been constructed around the fundamental parts. Part I (Evolutionary Theory Historical Trajectories), focuses on the use of evolutionary tools in order to explain the historical development of certain specific legal and economic phenomena. In his contribution, Joel Mokyr, provides an astute analysis of the varied impact that the Enlightenment had on the development of economic growth in Europe in the nineteenth century. Central to his argument is the contention that the role played by both attitude (towards technology) and institutions was crucial for the different trajectories in Britain on the one hand and continental Europe on the other. 'The Enlightenment changed the outlook of key persons on their natural environment, and their inventions and discoveries turned what might have become another technological efflorescence into a sea change in economic history.'[135] By insisting on the layered, complex nature of the Enlightenment, Professor Mokyr argues for the need to take into account the long-term development of mind-sets, institutional frameworks and conditions in countries that would otherwise be considered to be affected by the industrial revolution in the same manner. Drawing on scholarship that traced the emergence of a knowledge society in eighteenth-century Europe[136] and, in particular, the rising recognition and importance

---

134 See Sassen (2000), 109–116. See also Schepel (2005); and Slaughter (2004), 159–90.
135 Mokyr, in this volume.
136 See, e.g., Burke (2000).

of 'useful knowledge', Mokyr shows how of all the facets of the Enlightenment the development and consolidation of research-driven knowledge would eventually become the key factor in determining whether or not a country would be able to benefit from and ultimately to drive the revolutionary forces. This process, which Professor Mokyr describes as one of an interaction of prescriptive ('What?') and prepositional ('How?') knowledge, he sees as central to a country's ability to gain competitive advantage (M. Porter). While, in the beginning, somewhat naïve ideas regarding an allegedly unpolitical, scientific debate, that was unfolding on a 'market for ideas' circulated, it quickly became apparent how the quality assessment of offered information was indeed not only central to the development of a sophisticated, knowledge-driven society – and the corresponding political system – but also intimately correlated with its development.

Providing an inspiring contribution to the core challenge of the project informing this collection, i.e. how evolutionary theory can be used as a bridge to make economists and legal scholars speak to each other, Thrainn Eggertsson starts from the premise that economists generally agree that new technologies are the necessary source of long-term economic growth. Based on Solow's contribution to modern (neo-classical) growth theory, and his uses of the letter *A* to symbolize the stock of technology, Eggertsson stresses how in economic theory, *A* has a long history of being a nondescript exogenous long-term variable. This disregard is quite peculiar since increasing in *A* is the basic source of a sustained rise in living standards, but only when new production techniques are supported by complementary social institutions. The application of new production techniques usually requires investment in physical and human capital, which will not be forthcoming in the absence of secure property rights, enforceable contracts, and supportive organizations. Moreover, concludes Eggertsson, appropriate institutions and incentives are required for creating new knowledge since new knowledge and new methods of production are scarce assets that are costly to produce.

With a particular focus on law, Bruce Benson, in his *The Law Merchant Story: How Romantic is It?*, analyses the use of the term *Lex Mercatoria* in various historical documents from the Middle Ages in the face of growing criticism, arguing that the descriptions of medieval Law Merchants is either a romantic idea or a pure *ex post* reconstruction. This contribution then continues by pointing out how the controversy over the Law Merchant actually is definitional, i.e. those who contend that *Lex Mercatoria* did not exist start from the assumption that the normative system known as 'law' only exists when it is imposed or at least recognized by a sovereign with coercive power. Based on a detailed overview of the medieval *Lex Mercatoria*, Benson shows how various criticisms of the Law-Merchant literature, for the most part, are much more flawed than the Law Merchant descriptions they attack.

In Part II (Evolutionary Theory in Law and Economics), the contributors investigate, from different doctrinal and normative perspectives, the possible inputs coming from an evolutionary approach in law and legal theory. Taking an example from corporate governance, one of the most dynamic and innovative legal fields in recent years, Fabio Carvalho and Simon Deakin explore the correlations between evolutionary theory and systems theory, in particular the scope for synthesis between systems theory and new institutionalist approaches within economics. While the authors concede that, at first sight, it may seem that the methodological assumptions of economics are too far removed from those of systems theory for any kind of synthesis to be feasible, they argue that economics describes itself as a behavioural science which studies the logic of choice under conditions of scarcity. At the same time, systems theory focuses on the communicative processes through which social order is reproduced over time. As economics becomes increasingly concerned with the role institutions play in coordinating the behaviour of economic agents, it encounters a set of issues, which are central to systems theory. According to Carvalho and Deakin, the interdisciplinary field of 'law and economics' provides the terrain on which rival conceptions of the evolutionary process are being advanced and accessible through critical scrutiny. By using examples taken from company law and corporate governance, they suggest that mainstream law and economics approaches treat legal rules as surrogate prices, and contrast this with a conception of law as a cognitive resource upon which agents draw when engaging in production and exchange. By considering the function of the legal system in terms of the reduction and organization of complexity, systems theory provides, according to the two authors, a further dimension to the notion of law as a cognitive resource. In particular, system theory directs attention to the discontinuous and asynchronic quality of legal change where the legal system will maintain a set of 'foundational' concepts which are to a large extent free from immediate evolutionary pressures, and which tend to be manifested in the form of mandatory legal rules which leave little or no room for bargaining between the parties.

In his contribution entitled *Constitutional Possibility and Constitutional Evolution*, Eric Posner uses evolutionary game theory to explore and tackle recurrent questions about constitutionalism and the United States Constitution. Posner argues that the United States Constitution is a set of self-enforcing conventions that govern how people interact in important ways: the Constitution constrains the government in the same sense that conventions constrain individuals and prevent them from pursuing their immediate self-interest. It is true, continues the author that the Constitution evolves, but it does it at a slow and discontinuous pace, because conventions, by virtue of the fact that they coordinate behaviour, are, in Posner's terminology, 'sticky'. As to the Supreme Court, this body has authority because people believe that it identifies and enforces existing (or hypothetical) conventions. Therefore, justices sitting in the Supreme Court do not always implement their political preferences since otherwise people would stop believing that the Supreme Court enforces conventions, and then the binding force of its decision would decrease to the advantage of other branches.

Richard McAdams, in his chapter, explores what he refers to as a 'third way' of understanding compliance with adjudication. While the two conventional theories are economic – that people fear threatened sanctions – and sociological – that people defer to perceived legitimacy, McAdams invites us to explore an alternative approach which is grounded in social norms theory. Without denying the importance of these mechanisms, McAdams sets out to supplement them with a new causal story for the effect of adjudication. To explain how courts influence behaviour independent of their perceived legitimacy and the sanctions they wield, he argues, one must engage in a peculiar thought experiment imagining a court without these two typical characteristics. The theory of 'expressive adjudication' arises from a previously neglected synergy among three expressive concepts in game theory – 'correlated equilibrium', 'focal point', and 'signal'. McAdams identifies the circumstances in which adjudicative expression can, by itself, influence the behaviour of existing disputants and of future potential disputants. In each case, ambiguity as to the relevant facts or the concepts underlying intentional and spontaneous order can cause a conflict that is resolved by clarifying expression. According to McAdams, this expressive power explains otherwise puzzling instances of compliance with tribunals that lack the power of sanctions and unifies theories of third-party norm enforcement with a theory of legal sanctions. Finally, McAdams examines certain normative implications of the expressive theory, including a novel function of adjudicative impartiality, a new justification for the system of public adjudication, and a trade-off between dispute resolution and dispute avoidance. The core of the chapter then consists of a description of an expressive influence that any third party might have over two parties in a dispute. By focusing on the way that the court – here perceived as a third party in correlation to a conflict between two parties – McAdams' chapter provides important insights into the microstructures of institutional development in adjudication, an area that has often only been studied against the backdrop of critical engagements with legal interpretation and judicial activism.

Adopting a perspective similar to that of Richard McAdams but focusing specifically on private regulatory regimes, Amitai Aviram, in his contribution, points out how 'private legal systems', while they tend to be less visible through the traditional institutionalist legal lens, can be studied with regard to their impact on individuals' behaviour and by their interaction with the public legal system. These private legal systems expand to fill voids where the public legal system cannot or does not wish to enforce norms. Together with the public legal system, continues Aviram, two other forces shape the course of the development of private legal system: the 'incumbent's enforcement advantage' (which affects the identity of the private legal system that will enforce the norm) and the 'bias arbitrage' (which impacts the type of norms the private legal systems would choose to enforce). Due to the influence of incumbent's enforcement advantage, private legal systems tend to begin their life enforcing a core norm that has very low enforcement costs. Once this core has developed, Aviram argues, private legal systems may choose expansion norms that can be more expensive to enforce. These expansion norms can benefit from the private legal system's capacity to compel compliance with the new norm by denying a member the benefits of its enforcement of the core norm (and any expansion norms already successfully enforced).

Martina Eckardt's chapter relies on an 'evolutionary economics' perspective to explain legal change. She starts with an overview of typical evolutionary explanations of legal change and identifies the main actors, the key determinants, and the central mechanisms of the different approaches that bring about such change. From an evolutionary economics point of view legal change takes place through the generation and dissemination of legal innovations over time and the main mechanisms are statutory and judge-made legal change. While statutory legal change relies on legislation and thus on collective action, judge-made legal change is brought about by the judiciary through individual lawsuits. Therefore, while to explain legal stability over time the literature stresses the concepts of legal paradigms and of path dependence, with a particular emphasis on legal lock-ins, in this contribution Eckardt discusses also the main mechanisms that bring about break outs from such legal lock-ins. This enlargement, concludes the author, is done in order to provide a more comprehensive view on legal evolution between stability and change.

In his contribution to this volume, Marc Amstutz, too, adopts an evolutionary perspective on the law-making process but does so by pointing out how systems theory neglects to investigate the origin of the law. Law, according to Amstutz, is assumed to have always existed, usually by hiding behind myths produced within the system itself or by the introduction of new categorical differences. However, this assumption cannot be true with regard to law operating in anomy, an example for such a case being transitional justice. Using the Derridian idea of *supplément* and bringing into relation to Luhmann's idea of law's function consisting in the stabilization of social expectations, it is possible – according to Amstutz – to elaborate a decidedly more complex notion of origin of law. In particular, this Derridian-Luhmannian notion allows, according to Amstutz, the analysis of transitional law on a 'law and society' basis, for instance by revealing the genesis and evolution of the prohibition of crimes against humanity as applied during the Nuremberg trials.

The last two contributions of Part II provide another critical engagement with the promise of evolutionary theory for law and legal theory. Bart Du Laing, in his *Gene-Culture Co-Evolutionary Theory and the Evolution of Legal Behavior and Institutions*, suggests that in explaining institutional change we should draw more attention to its original source, i.e. *biological* evolutionary theory. The behavioural approach of 'dual inheritance theory', he argues, might prevent legal theory (especially that informed by systems theory) from losing sight of what is happening at lower levels of organization like the behavioural one, including human socio-cultural behaviour. Based on the contemporary evolutionary approach known as 'gene-culture co-evolutionary theory' or 'dual inheritance theory', Du Laing shows how evolutionary analysis in law could benefit from incorporating it into its theoretical framework, in particular by using examples of the field of contract law. After a digression into evolutionary economics and systems theory, the author points out the possible input gene-culture co-evolutionary theory can offer to the study of the transformations of commercial law and its institutions that are of central concern to the research project giving rise to this edited volume.

In his contribution *Let's go Normative! Making Evolutionary Theory Useful also for Legal Actors*, Mauro Zamboni starts by pointing out the generally sceptical attitude of a large sector of legal scholarship towards the evolutionary approach. In order to make evolutionary theory more useful for and therefore sympathetic to lawyers and legal actors in general, the author suggests shifting evolutionary theory from the position of mere external investigation of the legal phenomenon to being a fundamental contributor to the legal discourse also in its normative parts. The focus in particular is to understand why, though the evolutionary theory approach to law has been around quite a while in the legal scholar's discussion, the legal world has left it at the front step of the legal house. Based on this analysis, Zamboni aims at investigating whether it is possible, after certain adjustments, to invite evolutionary theory into the larger family of legal thinking, in particular as part of the legal theories of law-making. This invitation to join the legal discourse can be done, according to Zamboni, by convincing legal evolutionary scholars to bring the normative components of the evolutionary approach to the surface of their legal discussion in the form of explicit guidelines for future law-making and law-applying.

The first contribution to the third part dealing with the contribution of evolutionary theory to a theory of transnational law and (economic) governance by Wolfgang Kerber focuses on transnational commercial law from an evolutionary economics perspective. After presenting a general introduction into evolutionary economics, Kerber emphasizes the evolutionary concept of competition as innovation-imitation process as well as an overview about approaches for explaining institutional change from the perspective of evolutionary economics. In the main section, Kerber aims at demonstrating that both the evolution of public/private governance solutions as well as horizontal and vertical processes of regulatory competition within a multi-level legal system can contribute to the explanation of the evolution of 'transnational commercial law'. In this context, he also emphasizes the importance of conflict/choice of laws rules for this evolution. Kerber concludes that transnational governance solutions are the outcome of complex and interrelated evolutionary competition processes between private and public solutions on one hand and between public solutions of different jurisdictions on the other hand.

Jan Smits, in his chapter, begins by exploring the feasibility of applying evolutionary concepts to the explanation of change in transnational and European private law. His contribution aims at applying insights from evolutionary theory to transnational private law. The goal is to offer a framework for answering in particular to the issue of how it is possible to explain the evolution of law beyond the State (of which transnational commercial law and European private law are prime examples). In this spirit, Smits sets out Darwin's idea of natural selection as the analytical presuppositions underlying the application of evolutionary ideas to the development of private law. He subsequently goes on to apply this idea to legal change (looking at law as an organism) and, in particular, to transnational commercial law and European private law. Smits, finally, points out how, in this respect, the concepts of path dependency, adaptation, and co-existence (diversity) can be extremely helpful.

Following the same path traceable in Smits' contribution, Erich Schanze's chapter explores a variety of 'linkage mechanisms' between law and extra-legal norms, notably national and international standards, which can be found in a number of technical contexts of law ('reference norms'). All reference norms are styled from a legal centrist perspective, i.e. the judicial one starting from the premise that extra-legal norms are relevant only to the extent that a legal norm permits their application. According to Schanze, this perspective is essentially a backward-looking one, taking both legal and extra-legal norms for granted and using legal norms to determine their reciprocal relevance. Since the planning of business transactions requires a different approach, Schanze points out that a shift of perspective is necessary for understanding the relation of law and extra-legal norms. In particular, he proposes to look at the relation between legal and extra-legal norms from a drafting perspective, i.e. a forward-looking perspective, which is complementary to the backward-looking investigation of the linkage mechanisms in their applicative moments and which is largely uncommon to Continental European legal systems.

The last contribution to this part is authored by Gralf-Peter Calliess, Jörg Freiling and Moritz Renner. The authors show how the different perspectives of evolutionary economics and systems theory might complement each other in an interdisciplinary endeavour to explaining institutional change in the governance of cross-border commercial transactions. The aim of Calliess, Freiling and Renner is to outline elements of a consistent conceptual framework, combining elements from both strands of theory, and tie it to the specific field of transnational commerce. Starting from the assumption that international trade operates under circumstances which can appropriately be described as a state of 'lawlessness', the three authors stress how a plethora of private governance mechanisms are available to international commerce. This availability creates a form of economic governance, i.e. provision of 'good order and workable arrangements' for business purposes, which is at the same time internationalized and privatized. Nevertheless, they argue, legal regulation is not made obsolete by societal norm-generation, but complements it, competes and interacts with those new modes of governance in many different ways. Calliess, Freiling and Renner conclude their inquiry with an outlook on the possibilities and the problems of integrating evolutionary theory into a social science analysis of institutional change in the transnational arena.

BIBLIOGRAPHY

Aaken, A. van (2009), 'Effectuating public international law through market mechanisms?', *Journal of Institutional and Theoretical Economics*, **165**.

Aguilera, R., C. Rupp, C.A. Williams, and J. Ganapathi (2004), 'Putting the S back in corporate social responsibility: A multi-level theory of social change in organizations', *Academy of Management Review*, **32** [http://[papers.ssrn.com/sol3/papers.cfm?abstract_id=567842].

Alchian, A.A. (1950), 'Uncertainty, evolution, and economic theory', *Journal of Political Economy*, **58**, 211–21.

Alchian, A.A. and H. Demsetz (1972), 'Production information costs, and economic organization', *American Economic Review*, **62**.

Aman, A.C. Jr. (2001), 'The limits of globalization and the future of administrative law: From government to governance', *Indiana Journal of Global Legal Studies*, **8**.

Aman. A., Jr. (2007), 'Law, markets and democracy: A role for law in the neo-liberal state', *New York Law School Review*, **51**.

Arthur, B.W. (1989), 'Competing technologies, increasing returns, and lock-in by historical events', *The Economic Journal*, **99**.

Arthur, B.W. (1994), *Increasing Returns and Path Dependence in the Economy*, University of Michigan Press.

Baldus, M. (1995), *Die Einheit der Rechtsordnung. Bedeutungen einer juristischen Formel in Rechtstheorie, Zivil- und Staatsrechtswissenschaft des 19. und 20. Jahrhunderts.* Dunker & Humblot.

Baumol, W.J. (1986), 'Productivity growth, convergence, and welfare: What the long-run data show', *American Economic Review*, **76**.

Beck, U. (2009) *World at Risk [orig. German 'Weltrisikogesellschaft' (Frankfurt: Suhrkamp); Cronin, C. trans]*, Polity.

Beckert, J. (2007), 'The great transformation of embeddedness. Karl Polanyi and the new economic sociology', *Max-Planck-Institut für Gesellschaftsforschung/Max-Planck-Institute for the Study of Societies.*

Beckert, M.J. (2009), 'The social order of markets', *Theory and Society*, **38**.

Beckert, J. and W. Streeck (2008), 'Economic Sociology and Political Economy. A Programme Perspective', *MPIfG Working Paper 08/4* [http://www.mpifg.de/pu/workpap/wp08-4.pdf]

Berman, P.S. (2005), 'From international law to law and globalization', *Columbia Journal of Transnational Law*, **43**.

Bernstein, L. (1992), 'Opting out of the legal system: Extralegal contractual relations in the diamond industry', *Journal of Legal Studies*, **21**.

Black, J. and D. Rouch (2008), 'The development of global markets as rule-makers: engagement and legitimacy', *Law and Financial Markets Review*.

Bowler, P.J. (2003), *Evolution: The History of an Idea* (3rd ed), University of California Press.

Branson, D.M. (1989), 'A corporate paleontologist's look at law and economics in the Seventh Circuit', *Chicago-Kent Law Review.*

Bratten, W.W. and J.A. McCahery (2001), 'Incomplete contracts theories of the firm and comparative corporate governance', *Theoretical Inquiries in Law*, **2**.

Brown, W.J. (1919), 'Law and evolution', *Yale Law Journal*, **29**.

Brunkhorst, H. (2005) *Solidarity. From Civic Friendship to a Global Legal Community* [Flynn, J. trans], MIT Press.
Brunkhorst, H. (ed.) (2009), *Demokratie in der Weltgesellschaft*, Nomos.
Burke, Peter (2000), *A Social History of Knowledge: From Gutenberg to Diderot*, London: Blackwell.
Burris, S., M. Kempa and C. Shearing (2008), 'Changes in governance: A cross-disciplinary review of current scholarship', *Akron Law Review*, **41**.
Buxbaum, R. (1996), 'Die Rechtsvergleichung Zwischen nationalem Staat und internationaler Wirtschaft', *RabelsZ*, **60**.
Calliess, G.-P. (2001), 'Lex Mercatoria: A reflexive law guide to an autonomous legal system', *German Law Journal*, **17** [http://www.germanlawjournal.com/article.php?od=109]
Calliess, G.-P. and M. Renner (2009), 'Between law and social norms: The evolution of global governance', *Ratio Juris*, **22**.
Calliess, G.-P. and P. Zumbansen (2010), *Rough Consensus and Running Code: A Theory of Transnational Private Law*, Hart Publishing.
Campbell, D. (1997), 'The relational constitution of contract and the limits of "economics": Kenneth Arrow on the social background of markets', in S. Deakin and J. Michie (eds), *Contracts, Co-operation, and Competition. Studies in Economics, Management and Law*, Oxford University Press.
Campbell, D. (2004), 'The incompleteness of our understanding of the law and economics of relational contract', *Wisconsin Law Review.*
Catá Backer, L. (2009), 'The OECD Guidelines for Multinational Corporations: Using Soft Law to Operationalize a Transnational System of Corporate Governance'. *Law at the End of the Day (blog)* [http://Icbackerblog.blogspot.com/2009/03/oecd-guidelines-for-multinational.html].
Charny, D. (1996), 'Illusions of a spontaneous order: "Norms" in contractual relationships', *University of Pennsylvania Law Review*, **144**.
Cheffins, B.R. (2001), 'Does law matter? The separation of ownership and control in the United Kingdom', *Journal of Legal Studies*, **XXX**.
Cheffins, B.R. (2004), 'The trajectory of (corporate) law scholarship', *Cambridge Law Journal*, **63**.
Clark, G.L., M.P. Feldman and M.S. Gertler (eds) (2003), *Oxford Handbook of Economic Geography*, Oxford University Press.
Coase, R. (1937), 'The Nature of the Firm', *Economica*, **4**.
Coase, R.H. (1996), 'Law and economics and A.W. Brian Simpson', *Journal of Legal Studies*, **25**.
Cohen, M.R. (1927), 'Property and Sovereignty', *Cornell Law Quarterly*, **13**.
Cotterrell, R. (2008), 'Transnational communities and the concept of law', *Ratio Juris*, **21**.
Darwin, C. (1859), O*n the Origin of Species by Means of Natural Selection, or the Preservation of Favoured Races in the Struggle for Life (1st edn)*.
David, P.A. (1985), 'Clio and the economics of QWERTY', *American Economic Review*, **75**.
David P.A. (2000), 'Path dependence, its critics and the quest for "historical economics"', in P. Garrouste and S. Ioannides (eds), *Evolution and Path Dependence in Economic Ideas: Past and Present*, Edward Elgar.
David, P.A. (2008), 'Path dependence in economic processes: implications for policy analysis in dynamical systems contexts', in K. Dopfer (ed), *'The Evolutionary Foundations of Economics*, Cambridge University Press.
Davidson, P. (2009), *The Keynes Revolution. The Path to Global Economic Prosperity*, Palgrave Macmillan.
Dawson. J.P. (1968), *The Oracles of the Law*, The University of Michigan Law School.
Demsetz, H. (1967), 'Towards a theory of property rights', *American Economic Review*, **57**.
Dimaggio, P. (ed.) (2001), *The Twenty-First Century Firm. Changing Economic Organization in International Perspective*, Princeton University Press.
Dopfer, K. (2005), 'Evolutionary economics: a theoretical framework', in K. Dopfer, *The Evolutionary Foundation of Economics*, Cambridge University Press.
Dosi, G. and F. Malerba (2002), 'Interpreting industrial dynamics twenty years after Nelson and Winter's *Evolutionary Theory of Economic Change*', *Industrial and Corporate Change*, **11**.

Drahos, P. and J. Braithwaite (2001), 'The globalisation of regulation', *Journal of Political Philosophy*, **9**.
Drobak, J.N. (ed) (2006), *Norms and the Law*, Cambridge University Press.
Eggertsson, T. (1990), *Economic Behaviour and Institutions*, Cambridge University Press.
Eggertsson, T. (1996), 'A note on the economics of institutions' in L.J. Alston, T. Eggertsson and D.C. North (eds), '*Empirical Studies in Institutional Change*, Cambridge University Press.
Eidenmüller, H. (1995), *Effizienz als Rechtsprinzip. Möglichkeiten und Grenzen der ökonomischen Analyse des Rechts*, Siebeck Mohr.
Ellickson, R.C. (1991), *Order without Law: How Neighbors Settle Disputes*, Harvard University Press.
Ellickson, R.C. (1998), 'Law and economics discovers social norms', *Journal of Legal Studies*, **27**.
Elliott, E.D. (1985), 'The evolutionary tradition in jurisprudence', *Columbia Law Review*, **85**.
Fama, E. (1970), 'Efficient capital markets: A review of theory and empirical work', *Journal of Finance*, **31**.
Fama, E. (1998), 'Market efficiency, long-term returns, and behavioral finance', *Journal of Financial Economics*, **49**.
Fama, E. and M.C. Jensen (1983), 'Agency problems and residual claims', *Journal of Law and Economics*, **26**.
Felix, D. (1998), *Einheit der Rechtsordnung. Zur verfassungsrechtlichen Relevanz einer juristischen Argumentationsfigur*, Mohr Siebeck.
Fligstein, N. (2001), *The Architecture of Markets. An Economic Sociology of Twenty-First-Century Capitalist Societies*, Princeton University Press.
Frankenberg, G. (1985), 'Critical comparisons: Re-thinking comparative law', *Harvard International Law Journal*, **26**.
Frazzetto, G. (2004), 'Who's afraid of Darwin?' *European Molecular Biology Organization*, **5**, 662–5.
Gilson, R.J. and R. Kraakman (1984), 'The mechanisms of market efficiency', *Virginia Law Review*, **70**.
Gilson, R.J. and R. Kraakman (2003), 'The mechanisms of market efficiency twenty years later: The hindsight bias', *Journal of Corporate Law*, **28**.
Glenn, H.P. (2005), 'Doin' the transsystemic; Legal systems and legal traditions', *McGill Law Journal*, **50**.
Gourevitch, P.A. (2003), 'The politics of corporate governance regulation', *Yale Law Journal*, **112**.
Greif, A. (2006), *Institutions and the Path to the Modern Economy. Lessons from Medieval Trade*, Cambridge University Press.
Guzman, A.T. (2008), *How International Law Works. A Rational Choice Theory*, Oxford University Press.
Guzman, A.T. (2009), 'Symposium', *International Theory*, **1**.
Hadfield, G.K. (2001), 'Privatizing commercial law', *Regulation*.
Hadfield, G.K. and E. Talley (2006), 'On public versus private provision of corporate law', *Journal of Law, Econ. & Org.*, **22**.
Haferkamp, H. and N.J. Smelser (1992), 'Introduction' in H. Haferkamp and N.J. Smelser, *Social Change and Modernity*, University of California Press.
Haken, H. (2005), 'Synergetics: From physics to economics' in K. Dopfer (ed), *The Evolutionary Foundation of Economics*. Cambridge University Press.
Hale, R.L. (1923), 'Coercion and distribution in a supposedly non-coercive state', *Political Science Quarterly*, **38**.
Hall, P.A. and D. Soskice (eds) (2001), *Varieties of Capitalism. The Institutional Foundations of Comparative Advantage*, Oxford University Press.
Hardos, P. and D. Rahoc (2008), 'Blundering into wisdom? The Missing elements of Hayek's spontaneous order liberalism. *Working Paper* [http://ssrn.com/abstract.=1261873].
Harvey, D. (2009), *Cosmopolitanism and the Geographies of Freedom*, Columbia University Press.
Hayek, F. (1945), 'The use of knowledge in society', *American Economic Review*, **35**.
Hayek, F.A. (1949 [1996]), *Individualism and Economic Order,* Routledge and Kegan Paul.

Hayek, F.A. (1968 [2002]), 'Competition as a discovery procedure', M.S. Snow, trans, *Quarterly Journal of Austrian Economics*, **5**, 9–23.
Hayek, F.A. (1960 [2006]), *The Constitution of Liberty*, Routledge.
Hesselink, M.W. (2008), 'A spontaneous order for Europe? Why Hayek's libertarianism is not the right way forward for European private law', *Centre for the Study of European Contract Law, Working Paper Series No 2008/07* [http://ssrn.com/abstract=1270566]
Hollingsworth, J.R. (1997), 'The institutional embeddedness of American capitalism' in C. Crouch and W. Streeck (eds), *Political Economy of Modern Capitalism. Mapping Convergence and Diversity*, Sage.
Holmes, O.W. (1881), *The Common Law*, chapters 1 and 2.
Holmes, O.W. (1899), 'Law in science and science in law', *Harvard Law Review*, **12**.
Hovenkamp, H. (2009), 'The Coase theorem and Arthur Cecil Pigou,' *Arizona Law Review*, **51**.
Hull, D.L. (1988), *Science as a Process. An Evolutionary Account of the Social and Conceptual Development of Science*, University of Chicago Press.
Hull, D.L. (1995), 'Die Rezeption von Darwins Evolutionstheorie bei britischen Wissenschafts-philosophen des 19. Jahrhunderts', in E.-M. Engels (ed), *Die Rezeption von Evolutionstheorien im 19. Jahrhundert,* Suhrkamp.
Jensen, M.C. (1970), 'Some anomalous evidence regarding market efficiency', *Journal of Financial Economics*, **6**.
Jessup, P.C. (1956), *Transnational Law,* Yale University Press.
Johns, F. (2007), 'Performing power: The deal, corporate rule, and the constitution of global legal order', *Journal of Law and Society*, **34**.
Johnson, D.P. (2008), 'The historical background of social Darwinism', in D.P. Johnson, *Contemporary Sociological Theory: An Integrated Multi-level Approach*.
Kaldor, M. (2003), *Global Civil Society: An Answer to War*, Polity.
Keller, A.G. (1918), 'Law in Evolution', *Yale Law Journal*, **28**.
Kennedy, D. (1981), 'Cost-reduction as legitimation', *Yale Law Journal*, **90**.
Kennedy, D. (1982), 'Distributive and paternalist motives in contract and tort law, with special reference to compulsory terms and unequal bargaining power', *Maryland Law Review*, **41**.
Keohane, R.O. and J.S. Nye (2000), 'Introduction' in J.S. Nye and J.D. Donahue (eds), *Governance in a Globalizing World*, Brookings Institution.
Klöhn, L. (2006), *Kapitalmarkt, Spekulation und Behavioural Finance. Eine interdisziplinäre und vergleichende Analyse zum Fluch und Segen der Spekulation und ihrer Regulierung durch Markt und Recht*, Duncker & Humblot.
Koven Levit, J. (2007), 'Bottom-up international lawmaking: Reflections on the New Haven School of International Law', *Yale Journal of International Law*, **32**.
Kreide, R. (2009), 'The ambivalence of juridification. On legitimate governance in the international context'. *Global Justice: Theory Practice Rhetoric*, **2**.
Krugman, P. (1992), *Geography and Trade*, MIT Press.
Krugman, P. (1998), 'What's new about the new economic geography?', *Oxford Review of Economics & Politics*, **14**.
Ladeur, K.-H. (2000), *Negative Freiheitsrechte und gesellschaftliche Selbstorganisation*, Mohr Siebeck.
Ladeur, K.-H. (2009), 'The law of the network society' Viellechner L. et al. (eds) *German Law Journal.* [http://www.germanlawjournal.com/pdf.Vol10No04/pdf_table_of_contents_Vol_10_No_04.pdf]
Leiter, B. (1996), 'Legal realism', in D. Patterson (ed), *A Companion to Philosophy of Law and Legal Theory*, Blackwell.
Levi-Faur, D. (2004), 'The global diffusion of regulatory capitalism', *The Annals of The American Academy of Political and Social Science*, **598**.
Lie, J. (1997), 'Sociology of markets', *Annual Review of Sociology*, **23**.
Lindblom, C.E. (1995), 'Market and democracy, obliquely', *Political Science and Politics*, **28**.
Lobel, O. (2004), 'The renew deal: The fall of regulation and the rise of governance in contemporary legal thought' *Minnesota Law Review*, **89**.

Luhmann, N. (1975), 'Evolution und Geschichte', in: ders., *Soziologische Aufklärung* **2**.
Luhmann, N. (1978), 'Geschichte als Prozeß und die Theorie sozio-kultureller Evolution' in K.-G. Faber and Mayer (eds), *Historische Prozesse*, Deutscher Taschenbuchverlag.
Luhmann, N. (1982), 'The world society as a social system', *International Journal of General Systems*, **8**.
Luhmann, N. (1985), *A Sociological Theory of Law*, Routledge Kegan & Paul.
Luhmann, N. (1989), 'Verfassung als evolutionäre Errungenschaft' *Rechtshistorisches Journal*, **9**.
Luhmann, N. (1992), 'Operational closure and structural coupling; the differentiation of the legal system', *Cardozo Law Review*, **13**.
Luhmann, N. (1996), *Social Systems* [German orig: Bednarz, J. & Baecker, D. (1984) Transl.], Stanford University Press.
Luhmann, N. (2004), *Law as a Social System*, K. Ziegert, transl., F. Kastner, D. Schiff, R. Nobles and R. Ziegert (eds), Oxford University Press.
Mahoney, J.T. and J.R. Pandian (1992), 'The resource-based view within the conversation of strategic management', *Strategic Management Journal*, **13**.
Maine, H.S. (1861), *Ancient Law*, chapter 2.
Marazzi, C. (2010), 'The Violence of Financial Capitalism', Edizioni Casagrande.
Maus, I. (1980), *Bürgerliche Rechtstheorie und Faschismus. Zur sozialen Funktion und aktuellen Wirkung der Theorie Carl Schmitts (1976)*, Wilhelm Fink.
Mokyr, J. (2002), *The Gifts of Athena. Historical Origins of the Knowledge Economy*, Princeton University Press.
Mokyr, J. (2005a), 'The Knowledge Society: Theoretical and Historical Underpinnings', faculty.wcas.northwestern.edu/-jmokyr/Unitednations.pdf.
Mokyr, J. (2005b), 'Is there a theory of economic history?' in K. Dopfer (ed), *The Evolutionary Foundation of Economics*, Cambridge University Press.
Möllers, C. (2006), 'European governance; Meaning and value of a concept', *Common Market Law Review*, **43**.
Nee, V. and R. Swedberg (eds) (2005a), *The Economic Sociology of Capitalism*, Princeton University Press.
Nee, V. and R. Swedberg (2005b), 'Economic sociology and new institutional economics' in C. Ménard and M.M. Shirley (eds), *Handbook of New Institutional Economics*, Springer.
Nelson, R. (2006), 'Economic development from the perspective of evolutionary economic theory', *Working Papers in Technology Governance and Economic Dynamics 2* [http://hum.ttu.ee/wp.paper2/pdf]
Nelson. R.J. (1995), 'Recent evolutionary theorizing about economic change', *Journal of Economic Literature*, **33**.
Nelson, R.R. (2007), 'Understanding economic growth as the central task of economic analysis' in F. Malerba and S. Brusoni (eds), *Perspectives on innovation*, Cambridge University Press, 27–41.
Nelson, R. and S. Winter (1973), 'Toward an evolutionary theory of economic capabilities', *American Economic Review*, **63**.
Nelson, R. and S. Winter (1974), 'Neoclassical vs. evolutionary theories of economic growth: Critique and prospectus', *American Economic Review*, **84**.
Nelson, R. and S. Winter (1982), *An Evolutionary Theory of Economic Change*, The Belknap Press of Harvard University Press.
Neumann, F.L. (1964), 'The change in the function of law in modern society' in F.L. Neumann (1957), *The Democratic and the Authoritarian State.*
Nieson, P. and B. Herborth (2007), *Anarchie der kommunikativen Freiheit. Jurgen Habermas und die Theorie der internationalen Politik*, Suhrkamp.
North, D.C. (1981), *Structure and Change in Economic History*, Norton.
North, D.C. (1990), *Institutions, Institutional Change and Economic Performance*, Cambridge University Press.
North, D.C. (1991), 'Institutions', *Journal Econ. Persp.*, **5**.
North, D.C. (1994), 'Economic performance through time', *American Economic Review*, **84**.
North, D.C. (2005), *Understanding the Process of Economic Change*, Princeton University Press.
Ostrom, E. (2005), *Understanding Institutional Diversity*, Princeton University Press.

Ostrom, E. (2007), 'Challenges and growth: the development of the interdisciplinary field of institutional analysis', *Journal of Institutional Economics*, **3**.
Posner, E.A. (1998), 'Creating a legal framework for economic development', *The World Bank Research Observer*, **13**.
Posner, E.A. (2000), *Law and Social Norms*, Harvard University Press.
Priest, G.L. (1977), 'The common law process and the selection of efficient rules', *Journal of Legal Studies*, **6**.
Reimann, M. (2002), 'The progress and failure of comparative law in the second half of the twentieth century', *Am. J. Comp. L.*, **50**.
Riles, A. (2005), 'A new agenda for the cultural study of law: Taking on the technicalities', *Buffalo Law Review*, **53**.
Roe, M.J. (1996), 'Chaos and evolution in law and economics', *Harvard Law Review*, **109**.
Roe, M.J. (2002), 'Corporate law's limits', *Journal of Legal Studies*, **31**.
Rosenbaum, E.F. (2000), 'What is a market? On the methodology of a con-tested concept', *Review of Social Economy*, **LVIII**.
Rubin, P.H. (1977), 'Why is the common law efficient', *Journal of Legal Studies*, **6**.
Ruttan, V.W. (1997), 'Induced innovation, evolutionary theory and path dependence: Sources of technical change', *The Economic Journal*, **107**.
Sacco, R. (2002), 'Souvernirs d'un vieux comparatiste', *ZEuP*.
Sassen, S. (2000), 'The State and Economic Globalization: Any Implications for International Law?' *Chicago Journal of International Law*, **1**.
Sassen, S. (2003), 'Globalization or denationalization?', *Review of International Political Economy*, **10**.
Schepel, H. (2005), *The Constitution of Private Governance. Product Standards in the Regulation of Integrating Markets,* Hart Publishing.
Schulte, M. and R. Stichweh (eds) (2008), *Weltrecht*, Duncker & Humblot.
Schumpeter, J. (1934 [1983]), *The Theory of Economic Development. With a New Introduction by Elliott, J. E.*, Transaction Publishers.
Schumpeter, J. (1942 [2008]), *Capitalism, Socialism and Democracy with a new introduction by T. McCraw*, Harper Perennial Modern Thought.
Scott, C. (2005), A core curriculum for the transnational legal education of JD and LLB students: Surveying the approach of the International, Comparative and Transnational Law Program at Osgoode Hall Law School', *Penn State International Law Review*, **23**.
Scott, R.E. (2004), 'The death of contract law', *University of Toronto Law Journal*, **54**.
Simpson, A.W.B. (1996a), '"Coase v. Rigou" reexamined', *Journal of Legal Studies*, **25**.
Simpson, A.W.B. (1996b), 'An addendum: [A Response to Law and Economics and A.W.B. Simpson by R.H. Coase], *Journal of Legal Studies*, **25**.
Singer, J.W. (1988), 'Legal realism now', *California Law Review*, **76**.
Skidelsky, R. (2009), *Keynes. The Return of the Master*, Allan Lane.
Slaughter, M. (2004), 'Disaggregated sovereignty: Towards the public accountability of global government networks', *Government and Opposition*, **39**.
Smits, J. (2006), 'European Private Law: a Plea for a Spontaneous Legal Order', in D. Curtin, J. Smits, A. Klip and J. McCahery (eds), *European Integration and Law*, Intersentia.
Soskice, D. (1999), 'Divergent production regimes: Coordinated and uncoordinated market economies in the 1980's and 1990's' in H. Kitschelt, P. Lange, G. Marks and J.D. Stephens (eds), *Continuity and Change in Contemporary Capitalism*, Cambridge University Press.
Sousa Santos B. d. (2008), 'The world social forum and the global left', *Politics & Society*, **36**.
Stehr, N. (2002), *Knowledge and Economic Conduct: The Social Foundations of the Modern Economy*, University of Toronto.
Stehr, N. (2005), 'Knowledge Societies' in N. Stehr and V. Meja (eds), *Society & Knowledge. Contemporary Perspectives in the Sociology of Knowledge and Science*, Transaction Publishers.
Stehr. N. and Meja, V. (eds) (2005), *Society & Knowledge. Contemporary Perspectives in the Sociology of Knowledge & Science*, Transaction Publishers.
Stone Sweet, A. (2009), 'Constitutionalism, legal pluralism, and international regimes', *Indiana Journal of Global Legal Studies*, **16**.

Stout, L. (2003), 'The mechanisms of market inefficiency: An introduction to the new finance', *Journal of Corporate Law*, **28**.
Streeck, W. (2001), 'Introduction: Explorations into the origins of nonliberal capitalism in Germany and Japan' in W. Streeck and K. Yamamura (eds), *The Origins of Nonliberal Capitalism*, Cornell University Press.
Sugden, R. (1989), 'Spontaneous order', *Journal of Economic Perspectives*, **3**.
Sunstein, C. (ed) (2000), *Behavioural Law & Economics*, University of Chicago Press.
Swedberg, R. (1998), *Max Weber and the Idea of Economic Sociology*, Princeton University Press.
Swedberg, R. (2003), 'The case for an economic sociology of law', *Theory and Society*, **32**.
Teubner, G. (1983), 'Substantive and reflexive elements in modern law', *Law & Society Review*, **17**.
Teubner, G. (1984), 'Autopoiesis in law and society: A rejoinder to Blankenburg', *Law and Society Review*, **18**.
Teubner, G. (1992), 'The two faces of Janus: Rethinking legal pluralism', *Cardozo Law Review*, **13**.
Teubner, G. (1997a), 'The king's many bodies: The self-deconstruction of law's hierarchy', *Law & Society Review*, **31**.
Teubner, G. (1997b), '"Global Bukowina": Legal pluralism in the world society', in G. Teubner (ed.), *Global Law Without a State*, Ashgate.
Teubner, G. (1999a) *'Eigensinnige Produktionsregimes: Zur Ko-evolution von Wirtschaft und Recht in den varieties of capitalism'*, *Soziale Systeme*, **5**.
Teubner, G. (1999b), 'After Privatisation? The Many Autonomies of Private Law', in T. Wilhelmsson and S. Hurri *From Dissonance to Sense: Welfare State Expectations, Privatisation and Private Law*, Ashgate.
Teubner, G. (2002), 'Idiosyncratic production regimes: Co-evolution of economic and legal institutions in the varieties of capitalism', in J. Ziman (ed), *The Evolution of Cultural Entities; Proceedings of the British Academy*, Oxford University Press.
Teubner, G. (2006), 'Dealing with paradoxes: Derrida, Luhmann, Wiethölter' in O. Perez and G. Teubner (eds), *Paradoxes and Inconsistencies in Law*, Hart Publishing.
Teubner, G. (2009), 'Self-subversive justice: Contingency or transcendency formula of law?' *Modern Law Review*, **72**.
Thaler, R. (1987), 'Anomalies – The January effect', *Journal of Economic Perspectives*, **1**.
Thaler, R. (1999), 'The end of behavioral finance', *Financial Analysts Journal*, **55**.
Thaler, R. and C. Sunstein (2008), *Nudge. Improving Decisions about Health, Wealth and Happiness*, Yale University Press.
The World Bank (2009), *World Development Report. Reshaping Economic Geography.*
Tiebout, C.M. (1956), 'A pure theory of local expenditures', *Journal of Political Economy*, **64**.
Valverde, M. (2003), *Law's Dream of a Common Knowledge,* Princeton University Press.
Voigt, S. (2002), *Neue Institutionenökonomik*, Siebeck (UTB).
Watson, A. (1982), 'Legal change: Sources of law and legal culture', *University of Pennsylvania Law Review*, **131**.
White, H.C. (1981), 'Where do markets come from?', *American Journal of Sociology*, **87**.
Whittington, R., M. Mayer and F. Curto (1999), 'Chandlerism in post-war Europe: Strategic and structural change in France, Germany and the UK, 1950-1993', *Industrial and Corporate Change*, **8**.
Wiethölter, R. (1972), 'Artikel Wirtschaftsrecht' in A. Görlitz (ed), *Handlexikon zur Rechtswissenschaft*, Wissenschaftliche Buchgesellschaft.
Williamson, O.E. (1975), *Markets and Hierarchies. Analysis and Antitrust Implications,* Free Press.
Williamson, O.E. (1981), 'The modern corporation: Origins, evolution, attributes', *Journal of Economic Literature*, **19**(4).
Williamson, O. (1985), *The Economic Institutions of Capitalism*, New York, London: Free Press/ Macmillan.
Williamson, O.E. (1996), 'The Institutions and Governance of Economic Development and Reform', Oliver Williamson, the Economics of Governance. 322–343 Oxford University Press.
Williamson, O.E. (2000), 'The new institutional economics: Taking stock, looking ahead', *Journal of Economic Literature*, **38**.
Williamson, O.E. (2005), 'The economics of governance', *American Economic Review*, **95**.
Willke, H. (2007), *Smart Governance. Governing the Global Knowledge Society*, Campus.

Zerbe, R.O. Jr. and H. McCurdy (2000), 'The end of market failure', *Regulation*, **23**.
Ziman, J. (2002), *The Evolution of Cultural Entities: Proceedings of the British Academy*, Oxford University Press.
Zollo, M. and S. Winter (2002), 'Deliberate learning and the evolution of dynamic capabilities', *Organization Science*, **13**.
Zumbansen, P. (2002), 'Piercing the legal veil: Commercial arbitration and transnational law', *European Law Journal*, **8**.
Zumbansen, P. (2006), 'Spaces and places: A systems theory approach to regulatory competition in European company law', *European Law Journal*, **12**.
Zumbansen, P. (2007a), 'The law of society: Governance through contract', *Indiana Journal of Global Legal Studies*, **14**. http://ssrn.com/abstract=988610
Zumbansen, P. (2007b), 'Varieties of capitalism and the learning firm. Corporate governance and labor in the context of contemporary developments in European and German company law.' [http://ssrn.com/abstract=993910] *European Business Organization Law Review*, **8**.
Zumbansen, P. (2007c) 'Introduction: Private Ordering in a Globalizing World: Still Searching for the Basis of Contract', *Indiana Journal of Global Legal Studies*, **14**.
Zumbansen, P. (2008a), 'Law after the Welfare State: Formalism, functionalism and the ironic turn of reflexive law', *American Journal of Comparative Law*, **56**.
Zumbansen, P. (2008b), 'New governance in European corporate governance regulation as transnational legal pluralism', *European Law Journal*, **15**. http://ssrn.com.abstract=1128145.
Zumbansen, P. (2009), 'The state as black box and the market as regulator', *Journal of Institutional and Theoretical Economics*, **165**, http://ssrn.com/abstract=1292789
Zumbansen, P. and A. Skordas (2009), 'The Kantian Project of International Law: Engagements with Jürgen Habermas' "The Divided West"', *German Law Journal*, **10**. http://www.germanlaw-journal.com/index.php?pageID=2&vol=10&no=1

PART I

Evolutionary theory and historical trajectories

1. The European Enlightenment, the Industrial Revolution, and modern economic growth

Joel Mokyr

1. INTRODUCTION

The issue of the emergence of modern economic growth in the nineteenth-century West has once again resumed its rightful place at the center of attention of a large group of scholars, coming from economics, history, and the other social sciences. While different approaches have been taken to understand the causes of the Great Divergence, they all share two fundamental assumptions. One is that modern economic growth started in the 'West' – that is, selected economies in the northern Atlantic region. The other is that in this process Britain was a leader, while Continental Europe was a follower, if a rather quick one.

This chapter is primarily about the former assumption. It argues that most of the countries that in 1914 belonged to the 'convergence club' – countries that were industrialized, urbanized, educated, and rich – were countries that in the eighteenth century were subject to the European Enlightenment. This strong correlation is not in and of itself proof of causality, we need at the very least establish the mechanisms through which the Enlightenment affected the 'real economy' and show that they mattered. In doing so, I will deal only with part of the story. The Enlightenment affected the economy through two mechanisms. One is the attitude toward technology and the role it should play in human affairs. The other has to do with institutions and the degree to which rent-seeking and redistribution should be tolerated. This is an interpretation of the Enlightenment that will surely not cover everything we know about it, but it may be what mattered most from the point of view of economic growth. The second set of problems, dealing with the impact of institutions, has been dealt with elsewhere and will not be the subject of this chapter (Mokyr 2006a, 2007a; Mokyr and Nye 2007).

Do beliefs and attitudes matter to economic outcomes? The debate goes back at least to Marx, who famously argued against it.[1] Keynes, on the other hand, went on record in

[1] 'It is not the consciousness of men that determines their being, but, on the contrary, their social being that determines their consciousness' (1859, p. 4). This view is reflected in the thinking of current-day economists, who are as far from Marxism as can be. For instance, 'Ideology may perhaps be considered a random shock in a model of institutional change, . . . but the absence of any positive theory of idea formation or role for ideology leads us to support economizing activity as the primary explanation for institutional change . . . Ideology may usefully be thought of as a "habit of mind" originated and propelled by relative costs and benefits. As an explanation for events or policies, it is a grin without a cat' (Ekelund and Tollison 1997, pp. 17–18).

his well-known last chapter of the *General Theory* arguing that ideas had the power to affect economic outcomes. In this debate, the answer the economic historian must give is that it all depends on the circumstances. But in the eighteenth century the circumstances were correct for changes in beliefs to affect economies as a whole. The Enlightenment changed the outlook of key persons on their natural environment, and their inventions and discoveries turned what might have become another technological efflorescence into a sea change in economic history.

The importance of the Enlightenment to the subsequent economic development of Western Europe is consistent with both the temporal and geographical pattern of growth. The economic transformation occurred at the end of the Enlightenment and after it, and it was entirely confined to nations that had been exposed to it, although timing patterns were variable. By 1914, the convergence club of industrialized and rich economies consisted almost entirely of countries that had been exposed to it two centuries earlier. Such correlations do not constitute proof. What is needed is to unpack the mechanism that created modern economic growth and link it to the intellectual developments that preceded it.

2. THE INDUSTRIAL REVOLUTION AND MODERN GROWTH

The Industrial Revolution itself, in its classical definition, did not suffice to generate sustained economic growth. It is easy to imagine a counterfactual technological steady state of the techniques that had emerged between 1750 and 1800 of throstles, wrought iron, coke-smelting, and stationary steam engines, in which there was a one-off shift from wool to cotton, from animate power to low-efficiency steam engines and from expensive to plentiful wrought iron. It is easy to envisage the economies of the West settling into these techniques without taking them much further. Such a development would have paralleled the wave of inventions of the fifteenth century with the printing press, the three-masted ship, and iron-casting settling into dominant designs and the process of improvement subsequently slowing down to a trickle.

Why did this not happen? The fundamental reason is that before the Industrial Revolution all techniques in use were supported by very narrow epistemic bases. That is to say, the people who invented them did not have much of a clue as to why and how they worked.[2] The pre-1750 world produced, and produced well. It made many path-breaking inventions. But it was a world of engineering without mechanics, iron-making without metallurgy, farming without soil science, mining without geology, water-power without hydraulics, dye-making without organic chemistry, and medical practice without microbiology and immunology. The main point to keep in mind here is that such a lack of an epistemic base does not necessarily preclude the development of new techniques through trial and error and simple serendipity. But it makes the subsequent wave of microinventions that adapt and improve the technique and create the sustained productivity growth much slower and more costly. If one knows *why* some device works, it becomes easier to manipulate and debug it, to adapt to new uses and changing circumstances.

---

[2] I have developed this framework in some detail in Mokyr (2002) and (2005).

Above all, one knows what will *not* work and thus reduce the costs of research and experimentation. The Industrial Revolution, in short, would have been eventually constrained by the narrowness of useful knowledge and ground to a stop.

And yet, a simple connection between the Scientific Revolution of the seventeenth century and the Industrial Revolution that followed it has proven remarkably elusive.[3] Scholars have found it difficult to link the main technological breakthroughs of the Industrial Revolution to the scientific discoveries of its time, although some notable exceptions to this rule can be pointed out. The solution consists of two components. One is simply a matter of timing: while the main advances during the first stage of the Industrial Revolution (say, 1760–1800) were only weakly based on science, its subsequent momentum increasingly came to depend on the better understanding of the propositional knowledge underlying the invention. The second is that the epistemic base of inventions does not only include a modern definition of science, but a broader definition of knowledge including simply catalogs of phenomena and regularities that could be relied upon even if the underlying processes were not quite understood. Thus tables of the efficiency of steam power were already formulated in the 1710s and widely used in the eighteenth century long before scientists formulated the laws of thermodynamics.[4] Lists and detailed descriptions of practices in fields as far apart as farming, geology, and the performance of water mills helped engineers and producers improve their practices.

The centrality of technology in the emergence of modern economic growth is not really contested. Growth was possible through capital accumulation, increasing trade, better internal allocations, freer markets, and improved institutions. But all of those processes would eventually run into diminishing returns. It is technology that remains at the foundation of modern economic growth. Indeed, the various other definitions of the Industrial Revolution, such as a growing reliance on formal markets and a change in production organization toward the factory system were all endogenous to the changes in technology. A full explanation will need to deal with both the growth of useful knowledge and with the incentives and opportunities to take full advantage of it. Below I will cover only one aspect of it, namely the role played by the Enlightenment in generating this knowledge.

The European Enlightenment was a multifaceted phenomenon, much of it concerned with natural law and justice, religious and political tolerance, human rights and freedom, inequality, legal reform, and much else. At the deepest level, however, the common denominator was the belief in the possibility and desirability of human progress and perfectibility through reason and knowledge. Kant's famous suggestion for the motto of the Enlightenment as 'dare to know' is particularly apposite in this context. The material

---

[3] The opus classicus arguing the case for such a connection remains Musson and Robinson, 1969. Critical of this approach are Mathias 1979; McKendrick 1973; and Hall 1974. A more recent assessment is Cohen 2004. For recent attempts to rescue the importance of the rise of modern science in the eighteenth century see Lipsey et al. 2005 and Jacob and Stewart 2004.

[4] In 1718, Henry Beighton published a table entitled *A Calculation of the Power of the Fire (Newcomen's) engine shewing the Diameter of the Cylinder, for Steam of the Pump that is Capable of Raising any Quantity of Water, from 48 to 440 Hogsheads an Hours; 15 to 100 yards.* Beighton's Table was reproduced in Jean T. Desaguliers's widely read textbook, *Course of Experimental Philosophy*, p. 535. Desaguliers remarked that 'Mr. Beighton's table agreed with all the experiments made ever since 1717.'

aspect of this belief followed in the footsteps of Francis Bacon's idea of understanding nature in order to control her and has been named in his honor the Baconian Program, although its parentage was of course far more complex than that. In the words of one scholar 'The major purpose of Baconian natural philosophy is to produce innovations of which nature unaided is not capable' (Zagorin 1998, p. 97). The program that Bacon suggested to attain material progress through technological progress consisted of the application of the inductive and experimental method to investigate nature, the creation of a universal natural history, and reorganization of science as a human activity (Gillespie 1960, p. 78). Interestingly enough, Bacon has been heavily criticized by modern critics of industrial society. It is ironic that those who were born late enough to have benefited the most from advances inspired by his insights have heaped the most scorn on his 'disastrously mistaken belief that nature and the creation are ordained for man's benefit and rule' (Zagorin 1998, p. 121). It is even more striking that those who regard the Industrial Revolution and the subsequent process of economic growth as fundamentally a positive development (that is to say, economic historians) have never given the Baconian Program much credit for this development. It is this omission that I hope to rectify below.

Useful knowledge became the buzzword of the eighteenth-century Enlightenment. The term should not be associated simply with either 'science' or 'technology.'[5] It meant the combination of different kinds of knowledge supporting one another. The eighteenth century marked both an acceleration of the pace of research and a growing bias toward subject matter that, at least in principle, had some practical value. Indeed, Peter Burke (2000, p. 44) has argued that the eighteenth century saw the rise of 'the idea of research' and the sense that this knowledge could contribute to economic and social reform, a notion directly attributable to Bacon. The change in the pace of progress of knowledge after 1680 was indebted to the influence of Bacon but equally to the triumph of Newtonianism in the first half of the eighteenth century. The achievement of Newton did more than anything else to establish the prestige of formal science in the world of learning (Jacob and Stewart 2004).

The fundamental assumption of the Enlightenment, then, was that the growth of useful knowledge would sooner or later open the doors to prosperity. The belief was that the expansion of useful knowledge would solve technological problems and that the dissemination of existing knowledge to more and more people would have what we could call today substantial efficiency gains. These two notions formed the core of Denis Diderot's beliefs and his admiration for Bacon permeates his writing as it does that of many other eighteenth-century *philosophes* and scientists. In Britain, of course, this belief was not only widespread, but formed the explicit motive for the foundation of organizations and societies that were designed to advance it, above all the Royal Society, and the Society of Arts.[6] It was the triumph of hope over experience.

---

[5] This point has been well-made by Inkster (2006), whose analysis parallels what follows in certain respects. Inkster proposes the term URK ('Useful and Reliable Knowledge'), which is much like the term proposed by Kuznets, who preferred 'testable'. In my view *reliability* is an important characteristic of useful knowledge, but it seems less crucial than *tightness*, that is, the confidence and consensualness with which certain knowledge is held to be 'true'.

[6] William Shipley's credo is summed up in his 'plan' for the establishment of the Society of Arts (1754): 'Whereas the Riches, Honour, Strength and Prosperity of a Nation depend in a great

Not all of it was abstract science: the taxonomic work of Linnaeus and the descriptive writings of Arthur Young increased useful knowledge just as much as the abstract mathematics of Laplace and the experiments of Priestley and Lavoisier. But it was also clear that this growth could only be carried out collectively, through a 'division of labor' in which specialization and expertization were carried out at levels far higher than before, just as Bacon had foreseen in his *New Atlantis* in which Salomon's House is a visualization of a modern research academy.[7] All the same, the way useful knowledge increased in the eighteenth century was a far cry from the processes of R&D (corporate and government) of today. It might be better to say that much of it was by way of exploration and discovery, trial-and-error processes minimally informed by an understanding of the natural processes at work, inspired tinkering, and a great deal of serendipity and good fortune, albeit favored by prepared and eager minds. Over the eighteenth century these research processes became more systematic, careful, and rigorous. By the early nineteenth century the interaction between knowledge 'what' (propositional) and knowledge 'how' (prescriptive) became much tighter. It is this phenomenon, more than anything else, that prevented the early Industrial Revolution from fizzling out and enabled it to become the taproot of modern growth.

3. THE ENLIGHTENMENT AND TECHNOLOGICAL PROGRESS

How, then, did the Enlightenment affect the nature of invention and innovation in the eighteenth century? The Enlightenment was an intellectual process and it was primarily about persuasion. The assumption was that society was improvable, and that a complete program of how to bring this about was worked out and needed to be accepted. The process can be more readily understood if we distinguish four separate headings under which the Enlightenment made a difference to the growth of useful knowledge: agenda, capabilities, selection, and diffusion.[8]

3.1 Agenda

As already noted, the 'Baconian Program' increasingly served as the key to the agenda of researchers. The idea was that knowledge was supposed to be 'useful' – morally, socially, and increasingly, materially. Society was *improvable* through knowledge, and the purpose of the study of nature and experimentation was to help solve practical problems just as much and eventually more so than to satisfy human curiosity or to demonstrate

---

Measure on Knowledge and Improvement of useful Arts, Manufactures, Etc . . . several [persons], being fully sensible that due Encouragements and Rewards are greatly conducive to excite a Spirit of Emulation and Industry have resolved to form [the Society of Arts] for such Productions, Inventions or Improvements as shall tend to the employing of the Poor and the Increase of Trade.' (Allan 1979, p. 192).

[7] Priestley 1768, p. 7. Adam Smith, in the 'Early Draft' to his *Wealth of Nations* ([1978] 1757, pp. 569–72) believed that the benefits of the 'speculations of the philosopher . . . may evidently descend to the meanest of people' if they led to improvements in the mechanical arts.

[8] The following pages are based on Mokyr 2007b.

the wisdom of the creator.[9] Many, if not most, of the natural philosophers of the age of Enlightenment agreed with Bacon's notions and acknowledged their intellectual debt to his ideas, including Diderot, Lavoisier, Davy, and the astronomer John Herschel (Sargent 1999, pp. xxvii–xxviii).

Consequently, many eighteenth-century scholars better known for their contributions to science used their analytical rigor and formal training to attack practical problems of production even if the direct connection of their discoveries to science is not always apparent. Among them were the greatest minds of the scientific Enlightenment. Leonhard Euler was concerned with ship design, lenses, the buckling of beams, and (with his less famous son Johann) contributed a great deal to theoretical hydraulics. The great Lavoisier worked on assorted applied problems as a young man, including the chemistry of gypsum and the problems of street lighting. Gottfried Wilhelm Leibniz, William Cullen, Joseph Black, Benjamin Franklin, Joseph Priestley, Humphry Davy, Tobern Bergman, Count Rumford, and Johann Tobias Mayer were among the many first-rate minds who unabashedly devoted some of their efforts to solving mundane problems of technology: how to design calculating machines, how to make better and cheaper steel, increase agricultural productivity and improve livestock, how to build better pumps and mills, how to determine longitude at sea, how to heat and light homes and cities safer and better, how to prevent smallpox, and similar questions.[10]

The idea of turning research into useful knowledge was larger than the discovery of underlying general laws. Description and organization mattered as much, precisely as Bacon had argued. Many of the investigations of the eighteenth century were in the style of the 'three C's': counting, cataloguing, classifying. Knowledge could only be useful if it was organized (Yeo 2003). Taxonomy, often dismissed as a form of knowledge, was quite central to the market for ideas in the eighteenth century. The great figures were the Swedish botanist Carl Linnaeus and his French rival Georges-Louis Buffon, but many contemporaries followed them in attempts to gather more information about living beings so that farming and husbandry could be improved. In Britain the paradigmatic figures were Erasmus Darwin and Joseph Banks, the authors of voluminous books on plants and animals, and Arthur Young and John Sinclair, who wrote extensively on agriculture. These highly descriptive writings did not have immediate results: agricultural productivity increased only slowly in the period of the classical Industrial Revolution,

---

[9] The 'business of science,' John T. Desaguliers noted in the 1730s, was 'to make Art and Nature subservient to the Necessities of Life in joining proper Causes to produce the most useful Effects' (1763, Vol. 1, p. iii). This was spoken by one of the leading Newtonians of the time, a man who made a career out of selling knowledge to others, a professional lecturer, a textbook writer, and a consultant to business.

[10] Of the many examples one could pick here, the career of René Réaumur (1683–1757) is most telling as the embodiment of the Enlightenment ideals. Although one of the most recognized scientists of his day (he was president of the French Académie Royale) his reputation today has been eclipsed by others. Yet in his day he worked on a variety of problems concerning the nature of iron and steel (he was first to suggest the chemical properties of steel), on problems of porcelain and glazing, he showed the feasibility of glass fibers and suggested that paper could be made from wood. He carried out a huge research program on entomology and pests, egg incubation, and worked on meteorology and temperature measurement (hence the temperature scale still named after him).

and insofar that it did, it was probably not much due to agricultural writings.[11] And yet, the demand side of the market for ideas was there, and the supply was on the way. The market was supported by the belief that more and better knowledge would eventually lead to human progress.

How effective were these efforts? The scholarly debate alluded to above, between those who feel that modern science played a pivotal role in the Industrial Revolution and those who do not, is more than the hackneyed question whether a glass is half full or half empty, because the glass started from almost empty and slowly filled in the century and a half after 1750. Scientists and science (not quite the same thing) had a few spectacular successes in developing new production techniques, above all the chlorine bleaching technique, the lightning rod, and the mining safety lamp. It did broaden the epistemic base of some techniques that had been in use for centuries, explaining – in part – why the things that were known to work actually did so.[12] The efforts made by Europe's most eminent learned men to improve practical techniques demonstrate that by the second half of the eighteenth century most scientists felt an acute responsibility to help improve the material world, and made a sincere effort to learn which problems bothered people toiling in the workshops and the fields. These efforts were reinforced by commercial interests, which created a literal market in knowledge. An increasing number of British natural philosophers and learned persons found it remunerative to rent out their services to manufacturers as consultants.[13]

3.2 Capabilities

The age of Enlightenment was the period in which the interaction between prescriptive knowledge and propositional knowledge started in earnest. Progress in science, it has

---

[11] Voltaire in his famed *Philosophical Dictionary* (1816, Vol. III, p. 91) caustically remarked that after 1750, many useful books written about agriculture were read by everyone but the farmers.

[12] At times, major breakthroughs remained barren for many years. Thus, the most spectacular insight in metallurgical knowledge, the celebrated 1786 paper by three of France's leading scientists, Monge, Berthollet, and Vandermonde that established the chemical properties of steel, had no immediate technological spin-offs. It was 'incomprehensible except to those who already knew how to make steel' (Harris 2001, p. 220). Harris adds that there may have been real penalties for French steelmaking in its heavy reliance on scientists or technologists with scientific pretensions. This dismissive remark seems exaggerated. Without the knowledge that carbon content determined the characteristics of steel, it would have been rather hard to make progress in this industry – though it took many years from that paper to Henry Bessemer and Robert Mushet. The knowledge, however, had clearly diffused to Britain by the 1820s, and was cited in widely available sources (e.g. *The Repertory of Arts, Manufactures and Agriculture*, London: J. Wyatt, 1821, p. 369; Edward James Wilson, *The Artist's and Mechanic's Encyclopaedia*, Vol. 2, Newcastle upon Tyne: Mackenzie and Dent, 1830, p. 67). In France, the Committee for Public Safety instructed the three scientists to write a 34-page pamphlet depicting how to make steel and distributed 15 000 copies. See Horn 2006, pp. 147–48.

[13] Among the best-known ones in the early eighteenth century were the Scottish chemist William Cullen and the itinerant lecturer and Newtonian John T. Desaguliers. During the Industrial Revolution, the number of these consulting engineers expanded and they organized into the Smeatonian society named after John Smeaton, Britain's leading engineer. Among the consultants in high demand were John Whitehurst and Joseph Priestley, two members of the Lunar Society.

long been noticed, is often constrained by limited instruments and research techniques. The scientific revolution advanced in part because new tools such as the telescope, the barometer, and the air pump allowed new observations and made new experiments possible. Price (1984) refers to scientific advances made possible by better tools as 'artificial revelation.' In the eighteenth century this process accelerated. As a result, the rate of scientific discovery was stimulated by technological advances and in turn could help widen the epistemic base of techniques. It is this positive feedback effect that in the end led to the phased transition during which the entire dynamic of useful knowledge changed to produce sustained technological progress.

Examples are easy to find. The great advances made by Lavoisier and his pupils in debunking phlogiston chemistry were made possible by the equipment manufactured by his colleague Laplace, who was as skilled an instrument-maker as he was brilliant a mathematician. The invention of the first battery-like device that produced a steady flow of direct current at a constant voltage, namely Alessandro Volta's pile of 1800, made it possible to separate elements in the newly proposed chemistry which in turn filled in the details of the landscape whose rough contours had been outlined by Lavoisier and his students.[14] Improved instruments and research tools played important roles in a range of 'Enlightenment projects' that might be seen as technological improvements with poetic license. One such improvement was the use of geodesic instruments for surveying.[15] Time was measured with increasing accuracy, which was as necessary for precise laboratory experiments as it was for the solution to the stubborn problem of longitude at sea, one of the age of Enlightenment's proudest successes. Experimental engineering also made methodological advances. John Smeaton was one of the first to realize that improvements in technological systems can be tested only by varying components one at a time holding all others constant (Cardwell 1994, p. 120). In such systems, progress tends to be piecemeal and cumulative rather than revolutionary, yet Smeaton's improvements to the water mill and steam engine increased efficiency substantially even if his inventions were not quite as spectacular as those of James Watt.

Another increased capability came from mathematics. The use of mathematics in scientific research was an ancient tradition, but advances in mathematics added new tools to the arsenal of engineers, and theoretical work in engineering advanced consequently and – with a considerable lag – expanded the supply of good ideas. Mathematics increasingly became a problem-solving technology and many great mathematicians lent their skill to computations that had useful applications in ballistics, engineering, astronomy, and navigation. Copernicus's student, Rheticus, prepared complete tables for all six trigonometric functions, and Napier developed logarithmic tables. Computing tools such as Galileo's 'compass' and Pascal's early calculating machine were designed, though the inability of mechanics to construct them at low prices limited their use. The input of formal

---

[14] As Humphry Davy, perhaps the most accomplished practitioner of the new electrochemistry, put it: Volta's pile acted as an 'alarm bell to experimenters in every part of Europe' (cited by Brock 1992, p. 147).

[15] Jesse Ramsden designed a famous theodolite that was employed in the Ordnance Survey of Britain, which commenced in 1791. A comparable tool, the repeating circle, was designed by the great French instrument-maker Jean-Charles Borda in 1775, and was used in the famed project in which the French tried to establish with precision the length of the meridian.

mathematics into technical engineering problems in hydraulics and the design of better waterwheels was remarkable in the late eighteenth century. These attempts reflect both the potential and the difficulties of the learning process in applying the newly invented calculus to the dynamic problem of hydraulics.[16] Calculus, developed in the late seventeenth century, eventually found many applications in mechanical engineering as well as in construction.[17] Calculus, indeed, may be regarded a 'General Purpose Principle,' in the terminology of Lipsey et al. (2005): a multi-purpose tool that allowed for any function to be maximized and laws of dynamics written down and solved. Again, the French led their more pragmatic and less formal British colleagues. The three great French polytechniciens of the early nineteenth century, Gustave-Gaspard Coriolis, Jean-Victor Poncelet, and Louis Navier, placed mechanical and civil engineering on a formal base, and while the immediate impact of these advances on productivity is difficult to discern, it is hard to see how sustained progress in the longer run could have been made without it. The same holds for the study of electricity: eighteenth-century science grappled bravely with the topic, combining experimental work with theory. The mathematical work of Franz Aepinus (1759) provided the first theoretical epistemic base for the findings of experimentalists such as Musschenbroek, starting a long chain of investigation that would bear fruit more than a century later.

3.3 Selection

Ideas, small and large, are selected from larger menus of ideas that are proposed to people (Mokyr 2006a). The selection process is determined by persuasion, and persuasion in free selection environments follows a set of criteria based on the rhetorical conventions of the time, these rhetorical conventions themselves a result of a selection process. Society constructs certain rhetorical conventions by which logic, evidence, and authority are admissible in arguments about ideas, and these conventions set the rules of the game, or the underlying institutions, in the competition between ideas to be accepted. A naive view of this process would only select among competing alternatives by the criterion of the maximal likelihood that they were 'true.' By that logic, astrology would have disappeared centuries ago. Once established, however, they tend to determine the prevailing ideology in society, including its religious beliefs as well as the scientific dominant doctrines.

What is left out here is coercion. Existing knowledge and ideas tend to develop into orthodoxy, and incumbents are defensive and jealous. Many entrenched elites found ingenious ways to perpetuate the status quo, so that intellectual innovation would only be admissible if it did not contradict the existing orthodoxy. Conservative establishments in science, religion, and political thinking argued that the predominant criterion for the

---

[16] The French mathematician Antoine Parent calculated that the maximum useful effect of a waterwheel was only 4/27th the natural force of the stream and that the optimal speed of the waterwheel was 1/3 that of the stream. These calculations were widely accepted, although they were incorrect and did not square with empirical observations. They were subsequently revised and corrected. Experimental work remained central and at times had to set the theorists straight (Reynolds 1983).

[17] A celebrated example is the development of the theory of beams, in Charles Coulomb's celebrated 1773 paper 'Statical Problems with Relevance to Architecture.'

acceptance of novel knowledge was that it be consistent with existing ideas. New ideas and techniques that were inconsistent with the intellectual or technological status quo, and could thus threaten the human capital of those who were in control of the existing knowledge, were to be suppressed, by force if necessary.[18] Intellectual innovation could only occur in tolerant societies in which possibly outrageous ideas proposed by sometimes highly eccentric men would not incur violent responses against 'heresy' and 'apostasy.' This was especially true in a world in which science, philosophy, and religion were inextricably connected. In the late Middle Ages, the intellectual innovations of the 12th and 13th centuries had rigidified into a Ptolemaic-Aristotelian canon that became increasingly intolerant of deviants. Cosmology and theology in the picture of the world that emerged were deeply intertwined and provided an intellectual foundation of the religious establishment. 'The resulting system of the Universe was considered impregnable and final. To attack it was considered blasphemy' (Lipsey et al. 2005, p. 237). Yet from 1500 on, this system came under increasing pressure and eventually collapsed.

How and why it did so is discussed elsewhere (Mokyr 2005; 2007b), but it is important to see the Enlightenment as part of this changing set of criteria. Knowledge and beliefs were regarded as contestable at every level, and tolerance was raised to a level of a principle. Free entry into the market for ideas and the absence of repression were a high priority on which all Enlightenment thinkers were united. The ideals of tolerance and persuasion by argument and evidence, in which ideas were selected freely by individuals on merits other than acceptability by the ruling orthodoxy, eventually emerged successful. It held, somewhat naively, that selection among competing theories or observations was to be determined by criteria unrelated to politics, with acceptance exclusively determined by the rhetoric of knowledge itself: logic, rigor, experimental evidence, and observation. The triumph of this model became closely associated with the concept of the Enlightenment. All science and knowledge were riven with politics and their separation remained an ideal that in practice was never achieved, but degree is everything, and the politics of science changed considerably. What was determined in the age of Enlightenment was the principle of how scientific disputes were to be resolved when new information or insights emerged. In that regard, Lavoisier and Adam Smith were subject to the same rules. Consistency with earlier theories and respect for the knowledge of previous generations was to have little impact on selection, at least in theory.[19]

The main insight regarding the nature of new useful knowledge that Francis Bacon –

---

[18] The explanations of how such intellectual conservatism can be a rational response can vary (Kuran 1988). It was often felt that a free marketplace for ideas might lead to subversion that threatened political stability (that is, the power base of the status quo), or that they might cause economic disruption such as unemployment. In other cases, still not entirely absent in our own age, disrespect toward the wisdom of elders or the presumption of appropriating powers that belong to a higher being ('playing God') are also resented. Symbolic tales like the sorcerer's apprentice and Prometheus embody the notion that innovation could be dangerous and should be contained and controlled.

[19] John Taylor, a teacher at one of Britain's dissenting academies, Warrington Academy, told his pupils in 1757 that 'if at any time hereafter any principle or sentiment by me taught or advanced, or by you admitted and embraced, shall upon impartial and faithful examination appear to you to be dubious or false, you either suspect or totally reject that principle or sentiment' (cited by Reid 2006, pp. 8–9).

himself no scientist – left to his Enlightenment admirers was the legitimacy of experimental research in progress. In that regard, perhaps, his philosophy in part formalized what was already carried out by many natural philosophers and alchemists in practice, but his thinking clearly helped place experimental science at center stage of scientific progress. Whenever the orthodoxy was contradicted by experiment, the orthodoxy was challenged, and Gillespie (1960, p. 79) has stated that experimental science has become practically a synonym for 'modern science.' The importance of experimental work to the Industrial Revolution was enormous: the careers of James Watt, John Smeaton, James Keir, John Roebuck, Humphry Davy, Joseph Priestley, Count Rumford, Michael Faraday and countless other inventors cannot be imagined without experimental work guiding them. Especially when the epistemic base of a technique is quite narrow so that the outcome of a procedure cannot be predicted, there is no real substitute for experimental work to guide the selection process of useful knowledge.

The other element in selection is the concept of 'open science' to which I will return below. The Scientific Revolution saw the emergence of a set of norms and customs in which discoveries and advances in natural philosophy were placed in the public domain as soon as possible, with the author demanding credit for priority. One consequence of this procedure is the concept of peer review, whether before or after publication. For non-experts, selection was made more efficient because one could make a reasonable presumption that new knowledge had been vetted by other specialists. That such presumptions are often mistaken does not reduce the effect; without it, there is always no way such selection can be made. Some periodicals, especially the proceedings of the Royal Society and other official academies and, much later, high-prestige periodicals such as Nicholson's *Journal* and François Rozier's *Observations sur la Physique, sur l'Histoire Naturelle, et sur les Arts* fulfilled a similar function.

3.4 Diffusion

As Dasgupta and David (1994) have noted, knowledge requires an institutional set-up unlike any other market because the market for ideas in many ways resembles an open-source technology. Open science, as many scholars have stressed, was the key to the rapid changes in the market for ideas because its very purpose was to disseminate new ideas and offer them to the marketplace. The incentives in such a market work quite differently from those in other markets, and are most comparable to modern open-source technology networks (Lerner and Tirole 2004). In such networks, all new knowledge is placed in the public realm and judged by peers. Success is mostly a result of a signaling contest, in which reputations are maximized. Such reputations are then correlated with a variety of benefits, but also appear in the preferences of the actors directly. In seventeenth- and eighteenth-century Europe, such reputations were critical both for appointments at universities and patronage (David 2004), and contributed materially to the emergence of open science.

The Enlightenment picked up on this trend. It was, in large part, about communication. From the point of view of economic history, what is most interesting here is the reduction of access costs. Knowledge is a non-rivalrous good, and in theory, the source can share it costlessly. No such argument can be made for the recipient, who incurs a variety of search, transfer, and verification costs. These costs depended on both technological and cultural factors. Inventions such as paper, printing, and the telegraph, as well as improvements in transportation and postal services were an important factor. There can be no question, however, that institutions played a major role here, and that the emergence of open science and a culture of sharing knowledge as well as a growing aversion to the secrecy associated with useful knowledge in earlier times, so typical of the age of Enlightenment, were critical in reducing access costs (Eamon 1994). If knowledge were to grow, it needed specialization, a 'division of knowledge.'[20] Yet such a specialization depended crucially on low access costs.

Access costs were also important because they governed, so to speak, both the vertical and horizontal movements of useful knowledge. By vertical movements I mean the signals sent between those who controlled propositional knowledge, the *savants*, and those who were concerned with prescriptive knowledge, *fabricants*. As I emphasized elsewhere (Mokyr 2002), the connection between those two social spheres is critical to the question of which segments of propositional knowledge will end up being 'mapped' into the set of available techniques, in other words, what kind of inventions is one to expect? This, indeed, is among the hardest problems in economic history. Horizontal movement of useful knowledge provides would-be inventors and implementers with best-practice scientific knowledge underlying the technique in question (which may not be very good), and it sends would-be scientists and experimentalists signals about the needs of those in the workshops and the fields.

Indeed, it is astonishing that in many cases societies seem to have had technological opportunities that they could have exploited given the knowledge they had, but for one reason or another the mapping does not seem to have taken place. Why, for instance, did the Romans never invent eyeglasses despite their knowledge of glass or optics, or succeed in casting iron or use navigational instruments at sea? Part of the answer must be the point I made above: the communications (or *passerelles* as Hilaire-Pérez (2000) has called them) between those who make things and have a 'feel' for what is needed, and those with the mathematical or scientific knowledge to realize how the problem is to be solved needs to be tight and effective for this horizontal signaling.[21]

But there were other reasons why declining access costs played such a central role in the

---

[20] Smith ([1978] 1757, p. 570) argued outright that 'speculation in the progress of society . . . like every trade is subdivided into many different branches . . . and the quantity of science is considerably increased by it.' The idea caught on. Joseph Priestley wrote in 1768 that 'If, by this means, one art or science should grow too large for an easy comprehension in a moderate space of time, a commodious subdivision will be made. Thus all knowledge will be subdivided and extended, and knowledge, as Lord Bacon observes, being power, the human powers will be increased . . . men will make their situation in this world abundantly more easy and comfortable' (Priestley 1768, p. 7).

[21] Stewart (2007, p. 13) notes that Enlightenment thinkers considered the distinctions between scholars and craftsmen downright harmful 'to the philosophical enterprise' though they were regarded equally harmful to material progress in general. Some were optimistic: Humphry Davy wrote in 1802 that 'in consequence of the multiplication of the means of instruction, the man of science and the manufacturer are daily becoming more assimilated to each other' (Davy 1840, vol. 2, p. 321). Count Rumford, however, noted impatiently in 1799 that 'there are no two classes of men in society that are more distinct, or that are more separated from each other by a more marked line, than philosophers and those who are engaged in arts and manufactures' and that this prevented 'all connection and intercourse between them.' (Thompson 1876, pp. 743–745).

economic transformation of Europe. Much invention takes the form of analogues to and combinations of existing techniques, or combined knowledge from diverse fields in what we might call technical hybrids or recombinations.[22] It was thus critical that knowledge of techniques in use in other industries and regions be made accessible. Furthermore, such knowledge would help prevent inventors from entering blind alleys, both in terms of re-inventing the wheel and from trying things that would not work (though the latter, of course, could be quite ambiguous).

Access to knowledge can be usefully analysed by distinguishing between codified and tacit knowledge. The former depended crucially on the written word, especially on print. The eighteenth century experienced a veritable explosion of books that made useful knowledge accessible. The discovery that information could be made more accessible by alphabetization was exploited in full in the eighteenth century. The document most widely associated with the Enlightenment, Diderot and d'Alembert's *Encyclopédie*, contained numerous articles on technical matters, lavishly illustrated by highly skilled artists who, in most cases, were experts in their fields.[23] Encyclopedias and indexes to 'compendia' and 'dictionaries' were the search engines of the eighteenth century. In order to be of practical use, knowledge had to be organized so that it could be selected from. Alphabetization was one way to do this, the organization of science into categories another (Yeo 2003). Some encyclopedias and dictionaries were designed to be efficient search engines and to reduce access costs.[24] The number of scientific periodicals in the eighteenth century soared. In the early decades the number of learned periodicals (all areas) in all of Europe was still fairly modest: an average of 21 per year in the first decade of the eighteenth century, 34 in 1721–30, and 77 in 1741–50. In the 1790s, this number had soared to 531 (computed from Kronick 1991; see Mokyr 2005).

Tacit knowledge, passed in person, went through a similar flourishing. Stewart (1992), has described in great detail how science became 'public,' sold to the public in coffee houses, country inns, and a variety of societies and academies in which public lectures and meetings were held. In 1700 there were 2000 coffee houses in London alone, many of which were the locations of lectures. Over the course of the century, both formal and informal meeting places increased exponentially, the most famous being the Birmingham Lunar Society and the London Chapter coffee house. The Royal Institution, founded by Count Rumford and Joseph Banks in 1799, provided public lectures on scientific and

---

[22] This phenomenon was already realized on the eve of the Industrial Revolution: Joseph Moxon wrote in the 1670s that 'The Trades themselves might, by a Philosopher, be Improv'd . . . I find that one Trade may borrow from many Eminent Helps in Work of another Trade' (Moxon 1703, preface).

[23] Pannabecker (1996, 1998) points out that the plates in the *Encyclopédie* were designed by the highly skilled Louis-Jacques Goussier who eventually became a machine designer at the Conservatoire des arts et métiers in Paris. They were meant to popularize the rational systematization of the mechanical arts to facilitate technological progress.

[24] Croker et al., 1764–66 serves as an interesting example. The title page of their book reads 'in which the whole circle of human learning is explained and the difficulties attending the acquisition of every art, whether liberal or mechanical, are removed in the most easy and familiar manner.' The topics covered ranged from heraldry and rhetoric to hydraulics and pneumatics. Many of the articles were quite advanced and required considerable prior knowledge if the reader were to benefit from them.

technological topics. Its stated purpose in its charter summarizes what the Industrial Enlightenment was about: it was established for 'diffusing the knowledge, and facilitating the general introduction, of useful mechanical inventions and improvements; and for teaching, by courses of philosophical lectures and experiments, the application of science to the common purposes of life.'[25]

4. INTELLECTUAL PROPERTY RIGHTS AND THE ENLIGHTENMENT

Enlightenment thought was reasonably unanimous about its belief that progress through expanded and accessible useful knowledge was possible and desirable, Jean-Jacques Rousseau being perhaps the most noticeable exception. When it came to Intellectual Property Rights (IPRs), however, the new ideology found itself painfully torn between a number of conflicting views. One was the visceral opposition to monopolies and restrictions of any kind on free entry. This instinct was reinforced by the Baconian notion that useful knowledge should be shared and that its accumulation was a fundamentally cooperative endeavor. In such an ideal world, a patent system which limits usage is not desirable. At the same time, *philosophes* had to confront the notion that if a society wished to promote technological change, it needed to create the economic incentives for inventive activities to take place. Moreover, the belief in the sanctity of private property was profound, and considered a natural law, a fundamental human right, an idea that found its way into a declaration made by the French National Assembly in 1790 and the United States Constitution a few years earlier. The latter, perhaps, more than anything else, has helped establish IPRs as a paradigmatic Enlightenment institution, but such an inference would be rash.

Opponents of the patent system identified it as a rent-seeking device, often used to block new entry, conveniently ignoring the fact that those who resisted patents were sometimes motivated by protecting their own incumbency from unwelcome entrants. Among those opponents, guilds were uppermost (MacLeod 1988, pp. 83, 113). It was also noted in the late seventeenth century that patentees often were not the best qualified persons to exploit the inventions.[26] A different critique, but equally telling, was made by J.T. Desaguliers, who pointed out (1763, Vol. 2, p. viii) that a patent was often interpreted by investors as an official imprimatur of the quality of an invention (much like modern venture capitalists), and that there were 'several persons who have money, ready to supply boasting Engineers with it in the hope of great Returns, and especially if the project has the Sanction of an Act of Parliament to support it, and then the Bubble becomes compleat and ends in Ruin.' The problem remained how society should reward those who gave their time and money to develop knowledge that was of great benefit to the rest of society. Such rewards, it was understood, needed to be established if society was to enjoy the fruits of sustained technological progress.

---

[25] The lectures given by Humphry Davy were so popular that the carriages that brought his audience to hear him so clogged up Albermarle Street in London that it was turned into the first one-way street of the City.

[26] Andrew Yarranton, a tin-plater, found his business harmed by a patentee incapable of working it properly (MacLeod 1988, p. 184).

Of those incentives, the patent system was one option but by no means the only one. Many economists still think of it as the cornerstone of such an incentive system (Khan 2004) but the notion has come under criticism. The debate is far from new. Goethe may have been somewhat naive when he wrote that the British patent system's great merit was that it turned invention into a 'real possession, and thereby avoids all annoying disputes concerning the honor due' (cited in Klemm 1964, p. 173). In his *Lectures on Jurisprudence* (1762–66 [1978], pp. 83, 472), Adam Smith admitted that the patent system was the one monopoly (or 'priviledge' as he called it) he could live with, because it left the decision on the merit of an invention to the market rather than to officials. Smith thought, somewhat unrealistically, that if an 'invention was good and such as is profitable to mankind, [the inventor] will probably make a fortune by it.'

Not all inventors sought such rewards, and certainly not many actually attained them. Many inventors in the Industrial Revolution placed their inventions at the public's disposal, and others for one reason or another, failed to secure a patent or subsequently lost it.[27] Yet the politicians had come to realize that rewarding inventors who made significant contributions to the nation's technological capabilities was good public policy. Both Samuel Crompton, the inventor of the mule, and Edmund Cartwright, the inventor of the power-loom, were rewarded by Parliament with considerable sums, though they captured but a minute fraction of the social surplus that their inventions eventually created. A petition for the estate of Henry Cort was denied by Parliament, but the fact that other ironmasters entered a subscription for the benefit of Cort's widow demonstrates that contemporaries sensed significant spillovers here. The pioneers of paper-making machines, Henry and Sealy Fourdrinier, too, were awarded a grant of £20000 by a Parliamentary committee (after many manufacturers testified that the continuous paper machines had been of huge benefit to their respective branches), though this amount was later reduced to £7000 and paid as late as 1840, when Henry was already in his seventies. The scientist William Sturgeon, one of the pioneers of electrical technology in the 1830s, fell on hard times toward the end of his life, and was awarded a one-off payment of £200 plus a small pension by Lord John Russell's government. In all these cases, and many others, there was an explicit recognition that these people had added to the well-being of the realm; in other words, they had produced positive externalities. But they also reflect a recognition that invention was costly and risky, and that if society wanted to generate a continuous stream of technical improvements, it had to make the activity that generated innovation financially attractive.

Britain was not the only Western nation to take this view. France and the Netherlands had patent systems in which innovations could yield considerable benefits to their propagators. In Britain, however, the state only recognized and enforced the inventor's right (Hilaire-Pérez 2000). It did not normally take it upon itself to evaluate the invention's

---

[27] Scientists who made inventions of considerable importance, such as Count Rumford, Benjamin Franklin, Joseph Priestley, or Humphry Davy, usually wanted credit, not profit. Some entrepreneurs, too, refused to take out patents out of principle. The great engineers, too, largely stayed away from the patent system. Abraham Darby II declined to take out a patent on his coke-smelting process allegedly saying that 'he would not deprive the public from such an acquisition' (cited by MacLeod 1988, p. 185), although his father, the founder of the dynasty, did take out a patent on his sand-casting process (1708).

contribution to society. The type of encouragement given to inventors in Britain differed thus from the French system during the *ancien régime*, where government agents were put in charge of evaluating the contribution of certain inventions to the realm. The difference between the two systems can be overstated: at times the British authorities recognized the national interest and were willing to act to pursue it aggressively. An example was the Board of Longitude, established in 1714 by Parliament, which promised a large sum to the person who successfully cracked the age-old problem of measuring longitude at sea.

It seems that the main effect of the patent system on innovation was to goad potential inventors into believing that they, too, could make as much money as the Lombe brothers or James Watt. In point of fact, precious few ever did, but the expectation may have been enough for many. Britain's patent system was not exactly inviting: it charged a patentee £100 for the right to patent, not counting the costs of traveling to and staying in London (Khan and Sokoloff 1998). Moreover, many patents were infringed upon and judges were often hostile to patentees, considering them monopolists.

The exact impact of the patent system and other positive incentives on the technological creativity that eventually helped produce a more prosperous nation is hard to establish. Recently some economists have gone so far as to dismiss it altogether. Boldrin and Levine have argued that intellectual property rights have been unimportant in bringing about economic growth, and have specifically pointed to the Industrial Revolution as a period that provides 'a mine of examples of patents hindering economic progress while seldom enriching their owners and of great riches and economic successes achieved without patents' (Boldrin and Levine, 2005, chapter 4, p. 7). Such an extreme position neglects the important qualification that what the patent system was important *ex ante* in giving would-be inventors was hope for success, in a fashion not dissimilar to why people purchase lottery tickets. If no one ever won the lottery, people would stop buying tickets; but the number of winners need not be very large to keep hope alive. Yet it exemplifies the complexity of the institution.

The patent system also was a means for the diffusion of useful knowledge: once a patentee filed, he or she had to divulge the existence of the invention and in principle forewent the protection of secrecy. After *Liardet v. Johnson* (1778), the patentee was required to explain the invention in such a manner than anyone familiar with the technique could understand and reproduce it. While access to the filed patent remained cumbersome, it was easier than industrial espionage or reverse engineering.

The problems with IPRs underline the difficulty in separating exactly those elements we think of as 'institutional' and those that properly belong to the category of 'technological creativity.' Such categories are creations of our minds, which help us sort out complex historical relations, but they do not have a historical 'reality' of their own. Yet if we are to understand the Industrial Revolution and the germination and birth of the British economy, some kind of analytical framework that classifies different phenomena is necessary.

5. THE EMERGENCE OF MODERN ECONOMIC GROWTH

For many decades, the Enlightenment had little palpable impact on production. What is astonishing, in retrospect, is that the belief in the value of useful knowledge survived so long in the face of a lack of results. The world turned out to be more messy and complex than the early and hopeful proponents of the Baconian Program realized, as H.F. Cohen (2004, p. 123) has suggested. The natural philosophers on whom so many placed their hopes did not know enough and lacked the tools to solve most of the pressing problems quickly, and many of the early inventions, especially in textiles, were driven by mechanical dexterity, intuition, experience-driven insights, and similar abilities. Indeed, while the results of the Industrial Enlightenment in the eighteenth century were few and far between, those of the agricultural and medical Enlightenments were even less impressive. Farming practices, with some exceptions, were largely unaffected by the huge literature that Enlightenment writers interested in agriculture, known as *agronomes*, produced.[28] Things were no better in medicine, where high hopes that increased knowledge would cure the worst ills afflicting mankind were sorely disappointed. Again, there were some successes, but they remained local and limited triumphs until the epistemic base of medical techniques was expanded so that infectious disease was better understood.[29]

It is remarkable that belief in the mission remained indefatigable in the face of continuous frustration and disappointment (although the Royal Society itself lost its fascination with technology after 1700). And there was plenty of frustration and disappointment. A case in point is William Cullen, a Scottish physician and chemist. His work 'exemplifies all the virtues that eighteenth-century chemists believed would flow from the marriage of philosophy and practice' (Donovan 1975, p. 84). Ironically, however, this marriage remained barren for many decades. Cullen's prediction that chemical theory would yield the principles that would direct innovations in the practical arts remained, in the words of the leading expert on eighteenth-century chemistry, 'more in the nature of a promissory note than a cashed-in achievement' (Golinski 1992, p. 29). Manufacturers needed to know why colors faded, why certain fabrics took dyes more readily than others, and so on, but as late as 1790, best-practice chemistry was incapable of helping them much (Keyser 1990, p. 222). Before the Lavoisier revolution in chemistry, it just could not be done, no matter how suitable the social climate: the minimum epistemic base simply did not exist.

In many other areas, despite the best of efforts and intentions, the new research agenda yielded few tangible results. Another example is the exploration of electricity. The eighteenth-century natural philosophers were fascinated by this strange force, and believed that once tamed, it held great promise. While advances in electricity such as the Leyden jar (invented in 1746), the discovery of different levels of conductivity, and the finding that electricity could be transmitted over considerable distances all stirred many an imagination, and some entertaining uses were found for the mysterious phenomenon,

---

28 An exception was the success that animal breeders such as Robert Bakewell had in producing improved varieties of sheep and cattle, such as the New Leicester sheep and the Yorkshire shorthorn and the introduction of improved plough designs.

29 Among those were the discovery by British naval officers that fresh fruits and vegetables could prevent scurvy, the use of cinchona bark (quinine) to fight off the symptoms of malaria, the prescription of foxglove (now known as digitalis) as a treatment for edemas and atrial fibrillation (first recommended by Dr. William Withering, a member of the Lunar Society, in 1785), the consumption of cod liver to prevent rickets, and above all the miraculous vaccination against smallpox discovered by Jenner in 1796.

practical applications had to await the breakthroughs of Oersted, Faraday, and Ampère in the first half of the nineteenth century. An exception was Franklin's lightning rod (1749), one of the first useful pragmatic applications of experimental science.

It is important to realize how much effort was spent in this age on unsuccessful, or what may seem to us completely useless, research in chemistry, medicine, botany, electricity, and many other areas. Rather than indicating an inefficient allocation of resources, this shows of course that new knowledge creation is inherently wasteful. Yet the belief that somehow the systematic study of nature could yield insights that would eventually enrich and improve industry and agriculture never faded, no matter how remote the chances were. Such was the profound influence of the Enlightenment.

Although the Enlightenment is commonly considered to have ended in 1789, its effects on the economy were, as already indicated, most pronounced in the nineteenth century. The triumph of Enlightenment thought came in the growing influence of liberal political economy, which gradually dismantled the regulatory state in the first half of the eighteenth century, and between 1780 and 1830 repealed many of the limitations on the free market and reduced rent-seeking. But more than anything else, the momentum of technological progress was preserved rather than dissipated. While economic historians have not found much productivity growth during the classical Industrial Revolution (Antrás and Voth 2003), after 1830 productivity starts to increase and by 1850 its effects on real wages and the standard of living become apparent.

The second stage of the Industrial Revolution adapted ideas and techniques to be applied in new and more industries, improved and refined earlier inventions, extended and deepened their deployment, and eventually these efforts showed up in the productivity statistics. Among the remarkable later advances we may list the perfection of mechanical weaving after 1820; the invention of Roberts's self-acting mule in spinning (1825); the extension and adaptation of the techniques first used in cotton and worsted to carded wool and linen; the improvement in the iron industry through Neilson's hot blast (1829) and related inventions; the continuous improvement in crucible steelmaking through coordinated crucibles (as practiced for example by Krupp in Essen); the pre-Bessemer improvements in steel thanks to the work of Scottish steelmakers such as David Mushet (father of Robert Mushet, celebrated in one of Samuel Smiles's *Industrial Biographies*), and the addition of manganese to crucible steel known as Heath's process (1839); the continuing improvement in steam power, raising the efficiency and capabilities of the low pressure stationary engines while perfecting the high pressure engines of Trevithick, Woolf, and Stephenson, and adapting them to transportation; the introduction of ever-more efficient water mills, including the invention of the turbine by Benoît Fourneyron in 1837; the advances in chemicals before the advent of organic chemistry (such as the breakthroughs in candle-making and soap manufacturing thanks to the work of Eugène-Michel Chevreul on fatty acids); the introduction and perfection of gas-lighting and its subsequent dissemination; the breakthroughs in high-precision engineering and the development of better machine-tools by Maudslay, Whitworth, Nasmyth, Rennie, the Brunels, the Stephensons, and the other great engineers of the 'second generation'; the growing interest in electrical phenomena leading to electroplating; and the work by Hans Oersted and Joseph Henry establishing the connection between electricity and magnetism, leading to the telegraph in the late 1830s. In other industries such as cement, glass, paper, and food processing, there were major improvements. Many of those depended in ever-growing degrees on wider epistemic bases: the knowledge base was growing and those who needed it, whether they were inventors or engineers, had access to that knowledge.

While the years between 1830 and 1870 were the age of the railroad and the telegraph and witnessed the triumphs of British technology at the Crystal Palace exhibition in 1851, the full triumph of technology was only secured after 1870 with the arrival of cheap steel, electrical power, chemicals, and other advances associated with the second Industrial Revolution. Yet historians, celebrating the second Industrial Revolution as the central event of economic history and the true beginning of modern technological society (e.g. Smil 2005), need to confront the importance of the precedence of the first Industrial Revolution and the Enlightenment that made it possible.

BIBLIOGRAPHY

Allan, D.G.C. (1974), 'The society of arts and government, 1754–1800: Public encouragement of arts, manufactures, and commerce in eighteenth-century England,' in *Eighteenth-century Studies* **7**, No. 4, pp. 434–52.

Allan, D.G.C. (1979), *William Shipley: Founder of the Royal Society of Arts*, London: Scholar Press.

Antrás, Pol and Joachim Voth (2003), 'Factor prices and productivity growth during the British Industrial Revolution,' *Explorations in Economic History*, **40**, 52–77.

Boldrin, Michele and David K. Levine, *Against Intellectual Monopoly*, Cambridge University Press.

Brock, William H. (1992), *The Norton History of Chemistry*, New York: W.W. Norton.

Burke, Peter (2000), *A Social History of Knowledge: From Gutenberg to Diderot*, London, Blackwell.

Cardwell, Donald S.L. (1994), *The Fontana History of Technology*, London: Fontana Press.

Cohen, H. Floris (2004), 'Inside Newcomen's fire engine: The scientific revolution and the rise of the modern world,' *History of Technology*, **25**, 111–132.

Croker, Thomas (1764–66), *The Complete Dictionary of Arts and Sciences*, 3 vols., London: printed for the authors, and sold by J. Wilson & J. Fell.

Dasgupta, Partha and Paul A. David (1994), 'Toward a new economics of science,' *Research Policy*, **23**, 487–521.

David, Paul A. (2004), 'Patronage, reputation, and common agency contracting in the scientific revolution,' unpub. ms., Stanford University.

Davy, Humphry (1840), 'A discourse, introductory to a course of lectures on chemistry,' in *The Collected Works of Sir Humphry Davy*, John Davy, ed., London: Smith, Elder & Co.

Desaguliers, Jean Theophile (1763), *A Course of Experimental Philosophy*, third edition, London: Printed for A. Millar (2 vols.).

Donovan, A.L. (1975), *Philosophical Chemistry in the Scottish Enlightenment*, Edinburgh: Edinburgh University Press.

Eamon, William (1994), *Science and the Secrets of Nature*, Princeton, NJ: Princeton University Press.

Ekelund, Robert B. Jr., and Robert D. Tollison (1997), *Politicized Economies: Monarchy, Monopoly, and Mercantilism*, College Station: Texas A&M University Press.

Gillespie, Charles Coulston. (1960), *The Edge of Objectivity: An Essay in the History of Scientific Ideas*, Princeton, NJ: Princeton University Press.

Golinski, Jan (1992), *Science as Public Culture: Chemistry and Enlightenment in Britain, 1760–1820*, Cambridge: Cambridge University Press.

Hall, A. Rupert (1974), 'What did the Industrial Revolution in Britain owe to science?' in Neil McKendrick (ed.), *Historical Perspectives: Studies in English Thought and Society*, London: Europa Publications.

Harris, John R. (2001), *Industrial Espionage and Technology Transfer*, Aldershot: Ashgate.

Hilaire-Pérez, Liliane (2000), *L'invention technique au siècle des lumières*, Paris: Albin Michel.
Horn, Jeff (2006), *The Path not Taken: French Industrialization in the Age of Revolution*, Cambridge, MA: MIT Press.
Inkster, Ian (2006), 'Potentially global: "Useful and reliable knowledge" and material progress in Europe, 1474–1914', *The International History Review*, **28**(2), 237–86.
Jacob, Margaret C. and Larry Stewart (2004), *Practical Matter: Newton's Science in the Service of Industry and Empire, 1687–1851*, Cambridge, MA: Harvard University Press.
Keyser, Barbara Whitney (1990), 'Between science and craft: the case of Berthollet and dyeing,' *Annals of Science*, **47**(3) (May), 213–60.
Khan, B. Zorina (2004), *The Democratization of Invention: Patents and Copyrights in American Economic Development, 1790–1920*, Cambridge: Cambridge University Press.
Khan, B. Zorina and Kenneth L. Sokoloff (1998), 'Patent institutions, industrial organization, and early technological change: Britain and the United States, 1790–1850,' in Maxine Berg and Kristin Bruland (eds), *Technological Revolutions in Europe*, Cheltenham: Edward Elgar, pp. 292–313.
Klemm, Friedrich (1964), *A History of Western Technology*, Cambridge, MA: MIT Press.
Kronick, David A. (1991), *Scientific and Technical Periodicals of the Seventeenth and Eighteenth Centuries: A Guide*, Metuchen, NJ: Scarecrow Press.
Kuran, Timur (1988), 'The tenacious past: Theories of personal and collective conservatism', *Journal of Economic Behavior and Organization*, **10**, 143–71.
Lerner, Josh and Jean Tirole (2004), 'The economics of technology sharing: Open source and beyond', NBER Working paper 10956 (Dec.).
Lipsey, Richard G., Kenneth I. Carlaw and Clifford T. Bekar (2005), *Economic Transformations: General Purpose Technologies and Long-term Economic Growth*, Oxford: Oxford University Press.
MacLeod, Christine (1988), *Inventing the Industrial Revolution*, Cambridge: Cambridge University Press.
Mathias, Peter (1979), *The Transformation of England: Essays in the Economic and Social History of England in the Eighteenth Century*, New York: Columbia University Press.
McKendrick, Neil (1973), 'The role of science in the Industrial Revolution,' in Mikuláš Teich and Robert Young (eds), *Changing Perspectives in the History of Science*, London: Heinemann, pp. 274–319.
Mokyr, Joel (2002), *The Gifts of Athena: Historical Origins of the Knowledge Economy*, Princeton, NJ: Princeton University Press.
Mokyr, Joel (2005), 'The intellectual origins of modern economic growth,' *Journal of Economic History*, **65**(2) (June), 285–351.
Mokyr, Joel (2006a), 'Mercantilism, the Enlightenment, and the Industrial Revolution,' Presented to the Conference in Honor of Eli F. Heckscher, Stockholm, May 2003, in Ronald Findlay, Rolf Henriksson, Håkan Lindgren and Mats Lundahl (eds), *Eli F. Heckscher (1879–1952): A Celebratory Symposium*, Cambridge, MA: MIT Press, pp. 269–303.
Mokyr, Joel (2006b) 'Useful knowledge as an evolving system: The view from economic history,' in Lawrence E. Blume and Steven N. Durlauf (eds), *The Economy as an Evolving Complex System, Vol. III: Current Perspectives and Future Directions*, New York: Oxford University Press, pp. 307–337.
Mokyr, Joel (2007a), 'The institutional origins of the Industrial Revolution,' Unpublished, Northwestern University, May.
Mokyr, Joel (2007b), 'The market for ideas and the origins of economic growth in eighteenth century Europe,' *Tijdschrift voor Sociale en Economische Geschiedenis*, **4**(1), 3–38.
Mokyr, Joel and John Nye (2007), 'Distributional coalitions, the Industrial Revolution, and the origins of economic growth in Britain', *Southern Economic Journal*, **74**(1), 50–70.
Moxon, Joseph (1703), *Mechanick exercises: or the doctrine of handy-works. Applied to the arts of smithing joinery carpentry turning bricklayery*, third ed. (orig, pub. in 1677), London: Dan. Midwinter and Thomas Leigh.
Musson, Albert E. and Eric Robinson (1969), *Science and Technology in the Industrial Revolution*, Manchester: Manchester University Press.

Pannabecker, John R. (1996), 'Diderot, Rousseau, and the mechanical arts: Disciplines, systems, and social context,' *Journal of Industrial Teacher Education*, **33**(4), 6–22.
Pannabecker, John R. (1998), 'Representing mechanical arts in Diderot's Encyclopédie', *Technology and Culture*, **39**(1) (Jan.), 33–73.
Price, Derek J. de Solla (1984), 'Notes towards a philosophy of the science/technology interaction,' in Rachel Laudan (ed.), *The Nature of Knowledge: Are Models of Scientific Change Relevant?*, Dordrecht: Kluwer.
Priestley, Joseph (1768), *An Essay on a Course of Liberal Education for Civil and Active Life*, London: J. Johnson.
Reid, David (2006), 'For the benefit of knowledge: charity, access costs, and education in pre-industrial Britain', Paper presented for the workshop on 'History, Technology, Economy,' Appalachian State University, April 24.
Reynolds, Terry S. (1983), *Stronger Than a Hundred Men: A History of the Vertical Water Wheel*, Baltimore Johns Hopkins Press.
Sargent, Rose-Mary (ed.) (1999), *Francis Bacon: Selected Philosophical Works*, Indianapolis, IN: Hackett Publishing Co.
Smil, Vaclav (2005), *Creating the Twentieth Century: Technical Innovations of 1867–1914 and their Lasting Impact*, Oxford: Oxford University Press.
Smith, Adam ([1978] 1757), *Lectures on Jurisprudence*, Oxford: Clarendon Press.
Stewart, Larry (1992), *The Rise of Public Science*, Cambridge: Cambridge University Press.
Stewart, Larry (2007), 'Experimental spaces and the knowledge economy,' *History of Science*, xlv, pp. 155–77, available at: http://industrialization.ats.ucla.edu/publications/Experimentalspaces.pdf.
Thompson, William and Count Rumford (1876), *The Compete Works of Count Rumford*, London: the American Academy of Arts and Sciences, Macmillan & Co.
Voltaire (1816), *Dictionnaire philosophique: dans lequel sont réunis les questions sur l'encylcopédie, l'opinion en alphabet, les articles insérés dans l'encyclopédie*, Paris: Didot.
Yeo, Richard (2003), 'Classifying the sciences,' in Roy Porter (ed.), *The Cambridge History of Science, Vol. 4: Eighteenth-century Science*, Cambridge: Cambridge University Press, pp. 241–66.
Zagorin, Perez (1998), *Francis Bacon*, Princeton, NJ: Princeton University Press.

2. The unbearable lightness of A – useful knowledge and economic growth

Thráinn Eggertsson

1. INTRODUCTION

Economists usually sing with the same hymn sheet when they are questioned about the role of technology in economic growth. They generally agree that sustained long-term growth in productivity, which began in Western Europe some two centuries ago, could not have been maintained in an environment of stagnant production technologies. Whether we consult Karl Heinrich Marx, Joseph Alois Schumpeter or Robert Merton Solow, the answer is the same: new technologies are the source of long-term economic growth. Economists, as we know, usually argue that the production and utilization of new technologies depend critically on appropriate social institutions, such as competition, decentralized markets, secure property rights, enforceable contracts, and norms of trust and reciprocity. Yet virtually no one argues that long-term growth in output per worker is possible in an economy with stationary production techniques.[1]

In his pioneering contribution to modern (neo-classical) growth theory, Solow (1956; 1957) uses the letter A to represent technology. Specifically, in Solow-type growth models the letter A symbolizes the stock of technology, which for convenience is assumed to increase with time at a fixed rate. The exogenous increase in A is assumed to be labor saving, which means that technical change makes it possible to produce a given level of output by using fewer labor units than before and the same amount of capital. In equation (1) y, average output per capita for an economy, is a function of the state of technology, A, and the ratio of capital to labor, k:

$$y_t = A_t; k_t^{\alpha} \tag{1}$$

In any time period, t, output per unit of labor, y_t, is determined by the value of the capital-labor ratio, k_t. Note that A_t is fixed as well as the technical parameter α, which is a positive fraction. With A_t and α given, there exists an optimal value for k_t that maximizes output per unit of labor (or income per capita). In a competitive economy with flawless market institutions, the forces of supply and demand spontaneously establish global equilibrium involving optimal value for k. If for some reason the autonomous increase in

[1] Growth laggards are of course able to increase output per worker by simultaneously reforming their social institutions and obtaining advanced technologies from abroad. Long-term growth, however, requires new additions to the stock of existing knowledge and technologies.

A would come to an end, in Solow growth models the assumption of sharply diminishing marginal product of capital takes away the possibility of propelling long-term growth of y via capital accumulation (by steadily raising k). Finally, Solow's growth theory is admired for its formal elegance and bold predictions, particularly the famous convergence hypothesis, which states that in the long run, regardless of their starting points, all economies will converge on the same per-capita income, y, and realize the same steady-state rate of growth.

It is well known that in modern times economic growth has not equalized living standards around the world but instead opened an extraordinary income gap between rich and poor countries. If at time t all countries share the same technology, A, as the Solow model assumes, in theory differences in incomes per capita must be caused by country differences in the capital-labor ratio, k. In practice, we cannot use the variation between countries in k ratios to explain the income gap. Given a range of values for α in equation (1) that is empirically reasonable, differences in y between rich and poor countries can only be explained by assuming absurdly large differences in their capital-labor ratio, k (Romer 1994). We therefore must either throw away the Solow approach or modify the assumption that all countries share the same A_t. But now we have a new problem. Neoclassical growth theory assumes that A, technical knowledge, is a pure public good that is instantly available to all nations. To escape the quandary we can recognize A as having many attributes of an international public good (non-excludable and non-rival) but as being strongly dependent for its effects upon specific complementary goods: appropriate social institution. Moreover, we can argue that, unlike A, social institutions are generally local public goods with weak international public goods properties.[2] Along these lines, in a recent book I distinguish between social technologies and production technologies (Eggertsson 2005). The concept 'social technologies' refers to knowledge or understanding of the social mechanisms that give institutions their properties. Social institutions are bundles containing several elements: formal rules, social norms, beliefs, and enforcement mechanisms. The term 'social technologies' implies knowledge of how institutions emerge, how they function and how they change (spontaneously or by design). It is fair to say that we have more knowledge of physical technologies than social technologies, and in the domain of social technologies we know more about static than dynamic properties of institutions. We know more about the market response to harvest failures than about the path from insecure to secure property rights.

In sum: Long-term increase in A is the basic source of a sustained rise in living standards but only when new production techniques are supported by complementary social institutions – and therefore by appropriate incentives. The application of new production techniques usually requires investment in physical and human capital, which will not be forthcoming in the absence of secure property rights, enforceable contracts, and supportive organizations. Moreover, appropriate institutions and incentives are required

---

[2] For instance, shared history and common characteristics make it relatively easy for the Scandinavian countries to import laws and regulations from each other. Countries far away from the Scandinavian perimeter, however, would find it harder to import the same bundles of rules and enforcement mechanisms and put them to effective use.

for creating new knowledge. New knowledge and new methods of production are scarce assets that are costly to produce. Also, it is important to note that new knowledge, even new technical knowledge, is not always wealth augmenting. For instance, social institutions that create incentives to develop technologies for capturing resources through theft or warfare do not contribute to economic growth (at least not directly). Finally, it is fair to say that the economics of knowledge is one of the least developed branches of our science. In economic theory, A has a long history of being a nondescript exogenous variable.[3]

2. SOCIAL ORGANIZATION AND A

A, physical technology, is a critical input both in the traditional processes of producing commodities as well as in the production of institutions such as secure property rights or enforceable contracts. At the risk of oversimplifying we can write

$$I = f(A; Z; X) \tag{2}$$

In equation (2) each symbol represents a vector of variables. The letter I stands for the set of technically available forms of social institutions or organization, A represents physical knowledge and technologies, Z social knowledge and social technologies, and X stands for various background factors such as geography and natural resources. Equation (2) defines the choice set of institutional forms that are theoretically available to a particular community.[4] Communities select or acquire a set of social institutions, S, that belongs to the larger I set. The empirical evidence does not give us reasons to think that communities or nations optimize in the sense of always selecting the wealth-maximizing subset S from I. Various forces intervene, such as failures of collective action, narrow self-interests of ruling groups, beliefs, values and cognitive limitations. We argue, however, that I, the choice set of institutions, becomes larger as A increases. It follows that a social group that only knows and uses primitive physical technologies has relatively few choices when it comes to institutions.

Let us consider in some detail the case of primitive, isolated and preliterate farming societies. In such societies the capacity to organize is critically constrained by the limited availability of physical technologies of communication, measurement, monitoring and

---

[3] Relatively few mainstream economists have extensively studied economics of science, knowledge, and technological change whereas these topics appear to be more popular among evolutionary economists (Nelson and Winter 1982). Fritz Machlup (1962), a mainstream economist, is a classic reference. In addition to Machlup, the small but distinguished set of economists exploring the economics of knowledge contains, for instance, Adam Smith, Karl Marx, Joseph A. Schumpeter, Friedrich A. Hayek, Kenneth J. Arrow, Herbert A. Simon, and Paul A. David. So-called new or endogenous growth theory attempts to make A endogenous in macroeconomic growth models. To my knowledge, the new growth literature has not yet produced important new insights into the nature of A – perhaps because macroeconomic models are not a productive venue for studying the phenomenon (Nelson 1997).

[4] The simple formulation in equation (2) does not recognize that the choice of new institutions is constrained by already prevailing institutions, including formal rules and social norms.

enforcement. Primitive societies that have a long history of survival are likely to have set up relatively efficient social institutions, *S*, given their small *I* set, because the opportunity cost of inefficient institutions is high. Primitive societies live close to extinction and nature filters out the most inefficient ones. In a thoughtful essay Richard A. Posner (1980) works his way through organizational forms that are likely to be available in traditional societies with no written records, scant knowledge of the laws of nature, and access to only the most elementary techniques of farming and agriculture. In an ideal-type primitive society, he asks, what social institutions do we expect to find in the spheres of politics, property rights, insurance against hunger, protection of order, economic exchange and religion? Posner then appeals to high information and transaction costs to explain why preliterate and low-*A* societies usually are stateless, lack specialized organizations such as firms and government bureaus, are elaborately organized into clans, rely on communal property rights, strict liability in torts, gift exchanges, joint or interrelated institutions for production, government, and religion, and even have institutions that block the accumulation of surpluses by fortunate individuals.

Hull and Bold (1994) use an approach similar to Posner (1980) to explore the structure of religion in primitive societies, particularly their reliance on the promise of heaven and the threat of hell as social mechanisms for maintaining public order. In the production of social order, Hull and Bold assume diminishing returns to both threats and promises and hypothesize that primitive societies with relatively weak worldly governance mechanisms rely heavily on religion to maintain order, evoking both heaven and hell because of diminishing returns to each method. Societies with more advanced administrative control mechanisms rely either on heaven or hell, not on both. Hull and Bold (1994) then find statistical support for their thesis in an empirical test using data drawn from preliterate communities.

I conclude by suggesting two related explanations of the relatively high variance in *y*, *A*, and *S* across countries in modern times. First, the emergence of growth-compatible *S* (social institutions) is associated with the separation of political and economic institutions to a degree where (a large segment of) the population is free to enter (almost) all economic activities and compete in the economic sphere. In history, the alternative arrangement is for the rulers, in payment for political support, to allocate economic opportunities and monopoly rights directly to a small minority, the leading members of the rulers' winning coalition. Successful economic reforms require opening access to the economic sphere and providing investors with fairly secure rights. Second, reformers who rapidly overcome political barriers and attempt to move quickly by importing modern *A* and growth-friendly *S* come up against complementarities at two levels: the dependence of high-level *A* on appropriate *S*; and, within the *S*-set, the dependence of imported formal institutions on pre-existing local institutions, particularly on informal institutions or social norms. Imported constitutional, commercial, contract, and corporation laws tend to be dysfunctional unless supported by social norms involving legitimacy, trust, reciprocity, and basic standards of honesty. Informal institutions are rooted in history and do not adjust automatically to rapid changes in the environment.

In sum: Moves to qualitatively different new political equilibrium are associated with major changes in political power; and the social mechanisms governing rapid changes in social norms are poorly understood. The political balance and social norms are usually outside the reach of economic reformers (Eggertsson 2005).

3. SMITH AND THE BRITISH *A* REVOLUTION

The consensus on the critical role of *A* in economic progress has not stimulated comparably great interest among researchers in the economics of knowledge. In fact economists (and others) are not particularly good at recognizing industrial revolutions in their early stages.[5] We do best when predicting technological watersheds after the fact because the consequences of general-purpose technologies, such as steam power, electricity or electronics, are essentially unforeseen or unforeseeable. Revolutionary general-purpose technologies reshape production methods, economic institutions (rules and norms), economic organizations (the structure of firms and contracts) and our life styles, but these transformations occur gradually and sequentially. At the outset, most travelers cannot see whither their path will lead.

Adam Smith first published his *Wealth of Nations* in 1776. The third revised edition of the book appeared in 1782, the year in which, according to the English economic historian Thomas S. Ashton (1997 [1964]), the pace of output in England quickened, ushering in the British Industrial Revolution. Yet the Industrial Revolution does not play a role in Smith's masterpiece (Koebner 1959). Smith apparently did not foresee the rise of British industry driven by mechanization of production and transport; he was not a prophet of entrepreneurship and industrialization. Unlike Schumpeter writing some 150 years later, Smith was doubtful about the contribution of daring industrial innovators and entrepreneurs, referring to them as speculators and projectors (Koebner 1959). If we want to give Smith the benefit of doubt, it is possible (but unlikely), that he understood the significance of contemporary industrial developments but for strategic reasons decided to ignore them. Smith's practical aim with the *Wealth of Nations* was to lay bare the economic weaknesses of the Mercantile System and promote the use of free markets. Speculations about an industrial revolution could have complicated his message. Smith's well-known argument is that economic freedom increases the size of markets, promotes specialization, raises productivity (the pin example), and improves the standard of living. Taking *A* as given, Smith's eyes were on complementary social institutions and organizations.

4. *A*, THE ENLIGHTENMENT, AND MODERN ECONOMIC GROWTH

DNA evidence indicates that humans emerged in Africa, perhaps some 200 000 years ago. Modern production technology and modern economic growth span the last 200 years or thereabouts, which equals approximately only 0.125 percent of mankind's time on Earth. We know also that in the second half of the seventeenth century in Western Europe

[5] Few issues receive greater attention in modern economic theory than the relative efficiency of various market structures but theory usually assumes stationary *A* when analysing various mechanisms for allocating resources. The mainstream literature recognizes as such the concept of 'dynamic efficiency,' sometimes with a nod toward Joseph Schumpeter (2005 [1939]), who in his work explored the dynamics of capitalism. Yet it is fair to say that dynamic efficiency plays a trivial role in modern mainstream economic analysis.

the stock of useful knowledge, the source of modern production technology, started to expand rapidly and has since then grown at an accelerating rate. Why did this happen? Why in Western Europe?

Joel Mokyr (2005a, 2005b), the distinguished economic historian who specializes in the history of knowledge and the British Industrial Revolution, associates the rapid expansion in the stock of useful knowledge during the late seventeenth and eighteenth centuries with the Age of Enlightenment in Europe. If new production technology is to emerge and spread rapidly within a large geographical area, two conditions are required: (a) emergence of strong incentives for producing useful knowledge, and (b) falling costs of accessing and disseminating new knowledge. Mokyr finds evidence that both conditions were present during the Enlightenment in the latter half of the seventeenth and eighteenth centuries.[6] The period saw the gradual redirection of a significant component of the West European research program away from knowledge for its own sake with emphasis on theological and metaphysical issues toward knowledge useful for solving practical problems and raising living standards. The work and ideas of Sir Francis Bacon (1561–1626) symbolize the redirection of research toward modern science and technical change. Yet ideological incentives are only one part of the story. A scientific revolution also requires political conditions that do not punish and actually encourage those who seek practical knowledge. The travails of Galileo Galilei (1564–1642) and Giordano Bruno (1548–1600) are cases in point. We discuss the political environment below.

The latter of the two requirements is low costs of accessing new knowledge. Mokyr (2005a) documents how in the seventeenth century various methods for codifying and storing knowledge and information began to appear. The Age of Enlightenment saw a rapid increase in the publication of scientific pamphlets and periodicals; the evolution of informal networks of scholars; and the establishment of formal science academies, the first national academy being Royal Society of London for the Improvement of Natural Knowledge, established 1660, and the second Académie des sciences in Paris founded in 1666 by Louis XIV. Figure 2.1 reproduces one of the many indicators that Mokyr presents in support of his thesis: Scientific periodicals in Europe by year of first appearance.

Figure 2.1 shows that until around 1650 virtually no scientific periodicals had appeared; in the period 1741–50 approximately 100 new periodicals appear; and during the years 1791–1800 the number of new periodicals exceeds 500.

The evidence is hardly in doubt. Several reliable indicators show that in Western Europe during the Age of Enlightenment the production of useful knowledge surged and the costs of access fell. We have already mentioned the symbolic role of Francis Bacon in emphasizing useful knowledge. Yet an important issue remains unexamined: the political dimension. Why did the ruling elites of Western Europe tolerate relatively free scientific inquiry? In history, powerful rulers have been wary of new ideas about the social, spiritual and physical worlds and tried to control or repress scholarship. The rulers fear with some reason that unbridled new ideas may undermine the status quo and challenge their authority. What developments then opened a window of opportunity for independent

[6] Many scholars refer to the seventeenth century in Europe as Age of Reason and the eighteenth century as Age of Enlightenment. Others, as is done here, use the term Age of Enlightenment to represent the entire 200-year period.

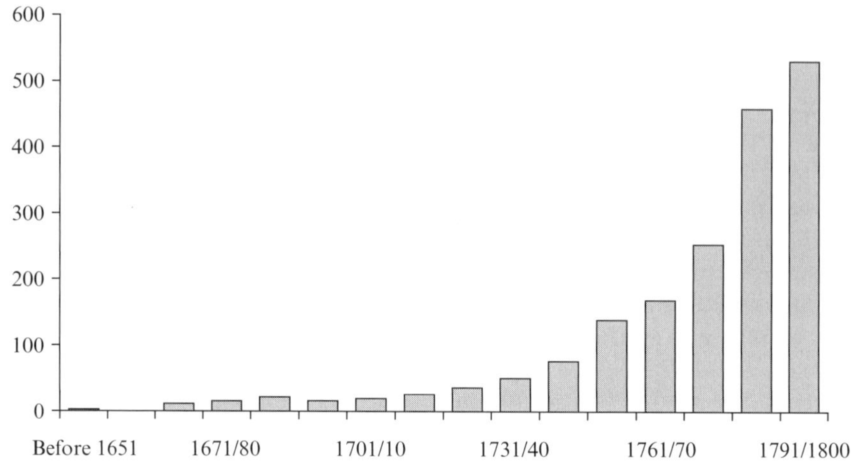

Source: Kronick, *Scientific and Technical Periodicals*; Mokyr 2005a, 331.

Figure 2.1 Scientific periodicals by year of first appearance

scholarship in Western Europe in the late seventeenth and eighteenth centuries? Mokyr (2005b) finds the answer in the political fragmentation of the region.

In this period Western Europe was politically fragmented and without an overarching and synchronizing center of power because of the diminished role of the Catholic Church.[7] With central authority absent, intellectuals and scholars who felt threatened by their local authorities had the option of moving between political units and playing one regime against another. Again Mokyr (2005b) presents data, now recording the movement of European intellectuals and scholars between European political units during the Enlightenment period. The data show high rates of mobility of scholars between European centers of learning but toward the end of the period mobility rates appear to fall in spite of a sharp reduction in transportation costs. Mokyr associates the decline in mobility with a gradual increase in the tolerance of new ideas in Western Europe, which would have lowered the demand for political refuge.[8]

The exponential rise of science and useful knowledge during the Enlightenment is often associated with the social norm of open science, which emerged in this period, replacing the institution of secrecy, which was the dominant strategy of medieval craft guilds as well as of scholars in general.[9] The economic rationale of secrecy was comparable to the motives behind the current phenomenon of trade secrets: they are attempts to privatize

---

[7] For instance, when Germany under the leadership of Prussia emerged as a nation state in 1871, it was through the unification of 39 independent states.

[8] Greater tolerance of scholars toward the end of the period could be related to rising opportunity cost of oppressing science and technology as the value of new discoveries steadily increased and became more obvious.

[9] Robert K. Merton (1973) in his book *The Sociology of Science* provides a classic analysis of the social norms that govern open science in an ideal world. He identifies four norms: universalism, communism, disinterestedness, and organized skepticism.

or internalize knowledge. The term 'open science' involves the practice of pursuing knowledge for its own sake (rather than for strategic motives), sharing findings with other members of the scholarly community, and submitting findings to peer reviews. Using my term, open science is a social technology with a history of being effective mechanism for organizing the production of scientific knowledge. Paul David (2007), the distinguished expert on the economics of science and technology, offers an interesting explanation of the historical origins of open science, which overlaps partly with Mokyr's (2005b) study of the intellectual origins of modern economic growth. Once again the argument centers on political fragmentation in early modern Europe, but David focuses his explanation on competition among princes and elites who sought prestige by surrounding themselves at court with artists, writers and scholars. A brief account of David's elaborate thesis must necessarily leave out many of his theoretical arguments and historical detail, including an elaborate explanation of the emergence in the late seventeenth century of formal scholarly societies and academies. His main argument, however, focuses on information asymmetry and problems of agency in the relationship between scientists or natural philosophers and their elite patrons.

The sixteenth and seventeenth centuries saw explosive growth in mathematical ideas. Leading scholars became increasingly involved with basic research in mathematics, which advanced rapidly, and moreover, natural scientists came to favor the language of mathematics in their studies. These producers of a public good, knowledge, needed somehow to make a living and the evolving system of court-patronage of the arts and sciences was a major source of support. In fragmented Western Europe competition among the princes for respect and awe took many forms. The princes built magnificent palaces and public buildings; they supported sculptors, painters and musicians and displayed their art; and they served as patrons to the prominent scientists of the day. However, the new math aggravated the information asymmetry between scientists and their patrons. The princes and their advisers were incapable of evaluating scholars who used complex mathematics, which meant for the elites that their risk of offering patronage to charlatans had substantially increased.[10] David (2007) theorizes that the social norm of open science and peer review emerged to ease the measurement problem of overseeing scholars. Facing serious problems in measuring directly the quality of scholarly services, the elites were willing to support the norm of open science and rely (at least partly) on indirect measurement by the scholarly community or peer review. Yet direct measurement did not entirely disappear. The circumstances sometimes permitted the rulers to get direct impressions of the importance of scientific findings. David (2007) cites the case of Galileo Galilei who advanced his career by strategically presenting rulers with powerful telescopes, a new invention, so they could see for themselves. It has even been suggested that Galileo's troubles with the Church were brought on not only by the Jesuit Order but also by fellow professors who were jealous of Galileo's aggressive pursuit of patrons and his successful career moves (David 2007, 44–9; Westfall 1985).

---

[10] Scientists were also hired for outright practical purposes. They were sought for technical contributions or problem solving, for instance, in military engineering, hydraulic engineering (canals, irrigation systems, aqueducts), navigation, and the new scientific cartography. Information asymmetry between agents and patrons was also increasing in practical applications of science (David 2007).

The Mokyr mechanism for allowing scholars to avoid political repression and the David mechanism for lowering the cost of agency are not mutually exclusive explanations of the rise of *A*; in fact the two explanations reinforce each other. Not all rulers would see scholar X or discovery Y as a threat to their regime; scholars who felt threatened could exploit the elites' competition for prestige and move to a friendly jurisdiction; open science and peer review made it easier for a prince to evaluate immigrating scholars.

For more than three centuries the accumulation of useful or practical knowledge in the Western World has been a monotonic process; we have neither seen stagnation nor reversals that were common in earlier historical settings, for instance in China. Various factors have prevented major reversals: the codification of knowledge through various means, its diffuse possession, competition, and the Western entrepreneurial spirit. David (2007) and Mokyr (2005a) both recognize that if their speculations are correct, namely that the *A* revolution in Western Europe is rooted in political fragmentation prior to the consolidation of the nation state, modern prosperity is a delayed gift to the modern era by West European feudalism and the ruins of the Roman Empire.

The steady increase in *A* has raised living standards in a major way but only for one segment of the human population, the inhabitants of the industrial countries. The gap between rich and poor countries is a measure of our limited knowledge and control of social technologies. Relative to the growth in *A*, social science knowledge has grown at a modest pace in the last 300 years. We understand only imperfectly how power politics and inhospitable social institutions block economic progress and make some countries fall behind. Even less is known about appropriate social technologies for reforming imperfect institutions and neutralizing destructive political systems. There is a fundamental uncertainty about possibilities and limits of reform.

5. FICKLE, FLIGHTY *A*: LESSONS FROM THE SECOND INDUSTRIAL REVOLUTION 1860–1914

In this section I discuss two important lessons from the Second Industrial Revolution. First I briefly introduce the dramatic experience of England toward the end of the nineteenth century when the country lost its industrial leadership. The other lesson concerns the uncertain and delayed impact of general-purpose technologies caused by time lags in discovering and implementing useful applications. Electricity and digital electronics are prime examples of general-purpose technologies, representing two different epochs.

To maintain worldwide leadership in *A* over a span of several generations a country requires not only foresight but also and above all adaptable social institutions. In the early stages of an industrial and technological revolution special interests typically emerge and gradually acquire enough power and authority to safeguard the status quo. These forces see it in their interest to oppose new industrial developments that could undermine their economic base. Economic success can also make the political and industrial leadership of a country complacent and inattentive to new opportunities. During the so-called Second Industrial Revolution 1860–1914, social rigidities and complacency swiftly and unexpectedly deprived England of its leadership in *A* and gave it to Germany and the United States.

Consider the new chemical industries that played a critical role in the Second Industrial

Revolution. Alfred DuPont Chandler, Jr. (1992), sometimes considered the father of modern business history, has examined how England lost its leadership in synthetic dyes. British scientists and entrepreneurs pioneered the technology for synthetic dyes and the huge British textile industry was the largest market in the world for dyes. The production of synthetic dyes required high quality coal and Britain was the largest supplier in Europe of this input. In the 1870s the new dye industry in Britain had almost every advantage. Germany, however, was more flexible, relying on foresighted cooperation between industry, government and technical universities. The provision of appropriate technical education was one of the key elements in Germany's success; novel business organization (new social technology) was another. By 1900 the leadership in synthetic dyes had moved to Germany. In 1913 some 160 000 tons of dyes were produced worldwide. Thereof German firms made 140 000 tons or 88 percent. The British produced only 4100 tons (Chandler 1992, 90–91). The synthetic dyes story and countless similar lessons tell us that A is a fickle visitor.

Industrial revolutions involve both limited-purpose and general-purpose technologies. The discovery of potential applications of new general-purpose technologies and their implementation is a long process that usually spans decades. The lags between invention and application are caused by many factors, including long and uncertain learning processes, high adjustment costs, and perhaps mental inertia. Electric power, a general-purpose technology, is the symbol of the Second Industrial Revolution. Historians of electricity have established that in the United States it took about half a century of innovations and costly investments before electricity had made its full impact on productivity. For instance, prior to electrification factories relied on the power of water or steam, which usually involved a centralized power source. Electric power made it often efficient for factories to equip each machine with its own electric motor, which provided opportunities for reorganizing the entire layout of the production process. The adjustments could be very costly, requiring new factory buildings and major learning and training efforts by management and workers (Devine 1983; David 1990).

6. WHITHER A? ARE WE IN THE EARLY STAGES OF A NEW INDUSTRIAL REVOLUTION?

The last half of the twentieth century saw major innovations that include both specific and general-purpose technologies. It is often said that new information and communication technology is the symbol of our era but, as often before, we do not really know where we are heading. Are we at the dawn of an economic revolution, somewhat like the innocent Adam Smith was at the end of the eighteenth century, or is recent talk about the Knowledge Economy only empty words? Robert Solow (1987, 2002) has said: 'You can see the computer age everywhere but in the productivity statistics.'[11] Was he right?

History tells us that the impact of an A revolution is not limited to raising y, average

---

[11] Solow made this famous statement in *New York Review of Books* on 12 July 1987. In a 2002 interview in *The Region*, a publication of the Federal Reserve Bank of Minneapolis, Solow had not changed his mind.

output per worker. Revolutionary new technology lowers costs and raises the quality of many existing products, gives us new goods and services, and transforms the organization of business, politics, and social affairs. The new information technology gathered momentum in the last decades of the twentieth century and is gradually transforming a variety of products and industries, ranging from automobiles to biotechnology. The distinguished economist Robert Gordon (2000) argues that recent changes in *A* are qualitatively less significant than the inventions of the Second Industrial Revolution, 1860–1914, which profoundly changed living conditions in the West with novelties such as electricity, the telephone, radio, and the internal combustion engine. Is Gordon right? Can he forecast what innovations in commodities and organization the next half-century will bring? I doubt it. In fact, economists and other social scientists can do little more than speculate about marginal changes in technologies, products, and organization. In recent decades various studies have emerged that tentatively examine implications of the new information technology. I conclude by introducing a few research questions that the new *A* has inspired.

In advanced industrial countries the structure of property rights is usually clearly defined, well enforced and relatively efficient. Major technological change, however, may require substantial revision of property rights in significant sectors of the economy; adjustments to new and uncertain circumstances that often involve trial by error. Intellectual assets are non-rival in use; they often involve huge fixed or set-up costs (for instance genetics-based drugs or computer software) but low (often close to zero) marginal costs of reproduction. An optimal regime for intellectual property must solve a complicated dilemma: to create incentives for the inventors of knowledge assets, for instance through patents (monopoly rights), and also secure efficient allocation of the knowledge assets through pricing close to marginal costs (competitive conditions). Posner (2005) argues convincingly that the task of creating optimal regime for intellectual property goes far beyond our cognitive capacities.[12] Posner is more optimistic about the capacity of scholars to evaluate marginal changes in intellectual property regimes: whether particular changes are likely to increase or decrease the efficiency of the system.

The recent extension of patents to basic research, even to research undertaken in laboratories at publicly funded universities, has created intense controversy among experts. The critics of recent laws extending patent rights claim that over-patenting will create anticommons effects, a problem that is symmetric to the well-known open commons effects that involve waste through over-utilization of resources (Heller and Eisenberg 1998; Buchanan and Yoon 2000). The anticommons condition involves excessive property rights and occurs when a large number of owners hold various rights to the same asset and potential users cannot make efficient use of the resource because of high transaction costs in acquiring the necessary rights.[13] In theory and depending on the cost of transacting, it is sometimes possible for firms to act strategically and limit

[12] An optimal intellectual property regime would probably require a large number of subsystems designed separately for each type of knowledge assets.

[13] Heller (1998) was the first to develop the anticommons concept in a paper entitled 'The Tragedy of the Anti-Commons: Property in the Transition from Marx to Markets.' In developing the concept, Heller was inspired by the puzzle of empty storefronts and full kiosks in Moscow during the early and mid-1990s.

the anticommons effects of new laws and regulations. The literature provides evidence of firms in the biotechnology industry that have actually invested in antiproperty by organizing open access commons for patentable findings in their sector, particularly for potential inputs located upstream in the production chain (Merges 2004).

Rapid technical change can also challenge the system of property rights by suddenly creating strong demand for resources that until recently had little commercial value and were therefore not subject to clearly specified property rights. In these situations new legislation or judicial rulings often have vast implications for new industries, and those implications are not always well understood *ex ante*. The biogenetics industry, it is often claimed, owes its existence in no small part to divided court decisions concerning ownership of biological materials.[14]

Network industries with scale economies on the demand side are relatively common among the new growth industries (Varian et al. 2005). With strong demand-side economies of scale, the demand curve for the output has initially an upward slope because the commodity becomes more valuable as more customers use it. These conditions hold for computer operating systems but also for fax machines. Economic analysis shows that in network industries welfare may fall as the number of new entrants increases, if the products of the various firms are incompatible in use. In these industries competition *for* the market becomes more important for welfare than competition *in* the market. Standardization is also a question of great importance. The special features of the new network industries seem to call for some rethinking of standard competition and antitrust policy (Economides 2006).

The economics of Internet markets is an emerging field of research (Ellison and Ellison 2005). It is reasonable to ask, for instance, whether exchange on the Internet or exchange in the regular market place more resembles the model of perfect competition. We may also want to know whether Internet marketing is likely to enable fine-tuned price discrimination or whether through anonymity it protects buyers who belong to social groups that traditionally pay relatively high prices, for instance for new automobiles or groceries. When combined with the Internet, digitalization of music, pictures and printed matter creates a whole range of issues concerning adjustments in property rights and business organization. The new technology has rekindled passionate debates about private, public and communal ownership, a common theme during the Second Industrial Revolution, although now the debate focuses on knowledge assets and not on coal and steel factories. Many scholars worry about privacy issues; whether digital technology in the hands of the state or large corporations will eventually undermine our privacy and freedom (Benkler 2006). Concurrently, diligent bloggers invite the world into their personal life.

The new technology also raises new questions in economic geography, for instance about urbanization and location of industry. The British Industrial Revolution introduced centralized manufacturing plants; for most people it separated the home from the workplace; and it moved workers from rural areas into urban centers, depopulating the countryside. Theoretically the new information and communications technology may gradually reverse the urbanization trend and send a substantial part of the workforce back home and into rural areas, away from the cities. Relocation to the home and away

---

[14] See essays by various authors in Ginsburg and Dreyfuss, eds. (2006).

from offices, factories and other external work places is an efficient alternative only for workers who can work at home approximately as effectively as they now do in centralized workplaces. Such relocation is obviously not an option for all job categories; for instance, most service employees cannot work at home. For potential home workers the critical question is whether new communication technologies, such as the Internet and video conferencing, substitute effectively for the synergy of direct contacts when joint tasks are involved (Leamer and Storper 2001). The answer depends on the psychology of learning and group dynamics but also on the quality of the communications technology, social norms and the nature of joint tasks.[15] Those who are able and willing to work at home may or may not desire to relocate outside major urban areas. The decision to leave the city depends in part on how the new communication technology affects the relative costs and benefits of living (and consuming) in rural and urban areas. The Internet, for instance, can provide various forms of entertainment in remote areas but it can also make consuming in the city more efficient and enjoyable, for instance through homepages of restaurants, theaters, and specialty stores (Sinai & Waldfogel 2003). Finally, the new technology affects economic geography on a global scale by lowering the cost of outsourcing across national borders. The economic, political and social consequences of the recent Globalization are only partly understood.

7. CONCLUSION

The unbearable lightness of *A* blurs our vision of the road ahead. We can see the big picture only when looking back and then not very clearly. Yet it is obvious, to cite the Chinese, that we live in interesting times.

BIBLIOGRAPHY

Ashton, T.S. (1997 [1964]), *The Industrial Revolution 1760–1830*, Oxford: Oxford University Press.

Benkler, Y. (2006), *The Wealth of Networks: How Social Production Transforms Markets and Freedom*, New Haven, CT: Yale University Press.

Buchanan, J.M. and Y.J. Yoon (2000), 'Symmetric tragedies: Commons and anticommons', *Journal of Law and Economics*, **43**(1), 1–13.

Chandler, A.D. (1992), 'Organizational capabilities and the economic history of the industrial enterprise', *Journal of Economic Perspectives* , **6**(3), 79–100.

Clement, Douglas (2002), 'Interview with Robert Solow', *The Region (the Publication of the Federal Reserve Bank of Minneapolis)*, September.

David, P.A. (1990), 'The dynamo and the computer: A historical perspective on the modern productivity paradox', *The American Economic Review*, **80**(2), 355–61.

David, P.A. (2007), 'The historical origins of "open science". An essay on patronage, reputation, and common agency contracting in the scientific revolution', Stanford University and University of Oxford. Stanford: Working Paper.

Devine, W.D. (1983), 'From shafts to wires: historical perspectives on electrification', *Journal of Economic History*, **43**(2), 347–72.

[15] The new technology raises of course questions about reorganization of education and the extent to which the new communications technology can effectively replace the classroom.

Economides, N. (2006), 'Public policy in network industries'. Law and Economics Research Paper, New York University, School of Law, New York.
Eggertsson, T. (2005), *Imperfect Institutions: Possibilities and Limits of Reform*, New York: Cambridge University Press.
Ellison, G. and S.F. Ellison (2005), 'Lessons about markets from the Internet', *Journal of Economic Perspectives*, **19**(2), 139–58.
Ginsburg, J. and R. Dreyfuss, eds. (2006), *Intellectual Property Stories*, New York: Foundation Press.
Gordon, R.J. (2000), 'Does the new economy measure up to the great inventions of the past?' *The Journal of Economic Perspectives*, **14**(4), 49–74.
Heller, M.A. (1998), 'The tragedy of the anticommons. property in the transition from Marx to markets', *Harvard Law Review*, **111**(3), 622–88.
Heller, M.A. and R.S. Eisenberg (1998), 'Can patents deter innovation? The anticommons in biomedical research', *Science*, **280**, 698–701.
Hull, B.B. and F. Bold (1994), 'Hell, religion and cultural change', *Journal of Institutional and Theoretical Economics*, **150**, 447–64.
Koebner, R. (1959), 'Adam Smith and the Industrial Revolution', *Economic History Review*, **11**, 381–91.
Kronick, D.A. (1961), *Scientific and Technical Periodicals of the Seventeenth and Eighteenth Centuries*, Lanham, MD: Scarecrow Press.
Leamer, E.E. and M. Storper (2001), *The Economic Geography of the Internet Age*, Cambridge, MA: National Bureau of Economic Research.
Machlup, F. (1962), *The Production and Distribution of Knowledge in the United States*, Princeton, NJ: Princeton University Press.
Merges, R.P. (2004), 'A New Dynamism in the Public Domain', *University of Chicago Law Review*, **71**, 183–203.
Merton, R.K. (1973), *The Sociology of Science*, Chicago, IL: University of Chicago Press.
Mokyr, J. (2005a), 'The intellectual origins of modern economic growth', *The Journal of Economic History*, **65**(2), 285–351.
Mokyr, J. (2005b), 'Mobility, creativity, and technological development: David Hume, Immanuel Kant and the economic development of Europe. Working Paper. Evanston, IL: Departments of Economics and History, Northwestern University.
Nelson, R.R. (1997), 'The agenda for growth theory: A different point of view', *Cambridge Journal of Economics*, **22**, 497–520.
Nelson, R.R. and S.G. Winter (1982), *An Evolutionary Theory of Economic Change*, Cambridge, MA: Harvard University Press.
Posner, R.A. (1980), 'A theory of primitive society, with special reference to law', *Journal of Political Economy*, **23**(1), 1–53.
Posner, R.A. (2005), 'Intellectual property: The law and economics approach', *Journal of Economic Perspectives*, **19**(2), 57–73.
Romer, P.M. (1994), 'The origins of endogenous growth', *Journal of Economic Perspectives*, **8**(1), 3–22.
Schumpeter, J.A. (2005 [1939]), *Business Cycles: A Theoretical, Historical, and Statistical Analysis of the Capitalist Process*, 2 vol., Eastford, CT: Martino Publishing.
Sinai, T. and J. Waldfogel (2003), *Geography and the Internet: Is the Internet a Substitute or a Complement for Cities?*, Cambridge, MA: National Bureau of Economic Research.
Solow, R.M. (1956), 'A contribution to the theory of economic growth', *Quarterly Journal of Economics*, **70**, 65–94.
Solow, R.M. (1957), 'Technical change and the aggregate production function', *Review of Economics and Statistics*, **39**, 312–20.
Varian, H.R., J. Farrell, and C. Shapiro (2005), *The Economics of Information Technology: An Introduction*, New York: Cambridge University Press.
Westfall, R.S. (1985), 'Science and patronage: Galileo and the telescope', *Isis*, **76**, 11–30.

3. The Law Merchant's story: how romantic is it?

Bruce L. Benson

Lex Mercatoria, the 'Law Merchant,' usually refers to the rules and procedures developed within merchant communities to support trade in medieval Europe, without the assistance of government.[1] While a very large literature describes and analyses *Lex Mercatoria*, an expanding literature argues that these descriptions are significantly over-romanticized stories, if not outright fabrications.[2] Some of the controversy reflects an apparent lack of familiarity with or misinterpretation of historical context or evidence, but much of the conflict appears to be definitional (Coquillette 1987: 291–2; Epstein 2004: 3–4).[3] The following presentation offers a focused examination of key aspects of *Lex Mercatoria* in an attempt to direct the debate toward actual tenets of and evidence supporting the story.

Section 1 below focuses on definitions of law, customary law, merchant, and Law Merchant that generally apply in the literature. After that, an overview of the medieval *Lex Mercatoria* is presented in Section 2. Section 3 concludes.

1. WHAT IS THE LAW MERCHANT?

Epstein (2004: 3) notes that those:

---

1 *Lex Mercatoria* also labels certain rules and procedures of modern international commercial activity. This modern Law Merchant is not discussed, but see Benson (2009).

2 E.g., Volckart and Mangels (1999), Donahue (2004), Kadens (2004), Drahozal (2005), and Sachs (2006).

3 The controversy actually appears to be part of the wider ideological debate about law, politics and legal regulation. The underlying issue is, *should* private substitutes for government law be allowed? Drahozal (2005: 525), for example states: 'Customary law, Benson contends, is superior to publically produced law because "politically dictated rules are not designed to support the market process; in fact, government made law is likely to do precisely the opposite".' This is only one of the reasons I offer to 'contend' that customary law is superior, but without recognizing others, Drahozal dismisses this *deduction* with arguments that the Law Merchant is actually an example of 'lawlessness' as merchants 'usurp' or 'undercut the regulatory authority of national governments and may result in underenforcement of national law.' Then he contends that the modern Law Merchant is largely irrelevant anyway, by defining the term in a different way than I do. The normative issue is not directly addressed here. Instead, relevant definitions are clarified and evidence is presented to show that the Law Merchant was a very important institutional arrangement. Hopefully, this will force those who claim to refute the Law Merchant story, to criticize the actual story rather than redefining 'Law Merchant' to create a 'straw man' that never existed. Benson (2009) directly rebuts critics, in part by revealing these straw men.

> who deny the independent existence of the Law Merchant are those who adopt, often implicitly, some version of Austinian theory that marks law as a general command of the sovereign. Those who support it tend to take . . . a different view of law which looks at it as a set of immanent principles that is so powerful that all sovereigns feel obliged to adopt it. So framed, the debate is as much about the definition of law as it is about the historical origins and development of the Law Merchant itself.

Despite recognizing this fundamental definitional issue, however, Epstein implies that these 'powerful' principles are not 'law' until they are recognized by sovereigns. Under this assumption, stateless customary-law systems, widely examined in the anthropology of law (e.g., Pospisil 1971, 1978), cannot be 'law,' by definition. Nonetheless, the rules and procedures labeled 'customary law' significantly influence behavior. Understanding *Lex Mercatoria* requires an understanding of customary rules and procedures.

1.1 Customary Law

Hayek (1973: 96–97) explains that many issues of 'law' are not:

> whether the parties have abused anybody's will, but whether their actions have conformed to expectations which other parties had reasonably formed because they corresponded to the practices on which the everyday conduct of the members of the group was based. The significance of customs here is that they give rise to expectations that guide people's actions, and what will be regarded as binding will therefore be those practices that everybody counts on being observed and which thereby condition the success of most activities.

Similarly, Fuller (1981: 213) notes that, 'We sometimes speak of customary law as offering an unwritten code of conduct. The word *code* is appropriate here because what is involved is not simply a negation, . . . but of this negation, the meaning it confers on foreseeable and approved actions, which then furnish a point of orientation for ongoing interactive responses.' Customary law involves more than rules of behavior, however (Pospisil 1978). Indeed, customary rules and procedures often can be characterized as 'legal systems' from Hart's (1961) positivist perspective (Benson 1989, 1990), with primary rules of obligation, as well as secondary rules of change, adjudication and recognition.

Flexibility and change often characterize customary systems (Pospisil 1971; Fuller 1981; Benson 1989, 1990). For instance, if conditions change and a set of individuals decide that, for their purposes, a new behavior rule will support more benefits than the current rule, they can voluntarily agree to follow (contract to adopt) the new rule within their own interactions. Thus, an existing rule is replaced by an obligation, but only for the contracting parties. This change occurs without prior consent of, or simultaneous recognition by, anyone else. Individuals who interact with these parties learn about their contractual innovation, however, and/or members of the community observe its results. If the results are more desirable than outcomes under older custom, the rule can be rapidly emulated. As Fuller (1981: 224–5) explains, 'If we permit ourselves to think of contract law as the "law" that parties themselves bring into existence by their agreement, the transition from customary law to contract law becomes a very easy one indeed.' In fact, contract and custom are intertwined:

> if problems arise which are left without verbal solution in the parties' contract these will commonly be resolved by asking what 'standard practice' is with respect to the issues . . . In such a case it is difficult to know whether to say that . . . the parties became subject to a governing body of customary law or to say that they have by tacit agreement incorporated standard practice into the terms of the contract.
>
> . . . [In fact,] . . . the parties may have conducted themselves toward one another in such a way that one can say that a tacit exchange of promises has taken place. Here the analogy between contract and customary law approaches identity (Fuller 1981: 176).

Negotiation (contracting) also is the most important method for initiating change in customary law (Fuller 1981: 157).

As conditions change, a gap in existing customary rules can be revealed because a dispute arises. Negotiation is the primary means of dispute resolution, reinforcing the contention that contracting is a primary mechanism for initiating change in customary law. If direct negotiation fails, however, the parties to a dispute often turn to arbitration or mediation. Many different procedures are observed in different customary communities (Benson 1990), so rather than explore all possibilities, medieval Law Merchants procedures are described in Section 2. Nonetheless, a new customary rule might be suggested by resulting third-party dispute resolution (Fuller 1981: 110–111). Unlike modern common law precedent, however, the resolution only applies to the parties in the dispute. If it suggests behavior that effectively facilitates desirable interactions, the implied rule can be adopted and spread through the community. In situations where contract is widely employed, however, adjudication can be a trivial source of change. Arbitrators may simply apply general default rules based on equity considerations.

Both 'positive' and 'negative' incentives to recognize rules and accept dispute resolutions arise in customary law. These include bilateral repeated dealing which creates both trust and the ability to threaten punishment with tit-for-tat strategies. Multilateral webs of interactions based on reciprocities accompanied by development of communications mechanisms and investments in reputations, also enhance the potential for voluntary interaction while simultaneously creating threats of punishment by the spread of information about misbehavior, leading to social sanctions including ostracism. Examples are detailed in Section 2.

Even in primitive societies, entrepreneurs establish extensive trade networks that cross community boundaries. Institutionalized rules and procedures also facilitate the expansion of inter-community interaction (Benson 1988). Groups need not formally 'merge' and accept a common set of rules. Individuals only have to expect each other to recognize specific rules pertaining to the types of inter-group interactions that evolve. Indeed, a 'jurisdictional hierarchy' may arise wherein each group has its own rules and procedures for intra-group relationships, with separate and possibly different rules and procedures applying for inter-group relations (Pospisil 1971; Benson 1988, 1990). This hierarchy does not create appellate courts, however, as the inter-group institutions have no role in any community's internal relationships. Communities also generally become mutual support groups with reciprocal obligations to assist each other in the pursuit of justice against outsiders, but they also provide insurance for one another in order to pay outsiders who are victimized by a member, thereby maintaining the group's reputation, and increasing the credibility of members' promises. Intra-community recognition is largely based on reciprocities, trust, and reputation, while inter-group recognition may also require bonding, group reputations, and surety commitments. Thus, customary law often is 'polycentric,' with multiple parallel 'local' jurisdictions, as well as overlapping jurisdictions supporting inter-community interactions. Many intra-group rules will be commonly held, of course, and emulation also will occur where differences initially exist but individuals perceive superior arrangements among other groups (Benson 1988, 1989), so many common customs can exist in an extensive polycentric web of communities (Benson 1988).

A crucial implication of this discussion is that understanding customary law requires consideration of different sources of information than those used to understand government law. A relatively good picture of government-imposed rules might be obtained by reading legislation, administrative documents, and court opinions, but customary rules generally are not recorded, either as codes or judicial opinions. Some obligations may appear as standard contract clauses, but contracts typically do not specify widely understood practices and usage. Therefore, behavior has to be observed to conceptualize customary rules. When observation is not possible (e.g., historical systems), the best one can generally do is to read contracts, letters and other documents that might reveal behavior. Such documents only provide an incomplete snapshot of customary law, however, so even if they are available, a more complete understanding requires theoretical analysis informed by examinations of other customary law systems.[4]

1.2 Custom versus Authority

Pospisil (1971, 1978) distinguishes between 'legal' arrangements that evolve from the top down through command and coercion (e.g., Austinian law), which he calls 'authoritarian law,' and customary law systems that evolve from the bottom up through voluntary interaction. Pospisil's distinction suggests that customary law may conflict with authoritarian law. When this occurs, an authority backed by coercive power may attempt to assert jurisdiction, but this can have very different impacts, depending on the options the customary-law community has. If the authority is strong enough, the customary community might be forced to accept the commands. Another possibility is that customary rules and procedures evolve that allow the customary community to avoid authoritarian supervision (Bernstein 1992; Benson 1995, 2006). This may involve moving 'underground,' making its rules and procedures difficult to observe in order to raise the costs of enforcement for the authority. If the customary community (and its wealth) is geographically mobile, however, members may simply move outside the authority's jurisdiction. The threat to move can significantly constrain authoritarian attempts to displace a customary system. If the sovereign wants to avoid an exodus, she may even offer to assist in enforcing the customary rules, or explicitly codify them. She still may capture benefits including revenues, either directly from taxes on the customary law community, or indirectly because of a positive impact of that community on other less-mobile sources of wealth. Once custom is absorbed, and the customary procedures atrophy, however, the authority

[4] See Benson (1990) where well-documented customary systems are discussed to establish basic principles about customary law, before examining historical systems including the medieval Law Merchant.

may amend or replace customary rules, although the ability to do so depends on the costs of reinvigorating customary institutions, and on the mobility of the community.

One of Berman's primary purposes is to illustrate that there was a plurality of distinct but interdependent legal systems in medieval Europe, some authoritarian and some customary, and that an understanding of their various behavioral implications leads to important insights about the interactions between them and the influence each has on the others (Berman 1983: 10):

> The very complexity of a common legal *order* containing diverse legal *systems* contributes to legal sophistication. Which court has jurisdiction? Which law is applicable? How are legal differences to be reconciled? Behind the technical questions lay important political and economic considerations. . . . The pluralism of . . . law, . . . has been . . . a source of development, or growth – legal growth as well as political and economic growth.

Also note that many of these legal systems were polycentric. Different royal law, manorial law, and local custom applied in different areas although they often had similar rules.

1.3 Lex Mercatoria

Now we can begin to define the Law Merchant, although additional characteristics are revealed in the next section.[5] *Lex Mercatoria* is:

> (1) a distinct, but not independent, system of polycentric customary law evolving spontaneously from the bottom up through the interactions of merchants in pursuit of the universal objective to enhance opportunities for voluntary trade, consisting of
> (2) primary rules of obligation including both long-standing custom and evolving commercial practices and usage that increase opportunities to contract by increasing the credibility of promises, as well as secondary rules of
> (3) change initialized through negotiation, and perhaps dispute resolution, followed by voluntary emulation of those practices that best enhance opportunities to engage in trade;
> (4) adjudication through processes like mediation, arbitration, participatory courts, and other available courts willing to quickly and equitably apply its rules (see below), and
> (5) recognition arising from positive incentives to expand trading opportunities (and merchant well-being) through repeat-dealing, reciprocities, reputation and surety mechanisms, and the accompanying negative incentives created by spontaneous sanctions like varying degrees of ostracism (see below), but
> (6) the Law Merchant's jurisdiction is functionally defined rather than geographically defined, so
> (7) this system applies across boundaries of geographically focused but functionally broad political jurisdictions that support objectives differing from those supported by the Law Merchant, so
> (8) these different legal systems often interact in various complementary and/or competitive ways over time and space, so the Law Merchant's primary and secondary rules both influence and are influenced by other legal systems.

The jurisdiction of the Law Merchant is limited to the commercial interactions between merchants, so one more definitional issue arises.

---

[5] *Lex Mercatoria* had many names in literature about or from the medieval period, including 'merchants' law,' 'custom of merchants,' 'customary law of merchants,' 'method of merchants,' 'mercantile law,' 'the way of the trade,' and 'law of the fair.' There also are many definitions of *Lex Mercatoria*, particularly by critics of the Law-Merchant literature. These definitions are not examined here, but see Benson (2009).

1.4 Merchants

As Bewes (1923: 15) explains, 'there would be less confusion if it were always realized that the law merchant only applies as between merchants when concerned in mercantile transactions.' Who are these merchants? In medieval Europe they were individuals repeatedly engaged in long-distance trade as middlemen wholesalers (Kadens 2004: 45).[6] Their business activities typically involved border crossing so they bought and sold in different geographic (royal, manorial, urban) jurisdictions. Local craftsmen who sold to wholesalers, and local retailers who purchased from middlemen, were not 'merchants.'[7]

As Greif (2006: 61) reports, 'eleventh-century trade was free, private, and competitive. . . . [T]here were few official restrictions that fettered migration or the transfer of raw materials, finished goods, or money across the Mediterranean.' Freedom continued to characterize merchants for several centuries in many parts of Europe (Volckart and Mangels 1999, 437). This point has significant implications for interpreting various actions by medieval kings and other authorities in their relationships with merchants.

2. MEDIEVAL *LEX MERCATORIA*

Substantial technological change in agricultural production occurred in Europe during the eleventh and twelfth centuries. Less labor was needed to produce sufficient food and clothing, individuals increasingly specialized, and many moved into towns. Trade is required with specialization. As wealth increased demands for spices, dye-stuff, cordovan and other 'luxury' items available in the Mediterranean (generally through trade with Middle-Eastern merchants) increased in other parts of Europe. Similarly, the demand for cloth and other products from Northern Europe increased in more southerly regions. As long-distance trade in these goods expanded, growing numbers of merchants from widely dispersed parts of Europe began trading with one another at fairs (Face 1958). These merchants often spoke different languages and had different cultural and ethnic backgrounds. In addition, geographic distances often inhibited direct communication between merchants, as agents represented them at fairs. Such transactions costs had to be reduced so merchants could insure credibility of promises and engage in contractual trading. 'Markets do not necessarily spontaneously emerge in response to opportunities for profitable exchange. For exchange to transpire, institutions that protect property rights and provide contract enforcement must be in place' (Greif 2006: 56).

Credibility can be established through knowledge, trust, or recourse (Benson 1999), and merchants pursued improvements in all three. While the following discussion has examples of innovations to increase knowledge and enhance trust, the focus is on

---

[6] By the late 1600s the term 'had begun to be applied to all those who bought and sold for a living: retailers, wholesalers, and craftsmen, whether they were involved in local or intercommunal commerce' (Kadens 2004: 45).

[7] Non-merchants could *choose* the Law Merchant's jurisdiction (Bewes 1923): 'The word "merchant" strictly meant a person dedicating himself to commerce, but commercial courts often tried cases where one solitary act of trading had taken place; though this was an assumption of jurisdiction contrary to the claims of the civil courts.'

recourse: law, essentially to substitute for limited knowledge and trust. As Berman (1983: 333) emphasizes, 'the basic concepts and institutions of . . . *lex mercatoria* . . . were formed' during the eleventh and twelfth centuries.[8]

2.1 Documentary Evidence

Evidence of the early emergence of the medieval Law Merchant is sparse, in large part because it was customary law, unrecorded and not understood by many outside observers. Writing around 1020, for instance, Alpert of Metz described merchants in the town of Tiel as 'men unaccustomed to discipline, who judge suits not according to law but according to inclination . . .' (Pertz 1925: 118). In other words, merchants did not follow what Alpert considered to be law.[9] In addition, Alpert, who was a monk, clearly did not understand the rules that formed the basis of merchant dispute resolutions. Nonetheless, merchants clearly played by their own rules.

There are even earlier documents from the first half of the ninth century suggesting that merchants were using different legal procedures than those employed in the local communities (Kadens 2004: 43, note 17). Similarly, Greif (2006: 58–77) examines eleventh-century documents produced by Maghribi traders, a group of Jewish merchants who moved to Tunisia, part of the Maghrib or Muslim West, in the tenth century because of political insecurity in Baghdad. When the Maghrib capital relocated to Cairo near the end of the tenth century, Jewish traders who followed became known as Maghribi traders. They deposited thousands of contracts, price lists, letters between traders, accounts and other documents in the *geniza* of a synagogue in Fustat (old Cairo). Quoting from various Maghribi documents, Greif (2006: 70) explains that,

> Given the state of communication and transportation technology in the eleventh century, it is not surprising that the Maghribi traders . . . employed a set of cultural rules or behavior – merchants' law . . .
>
> The importance of the merchants' law in determining expectations about and attitudes toward an agent's behavior is reflected in the letter written by Maymum ben Khalpha to Naharay ben Nissim. In discussing the conflict between Naharay and his agent, Maymum justifies the agent's actions by arguing that the agent 'did something which is imposed by the trade and the communication [system; what you asked him to do] contradicts the merchants' law.' . . . In another letter a 'very angry' merchant accused his business associate of taking 'actions [that] are not those of a merchant.'

Greif (2006: 71) also notes that numerous early Islamic documents indicate that Islamic law was not applied to merchants because of the 'custom of the merchants.' Clearly, 'merchants' law' was not unique to the Maghribi.

Similarly, Face (1958: 438) draws from twelfth-century documents from Genoa and finds that many substantive merchant rules (e.g., how to develop and interpret credit instruments, partnership arrangements, contracts with agents and with transportation specialists) were

---

8 The foundations of the medieval Law Merchant arose much earlier (Bewes 1923; Benson 2009).

9 Perhaps he was referring to Canon law, local manorial, or early royal law; see Berman (1983).

> fully developed by the year 1180. [But] *One must look far behind that date to discover the origin of these practices.* The pattern of the fair, with all its concomitant devices of business and financial organization, was worked out at some time too early for any written records to have survived. . . . A system so complex, so carefully worked out, could not have sprung up within a few years. [Emphasis added]

2.2 Universal and Polycentric

At any point in time, variation in some rules and practices existed across merchant communities (Benson 1999; Kadens 2004). The foundational principles of the Law Merchant were universal, however:

> within the appointed area of the Law Merchant no one wants to depart from the norm of freedom of contract . . . With that concurrence as to ends, huge sources of potential disagreement just disappear from view . . . There might not be perfect agreement among the practitioners . . . [about] what ideal customs are. But this fundamental agreement on ends was universal . . . Any differences in local culture could not push anyone away from basic principles (Epstein 2004: 8–9).

Kadens (2004) depicts the customs of medieval merchants as layered, and notes that the 'top layer' was 'similar across Europe' (Kadens 2004: 56). Furthermore,

> The fact that customs were local or trade-specific did not mean that they had no effect on commerce in general. The Italian wool buyer in England followed English custom; the Fleming who purchases a bill of exchange in Paris followed the local *usance*. One of the prevailing tropes in works by merchants on trade practices is the discussion of the rules one must follow in different locales. Knowing those rules and working within them was part of how a trader abided by the law merchant (Kadens 2004: 62–3).

Indeed, since some rules varied from place to place, itinerant consul often travelled with groups of traders of a particular nationality, specializing in determining the rules and practices in the markets and fairs they visited, and watching over the community's interests (Bewes 1923: 85). Merchants also retained agents who spent much more time at fairs than the merchants themselves (Face 1958; Greif 2006), gaining an understanding of local practice and usage.

2.3 Incentives to Recognize the Law Merchant

Note that 'For diversifications, traders were associated with many traders residing in different trade centers. It was [or, at some point, became] customary for merchants to supply their business associates with trade-related information, which was crucial to business success' (Greif 2006: 64). This has important implications. First, incentives to behave as expected by other merchants become stronger, so behavioral rules and resulting expectations tends to spread through the network. Second, reputation for honesty becomes valuable. In discussing relationships between Maghribi merchants and agents, for instance, Greif (2006: 62–5) notes that there is a serious credibility problem because monitoring an agent conducting business with a merchant's capital in a distant location is costly, creating an opportunity for agent embezzlement. The flow of information allowed merchants to more effectively monitor agents, however, and it also provided a mechanism for agents to signal honesty: 'eleventh-century Maghribi agents generally conducted important business in the presence of other coalition members. In their reports they included the names of witnesses the merchant knew, thus enabling the merchant to verify the agent report' (Greif 2006: 65). Merchants hired the same agents repeatedly as long as information indicated agent honesty. Indeed, honest agents earned a premium.

Maghribi traders 'share the belief that coalition merchants . . . will reward his agent enough to keep him honest. All coalition merchants, however, are expected never to employ an agent who cheated while operating on behalf of a coalition member' (Greif 2006: 66). Greif (2006, 69) stresses that this ostracism process was an 'uncoordinated response of the merchants located in different trade centers.' It arose as a result of the common practice of sharing information, and observation of the behavior of merchants when they received information about dishonesty. Despite the lack of a coordinated response, Greif (2006: 66–9) cites several Maghribi documents illustrating this unorganized sanction's impacts. For instance, letters written in 1055 discuss an agent in Jerusalem accused of embezzling from a Maghribi trader. As word spread, merchants 'as far away as Sicily' canceled their agency contract with the individual.

Agents and merchants also were willing to sacrifice immediate gains to maintain their reputations. One revealing incident involved a contract for flax purchase. The parties' agreed price was 13 dinar per load, but before the flax arrived, the price fell to eight dinar. The buyers initially refused to pay 13 dinar, but ultimately did so. Greif (2006: 68) quotes a seller's letter: 'if not [for their fear of losing their] honor . . . we wouldn't have received a thing.' Similarly, a merchant had two loads of pepper to sell, one that he owned, and one owned by a temporary partner. The pepper price was very low and falling, so he sold his partner's load for 133 quarter dinars, but not his. The night before his pepper was to be shipped to another location, new buyers arrived, bidding up the price, and he sold at 140–142 quarter dinars. He shared the profit with the partner even though the partnership was not being renewed: 'the merchant acted honorably solely to maintain his reputation with other coalition members' (Greif 2006: 69). Greif (2006: 63) reports that 'Despite the many opportunities for agents to cheat, only a handful of documents contain allegations of misconduct.' In fact, positive incentives associated with reputation building and/or reciprocities are the primary reasons for recognition of the Law Merchant (Trakman 1983: 10).

While the Maghribi traders quickly boycotted dishonest merchants and agents, partial or conditional ostracism also is possible. Merchants might continue trading with someone accused of misbehavior, but only if certain conditions are met that reduce the expected risk, perhaps by demanding relatively high returns (e.g., requiring higher prices if selling, or lower prices if buying) or that bonds be posted. These conditions punish the offender by raising his costs of doing business.[10]

An obligation to spread information was not the only rule that helped deter misbehavior. Reciprocal support in the pursuit of justice was generally an intra-group obligation.

---

[10] A modern example is the eBay reputation mechanism where sales, prices, and survivability vary significantly across sellers, depending on their feedback records, with negative feedback producing significant 'punishment' (Cabral and Hortacsu 2004: 1–2).

Thus, as *The Little Red Book of Bristol* explains, a 'hue and cry' could be raised if an offender refused to abide by a court decision, resisted efforts to collect debts, removed or reduced the value of disputed assets, or fled (Basile 1998 [c1280]: 25). Such cooperation does not mean that the relevant threat was violent physical punishment, however, as the purpose was to induce performance of promises or payment of debts.

As communications about reputations become more effective much larger inter-community trading networks develop. When members of different groups trade, however, ostracism threats become weaker. As a result, the reputation of trading communities also becomes valuable, creating incentives to develop surety arrangements to protect group reputations and increase the credibility of members' promises. As Malynes (1622 [1686]: 93) explains,

> Faith or trust is to be kept between merchants, and that also must be done without quillets or titles of the law to avoid interruption of traffic, where in his Suretiship is to be considered according to the promise; for if it be conditional if such a man do not pay, the other to pay the same within a time, or to save him harmless: it is first to be demanded of the Principal, and if he do not pay, the Surety is to pay it without any course of law, unless he be ordered by the Court of Merchants to perform the same . . .

All of these developments certainly do not mean that opportunism never occurred, of course. No legal system is perfect.

2.4 Dispute Resolution

'As any practicing commercial lawyer knows, there are many ways of enforcing fair practices, and punishing unfair practices, outside the [government's] courtroom. These patterns of informal enforcement are "law" to those who operate in that context, and have been called "law" for centuries' (Coquillette 2004: 298). For instance, arbitrators, generally chosen from the merchant community, were an important option (Malynes 1622 [1686]: 447–54). Each group of merchants at a fair appointed a captain or consul to perform various administrative duties, for instance, but these individuals also arbitrated disputes between group members (Bewes 1923: 14; Kaden 2004: 59).[11] Merchants also inserted arbitration clauses in contracts. Face (1959: 243) discusses two fairly complex contracts from 1191 between an individual who rented horses to a caravan merchant, for example; these contracts specified that if a horse was injured the degree of injury was to be determined by a board of arbitrators. Arbitration also was chosen after disputes arose. Consider the 'Memorandum of Arbitration Concerning a Freight Charge' about a 1229 dispute in Marseilles (quoted in Blancard 1884, Vol. 1: 29):

> Upon the complaint or petition which existed between Martin Castagne . . . and Stephen de Manduel . . . on behalf of himself and his son Bernard, about the freight charge of thirty-one bundles of skins, which belonged to Paul Sicard, concerning which skins the said Martin and his associates said that they had retained them until the charge they demanded was paid; but on the other hand the said Stephen said that the charge should be paid by Paul Sicard, or by someone

---

[11] Bewes (1923: 14) also notes that in the cities with major markets each group of merchants 'appointed consuls [who] had permanent jurisdiction over their nationals.'

on his behalf, and that Bernard de Manduel, son of Stephen, had bought or otherwise acquired the said thirty-one bundles free from freight charges . . . and free from all other burdens, for which charge Stephen placed twenty-four pounds in the keeping of Bernard Peter . . . This money ought to be in the possession of Bernard Peter, for the charge on the thirty-one bundles if it appears that the said charge was not paid. For this charge or for the complaint about the charge Stephen and Martin have agreed before Bernard Peter and John of St. Maximin, judges chosen freely by both contestants . . . both promised to submit to the judgment or decision of the judges, however the judges might wish to settle the matter according to equity, requiring the truth, and, according to what appeared from the hearing of the complaint, to disregard the due order of legal process and the solemnity of the law. The said judges, having required the truth, and having heard the testimony . . . according to the wish of both parties, and having . . . the said judges agreed and gave their decision as below . . . according to what seemed just and honest to them. Wherefore the said Bernard Peter and John of St. Maximin, the said judges . . . absolved Stephen for himself and his son from paying the freight, ordering besides that the twenty-four pounds, which Bernard Peter had in his possession, should be restored to Stephen by Bernard, without objection by any one . . .

This decision was made by the said judges in the shop of William Aicard . . .

This is an unusual document since arbitration rulings were rarely recorded in any detail. In fact, as Malynes (1622 [1686]: 450) notes, medieval 'Arbitrators have a determinate power to make an end of controversies in general terms, without declaration of particulars.' This was the case because of the merchants' need for quick solutions to their disputes, discussed below, and the fact that arbitrators chosen to resolve disputes had 'skill and knowledge of the Customs of Merchants, which always does intend expedition' (Malynes 1622 [1686]: 450).[12]

Participatory merchant courts were also established at fairs, particularly during the early years of the medieval Law Merchant. While the origins of these fairs courts, called *Piepoudre* or Pie Powder courts, are difficult to determine, surviving records from the tenth through the twelfth century do not indicate that kings or local lords created these courts, and judges often were the captains or consuls chosen by each merchant group attending a fair (Bewes 1923: 14). *The Little Red Book of Bristol* (Basile 1998 [c. 1280]) stresses that one important difference between the Law Merchant and the common law was that Law Merchant disputes were resolved quickly, as suggested above, because most merchants had to complete transactions at one fair quickly to move to the next. This is one reason for choosing Pie Powder judges from among merchants attending the fair or market (e.g,, group captains/consuls). Another is that clerics, lawyers, local lords, and royal judges might have little knowledge of many commercial issues, so the risk of judicial error was lower with merchant judges, particularly when highly technical commercial issues were involved. In addition, non-merchant judges might not accept evidence that merchant judges respected, as Zouche (1663: 128) observed,

At the Common Law no mans Writing can be pleaded against him, as his Act, and Deed, unless the same is sealed, and delivered: But in Suites between Merchants, Bills of Lading, and Bills of Exchange, being but Tickets, without Seals, Letters of advice, and Credence, Policies of

---

[12] Malynes (1622 [1686]: 447) discusses methods of choosing arbitrators to insure unbiased adjudicators with appropriate expertise. Such expertise was also important in merchant arbitration because 'good orders and customs are to be maintained as laws, and nothing is to be admitted that may infringe the Law of Merchants' (Malynes 1622 [1686]: 452).

> assurance, Assignments of Debts, all which are of no force at the Common Law, are of good credit and force by the Law-Merchant. To which may be added, what Malines observes, that the bearer of such Bills, by the course amongst Merchants, shall be admitted to demand, and recover the Contracts, without Letters of Attorney, which is not admitted in the Common Law.

Pie Powder courts did not leave significant records, but this is not surprising since their purpose was to provide quick and equitable dispute resolution. Merchant judges had no precedent setting power, so as with arbitrators, these judges had 'a determinate power to make an end of controversies in general terms, without declaration of particulars' (Malynes 1622 [1686]: 450).

Local authorities who successfully maintaining important annual fairs or markets over time allowed Pie Powder courts to function without interference. The Champagne fair courts operated for close to a century (and probably longer), for instance, before the Count appointed wardens to deal with administrative and judicial issues, an action that set the decline of these fairs in motion, as explained below. Similarly, Piergiovanni (1995, 1998), drawing on information from fifteenth century *consiia*, concludes that merchant courts in Italy operated independently from other tribunals, following their own procedures. This apparently did not change significantly until the sixteenth century.

Kadens (2004, 64) notes that 'merchants, at least in northern Europe, also used a second sort of court – that of the town, the prince, or the Church, in other words, non-commercial court.' Some of the other legal systems that were evolving during the medieval period (see Berman (1983)) had relevant rules in common with the Law Merchant or their judges offered to apply Law Merchant rules, so if the court was willing to try the case quickly, and the court had a reputation for fair unbiased decisions, merchants certainly could choose to use it.

Ecclesiastical courts were often available because many of the major fairs were held at important priories and abbeys. Furthermore, as Bewes (1923: 9) notes, 'the Canon law . . . was the prevailing authority and would tend . . . to favour simple good faith unhampered by formalities, and thus would extend its influence to the law merchant which, until damaged by legislation, rested on mutual confidence and good faith to an extent unknown in civil life. In this connection it should be remembered that in the Middle Ages the Church was a very considerable trader.' Indeed, it was in the interests of Church leaders to maintain good relationships with merchants by offering them quick and equitable dispute resolution.

As suggested above by the appointment of wardens for the Champagne fairs, Pie Powder courts also were taken over by authorities: 'a mayor of a corporate town. Sometimes they belonged to a lord' (Holdsworth, 1903: 331). Even when Pie Powder courts were explicitly replaced by a manor (or urban) court, merchants often dominated dispute resolution, as the *Little Red Book of Bristol* (Basile 1998 [c. 1280]: 20) explains,

> In every market court, every judgment ought to be rendered by Merchants of the same court and not by the mayor or by the seneschal of the market.
>
> And if such a mayor and seneschal take it upon themselves in any way to render judgments, although judgments do not belong to them in a court of this court, and [if] they execute the judgments or have them executed in any way whereby anyone feels aggrieved by such judgment and its execution, whether the judgment was just or unjust itself . . ., the aggrieved person should have his recovery both against the mayor, seneschal, or other reeve of the same market who acted thus and against those who execute such a judgment on their order, by a writ of

> trespass of the lord king, as of a matter done of their own wrong and against law and custom and against mercantile law.

A local lord might impose his court on a fair, but resolve merchant disputes quickly using merchant juries, or at least, advice from merchants. He might also enforce court rulings. Merchants were often more than willing to have authorities enforce their law, thereby reducing costs that they might bear personally, like responding to the hue and cry (Benson 1989). Such courts should not always be characterized as Law Merchant courts, however. In fact, as commerce developed and merchant communities gained wealth, local authorities and kings increasingly attempted to assert authority over various aspects of commerce, including merchant courts, in order to increase their abilities to collect revenues or other benefits.

Fairs were gradually replaced by permanent market towns, and many of these towns were able to exert considerable political influence because of the wealth that accumulated in them. Kings often granted special privileges to these towns' governments, which were dominated by domestic merchant guilds. Privileges include the power to make their own law, and establish urban courts. Citing letters reported in *The Little Red Book of Bristol* (c. 1280), Coquillette (1987: note 21) explains that 'surviving correspondence forms between one fair court and another, even fair courts of different countries, show a formula that clearly distinguishes between the law merchant . . . and the town customs.' In fact, urban governments began discriminating against some foreign trading communities while simultaneously granting other merchants special access. As Holdsworth (1903: 302) explains, when this occurred,

> It was only those who belonged to the Guild Merchant who could trade freely within the town. Its conduct was sometimes so oppressive that trade was driven from the town. In fact all the various privileges, jurisdictional and administrative, which the towns possessed could be, and often were used in a manner adverse to the commercial interests of the country. The foreign merchant was hampered at every turn by the privileges of the chartered towns. They were averse to allowing him any privileges except those which they had specifically bargained to give him.

Agreements between market towns became increasingly common with each granting certain exclusive privileges to merchants from the other. Some agreements became part of multilateral and geographically extensive coalitions that discriminated in favor of merchants from the coalition. The most obvious example is the Hanseatic Cities of Northern Europe.

While urban and manorial (and royal) law supported many Law Merchant rules, they also clearly imposed top-down discriminatory additions or alterations to extract revenues and/or provide special privileges and powers to selected individuals or groups: 'once in a civil court, the hierarchy of applicable law appears to have altered' (Kadens 2004: 64). Thus, these courts were not customary Law Merchant courts even if they dealt with merchant issues at fairs and in markets.

The success of authoritarian efforts to capture benefits by controlling commerce, including merchant law, depended on several factors, including the degree of competition between jurisdictions (the availability of fairs or markets in other jurisdictions which were more receptive to the Law Merchant), the mobility of merchants and their wealth, and the locational advantages enjoyed by particular markets or fairs. If competition was severely limited, merchants might be forced to use authoritarian courts despite a preference for some other method of dispute resolution. As Jones (1987: 89–90) explains, however, 'the ability of the market to free itself from the worst interferences by the authorities' was a distinctive characteristic of European trade. Arbitration could be used, for instance. Also recall that ancestors of the Maghribi traders moved from Baghdad to Tunisia in the tenth century because of the political situation in Baghdad (Greif 2006: 61). Similarly, German merchants representing the Hanseatic League moved out of Bruges, the Flanders trading hub, in 1288 because Bruges' appointed weighers fraudulently falsified weighings (Kadens 2004: 51). Bruges' government had to promise to prevent the fraud in order to get the German merchants to return.

A more significant example of merchant mobility in the face of authoritarian efforts to tax or regulate is the decline of the fairs of Champagne. The Count of Champagne did not interfere with the fairs through the eleventh and most of the twelfth century, but toward the end of that century, wardens were appointed (Kadens 2004: 53). While the Count's wardens apparently continued to apply merchant law, Champagne became dependent on the King of France in 1285. The institutions established by the Count were dominated by or replaced by the king, and fiscal exactions increased. When the Hundred Years War started in the following century, French kings required more revenues, and the fairs were seen as a revenue source. In addition, the black plague hit Europe shortly before the middle of the fourteenth century. Jews were widely blamed for the plague, and Jewish merchants were expelled from many fairs and markets, including those in Champagne. Extraction of revenues for war and the Jewish expulsion are just two examples of the growing authoritarian control over these fairs. The result was that 'The Rhone was deserted for the Rhine, the caravan for the convoy, and so the Flemish and British markets were reached . . . but . . . the greatest part of this trade became waterborne and direct' (Bewes 1923: 111). The merchant exit did not occur immediately, however. A relatively gradual decline of these fairs occurred as alternative fairs expanded on the Rhine, and as reliable sea transportation became available. Thus, the French kings could get away with imposing rules that were not consistent with the Law Merchant for some time before the full consequences materialized.

As increasing numbers of political jurisdictions imposed themselves on commerce, opportunities for merchants to escape by fleeing a jurisdiction declined, making it more difficult to maintain Law Merchant rules and institutions. Even so, 'Opposition norms' inevitably evolve as the incentives created by formal institutions and sanctions are weak relative to the incentives to pursue personal interests (Nee 1998: 88). As European governments attempted to control and tax maritime trade, for instance, the 'average merchant and seaman responded with piracy and smuggling, and a substantial part of maritime commerce was carried out in violation of the laws of some nation-state' (Rosenberg and Birdzell 1986: 92–6). Similarly, craft guilds attempted to monopolize production within their urban jurisdictions, but 'illegal' production flourished outside the urban boundary (Jones 1987: 99). As Jones (1987: 96) notes, 'Rigidities impeding the movement and use of goods and factors of production had to be removed for economies to work efficiently. The lure of profit was sufficient in already commercialized economies to bite into the "cake of custom" or to get around the regulations.' Clearly, royal and urban courts would not enforce contracts arising from illegal transactions. Contracts still arose, however, no doubt subject to an underground Law Merchant. These processes and rules were not easily observable, of course, but some practices and usage probably were stifled in various ways, making the system relatively less effective than systems with freer trade.

2.5 The Law Merchant's Rules

The preceding discussion of the incentives to recognize the Law Merchant, the procedures for resolving disputes, and interaction between the customary Law Merchant and various sources of authoritarian law, reveals many of the universal rules of the Law Merchant (and helps distinguish these rules from the many non-Law-Merchant rules that were imposed on merchant activity over time). These universal rules included [my characterization of such rules follows; this is not a list derived from a medieval source]:

(1) merchants' property rights must be respected;
(2) merchants have freedom of contract, which also means that they are free not to contract (thus, a contract agreed to under duress is not valid);
(3) merchants must be honest in dealings with one another, so merchandize must be accurately represented when an exchange is negotiated (therefore, a contract agreed upon because of fraudulent misrepresentation is not valid);
(4) if an agreement is achieved without duress or fraud then parties to the agreement must do what they promise to do, unless both parties subsequently voluntarily agree to alter the first contract (e.g., merchants must not engage in opportunistic behavior by demanding changes in a contract to capture a larger portion of the gains from trade);
(5) truthful information about the behavior of individual merchants must be passed on to other merchants;
(6) foreign merchants and domestic merchants from other regions must follow local practice and usage when trading, unless all parties to an exchange agree to behave otherwise for the term of their contract, so merchants are responsible for learning local rules relevant to their transactions;
(7) when local merchants trade with foreign merchants or domestic merchants from other regions, they must provide accurate information about local practice and usage relevant to the transactions;
(8) all merchants attending a fair or market must be treated equitably;
(9) if a dispute arises, an arbitrator(s) or judge(s) agreed to by both parties or chosen by the relevant group of merchants (e.g., those attending a fair) must be asked to resolve the dispute;
(10) the dispute must be resolved quickly and equitably;
(11) arbitrators/judges must consider any relevant evidence (documented terms of a contract, related documents, testimony of witnesses of an agreement) if such evidence is available;
(12) if a contract does not suggest a resolution, arbitrators or judges must turn to the customs, practices and usage that each party should be familiar with – the universal rules that everyone knows (such as those suggested here), along with relevant local practices and usage;
(13) if necessary to reach a quick decision, evidence about the reputation of the parties (oaths – recall number (5)) can be employed, with the number of oath-helpers varying according to local practices regarding relevant circumstances;[13]
(14) arbitrators or judges chosen by the parties or the community can be merchants or other adjudicators who agree to provide a resolution reflecting points (10), (11), (12) and (13);
(15) parties to a dispute must accept and abide by a dispute resolution proposed by the arbitrator or judge (appeals must not be made);

---

[13] Trial by oath was widely practiced in Europe at this time. The Law Merchant did not employ trial by ordeal or by combat, however, even though both were frequently used under other legal systems.

(16) a dispute resolution applies only for the parties in the dispute for the term of the relevant contract; arbitrators and merchant judges have no authority to create or impose rules so their resolutions are default rules that can be ignored in future contracts;[14]
(17) all merchants are free to negotiate contracts that conflict with the implications of court and arbitration rulings;
(18) merchants must support the reputable merchants in their own merchant community (guild, caravan, ethnic or national group) if called upon to protect property or assist in pursuit and collection efforts; and
(19) merchants must provide financial backing to reputable merchants from their community, but any surety loan of this type must be repaid in a timely fashion.

As with any legal system, rules were violated. Appeals to some authoritarian courts occurred, fraud was practiced, local merchants did not always inform foreign merchants about local practices and usage, and so on. The flow of information about such violations was vital (number (4)), as this allowed individual merchants to decide how to treat violators. There were probably other universal rules, and the importance of some of those listed probably varied over time and space. Importantly, by accepting these kinds of fundamental overarching general rules, many more specific behavioral requirements can be generated through negotiation and contracting.

As suggested above, customary law has no legislative authority, and there is little reason to record either well known or rapidly evolving rules. An understanding of a customary law system by an outsider requires consideration of actual behavior, but when behavior cannot be observed, contracts, letters, and other documents might reveal some kinds of behavior. Let us turn to some of these records to see what they reveal about the medieval Law Merchant.

The major focus of the medieval Law Merchant was contracting. Contracts arise when some terms of the exchange do not occur immediately, hence the importance of credibility. Successful contractual exchanges often require the use of credit. Indeed, the *Little Red Book of Bristol* (Basile 1998 [c. 1280]: 11) states that 'it is well known to all that merchants sell their goods and merchandize on credit . . . and also that servants and apprentices of such merchants [sell on credit] the goods and merchandise of their lords to other men in the same way . . .' (parenthetic in the translated quote). Consider the role of contracts and credit in the medieval fairs and their implications for the credibility achieved under the Law Merchant.

Face (1958: 428) reports that 'Even the most superficial examination of the Genoese documents [notarial entries from 1180 through the thirteenth century] . . . indicates that as early as 1180 . . . the yearly cycle of the six fairs of Champagne was fully developed, and that the internal divisions of the order of business at each of these fairs had *evolved at some time long before*, and continued to regulate and to dominate all business activity' [emphasis added]. The cycle of six fairs in different Champagne towns, each lasting about 52 days, took place every year. These fairs all were organized as follows: (1) eight days of 'entry' when merchants set up their shops, (2) ten days during which only cloth was traded, (3) eleven days during which cordovan (leather) goods were traded, (4) nineteen days for the trading of goods that were sold by weight, such as spices and dye-stuffs, and when accounts began to be settled, and (5) four days during which the 'letters of the Fair'

[14] This was also the case for Common Law courts during this period (Zywicki 2003).

(credit instruments; e.g., to deal with unsold goods that might be stored, or individuals who purchased more than their revenues would cover) were drawn (Face 1958: 427 and note 2). Cloth was exchanged for promises to pay later, in the form of promissory notes or letters of credit from money lenders, because the buyers of cloth did not sell their spices and other goods until after the cloth exchange ended. These instruments could then be used by cloth sellers to purchase spices and other items later in the fair (many credit instruments were also negotiable). Trading with credit instruments was the norm, so credibility had to be well established.

Face (1958: 429) also reports that Genoese 'caravan' merchants who traveled to the fairs, bought spices and/or cordovan on credit from Genoese importers. When they returned after Champagne, they made large numbers of sales of varieties of woolen and linen cloth to Genoese '*draperii*,' again on credit. Furthermore, Genoese caravan merchants often did not even arrive at the fair in time to buy cloth. Instead, merchants generally contracted with agents or partners who established themselves at the fairs in Champagne (Face 1958: 433). The promises of merchants' agents also had to be very credible. Merchants who traveled to the fair also left agents or partners to tend their affairs in Genoa, and they had additional agents and procurators representing them in other places in the north (Face 1958: 432). In fact, documents suggest that some merchants simply stayed in Genoa, continually selling northern cloth purchased by agents and making large purchases of spices and other commodities on credit to be sold by agents in Champagne (Face 1959: 245). To carry out such activities, merchants also contracted with professional freighters or '*Vectuarii*' who transported trade goods to and from the fairs. Clearly, freighters' promises to deliver were credible. And importantly, clauses 'repeated word for word in four separate contracts, seems a reliable indication that by 1248 a substantial and generally known set of obligations existed to which *vectuarii* were required to adhere by custom . . . in their professional dealings with merchant' (Face 1959: 240–241). In fact, documents from much earlier indicated that a substantial over-land freight business existed (Face (1959: 242) cites several 1191 documents), and that over time, new clauses were added to these contracts. For instance, freighters might guarantee that the goods would arrive undamaged, that packages or bales would not be opened, that delivery would take place within a specified number of days, and so on.

Face (1958: 430) explains that twelfth- and thirteenth-century merchants employed 'A group of advanced and polished techniques of business [that] enabled them to carry out a seemingly impossible task with the utmost regularity and precision. These techniques are hinged on three factors: first, the ingenious use of partnerships, agency, and procuration; second, the integration of these devices with communication and transportation; and third, the extensive use of credit instruments in the trade.' These techniques clearly had to be based on contracts, which in turn require credibility. In this context, Berman (1983: 350) concludes that, 'a great many if not most of the structural elements of the modern system of commercial law were formed' prior to and during the period when the documents examined by Face were produced. Berman's (1983: 341) conclusion that the rights and obligations of merchants in their dealings with each other 'became substantially more objective and less arbitrary, more precise and less loose' by 1200, and probably by 1150, appears to be quite consistent with evidence provided by Face (1958, 1959), and by Greif (2006). Essentially, a widely accepted (universal) set of fundamental rules substantially lowered the cost of interpreting local rules, because all of the local practices and usage could be expected to be consistent with the fundamental rules. Many of the local practices and usage also would have to be very similar, if not identical, particularly after inter-community trade had been going on for awhile, as profit-seeking merchants would naturally look for rules that minimized their transactions costs.

3. CONCLUSIONS

The medieval Law Merchant was a complex system of polycentric customary law that evolved under a universal set of fundamental customary rules. Some writers have presented simplified pictures of this system, generally in order to emphasize particular points. For example, Berman (1983) did so as part of his demonstration that the foundation of Western legal tradition was established during a period when multiple distinct but interdependent systems of rules and procedures were interacting with each other. Similarly, Benson (1989, 1990, etc.) did so in order to illustrate that both primary and secondary rules can be and have been developed spontaneously without government involvement or enforcement, and to illustrate that government involvement in commercial law did not arise in order to solve market failure. Instead, competition for jurisdiction over merchant communities was motivated by a combination of power-seeking and rent-seeking by both legal authorities and politically-powerful domestic merchants. These kinds of descriptions, particularly when constrained in length by journal or book editors, certainly might appear to be romanticized and inaccurate, rather than just simplified in order to focus on particular issues. Indeed, some may be romanticized, at least to a degree, but that does not mean that the distinct rules and procedures did not exist. This presentation attempts to detail various aspects of the Law Merchant that probably were not necessary for some earlier focused presentations, and therefore, were not examined as carefully as other aspects of the system. Hopefully this will help direct the debate toward the actual tenets of and evidence supporting the Law Merchant story.

BIBLIOGRAPHY

Basile, M. ed. ([c. 1280] 1998), 'Lex Mercatoria from The Little Red Book of Bristol' in *Lex Mercatoria and Legal Pluralism: A Late Thirteenth Century Treatise and its Afterlife*, Cambridge: The Ames Foundation.

Benson, B. (1988), 'Legal evolution in primitive societies', *Journal of Institutional and Theoretical Economics*, **144**, 772–8.

Benson, B. (1989), 'The spontaneous evolution of commercial law', *Southern Economic Journal*, **55**, 644–61.

Benson, B. (1990), *The Enterprise of Law: Justice Without the State*, San Francisco: Pacific Research Institute.

Benson, B. (1995), 'An exploration of the impact of modern arbitration statutes on the development of arbitration in the United States', *Journal of Law, Economics, & Organization*, **11**, 479–501.

Benson, B. (1999), 'To arbitrate or to litigate: That is the question', *European Journal of Law and Economics*, **8**, 91–151.

Benson, B. (2006), 'Contractual nullification of economically-detrimental state-made laws', *Review of Austrian Economics*, **9**, 149–87.

Benson, B. (2009), 'Yes Virginia, there is a law merchant', Working Paper, Department of Economics, Florida State University.

Berman, H. (1983), *Law and Revolution: The Formation of Western Legal Tradition*, Cambridge, MA: Harvard University Press.

Bernstein, L. (1992), 'Opting out of the legal system: extralegal contractual relations in the diamond industry', *Journal of Legal Studies*, **21**, 115–58.

Bewes, W. (1923), *The Romance of the Law Merchant: Being an Introduction to the Study of International and Commercial Law With Some Account of the Commerce and Fairs of the Middle Ages*, London, Sweet & Maxwell.

Blancard, L. ed. ([1884] 1965), 'Documents Inédits sur le Commerce de Marseille au Moyen Age' (Marseilles: Barlatier-Feissat, Pere et Fils, 1884), 29; reprinted in Roy C. Cave & Herbert H. Coulson, eds., *A Source Book for Medieval Economic History*, New York: Biblo & Tannen.

Cabral, L. and A. Hortacsu (2004), 'The dynamics of seller reputation: Theory and evidence from eBay', National Bureau of Economic Research, Working Paper 10363.

Coquillette, D. (1987), 'Ideology and incorporation III: Reason regulated – the post-Restoration English civilians, 1653–1735', *Boston University Law Review*, **67**, 289–361.

Coquillette, D. (2004), *The Anglo-American Legal Heritage*, Carolina Academic Press, 2nd ed.

Donahue, Charles (2004), 'Medieval and early modern lex mercatoria: An attempt at the probation diabolica', *Chicago Journal of International Law*, **5**, 21.

Drahozal, C. (2005), 'Competing and complementary rule systems: Civil procedure and ADR: Contracting out of national law: An empirical Look at the New Law Merchant', *Notre Dame Law Review*, **80**, 523–52.

Epstein, R. (2004), 'The empirical and theoretical underpinnings of the Law Merchant: Reflections on the historical origins and economic structure of the Law Merchant', *University of Chicago Journal of International Law*, **5**, 1–20.

Face, R. (1958), 'Techniques of business in the trade between the fairs of Champagne and the South of Europe in the twelfth and thirteenth centuries', *Economic History Review*, **10**, 427–38.

Face, R. (1959), 'The Vectuarii in the overland commerce between Champagne and Southern Europe', *Economic History Review*, **12**, 239–46.

Fuller, L. (1981), *The Principles of Social Order*, Durham, NC: Duke University Press.

Greif, A. (2006), *Institutions and the Path to the Modern Economy: Lessons from Medieval Trade*, New York: Cambridge University Press.

Hart, H. (1961), *The Concept of Law*, Oxford: Clarendon.

Hayek, F. (1973), *Law, Legislation, and Liberty, Vol. 1*, Chicago: University of Chicago Press.

Holdsworth, W. (1903), *A History of English Law, Vol. 1*, London: Methuen & Co.

Jones, E. (1987), *The European Miracle*, Cambridge: Cambridge University Press.

Kadens, E. (2004), 'The empirical and theoretical underpinnings of the Law Merchant: Order within law, variety within custom: the character of the medieval merchant law,' *University of Chicago Journal of International Law*, **5**, 39–65.

Malynes, G. (1622 [1686]), *Consuetudo, vel, Lex mercatoria or, The ancient law-merchant, in three parts, according to the essentials of traffick: necessary for statesmen, judges, magistrates, temporal and civil lawyers, mint-men, merchants, mariners, and all others negotiating in any parts of the world*, London: Printed for T. Basset, R. Chiswell, M. Horne, and E. Smith.

Nee, V. (1998), 'Norms and networks in economic and organizational performance,' *American Economic Review Papers and Proceedings*, **88**, 85–9.

Pertz, G. ed. (1925), *Movmenta Germaniae Historica, Scriptorum Tomus IV*, Hanover: Hahn.

Piergiovanni, V. (1995), 'Statito. Diritto commune e processo mercantile', in *l Dret Comu I Catalunya: Actes del VII Simposi International*, Barcelona: Fundacio Noguera.

Piergiovanni, V. (1998), 'Diritto e giustizia mercantile a Genova ne xv secolo: i consilia di Bartolomeo Bosco' in *Consilia im Spaten Mettlelalter: zum Histoischen Aussagewert einer Quellengattung*, I. Gaumgartner, ed. Thorbecke, 13 Schrifenreihe des Deutschen Studienzentrums in Venetia.

Pospisil, L. (1971), *Anthropology of Law: A Comparative Theory*, New York: Harper and Row.

Pospisil, L. (1978), *The Ethnology of Law, 2nd Edition*, Menlo Park, CA: Cummings Publishing.

Rosenberg, N. and L. Birdzell, Jr. (1986), *How the West Grew Rich: The Economic Transformation of the Industrial World*, New York: Basic Books.

Sachs, S. (2006), 'From St. Ives to cyberspace: the modern distortions of the medieval law merchant', *American University International Law Review*, **21**, 685–812.
Trakman, L. (1983), *The Law Merchant: The Evolution of Commercial Law*, Littleton, CO: Fred B. Rothman and Co.
Volckart, O. and A. Mangels (1999), 'Are the roots of the modern Lex Mercatoria really medieval?', *Southern Economic Journal*, **65**, 427–50.
Zouche, R. (1663), *The jurisdiction of the Admiralty of England asserted against Sr. Edward Coke's Articuli admiralitatis, in XXII chapter of his jurisdiction of courts*, London, Printed for Francis Tyton and Thomas Dring.
Zywicki, T. (2003), 'The rise and fall of efficiency in the common law: A supply-side analysis', *Northwestern Law Review*, **97**, 1551–1634.

4. Path dependence: a foundational concept for historical social science

Paul A. David[1]

1. PATH DEPENDENCE: WHEN 'HISTORY MATTERS'

'Path dependence' is an important concept for social scientists engaged in studying processes of change, as it is for students of dynamic phenomena in nature. A dynamic process whose evolution is governed by its own history is 'path dependent'. The concept, thus, is very general in its scope, referring equally to developmental sequences (whether in evolutionary biology or physics) and social dynamics (involving social interactions among economic or political agents) that are characterized by positive feedbacks and self-reinforcing dynamics.

Although the assertion that 'history matters' has come to be coupled frequently with references to the concept of path dependence, the precise meaning of the latter term – and hence the significance of the former expression – more often than not remains rather cloudy. This is unnecessary as well as unfortunate. The fundamental idea is straightforward enough to be intuitively grasped without any instruction in economics; indeed, a thorough training in modern economics actually might interfere with human intuitions about history, and especially about processes involving historically contingent evolution. Even the formalizations of the concept of path dependence (to be introduced subsequently) are far from forbidding and readily will repay the effort spent in absorbing them. They will be seen to lend a useful measure of precision to descriptions of the special class of dynamical systems that are neither completely deterministic nor purely random in

[1] The general shape of this chapter took form as the Invited Lecture presented to the Symposium on *Twenty years 'QWERTY-effects' and path-dependence studies*, which was convened at The State University – Higher School of Economics, on 13 May 2005 in Moscow, Russia. I am grateful to Nureev Rustem (SU-HSE) for that invitation, and for his role with Leonid Borodkin (Moscow State University) and other Symposium participants, including V. Polterovich (Russian Academy of Sciences), in making the entire occasion both memorably enlightening and enjoyable. [An account of the symposium is available at: http://www.hse.ru/temp/2005/05_13_simpo.shtml, for those who read Cyrillic.] A subsequent presentation of the paper to the First BETA-Workshop on Historical Economics, held on 20–21 May 2005 at the Université Louis Pasteur de Strasbourg, provided opportunities for memorable discussions with Kristine Bruland, Claude Diebolt (the Workshop's organizer), James Foreman-Peck, Patrick Llerena, and Steve Redding, which contributed further to improving the exposition in the present version. This chapter is a lightly revised version of an article published in *CLIOMETRICA* (2007), **1**(2), 91–114 under the same author and title, reproduced with kind permission of the original publisher, Springer Science and Business Media.

their workings, and in which the specific details of history govern the unfolding course of development.

A clearer grasp of what the term 'path dependence' is about therefore ought to be part of the historical social scientist's toolkit. One would expect it to figure especially prominently in the analytical consciousness of economic historians, and to be equally familiar to all who are concerned to study the evolution of technologies, institutions, firms' strategies and industry structures.

2. EMPIRICAL RELEVANCE

The foregoing prescription is not a full measure of the extent of the social and behavioral science domains that would be further illuminated by a working knowledge of the meaning and implications of this strong formulation of the idea that 'history matters.' As the term is employed here, 'path dependence' is merely the label for a particular class of dynamic phenomena, not a theory to account for the way that such systems behave. One may develop theories and frame hypotheses regarding the economic circumstances in which path dependent dynamics are likely to appear, and where the consequences of past events can be expected to exert the greatest and most enduring influence. Whether a particular dynamic process in a given economic setting is or is not path dependent remains an empirical question, and one that frequently is not so simple to resolve.

Much of the corpus of economic analysis upon which modern economic historians draw for their theoretical insights still envisages a form of dynamics that is path *independent*, in the sense that the unfolding sequence of events is not shaped in any significant and persisting way by particular events that occurred in the past. Such theories typically conceptualize change as continuous movement towards a prescribed outcome – upon which the details of the flow of events exercise no real causal influence. In its most elementary formulations, neoclassical theory encouraged economists to explain whatever patterns of resource allocation were observed by supposing each had emerged as a unique resultant of a particular set of given conditions. The (exogenous) 'givens' were those affecting tastes (consumption 'preferences,' including preference between present and future satisfactions), factor endowments (population, natural resources), technological knowledge, and some legal and other institutions that established rules governing market transactions. On this view, it was useful to study economic history because it was a source of observations on the basis of which certain invariant 'laws of economic motion' could be established; and also because history was seen – as Descartes saw it – to provide a fund of concrete examples that would illustrate the workings of those 'time-less laws.' Certainly there is ample space in which it is plausible to search for parsimonious theories of that kind, since, in some circumstances and over some intervals of time their simplified premises may correspond reasonably closely to the empirical realities. But, that will not be the case universally.

Indeed, there are good grounds for supposing that the opposite is true more often where one is concerned with the interplay of endogenous long-term changes in demography, in the state of technological knowledge, in institutional infrastructures, and in culturally formed tastes and the experientially conditioned mores and habits of individuals. These, of course, are the very stuff of economic and social history and the forces shaping the development and secular growth of economies. The elaboration of theories around the core concept of path dependent dynamics proves to be especially useful in those contexts. It encourages and enables the analytical historian and the economist alike to entertain the possibility that, in place of a unique-equilibrium-seeking dynamic, one should envisage a process that is seeking an evolving and historically contingent equilibrium. This provides a rationale for the methodology of *historical* social science, by indicating why it is that in order to uncover the logic (or illogic) of the world around us, we sometimes must first understand the details of how it got that way. A recognition of the existence of path dependence in economic processes – not simply as a possibility, but in some contexts as the more likely condition – thus accords a broader and more influential role for history, without sacrificing the rigor and precision to which modern economic analysis aspires.

3. PATH DEPENDENCE IN ANALYTICAL NARRATIVE HISTORY

Although the term can be defined precisely, and the concept of path dependence is amenable to further elaboration with the aid of tools from probability theory, it is possible also to grasp the core idea intuitively, by exercising common human understanding of the contingent character of seemingly inconsequential events that nevertheless set in motion a sequence of changes which make for an arresting outcome, and hence an interesting historical narrative. Any deterministic system's evolution will be governed by its initial conditions and its 'law of motion' (the dynamic relations). Thus, the most primitive 'plot structure' is presented by the familiar illustration of a simple physical system whose dynamics are path dependent: a drop of rain falling to one side of the continental divide eventually will reach the sea on that side; but had a gust of wind directed the falling droplet ever so slightly across the divide, it eventually would have joined the sea on the opposite edge of the continent. As stories go, however, this one has but a single moment of drama in it – the gust of wind. So we may turn to the no-less familiar yet rather more complicated parable related by Ben Franklin's *Poor Richard's Almanac* (1733) to illustrate to the homily that 'A little neglect may breed great mischief.' This is the 'tale of the horse-shoe nail,' for want of which a shoe was lost, then a horse was lost, and for want of a horse a rider was lost. The narrative need not be extended further – by allusion to the loss of a battle, and even a kingdom – in order to appeal successfully to the common intuition that it is quite possible for eventual outcomes to be shaped by the transmitted effects of remote and seemingly trivial occurrences, and for the magnitude of those effects to become magnified as each event leads to the next.

Reference to elementary historical narratives such as these, or, indeed, to the chain of Old Testament 'begats,' are a helpful first step in conveying the core idea that lately has been more formidably labeled as 'path dependent social dynamics' (Blume and Durlauf 2001; Durlauf and Young 2001). This phrase refers to systems of human social interaction, whose motions remain under the influence of conditions that are themselves the contingent legacies of events and actions played out within each system's history. In the realities of a social system's evolution, the events in question sometimes will be recent or obtrusive enough to be salient in the collective cultural identity of the society. That condition, however, is not essential; in other cases the critical events will have taken place in a past so remote that it has slipped from the conscious memories of the actors. Although economic agents' behaviors may be the deliberate resultants of rational calculation conditioned on currently prevailing circumstances, the particularities of that decision context itself may well be consequences of the contingent chain of events to which those remote critical events had given rise.

In order to delineate more precisely the dynamic properties that are referred to by the concept of path dependence, and to arrive at an analytical grasp of the main mechanisms that cause some economic and social processes to exhibit dynamic properties of that type, it is necessary now to go beyond the preceding rather loose evocations of the idea of path dependent change. The drama of an historical narrative becomes more acute when the presence of just such a critical juncture, 'a forking of the road' has been identified in the flow of events. In the tragic form of narrative, the action of the player or players when they reach that point are foreordained, and so it really does not matter whether or not they can be said to have seen what would befall them on each of the paths that lie ahead. This is not so in the stories that economic historians typically wish to tell. Economic analysis is essentially about human choices among what the philosopher William James termed 'real options,' and the question of what the actors knew, and when they knew it, sought to know it, or at least formed some expectations of it are of interest for the analytical narrative.

Consequently, the quintessential and most persuasive form for an 'historical' economic history narrative rightly involves those circumstances in which alternative local states of the world are plausible as well as merely conceivable. Articulating an entire counterfactual world is not what is called for here, but it nevertheless seems important for the narrator to show that when the traveler in the tale is paused at the putative 'critical' fork in the road, there was an open path which would have led to events quite different from those that eventually transpired. Furthermore, for a tale to emphasize the highly contingent nature of the eventual outcome, the actors who are being followed until their arrival at that critical branch-point, or perhaps others who might have been in their place, ought to have been capable of choosing either of the paths forward. Then, as a poem on that subject by Robert Frost relates, the actual choice can be seen to have 'made all the difference.'

Thus, among the most rhetorically satisfying narratives constructed by historians are those that identify and elucidate the role of critical human actions (or failures to act) that are shaped by transient and incidental circumstances – conditions that were not obviously pertinent to the principal issues of interest in the drama, yet from whose influence a succession of unanticipated and ultimately unwanted results unfolded. The masterful account of the debacle of the Spanish Armada by the English historian Garrett Mattingly (1959) is paradigmatic, in its reconstruction of the intricate chain of events that ensued from the Duke of Medina Sedona's being temporarily distracted from overseeing the proper provisioning of many ships in his fleet with adequate stores of fresh drinking water. This tale gains interest not only from the exquisite detail of Mattingly's chronicle and his sympathetic treatment of the Duke, but surely also from the implied historical counterfactual: were it not for the spoilt water in those cheaply made, rotting casks, the reign of Elizabeth I and the destiny of England among the European powers well might have turned out to be far less 'Glorious.' (Again, this is a story in which, when told from the Spanish side, 'a little neglect' is seen to breed 'great mischief.')

Another, more explicit and possibly more compelling presentation of the way that remote and transient circumstances left a profound and persisting impression upon national development emerges in the story of the separation of the Netherlands from

Belgium, as told by the great Dutch historian, Pieter Geyl (1936, 1961–1964). Geyl begins with the observation that the northern and southern Netherlands originally were neither politically nor religiously differentiated: they were a set of fiefs held jointly under Spanish dominion, and within each territory there was a similar division between Catholics and Protestants. The regional topographies were different, however. This turned out to matter when the Spanish sought to put down the revolt in the south, because Protestant refugees fled northward toward the safer havens afforded by that region's convoluted coastline. That shifting of the religious balance transformed the north into the center of Protestantism and successful resistance against Spanish sovereignty. When Spain ceded independence to the north, the divergence of religious and cultural orientations that had emerged between the regions' populations was further reinforced. Eventually, two centuries later, when, following the defeat of Napoleon, the Congress of Vienna decided to restore the unity of the Netherlands, the reunified state proved impossible to maintain in the face of the persisting divergence of religious and national sentiments.

One might see in Geyl's narrative a parallel with the biological process in which the separation of a land mass due to geological or climatological change allows genetic drift to create new traits which become fixed in a small, isolated segment of the animal species that originally was distributed throughout the entire territory. Had the carriers of those mutations been able to inter-mix and breed with the main population, it is likely that the recessive traits would have disappeared. But, the mutant strain could become fixed in an isolated sub-population and therefore could attain evolutionary stability: at a future date when the land mass became unified again (say, by the receding of waters and the emerging of land bridges), speciation would have proceeded to the point that interbreeding became biologically impossible. In a similar vein, the deep structure of Mattingly's story of the Armada could be held to bear a resemblance to the 'tale of the horse-shoe nail,' even to the appended moral about the adverse consequently that may come from 'a little neglect.'

To be sure, the fixing of a dominant religious orientation and the development of regional (and hence, ultimately national sentiment) is not a matter of biological replication. Likewise, in the simple physical model of the rain-drop paused above the continental divide, the action of the random zephyr on the water-droplet is the only bit of 'history' that matters, and that story is at once too contrived and mechanical to provide interesting insights into the determinants of the course of a major battle at sea, let alone the complex forces that shaped the development of the Tudor State.

Even with this important caveat, however, the foregoing brief narratives serve to impart a positive message. The possible existence of a multiplicity of locally stable equilibria (dynamic attractors of the system) is seen to pose two generic explanatory challenges for the historian. First, what reason is there to suppose that there is more than a single equilibrium, especially when the apparent stability and continuity observed around us would suggest that there is only one? This is the part of the challenge that requires analysis of the existing structure to demonstrate the plausibility of a counterfactual state. Second, if another state might have obtained, how did we arrive in this one? This is the problem of identifying the mechanism(s) of 'selection' – which, in the conceptualization of path dependence as a branching process, corresponds to looking for critical bifurcations in the sequence of development, and for the factors that conditioned the actions taken at those historical junctures.

One must emphasize that we are concerned here only with 'possibilities' and not with universal empirical certainties. The case for a more general appreciation of historicity in social and economic processes does not rest on the presumption that path dependence is ubiquitously present and of equal importance everywhere and in every historical epoch. Quite the opposite is true. Many of the problems that properly engage the attention of economists can be tackled perfectly well with the familiar tools for treating the familiar static equilibrium of supply and demand analysis, or with the analogous apparatus of 'steady state' dynamics – because the situations in question can reasonably be characterized as possessing a unique globally stable equilibrium. But, on the other hand, the latter condition cannot be held to be a reasonable simplification everywhere, and at all times.

To be able to answer the question of where the concept of path dependence properly comes into it own – and conversely where, in that sense, it is reasonable to proceed under the simplification that 'history does not really matter' – ought to be of interest both to economists and to historians seeking the right narrative modes to employ when relating their understandings of the past. In an important respect, identification of the respective properties of the many dynamic processes taking place in the world around us can be viewed as the very first thing one should try to establish, especially before undertaking actions intended to make a change for the better. Obviously, an elementary prerequisite for deciding such matters is the simple recognition of the question's existence and pertinence, which is to say, the possibility that some economic processes are characterized by path dependence whereas others are not.

4. PRECISE DEFINITIONS

Path dependence may be defined with regard to the relationship between a system's process dynamics and the limiting configuration(s) that it ultimately takes on. This is one of two mutually compatible conceptualizations, and it is most straightforwardly employed when a deterministic process is said to have 'led to a path dependent outcome,' i.e., a particular equilibrium among a number of potentially attainable limiting states. Alternatively, the property of path dependence may be defined for the class of stochastic processes, by referring not to 'an outcome,' but instead to the nature of the limiting probability distribution that eventually will govern the movements of the system under examination.

One route to a precise definition of the term starts by distinguishing between path dependent dynamics, and all the rest. The latter appropriately are labeled 'path independent,' because their dynamics guarantees that they converge to a unique globally stable equilibrium configuration regardless of where they started, or how they approached that eventual outcome. Models of deterministic convergence to a limiting position are very familiar in the literature of economic dynamics, much of which has been patterned on classical mechanics. In the case of a stochastic system, however, the eventual limit of the convergent process will be an invariant (stationary) asymptotic probability distribution that is continuous over the entire feasible space of outcomes. Putting this somewhat differently, in the limit a unique positive probability is assigned to every one of the configurations it could assume, or to every imaginable position the system can visit within some well-defined space. Thus, the probability of the non-recurrence of any one among the feasible states during the path independent system's history is zero. No matter where it starts, a system of this kind will visit all of its states eventually – some of them more frequently than others; quite evidently it is able in due time to shake free from the influence of the initial conditions or of any among the past state(s) that it attained. Were that not the case, the system's limiting behavior would not remain invariant throughout the course of its movements.

The technical term for the conditions just detailed is 'ergodicity.' In physics, ergodic systems are said to be 'connected,' precisely because it is possible for them to transit directly or indirectly between any arbitrarily chosen pair of states, and hence for the process eventually to re-visit all the states that are compatible with the energy of the system. With that model as a reference point, path dependence may now be defined in negative terms as the property of systems whose dynamics are 'non-ergodic.' The latter constitute the exceptions to the foregoing class of processes – where details of the system's past motions were seen not to matter in the long run. Where the condition of non-ergodicity rules, however, random movements and other perturbations that disturb the system will not necessarily be 'averaged away' with the passage of time. The Central Limit Theorem of statistics ceases to hold in this world, and random, transient perturbations can exert a lasting influence upon the movements of the system. This is the domain where the time series tracing the movements in, say, levels of economic activity would be found to possess 'unit roots' (Durlauf 1993).

Framing matters purely in these negative terms might suggest that path dependence is something of an 'aberrant property' that contravenes the (ergodic) norm by leaving the system unable to shake free from the influence of events in its past. To avoid imparting such an anti-historical bias, it is helpful also to supply a positive definition, one stating what a path dependent process is, instead of what it is not. This is simple enough to do: a path dependent stochastic system is one possessing an asymptotic distribution that evolves as a consequence (function) of the process's own history. Historians should be reassured to notice (from the contrasting definition of a stochastic ergodic process) that the conceptualization of a contingent, path dependent dynamics as 'non-ergodic' is one that accommodates their traditional doubts regarding the likelihood of 'history repeating itself' in any strict sense.

5. FORMAL REPRESENTATIONS IN STOCHASTIC SYSTEMS

The preceding definitions of path dependence subsume properties that are shared by a variety of deterministic and stochastic processes that in other respects possess quite distinctive features. Among the simplest representations are those stochastic systems that are formulated mathematically by an invariant set of finite (positive) 'transition probabilities' that are state-dependent. The latter probabilities express the likelihood of being in any state (or category) i at time $t+1$, conditional on having been in any state j (including $j = i$) at time t. Such probabilities can be concisely arranged in matrix form by listing horizontally all the states where the system could be observed at time t, and listing vertically the (same) set of states to which it could have moved by time $t+1$. Transition probability matrices of this kind define what are referred to as 'first order' or homogeneous Markov chains. (Their 'first order' character signifies that it is only the current state occupied by the system, and no anterior states in its history, that affects the probability of where it will go next.) Homogeneous Markov chains are familiar constructs in economic models of the evolving distribution of workers among employment states, firms among size categories, family lineages among wealth-classes or socio-economic (occupational) strata, and the rankings of whole economies in the international distribution of per capita income levels.

In such applications, it is quite common for the transition matrix formed by those probabilities to be specified in such a way as to ensure that the dynamic process is ergodic. The states of a Markov chain are said to be ergodic when they are *persistent*, *aperiodic* and *not null*. For a state that is ergodic, the probability of remaining in that state converges at the limiting, infinite step in the process to a positive constant – which is the inverse of the state's 'mean recurrence time.' From this definition of ergodicity, it follows that the distribution of the system's position among its possible states will be governed by the repeated iteration of the transition probability matrix, and will therefore converge eventually to an invariant asymptotic probability distribution in which positive probabilities are assigned to all the possible states.

When there is a single 'absorbing state' or subset of connected states from which there is zero probability of escape to the subset of transient states, the Markov chain will converge weakly to that particular 'attractor.' Nonetheless, it remains ergodic – in the sense that regardless of where it may have started, the motion of the system eventually shakes off its initial conditions and goes to that unique absorbing state. On the other hand, when there are two or more absorbing subsets (distinct states, or regions of equilibria that are locally stable), the homogeneous Markov chain is *non-ergodic*: both the process represented by the chain of transitions, and the eventual outcomes can be said to be path dependent.

One may see readily enough that in a system governed by a homogenous Markov process, if there exists at least one transient (non-absorbing) state from which (whether directly or indirectly) any of the multiple absorbing states can be reached, the realization of the random process of the system when it has arrived at such a point in its history – i.e., at the critical 'forking of its path' – will 'select' probabilistically among the alternative locally stable attractors. Thus, even within the class of probabilistic (Markov) models that has found wide application in the hands of conventional ('mainstream') social scientists, it is necessary to acknowledge the empirical possibility of limiting outcomes being contingent upon improbable transitions that occur at some historically remote moment on the developmental path.

The foregoing definitions of path dependence also subsume other stochastic processes that possess a multiplicity of limiting distributions – which generally is the case for 'branching processes' or 'branching systems.' In the latter class of non-Markovian probabilistic systems, the prevailing probabilities of transitions among states are functions of the sequence of past transient states that the system has visited. When a branching process is subject to local irreversibilities, it takes on the property of non-ergodicity. That is the case most familiarly in biological evolution, because speciation is a non-reversible action. Of course, as the previous metaphorical allusion to the 'fork in the road' implies, there are other, analogous physical systems that exhibit the same property. Indeed, observing certain physical systems, we are aware of the existence of critical conditions (such as externally controlled temperature levels) that can cause an irreversible 'phase change' in their macro states – as in the phenomenon of liquefaction of gases, and the sudden alignment of the electrons in an iron rod that makes it a ferromagnet.

Among the stochastic physical systems whose non-ergodic dynamics have been the subjects of extensive formal investigation, and therefore offer analogies that have caught the interest of students of social system dynamics, the 'reversible spin systems' studied in particle physics pertain to the dynamics of ensembles of interacting entities or agents that are finite in number (see e.g., Liggett 1985, particularly on the so-called 'voter model'; David 1988a, 1993a, 2005a, for applications). A contrasting case is the generalized Polya process, which envisages an urn containing colored balls that are being sampled with over-replacement, so that additional balls of the same color as the one drawn at each step, are returned to the urn. Here, convergence of one or another of the system's stable equilibria (attractors) for the distinction of colors is attained only when the size of the population also goes to the infinite limit (see Arthur 1994; building on Arthur et al. 1983, 1986).

Prediction *ex ante* of the limiting (equilibrium) configuration is not possible in the case of the frequently cited path dependent Polya-urn model. But, for other processes that are every bit as path dependent as the reversible spin systems, information about the initial configuration of the system is a sufficient basis for assigning probabilities to the elements of the sub-set of configurations that represent the system's potential equilibrium states (see e.g., David 1993a). We hardly need to enter further into such esoteric technical matters to extract the conclusion that path dependence is not a property that is tightly coupled with other, very specific attributes of dynamic systems, such as the feasibility of predicting their limiting states. As shall be seen below, there is similarly no tight coupling between the questions of whether or not the outcome of a dynamic process of resource allocation is non-ergodic and whether or not it will be economically optimal.

'Branching processes' or 'branching systems' constitute still another important and well-studied class of structures whose dynamics may be path dependent. It is interesting to notice the circumstances under which that condition will obtain, because they reveal what appears to be a more general condition that underlies this property. In a branching process the prevailing probabilities of transitions among states are functions of the sequence of past transient states which the system has visited. When a branching process is subject to conditions of local irreversibilities, however, it takes on the property of 'non-periodicity.' What is meant here by a local irreversibility is simply conveyed by the metaphor of a wanderer arriving at a 'fork in the road,' from which diverging trails lead to two or more distinct regions *between which there are no other connecting routes*. Suppose that if one continues along the right-hand path it would be possible to reverse direction and return to the fork; whereas traffic on the other path can only move forwards: this is the irreversibility. If the left-hand fork is taken, therefore, it will be impossible to return to the junction and so gain access to the right-hand branch. The wanderer's state space would have become 'disconnected,' and her future journey will be confined thereafter to positions reachable only along the left branch. This corresponds to the event of 'speciation' in biological evolution.

6. UNDERLYING CAUSES

The existence of a multiplicity of locally stable equilibrium (dynamic attractors of the system) therefore presents analysts with two generic explanatory challenges. First, what reason is there to suppose that more than a single equilibrium exists, especially when continuities and structures observed in the social world around us could suggest that there is only one? This part of the challenge requires examination of the existing structure of the system to demonstrate the plausibility of a counterfactual equilibrium state. Second, if another such state might have obtained, how did we arrive at the one we are in? This poses the problem of identifying the mechanism(s) of 'selection' – which, in the conceptualization of path dependence as a branching process, corresponds to looking for critical bifurcations in the sequence of development, and for the factors that conditioned the actions taken at those historical junctures. The selection mechanisms are manifold, and bewildering in their variety, which is why in formal modeling exercises their operation typically is represented by the stochastic part of the system.

Something more general and illuminating than that, however, can be said in regard to the nature of the structural conditions that underlie the non-ergodic property of dynamical systems. A fundamental condition, which appears to underlie all of the instances in which economic resource allocation processes exhibit path dependent dynamics, is presence of micro-level irreversibilities – as in branching systems where a path forks into several tracks that remain separated and un-retraceable irreversibility. There is a simple economic interpretation of 'irreversibility' in the foregoing context: a finite, and possibly substantial cost must be incurred to undo the effects of the resource allocation decision in question. Among the most readily recognizable economic irreversibilities are those associated with investment in durable assets, the cost of which are 'sunk,' i.e., not recoverable in some substantial part, even when the asset is not used. Under this broad heading one can list investments in the form of physical structures and equipment, in human capabilities acquired through education and training, in knowledge assets created by expenditures for discovery and invention. Similarly, one can view the reputations of individuals, firms and organizations as belonging to the 'assets' created by irreversible investments. Acquiring a deterrent reputation for readiness to engage in mutually destructive economic competition (e.g., price-wars), or credibility of commitment to a stated policy, usually requires undertaking some costly present resource expenditures that can be seen by others as a predictable response to a particular, externally recognizable situation. But actions that form 'bad reputations' also may share the property of being irreversible, since it is likely to prove costly to neutralize their effects.

In this connection, it is important to emphasize that the individual assets in question (whether they are productive or damaging to their possessors) need not be *infinitely* durable. Quite the contrary: a system that has been built up from complementary components all of which have finite but *overlapping* service lives, under certain conditions – may collectively display the property of indefinite self-replication (see David 1971, 1975: ch.5; Arrow 2004). This point sounds complicated and rather mysterious when it is expressed in these abstract terms, but one may grasp it quickly from a well-known parable of continuity in change: the story of 'the ship of Theseus.' In the course of that mythical vessel's long voyage, each timber, plank, and mast had to be replaced, one-by-one, so that when it returned there was not a single piece of the original structure which remained. Nonetheless, 'the ship' had survived unchanged.

Not only in branching systems, but in other deterministic and stochastic processes, the existence of micro-level irreversibilities alone is sufficient to give rise to path dependent dynamics (see, e.g., Fisher 1983; Arrow 2000, 2004; David 1997b, 2001). This establishes that there is *no necessary connection between non-ergodicity and the presence of indivisibilities* (or 'lumpiness') in the goods being produced, exchanged, and consumed in the system. Inasmuch as modern economic analysis attributes the phenomenon of increasing returns to scale in production or consumption activities to the presence of invisibilities in one or more of the required 'inputs,' a further proposition is implied: no necessary connection exists between conventionally defined 'increasing returns' and the phenomenon of path dependence.

Assertions to the contrary, which appear all too frequently in recent writings on the subject, simply are wrong, or stem from an unconventional usage of the term 'increasing returns' – applying it in reference to phenomena that actually do not involve indivisibilities. The latter is quite clearly the case in Arthur's (1989) use of the phrase 'increasing return to technology adoption.' The latter actually referred to self-reinforcing, positive feedback mechanisms governing decisions such as the choice whether to select one or another among alternative production techniques, or consumer goods, or geographical locations for production activities.

7. WHERE HISTORY MATTERS MOST, FOR 'MAINSTREAM' ECONOMISTS: MARKET FAILURES

It has been seen that the property of the large class of dynamic phenomena to which the term path dependence refers really is neither arcane nor esoteric, even when one is quite precise about its definition. This makes it rather puzzling that the intuitively natural representation of dynamics as being 'historical' should not feature in so many of the dynamical models that economics have developed and sought to apply in understanding or prescribing for the world around them. Stranger still has been the resolute resistance encountered by the idea of path dependence in some quarters of modern academic economics, where the phenomenon itself is dismissed as being devoid of any important economic consequences. Were that not sufficiently dismissive, path dependence as a conceptualization of the way that 'history matters' in the economy also has been denounced as harboring the contention that 'markets fail'; it therefore is suspect of being a sort of intellectual 'Trojan Horse' which harbors within it dangerous economic policy prescriptions derived from ideological doubts that the best course for society is to entrust almost all matters involving resource allocation to 'the workings of free markets' (see, e.g., Liebowitz and Margolis 1990, 1994, 1995).

The objection raised against giving attention to the economic implications of path dependence on the grounds that its consequences must be trivial would seem to put the cart before the horse: consequentiality of economic impact is an empirical matter that requires assessment of the findings of an extensive program of careful quantitative historical research, not a judgment arrived at by aprioristic arguments, much less than by tautologies fashioned by conveniently redefining what is meant by the concept of path dependence (see David 1997b, 2001).

The second style of objection (i.e., that 'path dependence' falsely implies that a decentralized competitive market process can result in a socially inefficient outcome) is a blatant logical *non sequitur*, because the concept (as understood here) itself carries no necessary implications whatsoever in regard to the existence or non-existence of 'market failure.' Nevertheless, frequent repetition of the contrary allegation has created considerable confusion on this point, a muddle that is best cleared up by examining it explicitly.

Before tackling that task, however, it may be remarked that the erroneous conflation that depicts the novel contribution of the idea that economic processes may be path dependent as residing in its implied theory of market failure is all the more peculiar because 'mainstream' economics has a quite elaborate theory of the sources of sub-optimality in the workings of decentralized, perfectly competitive markets. Indeed, that body of theory has been around for quite a long time, whereas the appearance of formal ideas about non-ergodic dynamics is a much more recent departure in the economics literature. Moreover, it was in the context of studying topics in *static* general equilibrium analysis that economists arrived at these fundamental theoretical propositions about the existence of 'market failure' – namely, that the Pareto optimality of allocations yielded via atomistic, competitive markets was not guaranteed when a stringent set of convexity conditions on production and preference sets was violated, and/or when markets for all extant and contingent commodities did not exist.

Now, one reasonably may question the usefulness for pragmatic policy purposes of defining market failure in a way that makes the fulfillment of those exacting conditions the relevant benchmarks for deciding when markets are performing efficiently. Nevertheless, it remains utterly bizarre to suggest that the key contribution in introducing formal ideas about path dependence – a property defined in reference to dynamical processes (both deterministic and stochastic) – consists in reiterating those familiar propositions concerning market failure, propositions that are usually taught to beginning students of economics in the context of purely static welfare analysis.

Turning then to the question of the connection between the two ideas that are in play here, the difference between them is apparent. One of them, the core content of the concept of path dependence as a dynamic property, envisages the possibility that historical change may take the form of an irreversible branching process. The other idea is that it is entirely possible for some 'branchings' in the course of a market-guided process to be deemed 'socially regrettable,' because they led to inextricable economic inefficiencies that could have been averted – in some counterfactual but equally attainable course of historical development. Since the two ideas are quite distinct, for them to become logically coupled requires an argument that the presence of phenomena to which the concept of path dependence refers *necessarily*, implies the existence of conditions that can be shown analytically to cause competitive market processes to 'fail' – yielding outcomes that are inefficient, and therefore sub-optimal from the societal viewpoint.

Economies of scale are among those troubling sources of competitive market failure, but it has be seen that path dependence *as such* may exist in the absence of invisibilities that give rise to economies of scale. So, it follows that path dependence does not imply that competitive markets fail. Indeed, quite the contrary proposition holds: under full conditions of convexity in preference and production sets a *non-tatonnement* general equilibrium process (in which costless re-contracting is not available to the agents) will converge in a strictly path dependent manner on one among the continuum of valid 'core' solutions. It thereby satisfies the criterion that the outcome is socially welfare-efficient in the Paretian sense. This well-known theoretical result (see Fisher 1983) should be sufficient to expose the analytical error of supposing 'market failure' to be among the necessary properties of a path dependent economic process.

Market efficiency, however, is not the only aspect of market outcomes that is of interest. In the process just envisaged, it is the distribution of the 'gains from trade,' and therefore the particular distribution of economic welfare among the trading parties – one such, among the many Pareto-efficient allocations at which the market process could have arrived – that will have been determined by the historical sequence of market transactions. To be sure, modern economic analysis devotes special attention to questions concerning allocative efficiency, because, in principle if not in practice, that is a goal which can be pursued without having to decide on whose welfare to reduce in order to raise the welfare of others. Given the centrality of that approach in classical welfare analysis, it does seem important to acknowledge that among the great variety of structural conditions that can give rise to the existence of multiple equilibria and path dependent dynamics, there are some that also would prevent the workings of competitive markets from arriving unerringly at allocations that are socially efficient in the sense of Pareto.

Prominent in that company are micro-level irreversibilities in the behavior of agents, due to learning by doing and the habituation of tastes, and externalities affecting non-market interactions in the spheres of consumption and production, including those which give rise to co-ordination games that end in 'co-ordination failures.' Consequently, while the logical relationship between path dependence and market failure is neither one of necessity nor sufficiency, there are indeed some potentially important underlying connections between the existence of path dependence and the welfare optimality of decentralized resource allocation in market economies.

The latter observation clearly raises the general policy relevance of historical research that would undertake to identify where and when economic processes exhibit the property of path dependence. This accounts for the fact that among economists at large most of the interest in path dependence has tended to fix upon possibilities that suboptimal equilibria will be 'selected' – almost to the exclusion of all other considerations. Nonetheless, as has been noticed, there is more to economic life than welfare losses due to static inefficiencies. Market structures in some areas of the economy – especially those where network externalities and bandwagon dynamics are especially important – are particularly susceptible to the shaping influence of specific historical events in the evolution of the industries concerned. Insofar as market structure itself strongly conditions entrepreneurial behavior and managerial strategies of innovation, path dependence then must be reckoned among the conditions that govern *dynamic* efficiency, as well as the static efficiency proprieties upon which traditional welfare analysis tends to focus.

But, questions about the distribution of welfare gains from trade and technological and institutional innovation surely do matter; these are not incidental issues that a socially useful discipline can afford to ignore, or to study with inadequate conceptual tools. Indeed, in private and public policy deliberations such questions often exert an influence far more powerful than that of narrow efficiency considerations. The identities of winners and losers in market rivalries understandably are matters of intense interest to the owners and employees of the affected enterprises, and to the governments of countries and regions where those agents are situated. More generally, all manner of political and social *sequelae*, as well as issues of equity and social justice, are attached to the dynamics governing the evolution of income and wealth distributions and related processes of socio-economic stratification. The analysis of positive feedback mechanisms that impart path dependent properties to those processes can significantly enhance economists' abilities to understand and predict distributional phenomena of the kind that recurrently have occupied the center of many economic policy debates, and most likely will continue to do so in the future.

8. PATH-CONSTRAINED AMELIORATION AND ITS POLICY IMPLICATIONS

There is, however, another way to look at the question of the policy significance of the conditions underlying path dependence as sources of the inefficiencies associated with 'market failure.' It may be that the selection of Pareto-dominated equilibria in positive feedback systems never results in inefficiencies that grow big enough (in the sense of Liebowitz and Margolis 1995) to impress contemporary observers, especially not those who can imagine a variety of clever, if costly, mechanisms for organizing collective escapes from locally sub-optimal situations. This, is a cogent empirical point to be made in objecting to highly simplified stories of 'lock-in,' particularly when a current sub-optimal local equilibrium is depicted as having been arrived at directly from some historically remote transient circumstances because a selection among alternatives available at that time irrevocably committed the system to develop along a particular path.

One surely should acknowledge and allow for the possibility that when economic or other disadvantages arising from past actions come to be properly perceived in an open social system, the self-interest of actors may be engaged to seize the opportunities it affords them to benefit by offering a more satisfactory solution. This could be a better product design, a new and more efficient technique of production, a different organizational structure, or even a reformed set of legal regulations. It is one thing, however, to glibly contemplate the possibility that effective responses of that sort would have been forthcoming, and quite another matter – indeed, a considerable challenge – to articulate the specific mechanisms by which one or another such response could be induced. The latter kind of historical research, however, is needed to establish the likelihood that under the prevailing circumstances particular corrective feedback mechanisms actually could come into play, and to determine how rapidly the 'repair' could be effected, if indeed it would be forthcoming at all.

The contention that the process of 'market competition' eventually works to rectify the mistakes of profit-motivated agents by harnessing the interests and capabilities of other profit-seekers – who will find opportunities for gain by eliminating existing sources of inefficiency – undoubtedly warrants serious consideration in this regard (see Liebowitz and Margolis 1990; Puffert 2002). But, that means it ought not be accepted on faith. Nevertheless, rather the opposite seems to be the position adopted by those who argue that it is implausible to suppose that market incentives will not operate rapidly to eliminate sources of substantial inefficiencies in the production and use of commodities, and that the burden of proof lies upon those who claim that sub-optimal outcomes of decentralized market-guided choices in the past might have saddled subsequent generations with quantitatively significant continuing economics costs.

The static framework of welfare analysis within this sort of argument is conducted, and in which too many economists are still being taught to think, carries an ahistorical if not an anti-historical bias. It tends to suppress the natural human disposition to conceptualize the whole flow of current economic life as contingent upon the results of antecedent actions. Seen in truly historical perspective, a great deal of human ingenuity, especially both of the sort that is said to be 'mothered by necessity' if not by opportunity, is devoted to trying to cope with the consequences of past mistakes whose economic costs are threatening to become 'serious'; to assuring, somehow, that the more pernicious effects will be moderated, if not entirely abated. Of necessity (because we live without perfect foresight) much of this effort is remedial. It is undertaken *ex post*, by contriving technological 'fixes' and 'patches'; by commandeering temporary task forces to handle emergencies that established organizational structures and routines are discovered to be handling badly, by sustained efforts at 'reforming' (not reinventing) long-standing institutions; and, yes, by concerted educational campaigns to 'un-train' people who have through historical circumstance learned habits of mind, or unthinking reactions that are proving in one way or another to be personally and socially dysfunctional.

From that vantage point it seems only reasonable to acknowledge that under conditions that create common sources of path dependence and potentials for market failure, the unfolding developmental process is likely to involve more-or-less continuous processes of 'path-constrained amelioration'. The latter is just a shorthand way of referring to incremental remedial resource allocation by intelligent, observant agents who are trying to cope with, and possibly gain something by removing unwanted features of the world left to them by the actions and inactions of their historical predecessors. This dynamic conceptualization certainly seems preferable to entertaining the fantasy that history somehow unfolds without anybody noticing what is happening, and that after some considerable passage of time, when an equilibrium appears to have been reached (how can one tell?), people gather round, assess its social efficiency and consider whether there is something in the system that is worth fixing.

Still, there is more than a whiff of heterodoxy about the foregoing line of considerations. A long and deeply rooted tradition in the West, one that is intimately connected with the eighteenth-century idea of 'Progress,' has pre-disposed us to refer to all of that corrective investment of resources as contributing in greater or lesser degree to 'economic welfare improvement.' Rightly so, because in a historically localized sense, that is just what it is – amelioration. The ameliorative options, however, are more often than not inherited from past decisions and are quite tightly bounded by the existing critical situation. It was the limited amount of lower memory on the mother-board of the first, hastily designed IBM PCs that created a need for devising clever software solutions to provide adequate temporary memory registers to execute the larger programs and larger data processing tasks that soon presented themselves. Another, more forward-thinking hardware specification with more lower memory surely was conceivable for the IBM engineers, and would for a while have obviated the recourse to compensating software creativity. Similarly, it was the existing software code that threatened to malfunction badly when the year 2000 dawned, not some other clock programs and data formats that had not been implemented, although those might well have been far more trivial to modify.

The resources spent in such perceived loss-avoidance activities are part of what we casually classify as productive investments that add to the net social product, and so should be included in the conventionally measured GDP. Yet, some part at least could just as well be thought of as the deferred costs of regrettable decisions made in haste to be remedied at leisure – albeit sometimes for great private profit. They might equally be labeled 'regrettable economic opportunities' (see David 1997b). To assess these imposed social costs it would be necessary to examine not only some eventual terminal situation, but the magnitudes of both the losses arising from the persisting inefficiencies, and the expenditures of resources in efforts to reduce them – whether or not such undertakings proved successful. Furthermore, it is important in considering situations where investment decisions involved choices among alternative technical standards or organizational rule-structures, that the persistence of un-removed diversity, and the consequent lack of interoperability in situations where there are potentially strong positive network externalities, can be a quantitatively greater burden than the selection of a technically sub-optimal standard (see Puffert 2002, 2004). Thus, the task of implementing a framework of analysis that takes account of the dynamics of path constrained amelioration is possible, but far from easy even when the historical case has been selected to render it less arduous.

The problem is that the selection of the more feasible cases is likely to bias the findings towards underestimation of the costs of path-constrained amelioration. Most of the situations in which the economic losses incurred by remaining stuck in a 'bad' coordination equilibrium really could be very large are those in which the particular institution, or technology, or complex of social norms that is being examined has become highly elaborated and deeply embedded in numerous activities throughout the economy and society. In a sense, it is that condition which makes the question attractive. But, to fully assess the impact of the course of development that was involved in such cases – for example, whether the outcome of the 'Battle of the Systems' between Edison's direct current and Westinghouse's alternating current was socially optimal (see David 1992c), one would have to imagine a counter-factual world in which the whole general equilibrium course of evolution could have been very different.

Thinking about the implications of general purpose technologies, and the effects of major social institutions is one of the ways in which economists today, and economic historians particularly, are seeking to come to grips with this sort of challenge to systems analysis. Description of what happened generally remains more readily within reach than measurement of causal effects, precisely because of the difficulty of specifying what a plausible alternative world would have looked like. Little wonder, then, that careful analytical and quantitative economic historians continue to draw back from attempting a full-scale counterfactual analysis when they approach such tempting questions as 'What was the contribution to economic growth of the steam engine, or of the railroad, of the electric dynamo, and what will be the economic impact of the modern digital computer?' And the same holds, when they try to think about how to assess the effects of the eighteenth-century codification of English common law, or the contribution of the corporate form of business organization to modern economic development.

9. 'ACCIDENTS OF HISTORY'?

In considering the nature of the policy lessons that might be drawn from the foregoing view of the incremental evolutionary development of complex technological systems, some remarks on the putative role played by 'historical accidents' in path dependent processes are now very much in order. Unfortunately, the use of that phrase itself is prone to cause misunderstandings. It is quite misleading to take it to suggest that some original economic irrationality or implementation error (accident) must be implicated whenever we find that positive network externalities have given rise to a sequence that turned out to be other than a globally optimal path. Indeed, only those who are hostile to the very idea of path dependence would repeatedly insist upon a literal interpretation of the phrase 'accidents of history.' Doing so suggests that the essential feature of such processes is that the original actors in the drama – whether as contributors to the design of a technical system, or an institutional rule structure, or a particular form of business organization, or as the initial adopters of such innovations – had to have been acting arbitrarily, or irrationally in the context of their economic circumstances. But, such an interpretation is not only logically unwarranted, it obfuscates an important and widely overlooked feature common to the histories of many network technologies, one that also has some bearing upon the way public policy might be approached in that and related areas.

The facts of all the technological instances recently under re-examination – QWERTY, 64K lower memory in the IBM PC, AC vs. DC electrical current, light-water reactors, and VCR formats (see David 2001 for discussion and references) are quite consistent with the view that the behavior of the initiating actors of the drama, generally, was quite deliberate and not at all random in the sense of remaining inexplicable to the historian. Furthermore, it was reasonably conformable to the urgings of the profit motive. Yet, generally, their actions were also bounded by a parochial and myopic conception of the process in which they were engaging – in the sense that these decision agents were not primarily concerned with whether the larger system that might be (and was eventually) built around what they were doing would be optimized by their choice. In most cases they can be held to have failed entirely to foresee the complementary innovations and investments that would be influenced by their initial commitment to one rather than another course of action. In other words, their 'failure of imagination' took the form of not thinking *systemically* about the technological and industrial structures that they were engaged in developing. Thomas Edison, of course, being a systems inventor *par excellence*, was an exception in that particular regard. Yet (as has been shown by David 1991, 1992c), Edison's business strategy in the context of the 'Battle of the Systems' – including his sudden decision to withdraw altogether from the flourishing electrical supply systems industry – appears to have been driven by quite different, rather myopic, but nonetheless rational economic considerations.

In general, what was difficult for the pioneers in any area to foresee were the complementaries that would emerge subsequently, and in so doing open the possibilities of developing a more complex, distributed system whose components were not produced or purchased in an integral system. The Remington Co. engineers who put the finishing touches on the first commercially successful typewriters to carry QWERTY into the world did not dream of the possibility of touch-typing manuals (David 1985, 1986); nor did Edison (perhaps because he was a designer of closed systems) anticipate that anyone would devise an efficient and economical converter to link DC electrical supply facilities with distant users by way of polyphase AC networks. Similarly, in more modern times, the IBM engineers in Texas, as they rushed to create a readily producible personal computer (the famous PC), were not concerned with the amount of random access memory that would be needed (remarkably soon thereafter) to load a word-processing program like WordPerfect whilst keeping an Excel spreadsheet and a LAN-modem connection open and running in the background. Likewise, neither of the rival vendor groups behind the Sony Betamax and VHS cassette formats in the early VCR market had anticipated the commercial importance of prerecorded movies and video rental stores. (For the latter case, one should refer to the detailed historical analyses of the VHS market in Baba and Imai 1990, Cusumano et al. 1992, and Grindley 1992, none among which are noticed by Liebowitz and Margolis 1994).

The point here is not that these inventors and entrepreneurs ought to have seen the shape of the future. Rather it is that the shape of the larger systems that evolved was built upon their work, and thus in each case preserved, and was in some respects much constrained by it – even in the way that those who came later coped with the problematic legacies of those initial decisions that had been taken quite deliberately but with quite other and considerably more evanescent considerations in mind.

10. CONCLUSIONS FOR POLICY

From the foregoing it may be seen that a proper understanding of path dependence, and of the possibilities of externalities leading to market failure, is not without interesting implications for economic policy. But those are not at all the sorts of glib conclusions that some critics have alleged must follow if one believes that history really matters – namely, that government should try to pick winners rather than let markets make mistakes. Quite the opposite view is closer to the policy position that I put forward more than 20 years ago, and have continued to argue in regard to technology choices among rival standards and institutional reforms that once taken were likely to develop 'excess momentum' (David 1987; David and Bunn 1988b; David and Greenstein 1990; David 2005b). If there is one generic course that public policy should pursue in such situations, it would be to counteract the 'excess momentum' of bandwagon movements in network product and service markets that can prematurely commit the future inextricably to a particular technical standard, before enough information has been obtained about the likely technological or organizational and legal implications of an early, precedent-setting decision.

In other words, preserving open options for a longer period than impatient market agents would wish is a major part of such general wisdom that history has to offer to public policy makers in all the applications areas where positive feedback processes are likely to be preponderant over negative feedbacks. Numerous dynamic strategies can and have been suggested as ways of implementing this approach in various, specific contexts where public sector action is readily feasible.

Still more sensible and practical approaches will be found if economists give up their exclusive obsession with traditional questions of static welfare analysis and, instead of pronouncing on the issue of where state intervention would be justified in the economy, begin to ask what kinds of public actions would be most appropriate to take at different points in the evolution of a given market process. Surely, bringing about that little shift toward 'thinking in time' is the really big contribution that a properly *historical* approach grounded on the concept of path dependent dynamics could make to the future of economics and other policy relevant social sciences.

BIBLIOGRAPHY

Arrow, K.J. (2000), 'Increasing returns: Historiographic issues and path dependence', *Eur J Hist Econ Thought*, **7**, 171–80.

Arrow, K.J. (2004), 'Path dependence and competitive equilibrium.' in T.W. Guinnane, W.A. Sundstrom, W.C. Whatley (eds), *History Matters: Essays on Economic Growth, Technology, Demographic Change*, Stanford, CA: Stanford University Press.

Arthur, W.B. (1989), 'Competing technologies and lock-in by historical small events', *Econ J*, **99**(1), 116–31.

Arthur, W.B. (1994), *Increasing Returns and Path Dependence in the Economy*, Ann Arbor, MI: University of Michigan Press.

Arthur, W.B., Yu.M. Ermoliev and Yu.M. Kaniovski (1983), 'A generalized urn problem and its applications' (in Russian; translated in *Cybernetics* **19**, 61–71), *Kibernetika*, **19**, 49–57.

Arthur, W.B., Yu.M. Ermoliev and Yu.M. Kaniovski (1986), 'Strong laws for a class of path-dependent urn processes,' in Arkin, Shiryayev and Wets (eds), *Proceedings of the International Conference on Stochastic Optimization, Kiev 1984*, New York: Springer.

Baba, Y. and K. Imai (1990), 'Systemic innovation and cross-border networks: The case of the evolution of the VCR systems,' Paper presented to the Schumpeter Society Conference on Entrepreneurship, Technological Innovation and Economic Growth, held at Airlie House, VA, USA, 3–5 June.

Blume, L. and S. Durlauf (2001), 'The interactions-based approach to socioeconomic behavior,' in S. Durlauf, and H.P. Young (eds), *Social Dynamics*, Cambridge, MA: MIT Press.

Cusumano, M.A., Y. Mylonadis and R.S. Rosenbloom (1992), 'Strategic maneuvering and mass-market dynamics: The triumph of VHS over Beta,' *Bus Hist Rev*, **66** (Spring), 51–94.

David, P.A. (1969), 'Transport innovation and economic growth: Professor Fogel on and off the rails,' *Economic History Review*, **22**(3), December, pp. 506–25.

David, P.A. (1971), 'The landscape and the machine: Technical interrelatedness, land tenure and the mechanization of the corn harvest in Victorian Britain,' in D.N. McCloskey (ed.), *Essays on a Mature Economy*, London: Methuen, pp. 145–205.

David, P.A. (1975), *Technical Choice, Innovation and Economic Growth: Essays on American and British Experience in the Nineteenth Century*, Cambridge: Cambridge University Press.

David, P.A. (1985), 'Clio and the economics of QWERTY', *American Economic Review*, **75**(2), May.

David, P.A. (1986), 'Understanding the economics of QWERTY: The necessity of history', in W.N. Parker (ed.), *Economic History and the Modern Economist*, London: Basil Blackwell.

David, P.A. (1987), 'Some new standards for the economics of standardization in the information age', in P. Dasgupta and P.L. Stoneman (eds.), *The Economics of Technology Policy*, London: Cambridge University Press.

David, P.A. (1988a), 'Path dependence: Putting the past into the future of economics', *Institute for Mathematical Studies in the Social Sciences Technical Report 533*, Stanford University, November.

David, P.A. and Julie A. Bunn (1988b), 'The economics of gateway technologies and network evolution: lessons from electricity supply history', *Information Economics and Policy*, **3**, Winter, 165–202. (French transl. published in *Flux: Cahiers due recherché au des reseaux*, 1989.)

David, P.A. (1989), 'When and why does history really matter?' *A Presidential Address to the Economic History Association*, delivered at the Smithsonian Museum of Science and Technology, Washington DC, September, Department of Economics Working Paper, Stanford University, October 1989.

David, P.A. and S. Greenstein (1990), 'The economics of compatibility standards: An introduction to recent research,' in *Economics of Innovation and New Technology*, **1**(1 & 2), Fall: 3–42.

David, P.A. (1991), 'The hero and the herd: Reflections on Thomas Edison and the "Battle of the Systems"', in P. Higonnet, D.S. Landes and H. Rosovsky (eds), *Favorites of Fortune: Technology, Growth, and Economic Development Since the Industrial Revolution*, Cambridge, MA: Harvard University Press.

David, P.A. (1992a), 'Path dependence and economics', The 1991–1992 Marshall Lectures delivered at the University of Cambridge, 28–29 April. Lecture I: 'The invisible hand in the grip of the past'; Lecture II: 'Models of non-ergodic economic dynamics, and their implications for policy', Center for Economic Policy Research Working Paper, Stanford University, August.

David, P.A. (1992b), 'Path dependence in economic processes: implications for policy analysis in dynamical system contexts,' *Background Paper – Rosselli Foundation Workshop on Path Dependence*, Torino, Italy, 29–30 May, Center for Economic Policy Research Working Paper, Stanford University, August; revised and published as David (2005a).

David, P.A. (1992c), 'Heroes, herds and hysteresis in technological history,' *Journal of Industrial and Corporate Change*, **1**(1), 129–80.

David, P.A. (1993a), 'Path dependence and predictability in dynamic systems with local network externalities: a paradigm for historical economics', in D. Foray and C. Freeman, (eds), *Technology and the Wealth of Nations*, London: Pinter Publishers. (French transl., in *Technologie et la richesse des nations*, Paris, 1993.)

David, P.A. (1993b), 'Historical economics in the long run: some implications of path dependence,' in *Historical Analysis in Economics*, London: Routledge.

David, P.A. (1993c), 'Intellectual property institutions and the panda's thumb: Patents, copyrights, and trade secrets in economic theory and history,' in M. Wallerstein et al. (eds), *Global Dimensions of Intellectual Property Protection in Science and Technology*, Washington, DC: National Academy Press.

David, P.A. and Dominique Foray (1993d), 'Percolation structures, Markov random fields and the economics of EDI standards diffusion,' in G. Pogorel (ed.), *Global Telecommunication Strategies and Technological Change*, Amsterdam: Elsevier Science Publishers.

David, P.A. and Dominique Foray (1994a), 'Dynamics of technology diffusion through local network structures,' in L. Leydesdorff (ed.), *Evolutionary Economics and Chaos Theory: New Developments in Technology Studies*, London: Pinter Publishers.

David, P.A. (1994b), 'Positive feedbacks and research productivity in science: Reopening another black box,' in O. Grandstrand (ed.), *Technology and Economic Change*, Amsterdam: Elsevier.

David, P.A. (1994c), 'Les standards des technologies de l'information, les normes de communication et l'état: Un problème de biens publics', in A. Orleans (ed.), *L'analyse économique des conventions*, Paris: Presses Universitaires.

David, P.A. (1994d), 'Why are institutions the "carriers of history"? Path dependence and the evolution of conventions, organizations and institutions', *Structural Change and Economic Dynamics*, **5**(2), 205–20.

David, P.A. and Warren C. Sanderson (1997a), 'Making use of treacherous advice: Cognitive progress, Bayesian adaptation and the tenacity of unreliable knowledge,' in J.V. Nye and J. Drobak (eds), *Frontiers of the New Institutional Economics*, San Diego, CA: Academic Press.

David, P.A. (1997b), 'Path dependence and the quest for historical economics: One more chorus of the ballad of QWERTY', University of Oxford Discussion Papers in Economic and Social History, No. 20 (November), available at: http://www.nuff.ox.ac.uk/economics/history/pap20.

David, P.A., Dominique Foray and Jean-Michel Dalle (1998a), 'Marshallian externalities and the emergence and spatial stability of technological enclaves,' *Economics of Innovation and New Technologies*, Special issue on Economics of Localized Technical Change, ed. C. Antonelli, **4**(2&3), 147–82.

David, P.A. (1998b), 'Communication norms and the collective cognitive performance of "invisible colleges"', in *Creation and Transfer of Knowledge: Institutions and Incentives*, G.B. Navaretti, P. Dasgupta, K.-G. Maier and D. Siniscalco (eds.), Berlin-Heidelberg: Springer-Verlag.

David, P.A. (1998c), 'From the economics of QWERTY to the millennium bug', *Stanford University Economics Department Newsletter*, Stanford, CA, Fall, 1998.

David, P.A. (1999a), 'At last, a remedy for chronic QWERTY-skepticism!' Discussion Paper for the European Summer School in Industrial Dynamics (ESSID), held at l'Institute d'Etudes Scientifiques de Cargèse (Corse), France, September, available at: http://www-econ.stanford.edu/.

David, P.A. (1999b), 'Krugman's economic geography of development: NEGs, POGs and naked models in space', *International Regional Science Review*, **22**(2), 162–72.

David, P.A. (2000a), 'Path dependence and varieties of learning in the evolution of technological practice', in John Ziman (ed.), *Technological Innovation as an Evolutionary Process*, Cambridge: Cambridge University Press.
David, P.A. (2000b), '"Just-in-time" for Y2K, and next, . . . for irreversible global warming?' *Invited Economic Memoranda for the President of the United States*, White House Office of Communications, 3 March.
David, P.A. (2000c), 'Path dependent learning, and the evolution of beliefs and behaviors,' in U. Pagano and A. Nicita (eds), *The Evolution of Economic Diversity*, London: Routledge.
David, P.A. (2001), 'Path dependence, its critics, and the quest for "Historical Economics"', in P. Garrouste and S. Ioannides (eds), *Evolution and Path Dependence in Economic Ideas: Past and Present*, Cheltenham: Edward Elgar.
David, P.A. and M. Thomas (2003) 'Thinking Historically About Economic Challenges: Editors' Introduction,' in P.A. David and M. Thomas (eds), *The Economic Future in Historical Perspective*, Oxford University Press for The British Academy, pp. 1–27.
David, P.A. (2005a), 'History Matters – QWERTY Matters,' The Tawney Lecture for the Economic History Society, presented at the EHS Conference in Glasgow, Scotland, 1 April 2001. (Revised 15 July 2005; expanded version under preparation for publication.)
David, P.A. (2005b), 'Path dependence in economic processes: Implications for policy analysis in dynamical systems contexts,' in Kurt Dopfer, (ed.), *The Evolutionary Foundations of Economics*, Cambridge: Cambridge University Press.
David, P.A. (2005c), 'Path Dependence and Historical Social Science: An Introductory Lecture.' An Invited Lecture to the Symposium on *Twenty years of 'QWERTY-effects' and path dependence studies*, held at State University-Higher School of Economics, Moscow, 13 May, 2005. SIEPR Policy Paper No. 04-022, available at: http://siepr.stanford.edu/papers/pdf/04-22.pdf.
David, P.A. (2006), 'Europe's universities and innovation – Past, present and future', SIEPR Discussion Paper, Stanford University (March), available at: http://siepr.stanford.edu/papers/pdf/06-10.html.
Durlauf, S.N. (1993), 'Nonergodic economic growth', *Rev Econ Stud*, **60**(2), 349–66.
Durlauf, S. and H.P. Young (2001), 'The new social economics,' in S. Durlauf and H.P. Young (eds), *Social Dynamics*, Cambridge, MA: MIT Press.
Fisher, F.M. (1983), *The Disequilibrium Foundations of Equilibrium Economics*, New York: Cambridge University Press.
Geyl, P. (1936), *The Netherlands Divided (1609–1648)* [Translated by S.T. Bindoff in collaboration with the author], London: Williams & Norgate.
Geyl, P. (1961–1964), *The Netherlands in the Seventeenth Century,* 2 vols, New York: Barnes and Noble.
Grindley, P. (1992), *Standards, Business Strategy and Policy: A Casebook*, London: London Business School.
Liebowitz, S.J. and S.E. Margolis (1990), 'The fable of the keys', *J Law Econ*, **33**, 1–25.
Liebowitz, S.J. and S.E. Margolis (1994), 'Network externality: An uncommon tragedy', *J Econ Perspect* **8**(2), 133–50.
Liebowitz, S.J. and S.E. Margolis (1995), 'Path dependence, lock-in, and history', *J Law Econ Org*, **11**(1), 205–26.
Liggett, T.M. (1985), *Interacting Particle Systems (Grundlehren der mathematischen Wissenschaftern 276)*, Berlin: Springer.
Mattingly, G. (1959), *The Armada*, Boston: Houghton-Mifflin.
Puffert, D.J. (2002), 'Path dependence in spatial networks: The standardization of railway track gauge', *Explor Econ Hist*, **39**, 282–314.
Puffert, D.J. (2004), 'Path dependence, network form and technological change', in T.W. Guinnane, W.A. Sundstrom and W.C. Whatley (eds), *History Matters: Essays on Economic Growth, Technology, and Demographic Change*, Stanford, CA: Stanford University Press.

PART II

Evolutionary theory in law and economics

5. System and evolution in corporate governance

Simon Deakin and Fabio Carvalho

1. INTRODUCTION

The aim of this chapter is to explore the scope for synthesis between systems theory and new institutionalist approaches within economics. Such a project has the potential to offer, among other things, a more fully rounded view of legal evolution. At first sight it may seem that the methodological assumptions of economics are too far removed from those of systems theory for any kind of synthesis to be feasible. Economics describes itself as a behavioural science which studies the logic of choice under conditions of scarcity. Systems theory, on the other hand, focuses on the communicative processes through which social order is reproduced over time. In most contexts the two disciplines address different questions and use mutually incompatible techniques. However, as economics becomes increasingly concerned with the role institutions play in coordinating the behaviour of economic agents, it encounters a set of issues which are also central to systems theory. The nature of the link between legal change and economic development is one of these issues, and the interdisciplinary field of 'law and economics' now provides the terrain on which rival conceptions of the evolutionary process are being advanced.

We begin our analysis by attempting to unpack the ontological assumptions made about law and the legal system within different strands of the law and economics literature, and to draw out their implications for both normative and positive analysis. We use examples taken from the economics of company law and corporate governance to illustrate our argument. We suggest that mainstream law and economics approaches treat legal rules as surrogate prices, and contrast this with a conception of law as a cognitive resource upon which agents draw when engaging in production and exchange. The focus then shifts to systems theory, which offers an account of the creation and reproduction of norms viewed from within the legal system itself. In explaining the function of the legal system in terms of the reduction and organization of complexity, systems theory provides a further dimension to the notion of law as a cognitive resource. We then examine in more detail how a systems approach can aid understanding of the evolution of legal norms. Where the standard law and economics analysis sees legal evolution as occurring through a linear process of adjustment to the external environment, systems theory stresses the notion of coevolution of law and the economy. In doing so it directs attention to the discontinuous and asynchronic quality of legal change. This offers an alternative normative perspective to the dominant contractualist and deregulatory tradition in law and economics, as well as a more complete positive theory of legal evolution.

2. ALTERNATIVE PERSPECTIVES WITHIN LAW AND ECONOMICS: COMPANY LAW AS CONTRACT, DEFAULT RULE, AND REFLEXIVE REGULATION

We begin by looking at divergent approaches to the conceptualization of law within the law and economics literature. The law and economics approach claims to offer a method for analysing the impact of law and regulation on behaviour. The economic impact of law is modelled as a particular illustration of a wider case. This is the one made familiar by neoclassical economics, which tells us how agents respond to price information in such a way as to maximize general welfare while simultaneously pursuing their individual well-being. On this basis, different types of law and regulation can be understood as inducing particular behavioural responses of agents. These lead to contractual outcomes which have a range of implications for allocative efficiency. Legal rules can enhance allocative efficiency by reducing transaction costs in various ways. But these cases aside, laws which interfere with the bargaining process prevent the achievement of equilibrium states in which allocative efficiency is maximized. As a result, there is a strong policy preference on the part of corporate law and economics scholars for 'default rules' of varying kinds which can be avoided or modified through contracting, and scepticism towards 'mandatory' rules which leave no such scope for bargaining (Easterbrook and Fischel 1991; Cheffins 1997). Mandatory rules often have the aim of redistributing resources from one group to another; but if they succeed in doing so, this can only be at the expense of aggregate well-being, thereby illustrating the inevitability of the 'big trade off' between equality and efficiency (Okun 1975).

The 'contractarian' model of Easterbrook and Fischel (1991) goes furthest in questioning the role of external regulation of corporate transactions. Here, the rules of company law approximate to the 'hypothetical bargain' which the parties would have made in a zero transaction cost environment. The rules operate as defaults which the parties can always modify or avoid through contract if they choose to. Alternative approaches see an extended role for defaults of various kinds – 'penalty' and 'strong' defaults – which do not necessarily represent the term which the parties 'would have wanted'. The role of penalty defaults is to induce information sharing and cooperation by penalizing parties who opportunistically exploit asymmetries of information, while strong defaults, which cannot easily be contracted out of, provide disincentives for the creation of negative externalities (Ayres and Gertner 1989).

Company law is replete with examples of default rules. Two particularly well known examples are the model corporate constitutions which, under legislation, apply in the absence of contrary agreement by the members of the company (in the UK context, the model articles set out in delegated legislation currently derived from the Companies Act 2006), and the rules governing self-dealing and conflicts of interest on the part of directors, many of which can be avoided through mechanisms of disclosure to and/or approval by various organs of the company (Law Commission 1999).

Whatever their differences, both the economic models just referred to make the same ontological move: they occupy the common theoretical ground of thinking about the rules of company law as *surrogate prices* (see Deakin and Hughes 1999). Law is thought of as a surrogate for prices in the sense that the agent's choice of behaviour is seen as a direct cause and consequence of rules – much in the same way that choices function in relation to prices in a market setting. The legal system (judges, legislators) 'supplies' a certain term through a default rule. Alternative terms simply set differential costs to contracting around the supplied default (Ayres and Gertner 1989). Agents will choose to behave either as the default term indicates (paying the lower price) or as the more expensive tailored term suggests (paying the higher price). Behaviour that is not consonant with the default is more costly, thus 'demand' will tend to concentrate on the default choice. But as the use of the more costly behaviour becomes widespread (hence in greater 'demand'), the equilibrium tends to shift the default to this kind of term, so that it becomes cheaper to use. The 'contractarian' view adopted by Easterbrook and Fischel (1991) relies on such dynamics to suggest that rule-making activity in company law should not interfere with the equilibrium. Ayres and Gertner's (1989) penalty default mechanism sees control of the default provision as a 'tool' through which the law induces certain kinds of behaviour, in much the same way as the control of prices induces consumer choices.

Conventional law and economics looks at the form of a legal rule – mandatory or default – and works out its likely economic consequences from there. However, this point of view is necessarily qualified if a 'procedural' or 'reflexive' conception of company law is adopted. The starting point now is the observation of the impossibility of complete, *ex ante* contracting over the terms upon which the different stakeholders (employees, shareholders, creditors) combine their inputs in the context of the firm. The adoption of an incomplete contracting framework represents an ontological move towards the notion of law as a 'cognitive resource'. In a world where private ordering is incomplete, the role of the law is to provide a resource of information about solutions to bargaining problems. The law assists the parties to achieve contractual cooperation through a process of collective or social learning. This move is important because it brings into the analysis a dimension lacking in the conventional law and economics account but which is essential to understanding the nature of law as a social practice, namely that of *interpretation*.

Contractual incompleteness *ex ante* gives rise to *ex post* bargaining among participants in the firm over the quasi-rents generated by cooperation between them. 'Corporate governance' is the term used to describe the architecture that shapes *ex post* bargaining processes (Zingales 1998). This is composed of rules agreed upon by the parties *ex ante* (such as the corporate constitution), and rules that are set out by the legal system to supply fill-in defaults which *ex ante* provisions fail to cover. Scattered across the system are mandatory rules in those situations where justifications such as those of paternalism, or externalities, have been deemed by the legal system to justify restraints on private ordering. So far this does not look unlike the standard law and economics approach. The difference made by the shift of perspective becomes clear when we ask the question: how do company participants interact with the governance system? While those who adopt the view of law as surrogate prices would probably answer 'they act *according* to it', the theory of reflexive law says 'they act *within* it'.

The theory of reflexive law lays two fundamental new assumptions which have knock-on effects on the way of thinking of not only the law-behaviour relationship, but also the behaviour-efficiency analysis. The first fundamental assumption-change relates to the expansion of the concept of efficiency as the object of the economic analysis of company law. Much of the conventional economic analysis of law focuses on *allocative* efficiency, whereby a given combination or allocation of resources is measured against alternative states in order to ascertain whether there has been an increase in the welfare or well-being of particular individuals or of society as a whole. Reflexive theory brings into the analysis of company law the concepts of *technical* efficiency and *dynamic* efficiency. The former comprises the assessment of economic gains not generated by the reallocation of resources but by improved use in its existing allocation, while the latter refers to the capacity of a given system (a company or, at a higher level, a sector or industry) to innovate and survive in a changing and uncertain environment. In other words, dynamic efficiency is concerned with the capacity of the system to maintain itself over time in a changing environment.

By analysing law beyond allocative efficiency, the economic function of company law ceases to consist in 'perfecting' the market through its influence on the price mechanism (through surrogate prices) to correct market imperfections. Efficiency now acquires a temporal dimension and is seen as a 'process'. Attempting to 'perfect' allocation by hypothetically imagining what such a state would be and designing rules to work the price mechanism towards that particular set-up, misses the point that it is only through certain imperfections that opportunities exist for competitive advantage to be achieved. Law then departs from a role of promoting allocative efficiency by correcting imperfections, to a more broadly considered task of fostering conditions under which risk and uncertainty can be effectively managed.

The theory of reflexive law also reconsiders the notion of economic agents' rationality. In place of the *substantive rationality* approach of mainstream law and economics, the theory of reflexive approach to company law assumes *procedural rationality*. Viewing law as surrogate prices relating to behaviour through the working of the price mechanism requires us to assume that agents possess the calculative and computational power needed to internalize and act upon the signals they receive from the contractual environment, so the laws, like prices, are to that extent self-enforcing. The theory of reflexive regulation drops such an assumption in favour of one of procedural rationality, whereby economic agents aim to bargain towards cooperative outcomes but cannot, *ex ante*, predict the results of the bargaining process (Deakin and Hughes 1999). Tackling head-on the consequences of limited information, procedural rationality brings to the theoretical agenda the understanding of behaviour as 'materialized intention', that is to say, as a product of individual (or group-shared) cognition based on available information, as opposed to seeing behaviour as a mechanical response to legal or contractual provisions.

From this point of view, legal rules are part of a wider set of 'social norms'. Social norms are rules of conduct derived from conventions that emerge from repeated interaction between members of a certain community, through a process of social learning. Over time, the adoption of certain conduct by individuals in certain types of situation proves to be more beneficial to those involved in the interactions. That is, in repeated situations with a prisoner's dilemma type of game dynamic, through observation of each other's behaviour, and cooperation on the basis of such observation, conventions emerge as 'tacit agreements' between the interacting agents. From this may be derived the understanding that through a process of 'social learning', social norms emerge from conventions (Sugden 1998a).

If we take the view that legal rules interact with social norms in guiding agents' conduct, the reception and implementation of legal rules is not a straightforward process. The analysis no longer takes for granted that agents fully understand the meaning (and objectives) of legal rules as a precondition of acting upon them. Instead, the influence of a set of constraints based on existing conventions will permeate the process of the reception and implementation of legal rules. The way in which legal rules are received and interpreted by the parties therefore needs to be understood at the level of the processes and procedures through which commercial relationships are sustained. Reception and implementation of legal rules will, indeed, be subject to 'second order' effects caused by the interaction of the new rule with an existing body of social conventions (whether socially or legally produced). There is, at the level of a group of agents, a 'collectively shared capital' which will serve as the basis for the reception of the positive legal rule, but also potentially undermine its implementation.

Viewing the economic analysis of law with regard to axioms of procedural rationality and to these extended definitions of efficiency invites a normative argument for the production of a certain type of legal rule – *reflexive law* – which is not based simply 'command and control', but which acts in conjunction with self-regulating mechanisms present within the 'community of experience' of the system being regulated, whether this is the industrial sector, the company, or the board of directors. Understanding the operation of the existing set of constraints of the system or object of the regulation, will provide the law-maker with the capacity to estimate the 'second order' effects and use such dynamics to 'steer' behaviour. At the level of company law, an understanding of self-regulatory mechanisms, in the form of social norms, which operate to shape the conduct of company participants, is therefore crucial to any consideration of economic efficiency to be generated by the introduction of a new legal rule of corporate governance, or any change in an existing one.

Working within procedural, or 'reflexive', regulation – that is, dismissing the assumption of a linear, causal relationship between legal rule and agent's conduct, and designing regulation aiming at 'second order effects' – also changes the way in which the default/mandatory rule distinction is analysed from a predictive or positive point of view. Mandatory or default rules only take effect as such after interaction with the other social norms which interface with the law at the level of 'steering' agents' behaviour. Therefore, default rules may acquire a near-mandatory character if underlying social norms deter 'contracting-out', while mandatory rules may be constantly defied by structures that attempt to avoid its effects, provided that social norms and conventions ratify such behaviour.

To sum up the argument so far: understanding legal rules as a cognitive resource available to bargaining parties invites a step back in the analysis of economics of company law to accommodate a change of focus. Within standard approaches to law and economics, the core of the analysis has been on the behavioural responses of economic agents to the law. The law is treated as a given, exogenous variable. This assumes that agents can rapidly and unproblematically process information concerning the legal rule. It is not simply the case that the contracting parties are endowed with 'substantive rationality' of the kind which orthodox neoclassical theory imputes to economic agents; in addition, the legal rules themselves are assumed to be clear and unequivocal in their application. When the notions of procedural rationality and law as a cognitive resource are introduced, a much closer focus on the precise ways in which the legal system operates to produce and convey information is required. This perspective leads to a consideration of the insights provided by systems theory.

3. AUTOPOIESIS: LAW AS SYSTEM

Law and economics analyses, even those which take a sophisticated view of the operation of law alongside social norms, focus on the behavioural effects of law. Systems theory radically inverts this perspective. Now, legal norms are viewed from within the legal process itself as linked elements of a systemic order (Luhmann 1995, 2004; Teubner 1993). The form in which a legal norm is expressed is a consequence of its place within that order. The overriding measure of the effectiveness or 'efficiency' of a particular norm is its contribution towards the continuity of the system, that is, its capacity to reproduce itself over time. This in turn depends on how far the system has the means to 'process' information which it receives from external environment in such a way as to make it internally meaningful.

The same goes for the capacity of the economic system to respond to the information which it receives from the law. Each system, the legal and the economic, forms the environment of the other; each one, through its own internal dynamic of self-reproduction, constructs an image both of itself and of the systems external to it. But a unity of viewpoints is impossible so long as systems remain autopoietically closed: '[t]he systems in a system's environment are oriented to their own environments. No system can completely determine the system/environment relations of another system, save by destroying them' (Luhmann 1995: 18). Thus the notion that economic agents respond to signals from the legal system *in the same way* as they do to movements in prices cannot be sustained.

This is of course not the same thing as saying that economic agents do not respond *at all* to changes in legal rules. Systems theory does not seek to deny the existence of causal interrelationships between law and the economy. The 'autopoietic closure' of systems implies simply that their constituent elements reproduce themselves without *direct* input from the external environment. These are systems which 'use their own output as input'. However, the form which these systems take over time is subject to external influence, through a process of environmental selection. Thus 'autopoietic closure does not mean that the system is independent of its environment' (Teubner 1993: 61). It does imply that the relationship of 'coevolution' between the two is likely be 'asynchronic', in the sense that 'a complex system, seen temporally, cannot rely on point-for-point correspondencies with the environment' (Luhmann 1995: 43).

From a law and economics perspective, this type of separation implies inefficiency: to the extent that law and the economy are out of synch with one another, legal rules will not be matched to the preferences and endowments of agents. But from a systems theory perspective, we can see that it would be not just pointless, but positively counterproductive, to think in terms of dissolving the system-environment boundary. This is because it is only through the emergence of systems that the 'unorganized complexity' of the world is capable of being organized:

> The concept of a self-referentially closed system does not contradict the system's openness to the environment. Instead, in the self-referential mode of operations, closure is a form of broadening possible environmental contacts; closure increases, by constituting elements more capable of being determined, the complexity of the system that is possible for the environment. This thesis contradicts . . . the classical opposition of open and closed systems . . . (Luhmann 1995: 37)

It in is this sense that system boundaries are 'an evolutionary achievement par excellence' (Luhmann 1995: 29).

The specific role of social systems, such as law, economy, politics and religion, is to contribute to the emergence of forms of *meaning* through which the complexity of the world can be understood. The evolution of 'meaning' marks 'a new way of combining closure and openness in constructing systems' (Luhmann 1995: 38) based on the aggregation and integration of information over time. Social systems are more or less effective according to the degree to which they can simultaneously increase the flow of information from the external environment, and their internal capacity to absorb and process that information. Thus '[t]he theory is not concerned, like classical theories of equilibrium, with returning to a stable state of rest after absorption of disturbances, but with securing the constant renewal of system elements – or, more briefly, not with static but with dynamic stability' (Luhmann 1995: 49).

To say, then, that the legal system functions as a cognitive resource means that it operates in a cycle of interaction with its external environment. The legal system receives information from the external environment, processes it in forms which are specific to the creation of legal or juridical meaning, and returns this information to the environment in the form of legal communications. The capacity of economic system, in its turn, to receive this information, depends on the existence of institutions capable of receiving and processing legal information. The idea that laws are like prices is *half* right, since prices embody highly complex information about supply and demand in 'coded' form which facilitates decision making by agents who may be distant in time and place from the initial market movements (Sugden 1998a). But just as the economy possesses its own particular mechanisms for the creation of information in the form of prices, so the legal system possesses its own internal logic, which is not that of the market. This requires us to consider more closely the internal logic of legal ordering.

4. THE INTERNAL LOGIC OF THE LEGAL ORDER

Consideration of the systemic properties of the legal system sheds light on the 'backstage' of a process of creation and conveyance of the cognitive resource of law, which has its own particularities and properties. Perhaps the most crucial notion contributed by systems theory to the economic analysis of company law is the idea that *only law produces law* (Teubner 1993), and that it does so through established processes. The legal system is *not independent* from its environment, but it is *operationally autonomous*. It 'sees' and 'understands' the environment through its own cognitive processes. Law is therefore to be understood as a product of a systemic order of thought, which draws from the interaction of agents a 'view' of the environment and uses this 'feedback' according to its own processes, which, in their turn, are constantly evolving on the basis of similar observational processes. The question to be asked in law and economics is not merely what does law do to behaviour, but what does behaviour do to law, and vice versa. The process is a cycle of inter-systemic interaction, a dynamic of *coevolution* between law and the economy.

Thus the essential characteristic of the order of the legal system as a system of communication is the importance of its *internal congruence*. It is on this basis that the legal system can be said to 'reproduce itself' over time. This figure of speech is another way of saying that the agents who participate in the making of legal communications do so on the basis of a set of shared understandings about the nature of the legal system. Most fundamentally, they operate on the basis of shared assumptions about 'boundary conditions' which demarcate the legal order from other forms of communication: what counts as a legal rule, and what does not. In addition, it is a feature of legal orders that the meaning which they create refers to a shared perception that individual legal communications are linked together to form a coherent body of norms. In other words, for the agents who operate within and by reference to it, an understanding of the legal system cannot be obtained from an analysis of isolated elements, but derives from the process of self-observation of the system as a 'whole'.[1] The 'logical harmony' between the several informational components directly influences the ability of agents to understand the system. Internal congruence among the elements of the legal system is thus a critical factor for its operational performance.

Thus the process of 'self-understanding' (as a unit of self-observation and self-description) which instructs self-reproduction, is a vital step in the systemic efficiency of law. As the system produces an infinite variety of legal communications, varying levels of understanding of the system as a whole will be necessary to instruct the production of each of them. Legal communications take place in day-to-day lives of individuals as well as in the day-to-day operations of a corporation. They are produced on the basis of recursive social interactions. Legal communications are to be found in legislatures and courts, but also in regulatory bodies, government departments, and in the interactions between legal practitioners and those they advise. These different types of legal communications demand different levels of self-understanding to instruct self-production. Legal communications produced in diverse situations differ in terms of relevance as far as the overall congruence of the systemic order is concerned. For instance, complete incongruence of the legal communications created during a transaction for purchase of a loaf of bread, is clearly less costly to the system than incongruence of legal communications generated in the meeting of a board of directors, within court proceedings, or during debates in the legislature. The degree of 'relevance' is determined by the systemic order's dependence on the 'congruence quality' of the legal communications being produced, that is, the level at which the overall order will be affected by any incongruent legal communications it produces.

To preserve and improve its order, the legal system has developed processes that act to provide the various actions of self-reproduction with a systemic informational background. Thus the existence of the law concerning the director's duty of care will 'instruct' the company's directors to consult with lawyers before undertaking amendments to the company's constitution. Parliamentary debates, a bicameral parliamentary system, judicial review, hierarchically ordered courts, the doctrine of precedent, and so on, will also act to improve congruence levels of legal communications. Arguably, all these processes can be seen to have been produced by the legal system to serve as mechanisms to ensure

---

1 More precisely, since the legal system has an order, and the patterns of the order make the acquaintance of a 'spatial or temporal part' of the system a source of reliable expectations about the functioning of the rest of the system (Hayek 1973), self-observation can be seen to be a process that covers 'partially' and not, literally, the 'whole' of the legal system.

that systemically-relevant legal communications (company constitutions, laws, statutory instruments, precedents) are produced in an internally congruent manner.

Internal congruence, in turn, is linked to the capacity of the system to provide legal certainty. Enhancing legal certainty can be thought of in terms of decreasing asymmetries of understanding of the legal instructions between agents. As such, it has a directly positive impact on the role of law as a cognitive resource. This is clear if we look at an ontological sub-level, where both the company and company law can be seen as social subsystems. The legal rules of corporate governance act as 'known variables' to be factored-in as part of the pay-offs of a network of cooperation games played among company participants. By applying their knowledge of legal rules, parties are able to rely on what other players within the games are more likely to do instead of having to rely on probable moves as a function of a pay-off matrix which is largely unpredictable. In the terms used by evolutionary game theory and information-theoretic economics, the result is that information asymmetry is reduced, risk is manageable, and moves can be taken towards the achievement of welfare-enhancing equilibria. Thus the more successful the legal system is in processing the complexity of its external environment, the more effective it will be, in its turn, in shaping cooperative outcomes in that environment.

Thus we might say that the congruent self-production, based on comprehensive self-observation and self-description, of the legal system, contributes to economic efficiency. It does so in the general sense of enabling the legal system to provide cognitive resources which, in their turn, facilitate economic transactions. Yet the legal system can only perform this role if it is separated from the economic system, and if distinctiveness of its internal processes of self-reproduction is maintained. The legal system cannot be subjected to the logic of economic exchange, if it is to retain its autonomy as a social subsystem. As Luhmann (2004: 391) puts it:

> A differentiated money economy makes high but (and this is crucial!) unpayable demands on the law. In order to make the economy possible in the form of its own autopoiesis, law has to fulfill its own function, not that of the economy, effectively. Law must not belong to the type of goods or services that can be bought in the economic system.

This leads us on to a consideration of the role played by legal concepts in the evolution of the law.

5. THE EVOLUTIONARY FUNCTIONS OF LEGAL CONCEPTS

Law and economics approaches to legal evolution focuses on the issue of selection, and sees adjudication and litigation as the selective mechanisms by which efficient rules emerge from the self-interested behaviour of actors. According to the model advanced by Rubin (1977) and Priest (1977), in a system of judge-made law, inefficient rules are more likely to be selected against than efficient ones because private parties have greater incentives to challenge them through litigation. In Priest's approach, it is not necessary to assume that judges will produce efficient rules most of the time. Even if, in a given population, rules were distributed entirely randomly with regard to their efficiency, selection through litigation would work to cull the less efficient ones. In other models, which focus on the supply side, efficiency could be improved if courts were to compete with one another, as they do in cases of multi-tiered or overlapping jurisdictions, and this model can be extended to legislatures operating in federal systems which allow for regulatory competition (Romano 1990).

Law and economics approaches see the legal system as open to external pressures which, over time, will ensure its alignment with the economy. This alignment might be prevented or delayed in given contexts where, for example, competition between courts is restricted, or litigation is unduly costly; however, these limitations can in principle be removed by appropriate institutional reforms. From a systems-theoretical perspective which sees law as operatively closed to its environment, the issue of legal evolution cannot be so straightforwardly resolved: 'if one has to start from the assumption that systems are closed and their structures are [internally] determined, it is far more difficult to understand (1) how structures can be changed at all, and (2) why it is possible at times . . . to detect the direction of those changes, for instance in the diversification of species or in the increased complexity of societies' (Luhmann 2004: 231).

The answer given by Luhmann in *Law as a Social System* is to make use of the Darwinian 'schema' or 'algorithm' of variation-selection-stabilization as a basis for understanding systemic evolution. From this point of view, the law and economics approach offers at best a partial analysis, which focuses on only one mechanism, selection, to the exclusion of the other two. To talk of a legal or institutional equivalent of 'natural selection' only makes sense, Luhmann suggests, if we first define exactly what is being 'exposed to selection by the environment' (Luhmann 2004: 232). A critical assumption made in law and economic approaches is that the legal system can produce the rules that the economy needs, leaving environmental selection to do its job. By contrast, a systemic view maintains that the capacity of the legal system for variation is channelled and, consequently, constrained by the need to ensure internal congruence as the condition of the system's self-reproduction or stabilization. Selection can only operate on that finite set of legal rules which the system, in the light of its historical development, has the capacity to produce. This is not to say that innovation, and hence variation, in legal rules does not occur, but to shift the focus of analysis on to those processes, internal to the legal system, which allow information from the environment to be assimilated and integrated in such a way as to make variation possible.

To organize the mass of legal information in a manner which can be efficiently processed, the legal system makes use of working variables in the form of legal concepts. Concepts are at the core of legal dogmatics, or systematic doctrinal thought, through which the elements of the legal order are stabilized; 'dogmatics guarantees that the legal system approves itself in its change as a *system*' (Luhmann 2004: 257). Concepts provide the means by which substantive rules are linked together to form the coherent whole of the legal order, and, in turn, the mechanism by which continuity, and hence system congruence through time, are maintained when one rule succeeds another. Concepts thereby perform the evolutionary function of inheritance or stabilization in a manner equivalent to that of genes in relation to living, biological systems (Teubner 1993: 51).

Concepts can be understood as memetic 'replicators' which are the institutional equivalent of genes, and substantive legal rules or norms as the 'interactors' in which they are embedded (Deakin, 2003; see Figure 5.1). The value of using the genetic model in this context, as Luhmann suggests, is not simply to invoke a potentially useful analogy, but to act 'as a pointer to a general evolutionary theory, which can have many different

	Replicator	*Interactor*	*Environment*
Biological evolution	Gene	Organism	Natural world
Social evolution	Meme (corporate culture)	Institution (enterprise)	Social world
Legal evolution	Concept (fiduciary duty)	Rule (No-conflicts rule)	Normative world

Source: Adapted from Deakin 2002.

Figure 5.1 Units of biological, social and legal evolution

applications (Luhmann 2004: 231). It need not be assumed that there is a precise match between biological and social (or legal) mechanisms, and the use of the model in the legal context should take into account what we know of the nature of the legal processes. In particular, whatever the value of a gene-centred view might be in the context of biological theory, the use of the idea of the 'meme' in the legal context should not be taken to imply that legal evolution is 'meme-centred' or 'memic' in the sense of being driven entirely by dogmatic structures. Concepts do not *dictate* legal outcomes; 'they make precise what is problematic in the *quaesito iuris* but do not establish an automatic device that leads to a decision' (Luhmann 2004: 342). They may *influence* the content of rules, but they are also influenced by that content and, at a further remove, by the environment in which the rules operate.

A systemic understanding of the Darwinian algorithm sees it in cyclical terms: it is through the interaction of variation, selection and stabilization that information flows between the system and its environment. In the context of legal evolution, information about the environment enters the legal system as rules are contested through the processes of litigation and legislation, among other things. By 'encoding' that information in a 'compressed' or 'compounded' form, concepts allow for its retention within the legal system. Concepts can be thought of as 'instructing' the production of rules in the same sense (loosely) that genes instruct the building of proteins and hence of organisms, but just as genes can be turned on and off by environment triggers, so the operation of concepts cannot be isolated from the social and economic context within which legal rules are applied, contested and enforced. As particular rules are selected and deselected through environmental pressures of various kinds, so the content of concepts will alter over time. Concepts cannot exist independently of the rules in which they are contained, any more than genes have an existence separate from their own interactors; thus changes in the population of rules will lead, although more gradually, to changes in conceptual structures.

The key to understanding the way in which legal concepts operate as evolutionary mechanisms is the idea of abstraction as a particular form of 'coding'. The difference between a concept and a rule, in this context, is the difference between an abstract idea such as the concept of 'fiduciary duty' and a specific rule such as the requirement that

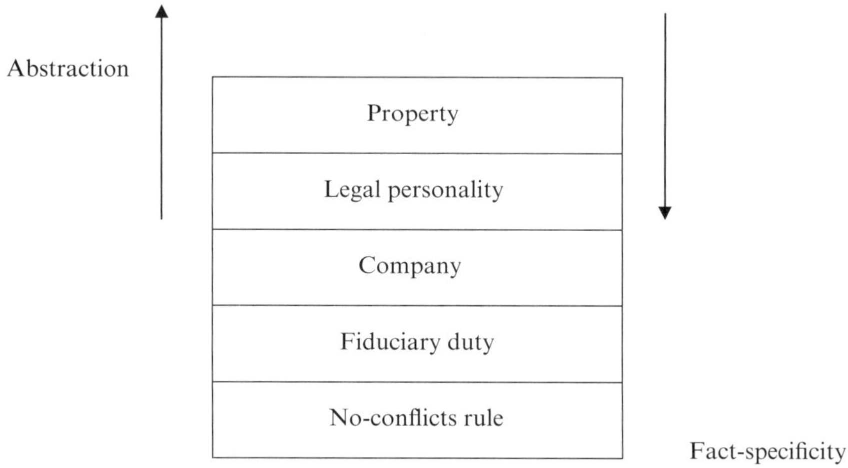

Figure 5.2 Degrees of abstraction and fact-specificity in company law concepts

a company director must not put herself in a position where her interests conflict with those of the company (the 'no-conflicts rule'). The notion of a 'fiduciary' is not itself a normative command, and can only be mobilized as such if it is embodied in a more specific norm such as the no-conflicts rule. It *informs* a family of linked rules on the duties of company directors and others in analogous positions, and is called on as an aid to interpretation at the point when, through adjudication or statutory drafting, the emergence of a new rule is in issue.

The analysis of doctrinal concepts in legal systems, in both the common law and the civil law, shows that concepts vary in levels of abstraction (as a counterbalance to levels of fact-specificity). This is illustrated in Figure 5.2. Legal concepts such as 'property' and 'legal personality' are highly abstract, while 'fiduciary duty' and 'conflict of interest' are specific to certain facts of the economic environment which are related to the emergence of the business enterprise as an organizational form. These concepts also display interdependence. The use of the legal concept 'fiduciary duty' as it operates in the company law context (in the sense of 'director's duty') is attached to the use of the legal concepts of 'property' and 'legal personality' among many others at similar, superior, and inferior abstraction 'levels'. Patterns of interdependence tend to show greater dependence of abstract-inferior concepts on abstract-superior legal concepts than vice versa. Thus a pattern of abstract-superiority and abstract-inferiority is revealed. Because the legal system works to convey legal instruction in the form of rules and because it has to be 'cognition-friendly' for procedurally rational agents, the information contained in legal concepts must be related to certain fact situations. Abstraction – *encoding* – makes legal concepts fact-neutral (Markesinis 1997), whereas interpretation – *decoding* – makes them fact-specific.

In principle, the more abstract a particular concept is, the less susceptible it is to change through evolutionary pressure. This is because legal concepts which are more fact-specific are thereby more 'exposed' to environmental selection. Although this suggestion may explain different patterns in 'mutation' rates, does it explain why is there a pattern of 'substantive dependence' of abstract-inferior to abstract-superior concepts? In part, yes. This is because the environmental 'selection' of legal rules will most strongly impact on self-reproductive 'mutation' at the level of fact-specific legal concepts, simply because environmental 'pressure' for change will most often arise at the point where there is 'legal rule-environmental fact' interaction. Because more fact-specific legal concepts are 'mutated' more often, abstract-superior concepts 'replicate' themselves over a longer period. Since the legal system undertakes successive self-referential analyses as a precondition of its self-reproduction, highly abstract concepts tend to accumulate more influence within the system's self-reproduction processes, diffusing their information throughout the system.

The importance of this observation lies in helping us to see that those concepts with the highest fact content (which are the ones that clearly indicate how the agent should proceed when faced with a certain set of facts) are a product of successive levels of 'coupling' of conceptual abstractions with social facts. High-level forms are brought down to 'ground level' application by matching concepts with facts. At some point, the information provided to agents derives from legal concepts that have enough fact-specificity to allow homogeneous interpretation. However, any legal concept with high fact-specificity is built up through a process of construction which means that it 'encapsulates' a whole 'chain' of abstract superior concepts, all the way 'up' to the most high-level principles. This coupling process enables information contained in a large number of legal rules to be 'condensed', as Luhmann puts it (2004: 341), in conceptual form:

> . . . the meaning of [legal] concepts is enriched in the process of repeat-use – among other things by a great number of rules that are formulated with the help of these concepts, or by legal problems which arise through the use of the concept and which are then solved in a particular way, which then co-characterizes the concept . . . Decisions and rules then become components of the concept . . . In this sense concepts store experiences and keep them on call, even though the concept does not formulate these experiences (otherwise it would become a text) but only re-actualizes them in a given instance.

The idea of abstraction also helps further to clarify the difference between legal concepts as the equivalent of the 'genotype' or replicator, and legal 'rules' operating as the phenotype or interactor. If highly abstract concepts provide the core of the system, it is the more highly fact-specific concepts (which effectively instruct their application to the facts of the environment) which agents receive as legal rules. Legal rules, in this sense, are not to be understood strictly or exclusively as written law ('script-coded' information). The legal rule is the information conveyed by the legal system, and comprises not just the relevant 'script-coded' information, but also the 'chain' of abstract-superior legal concepts which inform its interpretation. The key point here is that the expression 'legal rules' is not applied simply as a synonym for highly fact-specific 'ground-application' concepts, but also for the way in which these are viewed from 'outside' the legal system. The difference between them, used for purposes of this analysis, is that concepts are the working variables *within* the legal system and legal rules are the 'message' conveyed to the environment. The same informational unit can be viewed at the same time as a highly specific legal concept, from within the system, *and* as a legal rule with intended social or economic effects, from the side of the environment.

This dual aspect of legal concepts helps to clarify, in turn, their role as devices for achieving 'structural coupling' between the legal system and its environment. Although the legal and economic systems are 'operatively closed' in the sense of being reproduced through their own distinctive operations, without direct mutual reference, they are nevertheless 'cognitively open' in the sense of each being exposed to information, and thereby to environmental pressure, from each other. The presence within the legal system of concepts of varying levels of abstraction means that the legal system has not only 'a highly sensitive reception and transmission system for economic news' but also mechanisms for ensuring that 'a high level of mutual irritations in both systems can be absorbed' (Luhmann 2004: 390). Legal concepts combine what Luhmann refers to as 'redundancy of information', or those elements of conceptual form which, through repetition, serve to maintain the continuity of legal ideas over time and hence ensure the stabilization of the system, with the capacity to introduce new information through 'variety' and thereby permit variation to occur. Variety can only be given conceptual expression when combined with redundancy, and there is a trade-off between them which puts a limit on how much new information a given conceptual structure can absorb without losing its value as source of legal reliability and certainty. Thus it is through the relationship between redundancy (or continuity) and variety that the (limited) adaptation of the legal system to its environment is expressed (Luhmann 2004: 322).

6. EVOLUTION AND EFFICIENCY IN COMPANY LAW

We are now in a position to analyse more closely the process of evolution within company law. We have suggested that at any given time the legal system has its conceptual structures organized in a hierarchical pattern, the most abstract concepts at the 'top' and the most fact-specific (corresponding to legal rules) at the 'bottom'. In between, there is a whole range of legal concepts of varying levels of abstraction, exhibiting a more or less high degree of interdependence one with another as the precondition for system congruence.

The Darwinian theory of evolution, when applied to the social sphere, is often misunderstood to imply that those features of institutions which survive a competitive process of selection and deselection are necessarily optimal. As noted above, the argument that competition leads to the emergence of optimal norms is a mainstay of standard law and economics analyses of corporate governance; first applied in the context of interjurisdictional competition to attract incorporations in the USA (the 'Delaware effect': Romano 1990), it has been more recently invoked to support the prediction of global convergence around the 'standard shareholder model' of company law (Hansmann and Kraakman 2001). Even those law and economics writers who identify a prominent role for 'path dependent' effects in company law do not believe that these will lead to persistent suboptimal outcomes (Roe 1996; Bebchuk and Roe 1999).

Institutional forms may be functional and adaptive in the strictly qualified sense that features which are subject to selective pressures are well suited to the particular environmental contexts *in which they originally arose*. The process of natural selection in biology does not imply the inevitable discarding of those parts of the genetic code which hinder survival and the retention of those which assist it. Because selection occurs on the basis of *inherited* traits, the information encoded in the genotype is functional for *past* environments. Moreover, there is no means of ensuring that *only* those instructions which have current value endure; traits which have no useful function may persist as long as they do not actively impede survival to the point of being deselected. If the same were true of legal evolution, we would expect to find the persistence of doctrinal structures long after the point when the purposes for which they had first been invented had passed, a phenomenon for which there is indeed abundant evidence (Deakin 2003).

A consequence of the need for the legal system to maintain its internal order or system-congruence is that it is only through internal conceptual mutations that a 'new rule' can be generated in response to evolutionary pressures. Thus the process of 'adaptation' to the environment is neither automatic, nor optimal. The transformation must involve the *least* disturbance possible to the legal system's own internal congruence. The mutation process may cause the splitting, merger, recombination and/or dissolution of legal concepts. Mutation occurs by 'rearranging' the available components and coupling them with the 'new' informational components that represent the 'new facts' that caused the pressure for mutation. The resulting transformation is suboptimal in two aspects. Firstly, it is suboptimal in the sense that it ceases at the point where environmental pressure is overcome by internal transaction costs of legal change, and not at the point of the complete 'dissolution' of external pressure. Secondly, suboptimality occurs because the change will carry informational material from 'old' conceptual structures into 'new' ones, making use of components which are already there within existing conceptual 'units'.

The emergence of company law from the general body of contract and property law can be used as an illustration of this mechanism. The process can be reconstructed in functional terms as follows. As the evolution of the economic system brings about the emergence of firms as organizational forms for networked cooperation, the legal system is subject to pressures to adapt legal rules to the new economic dynamics that arise. Minor adaptations can be carried out by coupling the new facts to the existing concepts which instructed the legal rules of contract and property law. These conceptual changes are first manifested to the environment through changes in the relevant script-coded legal information (that is, new case law altering precedents and statutory changes) and through changes in the interpretation of script-coded legal information (that is, legal doctrine and case law).

As the firm as an organizational form matures, contractual relations among participants in the firm's cooperation network acquire particularities that create a distinction between intra-firm transactions and decentralized 'arms-length' exchanges. This growing distinction between the facts involved in 'intra-firm' commercial relations and those arising from decentralized exchange exerts corresponding pressure at the level of the legal system, 'demanding' legal rules that are able to cope with these distinctions. The legal system, after a certain amount of pressure, reaches a limit as to how far it can mutate concepts to the extent needed while working with the building blocks of property and contract. When this point is reached, in order to preserve internal congruence while also responding to environmental shifts, concepts of contract and property mutate, 'splitting' them into subconceptual forms. The result is the combination of ideas derived from 'property', 'legal personality', 'association' and 'contract' which come together to form the highly abstract concept of 'company'.

This mutation has knock-on effects on abstract-inferior concepts. The new notion of 'company' is now the abstract-superior concept that instructs successively abstract-inferior concepts of company law (such as the company limited by share capital, the company limited by guarantee, partnerships, and so on) all the way down to the most fact-specific 'company' concepts, which are the many and varied rules of company law. The contractual genealogy of company law is visible today in the way in which core concepts retain informational components that are present in the conceptual structures of general contract law. Thus section 33 of the (UK) Companies Act 2006 establishes that the company's memorandum and articles of association, when registered, 'bind the company and its members' as a contract that is 'signed and sealed' by all of them. Section 172 of the 2006 Act provides that directors shall have regard in the performance of their functions to the interests of a range of stakeholders including employees. While section 33 is generally recognized to be the most explicit recognition of company law's dependence on certain general contract law concepts, section 172 and its (partial) predecessor, section 309 of the 1985 Act, are often thought to be anomalous, politically-inspired insertions into the body of modern company law. But section 172 also has contractual roots. If company law emerged more effectively to regulate contractual relations between the different owners of inputs to the process of production, then in addition to provisions which protect shareholders from expropriation by managers, it is not surprising to find that rules aimed at protecting other company participants (including employees) take a form derived from core company law principles. Thus in addition to the origins of section 172 within the political system as a response to concerns, firstly at the end of the 1970s and early 1980s for some acknowledgement to be made of the role of employees within the corporate structure (see Wedderburn 2004 for discussion), and more recently as part of the stakeholder debate initiated by the Company Law Review in the late 1990s and early 2000s (Company Law Review Steering Committee 2000), this provision can also be understood as a manifestation of certain foundational principles of fiduciary law, adapted to the task of expressing the multi-stakeholder conception of the modern enterprise.

This perspective also helps us to understand the distinction between mandatory and default rules as distinct processes for the self-reproduction of law. 'Immutable' or mandatory rules can only be varied if the legal system undertakes self-production through 'formal' processes which are permeated by checks and balances aimed at preserving internal and constitutional congruence. Default rules, however, can be varied by the contracting parties themselves. Agents 'interpret' the legal rules ('reading' the background conceptual structure of the rule) and decide upon variations which would better suit their particular transactions.

However, the processes of interpretation which are available to the parties themselves in the context of privately ordered rule variation are different from the processes which order self-reproduction at the level of 'formal' legal change. Parties contract with the help of their advisers, while the 'formal' production process makes use of court system hierarchy, informed judges, litigation to determine the legality or constitutionality of certain processes, and so on. When parties alter the relevant rules in the context of a default term, they potentially affect the *internal* congruence of the legal rule and not simply its external application. Will the new rule reproduce, at the level of the parties' relationship, the foundational principles with which the legal system would have endowed such a rule had it been produced through the 'formal' process? Perhaps not. The scale of the potential disturbance to the internal legal order is a function of the foundational importance of the rule in question.

The effect does not end there. In the context of rapid and networked dissemination of information, 'private' variations of legal rules can rapidly become widely applied standards (Kahan and Klausner 1997; Whincop 2002). Ultimately, this process influences, through the means of repeated and recursive interactions of agents, the creation of social norms, setting in motion the evolutionary process which triggers change at the level of the legal system. In the same way that this mechanism can work positively, it can also work perversely.

We therefore have a new criterion for judging the efficiency of mandatory and default rules. Rather than focusing exclusively on the degree of contractual 'freedom' or 'restraint' which they seem to offer to agents, the importance of the distinction lies in the different processes for legal self-reproduction which they imply.

While analysing the economic efficiency of mandatory rules in company law or in general contract law, the law and economics literature generally concludes that they are almost always inefficient from a private cost perspective, and, only in certain cases, efficient from a social cost perspective. Put simply, when only private costs are considered, hardly any justification to the limitation of contractual freedom holds. Parties have incentives to know better. If they have found a better set-up, restraining it is inefficient. When a wider calculus of social costs is considered, the picture acquires more complexity (Ayres and Gertner 1989). The efficiency of mandatory rules is then measured by comparing the gains in social cost from protecting one of the contractual parties or a third party, with the private costs of limiting contractual freedom. But the basic method of comparison is the same. The private cost of default rules is understood as the cost to the parties of contracting around them. They will only fail to produce an efficiency improvement if the gain from such improvement is inferior to the cost of contracting around the default. The theory of reflexive company law more realistically understands the process as subject to rationality limitations and 'second-order' effects (see Deakin and Hughes 1999), but the general principle is maintained.

When, however, we view the same issue from the perspective of the operational workings of the legal system and their effects on economic efficiency, it is possible to argue that limitations on contractual freedom may well be economically efficient. Mandatory rules improve the efficiency of cooperation between corporate actors by sustaining their ability to deploy the cognitive resource of law. By supplying an 'immutable' framework, the law reduces the informational costs which are necessary to 'reinterpret' the legal system in order to 'understand' all the alterations in a context of legal congruence.

The use of default rules in company law (and contract law, generally) can therefore generate private costs that are greater than the 'friction' costs of contracting around them. These are the informational costs of maintaining legal congruence in the face of variations. When parties decide to contract around a given default and lay down a privately designed legal rule within the governance framework, all the systemic consequences of such an alteration must be assessed. Altering the default provision in the model articles of association which determines that 'the directors are responsible for the management of the company's business, for which purpose they may exercise all the powers of the company'[2] may change the way in which directors' duties are to be interpreted in relation to the

[2] Formerly Article 70 of the old Table A, which was worded slightly differently, this is now Article 3 of the Model Articles for (respectively) private companies limited by share capital, private

company. This could involve a considerable informational cost. Reliance on default rules creates another kind of cost. This is the cost represented by allowing parties to customize rules that may not carry into 'application' the foundational principles of the law to the same extent that a rule created through checks and balances of the 'formal' processes of self-production of the legal system would do. This cost is a function of the foundational relevance of a given default rule and the 'equilibrium' achieved with the environment to the extent that companies contract around, or not, such a default.

7. CONCLUSIONS

Evolutionary ideas play an important role in the contemporary corporate governance debate, being regularly deployed to support deregulatory initiatives and encourage belief in the likelihood of the global convergence of governance regimes. Close inspection suggests that many of these analyses are based on false analogies, drawn from misunderstandings of natural selection processes in the biological realm. They also suffer from a failure to address the issue of the social ontology of law. The key assumption in most law and economics analyses is that legal rules operate as surrogate prices. Given the importance of this step in law and economics reasoning, it is surprising that so little attention has been given to articulating and defending it. The effect, though, is severely to limit the value of the resulting analyses, by dissolving the distinction between the legal and economic systems.

Social systems theory offers an analysis which, while in some respects highly abstract, is more realistic than that of mainstream law and economics in the sense of being more faithful to the social practice and experience of law. At the same time, the focus of systems theory upon the role of *meaning* as the precursor to social interaction throws light on some of the questions addressed by new institutional economics. From the standpoint of a theory which accepts the bounded rationality of the individual economic agent, and which sees a role for norms and conventions in overcoming coordination problems, a new field of inquiry is opened up by an understanding of law as a complex, self-referential system of communication. From this point of view, the important methodological issue is not how to understand the law in the terms of the market, but to understand the distinctive and separate qualities of the legal and economic systems.

The most significant normative implications of a consideration of systems theory in this context is that the efficiency of the law cannot be measured solely in terms of the degree to which it 'interferes' with the autonomy of the contracting parties. Nor is it the role of the legal system to 'adjust to' changes in its external environment. Rather, the efficiency of the legal system is concerned with how successful it is in ordering the complexity of the external environment to which it relates. In order to undertake this task, the legal system must be able to maintain the principle of system congruence which is the precondition of its autonomy and self-reproduction. To that end, the legal system will maintain a set of 'foundational' concepts which are to a large extent free from immediate

companies limited by guarantee, and public companies (see the Companies (Model Articles) Regulations 2008, SI 2008/3229).

evolutionary pressures, and which tend to be manifested in the form of mandatory legal rules which leave little or no room for bargaining between the parties. In practice, there are many such rules, even in the common law systems which are said, above all others, to comply with the contractualist model of corporate governance. By enabling us to understand these rules, systems theory offers the possibility of a more complete positive theory of company law than any offered to this point by the law and economics literature.

BIBLIOGRAPHY

Ayres, I. and R. Gertner (1989), 'Filling gaps in incomplete contracts: a theory of default rules', *Yale Law Journal*, **99**, 87–130.
Bebchuk, L. and M. Roe (1999), 'A theory of path dependence in corporate governance and ownership', *Stanford Law Review*, **52**, 127–170.
Cheffins, B. (1997), *Company Law: Theory, Structure and Operation*, Oxford: Clarendon Press.
Company Law Review Steering Committee (2000), *Modern Company Law for a Competitive Economy: Developing the Framework*, London: DTI.
Deakin, S. (2003), 'Evolution for our time: a theory of legal memetics', *Current Legal Problems*, **55**, 1–42.
Deakin, S. and A. Hughes (1999), 'Economic efficiency and the proceduralization of company law', *Company Financial and Insolvency Law Review*, **2**, 169–89.
Easterbrook, F. and D. Fischel (1991), *The Economic Structure of Corporate Law*, Cambridge, MA: Harvard University Press.
Hansmann, H. and R. Kraakman (2001), 'The end of history for corporate law', *Georgetown Law Journal*, **89**, 439–68.
Hayek, F. (1973), *Law, Legislation and Liberty – Vol. I, Rules and Order*, London: Routledge & Kegan Paul.
Kahan, M. and M. Klausner (1997), 'Standardization and innovation in corporate contracting (or "the economics of boilerplate")', *Virginia Law Review*, **83**, 714–70.
Law Commission (1999), *Company Directors: Regulating Conflicts of Interests and Formulating a Statement of Duties*, Cm. 4436, Law Commission Report No. 126/Scottish Law Commission No. 173, London: TSO.
Luhmann, N. (1995), *Social Systems*, Stanford, CA: Stanford University Press.
Luhmann, N. (2004), *Law as a Social System* (trans. K. Ziegert, ed. F. Kastner, R. Noblfes, D. Schiff and R. Ziegert), Oxford: Oxford University Press.
Markesinis, B. (1997), *The German Law of Obligations, Vol. I – The Law of Contract and Restitution*, Oxford: Clarendon Press.
Okun, A. (1975), *Equality and Efficiency: The Big Trade-Off*, Washington, DC: Brookings Institution.
Priest, G. (1977), 'The common law process and the selection of efficient rules', *Journal of Legal Studies*, **6**, 65–82.
Roe, M. (1996), 'Chaos and evolution in law and economics', *Harvard Law Review*, **109**, 641–68.
Romano, R. (1990), *The Genius of American Corporate Law*, Washington, DC: American Enterprise Institute.
Rubin, P. (1977), 'Why is the common law efficient?', *Journal of Legal Studies*, **6**, 51–64.
Sugden, R. (1986), *The Economics of Rights, Co-operation and Welfare*, Oxford: Blackwell.
Sugden, R. (1998a), 'Conventions', in P. Newman (ed.), *The New Palgrave Dictionary of Economics and the Law*, London: Macmillan.
Sugden, R. (1998b), 'Spontaneous order', in P. Newman (ed.), *The New Palgrave Dictionary of Economics and the Law*, London: Macmillan.
Teubner, G. (1993), *Law as an Autopoietic System*, Oxford: Blackwell.
Wedderburn, Lord (2004), *The Future of Company Law: Fat Cats, Corporate Governance and Workers*, London: Institute of Employment Rights.

Whincop, M. (2002), 'An empirical investigation of the terms of corporate charters and influences on term standardization in a laissez-faire environment', *Journal of Corporate Law Studies*, **2**.
Zingales, L. (1998), 'Corporate governance', in P. Newman (ed.), *The New Palgrave Dictionary of Economics and the Law*, London: Macmillan.

6. Constitutional possibility and constitutional evolution

Eric A. Posner[1]

1. INTRODUCTION

This chapter uses evolutionary game theory to explore recurrent questions about constitutionalism and the United States Constitution. These questions are: (1) what is a constitution and how does it constrain a democratic government, if in fact it does; (2) does the United States Constitution 'evolve,' and if so, how does the Constitution, at any given moment, differ from whatever popular attitudes prevail at that moment; (3) why does an unelected Supreme Court have authority to enforce the Constitution in contradiction of the will of the majority in a democratic state; and (4) what prevents Supreme Court justices from implementing their political beliefs, if anything? The chapter argues that the United States Constitution is a set of self-enforcing conventions that govern how people interact in important ways. The Constitution constrains the government in the same sense that conventions constrain individuals and prevent them from pursuing their immediate self-interest. The Constitution evolves, but slowly and discontinuously, because conventions, by virtue of the fact that they coordinate behavior, are 'sticky.' The Supreme Court has authority because, or to the extent that, people believe that it identifies and enforces existing conventions or identifies hypothetical conventions that are superior to those that exist. Supreme Court justices do not always implement their political preferences because if they did, people would stop believing that the Supreme Court enforces conventions, and then they would stop paying attention to what it says, in which case it would lose its influence to the other branches.

The argument differs from most work in mainstream constitutional law, but it has several precursors as well. It departs from the mainstream literature by focusing on what is constitutionally possible rather than what is constitutionally desirable. Mainstream theorists focus on the desirable and downplay the problem of possibility. Ely, for example, argues that the Supreme Court should protect groups that are politically weak but does not explain why the politically strong tolerate such an infringement on their power.[2] Holmes argues that constitutions contain 'gag rules' that take politically sensitive

---

1 Thanks to Bruce Ackerman, Matthew Adler, Dan Farber, Beth Garrett, Jack Goldsmith, Richard McAdams, Steven Shavell, David Strauss, Cass Sunstein, and Adrian Vermeule, for comments and discussions. Also thanks to participants at a conference on Evolutionary Theories of the Law at Georgetown Law School, and at seminars at the University of Chicago Law School and Harvard Law School.

2 See John Hart Ely (1980).

issues off the table, but does not explain why people would submit to rules that prevent their government from regulating what they care about most.[3] Bork argues that the Supreme Court should enforce the original understanding of the Constitution but does not explain why the political branches and their constituents would tolerate an institution that frustrates popular legislation that departs from the original understanding.[4] Many scholars approve of constitutionalism on the ground that constitutions provide the basic conditions for democracy,[5] but they do not explain why the public would not sweep away any institution that barred changes when the public believes that the Constitution stands in the way of its immediate interests. Mainstream scholars examine why people might want restrictions on democratic outcomes. But the plausibility of their arguments depends on a theory of what is constitutionally possible, of the circumstances under which citizens and politicians will tolerate institutional constraints on democratic action, on what they want now. If the public and the political branches will not defer to a Supreme Court that enforces the original understanding of the Constitution, but will defer to a Supreme Court that protects groups that are politically weak, then the originalist theory is simply off the table, cannot possibly be considered a desirable theory of constitutional interpretation whatever its other merits, while Ely's theory remains viable. The desirable is circumscribed by the possible. Constitutional possibility is the subject of this chapter.[6]

Mainstream constitutional theorists have not completely ignored the problem of constitutional possibility. Casual references to this problem are scattered throughout this literature;[7] and some authors have warned that judicial activism would produce a popular reaction against the Court.[8] But there have been few instances of sustained analysis.[9] A notable example is that of Alexander Bickel, or at any rate the later Bickel who wrote *The Supreme Court and the Idea of Progress*.[10] According to Bickel, the

> Supreme Court's judgments may be put forth as universally prescriptive; but they actually become so only when they gain widespread assent. They bind of their own force no one but the parties to a litigation. To realize the promise that all others similarly situated will be similarly bound, the Court's judgments need the assent and the cooperation first of the political institutions, and ultimately of the people.[11]

---

3 Holmes 1988.

4 See Bork 1990; see also Scalia 1997.

5 See the essays collected in Constitutionalism (Larry Alexander ed. 1998).

6 The economics and political science literature on this subject has some relevance but is in disarray. James Buchanan adheres to a social contract theory of constitutionalism. See, e.g., Brennan and Buchanan 1985. This view, like the others mentioned in the text, begs the question why subsequent generations submit to constraints imposed by an earlier generation. See Hardin 1988. Other scholars have focused on the role of conventions and so on, but have not used evolutionary game theory. For a survey, see Voigt 1997.

7 See, e.g., Ely (1980), 47–48 (raising but dismissing historical concerns that an antidemocratic Court would be destroyed).

8 See Kurland 1969 (warning that the Court will be destroyed because of its activism).

9 Historical accounts, such as that of Ackerman (1991 and 1998), do take this problem seriously, but do not address the analytic problems raised by defenders of originalism.

10 Bickel 1978.

11 Ibid., at 90.

Bickel confronts squarely the question why the public cares about what the Supreme Court says, but he does not provide a satisfactory answer. He argues that the Court's judgments are likely to be accepted when they predict the trend of popular attitudes, but this suggests that the Court has no power at all; that its version of the Constitution may sometimes precede public attitudes, but cannot shape them. The Constitution, as an independent constraint on popular action, disappears.

This is in fact close to the view of Michael Klarman,[12] and of a political science literature going back to Robert Dahl.[13] These scholars argue that the Supreme Court makes decisions in a way that maximizes or preserves its political power, and this means not offending the political branches of government and the groups that control them. This literature does focus on constitutional possibility and is exemplary in its determination to explain how the Supreme Court can maintain its power. But like in Bickel's account, the idea of a constraining Constitution disappears, as does the idea that the Supreme Court enforces it. This conclusion rings false. Although it is true that the Court has often appeared to succumb to political pressure, it is also true that frequently the Court renders politically unpopular decisions. The political scientists make nonsense of the claim that a Constitution exists at all. In their view, rather than constraining the government by applying a set of external rules, the Court endorses government action and dresses it in fancy rhetoric. But why do people believe this rhetoric? If there is no Constitution, how can the Court get away with saying that one exists?

The focus on constitutional possibility reveals a basic problem with normative constitutional theory and its assumption that the Constitution constrains government behavior. The problem is that there does not appear to be anyone who can enforce the Constitution. Of course, the Supreme Court is supposed to enforce the Constitution; but nothing ultimately prevents the public and the political branches from sweeping away a Court that violates their immediate goals. In this way a Constitution differs from ordinary laws. We can expect judges to uphold ordinary laws because the public wants these laws created and enforced. But less clear is the theoretical basis for expecting judges to uphold a Constitution that constrains ordinary government action, because by hypothesis the government and the public do not want to be constrained.

One approach in the constitutional law literature that provides a way out of this impasse can be found in the writing of David Strauss. His theory of common law constitutional interpretation takes as its starting point the claim that 'conventionalism' plays an important role in the interpretation of the United States Constitution.[14] The Constitution at any time consists in part of conventions that have evolved with changes in tastes and technologies. People obey conventions for the same reason that they obey the rules of the road: if they did not, they would come into conflict with other people who are obeying the conventions. Thus, there is a complexity about what we mean by popular attitudes. On the one hand, people obey conventions because they cannot do better by *independently* deviating from them. On the other hand, people might do better by *collectively* deviating from existing conventions and establishing new conventions that

---

[12] See, e.g., Klarman 1996.
[13] See Dahl 1957.
[14] See Strauss 1996.

better suit their tastes and the environment. If the idea of a constitution can be linked to conventions, then the problem of constitutional possibility is solved. The Constitution prevails, even in the teeth of popular attitudes, because it is self-enforcing. The role of the courts is also clarified. If courts can prevent legislative violations of desirable conventions, or can help legislatures overcome existing undesirable conventions, then the public will approve of the courts' behavior after the fact.

In this chapter, I introduce a framework for analysing the relationship between constitutionalism and conventions. The motivation is that the normative mainstream of constitutional theory, while interesting and provocative, simply cannot be evaluated without a theory of constitutional possibility. If the normative proposals are not self-enforcing – that is, cannot be sustained by a Supreme Court that is able to retain its political power – then they are of little value. The chapter builds on the insights of Bickel, Strauss, Klarman, Dahl, and others who stress the problem of constitutional possibility. It takes from Klarman, Bickel, and Dahl the assumption that an adequate theory of the Constitution must focus on the political incentives of Supreme Court justices. But it rejects the view that the Constitution does not constrain at all and only reflects changing public attitudes. It takes from Strauss the insight that conventions and constitutionalism are importantly linked, but its approach and conclusions diverge from Strauss' in many ways.[15] The chapter is also positive, unlike most mainstream constitutional theory, rather than normative or 'interpretive,' though it has some normative implications, examined below.[16]

Before beginning the argument, I should note that this chapter is not intended to provide a complete theory of constitutional possibility; it is meant to be suggestive. The focus is on constraints on government action, exemplified by the rights contained in the first ten amendments and the fourteenth amendment of the US Constitution, as well as rights that are not in the written Constitution, like the right to travel or to marry. But I do not discuss all of these rights; for example, I do not discuss freedom of speech and religious freedom. Although the approach can be used to shed light on these rights, there simply is not space to defend this view. In addition, I do not discuss the institutional structure of the government, including the separation of powers and the assignment of various powers to the three branches.

This chapter relies on evolutionary game theory, an offshoot of game theory that has been influential in evolutionary biology and (to a considerably lesser extent) economics.[17] Evolutionary game theory is useful for understanding how behavioral regularities arise and spread through populations, either by way of genetic inheritance (as in the original biological applications) or learning and imitation (as in the economic applications). So far this method has had little influence on legal scholarship except indirectly via the work

---

15 See infra.

16 On the interpretive approach, see Strauss (1996), at 888–9, n. 35.

17 The origin of the model is in the biological work of Maynard Smith and Price 1973. See Maynard Smith 1982. Sugden 1986; Hirshleifer 1982; and Young 1998 have applied related models to social phenomena. See also Binmore 1994. There is now a vast technical literature that focuses on biological applications, very simple (human) social interactions, and methodological issues in economics such as the appropriate equilibrium concepts in game theory. Useful textbooks include Jörgen Weibull (1995), and Colman (1995).

of Robert Axelrod on cooperation in prisoner's dilemmas,[18] but there has been increasing interest in recent years.[19] This paper is the first I am aware of to apply insights from evolutionary game theory to constitutional jurisprudence.

2. MODELING CONVENTIONS

2.1 A Simple Example: The Passing Game

A convention is a certain kind of self-enforcing behavioral regularity. Conventions arise spontaneously and persist despite the absence of the involvement of a central authority. They 'solve' a problem of coordination, although the concept of solution must be understood with care. The recurrent example is traffic behavior. Suppose that in some earlier time, before the creation of traffic laws, drivers faced the following coordination problem. When two drivers on a road come toward each other, they must decide whether to pass on the left or pass on the right. Both drivers are equally happy if they choose the same action (both passing on the right, or both passing on the left), and equally unhappy if they choose different actions and collide. Their payoffs might be represented as in Table 6.1.

The numbers in each cell represent the payoffs to each of the two players, who will be called 'Row' and 'Column.'

In the case of two particular drivers, who cannot communicate with each other in advance and who have no relevant prior experience, there is no obvious right way to play. Column, for example, wants to choose Pass on Right if Row chooses Pass on Right, but Column has no basis for believing that Row will choose Right rather than Left. There is a 50 percent chance that the drivers will fail to coordinate, so their average payoff is 0.5.

But consider the problem from a dynamic point of view. Suppose that the members of the local population drive and pass each other frequently, observe what happens to people who choose different strategies, and imitate those who are more successful (that is, who do not collide). Initially, people might choose strategies at random. Collisions occur half the time. But if people choose their strategies at random, then in any given round of play there is a chance that one strategy will be chosen more often than the other strategy. Suppose, for example, that in one round 55 percent of the people choose Right, and 45 percent of the people choose Left. That means in the next round people will observe that those who chose Right collided slightly less often than those who chose Left.

---

[18] Axelrod (1986). In legal scholarship, this book is frequently cited as support for the view that people can cooperate in the absence of legal intervention. The story is much more complex, however. See Jonathan Bendor and Piotr Swistak (1997).

[19] See Picker (1997) (using an evolutionary model to explore the relationship between law and social norms); Kraus (1997) (using an evolutionary model to discuss commercial law and norms); Cooter (1994) (similar); Roe (1996) (discussing some phenomena associated with evolutionary game theory); and McAdams (2000) (using evolutionary game theory to analyse the use of law to shift equilibria). I briefly discussed the implications of evolutionary models for the law in Posner (1996), 1715–16 and Posner (2000). Rubin (1977), Priest (1977), and others used somewhat different evolutionary models to analyse the development of the common law. For a broader historical and philosophical discussion of evolutionary approaches to the law, see Elliott (1985).

Table 6.1 The passing game

	Pass on Right	Pass on Left
Pass on Right	1, 1	0, 0
Pass on Left	0, 0	1, 1

What strategy will people adopt in this round? One possibility is that everyone will notice that Right-players are less likely to collide than Left-players. For any player, the expected payoff from playing Right is 0.55, which is higher than the payoff from playing Left (0.45).[20] If all players can calculate this payoff, then all would switch to R in the second round. Even if people are not calculating machines, but make decisions by mimicking the strategies of other people who receive high payoffs, everyone will switch to R.

Depending on how people evaluate competing strategies, and how much information is available to them, the R-strategy will gradually or quickly spread through the population.[21]

Whatever the decision rule, once the entire population coordinates on one move, there will be no deviations. Right-players will not switch because they do not have accidents, or because they realize that if they did switch, they would have accidents. Right-playing emerges as a convention. The emergence is spontaneous, the result of random behavior and simple boundedly rational thinking. It persists once created because one cannot improve one's payoff by deviating from the convention, given that all others follow the convention.[22] The convention 'solves' a coordination problem in the sense that everyone does better by following the convention, or imitating each other, than by choosing different moves. The convention is normatively superior to a failure to coordinate; but different conventions (All Play Right, All Play Left) are of equal value. It was not necessary to invoke a central authority in order to explain how a normatively desirable convention can emerge from anarchy.

2.2 The Static, 'Two-player' Assert-Defer Game

The Passing Game is too simple for understanding the conventions that are relevant to the evolution of constitutions. To understand these conventions, we introduce the Assert-Defer game, otherwise known as the Hawk-Dove game.[23]

Imagine that two individuals live near each other, and must go out into the local environment in order to acquire resources. These resources might include food, water, firewood, and so on. If a piece of food is lying about out in the open, it is easy enough to pick

[20] U(L)=.45(1)+.55(0). U(R)=.45(0)+.55(1). U(i) is the payoff from playing strategy i, where i is Left or Right.

[21] Thus, one does not need to assume that people are rational maximizers; instead, one can assume that they are boundedly rational, a more realistic if less tractable assumption.

[22] See Sugden (1986); Hirshleifer (1982). For historical evidence, see Young (1998), at 16–17.

[23] I have changed the vocabulary, because the terms 'Hawk' and 'Dove' tend to confuse people unfamiliar with the literature, as they denote a state of being rather than a choice of action. The vocabulary did not make much sense even in the biological context for which it was invented.

Table 6.2 The static assert-defer game

a. A general example

	Assert	Defer
Assert	(V − C)/2, (V − C)/2	V, 0
Defer	0, V	V/2 − T, V/2 − T

b. A numerical example (V=2, C=4, T=0)

	Assert	Defer
Assert	−1, −1	2, 0
Defer	0, 2	1, 1

it up and take it home. But what if each individual encounters this resource at the same time? Or what if one individual encounters another individual who already possesses the food; should the first try to grab it, or demand a share of it? The parties must decide whether to fight over the piece of food, which risks injury, or to let the other person take the piece of food, which means being deprived of a valuable resource. The strategic problem faced by the two individuals can be represented in a 2 × 2 matrix, like the Passing Game. Table 6.2 contains a general version, and then an example using numbers.

In the standard formulation, C>V. Suppose, then, that V = 2 and C = 4 (see Table 6.2b), and take the perspective of the Row player. Row can choose the aggressive move ('Assert') or the passive move ('Defer'). If he[24] chooses Assert, while Column chooses Defer, he receives his highest possible payoff, 2. In our story, Row charges up to snatch the food while Column stays back or retreats. If, instead, Column has chosen Assert as well, then the two players fight over the resource, incurring injuries in the course of splitting it up. Each receives a payoff of −1. If Row chooses Defer, while Column chooses Assert, then Row receives 0. If both players choose Defer, then they peacefully split the food, receiving 1 each.

It might also be the case that the passive move involves costs. If it takes time and effort to carve up the piece of food, or to negotiate an even division of it, the joint payoffs are likely to be less than when one party plays Assert and the other plays Defer. If so, T>0. However, in our numerical example, we assume that this is not the case, in order to keep things simple.

What should Row do? If Row believes that Column will play Assert, then Row should play Defer (and receive 0) rather than Assert (and receive −1). If Row believes that Column will play Defer, then Row should play Assert (and receive 2) rather than Defer (and receive 1). As in the Passing Game, Row has no basis for believing that Column will play Assert or Defer. Row might think that Column would choose Assert because Assert offers the highest potential payoff (2); but Row might also think that Column will not choose Assert because Assert offers her the lowest potential payoff (−1).

24 For clarity, Row will be designated 'he' and Column will be designated 'she.'

In a one-shot game, it is impossible to predict how the parties will play. Indeed, one might think that each player will choose randomly. We will discuss this possibility in greater detail below, but for now suppose that this is the case. Each player chooses Assert with probability 0.5 and Defer with probability 0.5. This is the Mixed strategy equilibrium of the game. For this equilibrium, we can calculate the players' expected payoffs. Each of the four outcomes will occur with probability of 0.25. This means that each player will receive $0.25(-1 + 2 + 0 + 1) = 0.5$. The expected joint outcome is 1.[25]

The application of the Assert-Defer game to constitutional law is straightforward. The resources at stake include anything of value, including money, land, commodities, the ability to speak or influence others, control over reproductive capacities, and offices in institutions. People want these resources but they also fear conflict. Unless people have settled expectations about how aggressively others will exert control over these resources, stochastic conflict will occur. This is the state of anarchy. Below we show that constitutions overcome anarchy by creating focal points around which people coordinate. But first we must develop the analysis.

2.3 The Dynamic, Two-Player Assert-Defer Game: The Bourgeois and Retaliation Strategies

Like the static Passing Game, the static Assert-Defer Game does not have an obvious solution. But we saw that analysis of the Passing Game from a dynamic perspective yields insights about how conventions form. A similar shift in perspective yields insights about the Assert-Defer Game.

Initially, to keep things simple, assume that there are only two players (rather than a large group, as in the dynamic Passing Game), but that they interact with each other repeatedly over time. Row and Column live near each other and expect to interact over time. For the moment, assume that they cannot communicate. They anticipate that every so often they will come upon a resource at the same time, and have to decide whether to fight or retreat, that is, play Assert or Defer. How might they behave?

One might imagine that each player will want to establish a strategy of always playing Assert. If the other player believes this, then the other player will always play Defer, and the first player will therefore receive the highest payoff in every round. The problem is that both players want to do this. If Row adopts this 'All-Assert' strategy in the first round and Column does as well, both players will lose 1 on the first round and every round that they persist.

However, it would also be a bad strategy to play Defer on the first round and then every round. Once the other player realizes the first player's strategy is 'All-Defer,' the other player will play 'All-Assert,' with the result that the first player would receive 0 in every round. There may be ways out of this dilemma but they are by no means obvious. If the players can communicate, they might agree that each will play All-Defer, but every round each player has every incentive to deviate and play Assert, so as to obtain 2 rather than 1.

---

25 Technically, the Mixed strategy equilibrium described above and two pure-strategy equilibria (in which one person plays Assert and the other Defer, and vice versa) are all Nash equilibria (see infra note 30). In the present context, however, this is not a particularly useful observation.

If the players cannot come to such a self-enforcing agreement, they may well decide to randomize, in order to avoid being exploited by the other player. If Row plays Assert with probability 0.5 – and Column knows this – then Column gains nothing by always playing Assert or always playing Defer. Column may play the same Mixed strategy, in which case both players end up with an expected gain of 0.5 per round. Row or Column gain nothing from switching to All-Assert or All-Defer. Each player uses the Mixed strategy, and the result is a Mixed strategy equilibrium. Expected payoffs are, as in the static Assert-Defer game, 0.5 for each player in each round.

The Mixed strategy equilibrium is, not, however the only possible outcome. Consider two further strategies.

Bourgeois: if one possesses or is very near the resource, play Assert; otherwise play Defer.
Retaliator: play Defer only as long as the other person plays Defer; otherwise play Assert.

The Bourgeois strategy exploits an asymmetry in the environment. Unless the two parties arrive at the resource at exactly the same time, one will always be in the position of possessor, the other the non-possessor. If one party expects the other to play the Bourgeois strategy, then the first party does best by also playing the Bourgeois strategy. To see why, imagine that Column believes that Row plays the Bourgeois strategy. If Column encounters Row when Row possesses the property, Column expects Row to play Assert. Given that Row will play Assert, Column receives a higher payoff from playing Defer (0) than from playing Assert (−1). Now suppose that when Column encounters Row, Column possesses the property. Given that Row will play Defer, Column receives a higher payoff from playing Assert (2) than from playing Defer (0).[26]

The Retaliator strategy depends on the assumption that in any given round, a player can start off by playing Defer but switch to Assert if the other player does not reciprocate. If Column believes that Row plays Retaliator, then Column cannot do better than play Defer (and receive 1, rather than −1). The same is true of Row. Of course, Column could receive just as high a payoff by adopting All-Defer; but that assumes that Row would not switch from Retaliator to All-Assert in subsequent rounds, when in fact Row would do better by switching to All-Assert.[27]

Each player can choose among the five strategies discussed so far: All-Assert, All-Defer, Mixed, Bourgeois, and Retaliator. Table 6.3 shows the possible outcomes in any single round.

There are many Nash equilibria, that is, equilibria in which neither player has an incentive to deviate from the equilibrium strategy given that the other player uses that strategy.[28] For example, Bourgeois-Bourgeois is a Nash equilibrium. Given that Column has chosen Bourgeois, Row can do no better by deviating from Bourgeois – and vice versa. Retaliator-Retaliator and Mixed-Mixed are also Nash equilibria, but they are weaker in the sense that one can deviate and do no worse (for example, given that Column chooses

---

[26] The Bourgeois strategy is apparently used by many different animal species. See Maynard Smith (1982).

[27] I will say little about the Retaliator strategy, which does not seem plausible, and mention it because it provides a contrast and because it is prominent in the literature.

[28] For the definition of Nash equilibrium and a clear discussion, see Baird et al. (1994), 19–23.

Table 6.3 The Two Player Dynamic Assert-Defer Game[29]

	All-Assert	All-Defer	Mixed	Bourgeois	Retaliator
All-Assert	−1, −1	2, 0	0.5, −0.5	0.5, −0.5	−1, −1
All-Defer	0, 2	1, 1	0.5, 1.5	0.5, 1.5	1, 1
Mixed	−0.5, 0.5	1.5, 0.5	0.5, 0.5	0.5, 0.5	0, 0
Bourgeois	−0.5, 0.5	1.5, 0.5	0.5, 0.5	1, 1	0, 0
Retaliator	−1, −1	1, 1	0, 0	0, 0	1, 1

Retaliator, Row could deviate to All-Defer and receive the same payoff of 1). Finally, there are two Nash equilibria with asymmetric payoffs – All-Assert-All-Defer, and All-Defer-All-Assert.[30]

The analysis so far has established only that if two players face the payoffs in the Assert-Defer Game, and have repeated interaction, several combinations of strategies are likely to persist, while the other combinations of strategies are likely not to persist. Nothing has been said about how parties might choose one strategy rather than another, and why one Nash equilibrium rather than another might emerge. Nor has anything been said about what would happen in a group of more than two people, as in the Passing Game. But the outline of a theory of constitutions should be evident. When two players arrive at a Bourgeois equilibrium, conflict is avoided and property becomes secure. The question is whether they can come to this equilibrium, and whether the analysis can be generalized from two players to the sorts of societies and groups that are governed by constitutions.

2.4 The Dynamic, Multi-Player Assert-Defer Game: The Emergence of Conventions

Assume now that the game involves more than two people. For expository purposes, assume that there are 100 people, although the general conclusions of the model hold for any number of people (about which more below). Suppose that every round (maybe a round is a day or a week or a month), each person is randomly paired with another person – a total of 50 interactions. Over the course of several rounds, a person may be paired with a different person every round. In every interaction, the person has the basic choice between playing Assert or Defer, though we may interpret this in many ways. If the 100 people belong to a tribe that is foraging in the wilderness, the analogy is straightforward.

29 Payoffs assume that the Mixed strategy involves choosing Assert and Defer with 50 percent probability, but any combination of probabilities equaling 100 percent can be used; indeed, one could adopt a Mixed strategy involving Bourgeois and Retaliator as well. Payoffs also assume that each player has a 50 percent chance of being a 'possessor' for purposes of the Bourgeois strategy.

30 There are other possible strategies, some of which produce equilibria. For example, there is the opposite of the Bourgeois strategy, where the possessor plays Defer and the non-possessor plays Assert. There are many reasons outside the model for thinking that this equilibrium is implausible. If the possessor values the resources more or can defend them more cheaply, the equilibrium would be unlikely to occur. Maynard Smith (1982) says that it has been found in only one case in the natural world, a species of spider.

When two people come upon the same resource, they must choose between aggressive and passive action. But the 100 people might belong to a merchant group whose members trade with each other. Assert, then, refers to aggressive trading behavior, like insisting on timely delivery despite the other person's production problems or delaying delivery despite the other person's urgent need for the product. Defer refers to a willingness to compromise, to make adjustments in the order in response to a special request, to deliver on time even though it is more costly, and so on. Or Assert/Defer behavior might refer to the aggressiveness with which neighboring ranchers drive off trespassing cattle or fail to respect the boundaries of someone else's land.

The next assumption is that players are *boundedly rational*. This assumption is an important departure from the assumption about rationality in the two-player Assert-Defer Game. In that game, players *optimize*: each player knows all possible moves that it can make, all possible moves that the other player can make, all relevant payoffs; and each player correctly calculates its own payoffs on the basis of this information. The new assumption is that players have limited information, and mimic apparently successful strategies that they have observed others using; and that players make errors.

There are many ways to model bounded rationality. I rely mainly on the model introduced by Maynard Smith,[31] and secondarily on a model used by Young.[32]

Bounded rationality means that in every round most players use the strategy that they used in the previous round, but that a small fraction of the population – say, 10 percent or less[33] – will randomly choose a new strategy every round. One can interpret this pattern of deviation as experimentation or as error or as both. If these deviating players receive a higher payoff than the other players, then in the next round these players will continue with their new strategy, while 10 percent of the remaining group also switch to this strategy. Thus, after two rounds 19 percent of the population will be playing the alternative strategy. However, if the players who deviate receive a lower payoff than the players who do not deviate, then in the subsequent round they abandon the strategy and no other players imitate it. Whether or not the deviators do better or worse, there will always be some experimentation in every round.[34]

The approach is best illustrated by example. Suppose that in the first round all the players play Defer. Each player initially receives a payoff of 1. (See Table 6.2b.) One player decides to experiment by playing Assert in the next round. This player receives a payoff of 2. Because this payoff exceeds 1, other players might imitate the first player. If a few more players join the first deviator, they will also receive more than 1, while the remaining Defer-players will receive less than 1. The reason is that although the Assert-players receive low payoffs when they match up with each other, they receive high payoffs when they match up with Defer-players, and there are many more Defer-players than

---

[31] See Maynard Smith (1982).

[32] See Young (1998).

[33] It must be kept in mind that on this interpretation of bounded rationality the fraction of the population must be allowed to be arbitrarily low – not just 10 percent, but 1 percent or 0.0001 percent. When I say '10 percent' for expository purposes, I mean any arbitrarily small fraction of the population.

[34] For a discussion of alternative models of replication, see Bendor and Swistak (1997), 295–6.

Assert-players.[35] Because Assert-players continue to receive more than Defer-players, in future rounds more people will switch from Defer to Assert. Meanwhile, the payoff from playing Defer falls as the probability of matching up with an Assert-player climbs.

Suppose, instead, that at the first round all players play Assert. Each player initially receives a payoff of −1. One player experiments by playing Defer in the next round. This player receives a payoff of 0, which is higher than −1. If a few more players join the deviator and play Defer, they will receive more than 0, while the remaining Assert-players will receive less than 0. The reason is that the Defer-players receive 1 when they match up with each other, and 0 when they match up with Assert-players. While Assert-players receive 2 when they match up with Defer-players, there are so few Defer-players initially, that this large amount does not compensate the Assert-players for their payoffs of −1 when they match up with each other.[36] Because Defer-players continue to receive more than Assert-players, in future rounds more people will switch from Assert to Defer.

Further reasoning along these lines would show that the fraction of Assert-players will steadily rise (in the first case) or fall (in the second case). A population of 100, 81, 19, or 0 percent Assert-players is not 'stable,' in a sense to be described below.

Consider now the case in which half the people play Assert and half play Defer (the 'Mixed' strategy). An Assert-player matches up with another Assert-player half the time and receives −1, and matches up with a Defer-player half the time and receives 2; thus on average the Assert-player receives 0.5. A Defer-player matches up with another Defer-player half the time and receives 1, and matches up with an Assert-player half the time and receives 0; thus on average the Defer-player receives 0.5. It follows that a person who plays Defer half the time and Assert half the time will also on average receive 0.5.[37] If a portion of the population deviates in either direction, the deviators will receive lower payoffs than the remaining conformists. For example, if a portion of the population switches from playing Assert half the time, to playing Assert all the time, its payoffs will decline more rapidly than the payoffs of those who continue with the Mixed strategy. The reason is that the Assert-players match up with Assert-players more often, and their payoffs fall dramatically from 0.5 to −1, whereas the Defer-players, who also match up with Assert-players more often, suffer a decline of only 0.5 to 0. A similar argument shows that people do worse if they deviate by playing Defer more often.[38]

---

[35] If, say, 11 players play Assert in a population of 101, then the Assert-players expect to receive (10/100)(−1) + (90/100)(2) = 1.7. (An Assert-player is one of the 11 Assert-players, so there are ten remaining Assert-players and 90 Defer-players out of the remaining 100 players.) The Defer-players expect to receive (11/100)(0) + (89/100) = 0.89.

[36] If 11 players play Defer, these players receive an expected payoff of (90/100)(0) + (10/100)(1) = 0.1. The other players receive (89/100)(−1) + (11/100)(2) = −0.67. Because those playing Defer receive more than those playing Assert, in the next round 10 percent of the Assert players switch to Defer, while the original Defer players continue to play Defer. In the next round, the proportion of Defer players in the population rises to 19 percent, and so on.

[37] Their payoffs are (0.5)(−1) + (0.5)(2) = (0.5)(0) + (0.5)(1) = 0.5. (Technically, if half the population plays Assert and half plays Defer, an individual entering the population will receive the same payoff of 0.5 regardless of whether this person plays Assert or Defer.)

[38] If, for example, 51 percent play Assert, their payoff will fall to (0.51)(−1) + (0.49)(2) = 0.47, while the Defer-players' payoff remains higher at (0.51)(0) + (0.49)(1) = 0.49. If 51 percent play Defer, their payoff rises to (0.51)(1) + (0.49)(0) = 0.51, but the Assert-players' payoff rises more

A population consisting entirely of Assert-players or Defer-players is not stable in the sense that players who deviate and play a different strategy will receive higher payoffs than those who do not. A population consisting of 50 percent Assert-players and 50 percent Defer-players is stable, in the sense that deviators will do worse than those who do not deviate. The equilibrium concept being used is known as an evolutionary stable strategy, or ESS. ESS refers to behavioral regularities that emerge in populations that are robust against 'mutations' or (in our case) experimental or accidental variations in strategy by a small portion of the population.[39] The idea of ESS is to allow one to predict or describe patterns of behavior that are relatively stable over time, which means that they will not undergo radical changes in response to slight changes in environmental conditions. An important point is that a population is said to be in an ESS equilibrium only with respect to alternative strategies being considered, not with respect to all possible or conceivable strategies. The Mixed ESS equilibrium is not robust against the Bourgeois strategy.

To see why, suppose that some people deviate and play the Bourgeois strategy, and suppose further that every player has a 50 percent chance of being the 'possessor' and a 50 percent chance of being the 'non-possessor.' An individual deciding on a move in such a population would make the following calculations. If this person plays Bourgeois, some of the time this move will be against another Bourgeois player. Half the time the first is the possessor and the second is the non-possessor, and half the time the situation is the reverse, producing payoffs of 2 and 0, or on average 1 (see Table 6.3). Most of the time the individual encounters someone playing the original Mixed strategy, in which case the payoff is 0.5 (see Table 6.3). The Bourgeois-players do as well against Mixed-players as Mixed-players do against Mixed-players (0.5 in both cases), but the Bourgeois-players do better against other Bourgeois-players (1) than the Mixed-players do against Mixed-players (0.5). This means that a person who plays Mixed can only do better by playing Bourgeois, and cannot do any worse.[40] The Mixed strategy is not an ESS against the Bourgeois strategy.

But the Bourgeois strategy *is* an ESS against the Mixed strategy. Suppose everyone plays Bourgeois, then a few people deviate to Mixed. The remaining Bourgeois-players continue to receive a high payoff with other Bourgeois-players (1) while receiving a lower payoff when interacting with the deviating Mixed-players (0.5). By contrast, the Mixed-players receive the lower payoff *both* when they match up with the Bourgeois-players (0.5) *and* when they match up with the other deviating Mixed-players (0.5). Thus, the deviating Mixed-players can only do worse.[41] No one will imitate, and the population will tend back

---

rapidly to $(0.51)(2) + (0.49)(-1) = 0.53$. Because the deviators receive lower payoffs than they did before they deviate (or, alternatively, since they observe that those who do not deviate receive higher payoffs than they do), they return to their earlier strategies, and the population tends back to 50 percent Assert and 50 percent Defer.

[39] The formal definition of an ESS equilibrium is as follows. Let E(I,J) equal the payoff of an individual playing I against someone who plays J. Strategy I is an ESS vis-à-vis strategy J if $E(I,I) > E(J,I)$, or $E(I,I) = E(J,I)$ and $E(I,J) > E(J,J)$. See Maynard Smith (1982), at 13–14.

[40] If, say, 10 percent deviate, $E(B) = (0.1)(0.5(2) + 0.5(0)) + (0.9)(0.5(0.5) + (0.5)(0.5)) = 0.1 + 0.45 = 0.55$. $E(M) = (0.1)(0.5(0.5) + 0.5(0.5)) + (0.9)(0.5) = 0.05 + 0.45 = 0.5$.

[41] $E(B) = (0.9)[(0.5)(2) + (0.5)(0)] + (0.1)[(0.5)(0.5) + (0.5)(0.5)] = 0.95$. $E(M) = (0.9)[(0.5)(0.5) + (0.5)(0.5)] + (0.1)[(0.5)(0.5) + (0.5)(0.5)] = 0.5$.

toward the Bourgeois strategy. As long as there is more than one Bourgeois-player, the Bourgeois strategy yields a higher expected payoff for any population.

The Bourgeois strategy also is an ESS equilibrium versus All-Assert, All-Defer,[42] and Retaliator.[43]

2.5 Defining Conventions

Conventions are behavioral regularities that result when (1) the environment creates opportunities for gain when individuals coordinate their behavior and avoid conflict; and (2) individuals cannot improve their payoffs by deviating from existing behavioral regularities, even when small groups (rather than single individuals) simultaneously deviate, where (3) the ability to experiment with deviations is constrained by limited knowledge of alternative strategies and of the payoffs received by other players under current conditions (bounded rationality).[44] In the multi-player dynamic Assert-Defer Game, a convention refers to strategies in ESS equilibria.

Conventions are defined endogenously; it is a mistake to say that individuals are constrained by conventions. They are really constrained by what they perceive to be the actions of others. A convention is just a label that we attach to equilibrium behavior. To be sure, individuals might prefer to live in a world in which conventions (that is, equilibrium behavior) were different. An individual might prefer to live in a world in which all people played Defer, but as long as others play the Bourgeois strategy, this individual does better by playing Bourgeois than by playing All-Defer. Conventions do not constrain in the sense that a law might constrain a person who fears a legal sanction. Third parties do not enforce conventions in the sense of self-consciously punishing those who deviate from them. Conventions persist because those who might prefer alternatives fear that if they deviate from the convention, they will fail to coordinate with others, and value will be lost.[45]

Conventions can be more or less fluid. In the evolutionary model, it is not the case

---

[42] To see why, observe that in a population of 100 percent Bourgeois players, the per-round average payoff of 0.5(2) + 0.5(0) = 1, for the reasons given above. If 10 percent of the population deviates to All-Assert, then a new player trying to decide what to play will do better by playing Bourgeois (E(B) = (0.9)(1) + (0.1)(−0.5) = 0.85) than by playing All-Assert (E(A) = (0.9)[(0.5)(−1) + (0.5)(2)] + (0.1)(−1) = 0.35).

[43] If 10 percent of the population of Bourgeois-players choose Retaliator, and someone enters the population, then E(R) = (0.1)(1) + (.9)[0.5(−1) + 0.5(1)]=.1, whereas E(B) = (0.1)[0.5(−1) + 0.5(1)] + (0.9)(1)=.9. So the Bourgeois strategy is an ESS with respect to the Retaliator strategy. In addition, the Retaliator strategy is an ESS. Retaliators expect a payoff of 1 when they play each other. Suppose 10 percent deviate and play Assert. E(A) = (0.1)(−1) + (0.9)(−1)= −1, whereas E(R) = (0.1)(−1) + (0.9)(1) = 0.8, and E(B) = (0.1)(1) + (0.9)[(0.5)(−1) + (0.5)(1)] = 0.1. By contrast the Retaliators receive E(R) = (0.1)[(0.5)(−1) + (0.5)(1)] + (0.9)(1) = 0.9. Similar reasoning shows that deviators who play Mixed or Defer receive lower payoffs than conformists who play Retaliator.

[44] Cf. David Lewis (1969), who pays more attention to problems of common knowledge and ignores evolutionary dynamics. Other useful discussions include Ullman-Margalit (1977), Schotter (1981), and the game theory literature cited in note 17, supra.

[45] In fact, the analysis is more complex. Some strategies are more likely to become evolutionarily stable than others; in the jargon, they have large 'basins of attraction.' See Young (1998), at 68–9.

that if a convention exists, everyone is conforming to it. On the contrary, the assumption of bounded rationality means that some fraction of the population is constantly violating it. They may violate it by mistake: they simply misunderstand other people's behavior, the relevant payoffs, and so on. Or they violate it deliberately: they are willing to risk low payoffs in the hope of matching up with others who have similar interests. Different conventions will have different levels of compliance. As the coordination payoff increases relative to the conflict payoff, as the fraction of conformists increases, and as information about other people's behavior spreads, there will be less deviation from the convention. The result is that although many conventions are quite clear, many others are quite unclear. People may try to reduce the ambiguity by consulting etiquette books or authoritative institutions, but often the ambiguity results not from lack of information but from the fact that people are engaging in mutually inconsistent actions, and behavior has not yet settled down into a pattern. When this is the case, people will often (though not always) benefit if some outside institution can dictate the convention.

3. THE CONSTITUTION AND CONVENTIONS

Recall the four questions with which we began. The first is how a constitution can constrain a government, and the second is how such a constitution could evolve. The third and fourth questions are what prevents the other branches of government from ignoring the Supreme Court's decisions, and what prevents Supreme Court justices from abusing their power.

Most constitutional scholars ignore the first question, and assume that the Supreme Court constrains the rest of the government to obey the United States Constitution. We will examine this assumption below; for the moment, let us accept it. Then the question is what is the constitution that the Supreme Court enforces. Originalists say that the constitution is the written United States Constitution, as originally understood. Anti-originalists say that the Constitution consists of evolving norms or traditions, but they have been hard pressed to explain what they mean. The evolving Constitution cannot be the same as popular attitudes at any given time; if that were so, there would never be a conflict between the Constitution and (barring extreme political failure) the legislation that it is supposed to govern. But if the Constitution is not the same as popular attitudes, then what is it? Critics of the originalists appeal to political theory, moral philosophy, institutional exigencies, and traditional values, but these phenomena are so controversial and spongy that it seems unlikely that they could constrain judges.[46]

Before dealing with this problem, return to the originalists. They claim that the judges can enforce the original meaning of the Constitution. The problem with this argument is that the desirable Constitution (understood as a constraint on government power) will change over time as the environment changes, and there is no reason to believe that the amendment power is, or can be, well-calibrated to allow changes in the Constitution if

[46] For discussions, see, e.g., Scalia (1997), at 44–5; Paul Brest (1980); Daniel A. Farber (1989); Thomas C. Grey (1975); Rakove, ed. (1990). See generally Levinson ed. (1995).

and only if there are sufficient justifying changes in the social and political environment.[47] An even more serious problem is that as a positive theory of Supreme Court behavior it is wrong. The constitution of the United States has changed many times outside of the formal amendment process – in 1937, in the 1960s, and so on – and whatever one thinks of the desirability of these changes, it is hard to avoid the conclusion that the originalist view, taken as a description of the world, is false.

A recent version of the anti-originalist view illustrates its promise and its problems. David Strauss argues that courts engage in 'common law constitutional interpretation.' By this, he means that the Constitution is like the common law: it is a set of principles that evolve over time, a result of judicial interpretation. Like other anti-originalists, he points out that even the originalists must appeal to standards that lie outside the text of the Constitution, if only because no text is self-interpreting and one must get principles of interpretation somewhere.[48] But Strauss does not make a convincing case that the traditions and conventions to which he refers are in fact discoverable by courts and sufficiently determinate to provide guidance. In part this may be because Strauss thinks that the common law itself is sufficient evidence for this proposition. Judges who make the common law do not rely on a text, yet they seem to be constrained. Similarly, judges who make the Constitution do not (exclusively) rely on a text, yet seem to be constrained. The problem with this argument is that it pushes the question back from the Constitution to the common law rather than answering the question. What constrains common law judges? Some scholars doubt that anything does, and these scholars could argue that both the common law and the evolving Constitution are outcomes of judicial policy making.[49] Further, one is likely to be more comfortable with judges inventing common law rights which can be abrogated by statute than with judges overturning statutes enacted by democratically elected legislators. In the balance of this chapter, I fill this gap in Strauss' argument by using the evolutionary Assert-Defer model of conventions.

In the United States (and every other country) people's behavior is heavily governed by conventions that describe their property interests in various resources, including their ordinary goods, but also their bodies and speech and religious practices. These conventions arise more or less spontaneously, in the absence of government direction, in response to shifts in tastes, technology, demography, and other environmental factors. Conventions can be divided roughly into more foundational conventions and more superficial conventions, the two positions being extremes on a continuum. Foundational conventions are those that govern a large fraction of the population, and that govern resources that people value very highly (so V is very high) but are costly to seize and protect (so C is very high). Superficial conventions may govern everyone or small portions of the population, but the main point is that relatively little is at stake (like men wearing ties). The 'constitution' of a country at any given time consists of the foundational conventions.[50] When different segments of the population are governed by different and

---

[47] The insufficiency of the formal amendment power is pursued by Ackerman (1991 and 1998). It is implausible to think that people would allow themselves to be bound by it.

[48] See Strauss (1996).

[49] Similar skepticism meets the related claim that the constitution consists, in part, of 'traditions.' See Tushnet (1999), 86–9 (arguing that traditions are 'vacuous').

[50] That is why the United Kingdom and other countries can have unwritten constitutions.

conflicting foundational conventions, the country is deeply divided, and it does not make sense to talk of the country having a constitution.

Although the Assert-Defer model was developed to analyse traditional property rights, it can be used to analyse the more general liberty rights protected by the US Constitution as well. Indeed, liberty and property rights are subsumed in the definition of convention. When people confront each other in pairwise interactions, they must choose a strategy. The strategy might be to play Assert, Defer, Bourgeois, and so on. The interactions involve the assertion of control: over land or commodities or traditional property-like resources; or over reproductive capacities, or the ability to speak or influence, and similar liberty-like domains. When conventions are absent, people fail to coordinate and conflict results. Conventions evolve when people play the strategies that coordinate, such as the Bourgeois strategy. The convention describes the kind of control that each person expects the other person to exert.

The written constitutions of the United States and other countries usually attempt to describe the foundational conventions at the time of the writing, and also to provide a mechanism for amendment. They also establish political institutions that are consistent with, though not necessarily determined by, the foundational conventions. But foundational conventions develop independently of the writing. They may fill gaps in the text, and they may even supersede the text. This is not to say that the text has no force at all. The text may, by sharpening and publicizing existing conventions, enhance people's knowledge of these conventions, which reduces the incentive to deviate and increases the stability of the convention. But if the constitution gets the conventions wrong enough, citizens will ignore it. If citizens ignore it, so will democratic politicians. And if the social and political environment changes radically enough, citizens and politicians will ignore the written constitution, unless it is either amended or aggressively interpreted in light of changing understandings.[51]

The US Supreme Court strikes down statutes for 'constitutional' reasons under two conditions. First, the Court strikes down statutes when they depart from contemporary foundational conventions – whether or not the foundational conventions are stated in the written Constitution. The Court may be right or wrong (descriptively). When it is right, the decision will be accepted by the other branches and by the public. The convention will spread from those states where it is widely recognized to those states where it is fuzzier. When the Court is wrong, its decision will be ignored or challenged, and if it is challenged, the Court will eventually backtrack or risk losing its legitimacy. By this I mean that people will stop taking seriously the court's announcements about foundational conventions. The executive might be tempted to disobey the court's orders; the legislature may deny it resources. Think of the reactions to *Dred Scott v. Sandford*, the *Lochner* line of cases, and possibly *Roe v. Wade*.[52] By contrast, it is clear that cases establishing rights to travel and vote, for example, identified foundational conventions, and this is clear not

[51] A theme of Ackerman; see Ackerman (1991 and 1998).

[52] Another interesting example is that of religion. There are some clear foundational conventions in this area, including the right not to be forced to practice a particular religion; but also many conventions that are under great pressure, such as bans on school prayer and on the construction of religious displays on public property. See, e.g., *Lee v. Weisman*, 505 U.S. 577 (1992) (forbidding school prayer at graduation ceremony); *Lemon v. Kurtzman*, 403 U.S. 602 (1971) (establishment

just because the precedents were never overturned by subsequent decision or constitutional amendment; but because legitimate scholars cannot question these precedents, judicial nominees must praise them, and the political branches have independently tried to legislate and enforce the foundational convention that it reflects.[53]

Second, the Court may strike down statutes when they are consistent with current foundational conventions which, the Court believes, are undesirable. The Court can do this when everyone avoids deviating from a convention because they fear a failure to coordinate, but everyone knows or realizes, after the Court's decision, that the convention is inferior to an alternative. Few people with real political power supported – at their earliest stages of development – civil rights for blacks, or contraception or abortion rights for women, or procedural rights for criminal defendants, or speech rights for war protestors; because support for these unconventional causes would provoke, just because the causes were unconventional, dismay and opposition from constituents. But if large segments of the population do not like these conventions, or would be better off if the conventions were changed, the Supreme Court can in theory change behavior simply by announcing the new convention. This is a possible explanation for what happened when it decided *Brown v. Board of Education*,[54] although it took many years for the new convention – tolerance of racial differences – to spread.

There is an intermediate case where behavior has not yet settled into a consistent pattern, and so conventions are weak or nonexistent. Consider again abortion. It might plausibly be said that sometime in the 1960s and early 1970s in certain communities there was no convention about whether women could obtain abortions.[55] The result would be Mixed strategies, with plenty of conflict and low payoffs. A judicial decision that announced one convention or the other – that is, a decision that approved or struck down an abortion statute – might (or might not) create a convention by persuading enough people that sufficient numbers had already adopted one strategy or the other. In this case, the decision would not so much violate or confirm a foundational convention as contribute to its formation.

Table 6.4 summarizes the argument, ignoring the intermediate case. The Supreme Court might uphold a statute. If the statute conforms to a convention, then the decision is 'convention-consistent'; if not, the decision is 'convention-inconsistent.' If the Court strikes down a statute, and the statute conforms to a convention, then the decision is 'convention-inconsistent,' and so on.[56] Further, a convention might be desirable or not in a loose or strong sense. A convention might be undesirable because an alternative allows coordination where payoffs for everyone or nearly everyone are higher; or it might be undesirable because an alternative allows coordination where payoffs for one group

clause requires laws to have secular purpose); *County of Allegheny v. ACLU Greater Pittsburgh Chapter*, 492 U.S. 573 (1989) (public display of creche violates establishment clause).

53 As discussed below.

54 347 U.S. 483 (1954).

55 See below.

56 Of course, conventions might be more or less widespread; we will say a decision is 'convention-consistent' if it conforms to a more widespread convention and not to a more isolated convention.

Table 6.4 Effect of Supreme Court decisions

Decision's relationship to convention	Social value of convention	
	Desirable	Undesirable
Conforms to convention	Decision may assist spread of convention (*Griswold*)	Decision may subsequently weaken court (*Bowers*?)
Violates convention	Decision will have no effect on behavior, may weaken Court (*Lochner* cases)	Decision may subvert convention (*Brown*)

Note: A decision conforms to a convention by either striking down a statute that violates the convention or upholding a statute that is consistent with the convention; similarly, for a decision that violates a convention.

are substantially higher, and for another group only slightly lower. We will avoid these complications, and speak generally.

Suppose that a convention is desirable. A convention-consistent decision may strengthen the convention. Assume that the Court has 'legitimacy,' or roughly that people believe that its decisions reflect actual conventions, that is, the strategies that are most common in the population.[57] If so, they will revise upwards their belief about whether other people obey the convention, and how many other people obey the convention. The result is that they are more likely to obey the convention: their expected payoff rises from conforming given their beliefs about the extent to which other people conform. If the Court is right, people will additionally believe that it is more likely to be right next time, and thus will adjust even more rapidly next time to the Court's decision. Convention-consistent decisions both strengthen conventions and enhance the Court's legitimacy, that is, its ability next time to influence people's behavior.

A convention-inconsistent decision might change behavior even when the convention is desirable. Assuming the Court has legitimacy, people will revise downward their belief about whether other people obey the convention. As people increasingly violate the convention, failures to coordinate will multiply. The result is that people will realize that the Court's decision violated the convention. Their behavior will change in response to this realization: they will be less likely to follow the Court in its next decision. The Court's legitimacy will decline.[58]

Suppose now that a convention is undesirable. If a legitimate Court makes a convention-consistent decision, people believe (correctly) that the Court has accurately revealed what other people's strategies are, and so their conformity to the convention is strengthened, and they are more likely to believe the Court in the next case. But one might think that in the long run the Court's legitimacy will be injured, at least if people believe that it should not merely reveal existing conventions, but also evaluate and change them. That brings us to the last box.

---

[57] Legitimacy is a complex concept; for further discussion, see below.

[58] One might distinguish a decision upholding a statute that violates a convention, and a decision striking down a statute that conforms to a convention. The former decision allows democratic change in conformity with convention; the latter does not. So there may be normative and positive implications to this distinction.

A convention-inconsistent decision might change behavior for the same reason as above, when the convention is desirable. There may as a result be a period of conflict, which will cause people to distrust the Court in the next case. But it is also possible that (1) eventually the convention shifts, after the period of conflict; (2) the new convention is superior to the old convention; and (3) the benefit justifies the transition costs. If all this is true, in the long run the legitimacy of the Court will rise rather than fall. But the meaning of legitimacy here is complex. People might believe that the Court will accurately reveal good conventions and misrepresent bad conventions. If so, they might be less likely to change their behavior in response to a decision than they would if the Court were always accurate about the existing convention. For a decision to change conventions, people must believe that all or most people will change their behavior when the Supreme Court declares a convention undesirable, but such a vast and rapid change in behavior by boundedly rational individuals in response to a mere announcement by a fallible institution seems unlikely. Although it is possible that the Court can effect desirable social change, there must be limits as well.[59]

Table 6.4 contains some illustrative cases (all of them highly contestable), which will be discussed in more detail below. How one interprets these cases depends on the conventions that one thinks prevailed at the time, but some possible interpretations are these. *Griswold* accurately expressed a widespread and growing convention about women's rights over their reproductive capacities.[60] The decision enhanced the Court's legitimacy. *Lochner* and especially later cases in the *Lochner* line tried to enforce old property conventions that had broken down.[61] These cases diminished the Court's legitimacy. *Bowers* might have enforced a convention that still existed but was on the cusp of change, and which had become undesirable.[62] If conventions in favor of tolerating homosexuality continue to spread *Bowers* might be seen as another *Plessy*;[63] *Romer* as a *Brown* that came too late, so that the court was in the wake of social change rather than in the vanguard.[64] And, as already mentioned, *Brown* might be seen as a convention-inconsistent decision that helped shift the population to a better convention.[65]

The Supreme Court's legitimacy can be understood as its reputational capital. When the Supreme Court strikes down statutes that violate 'good' or unobjectionable conventions, and when the Supreme Court strikes down statutes that are consistent with 'bad'

---

[59] 'The Court's effectiveness, it is often remarked, depends substantially on confidence, on what is called prestige. It is likely, therefore . . . that there is a natural quantitative limit to the number of major, principled interventions the Court can permit itself per decade, let us say. It is a matter of credibility.' Bickel (1978), 94.

[60] *Griswold v. Connecticut*, 381 U.S. 479 (1965). See also *Saenz v. Roe*, 526 U.S. 489 (1999) (right to travel); *Shapiro v. Thompson*, 394 U.S. 618 (1969) (same); *Zablocki v. Redhail*, 434 U.S. 374 (1978) (right to marry); *Loving v. Virginia*, 388 U.S. 1 (1967) (same).

[61] *Lochner v. New York*, 198 U.S. 45 (1905).

[62] *Bowers v. Hardwick*, 478 U.S. 186 (1986). See also *Buck v. Bell*, 274 U.S. 200 (1927) (upholding involuntary sterilization); *Korematsu v. United States*, 323 U.S. 214 (1944) (upholding internship of Japanese-Americans for security reasons).

[63] *Plessy v. Ferguson*, 163 U.S. 537 (1896).

[64] *Romer v. Evans*, 517 U.S. 620 (1996).

[65] Other examples might include voting rights (*Reynolds v. Sims*, 377 U.S. 533 (1964)) and the right to counsel (*Gideon v. Wainwright*, 372 U.S. 335 (1963)).

conventions, thus contributing to the demise of those conventions, it enjoys an enhancement in capital. This has a very specific meaning. People revise their beliefs about the Supreme Court's ability to discover and evaluate conventions. After the Court behaves in either of these two ways, people think that next time it is more likely that the court is right about the strategies that people play. Next time they are more likely to adjust their behavior in response to the Court's decision. When the Court upholds statutes that violate good conventions, and when the Court upholds statutes that are consistent with bad conventions, its capital diminishes. This means that next time people are less likely to adjust their behavior in response to the Court's decision, and are less likely to object if the political branches disregard the Court's decisions or those of the federal judiciary.[66] If justices want to act on their policy preferences or even on their jurisprudential commitments, and want their actions to be influential, they will be more interventionist during periods of high capital, and less interventionist during periods of low capital.[67] Capital is built up through minimalist intervention, or through dramatically correct interventions like *Brown*; it is diminished through maximal intervention, or through dramatically wrong failures to intervene like (possibly) *Bowers*.[68]

A few further points should be made. First, conventions frequently vary by location or region, and so do the statutes that reflect them. When a new convention has spread throughout the country except for isolated pockets, a Supreme Court decision striking down a statute that reflects the old convention will assist the spread of the new convention and will enhance the legitimacy of the Court. But when a new convention has not spread very far, so that different regions are governed by different conventions, the Court is in a difficult position. Any decision will polarize people and injure the Court. This is the difference between *Griswold* and *Roe*.[69]

Second, the written constitution has no particular authority compared to the unwritten constitution. By identifying some of the important contemporary conventions, it clearly serves an important purpose of disseminating information to individuals and judges. But these conventions can change, and the text cannot prevent them from changing. One interesting function of the text is that it supplies focal points, some of which – the right to counsel,[70] for example – diverge from the original intentions of those who drafted the constitution. As Strauss points out, this phenomenon is a rebuke to the

---

66 The well-known examples are Jackson's refusal to obey the Supreme Court's decision in *Worcester v. Georgia*, Lincoln's suspension of habeas corpus, and the Court's reversal of its *Lochner* jurisprudence after Roosevelt proposed his court-packing plan.

67 The view that Supreme Court justices might act strategically in order to enhance the influence of the Supreme Court is discussed in Baum (1997). He also examines various empirical studies, which, because of data limitations and the difficulty of generating testable predictions, are inconclusive. Id., at 119–23. The most famous anecdotal evidence is, of course, the 'switch in time' in 1937. See Leuchtenberg (1995), 82–162, for a discussion.

68 Backpedaling after it is too late (see *Romer*, supra, or, for example, *West Coast Hotel Co. v. Parrish*, 300 U.S. 379 (1937)) is perhaps a way of minimizing the loss of prestige but it looks bad. The Court effectively acknowledges that it follows, rather than leads, the public and the political branches; the embarrassment is such that the Court even refuses to acknowledge the earlier case. But the alternative – standing in the way of powerful political currents – is even worse.

69 See infra.

70 *Gideon v. Wainwright*, 372 U.S. 335 (1963).

claims of the originalist.[71] But Strauss cannot explain why the written Constitution has the authority that it has; why, for example, the Declaration of Independence does not have that authority, or the Magna Carta for that matter, or why there is no authoritative text as in the British system.[72] The barest sketch of an answer is that it was understood at the time that the drafters of the Constitution were recording existing conventions or at least creating institutions that were consistent with those conventions. The ratification of the Constitution by the states made it, like a statute, the natural place to turn in order to resolve political disputes. Further, the writers of the Constitution retained political influence for several decades after its ratification, so *they* naturally referred to the Constitution which they themselves created. Once this precedent of referring to the Constitution was started, each succeeding generation of politicians had to comply with this precedent or otherwise be interpreted to be mounting a revolutionary challenge to the state rather than to any existing government.

Third, the analysis sheds some light on legal reasoning used by the Court. When conventions change, the Court's jurisprudence must change with it. Originalists are right (as far as I can tell) to say that *Brown* and *Griswold* violate the Constitution as amended,[73] but if the Court overturned these precedents, it would lose its legitimacy. It would not lose its legitimacy because the public cares about *stare decisis*. The Court would lose its legitimacy, because the public regards the principles expressed in these opinions as Constitutional rules. There will always be some incoherence in judicial reasoning, because it must reconcile itself to exogenous, extralegal shifts in foundational conventions.

One might argue that if the present analysis is correct, the reasoning in legal decisions would look different. The Court would spend more time discussing whether conventions exist or are changing, and less time discussing the original meaning of the Constitution. In fact, the Court clearly does care about conventions, and openly discusses their importance. Especially in Eighth Amendment cases, it looks for social 'consensus,' which is different from merely the results of contemporary opinion polls, and so corresponds to the idea of conventions that underlie and sometimes conflict with current public attitudes.[74] Still, a complete theory of the Court would explain the rhetoric of the cases as well as

---

[71] See Strauss (1996), 919–20.

[72] See Strauss (1996), 913–16. He appeals vaguely to a number of possibilities – 'patriotic impulses and narratives, . . . American exceptionalism, . . . Protestantism,' id. 915 (footnotes omitted) – but these phenomena do not imply a commitment to a written constitution.

[73] But see McConnell (1995).

[74] See, e.g., *Stanford v. Kentucky*, 492 U.S. 361, 371, 377 (1989) (upholding imposition of death penalty on certain juveniles, noting that of 37 states with capital punishment, only 27 decline to impose it on 16- or 17-year old juveniles, and ignoring opinion polls); *Tison v. Arizona*, 481 U.S. 137 (1987) (upholding capital punishment for major participation in felony with reckless indifference to human life, noting that only 11 jurisdictions declined to impose capital punishment under these conditions); *Ford v. Wainwright*, 477 U.S. 399, 408 (1986) (striking down capital punishment of the insane, noting that no state imposed such a punishment); *Solem v. Helm*, 463 U.S. 277, 300 (1983) (striking down life sentence without parole for recidivist, noting greater severity than in any other state); *Enmund v. Florida*, 458 U.S. 782, 792 (1982) (striking down imposition of death penalty on participant in robbery whose accomplice committed a murder, noting that only eight jurisdictions impose the death penalty in such circumstances); *Coker v. Georgia*, 433 U.S. 584, 594 (1977) (striking down death penalty for rape, noting that only one state has such a punishment). A fourth amendment case is *Tennessee v. Garner*, 471 U.S. 1, 18 (1985) (striking down statute that authorized

the results. For now the only response is to concede the incompleteness of the theory and take some comfort in the fact that alternative theories that seek to rationalize Supreme Court decision making fail in this respect as well.

Fourth, one might ask the question, Why the Supreme Court? Even if there is a natural tendency for people to look to an authoritative institution to reveal conventions, and to coordinate their behavior around that institution's pronouncements, it does not follow that the Supreme Court ought to be that institution. It could be a charismatic or at least salient leader like the President; it could be a canny analyst of popular trends like Madison Avenue or Hollywood; it could be an imaginary board of notables or experts on social trends, rather than nine out-of-touch oldsters, a bit like the Federal Reserve Board, which has legitimacy because it consists of experts on macroeconomics who seem to know what they are doing. The answer to the question is a matter of historical conjecture, but I will say this. The Supreme Court, through design and evolution, has the last word on many disputes; has special authority in a law-centered society; has, unlike Congress and the President, institutional devices for separating itself from divisive, short-term politics;[75] and is composed of prominent people with life tenure. But the answer is also historical. John Marshall seized the opportunity to fill a gap in government – that of reviewing the constitutionality of government actions – and his successors have cannily maintained this role by, with some notable exceptions, paying attention to evolving conventions. The Supreme Court's role is, in the end, a historical accident, and so it is no surprise that its role is not what it would be in an ideal system constructed by academics.[76]

Finally, it is worth distinguishing this account from the view that the Constitution consists of traditions, a view that appears to be held by some Supreme Court Justices.[77] McConnell describes it thus:

> Courts should look to *experience* and to *stable consensus* as an objective basis for decision making. If a practice is adopted by many different communities, and maintained for a considerable period of time, this provides strong evidence that the practice contributes to the common good and accords with the spirit and mores of the people.[78]

The Assert-Defer game shows both why this view is attractive and incomplete. In Young's model persistence over time *is* evidence that the convention coordinates behavior effectively, but it is not conclusive evidence; it is also possible that an undesirable convention will persist for a substantial duration.[79] This is particularly true when the environment changes rapidly, which is true of the New Deal era and probably true about the 1960s as well. Practices that persist just because of their age may violate the common good,

---

police to use deadly force in order to stop nonviolent fleeing suspects, noting that 86.8 percent of police departments do not authorize the use of deadly force against any felon).

75 The 'passive virtues' – see Bickel (1962).

76 See Bickel (1978), 38 (Frankfurter believed that the judge had to act as 'historian, philosopher, and prophet . . . even though ill-equipped to do so').

77 See *Michael H. v. Gerald D.*, 491 U.S. 110, 127 n. 6 (1989) (Scalia, J.). Scalia also notes a kind of traditionalism in *Bowers* and *Roe*. Ibid.

78 McConnell (1997), 683 (emphasis in original).

79 On the problem of unattractive traditions, see Ely (1980), 60–63; Strauss (1996), 894–7; and on the question of their determinacy, see Tushnet (1999), 86–9.

and the 'spirit and mores' of the people will adjust rapidly when a superior convention, imposed from above, replaces a dysfunctional one. But the Assert-Defer game shows why traditions are attractive, despite the fact that they reflect the interests of 'yesterday's majority.'[80] Prior behavior is a focal point, and when behavior is coordinated around focal points, conflict is avoided. This does not mean that there are not superior focal points, ones that would produce fairer and more attractive patterns of behavior. But avoiding conflict is important, and when submission to tradition avoids conflict, that is a good in itself.

BIBLIOGRAPHY

Ackerman, Bruce (1991 and 1998), *We the People, vols. 1, 2.*
Alexander, Larry (ed.) (1998), *Constitutionalism.*
Axelrod, Robert (1986), *The Evolution of Cooperation.*
Baird, Douglas G., Robert H. Gertner, and Randal C. Picker. (1994), *Game Theory and the Law.*
Baum, Lawrence (1997), *The Puzzle of Judicial Behavior*, Ch. 4.
Bendor, Jonathan and Piotr Swistak (1997), 'The evolutionary stability of cooperation', *Amer. Pol. Sci. Rev.*, **91**, 290.
Bickel, Alexander M. (1962), *The Least Dangerous Branch,* Ch. 4.
Bickel, Alexander M. (1978), *The Supreme Court and the Idea of Progress.*
Binmore, Ken (1994), *Game Theory and the Social Contract, vol. 1.*
Bork, Robert H. (1990), *The Tempting of America.*
Brennan, Geoffrey and James M. Buchanan (1985), *The Reason of Rules: Constitutional Political Economy.*
Brest, Paul (1980), 'The misleading quest for the original understanding', *B.U.L. Rev.*, **60**, 204.
Colman, Andrew M. (1995), *Game Theory and its Applications in the Social and Biological Sciences*, 2nd ed.
Cooter, Robert (1994), 'Structural adjudication and the new law merchant: A model of decentralized law, *Intern'l Rev. Law & Econ.*, **14**, 215.
Dahl, R.A. (1975), 'Decision-making in a democracy: The Supreme Court as a national policy-maker', *J. Publ. L.*, **6**, 279.
Elliott, E. Donald, (1985), 'The evolutionary tradition in jurisprudence', *Colum. L. Rev.*, **85**, 38.
Ely, John Hart (1980), *Democracy and Distrust.*
Farber, Daniel A. (1989), 'The Originalism Debate: A Guide for the Perplexed', *Ohio St. L.J.*, **49**, 1085.
Grey, Thomas C. (1975), 'Do we have an unwritten Constitution?', *Stan. L. Rev.*, **27**, 703.
Hardin, Russell (1988), 'Review article: Constitutional political economy – agreement on rules', *British J. Pol. Sci.*, **18**, 513.
Hirshleifer, Jack (1982), 'Evolutionary models in economics and the law: Cooperation versus conflict strategies, *Research in Law & Econ.*, **4**, 1.
Holmes, Stephen, Jon Elster, and Rune Slagstad (eds) (1988), *Gag Rules or the Politics of Omission, in Constitutionalism and Democracy.*
Klarman, Michael J. (1996), 'Rethinking the civil rights and civil liberties revolutions', *Va. L. Rev.*, **82**, 1.
Kraus, Jody S. (1997), 'Legal design and the evolution of commercial norms', *J. Legal Stud.*, **26**, 337.
Kurland, Philip (1969), 'Toward a political Supreme Court', *U. Chi. L. Rev.*, **37**, 19, 20.
Leuchtenberg, William E. (1995), *The Supreme Court Reborn.*

[80] Ely (1980), 62.

Levinson, Sanford, ed. (1995), *Responding to Imperfection: The Theory and Practice of Constitutional Amendment.*
Lewis, David (1969) *Convention: A Philosophical Study.*
Maynard Smith, John (1982), *Evolution and the Theory of Games.*
Maynard Smith, John and G.R. Price (1973), 'The logic of animal conflict', *Nature*, **246**, 15.
McAdams, Richard (2000), 'A focal point theory of expressive law', *Va. L. Rev.*, **86**, 1649.
McConnell, Michael W. (1995), 'Originalism and the desegregation decisions', *Va. L. Rev.*, **81**, 947.
McConnell, Michael W. (1997), 'The right to die and the jurisprudence of tradition', *Utah L. Rev.*, 665.
Picker, Randal C. (1997), 'Simple games in a complex world: A generative approach to the adoption of norms', **64** *U. Chi. Law Rev.* 1225.
Posner, Eric A. (1996), 'Law, economics, and inefficient norms', **144** *U. Pa. L. Rev.*, 1697.
Posner, Eric A. (2000), *Law and Social Norms.*
Priest, George L. (1977), 'The common law process and the selection of efficient rules, *J. Legal Stud.*, **6**, 65.
Rakove, Jack N., ed. (1990), *Interpreting the Constitution: The Debate over Original Intent.*
Roe, Mark J. (1996), 'Chaos and evolution in law and economics', *Harv. L. Rev.* **109**, 641.
Rubin, Paul H. (1977), 'Why is the common law efficient?', *J. Legal Stud.*, **6**, 51.
Scalia, Antonin (1997), *A Matter of Interpretation*, 37–41.
Schotter, Andrew (1981), *The Economic Theory of Social Institutions.*
Strauss, David (1996), 'Common law constitutional interpretation', *U. Chi. L. Rev.*, **63**, 877, 906–16.
Sugden, Robert (1986), *The Economics of Rights, Co-operation and Welfare.*
Tushnet, Mark (1999), 'The Supreme Court – Forward: The new constitutional order and the chastening of constitutional aspiration', *Harv. L. Rev.*, **113**, 26.
Ullman-Margalit, Edna (1977), *The Emergence of Norms.*
Voigt, Stefan (1997), 'Positive constitutional economics: A survey', *Pub. Choice*, **90**, 11.
Weibull, Jörgen (1995), *Evolutionary Game Theory.*
Young, H. Peyton (1998), *Individual Strategy and Social Structure: An Evolutionary Theory of Institutions.*

7. The expressive power of adjudication in an evolutionary context

Richard H. McAdams

This chapter offers a 'third way' of understanding compliance with adjudication. The two conventional theories are economic – that people fear threatened sanctions – and sociological – that people defer to perceived legitimacy. Without denying the importance of these mechanisms, I offer to supplement them with a new causal story for the effect of adjudication. To explain how courts influence behavior independent of their perceived legitimacy and the sanctions they wield, one must engage in a peculiar thought experiment imagining a court without these two typical characteristics. I therefore devote much of the chapter to describing an expressive influence that any third party might have over two parties in a dispute.

The expressive theory of adjudication synergistically combines three ways that economics has of understanding communicative influences: (1) as a device for creating a 'correlated equilibrium;' (2) as a 'cheap talk' means of constructing a 'focal point' around which individuals coordinate; and (3) as a signal of private information. The synergy of these three forces gives the third party an expressive power to resolve the specific disputes subject to adjudication.

After discussing dispute resolution, I turn more clearly to a discussion of adjudication – to the ability of courts or quasi-judicial bodies to influence the behavior of those *not* a party to the dispute that prompts its decision. This part of the story requires an evolutionary approach. I discuss how informal order – conventions and norms – inherently contain ambiguity that the adjudicator can resolve expressively. The adjudicator's clarification of the convention or norm affects the expectations and therefore the behavior of parties other than the immediate disputants. Thus, adjudicative expression can both resolve existing disputes and, by articulating clear precedent, avoid future ones.

1. DIVERGENT ECONOMIC THEORIES OF ADJUDICATIVE EXPRESSION: A REVIEW AND CRITIQUE

Does economics offer any selfish reason for the parties to a dispute to obey a judicial declaration *other than* the threat of legal sanctions? The scant literature giving an affirmative answer suggests three different theories: that adjudication is a device for (1) achieving a 'correlated equilibrium,' (2) constructing a focal point, and (3) signaling information. In this section, I describe the existing literature and elaborate on each theory. I also provide a critique, finding each of the three expressive theories subject to serious objection.

1.1 Adjudication as a 'Correlated Equilibrium' Device

I begin with the most non-intuitive possibility. The idea of a 'correlated equilibrium' is that, in some strategic situations, it is a stable outcome for two individuals to condition their behavior on some observable, random feature of the world. I explain the relevance correlated equilibria may have to adjudication, extend the existing theory, and then describe some critical objections to it.

1.1.1 Existing literature

Game theory predicts behavior based on the idea of an equilibrium. An outcome is a 'Nash equilibrium' when, from that outcome, no individual has any incentive to switch strategies unilaterally; each is playing his best response to what the others have done. In any game, there may be one or multiple outcomes that satisfy this condition. Against this background, however, Nobel Laureate Robert Aumann noted that if the parties have rich opportunities to communicate, they can sometimes create the possibility of an *additional* 'correlated' equilibrium.[1] Under some conditions, if the individuals (technically, those in the game are 'players,' though I will also use the term 'parties' given my focus on disputes) mutually agree to observe some random event, they will benefit by basing their actions on the outcome of the event. For example, one player might flip a coin in the other's presence and each could then play a strategy that takes one action when the coin comes up heads and another action when the coin comes up tails. As a result, the parties now have strategic options that they did not have in the absence of communication. Sometimes these new strategies will make possible new correlated equilibria.

Jennifer Brown and Ian Ayres use this idea to explain one function of mediation.[2] They observe how a mediator could, by randomly choosing between alternative resolutions of a dispute, produce a mediate solution that enhances value for both disputants. They therefore claim to explain both why the disputants would hire a mediator and why they would tend to obey him. Brown and Ayres illustrate the point with the Battle of the Sexes Game in Figure 7.1. (As is standard, each cell lists the payoffs for, respectively, Player 1 and Player 2.) The players each choose between Strategy O and Strategy B where matching the strategies (OO or BB) produces a higher payoff for both players than failing to match (OB or BO). The two matching outcomes are equilibria (with payoffs of 1 or 5).[3] The two players each prefer reaching either equilibrium to either of the two non-equilibrium outcomes (with payoffs of 0). But the players also have conflicting preferences because each prefers a different equilibrium. Indeed, if each player selects the strategy necessary to produce his desired outcome (Player 1 picks O and Player 2 picks B), the result OB is one of the non-equilibrium outcomes that is worse for both.

Figure 7.1 offers a good model for bargaining impasse, where each threatens to walk away from negotiations and where there is some barrier to a simple 50/50 split. One might

---

1 See generally Aumann (1974, 1987).

2 See Brown and Ayres (1994).

3 At OO, either player would be worse off being the only one to switch strategies because the results OB and BO are worse for each. The same is true of BB.

		Player 2	
		O	B
Player	O	5,1	0,0
1	B	0,0	1,5

Figure 7.1 Battle of the Sexes game

imagine two divorcing spouses disputing the allocation of two jointly owned properties (or two siblings disputing jointly inherited property) where both prefer one to the other, but where the second best property is better than failing to agree because non-agreement forces a sale and loss of sentimental value. Or the game could represent two businesses contemplating a merger where the two owners have not yet agreed which of them will be the new CEO or what the new firm's name will be; the failure to agree blocks the merger. All of these individuals lose by failing to agree, but each may purposely risk impasse to get his preferred outcome.

Brown and Ayres claim that, in this situation, the parties would agree to have a mediator announce a recommendation before they simultaneously select their strategies. The key assumption is that each player has a sufficiently large probability of 'winning' from the mediator a message to play his preferred equilibrium. Brown and Ayres illustrate the point by assuming that the mediator randomly chooses between the two messages 'Play O' and 'Play B,' so that each party has a 50 percent chance of receiving the message he prefers. If so, then following the mediator's recommendation improves the players' expected outcome by giving each a 50 percent chance of his best outcome, a 50 percent chance of getting his second best outcome, and a zero percent chance of the non-coordinated outcome both wish to avoid.

The point can be made more precisely by comparing this result to the 'mixed strategy' equilibrium. In addition to choosing O or B, a party may play a 'mixed strategy' of choosing O with probability p and B with probability (1−p). There can be an equilibrium of mixed strategies. In Figure 7.1, the equilibrium occurs where Player 1 plays O 83 percent of the time and B 17 percent of the time, while Player 2 plays B 83 percent of the time and O 17 percent of the time. As a result, they fail to coordinate 72 percent of the time and the expected payoff for each is approximately .83. Now consider: if the parties know the mediator will flip a coin and, depending on the results, announce 'Play O' or 'Play B,' then mutually following the mediator will eliminate the non-coordinated outcome and produce an expected payoff of 3 for each, a 'more than a three-fold improvement over the unmediated mixed-strategy equilibrium.'[4] Thus, to solve a dispute that takes the form

[4] Brown and Ayres (1994), 375. Each has a 50 percent chance of receiving a payoff of 5 and a 50 percent chance of receiving a payoff of 1, for a total expectation of 3.

		Player 2	
		Dove	Hawk
Player	Dove	2,2	0,4
1	Hawk	4,0	–1,–1

Figure 7.2 Hawk/Dove game

of a Battle of the Sexes game, 'a mediator . . . only needs randomly to select one of two signals and transmit this signal to both parties.'[5]

As a terminological matter, I would not use 'signal' to describe what the mediator is doing here. What really matters to the Brown and Ayres analysis is that if each party perceives *ex ante* that the mediator will recommend the equilibrium he prefers with a 50 percent probability (or something close to it), and if each will then follow the mediator's advice, then each will prefer mediating the dispute to not mediating. But it does not matter how the mediator generates this perception, by promising to randomize in some formal way or just by being unpredictable. So the mediator's message is not a signal of his private knowledge of anything such as how a coin landed. It is, in game theory parlance, 'cheap talk.'[6]

1.1.2 Extending correlated equilibrium analysis

Now I want to extend the correlated equilibrium analysis to a similar game – called Hawk/Dove or Chicken – that I believe is better for modeling certain disputes. Here, each player chooses between an aggressive strategy – 'Hawk' – where one insists on getting one's way – and a passive strategy – 'Dove' – where one defers to others. In a two-person version, the game is Hawk/Dove when both players rank the four possible outcomes as follows, starting with the best: (1) playing Hawk against Dove; (2) playing Dove against Dove; (3) playing Dove against Hawk; and (4) playing Hawk against Hawk. The pure strategy equilibria are Hawk/Dove and Dove/Hawk; an example is Figure 7.2. The Dove/Dove outcome is attractive because it seems 'fair,' but it is not an equilibrium because each party would benefit by switching to the more aggressive strategy when the other plays Dove.

The Hawk/Dove Game does a better job than Battle of the Sexes of mapping onto real world situations whenever the different ways of failing to coordinate produce these different sorts of rankings. For example, imagine two drivers merging into a single lane, where each wants to proceed first. In this case, Hawk is the strategy of maintaining speed and Dove is the strategy of slowing down. There are two sorts of non-equilibrium outcomes

---

5 Id. at 375–6.
6 See Farrell and Rabin (1996).

– Dove/Dove means that both cars slow, while the Hawk/Hawk outcome is a collision.[7] Or, suppose two individuals are sitting near each other in a public place when one pulls out a cigarette and the other requests that the first not smoke it. At this point, Hawk is the strategy of insisting on getting one's way and Dove is the strategy of giving in to the other's preference. Here, Dove/Dove may represent each party moving slightly away from their current location, while the Hawk/Hawk outcome might be an embarrassing shouting match.

As the most general possibility, whenever the parties have a dispute Dove/Dove may represent some compromise while Hawk/Hawk represents violence. If two neighbors disagree about the precise location of their shared property boundary, for example, we can think of Hawk as the strategy of treating the disputed land as one's own and Dove as the strategy of deferring to the other's claim. Imagine that the Dove/Dove outcome is to split the disputed land equally, while Hawk/Hawk represents a physical fight. In this case, although the outcome of Hawk/Hawk for each player is uncertain – one might win or lose the fight – the expected value is the worst possible outcome for both players because the cost of fighting is high relative to the value of the disputed resource. Both parties, of course, are subject to criminal punishment for assault, but deterrence of violence is obviously highly imperfect, which is one reason that a significant amount of violent crime is a 'self-help' remedy to a perceived loss of honor or property.[8] The risk of costly but non-deterring criminal sanctions is merely another reason that the violent outcome is the worst for everyone.

Again, the players in this context will benefit if they correlate their strategies with a mediator's randomly selected recommendation of one of the two equilibria. Without anything to make either equilibrium focal, the players may use a mixed strategy and reach equilibrium (given these payoffs and assuming risk neutrality) only when each plays Dove with probability 1/3 and Hawk with probability 2/3. For each player, the expected value of the game at this equilibrium is .67. This payoff includes a 4/9 chance of the costly Hawk/Hawk outcome. By contrast, if the two players designate a third party to randomly select one of the two equilibria, and each player follows this recommendation, then the expected outcome for each is now 2.[9] Because the third party mediator never recommends that both players select Hawk, the mediator eliminates the possibility of a costly Hawk/Hawk clash. The third party thereby creates a substantial expected gain for each player.

In sum, the Brown and Ayres analysis appears to apply in a wide array of circumstances, where adjudicative expression can influence the behavior of disputants by creating a correlated equilibrium.

1.1.3 Two problems for the correlated equilibrium theory

Nonetheless, there are two important objections to the correlated equilibrium theory: (1) the theory is not actually sufficient to show why disputants would comply with the

---

[7] If both cars slow, the drivers have to then decide whether to take further action to get ahead or behind the other driver. The extended game is no longer Hawk/Dove but it still has multiple equilibria and is still subject to all the points made in the text.

[8] See e.g. Engle Merry (1981); Nisbett and Cohen (1996).

[9] Each has a 50 percent chance of receiving a payoff of 4 and a 50 percent chance of receiving a payoff of 0, for a total expectation of 2.

mediator; and (2) the theory implies that the disputants would resolve their dispute without a third party.

The first problem is a gap in the application of correlated equilibrium theory to mediation or adjudication. The theory demonstrates only the existence of a new equilibrium – one in which the two players correlate their strategy with an observable event. By itself, the theory does not demonstrate that the players will wind up at that equilibrium. To the contrary, whenever there are multiple equilibria, the theory tells us only that these are the possible outcomes, not which outcome will occur.

Brown and Ayres appear to avoid this problem by showing that it is in the interest of the players to follow the correlated equilibrium created by the mediator. But it is an error to think that the reason for compliance flows simply from the calculations of expected payoffs. Given their assumptions, Brown and Ayres only show that, prior to the mediator's announcement, each party would expect to improve his payoffs by hiring and following the mediator's message, assuming that the other player would follow it as well. But is there any reason for one player to assume that the other player will follow the announcement? Because the mediator's message does not change the payoffs, even after the mediator endorses a particular outcome, the unendorsed equilibria stubbornly remain.

Perhaps the answer is that, when there are multiple equilibria, the players tend to play the one that is mutually best, if there is one (and subject to other qualifications not relevant here). Thus, demonstrating that both players expect to gain the most by obeying the mediator's recommendation is arguably sufficient to show that they will obey him. But this does not follow. The expected payoff analysis says that each player will be better off obeying the mediator's recommendation given that the other player does so. Yet we could also say the opposite: each player will be better off doing *the opposite* of what the mediator recommended, given that the other player does so. The equilibrium of both players doing the opposite of what the mediator says has the same expected payoffs as both players following the mediator. Yet this equilibrium represents perfect noncompliance, which now makes it an odd representation of the power of mediation.

My point is not that Brown and Ayres are wrong about mediation, but that there is a gap in the theory. They do not explain what it is about the mediator's expression that will cause each player to expect the other to follow it, rather than its opposite and rather than some other third-party expression.[10]

The second problem with using correlated equilibria theory to explain adjudication is that it does not justify the need for a third party. If disputants merely need to correlate their strategies with dichotomous events they perceive as being (approximately) equally likely, then why can't the parties simply flip a coin? Obviously, it is more costly and time consuming for the parties to ask a mediator to randomly select between the equilibria than for the parties to do so themselves. So this explanation raises the question of why the parties would ever resort to a third party mediator or adjudicator to provide this service.

---

[10] Indeed, Brown and Ayres point to the precise answer I give in the next section when they say: '[T]he parties' agreement to bring the dispute before a mediator might allow the parties to look to the mediator's action as a focal point to coordinate their behavior.' Brown and Ayres (1994), 376. But they do not identify the problem for which focality is the necessary solution – the gap in the theory just described in the text.

1.2 Adjudication as Focal Point Construction

A second expressive theory is that an adjudicator uses cheap talk to construct a 'focal point' in a coordination game. Here I provide some basic background, describe the literature proposing that courts can construct focal points, and then provide a critique.

1.2.1 Background on focal points

Talk is said to be 'cheap' when it is 'costless, nonbinding and non-verifiable.'[11] *A*'s threat of harming anyone who fails to keep his promise to *A* is cheap talk if *A* bears no cost from uttering the statement, nothing binds *A* to follow through on the threat, and there is nothing to verify whether *A* has harmed past promise-breakers. That 'cheap' talk could ever influence behavior may seem puzzling within a rational-choice framework.

There is no puzzle, however, if the game has multiple equilibria. When a game has only one equilibrium, then by definition the payoffs determine the outcome. If the game has more than one equilibrium, however, then by definition something other than the payoffs may determine the particular equilibrium that results. A simple example is the pure coordination game, such as the choice of whether to drive on the left or right side of the road. Assume Players 1 and 2 choose between strategies L and R, where each receives a higher equal positive payoff if both coordinate at LL or RR than if they wind up at LR or RL. Merely from the payoffs, Player 1 cannot rationally determine whether to 'aim for' the LL equilibrium or the RR equilibrium; neither can Player 2. But if the players can communicate freely, they might 'agree' to each play L. Though the agreement is nonbinding cheap talk (it is not enforced by a third party and, let us assume, the players feel no moral obligation to keep their promise), it is likely the players will follow it. Even if the players cannot both communicate, if one can send a message to the other naming a particular equilibrium, it is likely the message will determine the behavior. Experimental data confirms the value of cheap talk to coordinating behavior.[12]

If players cannot communicate or fail to agree, Nobel Laureate Thomas Schelling identified an alternative mechanism for coordination – 'focal points.' An equilibrium is focal if it has some feature that, for reasons of psychology, history, or culture, draws attention to itself, making it 'stand out' among all equilibria. If the players are aware that one equilibrium draws special mental attention from all the players – is 'salient' to all – that fact alone can cause everyone to play their strategy associated with that equilibrium. For example, when Schelling asked individuals where they would go to meet someone on a map if they had been separated accidentally, most individuals identified topographically unique places on the map (such as the only bridge or only 5-way intersection).[13] In this context, expectations are self-fulfilling: once a player believes the other players are 'aiming for' a particular equilibrium, the player's best response is to play the strategy associated with that equilibrium. Experiments confirm that, in games of multiple equilibria, salient non-payoff features – i.e., focal points – significantly facilitate coordination.[14]

---

[11] Baird et al. (1994), 303.
[12] See generally Crawford (1998).
[13] Schelling, (1960), 54–55, 58.
[14] See Bacharach and Bernasconi (1997), 37–39; Mehta et al. (1994), 658, 672.

For purposes of law, Schelling's most interesting insight combines cheap talk and focal points. He discusses the ability of a third party – someone who is not a player in the underlying coordination game – to influence the players in the game merely by communicating in favor of a particular outcome. By publicly endorsing a particular outcome in view of the players, the third party makes that equilibrium 'stand out' from the rest, which may then create self-fulfilling expectations that others will play the strategy associated with that equilibrium. In contrast to 'natural' focal points, third-party cheap talk constructs a focal point.

One of Schelling's illustrations is useful. Suppose that two drivers approach a busy intersection on different roads when the traffic light is broken. Each prefers to maintain his or her speed and have the other driver slow down or stop, but each realizes that the drivers will collide in the intersection if neither slows down. In this Hawk/Dove context, Schelling observes the likely effect of 'a bystander who jumps into an intersection and begins to direct traffic.'[15] The bystander's suggestions do not change the payoffs because the bystander cannot sanction drivers for failing to comply. Nor does the bystander seem to enjoy authority or legitimacy of the sort that sociologists and psychologists attribute to law. Nonetheless, because 'coordination requires the common acceptance of some source of suggestion,'[16] one suspects that the bystander's directions will influence the drivers' behavior. By calling attention to one outcome, the relevant hand signals make that outcome focal. Experimental studies confirm Schelling's intuition.[17]

1.2.2 Using adjudication to construct a focal point: Existing literature and the connection to correlated equilibria

Several economic theorists and philosophers have suggested cheap-talk construction of focal points to explain the expressive effect of law.[18] Most of the prior work on legal expression as means of constructing focal points, including most of my own, has focused on legal rules of general application stated in advance of a particular dispute. In this chapter, however, my concern is whether this expressive effect can work retrospectively for adjudication, providing a tribunal with power to influence disputants after their dispute occurs.

Schelling himself first suggested that mediation and fact-finding might work to resolve disputes by making focal a particular outcome.[19] The first theorists to apply Schelling's idea to adjudication were apparently the political scientists Geoffrey Garrett and Barry Weingast, who offer a focal point explanation of the role of the European Court of Justice.[20] Garrett and Weingast claim that nations have a mix of common and conflicting interests that frequently create situations of multiple equilibria. Specifically, they imagine that nations seeking to cooperate in an iterated Prisoners' Dilemma (PD) game may enter into a potentially self-enforcing agreement that specifies what form their cooperation will

---

15 Schelling (1960), 144.

16 Id.

17 See McAdams and Nadler (2008), 865; McAdams and Nadler (2005), 87; Tyran and Feld (2006), 135.

18 See e.g. Garrett and Weingast (1993); Hardin (1989); McAdams (2000), 1649.

19 Schelling (1960), 62, 68.

20 Garrett & Weingast (1993).

take. Two nations, for example, may agree to limit their tariffs and sustain cooperation by threatening to breach if the other breaches. To the conventional point that iteration allows (but does not ensure) the parties to sustain cooperation, Garrett and Weingast add the point that there is often more than one way for parties to cooperate to achieve their best outcome. The parties therefore require an agreement to define what behavior constitutes 'cooperation' for purposes of their conditionally cooperative strategies (which effectively 'enforce' the agreement).

The problem is that contracts are inevitably incomplete. There are always ambiguities and unforeseen contingencies that create situations where the parties disagree on what behavior is required to cooperate. The parties may be drawn to pre-existing focal solutions but, in the absence of natural focal points, 'an institution can construct one by devising the required set of specifications (as to the nature of the agreement, and hence as to what constitutes cooperation and defection) and by making them known to the community.'[21] Similarly, I recently coauthored an article arguing that the International Court of Justice generates high compliance with its decisions in part by its ability to make focal the outcomes it endorses.[22]

None of this prior work, however, notes the vital connection of focal point construction to the idea of a correlated equilibrium. Focal points provide what I described in the previous section as the element missing from Brown and Ayres's discussion of correlated equilibria. A mediator's message tends to make salient the outcome he endorses, rather than the opposite outcome, and thus tends to generate self-fulfilling expectations that the endorsed outcome will occur, rather than the opposite one.

Thus, the missing element in the story of adjudication as correlated equilibrium is this ability of the designated coordinator's speech to make a particular outcome salient and the tendency of salience to produce self-fulfilling expectations that the salient outcome will result. Henceforth, I will combine the ideas of focal points and correlated equilibrium by saying that parties correlate their strategies on an equilibrium the arbiter makes focal. Note the synergy: while the focal point explains the special power of the arbiter's message, the ability of a correlated equilibrium to increase expected payoffs explains why the parties will seek out the message in the first place.

1.2.3 Two problems for the focal point theory

The idea of constructed focal points solves one of the objections I raised above to the idea of adjudication as correlated equilibria – that it did not actually explain compliance. But we are still left with the second problem – that disputants seeking a randomized solution do not need to hire a third party because they could randomize by themselves. If two parties need to correlate strategies on a constructed focal point, selected at random, they can create one without third-party assistance. The parties need only to select a future event with equal dichotomous outcomes (e.g., a coin flip) and to agree on how they will correlate their strategies on the two possible outcomes. Once the event occurs, the agreed-to solution will tend to be focal. Thus, the focal-point theory does not explain why two parties seek a third-party arbiter to resolve their dispute.

---

21 Garrett & Weingast (1993), 183.
22 Ginsburg and McAdams (2004), 1229.

There is now a second objection I want to raise with the idea of adjudication as a constructed focal point. The problem with randomly generated focal points is the strategic ability of one party to exploit randomization by the other. This point requires identifying an implicit assumption of the above analysis. The Brown and Ayres and the Garrett and Weingast analyses are static; they assume that the existence of a dispute is exogenous to and unaffected by the manner of dispute resolution, that the players can therefore resolve a dispute without affecting the likelihood of finding themselves in such a dispute again in the future. Put differently, existing models proceed as if all disputes are genuine – that is, based on actual differences in how the parties perceive the situation.[23] But when one allows for the dynamic possibility of strategic disputes – that is, the manufacturing of apparent disagreement about the nature of the situation to exploit the opportunities the dispute creates – then disputes will be endogenous to the method of dispute resolution. The number of times one must play a game may be determined by how one plays it. Of particular relevance, if an individual always randomizes to resolve his disputes, then he will have more of them.

This strategic problem is obscured if one focuses solely on the payoffs of the canonical Battle of the Sexes Game. That game is normally described as having only positive payoffs in equilibrium, zero payoffs for the non-equilibrium outcomes, and no negative payoffs. Under these circumstances, where one cannot lose, one wants to play this Battle of the Sexes (BOS) game as often as possible (at least as long as one does not thereby forgo playing other games with even higher expected payoffs). Therefore, there is no strategic danger in taking action that encourages others to create this BOS situation again in the future. Many disputes, however, involve negative payoffs for at least one party. Here, randomization may encourage disputes one wishes to avoid.

An example of the strategic problem is a property dispute modeled by the Hawk/Dove game. A person does not want to be in the situation in which others assert a claim to property he currently possesses and uses as his own. Losing property one has been enjoying causes a loss of utility. Yet if an individual is known to have used randomization in the past whenever others claimed property he was using, he will encourage such claims. Knowing that *A* will flip a coin to resolve ownership of what he currently regards as his house would prompt a long line of individuals to appear claiming to own the same property, in order to get a 50 percent chance of acquiring it. Eventually, *A* will lose his house and all of his property. To avoid this predicament, *A* may want to avoid randomization, or at least to cabin it in some way. My point is not that this strategic barrier is insurmountable; only that it remains to be shown how it can be solved.

2. ADJUDICATION AS SIGNALING

The strategic problem just discussed implies that there is a flaw in Garrett and Weingast's analysis of the European Court of Justice (ECJ). They find significant compliance with the decisions of the ECJ, yet I have claimed that disputants would not wish to resolve

---

23 Brown and Ayres (1994) explicitly assume, for this part of their analysis, that the parties have no private information, which means that the dispute is genuine.

their conflict by following randomly constructed focal points. Why would a group of nations create an institution for resolving disputes that would only encourage more disputes? Upon closer examination, Garrett and Weingast are implicitly relying on some feature of adjudication other than focal-point construction. Rather than describing the ECJ as endorsing outcomes arbitrarily or randomly, they have in mind that the institution mitigates the problem of ambiguity by 'making declarations or judgments about what occurred in the past.'[24] At one point, they give an example where the Danish government backed down prior to an ECJ ruling because the government 'fear[ed] an adverse judgment had it proceeded with a case "it probably would have lost".'[25] In other words, because the adjudicator engages the facts underlying the dispute, its decisions are made on some constrained, predictable basis. Despite the authors' claim, this is not (or not merely) focal point construction (nor is it a correlated equilibrium analysis). Garrett and Weingast are describing signaling.

In this section, I describe a theory of adjudicative signaling and then raise some objections.

2.1 A Signaling Model of Dispute Resolution

The third expressive possibility, within the assumptions of economics, is that adjudication provides disputants with an informational signal about some feature of the world. According to this idea, those receiving the signal will change (update) their belief about the feature of the world being signaled, and this change in beliefs can cause a change in behavior. I will eventually explain why the change in belief influences the behavior of disputants, but first I address the general idea of signaling.

Economists usually use signaling to describe inferences made from an individual's conduct. In the typical model, an individual reveals his 'type' ('good' or 'bad') by the degree to which he will engage in behavior that has different costs for different types. For example, one who earns a graduate degree may signal his having abilities that make such education less costly for him.[26] For my purposes, however, it is important to see how ordinary talk can also constitute a signal.[27] As an example, consider the expression of a critic or reviewer. A review (of theater, wine, stereo equipment, etc.) is cheap talk only if the reviewer doesn't value his reputation for providing reliable information for a consumer's purchasing decision. If the reviewer does value his reputation, deriving some monetary or other satisfaction from influencing these decisions, then his public statements are costly because they affect his reputation. For this reason, the expression of a reviewer (who values his reputation) can cause readers to change their beliefs about the reviewed item, which in turns changes their behavior.

Another analogy, closer to adjudication, is the informal sports referee, who lacks any power to sanction players for disobeying his rulings. Nonetheless, athletic competitors sometimes solicit individuals to serve as informal referees and often obey their rulings.

---

24 Garrett & Weingast (1993), 204.
25 Id. at 195.
26 See Spence (1973), 355.
27 See, e.g., Dharmapala and McAdams (2005), 93.

Among other possible reasons is signaling. If the players believe the referee cares about preserving his reputation for accurate rulings, then they will view his rulings as signals of his beliefs and update their beliefs accordingly. If such an informal referee signals a goal in a soccer game, members of the team ostensibly scored against would assign greater probability to the fact that the ball crossed the goal line, and expect the team that apparently scored also to assign greater probability to that fact. As a result, the former team is more likely to concede the goal. Like the reviewer, the informal referee has persuasive, rather than coercive, influence.

Of course, to cause individuals to update their beliefs about the state of the world, a reviewer, referee, or arbiter must have a certain ability and motive. To be able to form a relevant belief, the third party must first have private information about the relevant state of the world. That could be based on some independent observation, but more usually it is simply that the individual reviews existing evidence (perhaps provided by the parties) and evaluates it with his own unique experience and judgment. Obviously, individuals vary greatly in their experience and judgment, which from the disputants' perspective means they vary in signaling accuracy – the fit between the signal and the 'true value' of the variable being signaled. They also differ in their partiality toward the parties. The degree to which the disputants change their beliefs in the face of a signal depends on this perception of accuracy and partiality. Other things equal, a disputant will give greater weight to (and change his beliefs more in response to) a signal against his interests (i) having greater accuracy and (ii) being less biased against him.

So we come to the basic signaling story of adjudication I want to defend. Stated abstractly, the point is that even selfish players, or players motivated in a particular context by selfish interests, frequently choose strategies that depend, in part, on observed facts about the world. If so, then a third-party signal can change the players' beliefs and therefore their behavior.

For example, in an iterated Prisoner's Dilemma, one's best strategy may depend on whether one's counterpart 'cooperated' or 'defected' in the last round, and this may depend on narrower matters of observed fact. We might imagine two business partners who each prefer to shirk while the other works or two neighbors who each prefer to free-ride on the public-good investment of the other. Sustaining cooperation is possible if each side implements a reciprocal strategy that in some respect rewards past cooperation with cooperation and punishes defection with defection. An example is the strategy Tit-for-Tat, where a player cooperates in round one and then reciprocates whatever the other player did in the prior round. Suppose, however, that the underlying facts are ambiguous; the situation is 'noisy.'[28] Noise represents an impediment to cooperation because *A* may think it has cooperated in round n while *B* thinks *A* has defected. *B* may then defect in round n + 1, producing a cascade of alternating defection. In this context, a timely third party signal of the relevant facts of round n might cause *A* and *B* to update their beliefs in the same direction, such that they now agree as to what happened in the prior round.

The result is compliance. If the adjudicator rules in favor of *A* by saying '*A* cooperated in round n and therefore *B* should cooperate in round n + 1' (or some more contextually

---

[28] See, e.g., Sainty (1999), 421; Wu and Axelrod (1995), 183.

appropriate language), *B* may now update his factual belief sufficiently to believe that *A* did cooperate in round n. If so, then *B*'s strategy tells *B* to cooperate in round n + 1. In general, the losing player will then tend to comply with this expression, so long as the signal is strong enough to cause him to update his beliefs sufficiently. Thus, for very general reasons, adjudicative signaling about such facts can generally influence disputant's behavior, generating compliance independent of sanctions.

2.2 Two Problems for the Signaling Theory

There are two weaknesses in the signaling account of expressive adjudication. First, in many cases, disputants are so confident in their position that the third party's signal will not change their beliefs sufficiently to change their behavior. For example, the parties would presumably always have some doubt about their estimates, but they might play strategies based on their level of confidence. So, Party *A* might treat Party *B*'s behavior as defection, and act accordingly to punish *B*, if *A* believes it to be at least X% probable that *B* defected. If *A* begins believing it is far greater than X% likely that *B* defected, then even after a contrary signal from the third party, *A* may still believe it is X% (or more) likely that *B* defected. Stated more generally, both disputants may start out with such confidence in their beliefs and such doubts about the third party's perceptive abilities that, after adjudication, they do not change their beliefs sufficiently to avert conflict. In genuinely close cases, the parties may not be so confident in their beliefs, but the third party may also lack confidence and therefore form only a very weak belief about what the facts show. If the arbiter can only determine and signal that there is, say, a 51 percent probability that the facts favor party *A* then he will ordinarily fail to cause *B* to update his beliefs sufficiently to induce him to play a different strategy. Close cases are among the situations most likely to produce a dispute. Yet, again, a true signal here would do little to cause the disputants' beliefs to converge to a common understanding.

Of course, if a single third party's signal fails to resolve the dispute, it is always possible that additional third party signals may do the trick. But this possibility reveals the second problem with the signaling model: it implies that disputants would seek out too many third parties. If two parties to a dispute recognize the possible advantage of receiving the signals of others, so as to avoid conflict caused by ambiguous facts, then they would presumably prefer to seek signals of a great many third parties, who collectively have the potential for producing greater belief change and greater accuracy than any one individual. This is a problem because adjudication is typically centralized in a single tribunal or institution, often with a single member (perhaps with limited appeals) who provides the dispute resolution services. Disputants may choose between many different fora, and may appeal from one decision maker to a higher ranking one, but they do not just gather a large number of opinions and aggregate them as signaling implies.

The story thus far is pessimistic. There appears to be no room for expressive adjudication based on economic models of correlated equilibria, focal points, or signaling. But the story becomes more optimistic in the next section where I consider how these elements interact.

3. A RECONSTRUCTED THEORY OF ADJUDICATIVE EXPRESSION: THE SYNERGY OF CORRELATED EQUILIBRIA, FOCAL POINTS, AND SIGNALS

Adjudication can work expressively by combining in a particular way the different elements just discussed. An adjudicator will wield an expressive influence on disputants if he offers a signal where appropriate and a focal point for correlating strategies where appropriate. The synergy between these types of expression arises because each type works to address weaknesses in the other. Recall the two problems with seeking to correlate strategies around randomly constructed focal points: (1) disputants do not need a third party and (2) randomization invites strategic exploitation. Signaling, however, does necessitate a third party and, as explained below, signaling works to minimize the problem of strategic disputing. Recall also the two problems with signaling: (1) when the evidence of the relevant facts is closely divided, signaling will be too weak to cause disputants to agree on the facts; and (2) signaling does not explain centralization of dispute resolution into a single tribunal. The construction of focal points, however, does necessitate a centralized source of adjudicative expression and focal points can, as explained below, facilitate the correlation of strategies even when the signal is too weak to change the losing party's beliefs.

I now describe the synergy between these various expressive elements. I conclude that, in common circumstances, adjudicative expression can itself induce even selfishly motivated disputants to comply. This section shows only how third-party determination of *facts* can influence behavior. Then I turn toward the legal side of adjudication. I claim that ambiguities in the conceptual categories underlying evolved conventions generate conflict between individuals. I then show how adjudicative expression can influence behavior by clarifying these conventional categories.

3.1 Declared Fact-finding as a Focal Signal: The Basic Theory in Three Steps

Step one: The screening function of arbitral signals

I objected to the correlated equilibrium and focal-point theories because they invite strategic exploitation and they do not explain the need for a third party. Signaling overcomes both problems. First, by calibrating expression to the strength of the disputant's case, adjudicative signaling ameliorates the problem of strategic disputing otherwise caused by randomization. To see this point it will help to assume, for simplicity, that an arbiter will consider the evidence and reach one of only three beliefs: (i) that the facts clearly favor party *A*, (ii) that the facts clearly favor party *B*, or (iii) that the facts do not clearly favor either side because the evidence is closely divided. Assume for now that the third-party arbiter adopts a policy of signaling his particular belief to the parties, including his indecision in case (iii). If the disputants receive signal (i) or (ii), then they will both update their beliefs in light of this new information. This updating might cause the losing party to update his beliefs sufficiently to align them with the prevailing party, but I defer discussing these outcomes until the next subsection. By contrast, signal (iii) is unlikely ever to cause either party to update its beliefs sufficiently to align them with the other party. Signal (iii) seems too weak to cause the parties to change their behavior, and therefore too weak to avert conflict.

But signal (iii) is nonetheless important for its screening function. When the facts are closely divided, a signal of this fact raises the probability that the dispute is genuine because both sides actually believe the facts favor their position. Thus, the signal that the case is a close one provides some evidence to each party that the other side is not raising the dispute strategically. As such, while still refusing to randomize as a general mechanism for resolving disputes, the parties can benefit from following a strategy of randomizing in this kind of case. A player will not necessarily fear strategic exploitation from correlating his strategy with a random event in just those cases where a neutral arbiter has signaled that the facts do not clearly favor either side. Signaling screens out those cases where the parties would be exploited by using randomization and leaves those where they would not.

Put differently, to address the problem of strategic disputes, we need a mechanism that tends to resolve disputes against the party who raises a dispute strategically. A signal does this. The more probable one party believes it is that the facts favor the other party, the more the former will anticipate that the arbiter will signal in favor of the latter. Thus, although a party may not be able to tell whether the other party's claim of dispute is genuine or strategic (because he may be confident in his position in either case), he will still expect to win the adjudication far more often when the other side's claim is strategic. And a party expects to lose disputes when he decides to raise a dispute strategically. With these assurances in place, the parties may then agree to randomize in the cases where the arbiter believes the facts are unclear.

Of course, an arbiter will err on occasion, so this solution is not perfect. A party will still expect to win some small number of strategic disputes. If adjudication were costless, then any positive error rate would prevent expressive adjudication from working because the creation of a strategic dispute would have a possible upside (the favorable result when the adjudicator errs) and no possible downside. But adjudication is not free. One cost is any fee the arbiter charges. Another is the time and resources adjudication requires. A final cost is a loss of one's credibility before the set of possible arbiters. The danger here is that 'crying wolf' too often will earn one a reputation for inventing disputes – a reputation that will make one more likely to lose future adjudications. These costs constitute disincentives to inventing disputes because parties are certain to incur costs and yet unlikely to gain the benefits of winning the adjudication. The point is not that the system will necessarily, or even probably, deter all strategic disputes but that it can deter enough of them to make the parties want to randomize in disputes the arbiter says are 'close.'[29] Subsequently, the outcome selected at random is now focal, which creates self-fulfilling expectations this outcome will occur.

In addition, note that signaling requires a third party. A randomizing device such as a coin flip cannot signal. Because the parties do not know in advance whether or not they need a signal to screen out a strategic dispute, they require a third party in every dispute.

In sum, signaling solves the objections I raised to the focal point and correlated

[29] The concern over error rate, however, points again to the importance of the arbiter's accuracy. Signaling accuracy matters not only as it did in a prior section – where more accurate signals produce more updating which produces more behavioral change – but also because the arbiter is using signaling to identify the cases that are genuine disputes for which the parties can agree to randomize without fear of exploitation.

equilibrium theories. The next step is to address the objections I previously raised to signaling.

Step two: Disputants correlate strategies with the arbitral signal

With the threat of strategic disputing sufficiently limited, the parties can simply correlate their strategies with the arbiter's signal regardless of how much they update their beliefs. In other words, the disputants can benefit by treating the signal as if it were perfectly accurate even though they know it is not. The reason is simply the logic of the correlated equilibrium. I objected to that logic only because of the two problems that, as just indicated, signaling resolves.

To see the point, return again to the simplified assumption that the arbiter will consider the evidence and form one of three beliefs: the facts (i) clearly favor party *A*, (ii) clearly favor party *B*, or (iii) do not clearly favor either side. The last subsection addressed only signal (iii); now consider the effect of signals (i) or (ii). If an accurate arbiter sends these signals, the losing party will sometimes update his beliefs sufficiently to align them with the other party, thereby resolving the dispute. I noted two objections above: (1) that if a party's prior belief about the relevant facts is sufficiently strong, he will not change his belief enough to change his behavior (even though he does revise his estimate of the probabilities somewhat), and (2) that disputants would always seek signals from multiple sources and not from a centralized adjudicator.

The crucial point, however, is that, even if the parties are unpersuaded by an adjudicative signal, they may still benefit *ex ante* from correlating their strategies with this signal. This point rests on the logic of an efficient correlated equilibrium. And once they seek adjudication, the resulting declaration will make focal a particular outcome, creating self-fulfilling expectations that it will occur.

The parties will favor adjudication *ex ante* as long as the arbiter is unbiased; if so, then each party will expect to prevail in adjudication of genuine disputes about 50 percent of the time. As the Brown and Ayres example demonstrated, there are many situations where the parties are better off correlating their strategies with a random event because the parties then each have an equal chance at getting their preferred payoff, while at the same time reducing to zero the chance of noncoordinated outcome that harms them both. Put differently, prior to adjudication each party expects to be in the situation described above – unpersuaded by an adjudicative signal contrary to one's position – no more often than to be in the opposite position – the recipient of a favorable adjudicative signal that does not persuade the other party. In the set of cases we are considering, failing to resolve the dispute is costly to both sides. Thus, both parties are better off *ex ante* accepting this equal chance of prevailing, which means correlating their strategies with the arbiter's public signal. Thus, the idea of coordinating on a *focal signal* explains how adjudication works when the signal is too weak to influence behavior via its direct affect on beliefs.

Moreover, correlating strategies with a public signal requires identifying in advance the one and only signal that will serve as the focal basis for coordinating, which explains why the parties seek a centralized and hierarchical set of adjudicative signals (with possible but limited appeals). As explained above, the focality of the agreed-to adjudication is necessary to produce *ex post* compliance with the endorsed outcome rather than its opposite and rather than with some competing expression. That the expression has to be focal explains why adjudication tends to be centralized in a single actor or institution.

Step three: The arbiter sends an undifferentiated signal

Having completed the penultimate step in the argument, I reach a final objection. The process just described still does not map onto adjudication because adjudicators do not send signals like the third one described above that fail to favor either side. Courts do not say 'too close to call' (and disputants do not employ random devices after such signals). Here, I offer to explain how and why randomization is concealed.

Suppose again that an arbiter assesses the competing claims of the disputants, and concludes that the facts: (i) clearly favor party *A*, (ii) clearly favor party *B*, or (iii) do not clearly favor either side. But now suppose that the arbiter only sends one of two signals: that *A* prevails or that *B* prevails. The arbiter maps the signals to his beliefs by following this strategy: 'If I reach conclusion (i) then I will signal "*A* prevails." If I reach conclusion (ii) then I will signal "*B* prevails." If I reach conclusion (iii) then I will randomly choose between delivering the signal "*A* prevails" and the signal "*B* prevails."' In other words, the arbiter no longer differentiates in his signal between the cases where he perceives the evidence to be clear and those where he perceives the evidence to be unclear. Instead of publicly identifying the close cases where the disputants could gain by randomizing, the arbiter himself randomizes in those cases and then sends one of the signals he would send when the evidence actually favored a particular party.

From the parties' perspective, there is no difference in following a strategy that randomizes in certain cases the arbiter identifies and following a strategy that permits the arbiter to randomize in those same cases. If *A* and *B* are planning on correlating strategies with signals (i) and (ii) and randomizing after signal (iii), then they would also be willing to correlate strategies with signals (i) and (ii) and to allow the arbiter to randomize after reaching the decision that previously resulted in signal (iii). From the parties' perspective, nothing of importance changes in moving from the fully candid to the more discreet arbiter. At this point we reach a process that looks more like adjudication, where the arbiter purports to decide every case and resists full disclosure of his own uncertainties about the dispute.

The question arises, however, why arbiters rarely reveal their own indecision. If I am right in thinking that an arbiter occasionally reaches belief (iii), why do we observe a near universal refusal to signal this indecisiveness? One answer is that individuals are more likely to comply with decisions they regard as legitimate and that individuals are less likely to perceive as legitimate a decision where the arbiter admits uncertainty and randomizes. But there is a self-interested reason I want to identify if only because the idea of an undifferentiated signal cuts against my claim above that individuals competing for the job of arbiter will signal their actual beliefs. If that is true, why not signal one's actual indecision?

The answer is that the arbiter is concerned about revealing his fallibility. Disputants seek accurate adjudicators. The need for the arbiter to project accuracy (to obtain future opportunities) creates an incentive to conceal his failure to form a determinative belief, that is, to conceal the fact that he had to randomize. In a sporting event, for example, a referee who has to resort to randomization 20 times a game will seem less competent than a referee who has to resort to randomization only five times a game, other things equal. Even though everyone knows there are some calls that are too close for anyone to determine, those competing to be referees will understandably engage in a race to the bottom, where the bottom means the referee claims never to require randomization because, in every case, he has actually determined the relevant facts.

To summarize: the success of adjudication does not depend entirely on the sanctions law threatens nor the willingness of moral agents to defer to the judiciary's perceived legitimacy. In circumstances of multiple equilibria, individuals have an incentive to seek out and comply with adjudication, even when the arbiter lacks the power to sanction. There is a synergy between focal points, correlated equilibria, and signaling. Expressive adjudication can, therefore, generate some compliance because disputants benefit by correlating their behavior on the arbiter's focal signal.

4. FROM FINDING FACTS TO SETTING PRECEDENT: THE EXPRESSIVE POWER OF RULE ARTICULATION

As I have developed the theory, it seems that third-party expression can resolve only factual disputes and influence only the behavior of the disputants. In this section, however, I explain how third parties can also use expression to resolve disputes that arise from ambiguities in the formal or informal rules that govern behavior. Mere expression can influence behavior by sharpening the common understanding of what formal or informal rules require.

To some degree, existing theory already demonstrates the expressive power of rule articulation in the context of private contracts. Most commonly, scholars employ the idea of a potentially self-enforcing agreement arising from an iterated PD game.[30] When two individuals are in this situation they will benefit if they can sustain a cooperative equilibrium, as where each individual employs a strategy that conditions his cooperation on the other player's cooperation. For example, two nations might agree to restrain tariffs. But the players will not sustain the cooperative equilibrium if they do not have concordant expectations about what behavior will constitute cooperation as well as common beliefs in each round about whether the other has engaged in that behavior. In the example, they have to agree on what constitutes a tariff.

The problem with self-enforcing agreements is that expectations and beliefs inevitably diverge. Garrett and Weingast emphasize that there is often more than one way to cooperate to achieve the Pareto-optimal outcome.[31] To create concordant expectations, therefore, the parties must agree on what each will regard as cooperative and defective behavior. Yet the agreement they create will, like all contracts, be incomplete. Success may then depend on third-party adjudication to resolve ambiguities. Because the iterated PD game is generally thought to describe a common situation, this story suggests a broad role for expressive adjudication.

This analysis of formal order, however, omits half the story – arguably the more interesting half. Where other theorists have stressed the example of self-enforcing agreements, in this section I emphasize spontaneous order or evolved conventions that arise without agreement or other design.[32] To include the latter, I briefly describe some of the evolutionary game-theory literature about the emergence of conventions, using the iterated Hawk/

---

[30] See e.g. Goldsmith and Posner (1999), 1113, 1170–72.
[31] See Garrett and Weingast (1993).
[32] See McAdams and Rasmusen (2005).

Dove game to illustrate. I claim that expressive adjudication can resolve disputes about what behavior a convention requires in a given situation, and that such resolutions create effective precedent for future behavior in similar situations.

4.1 The Emergence of Informal Order

Even an informal understanding of evolutionary game theory provides a useful but neglected tool for understanding the relationship between law and custom. Evolutionary theory shows that, when a population of players repeatedly encounters a particular game, repetition can eventually produce a strong pattern of expectations about what strategies others will use. Thus, in the common situations where there is more than one possible equilibrium, a pattern of expectations can emerge that sustains a pattern of behavior because each person is best off conforming to the behavioral pattern given that he expects everyone else to do so. I will call the resulting pattern of expectations and behavior a 'convention.'

An obvious example is the problem of coordinating driving on the left or right side of the road; the practice that emerges is a convention. Once a conventional pattern of behavior spontaneously arises (e.g., driving on the right), it tends to be self-sustaining. That is, even though conventions arise without design, conformity to conventions is 'self-enforcing' because a person is worse off by being the only one (or one of a few) to deviate from the convention (as by driving on the left when everyone else drives on the right).

To illustrate, my primary example for the remainder of the article is property. The convention of property is perhaps the most discussed example in the evolutionary literature.[33] Here, I briefly describe one account.[34] Robert Sugden and Jack Hirshleifer (separately) used evolutionary game theory to explain David Hume's claim that property is conventional.[35] They posit that, in a 'state of nature,' with no state to enforce property rights, disputes over particular resources (e.g., a set of firewood) may be modeled by an Iterated Hawk/Dove ('HD') Game. In their models, Hawk refers to an aggressive claim to the resource, Dove is deference to the others' claim, the Hawk/Hawk outcome is violence, and the Dove/Dove outcome is an even split of the resource. The use of the Iterated HD Game is a plausible model for those cases where (a) the fighting capabilities of the players are roughly equal (otherwise there may be a dominant strategy for the better fighter to play Hawk and the weaker player to play Dove) and (b) the costs of fighting over the resource are large compared to the value of the resource (and hence, the worst outcome for both sides is a Hawk/Hawk fight).

If these assumptions are correct, one can view property as a complex set of expectations that emerges over time in the iterated game. According to Hirshleifer and Sugden, the key is that the individuals observe some feature of the repeated situation that distinguishes or labels their roles in the game.[36] One such asymmetry is the fact that one of

---

33 See Hirshleifer (1987), 223–34; Sugden (1986), 55–103; see also Maynard Smith (1982).

34 There are other theories of property but the point I develop in the text – that law clarifies ambiguities in informal order – applies whatever the specific theory one uses to explain property.

35 See Hume (1978) (1740, Book 3, Part 2, Section 2); see also Vanderschraaf (1998), 215, 230–45.

36 See Hirshleifer (1987), 223–34; Sugden (1986), 55–103.

them is currently in physical possession of the property in dispute and the other is not. By itself, this observation creates new possible strategies such as: (1) when possessor play Hawk and when nonpossessor play Dove, or (2) when possessor play Dove and when non-possessor play Hawk. Finally, the existence of these new strategies creates two new possible equilibria where everyone plays strategy (1) or everyone plays strategy (2). For example, if everyone else is playing strategy (1), then when you are the possessor, you expect the other player to play Dove, and when you are the nonpossessor, you expect the other player to play Hawk. Your best reply is then to play Hawk when possessor and Dove when non-possessor, which is to say to play strategy (1) like everyone else. The result is a first approximation of the convention of property.

Though nothing guarantees that this convention will arise (everyone playing strategy (2) is also possible),[37] the theory demonstrates that the social practice of property can emerge from the repeated interactions of individuals in a state of nature, without a third-party enforcer creating or protecting property rights. Significantly, the analysis does not require that individuals act morally or perceive property as legitimate. Moreover, as long as every player can perfectly determine whether he is a possessor or non-possessor in a given case, the property convention (or its opposite) will eliminate Hawk/Hawk fights.

Note also that the evolutionary process will not stop at such a simple convention (nor need it ever stop). Suppose the players notice not only the asymmetry of physical possession but also a temporal asymmetry – when physical possession occurs. The combination of these asymmetries – possession and time – produces a more complex set of roles the players can occupy: not just (1) the current possessor and (2) the current non-possessor, but (3) the original possessor and (4) the original non-possessor. The larger set of possible roles creates a larger set of possible conventions. One obvious (but not inevitable) possibility is the familiar idea of first possession.[38] The common expectation may be that everyone will play Dove against the original possessor, who will always play Hawk (and perhaps also that everyone but the original possessor will play Dove against the current possessor, who will play Hawk against everyone but the original possessor). In this fashion, individuals may come to expect that others will play Hawk or Dove depending on the asymmetry of first possession.

So stated, however, one can immediately discern a possible objection to an expressive theory of precedent. Given that this form of unintentional, spontaneous order can prevent Hawk/Hawk fights, why is adjudication necessary? Indeed, given settled expectations, how can pure expression influence behavior? On the one hand, if the policymaker favors the existing convention, then there is no need for any intervention, including adjudication. On the other hand, if a policymaker wants to change the prevailing convention, by redirecting settled expectations toward some other behavior (e.g., a switch to driving on the left), then mere expression is insufficient. Sanctions and/or legitimacy are strictly necessary to upset a self-sustaining convention. Thus, if I am going to explain a

---

[37] Sugden argues that the property convention is more likely to arise than is the opposite convention because of payoff differences between possessors and nonpossessors. See Sugden (1986), 89–91.

[38] See, e.g., Epstein (1979), 1221, 1241–2; Rose (1985), 73–5.

role for expression given these constraints – to prove the precedential power of adjudicative expression – I must explain why spontaneous forces do not fully coordinate behavior without the need for adjudication.

4.2 Conceptual Ambiguity in Informal Order

Despite the presence of a convention, there always remains the possibility that a situation will occur in which the players lack common expectations about what each other will do. As Gerald Postema describes it, while 'the standard situations needing coordination are provided for,' '[t]here may . . . be substantial differences of opinion in the community regarding what the convention requires in some specific instances.'[39] Without common expectations, the players will frequently fail to coordinate their behavior. Thus, expressive adjudication can effectively set precedents for conventional behavior before expectations are firmly settled, as in the non-standard cases. This is not a surprise because genuine disputes arise because expectations are not firmly settled, where residual ambiguity infects the conceptual categories the individuals use in forming their expectations. With enough time for endless trial and error, evolutionary game theory shows that individuals could resolve residual ambiguities without design. But ambiguity will cause conflict during the period of uncertainty, possibly a very long time, creating an advantage to intentional clarification of the convention.[40]

Garrett and Weingast make this point with respect to the contracts that define cooperation in an iterated Prisoner's Dilemma – a form of intentional order. Because contracts are always incomplete, some event for which the contract is not fully specified may cause the parties' expectations to diverge. Here, I extend the problem of ambiguity to explain the imperfection of spontaneous conventions (unintentional order). There are two problems: the convention may be ambiguous because (1) it is based on a fuzzy asymmetry or (2) there is uncertainty about its completeness.

I will illustrate these points with the property convention discussed above. Repetition of the HD Game may produce the convention of deferring to first possessors. This theory is useful for explaining why those claiming to own things often seek to communicate their claim to the world by various markings, such as boundary markings or other physical markers on land.[41] This sort of communication avoids misunderstandings about who is in possession, which in the HD Game described above is necessary and sufficient to avoid the Hawk/Hawk outcome. The problem, however, is that despite these efforts, possession often remains ambiguous, a point well made by the property scholar Carol Rose.[42] Where possession is ambiguous, the roles the players occupy will be ambiguous, and they may each expect the other to play Dove, with the result being a Hawk/Hawk conflict. Consider two types of ambiguity.

---

[39] Postema (1982), 165, 178.

[40] I leave aside the possibility that intentional resolution of the ambiguity will, on average, lead to better or worse conventions.

[41] See Ellickson (1993), 1315, 1328–30; Rose (1985), 81–2.

[42] See Rose (1985), 82–8.

4.2.1 Fuzzy boundaries

The convention may be ambiguous because the boundaries of the asymmetry underlying it are fuzzy, at least in part.[43] Recall that the convention arises because the players mutually observe an asymmetry that distinguishes their roles in each play of the game, and then play strategies based on what role they occupy. What asymmetries the players notice in their situation depends on the conceptual categories they use for understanding their situation.

As an example, consider an ambiguity in the property convention of first possession. When exactly does possession occur? One of the more famous property cases poses this question regarding a wild fox. In *Pierson v. Post*,[44] Post hunted a fox for a time and was about to shoot it when Pierson appeared, killed the fox, and took it. If possession required killing or physical grabbing, then Pierson was the first possessor; if some broader concept of control (or investment in acquiring control) is sufficient, Post was the first possessor.[45] The same issue arises in other cases where individuals attempt to transform other wild animals or gas reserves into property.[46] Similarly, nations disputing over a territory often have different versions of the precise point at which possession of the territory first occurred.[47]

In disputes of this sort, the boundary defining the convention is fuzzy, and therefore, the convention is (at the moment) ambiguous. The ambiguity prevents there being any clear expectation about what a given person will do. While the ambiguity lasts, the individuals may fail to coordinate and end up in a Hawk/Hawk fight. If the ambiguity in the roles of 'original possessor' and 'original non-possessor' were sufficiently severe, it would be unlikely that any convention would arise based on that asymmetry. But the convention might arise because the asymmetry works in what Postema calls the 'standard case,'[48] while ambiguity arises only in the residual case.

4.2.2 Potential incompleteness

The convention may be ambiguous for another reason. Even if the boundaries of the underlying asymmetries are perfectly clear, the convention is always potentially incomplete. That is, there may be uncertainty about whether the set of expectations constituting a convention is subject to exception. There are usually more asymmetries present in a situation than are likely to be relevant to the players' behavior. The question always arises: which asymmetries do not matter? We have already seen a possible evolutionary path the property convention may take: first the players play strategies based on the asymmetry of possession, then the players add the further asymmetry of time and play strategies based on first possession. But would the process stop at two asymmetries? Some asymmetries seem irrelevant – e.g., the names of the parties – but it is difficult to specify in advance the criteria by which some asymmetries are relevant and some are not. Without criteria for

---

[43] See Klir and Folger (1988); Zadeh (1965), 338–53.
[44] 3 Cai. R. 175 (N.Y. Sup. Ct. 1805).
[45] The Court ruled for Pierson, holding that one must bring the animal within 'certain control' before one possesses and therefore owns it.
[46] See Ellickson (1991), 191–206 (whaling); Rose (1985), 77 n.21 (oil and gas).
[47] See Ginsburg and McAdams (2004), at 1258–9.
[48] Postema (1982), 178.

relevance there can always be a divergence of expectations concerning new asymmetries. Every convention – every set of expectations – might be subject to an exception based on facts that have not previously occurred, at least not in the precise combination now present.

To illustrate, suppose that *A* is unquestionably the first occupier of a plot of land, but that he vacates the area, after which *B* occupies the land openly for 20 years. Suppose *A* is silent about *B*'s use of the land for this time, but then reasserts his claim, demanding that *B* vacate the plot. Given the first possession convention, will the non-original possessor (*B*) play Dove? *B* will play Dove if he assumes that the only asymmetries relevant to *A*'s behavior are those embodied in the concept of first possession. But it is possible that the players will take account of another time asymmetry (in addition to who possessed the territory first), which is how long the current possessor has been in possession. Even in a state of nature, it is possible that the players will adopt more complex strategies that render the original description of the convention – that it always favors first possessors – incomplete. The convention that eventually emerges might instead be deference to the first possessor except when the current possessor has occupied and claimed the territory for more than, say, 20 years, in which case everyone defers to the current possessor. In other words, we might get the convention similar to what the common law terms adverse possession.[49]

There is, however, no guarantee that the extended occupancy exception will arise. As a result, when these hypothetical facts – first possessor *A* tolerates *B*'s 20-year occupancy – first occur (or occur for the first time within memory), there will be uncertainty about whether the new asymmetry between the players – one being a current possessor of long duration and the other not – will matter. The ambiguity of potential incompleteness is common because new circumstances are pervasive and they inevitably raise the question of how the old convention now applies.[50] Although repetition may eventually resolve the ambiguity, conflicting beliefs about the relevance of the new asymmetry may produce conflict, as each plays Hawk expecting the other to play Dove.

4.3 Using Expressive Adjudication to Resolve Ambiguity and Create Precedent for Future Behavior

When conventional ambiguity causes conflict, a third party may influence the behavior of the two disputants by offering a clarification of the convention. Unlike the resolution of a factual dispute, however, a third party's clarification of a convention can, if sufficiently publicized, influence the future behavior of the disputants and others in the community in which the convention exists. An adjudicator's focal signal concerning the convention creates a precedent for future behavior by making salient to community members a particular solution to a recurring coordination game. Aligning expectations in this way is usually socially valuable because it works to avoid conflict without the need for future services of conflict resolution.

To begin, I should define the difference between a genuine and strategic dispute in this

---

[49] See Rose (1985), 79. See discussion of international examples in Ginsburg and McAdams (2004), 1260–61.

[50] Lawyers are familiar with the idea that the facts of two cases are never exactly alike. As a logical matter, there are an infinite (or at least large) number of 'circumstances' in a situation that may distinguish the roles of the two players. See Sugden (1998), 377.

context. A genuine dispute exists because the players actually have divergent expectations, which occur because there is either residual fuzziness in the asymmetry that defines the behavior for this circumstance, or uncertainty about the possible exceptions in the broader convention for this circumstance. A strategic dispute exists when the parties actually have consistent expectations, but one party pretends otherwise in an effort to gain some advantage from disputing.

At this point, all of the above analysis of factual disputes carries through to conceptual disputes. First, from the parties' perspectives, they would benefit from a randomized solution to their genuine disputes caused by fuzzy boundaries or potential incompleteness. But they do not want to commit to a strategy of randomizing all disputes because they would make themselves vulnerable to strategic exploitation. Signaling, however, can ameliorate this problem. What is different in this context – with disputes over the content of the convention – is what the third party signals: his beliefs, if any, about the existing state of expectations in the relevant community. For example, if an individual seeks to raise a strategic dispute by contesting the relevance of first possession to the expected behavior when in fact nearly everyone in the community expects the first possessor to play Hawk, then the third party can signal his belief that the existing convention clearly sides with the person who is the first possessor. Similarly, if one disputant claims to believe that there is an exception to the ordinary expectation (e.g., first possession does not apply when the first possessor is a minor), but the third party believes that the existing expectations clearly reject such an exception (e.g., because there are clear precedents applying first possession to cases involving minors), then he can signal his beliefs that existing expectations clearly sides with the first possessor.

Signaling lowers the returns to strategic disputing, which (as previously argued) makes it possible that the parties will benefit in the remaining cases by following the adjudicator's randomly selected recommendation – a constructed focal point. These genuine disputes are the cases of first impression where there really is some fuzziness in a conventional boundary or some uncertainty about a possible exception. As long as each party expects to win with a probability close enough to 50 percent, then both may benefit from correlating their strategy with the third party's recommendation, thereby reducing to zero the probability of the non-coordinated outcome each prefers to avoid.

As stated above, however, the additional significance of the adjudicator's resolution of conventional ambiguity is that it may serve as a precedent for the future behavior of the disputants and of other parties. The reasoning here is based on focal point analysis. The disputants tend to follow the third party's recommendation because their common knowledge that each is focusing unique attention on this message makes the third party's recommended outcome salient; salience tends to create self-fulfilling expectations that the salient outcome will occur. The same effect can occur for those not a party to the present dispute if the adjudicatory declaration is publicized sufficiently. When future disputants face the same situation of multiple equilibria, their best choice of behavior depends on what they expect the other to do. If nothing else creates determinate expectations, common knowledge of the outcome of a prior adjudication of this issue may suffice. Certain ritualistic qualities of adjudication can create common knowledge of the decision among parties other than the disputants.

Thus, a decision like the one in *Pierson v. Post*, if publicized, tends to support the expectations that a hunter in the position of Pierson (who is the first to kill the animal) will play Hawk and that a hunter in the position of Post (who came close but had not yet killed or captured the animal) will play Dove. If there had been no settled expectations at the time the court decided *Pierson v. Post*, because the case genuinely was one of first impression, the case could have created such expectations in parties involved in similar disputes in the future. When the issue is relitigated, the court may find that the current expectations support a particular outcome, and may then signal that fact. Focal signals thus provide a way of sharpening the convention for everyone.

Finally, when the case is one of first impression, I have proceeded up to now on the assumption that the adjudicator will randomly choose between the possibilities. But while randomization may be appropriate for resolving factual disputes when the evidence is evenly divided, there will usually be reasons to prefer one way of resolving the conventional ambiguity over another. More likely, considerations of efficiency or fairness justify resolving the ambiguity in a particular way. In general I have nothing to say about such matters here. Given the way I have described the problem, however, one general consideration for selecting a resolution is the degree of clarification that different resolutions permit. Some methods of clarifying a convention to resolve the existing dispute may work to align expectations for a broad range of future situations; others may provide minimal clarity beyond the precise situation.[51] The point is familiar to lawyers as the choice between bright-line rules and standards. Thus, in *Pierson v. Post*, the rule favoring the party who first kills and holds the animal provides a clearer demarcation of possession than would a rule favoring the one who hunted the animal for a 'sufficient time' or who came 'close' to capturing it.

In contrast to my original focus on the process of adjudicating facts, the process just described is the 'law' part of adjudication. Sharpening the definition and clarifying the completeness of a convention are what a court does when it precisely states the legal rule in a case of first impression. What I am adding here is an understanding of how the court, merely by expression, can influence behavior. Like the bystander-in-the-intersection, the third party who points to and makes salient one particular outcome (in a game of multiple equilibria) is likely to create self-fulfilling expectations that each player will select the strategy associated with that outcome. One of the parties in the present dispute, and one party in each future dispute, will want to resist the adjudicator's suggestion that he play Dove, but the third-party's cheap talk expression will cause him to do so anyway because he now expects the other party to play Hawk.

That an adjudicative announcement today can avoid or resolve disputes tomorrow is significant. Society may gain considerably from having the convention clarified in this manner by aligning expectations and avoiding conflict.

5. CONCLUSION

Where the conventional theories of adjudicative compliance emphasize threatened sanctions and perceived legitimacy, I emphasize the interest of disputants in correlating their strategy with the adjudicator's focal signal. There is a synergy among three roles

---

[51] See Rose (1985), 77–8.

that adjudicative expression serves: as a device for correlating strategies, as a means of constructing focal points, and as a signal of information. When the relevant facts or conventions are ambiguous, an adjudicator can resolve disputes by signaling his beliefs – which works by screening out strategic disputes with sufficient probability and then by providing a focal point that creates self-fulfilling expectations for how the individuals will proceed. When the ambiguity is conventional, the adjudicator's clarification of the convention can set a precedent and thereby affect the behavior of parties other than the immediate disputants. Thus, expressive adjudication can both resolve existing disputes and, by articulating clear precedent, avoid future ones. The latter role explains the co-evolution of formal and informal order.

My claim for the power of adjudicative expression has a limited domain – situations of multiple equilibria where the parties, despite conflicting over which equilibrium should prevail, mutually prefer to coordinate to avoid certain outcomes. Yet this domain is significant and the theory described here reveals an important new way in which adjudication achieves compliance, or more generally, of how law works.

BIBLIOGRAPHY

Aumann, Robert J. (1974), 'Subjectivity and correlation in randomized strategies', *J. Math. Econ.*, **1**, 67–96.

Aumann, Robert J. (1987), 'Correlated equilibrium as an expression of Bayesian rationality', *Econometrica* **55**, 1–18.

Bacharach, M. and Michele Bernasconi (1997), 'The variable frame theory of focal points: An experimental study', *Games & Econ. Behav*, **19**, 1–45.

Baird, Douglas G., Robert H. Gertner, and Randal C. Picker (1994), *Game Theory and the Law*, Cambridge, MA, Harvard University Press.

Brown, Jennifer Gerarda and Ian Ayres (1994), 'Economic rationales for mediation', *Va. L. Rev.*, **80**, 323–95.

Crawford, Vincent (1998), 'A survey of experiments on communication via cheap talk', *J. Econ. Theory*, **78**, 286–98.

Dharmapala, Dhammika and Richard H. McAdams (2005), 'Words that kill? An economic model of the influence of speech on behavior (with particular reference to hate speech)', *J. Legal Stud.* **34**, 93–136.

Ellickson, Robert C. (1991), *Order Without Law: How Neighbours Settle Disputes*, Harvard University Press.

Ellickson, Robert C. (1993), 'Property in land', *Yale L.J.*, **102**, 1315–1400.

Engle Merry, S. (1981), *Urban Danger: Life in a Neighborhood of Strangers*, Philadelphia, PA: Temple University Press, pp. 175–86.

Epstein, Richard A. (1979), 'Possession as the root of title', *Ga. L. Rev.*, **13**, 1221.

Farrell, Joseph and Matthew Rabin (1996), 'Cheap talk', *J. Econ. Persp.*, **10**, 103–18.

Garrett, Geoffrey and Barry R. Weingast (1993), 'Ideas, interests, and institutions: Constructing the European Community's internal market', in J. Goldstein and R.O. Keohane (eds) *Ideas and Foreign Policy: Beliefs, Institutions, and Political Change*, Ithaca, NY: Cornell University Press, 173–206.

Ginsburg, Tom and Richard H. McAdams (2004), 'Adjudicating in anarchy: An expressive theory of international dispute resolution', *Will. & Mary Law Rev.*, **45**, 1229–1339.

Goldsmith, Jack L. and Eric A. Posner (1999), 'A theory of customary international law', *U. Chi. L. Rev.*, **66**, 1113–1177.

Hardin, Russell (1989), 'Why a Constitution?', in Grofman & Wittman (eds), *The Federalist Papers and the New Institutionalism*, New York, NY: Agathon Press, pp. 100–119.

Hirshleifer, Jack (1987), *Economic Behaviour in Adversity*, Chicago, IL: University of Chicago Press.
Hume, David (1978 [1740]), *A Treatise of Human Nature*, L.A. Selby-Bigge (ed.), 2nd edn, Oxford: Oxford University Press.
Klir, George J., and Tina A. Folger (1988), *Fuzzy Sets, Uncertainty, and Information*, Englewood Cliffs, NJ: Prentice.
Maynard Smith, J. (1982), *Evolution and the Theory of Games*, Cambridge: Cambridge University Press.
McAdams, Richard H. (2000), 'A focal point theory of expressive law', *Virginia Law Review*, **86**, 1649–1729.
McAdams, Richard H. (2005), 'The expressive power of adjudication', *University of Illinois Law Review*, 1043–1121.
McAdams, Richard H., and Janice Nadler (2005), 'Testing the focal point theory of legal compliance: The effect of third-party expression in an experimental hawk/dove game', *J. Empirical Legal Studies*, **2**, 87–123.
McAdams, Richard H., and Janice Nadler (2008), 'Coordinating in the shadow of the law: Two contextualized tests of the focal point theory of legal compliance', *Law & Society Rev.* **42**, 865–98.
McAdams, Richard H., and Eric B. Rasmusen (2005), 'Norms in law and economics', in *The Handbook of Law and Economics 1573–1618*, A. Mitchell Polinsky and Steven M. Shavell, eds., Amsterdam: Elsevier Science Publishing.
Mehta, Judith, Chris Starmer, and Robert Sugden (1994), 'The nature of salience: An experimental investigation of pure coordination games', *Am. Econ. Rev.*, **84**, 658–73.
Nisbett, R.E. and Dov Cohen (1996), *Culture of Honor: The Psychology of Violence in the South*, Boulder, CO: Westview Press.
Postema, Gerald J. (1982), 'Coordination and convention at the foundation of law', *J. Legal Stud.*, **11**, 165–203.
Rose, Carol M. (1985), 'Possession as the origin of property', *U. Chi. L. Rev.*, **52**, 73–88.
Sainty, B. (1999), 'Achieving greater cooperation in a noisy Prisoner's Dilemma: An experimental investigation', *J. Econ. Behav. & Org.*, **39**, 421.
Schelling, Thomas C. (1960), *The Strategy of Conflict*, Cambridge, MA: Harvard University Press.
Spence, Michael A. (1973), 'Job market signalling', *Q. J. Econ.*, **87**, 355–74.
Sugden, Robert (1986), *The Economics of Rights, Co-operation and Welfare*, Oxford: Basil Blackwell.
Sugden, Robert (1998), 'The role of inductive reasoning in the evolution of conventions', *Law & Phil.*, **17**, 377–410.
Tyran, J. Robert, and Lars P. Feld (2006), 'Achieving compliance when legal sanctions are non-deterrent', *Scandinavian Journal of Economics*, **108**, 135–56.
Vanderschraaf, Peter (1998), 'The informal game theory in Hume's Account of Convention', *Econ. & Phil.*, **14**, 215–47.
Wu, Jianzhong and Robert Axelrod (1995), 'How to cope with noise in the iterated Prisoner's Dilemma', J. Conflict Resol., **39**, 183.
Zadeh, Lotti (1965), 'Fuzzy sets', *Info. & Control*, **8**, 338–53.

8. Forces shaping the evolution of private legal systems

Amitai Aviram*

1. INTRODUCTION

In a world with no transaction costs, perfect rationality, and complete information, not much could be gleaned from studying the evolution of private legal systems (PLSs),[1] nor could one predict with any accuracy the future evolution of PLSs. In this economic fantasy land, efficient norms are already known and recognized by all, and the PLSs' norm enforcement costs (which are a component of the total transaction costs) are zero. Thus, any institution – public or private – is likely to become a successful norm enforcer.

* I thank Ben Christenson and Lauren Ferrante for their diligent research assistance.

1 For the purposes of this chapter, I define a PLS as a multi-party institution that enforces norms through the use of network effects. This distinguishes PLSs from other norm-enforcing institutions, notably government regulation (which uses hierarchy and government's monopoly of force), and bilateral contracts (which rely on either government enforcement, repeated play or the exchange of collateral, but not on network effects). I prefer this definition to an alternative one that focuses on the non-government (i.e., private) character of the institution, because the dichotomy between public and private legal systems is not always a clear one. Some PLSs have a significant public backing and are very similar to public legal systems. For example, the King of England enacted in 1353 the 'Statute of the Staple,' which prohibited Common Law courts from hearing disputes arising from contracts made on the staple markets (markets for important commodities, such as wool). Instead, the statute created Staple Courts and instructed them to apply the (privately formed) law merchant. Thus, private law was given exclusive jurisdiction by public decree. See Zywicki (2003). Conversely, some public legal fora defer to private ordering (e.g., arbitration proceedings).

I also prefer a definition that focuses on network effects to one that focuses on the competitive environment of the institution (i.e., PLSs compete against each other while public legal systems enjoy a monopoly). Some public legal fora compete with other legal fora. For example, the common law developed in England from the rulings of judges of the Court of King's Bench. For centuries this court had competed with several other royal courts (notably the Court of the Exchequer and the Court of Common Pleas), the ecclesiastical courts, town and feudal courts, and merchant courts. Id. at 31–38. Though the courts had, in theory, limits to their jurisdictions, they each used legal fictions to expand their reach. Id. Similarly, today, American companies can incorporate in any of the states, and that state's corporate laws will apply to them. Much scholarship has examined the competition between states that results. See Cary (1974); Winter (1977). The enforcement mechanisms of, say, the Delaware court, bear a lot of resemblance to other public legal systems, and very little resemblance to PLSs. Thus, I find the definition of PLS that focuses on the competitive environment to be unhelpful in analysing the enforcement mechanisms of PLSs.

Indeed, as in the joke about the Chicago professor and the $20 bill,[2] if a norm is efficient, no measures to enforce it need be taken because someone must already be enforcing it.

Relax one assumption – that of complete information – and there becomes a need for a theory to explain and predict the behavior of PLSs: Now individuals potentially affected by the norm ('participants')[3] must discover which norms are efficient and persuade others of the norms' efficiency. Therefore, a particular PLS (as opposed to other PLSs or a public entity such as government) will enforce a norm if it is able to formulate a more efficient norm than other potential enforcers, and convince participants of the norm's efficiency. Much of the literature on private ordering investigates these questions, identifying the superior efficiency of a given PLS's norms or suggesting why a given PLS has greater ability than a public enforcer (or other PLSs) to formulate an efficient norm or to assure participants of this efficiency.[4]

Relax another assumption – that of no transaction costs in enforcing norms – and an explanatory or predictive theory must consider not only the efficiency of the norm, but also the efficiency of the PLS in enforcing it. Indeed, in most cases there are lower barriers to entry to identifying efficient norms than to enforcing them – many law professors identify, refine and optimize norms, though they would be unable to enforce them on participants – and therefore norm enforcement, rather than norm creation, is often the bottleneck to creating a PLS, and the PLS that is best suited to enforce a given norm – rather than the PLS or person formulating the norm – becomes that norm's enforcer. One of the two forces I will discuss in this chapter – incumbent's enforcement advantage – creates an enforcement advantage to a particular PLS that may outweigh rivals' advantages. The result, as I will explain later, is that PLSs tend to evolve in a particular pattern: a core PLS administering norms or activities that are self-enforcing, and gradually expands by adopting additional, expansion norms.

Finally, relax the third assumption, that of perfect rationality. A growing literature in the field of behavioral economics examines common patterns of irrationality called cognitive biases.[5] This chapter will not examine the biases themselves – there is a large literature doing this, and the broad examination of PLSs in this chapter does not lend itself to specific applications of the biases (such applications must be made in the context of a specific norm or group of norms). Rather, this chapter will focus on the impact on the PLS's choice of norms caused by a gap between an objective risk and the individual's perception of that risk (perception gap), which in turn is caused by the biases. As I will explain in section 3, people controlling the PLS can benefit privately (and sometimes also enhance total social welfare) by forming and enforcing norms that address risks that are

---

2 One version of this joke is as follows: A University of Chicago economics professor and his student stroll through the campus, walking past a $20 bill that is lying on the ground. The student asks the professor why he did not stop to pick up the money. 'If it were a real $20 bill,' replies the professor, 'someone would have already picked it up.'

3 I use the term 'members' (or 'PLS members') to refer to the individuals or firms who are subject to the norms enforced by the PLS. The broader group of 'participants' (or 'market participants') are the people who could potentially be PLS members (and who may currently be members of another PLS, another norm enforcement institution, or not currently subject to any norm enforcement institution).

4 See, e.g., Bernstein (1992); Ellickson (1991).

5 See, e.g., Kahneman *et al.* (1982); Pohl (2004).

subject to large perception gaps. The PLS's members, oblivious to their perception bias, value more highly norms related to over-estimated risks, and there is a certainty that an exaggerated perception of risk may be mitigated, while the reduction of a real risk is rarely certain. As a result of this force, rather than having the incentive to enforce only the most cost effective norms, PLSs have norm-enforcing incentives affected by changes in the perception gap of the risks that the norms aim to address. As explained in section 3, this tendency is not necessarily inefficient, though it may be.

The evolution of private legal systems is gradually receiving increased attention as rigorous evolutionary theory is introduced into the private ordering scholarship.[6] Traditional scholarship on private ordering examines predominantly either the social welfare impact of norms enforced by PLSs, or the processes by which the norm is applied. This analysis is typically static, in the sense that the facts or circumstances to which the norm is applied may change, but the institution that enforces the norm is assumed to be fixed. This assumption usually holds true in the short-term, but rarely does in the long-term. The addition of evolutionary theory to the PLS scholar's toolbox allows a more accurate explanation and prediction of the long-term behavior of PLSs, and thus a more complete evaluation of the impact of PLSs on the public legal system and on social welfare.

2. INCUMBENT'S ENFORCEMENT ADVANTAGE: WHICH PLS ADOPTS THE NORM?[7]

2.1 Which PLS? (The One with Lowest Transactions Costs, of course)

Nobel laureate Ronald Coase anticipated a significant role for PLSs. In a world with no transaction costs, states one form of the Coase Theorem, parties would renegotiate inefficient entitlements granted by law to achieve an optimally efficient allocation.[8] For example, suppose that tort law imposes liability on a rancher whose cattle trespass onto a farmer's land. This rule may be inefficient in regions with many ranchers and very few farmers, because it would be cheaper to fence out the few farms, and have the cattle roam freely in the pasture, than to fence in the cattle.[9] If transaction costs were negligible, having this inefficient rule would not result in an inefficient outcome. Instead, the ranchers would agree with the farmers to pay the farmers to fence themselves out, and the ranchers would let the cattle roam freely. This outcome would be feasible, since the cost for the ranchers to comply with the rule and fence their cattle in would be greater than the cost of fencing the farms in (which is why the rule was inefficient). As a result, the ranchers would be willing to bear the lesser cost of fencing out the farmers, plus a small premium to obtain the farmers' consent. The farmers, on the other hand, would agree to opt into the private regime in return for this small consent premium, since the private

---

6 See, e.g., Kerber (2008).

7 This section includes revised excerpts from: Aviram (2004). That article offers a more elaborate analysis of the incumbent's enforcement advantage.

8 See Coase (1960).

9 Private ordering of liability for cattle trespass is a central issue in Ellickson (1991); and in Ellickson (1986).

regime would not increase their exposure to trespass risk. Under the public (legal) regime, they would be compensated through tort law for the trespass; under the private regime the cattle would be fenced out, preventing the trespass from occurring.

In other words, in a world with no transaction costs, PLSs would form spontaneously, through ad hoc contracting. Of course, no such world exists. There are costs to identifying an efficient regime and negotiating its terms among its stakeholders. When there are many ranchers and many farmers, there might be free riding, holdout problems, or other forms of strategic (or irrational) behavior that could prevent an efficient bargain from being reached. And, of course, there are enforcement costs incurred to ensure that the parties abide by the agreed terms. Enforcement costs become significant when parties perform their parts of the bargain non-simultaneously. They may also be significant if the public regime (i.e., the law) does not defer to the private regime, allowing parties to instead opt out opportunistically by suing and receiving their entitlements under law at any time, even if they purported to contract those away.

Scholars recognized long ago that institutions form to reduce these transaction costs. No institution reduces transaction costs to zero. However, the lower the transaction costs, the closer the parties get to the efficient allocation of entitlements. Since transaction costs impede parties from reaching bargains that they would otherwise want to reach, such parties are likely to adopt the institutions that most reduce transaction costs. Therefore, prevalent institutions are likely to be ones that most reduce transaction costs.

2.2 The Paradox of Spontaneous Formation

2.2.1 The newly-formed PLS's enforcement disadvantage

While the private ordering literature examines PLSs and tracks the evolution of norms that are created and enforced by these systems, it pays scant attention to how the institutions themselves evolved to become PLSs. Perhaps drawing on the Coase Theorem and implicitly assuming negligible transaction costs, and perhaps expanding on Friedrich Hayek's theory of spontaneous order, most of the literature presupposes that PLSs emerge spontaneously in response to a governance need unfulfilled by government.[10] Even the private ordering literature that explicitly recognizes the high transaction costs borne by a PLS in enforcing norms focuses (with rare exceptions) not on the effects of these costs on the evolution of institutions but on what institutions eventually evolved.[11]

PLSs, however, do not form spontaneously but build on existing institutional infrastructure – networks that already facilitate low-enforcement-cost norms (i.e., norms that do not require coercion to effect compliance) to the same group of participants that has the potential of violating the new norm (and therefore needs to be deterred from such violation).

---

[10] The term 'spontaneous formation' of a PLS may be ambiguous. By 'spontaneous formation' I mean the creation of a PLS without reliance on a pre-existing foundation. In this chapter I claim that such patterns of PLS formation are rare. Some of the literature uses the term 'spontaneous formation' of private ordering to regard an evolution that is decentralized or private (i.e., not dictated by a government). I do not dispute that PLSs may evolve in a decentralized process.

[11] See, e.g., Ellickson (1986). But cf. Greif *et al.* (1994) (discussing the evolution of a specific institution that became a PLS: the merchant guild).

The reason for this pattern is driven by transaction costs: all else equal, transaction costs tend to be greater for norms enforced by newly-formed PLSs that are unassisted by existent enforcement mechanisms, due to a 'chicken and egg' paradox. This paradox, which I call the paradox of spontaneous formation, runs as follows: to enforce a norm efficiently, a PLS must ensure the cooperation of its members. But the effectiveness of the mechanisms used to secure this cooperation depends on the PLS's ability to confer benefits to its members – primarily the ability, not yet existing in a newly-formed PLS, to efficiently enforce norms.

Consider, for example, a PLS's most potent weapon – the ability to exclude. To enforce a norm, the PLS threatens its members with ostracism if they fail to conform. The significance of this threat to a member depends on what this ostracism would deny him – what benefits he currently derives from the PLS. An established PLS already provides benefits to the members. For example, a PLS that prevents opportunistic behavior will provide its members with a more amicable transacting environment once it is effective. But until the PLS has undertaken enforcement for a while and has assured members of its ability to function, its members may significantly discount (or not consider at all) any benefits of membership, and thus view exclusion as costless to them. This becomes a self-fulfilling prophecy as the more skeptical members ignore the threat of exclusion and act opportunistically, dissipating the PLS's benefits and persuading those members who initially had faith in the PLS that the benefit of the PLS, and hence the cost of exclusion, is negligible.

This paradox need not conclude with the default of all members, since members react differently to the perceived effectiveness of the PLS. Some find it almost costless to follow the norms and do so regardless of the perceived effectiveness of the enforcement mechanisms. Other members benefit so much from a PLS (as opposed to the next best alternative available to them) that they find it feasible to abide by the PLS's norm even when compliance with the norm is low. However, such circumstances apply to infra-marginal members; that is, the firms that benefit most from the PLS or find it least costly to follow the norms. The marginal firms, in contrast, will migrate to a less costly norm enforcer, reducing the scope of the PLS, and the utility derived from network effects of the PLS.

An alternative norm enforcer may be something other than a PLS, such as government regulation or bilateral contracts. But in many circumstances, PLSs' ability to harness network effects would make them more efficient enforcers than government or bilateral contracts.[12] In these circumstances, participants will seek another PLS that avoids the paradox of spontaneous formation. This quest for the least-cost regulator, in the face of the paradox that plagues newly-formed PLSs, results in a pattern of non-spontaneous evolution – the assumption of responsibility for enforcing a norm by PLSs that already facilitate other, low-enforcement-cost norms.

2.2.2 Bilateral bonding is expensive

The paradox of spontaneous formation could be resolved if there were an efficient bonding mechanism that deters violations of the norm by a member of a newly-formed PLS, while also assuring the member that other members will be similarly deterred and

---

[12] For an in-depth analysis of the mechanisms that enhance PLSs' efficiency as norm enforcers, see Aviram (2003).

will abide by the norm. Bonds are interests of the assuring party that are placed at the mercy of the assured party. Upon receiving a bond, the assured party may confiscate or destroy it at will, causing harm to the assuring party. Knowing that the assured party will use this power if the assuring party reneged on an obligation, the assuring party will not renege. This provides the assured party with peace of mind. But who will assure the assuring party? If a bond can be confiscated at will (rather than only upon default of the assuring party), then the assured party can confiscate the bond despite proper execution of the underlying obligation. To mitigate this risk (and to guarantee the reciprocal obligation in case of a transaction involving obligations from both parties), bonds can be exchanged.[13]

One such bond is created through the public legal system. Contract law exists for this very purpose – to allow each party to an enforceable agreement to use the state's enforcement machinery to force the other party to undertake the obligation (or better yet, to deter the other party from reneging). In some cases, criminal law intervenes, replacing private detection of violations with complete government control of both detection and enforcement. But using the public legal system to enforce a PLS's norms is often of questionable benefit: if the PLS is not as good a regulator as the public legal system, it might seem preferable to do away with it and have the law regulate directly. And, if the PLS is more efficient than the public legal system, the use of the public legal system to support the PLS would likely introduce the costs and inefficiencies of the public legal system.

PLSs often use reputation as a bond. Like other forms of collateral, reputation is an asset that affects the owner's utility (by influencing the owner's future transactions with others) and can be affected by others (who disseminate positive or negative information that impacts the reputation). Reputation bonds, however, are not a very useful tool for newly-formed PLSs that do not rely on pre-existing counterparts. For these PLSs one failed episode would lead to elimination, and hence members discount future interactions with the PLS. As discussed in the next subsection, reputation might still be an effective bond if the PLS's members interact with each other outside the PLS (e.g., are members of the same social circle), or if the PLS already enforces other norms that will survive its failure to regulate the new norm. But absent either of these, members will not value establishing a good reputation in a PLS that is expected to fail.

Bonding, whether using tangible or intangible collateral, is an expensive enforcement system, and usually a crude one. Non-reciprocal bonding (providing a bond without receiving one) leaves the party offering the bond vulnerable to the other party's ability to confiscate the bond without cause. Reciprocal bonding is subject to reciprocal confiscation, which may leave both parties worse off, but not by enough to deter an opportunist. For example, suppose that Jack agrees to sell to Jill his share of Acme stock for $10. In order to bond each other into performing their contract, each gives the other $100 in cash

---

[13] This practice has been termed an 'exchange of hostages'. See Williamson (1983) (citing Schelling (1956)). In fact, a literal exchange of hostages was among the early forms in which this mechanism was used to assure commitment to peace treaties. Gregory of Tours describes the use of this mechanism in the year 511: 'But Theoderic and Childebert entered into a treaty and each took an oath that neither would wage war upon the other. They took hostages so that they might the more firmly adhere to what they had promised. Many sons of senatorial families were thus given.' Gregory of Tours (1849).

as collateral. When Acme's share price drops to $5, Jill reneges on the agreement. When Jack retaliates by confiscating Jill's collateral, Jill can confiscate Jack's collateral, so that the bonds will offset each other without deterring Jill.

Another solution to this offsetting problem is in providing a bond that harms one party without providing the other party with any utility. A hostage exchange is one such example: killing a hostage harms the hostage's kin but does not directly benefit the murderer. Likewise, if person A sullies B's reputation, then B is harmed while A does not receive any benefit (indeed, if A were seen to benefit from the harm to B's reputation, the credibility of A's negative information about B would be undermined).

Even with such asymmetrical collateral, there is a risk of insufficient deterrence. First, destroying collateral upon suffering a perceived offense might be rational, even when the destruction of the collateral is not profitable, because such destruction maintains deterrence: it indicates that the same action may be taken again in the future if that person is offended again.[14] But while excessive sensitivity may provide increased deterrence, it also risks undoing a bond. Each party has an incentive to react to minor slights in order to deter the other party from attempting even minor opportunistic behavior at his expense. Therefore, parties are likely to over-react, confiscating the bond at the first perception of an offense (in the hope of greater deterrence of the other party in future transactions). But once a bond provided by the other party is confiscated, that other party may reciprocate by confiscating the bond it holds, eliminating the assurance mechanism and increasing the likelihood of a cycle of opportunistic (or outright malicious) behavior.

Second, collateral designed to be costly to one party but useless to the other party may be handled in ways that create utility to the latter party. For example, rather than killing a hostage, the hostage may be enslaved, providing the enslaving party with utility[15] (likewise, collateral useless to the possessing party but useful to a third party may be traded to the third party).

Third, even when exaggerated sensitivity can be avoided, the value of the collateral is often hard to determine. There is a cost to providing collateral, even when it is not confiscated (e.g., a work of art given as collateral does not bring joy to its owner while it is held by others). This cost creates an incentive to reduce the size of the collateral as much as possible. On the other hand, collateral only deters opportunistic action that is no more profitable than the collateral's value (otherwise, its owner would find it profitable to commit the opportunistic act, pocket the gain, and accept the loss of the collateral). Since gains from opportunistic behavior vary widely, it is hard to anticipate the optimal value of the collateral, and almost any value of collateral would fail to deter some extremely profitable opportunistic behavior. Furthermore, since parties exchanging bonds differ in the degree

---

[14] Indeed, as Richard Posner explains, this is the rational basis of the concept of revenge. See Posner (1998).

[15] This is precisely what happened in the hostage exchange between Theoderic and Childebert, mentioned *supra* note 13. Gregory of Tours describes: '[B]ut when a new quarrel broke out between the kings [the hostages] were reduced to servitude. . . . And those who had taken care of them now made slaves of them.' Besides deriving utility from the hostages, enslaving them (rather than killing them) may be intended to inflict some harm on the hostage's kin, while maintaining future deterrence through the ability to inflict additional harm (by killing the hostages).

to which each is vulnerable to the other party's opportunism, and in the loss of utility they suffer in providing the bond, parties might disagree on the optimal value of the bond.

Thus, bonding in a newly-formed PLS tends to be more expensive than the inherent bonding mechanism of a pre-existing PLS. As a result, in most cases bonding is not a practical solution to the paradox of spontaneous formation.

2.2.3 Which PLS? (A Pre-existing One)

2.2.3.1 Conditions for an effective PLS The solution to the problems that plague bilateral bonding lies in a centralized bonding mechanism, in which: (1) an independent party (the PLS) holds the collateral of all members and has control over its confiscation; (2) the collateral (i.e., the right of membership in the PLS) does not lose utility by being controlled by the independent party; (3) the independent party does not profit from confiscating the collateral (i.e., remaining members do not profit from excluding the expelled member); and (4) confiscation of the collateral by the PLS (i.e., expulsion from the PLS) is more costly to the member than most expected profits from defaulting on the norm.

Condition (1) eliminates the risk of retaliation confiscations (such as between Jack and Jill in the above example), and also places the confiscation decision at the hands of a frequent repeat player (the PLS) who may suffer if its decisions are arbitrary. Condition (2) reduces the costs of providing the collateral. Condition (3) eliminates the risk of opportunistic confiscation of the collateral. Condition (4) ensures that the threat of confiscating the collateral (i.e., expulsion) deters members from violating the PLS's norms.

Not all PLSs satisfy these conditions. Some PLSs (e.g., common social courtesy) are decentralized, lacking a centralized entity that decides whether to confiscate the collateral – failing to satisfy condition (1). If membership in the PLS does not provide enough value to be sufficient collateral, the PLS may demand additional collateral (such as money) that loses utility by being held by the PLS (since the member cannot use it) – failing to satisfy condition (2). Some PLSs' structures are such that members may profit from 'ganging up' on other members and expelling them. In these PLSs condition (3) is not satisfied, and the potential for opportunism hurts the credibility of the PLSs' expulsion decisions. Finally, newly-formed PLSs usually fail to satisfy condition (4), because they have yet to provide significant utility, and therefore expulsion from the newly-formed PLS is not very costly. Some pre-existing PLSs also fail to satisfy condition (4), either because the benefits they already provide are not sufficiently great to surpass the cost of enforcing the new norm,[16] or because they cannot effectively exclude a member. Such ineffectiveness may either be due to the PLS needing the member more than the member needs the PLS, or due to structural limitations of the PLS in ensuring all members complied with the decision to exclude a particular member. A social group, for example, may rely on negative gossip to ostracize a member. However, the PLS can only disseminate the negative gossip; the decision to ostracize is taken by each member individually. Some PLSs may have secondary exclusions of those members who fail to comply with the boycott. Those PLSs who do not (or cannot enforce the more expensive-to-enforce secondary boycott)

[16] This is a corollary to condition (2) for becoming an expansion norm, specified a few paragraphs below at 2.2.3.3.

have less credible threats of exclusion. For that reason, some PLSs form more centralized exclusion mechanisms, in which a member suspected of violating norms is judged by certain PLS officials, who may then decide to exclude the member, and their decision is binding on all other members. In yet more centralized PLSs, the PLS officials control an essential common facility of the PLS (e.g., a computer system used by the members to transact their common business), and therefore can affect an exclusion of any particular member by denying that member access to the facility, without having to rely on other members' adherence to the officials' decision.

2.2.3.2 The evolutionary process and PLS structure As a result of reliance on pre-existing PLSs, the evolutionary process that results in a successful PLS has three stages. First, a centralized bonding mechanism forms, most likely not as an end of its own but as a side effect of regulating a low-enforcement-cost norm (i.e., a norm to which members adhere without coercion). Then, at stage two, the centralized bonding mechanism expands its application to regulate a higher enforcement-cost norm, using its ability to deny members the benefit of the low-enforcement-cost norm to coerce members to abide by the higher-enforcement cost norm.[17] Once the PLS can successfully enforce the higher-enforcement-cost norm, the utility of membership in the PLS increases, and correspondingly the cost of exclusion from the PLS increases. The PLS now has a more powerful threat against its members, which enables it to regulate yet higher enforcement-cost norms.

2.2.3.3 Conditions for an effective expansion norm Seen in this way, PLSs have a core which gradually expands by annexing additional norms. The core is the centralized bonding mechanism that enforces a low-enforcement-cost norm. The additional norm ('expansion norm') needs to satisfy the following conditions:

(1) It must be attractive to enforce through the PLS, from the perspective of the members that direct the PLS's behavior. In other words, the net benefits to those members from enforcing the norm, after deducting the costs of enforcement borne by those members, are: (i) greater than zero; and (ii) greater than the net benefits to the same members from enforcing the norm via another regulator (another PLS, a government regulator, or bilateral contracts).

(2) Its enforcement costs must be lower than the utility to members, prior to expansion, from membership in the PLS. Thus, at an early stage of a PLS's evolution, while it enforces relatively few norms, it can expand only to slightly more expensive to enforce norms. However, each additional norm enforced, if it provides positive utility to the PLS members, adds to the net benefit the members derive from their membership. Therefore, it increases the deterrence of exclusion and allows the PLS to enforce additional norms with higher enforcement costs that were too expensive to enforce earlier. This creates economies of scale that encourage the expansion of those PLSs that are already larger (i.e., enforce more norms). However, this trend towards few, large PLSs is checked by condition (3) below.

(3) It must be successfully enforced if the PLS ensured that its current (pre-expansion)

---

[17] For a discussion of factors that affect the enforcement cost of a norm see Aviram (2004), at 23–26.

members complied with it. The threat of exclusion, even from a successful PLS, is only effective against the members who currently benefit from it. If another norm requires the cooperation of a different set of actors, then the PLS would not have a particular advantage in enforcing the latter norm. Suppose that two towns are situated on opposite sides of a small lake, and the residents of each town share a common religion or ethnicity that is different from that of the residents of the other town. If people from either town polluted the lake, all inhabitants of both towns would suffer. Suppose also that there already exists a highly successful PLS, the core norm of which is fostering a sense of community and kinship among the residents of Town A, based on the shared religion or ethnicity. That PLS now attempts to enforce an expansion norm prohibiting the pollution of the lake. Exclusion from the PLS (i.e., social ostracizing or excommunication) is a highly effective threat against residents of Town A, but does not at all deter residents of Town B (who are not members of the PLS and who do not share that PLS's norm). Thus, Town B residents will pollute the lake, harming both Town A and Town B residents. Now, the enforcement of the non-pollution norm becomes a tax on Town A residents. They are precluded from the utility of whatever actions pollute the lake, yet they suffer from the same pollution harms as the residents for Town B. The enforcement of this new norm *reduced* the net utility to the PLS's members, making it less able to enforce additional norms and making it more attractive for marginal members to leave the PLS. Thus, the PLS is likely to abandon the enforcement of this norm. A PLS, if it is to successfully enforce the non-pollution norm without external assistance, will need to have a pre-existing norm that it enforces on all the actors whose compliance is needed to gain from the norm's enforcement – in this case, all the residents of Towns A and B.

2.2.3.4 Common core norms The most ubiquitous PLS cores are social and religious norms. Social and religious groups provide members with a sense of community, social interaction, and spiritual guidance. These tend to have low enforcement costs – it is easier to get people to interact socially with their neighbors than to get them to keep their promises to the same neighbors. Social interaction benefits most people more than isolation, and most people would rather interact with some people even if others in the same group snub them. So there are few costs involved in getting people to cooperate in agreeing to interrelate. On the other hand, if some members break their promises, this will encourage other members to do the same so that they are not taken advantage of by the first group. In some cases, one would not commit to a promise even when she knows that everyone else is committing, in the hope of taking advantage of the others. In either of these cases, some enforcement costs are necessary to secure members' commitment to promises they have made.

Religious norms offer two additional benefits that enhance their ability to regulate believers. First, since they purport to be enforced by an omnipotent and omniscient god, a believer would view as certain both the detection of violations and the ability to punish. Second, in religions that include beliefs in an afterlife or reincarnation, both reward and punishment that comes after death may incentivize believers.[18] This is a particularly valuable feature in regulating in environments of high mortality, or when being taken advantage of may lead to death. For example, consider a norm prohibiting surprise attacks

[18] Richardson and McBride (2009).

of the enemy. If person A abides by the norm, while person B violates the norm and surprises A, then A may die. If punishment and rewards are limited to one's lifetime, then the risk of being taken advantage of may make this norm unenforceable, since A cannot be rewarded posthumously for complying with the norm. However, a reward in one's afterlife may be sufficient incentive for a believer to abide by the norm. Likewise, consider a norm of honoring one's promises, enforced at a time of very high mortality (e.g., during a plague). If A is to honor her promise, she forgoes the option of opportunistically reneging on a now unprofitable promise. In return, she may expect others to honor their promises in the future. But if A believes she may die soon, before others honor their promises to her, she may renege now. Again, if A believes that she would be rewarded in her afterlife (or be reincarnated in a manner that rewards her for her good deeds in her current life), then her death does not constrain the ability to incentivize her.

Initially, social and religious PLSs tend to rely heavily on reputation bonds. Reputation bonds are ineffective when individuals expect the PLS to fail, but many social groups continue to exist over long periods of time – one's neighbors, for example, will continue to affect one's social life indefinitely. By gossiping about each other within the social group, and by reacting to the gossip according to common norms, the PLS can align most members' responses to a member's deviant behavior.

Decentralized exclusion mechanisms of this sort, however, reduce the credibility of the PLS's exclusion threat. For that reason, as a social group expands and attempts to enforce higher enforcement cost norms, it is likely to develop a centralized body to determine whether a member is excluded; a secondary boycott norm (excluding those members who continue to transact with excluded members); or common facilities controlled by a centralized institution (e.g., a clubhouse, a centralized computer system, etc.) that the centralized institution can deny excluded members.

3. BIAS ARBITRAGE: WHICH NORMS DOES THE PLS ADOPT?[19]

3.1 Which Norms? (Those that Members Perceive as Good)

In the above section, I suggested a pattern in which PLSs evolve, starting from a core norm and gradually adding expansion norms. I offered several conditions that an expansion norm needs to satisfy, and which ensure that the norm is both desirable to the PLS and enforceable by it. In the following section, I will revisit the criteria that make a norm desirable to the PLS. As I will demonstrate, the members who control the PLS's actions may gain either pecuniary or electoral benefits from picking a norm that addresses an over-estimated risk and purports to mitigate it, even if this norm does not objectively reduce the risk in a cost-effective way.

This strategy – which I call bias arbitrage – is an important force shaping the PLS's choice of norms to enforce. In predicting or explaining the norms that a PLS enforces, a

[19] This section includes revised excerpts from Aviram (2007), adapted to the context of private legal systems. For a more detailed analysis of bias arbitrage see that article, as well as: Aviram (2006); Aviram (2008).

theory of PLS evolution should consider not just the objective efficiency of the norm (to society or to the PLS members), but also the misperceptions of the PLS's constituencies regarding the norm and the risks the norm addresses.

Before I describe bias arbitrage, I should point out a significant difference between public and private legal systems. In public legal systems, the system itself and adherence to the norms it enforces (i.e., laws) is backed with government's monopoly on violence. In contrast, a PLS has no assurance of its existence. Adherence to norms enforced by a PLS depends on the utility that constituents perceive they derive from the norm.

Of course, it would be a poor long-term strategy for a PLS to falsely claim that a norm is beneficial to its members, if the members will later discover it is not. This will undermine the PLS's credibility and may result in members abandoning the PLS upon discovering the truth.

However, the PLS can overstate the benefits of a norm if the members are unlikely to discover the norm's true effects. The strategy of bias arbitrage is based on identifying norms whose effects can safely (for the PLS) be overstated. As I will briefly discuss at the end of this part of the chapter, such overstating may even enhance (objective) social welfare. However, from the perspective of the PLS and those who control it, survival and prosperity depend on choosing (and then efficiently enforcing) norms that most enhance the long-term *perceived* benefit of members, rather than norms that enhance the long-term *actual* benefit of members.

3.2 What is Bias Arbitrage?

Bias arbitrage is a strategy in which an actor identifies a perception gap and acts in ways (such as creating or conspicuously enforcing a norm) that make the public re-evaluate the perceived risk in a way that mitigates the perception gap and provides private gains to the actor.[20]

Crucial to the feasibility of bias arbitrage is the assumption that we often misperceive risks. For example, after Hurricane Katrina battered the Gulf Coast in late August 2005 and subsequent levee failures resulted in the flooding of low-lying areas in New Orleans, reports from the city portrayed surreal mayhem.[21] In the city's Convention Center, SWAT teams were deployed to capture groups of men who were said to have taken over some of the halls.[22] Media reports included 'roving bands of armed gang members attacking the

---

[20] Bias arbitrage is a form of counter-biasing, not de-biasing. In other words, it does not address and eliminate the bias that created the risk misperception. Rather, it creates a new bias that is aimed to offset the original bias. Because the causes of the original bias are not addressed and because counter-biasing may overcorrect, or conversely, fail to fully offset the original bias, from a social welfare perspective, bias arbitrage is a second best solution. In ideal conditions, de-biasing would be preferable. However, de-biasing is often costly, impractical, and less likely to be employed because it frequently lacks the private incentives that bias arbitrage offers to those that engage in it.

[21] See e.g., *Thousands feared dead in lawless city*, Chicago Tribune, Sept. 1, 2005, at 1 (describing reports of crime, looting, and virtual anarchy).

[22] See Jim Dwyer and Christopher Drew, *Fear Exceeded Crime's Reality in New Orleans*, N.Y. Times, Sept. 29, 2005, at A1 (noting several examples of official response to reports of crime in New Orleans following Hurricane Katrina).

helpless, and dozens of bodies being shoved into a freezer at the Convention Center.'[23] New Orleans' police chief appeared on television and reported that 'little babies [were] getting raped' at the Superdome.[24]

These reports and numerous others were unfounded.[25] Hurricane Katrina caused a tremendous amount of suffering in New Orleans, but the tidal wave of violent crime that was reported in its wake was grossly exaggerated.

Severe misperceptions of risk are not limited to traumatic situations. They are an inevitable result of the human mind's use of heuristics – mental shortcuts that manifest themselves as 'gut feelings.' Heuristics facilitate immediate analysis of complex information, but like any analytical mechanism, heuristics sometimes fail. Failures that occur in predictable patterns are called cognitive biases. The specific biases that cause risk perception to deviate from actual risk in a particular case are not important for the purpose of predicting the norms selected by a PLS.[26] Rather, such predictions are affected by the perception gap that results from the operation of the various biases (which may well operate in opposite directions and interact with each other). The perception gap is the difference between a perceived risk and the actual risk.[27] Its existence offers an opportunity to some actors to benefit from actions that mitigate the gap.

The perception gap can be mitigated (or exacerbated) by norms. The creation and conspicuous enforcement of norms affect individuals' expectations about the behavior of those surrounding them. For example, a norm that prohibits lying creates an expectation that people will be less likely to lie, while a norm that casual attire is inappropriate for a professor teaching a class would cause one to be surprised if a professor taught a class dressed in shorts and a tank-top. Norms modify expectations not only for those parties to whom the norm applies (e.g., the professor), but also for parties who are affected by the behavior of those to whom the law applies (e.g., the students attending that class).

In a world without information asymmetries or cognitive biases, the change caused by a norm to the perception of a risk it addresses would be identical to the change in the objective risk. In other words, if a norm that prohibits lying reduces the risk of lying by 10 percent, it would cause a reduction of 10 percent in the perceived risk of lying. However, both information asymmetries and cognitive biases frequently cause misperceptions of the effects of a norm.

Misperceptions of the effect of a norm can either correct or exacerbate pre-existing

---

[23] Susannah Rosenblatt & James Rainey, *Rita's Aftermath: Katrina Takes a Toll on Truth, News Accuracy*, L.A. Times, Sept. 27, 2005, at A16.

[24] *Id.*

[25] In all of Louisiana, only four of the 841 recorded hurricane-related deaths were due to gunshot wounds. *Id.* (contrasting the actual violent crime in the Convention Center with the exaggerated media reports).

[26] For a discussion of different types of cognitive biases, see note 5, *supra*.

[27] For the sake of convenience, I will consider the perception gap, in hypothetical examples in this chapter, as a single number representing the subjective-objective discrepancy in a risk's probability. This is a simplification. A slightly more complex portrayal of a perception gap would consider subjective-objective discrepancies in two dimensions: the risk's average probability and its average magnitude. An even more complex portrayal of the perception gap would consider subjective-objective discrepancies in the distribution of possible outcomes of the risk (i.e., consider the entire array of possible outcomes rather than just their averages).

perception gaps. Consider the following example. A short sale of securities involves borrowing securities from another investor and selling them (with the intent to buy the securities again when they need to be returned to the other investor, profiting if the securities meanwhile dropped in price). One trading strategy known as 'naked short selling' involves selling the securities before they had actually been borrowed. Since stock exchange rules contemplate settling the trade (and delivering the securities to the buyer) within a few days rather than immediately, the naked short seller acts with the expectation that a lender of the securities will be found before the sale closes. This allows the short seller to act immediately (rather than postpone the sale until she finds a lender), but it raises the possibility of the seller defaulting on the trade if she does not find a lender by the time the trade is to be settled.

Suppose that government is irrelevant in regulating naked short selling on a stock exchange (there are jurisdictional or constitutional constraints limiting government's authority to regulate; the country in question does not have laws regarding naked short selling; it does not vigorously enforce these laws; or it enforces these laws only as a pretext for other actions such as to extract side payments or to suppress political opponents). The stock exchange itself may create and enforce norms regulating short selling, to assure buyers that short sellers will not default on a transaction. Suppose also that the probability of default on a given trade is 0.001 (1-in-100 000), but the public misperceives the risk to be 1 percent (perhaps as a result of some publicity given recently to a failed trade). At a 1 percent probability of default, most investors will avoid trading. Sensing a risk misperception that creates an opportunity for bias arbitrage, the stock exchange announces an initiative to monitor and prevent naked short selling (by requiring a seller to already possess the shares she offers to sell). Finally, suppose that the implementation of this norm has the effect of reducing the likelihood of default by 50 percent (to 1-in-200 000). If the stock exchange officials are modest and 'undersell' the initiative, so that the public perceives the initiative to have no effect, the result would be that the public will still believe that the probability of default is 1 percent and trading will remain low, significantly reducing the objective benefits of the initiative.

If the stock exchange officials were not modest, but merely honest, and persuaded the public that the initiative would reduce default by 50 percent (as it indeed does), then the public would perceive the probability of default as 0.5 percent, still a great risk that would deter most investors. The stock exchange will likely see some increase in trading, but because most investors still view the risk of default as excessively high, the initiative's effect would be limited.

Suppose, instead, that the stock exchange officials persuasively overstate the effects of the initiative, convincing investors that it reduces the probability of default by 99 percent. To a public that expects (prior to the initiative's implementation) default at a probability of 1 percent, the law's effect would be to reduce the perceived probability to 1-in-10 000. While the public would still over-estimate the likelihood of default by a magnitude of 20,[28] this reduced probability would likely result in a significant increase in trading.

Individuals who are skeptical of the stock exchange's claims (and still believe that the probability of default is 1 percent) may refrain from trading, but as they observe

28 Since the actual probability is, per our assumptions, 1-in-200 000.

others' trades they would notice that sellers default on far less than 1 percent of trades, supporting the exchange's claim of a probability of 1-in-10 000. Thus, even some of the skeptics are likely to eventually credit the exchange for the 'reduced' risk of seller default. Beyond the private benefit to the exchange, persuasively overstating the initiative's effects improved social welfare in this hypothetical because the perceived probability of default now more closely approximates the actual probability, resulting in less excessive avoidance of trading on the exchange.

3.3 Which Norms? (Those that Address the Largest Perception Gap)

This example points out why the opportunity for bias arbitrage affects a PLS's choice of what norm to enforce. An infinite number of norms cannot be enforced at once by the PLS, and resources devoted to creating and effectively enforcing one norm come at the expense of other norms that could be created or enforced. A PLS may benefit from enforcing a norm that addresses a correctly perceived risk and objectively reduces that risk. However, there would be some uncertainty as to whether enforcing the norm would indeed reduce the risk, and even if it did, objective solutions may reduce an objective risk more modestly than cognitive biases inflate perceived risks. In our hypothetical, the enforcement of the norm against naked short selling reduced the objective probability of default by 50 percent, so if (counter to the hypothetical's assumptions) the public correctly estimated the risk of default and the initiative's effects on that risk, the exchange would be credited with reducing the risk to 50 percent of its previous level. Instead, in our hypothetical, the exchange is credited with reducing the risk 50 times more, to 1 percent of its previous level.

Addressing a risk that is correctly perceived would also cause 'overselling' the norm to have adverse results, both to the PLS and to social welfare. If, in our hypothetical, the actual probability of default was identical to the probability perceived by the public (1 percent), and the exchange successfully persuaded investors that its initiative reduced the probability by 99 percent (to 1-in-10 000), while it in fact reduced the objective probability by only 50 percent (to 1-in-200), then the public would trade excessively, unwittingly over-exposing itself to the risk of default. In addition, over time the public will observe that sellers default more frequently than 1-in-10 000 trades. When notice of this spreads, the exchange's credibility will suffer, reducing its ability to receive credit for future actions and possibly causing members to abandon the PLS.

Therefore, enforcing norms that address risks that are over-estimated is likely to offer higher expected payoffs to the PLS and pose less risk to the PLS from 'overselling' than enforcing norms that address correctly estimated risks, let alone norms that address under-estimated risks. A rational PLS may choose to address an over-estimated risk that has less effective objective solutions over a correctly estimated risk (or an under-estimated risk) that has more effective objective solutions.

3.4 The Impact of Bias Arbitrage on PLS Members' Social Welfare

The bias arbitrage portion of this chapter challenged the notion that PLSs necessarily (or even most frequently) pick norms that maximize their members' self interest. A PLS's attempt to bias arbitrage would lead it to frequently choose to enforce norms that have the greatest potential for bias arbitrage (i.e., norms that address risks with sizable perception gaps). Are these norms different from the norms that maximize the (objective) social welfare of the PLS's members? If that is the case, then perhaps PLSs do pick the norms that are most efficient for their members, even though that is not what they attempt to do.

An answer requires additional analysis. Bias arbitrage can improve or reduce social welfare, depending on several circumstances, foremost of which is whether, prior to the PLS's enforcement of a norm, the PLS members had a biased perception of the risk that the norm addresses.

Bias arbitrage has direct and indirect effects on social welfare. The indirect effects have to do with the opportunity cost of enforcing a norm that creates bias arbitrage. While a PLS does not necessarily have a fixed number of norms that it can enforce, there is some rivalry between norms over enforcement resources. Thus, if one norm is chosen by the PLS for enforcement, this might reduce the resources available to enforce other norms. Indeed, some norms may conflict with others, so that choosing one norm precludes adopting certain other norms. Thus, the opportunity cost (or indirect effect of bias arbitrage on social welfare) is the impact on social welfare of the norms that are precluded from adoption, or that receive diminished enforcement resources, due to the adoption of the norm that is used to bias arbitrage.

The direct effects of bias arbitrage on social welfare are derived from bias arbitrage's effect on the behavior of those people whose perception gaps it manipulates. Individuals respond to risk in two ways: avoiding the risk, or, if avoidance is not feasible, expending resources to confront the risk. In our naked short selling hypothetical, investors had the choice of refraining from trading in the face of a high perceived risk of counterparty default, or confronting the risk by monitoring the trade and identifying risky counterparties.

Both activity avoidance and confrontation are costly, though either may be efficient if it is the least costly method for avoiding more costly harm from the risk. Given the expense and limited ability of an individual investor monitoring the quality of his counterparty, most investors would likely choose, in this case, to refrain from trading.

Absent information asymmetry and cognitive biases, an individual's decision to avoid or confront a risk should be efficient from the perspective of social welfare.[29] However, cognitive biases cause misperceptions of risk. When perceived risk exceeds actual risk, individuals excessively avoid or confront the risk, imposing unnecessary costs on themselves and others.[30] When perceived risk is lower than actual risk, individuals insufficiently avoid or confront the risk, imposing on themselves or others the cost of a higher probability of harm.

Looking to the short selling hypothetical, if the objective probability of a short seller

---

[29] An implicit assumption in this statement is that any externalities of the decision whether to avoid/confront the risk are internalized.

[30] Risk confrontation may internalize costs on others just as risk avoidance does. For example, heightened perception of risk of crime in New Orleans may cause a property owner who is patrolling his property to misperceive another's actions as hostile and attack that person. As with externalities of risk avoidance, there are internalization mechanisms (e.g., criminal law, tort law), and as with risk avoidance, these mechanisms sometimes become destabilized due to changes in perceived risk.

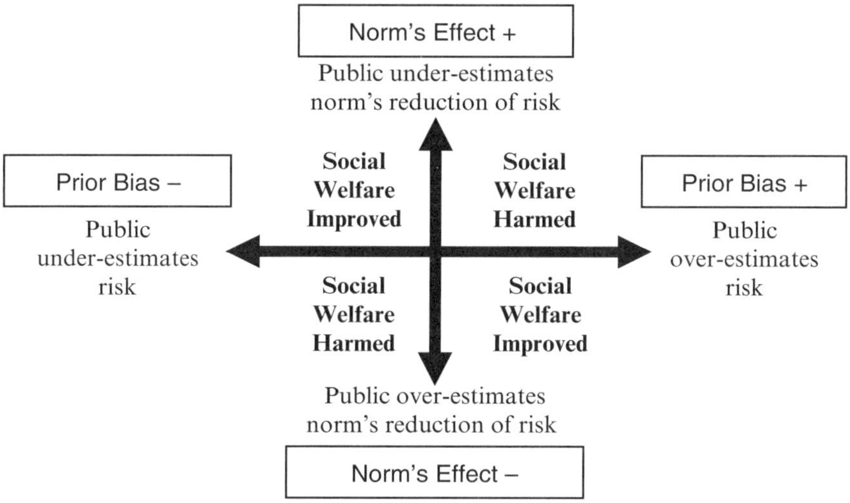

Figure 8.1 Direct effects of bias arbitrage on social welfare

defaulting on a trade is 1-in-100 000, but the public perceives the probability as 1 percent, then most individuals would avoid trading. On the other hand, if the objective probability of default were 1 percent, but cognitive biases caused the population to perceive the probability as 1-in-100 000, then too many people would trade and face counterparty default.

The loss of social welfare from excessive or insufficient risk avoidance or confrontation increases as the gap between objective and perceived risk (the perception gap) grows. Thus, if the creation or enforcement of a norm widens the perception gap, then its direct effect on social welfare will be negative. Conversely, if the creation or enforcement of a norm narrows the perception gap, then its direct effect on social welfare will be positive.[31] Figure 8.1 illustrates the direct effect bias arbitrage has on social welfare.[32]

4. CONCLUSION

The literature on private ordering has documented the effect of the public legal system on private legal systems. PLSs often emerge to address a demand for a norm that the

[31] For a more detailed analysis of the impact of bias arbitrage on social welfare see Aviram (2006) at 92–102. Note that even without the aid of bias arbitrage, perception gaps narrow over time as individuals track the occurrence of a risk and adjust their perceptions to what they observe. By speeding the process, bias arbitrage reduces the amount of time during which the misperception of a risk causes a reduction in social welfare.

[32] The axes in Figure 8.1 measure change in the perception gap. A positive value indicates an increase in perceived risk relative to actual risk. For example, 'Norm's Effect +' means that the norm increases the perception gap; i.e., causes perceived risk to increase relative to actual risk. This would be the case when the public under-estimates a norm's effect in reducing the risk.

public legal system fails to enforce (either because it is unable to or because it is unwilling to enforce the norm); PLSs can also be uprooted when the public legal system moves to displace them.

But the evolution of PLSs is not simply a derivative of the evolution of the public legal system. This chapter presented two important forces that have been neglected by the literature, yet help explain which norms a PLS chooses to enforce and which PLS ends up enforcing the norms. Bias arbitrage and the incumbent's enforcement advantage are not the only forces that determine which PLSs survive and which norms they enforce, but they are among the most significant yet least appreciated.[33]

The incumbent's enforcement advantage causes an evolutionary pattern, in which PLSs begin their life enforcing a core norm that has very low enforcement costs (typically, providing social or spiritual services). Once this core has developed, PLSs may then choose expansion norms that can be more expensive to enforce, and that benefit from the PLS's ability to compel compliance with the new norm by denying a member the benefits of its enforcement of the core norm and any expansion norms already successfully enforced.

Bias arbitrage affects the types of the norms that the successful PLSs will choose to enforce. Unlike the public legal system, a PLS's existence is tentative and depends on providing its members with more perceived benefits than do rival norm enforcers (other PLSs, the public legal system, or bilateral contracting). The extant scholarship focuses on a norm's objective impact on social welfare. This chapter suggests that the focus should be placed instead on long-term perceived benefits to the PLS members, and therefore on the size of the members' perception gap regarding the risk or opportunity the norm addresses. In other words, a norm is appealing for the PLS to enforce the more the public over-estimates the risk it addresses (or over-estimates an opportunity the norm exploits), in some cases even though the norm has very little objective effect on the risk.

BIBLIOGRAPHY

Aviram, A. (2003), 'Regulation by networks', *Byu L. Rev.*, 1179.

Aviram, A. (2004), 'A paradox of spontaneous formation: The evolution of private legal systems', *Yale L. & Pol'y Rev.*, **22**, 1.

Aviram, A. (2006), 'The placebo effect of law: Law's role in manipulating perceptions', *Geo. Wash. L. Rev.*, **75**, 54.

Aviram, A. (2007), 'Bias arbitrage', *Wash. & Lee L. Rev.*, **64**, 789.

Aviram, A. (2008), 'Counter-cyclical enforcement of corporate law', *Yale J. Reg.*, **25**, 1.

Bernstein, L. (1992), 'Opting out of the legal system: Extralegal contractual relations in the diamond industry', *J. Legal. Stud.*, **21**, 115.

Cary, W.L. (1974), 'Federalism and corporate law: Reflections upon Delaware', *Yale L. J.*, **83**, 663.

Coase, R. (1960), 'The problem of social cost', *J. L. & Econ.*, **3**, 1.

Ellickson, R.C. (1986), 'Of Coase and cattle: Dispute resolution among neighbors in Shasta County', *Stan. L. Rev.*, **38**, 623.

Ellickson, R.C. (1991), *Order Without Law: How Neighbors Settle Disputes*, Harvard University Press.

---

[33] Other forces include: government intervention in favor or against a PLS (i.e., interaction with the public legal system), the objective effects of a norm enforced by the PLS, the degree of competition among PLSs and between PLSs and other norm enforcers.

Gregory of Tours (1849), 'Enslaving noble families', *Patrologiae cursus Completus*, **71**, 255 (J.P. Migne, ed), reprinted in R.C. Cave and H.H. Coulson (eds), *A Source Book For Medieval Economic History* (1965), pp. 288–9.

Greif, A. et al. (1994), 'Coordination, commitment, and enforcement: The case of the Merchant Guild', *J. Pol. Econ.*, **102**, 745.

Kahneman, D., P. Slovic and A. Tversky (eds) (1982), *Judgement Under Uncertainty: Heuristics and Biases.*

Kerber, W. (2008), 'Institutional change in globalization: Transnational commercial law from an evolutionary economics perspective', *German L. Rev.* **9**, 411.

Pohl, R. (ed.) (2004), *Cognitive Illusions.*

Posner, R.A. (1998), *Law & Literature*, 2nd edn, pp. 49–60.

Richardson, G. and M.T. McBride (2009), 'Religion, longevity, and cooperation: The case of the Craft Guild', *Journal of Economic Behaviour and Organization.* **71**(2), 172–86.

Schelling, T.C. (1956), 'A essay on bargaining', *Am. Econ. Rev.*, **46**.

Williamson, O.E. (1983), 'Credible commitments: Using hostages to support exchange', *Am. Econ. Rev.*, **73**, 519.

Winter, R.K. Jr. (1977), 'State law, shareholder protection, and the theory of the corporation', *J. Legal. Stud.* **6**, 251.

Zywicki, T.J. (2003), 'The rise and fall of efficiency in the common law. A supply-side analysis', *Nw. U. L. Rev.* **97**, 1551, 1598–9.

9. Legal evolution between stability and change

Martina Eckardt

1. INTRODUCTION

Institutions can have a decisive impact on economic performance. The law is particularly important in shaping the institutional framework for economic activities. Legal rules can be viewed as socio-technological devices used to help individuals solve the coordination problems and conflicts that arise in an environment of scarce resources.[1] In such an environment, the law affects both the allocation as well as the distribution of resources, and is itself influenced and altered by economic evolution. However, our understanding of the determinants and mechanisms of legal change from an economic perspective remains rather weak.

The traditional neo-institutional economics and law and economics perspectives have made a measured contribution to our theoretical and empirical understanding of legal change.[2] Yet these two perspectives are deeply rooted in neoclassical microeconomics, and as such, they remain at their core concerned with the impact of given legal rules on economic activities. To a large extent, this reflects the inherent static nature of neoclassical microeconomics (stable preferences, rational choice behavior, and equilibrium),[3] wherein the economic problem is reduced to optimization (i.e., choosing the best option from a given set of alternatives). The decisive question of how the legal alternatives themselves are generated is thus not analysed and so novelty and change are assumed to be exogenous.

Change, on the other hand, is the main starting point of the evolutionary economics perspective. Calling into question the stable preferences on which the traditional premise of optimization is based,[4] evolutionary economics purports that innovation, uncertainty, and the 'constitutional lack of knowledge' are central characteristics of modern economies which have to be addressed in economic theorizing.[5] The perspective's very aim is

---

1 Eckardt (2001); Kerber and Heine (2003).

2 Cooter and Ulen (2007); Eggertsson (1990); Furubotn and Richter (1998); Posner (1998). The law is part of the formal institutions of a society. Nevertheless also informal rules, which are not considered in the following, play an important role for legal change. See, e.g., Hayek (1973); Hayek (1979); Knight (1992); North (1990a); Okruch (1999); Posner (1998).

3 Eggertsson, *id.*

4 Indeed, a number of different methods from different disciplines reflect recent interest in these issues. See Herrmann-Pillath (2002); Hodgson (1993); Metcalfe (1998); Nelson (1995); Nelson and Winter (2002); Witt (2003).

5 Hayek (1969); Schumpeter (1950).

the explanation of economic, technological, or institutional change over time; central issues include the generation of innovations and their diffusion through imitation and learning.

At the core of evolutionary economics lie three key assumptions or building blocks.[6] First, while mainstream neoclassical economics assumes a closed action space with homogeneous and representative actors, evolutionary economics assumes one that is open with undefined processes. To this end, evolutionary economics assumes heterogeneous actors that exercise bounded rationality due to limited information-processing capacities and create subjective cognitive models to make sense of the world as they perceive it.[7] Moreover, actors are assumed to be creative and able to generate novel activities in any domain in which they are engaged. The evolutionary economist thus seeks to explain the mechanisms that generate and transmit new action opportunities. Pursuant to Schumpeter's notion of 'creative destruction,' these mechanisms can be perceived as new ways of doing things by re-combining existing and well-known action possibilities as well as generating novel ones.[8] Hence, economic change is perceived as a trial-and-error process of experimentation with new economic activities, involving not only technological and organizational innovation, but also political and legal innovation.

However, it may be argued that a focus on the endogenous generation of new action states is at odds with our everyday lives and experiences. Indeed, our lives are often characterized by a certain degree of regularity and stability, as opposed to the chaos and unpredictability purported by the evolutionary economic perspective. There must be forces at work that limit the continuous generation of variety by heterogeneous creative actors. Hence, a second main building block of evolutionary economics is the study of the selection mechanisms, including the relevant selection environments, of the activities analysed.

Since evolutionary economics is concerned with economic evolution over time, the perspective's third main building block is the analysis of those mechanisms that lead to the patterned transmission of innovations from one period to the next. This includes not only mechanisms of differential 'reproduction,' but also mechanisms that generate path-dependencies. This is particularly important in regard to institutional, and consequently, legal change.

To date, however, evolutionary economics has dealt mainly with change in the technological and organizational domain, as opposed to institutional and legal evolution. While there are some promising approaches that seem to be a good starting point for further research efforts, a comprehensive evolutionary economic theory of legal change has not yet been articulated. To this end, this chapter begins with an overview of typical evolutionary explanations of legal change: its main actors, key determinants, and the central

---

[6] For some time now evolutionary arguments are prominent in the law and economics literature. Usually they refer to gradual innovations and changes in contrast to discrete ones. Note, however, that evolutionary economics cannot be reduced to this notion. It is more comprehensive in that it uses a process perspective, trying to broaden the static neoclassical approach to encompass the endogenous generation of novelty, be it gradual or discrete (Metcalfe, *id.*; Nelson, *id.*; Nelson and Winter, *id.*; Witt, *id.*).

[7] Denzau and North (1994).

[8] Schumpeter (1934); Schumpeter (1950).

mechanisms of the different approaches that bring about legal change are identified. By pointing out the evolutionary aspects of the different approaches, their contribution to the explanation of legal change becomes clear. The following analysis is confined to the change of specific legal rules. From an evolutionary economics point of view legal change takes place through the generation and dissemination of legal innovations over time.[9] The main mechanisms are statutory and judge-made legal change. While statutory legal change relies on legislation and thus on collective action, judge-made legal change is brought about by the judiciary through individual lawsuits. To explain legal stability over time the literature stresses the concepts of legal paradigms and of path dependence, with a particular emphasis on legal lock-ins. In this chapter we extend the analysis by discussing the main mechanisms that bring about break outs from such legal lock-ins, thus providing a more comprehensive view on legal evolution between stability and change.

Section 2 starts with a short account of the public choice approach to politics and thus to statutory innovations. It is followed by a cognitive-evolutionary approach to policy-making which analyses statutory legal change in the Schumpeterian tradition. Section 3 considers both Hayek's explicit evolutionary view[10] of judge-made legal change as a trial-and-error process as well as the law and economics literature that implicitly draws on evolutionary arguments. While the approaches discussed so far more or less exclusively deal with the generation and dissemination of single legal innovations, Section 4 widens the horizon by presenting an approach that deals with the co-evolution of legal rules, technology, and the economy. Section 5 turns to the notions of legal paradigms and of legal path-dependence and discusses their implication for legal evolution between stability and change. Finally, Section 6 concludes with a short summary and a brief outlook on further areas of future research.

2. STATUTORY LEGAL CHANGE AS AN INNOVATION PROCESS

2.1 The Public Choice Approach to Politics

Given that economic policy in modern democracies is implemented by a set of legal rules, the economic analysis of politics can be construed as a concurrent analysis of statutory legal change. The dominant approach to political economy is based on traditional neo-classical economics.[11] Its main focus is on equilibrium outcomes that are brought about

---

9 A comprehensive evolutionary economics theory of legal change has to further clarify its research object. For example, a legal rule can be defined as comprising the following three components: (1) the facts which decide to what economic activity it applies; (2) a legal norm which prescribes which actor is allowed to carry out what action; and (3) the burden of proof which states who has to bring the necessary information before the court in case of an action. See Eckardt (2001), 19–22.

10 For an overview of Hayek's reasoning on economic and legal theory, see Beaulier *et al.* (2004); Eckardt (2001); Okruch (1999).

11 Buchanan and Tullock (1962); Olson (1965); Olson (1982); Niskanen (1971); Rowley (1989); Rowley *et al.* (1988); Mueller (1997); Mueller (2003); Mercuro and Medema (1997); Tullock (1998); Breton (1998).

by marginal adaptations of rational utility-maximizing actors to changes in exogenous variables. The relevant actors in this paradigm include voters, special-interest groups, politicians or political parties, and bureaucracies; all of these parties seek to maximize rents, or in this case, votes. Under this model, there is an exchange of votes for election promises or for the expected legislation by the parties elected. In other words, politicians, political parties, and the government are largely conceived as only passively reacting to the demands expressed by voters or interest groups. Following this argument, it can further be asserted that the content of a statute is based on the interests of either the median voter, predominant interest-group, or government controlled bureaucracy. By specifying exogenously given restrictions, objective functions, and exchange mechanisms, empirical testable hypotheses can be tested against the outcome of the political bargaining processes and thus the typical content of statutory legal change. Note, however, that political markets – like any other economic market – are not immune to market failure, meaning that statutory legal change does not always lead to efficient outcomes.[12]

While the various strands of Public Choice deal with specific aspects of legislation, they all have in common that they usually assume the set of political options and thus the set of legal alternatives as given. Any deviations from the standard assumptions of neoclassical economics have, however, come under increased scrutiny in recent years. A prime example is that of the 'cognitive turn' by North, who deviates from the behavioral model of standard microeconomics.[13] Aside from assuming that individuals act under incomplete information and conditions of bounded rationality, North supposes that they also interpret the information received in the light of subjective theories and beliefs. For collective action to take place, communication transmits these subjectively held views of the world in commonly shared views (ideologies), which govern decisions and behavior.[14] As a consequence, the set of alternatives from which to choose is no longer a given. Thus, even under competition, feedback-effects to select out inefficient alternatives might not work because individuals do not hold the 'true' cognitive models about the cause-and-effect relations on which their decisions are based. This effect might even be intensified because of the path-dependent nature of institutional change.[15] Although Public Choice theories are based on Schumpeter's idea of democracy as competition for political power, it has taken quite some time before the Schumpeterian notion of creative entrepreneurs was also applied to the political arena.[16]

Thus, while the Public Choice literature provides us with rich insights into the

---

[12] However, supporters of the efficiency redistribution hypothesis argue that competition among different interest groups leads to efficient redistribution. See, e.g., Becker (1983); Bullock (1995); Wittman (1989); Wittman (1995).

[13] North (1990a); North (1990b).

[14] Denzau and North (1994).

[15] North also refers to the importance of entrepreneurs for creating innovations and for enhancing the adaptive efficiency of an economy and thus alludes to the Schumpeterian line of evolutionary economics. But so far he has not systematically integrated this notion in his transaction cost approach to politics. For a critical appraisal of the cognitive turn in Neo-Institutional Economics, see Lindenberg (1998).

[16] For academics that explicitly supplement traditional Public Choice analysis by integrating Schumpeterian ideas, see Breton (1998); Dunleavy (1991); Eichenberger and Serna (1996); Frey and Eichenberger (1991); Kirchgässner and Pommerehne (1993); Schumpeter (1950). For examples

determinants and mechanisms of different institutional settings for statutory legal change, it only superfluously deals with the question of how collective goods and thus how statutory legal innovations are actually generated and disseminated.

2.2 A Cognitive-evolutionary Approach to Policy-making

On the other hand, the cognitive-evolutionary approach to policy-making casts statutory legal change as an innovation process.[17] It applies Schumpeter's notion of the entrepreneur as creator of innovations to all participants in the political process. Politicians and the government are thus no longer modeled as merely passive actors that react to the demands of voters, interest-groups, or the bureaucracy. But rather, they are actively engaged in generating novel solutions to collective problems that ultimately leads to the drafting of new legislation. Moreover, it is assumed that even the problems themselves are not given, but are created in a collective process of cognitive construction. In contrast to Public Choice theories, both the set of alternatives from which a new statute has to be chosen and the very problem to which it provides a solution is not seen as objectively known *ex ante*.[18]

Obviously, endogenizing these hitherto exogenous variables limits the explanatory power of the traditional utility-maximizing economic approach, which assumes a given invariable and closed set of alternatives. The cognitive-evolutionary approach to policy-making applies a multi-level variation-selection concept which allows one to derive empirically testable hypotheses. Three main levels are distinguished, which are characterized by different variation mechanisms, selection environments and principles as follows: the individual, the collective, and the constitutional level. They are interlinked by the individual actors, who generate variations on each level – although through different mechanisms, and by the outcomes of the different selection processes which in turn affect the working of the other levels (Figure 9.1).

While the constitutional level defines the institutions, rules, and procedures that govern the problem-solving process on the collective level, the starting point for all statutory innovations is the individual.[19] Based on methodological individualism, this approach applies a cognitive model of action that incorporates elements from cognitive science. By assuming cognitive creativity, novelty can emerge endogenously. Continuously generated novel ideas and perceptions lead to innovations, which can be interpreted as being created by Schumpeterian entrepreneurs. But bounded rationality and satisfying behavior set a first limit on the ubiquitous generation of variety. Individual discontent with the actual situation and ambiguity with respect to the information received and the theories held lead individuals to the perception of problems that have to be solved.

The implementation of statutory innovation requires the passing of a four-stage collective problem-solving process. At the first stage, mobilization of other individuals and resources must be sufficiently high to convince others about one's own view of a

---

of how the process of collective opinion formation can be explored in more detail, see Wohlgemuth (2002a); Wohlgemuth (2002b).

17 Meier and Haury (1990); Meier and Slembeck (1998); Slembeck (1997); Slembeck (2003).

18 Slembeck (1997), 227.

19 Slembeck (1997), 230–231.

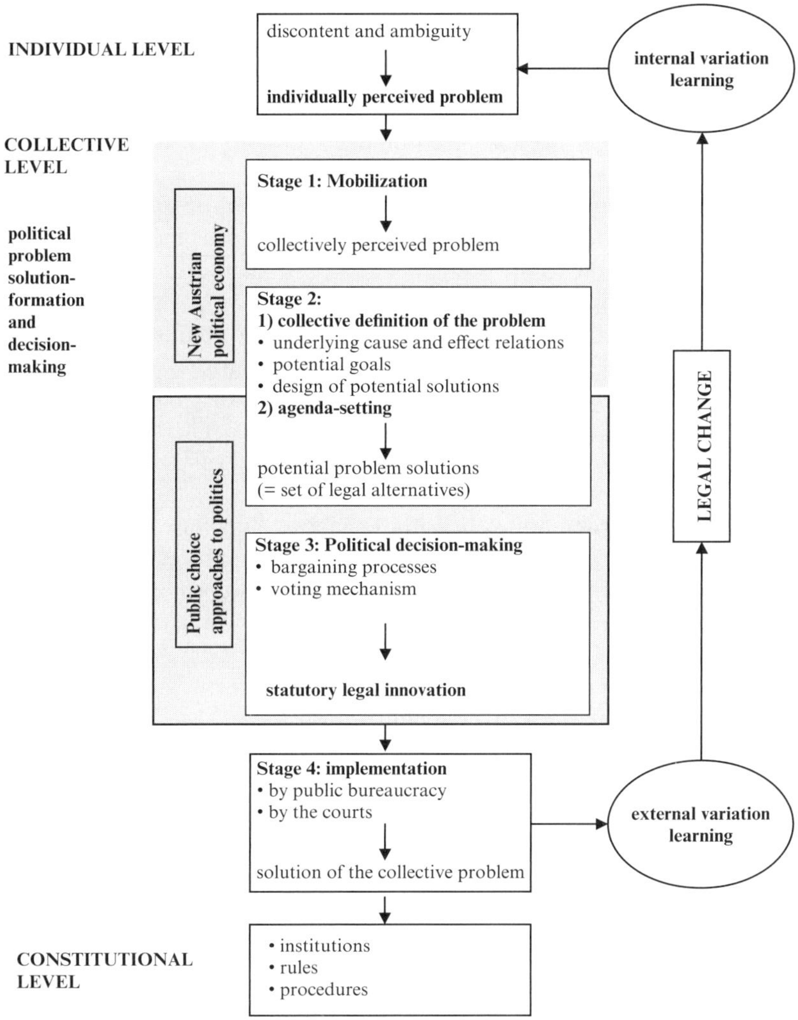

Source: Adapted from Slembeck (1997).

Figure 9.1 A variation-selection approach to statutory legal change

problem.[20] After successful mobilization, the problem enters the second stage in which a collective definition of the problem is generated through public debate and opinion formation.[21] It encompasses the underlying causes, their potential effects, the goals to

[20] The resources necessary to mobilize support and political pressure differ according to the number of potentially affected persons and the extent of the problem. Accordingly, elite problems, structural problems, interest group problems and crisis problems can be distinguished (Slembeck (1997), 231–3).

[21] Slembeck (1997), 233–8.

be pursued and the potential solutions. The more novel a problem is, the higher is its uncertainty and the more controversial its resulting debates. Due to the limited problem-solving capacity of legislation, which itself is a consequence of the limited resources and time, a number of different collective problems 'compete' with one another. If an issue is finally put on the political agenda, preliminary views about its proper definition, the goals, and the effective instruments have been reached.

On the decision-making stage, political exchange and thus bargaining processes dominate.[22] Here the questions dealt with by the Public Choice approach come into sharp focus. The resources available to the political decision-makers and the institutional setting such as the voting rules and the role of committees prove to be the decisive selection criteria for the finally enacted legal innovation. While traditional approaches to statutory legal change end with the passing of a statute, in the cognitive-evolutionary approach, its implementation is explicitly taken into account.[23] Both public administration and the courts have discretionary power to modify its content. Therefore, new processes of reinterpreting the underlying problem as well the meaning of the statute may start over again.

Statutory innovation thus implies hypotheses about the cause-and-effect-relations of the collectively perceived problem, which is based on the subjective theories and beliefs of the actors and that can thus potentially be wrong. As a consequence, both the underlying problem may remain unsolved and new problems originating from unforeseeable reactions to the new statute may emerge. The resulting external variation initiates new efforts that will perhaps lead to additional legal innovations. Moreover, learning takes place because the effects of the statutory innovation are assessed on the individual, the collective, and the constitutional level. Thus, there is an ongoing process of legal change.[24]

3. JUDGE-MADE LEGAL CHANGE AS A DISCOVERY PROCEDURE

3.1 Legal Change as a Trial and Error Process – The Austrian Perspective

Hayek's notion of competition as a trial-and-error process plays a prominent role in evolutionary economics. The starting point of his reasoning is the fundamental knowledge problem of human beings.[25] This is in stark contrast to the neoclassical assumption that preferences, tastes, information, resources, skills are already given as data before competition starts, which then works solely as an allocation mechanism. According to Hayek, the economic problem is exactly that the data and assumptions of neoclassical economics are not and cannot be known by anyone in advance. Therefore competition serves as a mechanism to discover and communicate information about the underlying variables.[26] It sets incentives for individuals to search for new knowledge. Since competition allows

22 Slembeck (1997), 238–41.
23 Slembeck (1997), 241–3.
24 Slembeck (1997), 245–8.
25 Hayek, *supra*, note 2, 11–15.
26 Hayek (1948a); Hayek (1948b); Hayek (1948c); Hayek (1968/2002).

for the parallel testing of different hypotheses, it makes more information available than could be used otherwise. Competition can be thus conceived as a permanent trial-and-error process in which new hypotheses are continuously generated and tested.[27] This notion of competition as a discovery procedure underlies also Hayek's reasoning about the evolution of societies and their institutions which he refers to as cultural evolution.[28] Consequently, he has also analysed judge-made legal change from this point of view.[29]

Like markets, Hayek regards the law as a spontaneous order which is the result of an ongoing evolutionary process.[30] He sees judge-made legal innovations as a mainly unintended outcome of administering the law.[31] The necessary precondition is that conflicts are brought to the courts. If conflicts arise out of novel economic situations, legal innovations have to be generated, since legal rules are always only a response to past conflicts. Because a judge cannot refer to an already established legal norm or convention, he or she has either to derive a legal innovation from higher legal principles or to create one from the start. But also in the case of already well-known situations, conflicting expectations of the actors involved about the relevant legal rule can result in an action by which it will be modified just by chance. By referring to informal legal norms and conventions a judge will derive the legal rule applicable to the case at hand. However, in the course of explicitly articulating an informal legal rule, it is inevitable that slight modifications or legal innovations occur; this also holds for routine cases. Accordingly, Hayek assumes that judge-made legal innovations are to some degree the result of chance.[32]

The variety of viable legal innovations is restricted by the selection and retention mechanisms inherent to the court system. In particular, a judge has to be able to defend his legal innovation according to the valid legal principles against other members of the judiciary. Thus for Hayek, the socialization of the judges is decisive.[33] He assumes that they acquire a preference for interpreting conflicts in accordance with the given legal order during their professional training. Therefore, each judge strives to decide cases in line with the legal principles handed down by legal tradition. In addition, he supposes that the same holds true for the application of statute-based law, even if the legislature had once intended that a statutory legal rule should be interpreted in a different manner.[34] In general, Hayek prefers judge-made legal rules since he assumes them to be better able to create stable expectations based on abstract legal rules, which are a prerequisite for the working of a market economy. But he also acknowledges that under specific circumstances statutory legal innovations are more advantageous. Because of the gradual

---

[27] The Austrian notion of competition as a discovery procedure is thus also compatible to Popper's idea of hypothesis testing and falsification (Popper (1972)).

[28] For his concept of cultural evolution see Hayek, *supra*, note 2; Hayek (1967), Hayek (1988). This concept has been extensively criticized. For a detailed analysis, see e.g., Hodgson (1993); Okruch (1999), 123–36; Vanberg (1994), 77–94, 95–106.

[29] Hayek discusses statutory legal change largely according to public choice theory (Hayek (1979), 1–40, 98–105).

[30] Hayek, *supra*, note 26; Hayek (1969); Hayek, *supra*, note 2.

[31] Hayek, *supra*, note 2, 94–123.

[32] See Hayek (1973), 78, 99–118. For a more elaborated discussion of this argument, see Eckardt, *supra*, note 1, 95–106; Okruch, *supra*, note 2.

[33] Hayek, *supra*, note 2, 65–67.

[34] Hayek, *supra*, note 2, 66.

evolution of judge-made legal rules, they may also result in an undesirable path, which cannot be reversed that easily and quickly by the courts. In addition, in case of novel conflicts, immediate legal action may be required, and the legislature requires less time to promulgate publicly known legal innovations than the judiciary.[35]

For Hayek, administering the law by the courts is a trial-and-error process in which hypotheses as to the proper interpretation of legal rules are continuously tested. The central selection mechanism of the finally applied legal rule is the socialization of the judges.[36] Gradual modifications and novel interpretations of well-established legal rules may lead to their application in varying economic situations in the future. In addition, novel conflicts may arise because of conflicting expectations of the individual actors regarding the valid legal rules, and again have to be decided by the courts.[37] As a consequence, the administration of law by judges entails a permanent process of trial-and-error that contributes to the evolution of the law.[38]

Hayek thus directs the attention to the knowledge-creating features of legal change, which is an ongoing task in an evolutionary environment. More recent research has emphasized that Hayek's concept of judge-made legal evolution cannot only be applied to the Anglo-Saxon common law system.[39] In the case of statutes, courts have to decide the precise content of a statutory legal rule while applying it to the actual case at hand as well. Thus, at any given point in time, there usually are quite a number of more or less differing interpretations of the same overall legal rule applied within a jurisdiction. However, legal heterogeneity is limited due to the selection and retention mechanisms inherent to legal systems. Thus, conceiving judge-made legal change as a trial-and-error process holds also for civil law systems.

3.2 The Law and Economics Approach to Legal Change

The law and economics approach to legal change has as its genesis neoclassical economics. There are two main lines of law and economics reasoning on the evolution of law. The first approach, which is outlined in greater detail in the following, analyses legal change within a given legal system. It sees the driving force of legal change in the frequency to litigate. In contrast, the second, more recent approach, sees the driving force for legal change in competition between different legal systems and thus in free choice of law.[40] Since Kerber provides an elaborate discussion of the latter's working mechanisms in this volume, it should suffice here to note that in contrast to the former one, competition among legal rules between different legal systems addresses not only the question of the selection mechanisms but also of the sources for novel legal rules.

---

35 Hayek also admits that sometimes judges may even destroy the legal tradition they had supported so far. However, he is not precise as to the underlying causes and mechanisms (Hayek (1973), 66).

36 Hayek, *supra*, note 2, 120.

37 Hayek, *supra*, note 2, 78, 120.

38 Hayek, *supra*, note 2, 65, 102.

39 Eckardt, *supra*, note 1; Okruch, *supra*, note 2; von Wangenheim (1993); von Wangenheim (1995).

40 Carbonara and Parisi (2007); Ogus (1999).

Table 9.1 Analogy between economic markets and courts

	Markets	Courts
Supply side Actors, behavioral assumptions	Firms, profit maximization	Judges, utility maximization (income, reputation)
Demand side Actors, behavioral assumption	Consumers, utility maximization	Litigants, income maximization
Objects of exchange	Goods and services vs. money	Legal rules (public good) and income (private good) vs. reputation (private good) and income of the judges (public costs)
Coordination mechanism(s)	Invisible hand of the market (price mechanism)	Impartiality of the judges

Source: Adapted from Posner (1998).

Judge-made legal change is, for the most part, an unintended byproduct of the ordinary administration of law by the courts. A statutory legal innovation is the outcome of a collective problem-solving process and is immediately binding for the whole jurisdiction once it is enacted.[41] In contrast, to be binding for the whole jurisdiction, judge-made legal innovations first have to be disseminated through the hierarchical court system. To explain the process of judge-made legal change in detail, the selection mechanisms driving the diffusion of legal innovations are an explicit topic in the law and economics literature.[42] Similar to the public choice approach to statutory legal change, the law and economics approach applies the main ideas of standard microeconomic theory to judge-made legal change (Table 9.1), but it also uses evolutionary arguments.

The typical reasoning of the law and economics literature is briefly illustrated with reference to Posner's.[43] On markets all relevant information is communicated through price signals, with the price mechanism as the decisive coordination mechanism. For Posner, the market mechanism guarantees an efficient resource allocation according to consumers' preferences, which are revealed by their willingness-to-pay. However, he assumes that in cases of high transaction costs, courts provide a more economical allocation of resources and thus work as a substitute for the market mechanism.[44]

Legal rules impose 'prices' on potential economic activities. It is assumed that

[41] At least, this is the usual idea. However, Aoki makes quite clear that it is not the wording of a statute, but people seeing it as binding for their actions that makes a legal rule an institution. In this way, the distinction between statutory and judge-made legal rules becomes somehow blurred (Aoki (2001)).

[42] Cooter and Ulen, *supra*, note 2; Fon and Parisi (2003); Fon *et al.* (2005); Mercuro and Medema, *supra*, note 11; Posner (2007). Note that Hayek remains rather unspecific in this respect.

[43] For a short summary of other approaches discussing judicial incentives and litigation as a selection mechanism, see Mialon *et al.* (2007).

[44] Posner, *supra*, note 2.

utility-maximizing individuals take these into account when they decide whether to carry out an activity or not; thus, the willingness-to-pay (for the sanctions imposed by certain legal rules) reflects the preferences of individuals. According to Posner, the impartial judge takes on the role of the invisible hand of the market.[45] Aside from specific ethics, which are learned by the judges in the course of their professional training, the hierarchical structure of the modern court system ensures the efficient allocation of property rights by the courts. Therefore, utility-maximizing self-interested judges will pass only decisions that are in line with the overall legal order, since the overruling of a judgment by a higher court would lead to a loss of reputation for the judge of the lower court.

Legal innovations are assumed to be unintentionally generated by judges through the application of given legal rules to the specific case at hand.[46] By chance a judge might slightly modify an existing legal rule. Such legal innovations, which at first only hold for the case at hand, are disseminated in two ways. Firstly, the party defeated might appeal to a higher court, which in turn might confirm the decision of the lower court, thus turning this legal innovation into a precedent. Secondly, similar conflicts might lead to a higher frequency to litigate; therefore, the underlying legal rule is brought to court more often. Hence, the probability rises that it will be modified more often by different courts of the jurisdiction.

These mechanisms inherently use evolutionary ideas. No longer a given set of legal alternatives is assumed, the process through which legal innovations and thus variety is created is explicitly modeled. Moreover, the selection mechanisms that restrict the range of viable legal rules are explored. The well-known and broadly discussed hypothesis that judge-made legal change tends to enhance the proportion of legal rules that promote economic efficiency entails a statement about the direction of judge-made legal change over time.[47] It implies that the court system should be able to perfectly mimic competitive markets.

This efficiency hypothesis has drawn a lot of attention and a number of objections have been raised.[48] They mainly concern the specification of the selection environment that is necessary to render the term 'efficiency' meaningful, and the common goods characteristic of efficient legal rules.[49] Since both litigants as well as judges are assumed to maximize their individual utility, a suboptimal production of efficient legal rules is to be expected as individual actors take into account only those costs and benefits which directly accrue to them. Thus, it is not that convincing that inefficient legal rules are brought to court more often than efficient ones since this would imply different incentives for individual actors for taking legal action.[50] It seems just as plausible that efficient legal rules are contested more often than inefficient ones due to their distributive effects, if certain actors are

---

45 Posner, *supra*, note 2, 581–4.

46 Posner, *supra*, note 2, 587–96.

47 Priest (1977); Rubin (1977); Landes and Posner (1979); Priest and Klein (1984); Aranson (1998); Posner, *supra*, note 42; Cooter and Rubinfeld (1989); Cooter and Ulen, *supra*, note 2; Hackney (2003).

48 For a discussion of what kind of efficiency makes sense as a principle to evaluate and guide legal change, see Parisi and Klick (2004). For a discussion of the law and economics approach from a behavioral perspective, see Jolls *et al.* (2001); Hayden and Ellis (2007).

49 Kerber (1996); Vanberg, *supra*, note 28.

50 Cooter and Kornhauser (1980); Cooter and Ulen, *supra*, note 2.

systematically burdened by an efficient legal rule, and if the costs of taking an action are relatively small compared to the potential gains.[51] Thus, Cooter and Ulen conclude that '(t)he problem with viewing a court as a market is that redistributive gains are frequently more important than inefficiencies in channeling litigation.'[52]

To sum up, the efficiency thesis of judge-made legal change cannot be supported from an evolutionary economics point of view. Nevertheless, the law and economics approach to judge-made legal change provides a good starting point for further elaboration. In contrast to the standard neoclassical model, it takes legal rules not as given, but explicitly deals with their generation and dissemination. The frequency to litigate and the hierarchical structure of the court system define the relevant selection environment, which influences the pace and direction of legal change. Moreover, in recent years the law and economics literature has not only broadened the scope of subjects analysed but also the methods used. So it not only relies on static maximization, but also draws on game theoretic approaches to model legal change. However, as Aoki impressively shows, these two approaches are still static in that they both assume a given action space from which the actors choose according to a given available selection of strategies.[53] In contrast to that, Aoki suggests a cognitive-constructivist view and formulates a subjective game theoretical approach. His concept of institution-induced, individual game-models no longer relies on a closed action space but allows for variety implying genuine novelty, and thus for one of the main ingredients of evolutionary approaches. Although he only implicitly deals with legal change, his approach might prove very fruitful for analysing the interrelationship of institutional change (comprising legal evolution) and economic change.

4. LAW, TECHNOLOGY AND ECONOMIC CHANGE

The approaches discussed so far have in common that they concentrate on the mechanisms of legal change that are inherent to the law. Although they assume changes in economic variables as one of the main driving forces for legal evolution, the impact of economic change, which is itself an evolutionary process, is not analysed in more detail. A more comprehensive framework for analysing the co-evolution of law and technology and its economic impact is presented in Eckardt (2001).[54] Technological, economic and legal change are viewed as the outcome of specific variation-selection processes. They are nevertheless linked to each other due to the wealth effects they cause, since the latter set incentives for individual actors to actively engage in the generation and dissemination of technological as well as legal innovations (Figure 9.2).[55]

The starting point of this approach is the appearance of novel negative technological

---

51 De Alessi and Staaf (1991); Hackney, *supra*, note 47.
52 Cooter and Ulen (1988).
53 Aoki, *supra*, note 41.
54 Eckardt, *supra*, note 1.
55 The fruitfulness of this approach is shown in several case studies which focus on the evolution of the German tort and accident law which was a result of the introduction of modern technologies like railroads and steam engines in the 19th century, see Eckardt, *supra*, note 1, 207–311; Eckardt (2004).

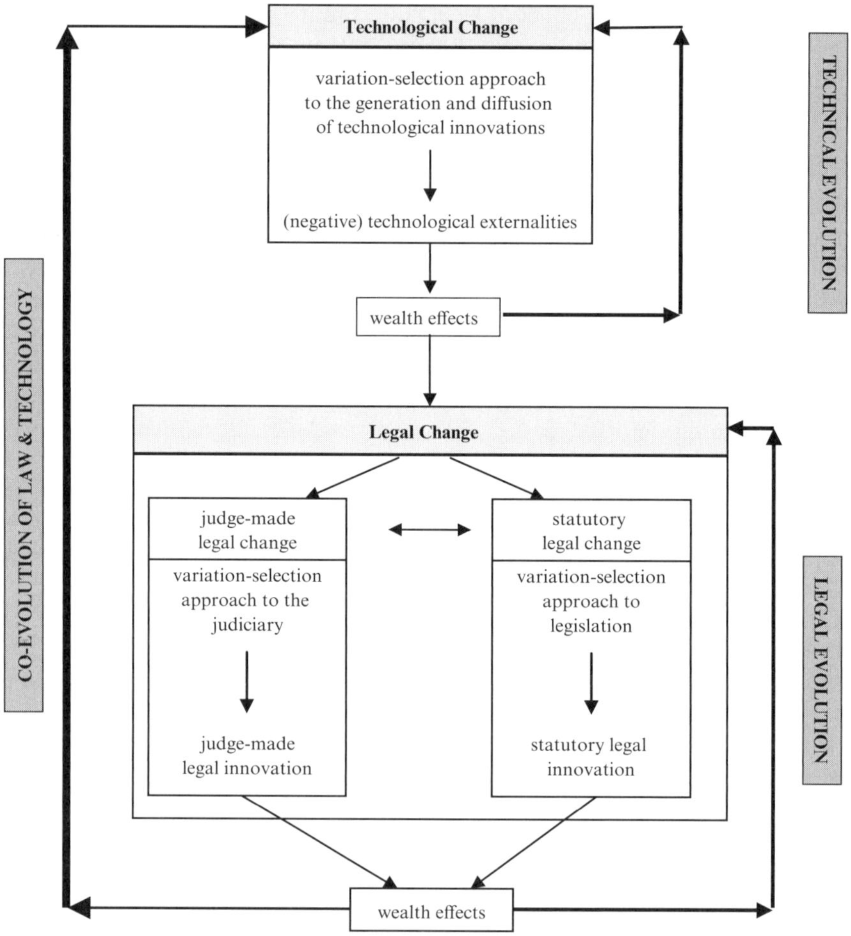

Source: Own composition.

Figure 9.2 Co-evolution of law and technology

externalities, which arise as an unintended, but inevitable by-product of technological innovations.[56] Similar to the variation-selection approach to statutory legal change discussed in Section 2.2, a cognitive model of human action is applied, according to which cognitive creativity is the main source from which novel ideas emerge.[57] The various variation and selection mechanisms finally lead to technological and legal innovations.

[56] Due to the complexity of the subject dealt with, this approach concentrates on the impact of negative technological externalities on legal evolution. However, it should become obvious that it can be easily modified to analyse other aspects of the co-evolution of law and technology as well.

[57] Eckardt, *supra*, note 1, 69–75.

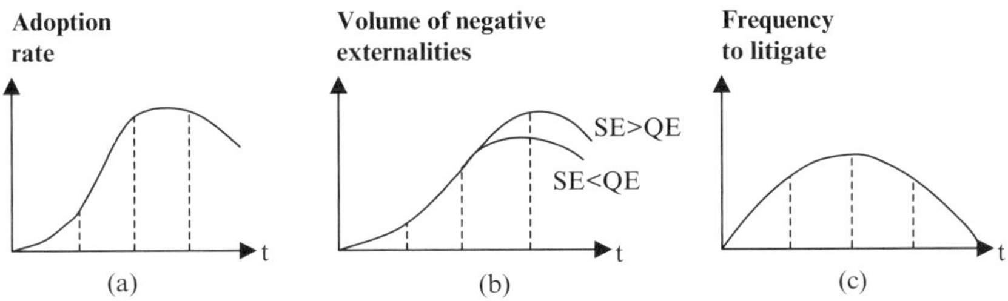

Note: *t = time; SE = scale effect; QE = quality effect*

Source: Own composition.

Figure 9.3 *Judge-made legal change over the industry life cycle*

To cope with the particularities of technological change the concept of the industry life cycle is used as an heuristic device.[58] It allows specifying the economic selection environment which changes over time due to the generation and dissemination of technological innovations. Several phases in the evolution of a market can be distinguished, each with its own constraints, behavioral incentives, and outcomes.

According to the concept of the industry life cycle, industries show some uniform patterns with respect to the rate of adoption of technological innovations, their improvements and market entries and exits, output growth, and changes in prices and qualities.[59]

Successful technological innovations, which are disseminated over time, usually have not only positive, but also negative effects. These arise as an unavoidable by-product of a new technology. However, their extent also changes over the industry life cycle.[60] It depends positively on the rate of adoption of the new technology (scale effect) and negatively on additional technological improvements which take place *inter alia* through learning-by-doing and learning-by-using (quality effect) (Figure 9.3 a, b). As a consequence, over the different market stages not only the volume of negative externalities but also the ensuing volume of wealth reduction varies systematically so that, in principle, empirically testable hypotheses can be derived.

Eckardt suggests that these wealth effects link legal change to technological change. Since judge-made and statutory legal changes are different mechanisms for generating legal innovations, they have to be discussed separately. However, the impact of technological innovations is incorporated in this approach in a consistent way through the industry life cycle, which constitutes the economic selection environment. It is assumed that wealth effects set incentives for individuals negatively affected by a new technology to turn to the law. They are induced so by the potential redistributive gains from legal innovations. Both statutory as well as judge-made legal innovations can be linked to technological change in a systematic way, which allows to identify regularities and thus again to derive testable hypothesis about the co-evolution of law and technology.

---

58 Eckardt, *supra*, note 1, 75–87.

59 Audretsch (1995); Cohen and Klepper (1992); Klepper (1996); Klepper and Graddy (1990).

60 Eckardt, *supra*, note 1, 112–116.

Judge-made legal innovations are linked to the industry life cycle since the incentives for individual actors to take legal action increase the more they are negatively affected by wealth reductions due to the use of the new technology (Figure 9.3 c). Individual actors can go to court to get either compensated and/or to prevent additional negative externalities. Judge-made legal change is modeled using a variation-selection approach, which is based both on the litigation frequency approach of the law and economics literature,[61] as well as on Hayek's view of judge-made legal change as a permanent trial-and-error process.[62] All actors involved (judges, litigants) are assumed to be creative. Because abstract legal rules are applied to particular cases, varying interpretations are inevitable so that the administration of the law by the judges inevitably generates legal innovations. The extent of the variety and heterogeneity of these legal innovations is positively correlated with the novelty of the underlying legal conflict. It is highest in the early stages of the industry life cycle of a new technology. It takes time until a specific legal innovation has passed the hierarchical structure of the court system and eventually has become a precedent, which then is binding for the decisions of lower courts in similar cases. It is assumed that the frequency to litigate positively varies with the wealth reductions caused by the new technology.

Thus, the diffusion of a legal innovation that at first only applies to the particular legal case at hand depends on (1) the selection mechanisms provided by the court system[63] and on (2) the economic selection environment which is represented through the industry life cycle and the resulting incentives to litigate. During the life cycle a legal problem-solving routine evolves, which leads to a growing homogeneity of court decisions.[64] As a consequence the frequency to litigate decreases since potential litigants can form more stable expectations as to the outcome of an action. Therefore out-of-court settlements become more attractive. In addition, interest groups can also influence judge-made legal change.[65] On the one hand, they can affect the frequency of litigation because generally they have more resources available for taking legal action. On the other hand though, they can provide more specialized information and thus can even influence the content of judge-made legal innovations. Since the costs for the formation of interest groups also vary over the market life cycle, again testable hypotheses about the potential impact of different kinds of interest groups on judge-made legal change in different stages of the life cycle can be derived.[66]

If actors are not content with the distributional results from judge-made legal innovations, they can try to alter them through the legislation. However, this requires the formation of interest groups. To analyse statutory legal innovations the variation-selection

---

[61] However, the notion that judge-made legal change is directed towards more efficiency is rejected.

[62] Eckardt, *supra*, note 1, 132–49.

[63] This is for example characterized by the juridical socialization, the rules of interpreting the law, legal theory, the hierarchical structure of the court system, the role of precedent (Eckardt, *supra*, note 1, 138–42).

[64] According to Nelson, 'routines can be understood as the behaviors deemed appropriate and effective in the settings where they are invoked' (Nelson, *supra*, note 4, 68). For a formal treatment of the impact of litigation on the generation of new legal remedies through judge-made legal change, see Fon and Parisi, *supra*, note 42; Fon *et al.*, *supra*, note 42.

[65] See also, Hutter (1986); Parisi (2002); Rubin *et al.* (1999).

[66] Eckardt, *supra*, note 1.

approach presented in Section 2.2 is applied. Again, technological and legal changes are linked through the wealth effects exerted by the new technology, which vary over its life cycle and constitute the economic selection environment. It is assumed that in the early market stages first a collective perception of the problem at hand must be generated. Successful statutory innovations require that the negative externalities produced as by-products of the new technology are collectively perceived as a problem which should be regulated by the law. In the later market stages, bargaining processes dominate, which can be analysed by employing the findings of the Public Choice approach to politics (Section 2.1)

In any case, however, creative political entrepreneurs play an important role. They not only react passively to the demand of voters or interest groups, but actively create commonly shared perceptions of the underlying problems and offer statutory innovations. Again the selection mechanisms of the legislative system limit the variety of viable statutory innovations. The rules laid down by the constitution define the relevant political selection environment. They determine what kind of problems can be treated by legislation and what actors are formally involved. Actors who are formally not allowed to take part in legislation have higher costs of putting through their interests than other parts of the population. The demand for statutory innovations is further influenced by the economic selection environment, since the costs of interest group formation vary according to the type of problem and the opportunity costs of the dominant interest groups.[67] Since these too change systematically over the industry life cycle, again testable hypotheses about the timing and the potential content of statutory innovations demanded for by interest groups can be derived.

Statutory and judge-made legal innovations and their resulting wealth effects not only affect the legal, but also the technological evolution, since the law is part of the selection environment under which technological change takes place (Figure 9.2). Who has to bear the costs of negative technological externalities, which arise as a by-product of technological innovations, is itself a consequence of the legal rules in force. For example, if the producers of the negative externalities have to bear these costs, they will have stronger incentives to invest in technological change which is aimed to reduce these externalities. But if the persons negatively affected have to bear them, they will have incentives to demand products which eventually may help to reduce them. There are incentives for additional technological innovations. However, they will lead to another path of technological change.

Although this approach to the co-evolution of law and technology needs further analytical and empirical elaboration,[68] it provides a uniform and consistent way to cope with the relationship of technological and legal change.

---

[67] The most relevant interest groups are the producers of the negative externalities, their competitors, and the persons negatively affected by the resulting wealth reductions (Eckardt, *supra*, note 1, 161–70).

[68] See for example, Eckardt, *supra*, note 1.

5. LEGAL PARADIGMS AND PATH DEPENDENCE

5.1 Stability Through Legal Paradigms and Path Dependence

With the exception of the last section, the approaches presented thus far focus on the mechanisms of either statutory or judge-made legal change. To derive hypotheses about the direction of legal change, additional complexity has to be taken into account.[69] For this, the concept of legal paradigms may prove helpful.[70] Legal paradigms allow for integrating on the one hand a model of human action, which includes cognitive creativity as an endogenous source of novelty and thus as a variation mechanism, and on the other hand the concept of path dependence, which serves as an additional selection and retention mechanism.

Both the notion of paradigms and of path dependence have been developed in the economic analysis of technological change. Therefore, they allow drawing from the rich insights gained in the evolutionary branch of innovation economics.[71] Legal paradigms can be defined analogous to technological paradigms. This latter concept was introduced by Dosi, who draws on Kuhn's notion of scientific paradigms.[72] Since legal rules can be conceived as socio-technological devices to cope with interpersonal coordination problems and conflicts as a consequence of scarce resources, legal paradigms can be defined as encompassing all positive and negative heuristics how to legally cope with particular problems as well as the specific legal rules generated by and applied to them.[73] A legal paradigm defines both the cognitive frame within which novel legal problem-solutions are looked for as well as the methods used to generate and disseminate legal innovations. A given dominant paradigm entails the prevailing way of perceiving and dealing with legal problems. Only if inconsistencies and contradictions prove too strong under the given legal paradigm, the underlying positive and negative heuristics will be scrutinized and eventually changed.

The legal paradigm in place also delimits the scope for viable legal innovations if a novel problem emerges or a given legal rule is modified. As a consequence, it also strongly influences the direction of legal change, however without prescribing the particular content of the legal rules applied. At any point in time there are a number of different legal rules that can solve the underlying socio-economic problem while at the same time being compatible with the overall legal paradigm. However, the actually applied legal rule is the outcome both of chance and of the contingencies (like the influence of different interest-groups) as well as the result of the legal rules applied in the past and thus of path dependence.

---

[69] Although the interdependence between statutory and judge-made legal change has been addressed by a number of authors, so far no coherent explanation as to the relative weight of these two main mechanisms of legal change has been developed. See, e.g., Boudreaux and Pritchard (1994); Eckardt, *supra*, note 1, 176–201; Hayek, *supra*, note 2; Landes and Posner, *supra*, note 47; Posner, *supra*, note 2.

[70] Eckardt, *supra*, note 1; Kerber and Heine, *supra*, note 1; Heine (2003).

[71] Dosi (1982); Metcalfe, *supra*, note 4; Nelson and Winter, *supra*, note 4; Saviotti (1996).

[72] Kuhn (1970).

[73] Eckardt, *supra*, note 1, 196–200; Kerber and Heine, *supra*, note 1.

Although the concept of path dependence was developed without reference to the notion of paradigms, the two concepts are complementary.[74] While the concept of legal paradigms might serve as a heuristic device that delimits the overall scope for legal innovations, the concept of path dependence helps to explain the mechanisms that link the applied legal rules to one another over time. Therefore, legal innovations are partly shaped by the previously applied legal rules.[75] So far no consistent classification of the factors that cause path dependences through positive feedback effects has been developed.[76] But it seems not to be controversial that sunk and switching costs due to set-up and fixed costs and institution specific-investment, dynamic economies of scale that result from network externalities and learning effects, and complementarities contribute to the persistence of a particular legal path.[77] Furthermore, the complexity and genuine uncertainty that characterize the process of legal change foster path dependence, since the actors involved will rather base their decisions on routines than taking an optimization approach.[78] Such routines are also part of the overall legal paradigm, since the positive and negative heuristics guide both the perception of the legal problem under consideration as well as the search for novel legal problem-solutions.[79]

5.2 Break-outs from Legal Lock-ins

While the literature on path dependence helps to explain legal stability over time, its focus is primarily on lock-ins. As a result, although a legal trajectory might have become inefficient, the path dependence literature provides a rather pessimistic view whether there is a chance of leaving it.[80] However, in the following we will discuss some mechanisms that might lead to break-outs from legal lock-ins.

Based on the neo-institutional economics approach, Woerdman's starting point are the very mechanisms that generate legal lock-ins and thus legal inertia.[81] By turning them upside down, he finds that additional information, decreasing set-up and/or switching costs and learning effects as well as external shocks are the main mechanisms that explain break-outs from lock-ins. There is also an interesting strand of political science literature which deals with path dependences and its underlying mechanisms.[82] It draws the attention on the mechanisms of the political process itself. Stabilizing a legal path once it has been reached involves permanent efforts. Thus by focusing in detail on the underlying

---

74 Arthur (1994); David (1985); Liebowitz and Margolis (1995); North, *supra*, note 13, 92–104.

75 The existing legal rules form a legal trajectory. According to Dosi, a technological trajectory is 'the pattern of "normal" problem solving activity . . . on the ground of a paradigm' (Dosi, *supra*, note 71, 152).

76 For a detailed formal treatment of legal path dependences by applying the concept of frequency-dependency, see Wangenheim, *supra*, note 9.

77 Eckardt, *supra*, note 1; Hathaway (2001); Heine, *supra*, note 70; Kerber and Heine, *supra*, note 1; Kiwit (1995); North, *supra*, note 2, 92–104; Ogus (2002); Woerdman (2004).

78 Nelson, *supra*, note 4; Nelson and Winter (1982), 96–136; Nelson and Winter, *supra*, note 4.

79 Eckardt, *supra*, note 1, 196–200; Woerdman, *supra*, note 7.

80 Kerber and Heine, *supra*, note 1.

81 Woerdman, *supra*, note 77; Crouch and Farrell (2004).

82 Ebbinghaus (2005).

processes which hinder or enable change, additional mechanisms explaining outbreaks from given legal paths can be derived as well as empirically testable hypotheses.

Within an evolutionary economics perspective, there are mechanisms at work which continuously cause both endogenous as well as exogenous variation, making a move from a given legal path more likely. Creative agents, that is political, legal and economic entrepreneurs permanently provide new ideas and novel actions. In this way they increase the internal heterogeneity and thus the likelihood of endogenous change. Besides, due to the complexity of the interaction between the different subsystems, also exogenous change is a permanent feature. It not only occurs in the form of discretionary shocks, but happens in a gradual fashion. Path dependence involves multiple equilibria, where moves from one path to another are at least partly due to frequency-dependency effects. In this way also incremental changes, be they endogenous or exogenous, can lead to a break-out from former lock-ins.

In addition, the more intense competition is within the political and economic sphere, the more variation is generated. Intra- and inter-jurisdictional competition not only serve as a 'discovery procedure', but also as a mechanism that helps to foster break-outs from given legal paths. There is an evolutionary strand of literature which deals with the different forms and different conditions that have to be fulfilled for inter-jurisdictional competition to produce the desired outcomes.[83] It cannot be assumed that all relevant solutions to political and economic problems are already known. In this view interjurisdictional competition is a mechanism which allows for parallel experimentation on which bundles of public goods and services best fulfill the preferences of the citizens. In contrast to mere sequential experimentation, the parallel testing of different hypotheses in various jurisdictions generates more knowledge about the possible design and outcome of legal innovations than could be obtained otherwise. Institutional competition is a trial and error process which, in principle, allows for a higher rate of learning. As a consequence unsuited legal rules and the related economic policies should be modified or sorted out more easily.

It seems to be useful to classify interjurisdictional competition according to the factors which are mobile between jurisdictions.[84] Depending on whether only information, or also goods and services, or even labor, capital and enterprises are mobile, we observe either yardstick competition or locational competition, each with its own mechanisms to bring about legal change. Furthermore, it has to be distinguished whether actors can choose merely between the whole bundle of legal rules offered by a jurisdiction or whether they are free to choose even single legal rules from various jurisdictions (free choice of law). Only in the latter case interjurisdictional competition is akin to market competition because in that case single legal rules directly compete with one another. In all other cases legal change is almost exclusively the result of intra-jurisdictional competition among the various political actors of the respective jurisdiction.

This short outline of interjurisdictional competition as both a discovery procedure and as a path-breaking mechanism shows its potential for gaining additional insights in legal evolution. However, both more analytical as well as empirical work has to be done to be

---

[83] Kerber (2008); Kerber and Budzinski (2003); Kerber and Heine (2003).
[84] Kerber and Budzinski, *supra*, note 83.

able to fully appreciate the contribution of this approach to our understanding of legal change.

The path dependence of a given legal trajectory might lead to lock-ins which prevent the application of superior legal rules.[85] Nevertheless, a given legal paradigm is compatible with various legal trajectories. Generated by creative actors legal innovations might be adopted which eventually lead to either ramifications of the given legal trajectory[86] or even to competing trajectories. Also shifts between legal paradigms are possible which would imply a change in the positive and negative heuristics applied to the search for legal problem solutions. Although the notion of both legal paradigms and legal path dependences seems to be a fruitful approach to derive additional statements about the direction of legal change over time, more conceptual and empirical work is necessary to explore its contribution to a comprehensive theory of legal change.

6. CONCLUSION AND OUTLOOK

Law matters – both for long-term economic evolution as well as for more short-termed economic performance. The approaches presented above give an overview of the main lines of reasoning about the central mechanisms of legal change from an evolutionary economics perspective. Evolutionary economics seems to be fruitful for explaining the generation and dissemination of legal innovations over time. The approaches discussed show that cognitive behavioral models, which stress creativity as a source for the endogenous generation of novelty, and various methods and concepts developed to explain technological and economic change are also appropriate for dealing with the peculiarities of legal stability and change. In addition, distributional conflicts prove to be a relevant determinant of legal change. Evolutionary economics thus extends the explanatory power of an economic approach to legal evolution.

We are, however, still far from a comprehensive theory of legal change. The most elaborated approaches deal either with statutory or with judge-made legal change. Although progress has been made in comparing different sources of statutory, judicial, and customary law, there is still room for further research, in particular in analysing the interdependence of statutory and judge-made legal change.[87] Moreover, the impact of public bureaucracy on legal change during the implementation and application of legal innovations has been largely neglected so far. An evolutionary economic approach to intra-jurisdictional competition might perhaps be a promising starting point for gaining further insights.

Besides, both legal history and current developments, however, show that legal change does not take place in isolation. Legal rules are often imitated from rules in other jurisdictions and even from quite different legal traditions. Additionally, due to the growing economic and political integration, institutional competition has become more intense

---

85 Kerber and Heine, *supra*, note 1.

86 Such ramifications might result when a legal innovation is generated to solve a particular aspect of the underlying socio-economic problem which so far has been addressed also by the original legal rule. As a consequence, both legal rules will form independent paths in the future.

87 Parisi (2001); Posner, *supra*, note 2.

over the last years. Moreover, both on a regional as well as on a global level there is a growing number of supranational bodies trying to solve coordination problems and internalize externalities among different autonomous jurisdictions. Thus the growing literature on *inter*-jurisdictional legal change seems to be quite promising in increasing our understanding of legal change.

Given intensifying economic integration, the continued analysis of the evolution of law, technology, and the economy remain on the research agenda. In this regard, using the framework provided by Aoki to explicitly integrate legal change in the analysis of institutional change may provide new insights. In addition, more empirical studies on the hypotheses presented by Eckardt can increase our knowledge regarding the utility of this line of reasoning for explaining the interdependences of technological and legal change.

BIBLIOGRAPHY

Aoki, Masahiko (2001), *Toward a Comparative Institutional Analysis*, Cambridge, MA.

Aranson, Peter H. (1998), 'Electoral competition and entrepreneurship', *Advances in Austrian Economics*, **5**, 183–215.

Arthur, Brian W. (1994), *Increasing Returns and Path Dependence in the Economy*, Michigan.

Audretsch, David B. (1995) *Innovation and Industry Evolution*, Cambridge, MA.

Beaulier, Scott A., Peter J. Boettke and Christopher J. Coyne (2004), 'Knowledge, economics and coordination: understanding Hayek's legal theory', *NYU Journal of Law and Liberty*, **1**, 209–223.

Becker, Gary S. (1983) 'A theory of competition among pressure groups for political influence', *Quarterly Journal of Economics*, **98**, 300–371.

Boudreaux, Donald J. and A.C. Pritchard (1994) 'Reassessing the role of the independent judiciary in enforcing interest-group bargains', *Constitutional Political Economy*, **5**: 1–21.

Breton, Albert (1998), *Competitive Governments. An Economic Theory of Politics and Public Finance*.

Buchanan, James M. and Gordon Tullock (1962), *The Calculus of Consent*, Ann Arbor.

Bullock, David S. (1995), 'Are government transfers efficient? An alternative test of the efficient redistribution hypothesis', *Journal of Political Economy*, **103**, 1236–74.

Carbonara, Emanuela and Francesco Parisi (2007), 'Choice of law and legal evolution: Rethinking the market for legal rules', University of Minnesota Law School, *Legal Studies Research Paper Series*, Research Paper No.07-38, http://ssrn.com/abstract=1011376.

Cohen, Wesley M. and Steven Klepper (1992), 'The anatomy of industry R&D intensity distributions', *American Economic Review*, **82**, 773–99.

Cooter, Robert D. and Lewis Kornhauser (1980), 'Can litigation improve the law without the help of judges?', *Journal of Legal Studies*, **9**, 129–63.

Cooter, Robert D. and Daniel L. Rubinfeld (1989), 'Economic analysis of legal disputes and their resolution', *Journal of Economic Literature*, **27**, 1067–97.

Cooter, Robert D. and Thomas Ulen (1988), *Law and Economics*.

Cooter, Robert D. and Thomas Ulen (2007), *Law and Economics*.

Crouch, Colin and Henry Farrell (2004), 'Breaking the path of institutional development? Alternatives to the new determinism', *Rationality and Society*, **16**, 5–43.

David, Paul A. (1985), 'Clio and the economics of QWERTY', *American Economic Review*, **75**, 332–7.

De Alessi, Louis and Robert J. Staaf (1991) 'The common law process: Efficiency or order?', *Constitutional Political Economy*, **2**,107–126.

Denzau, Arthur T. and Douglas C. North (1994), 'Shared mental models: Ideologies and institutions', *Kyklos*, **47**, 3–32.

Dosi, Giovanni (1982), 'Technological paradigms and technological trajectories. A suggested

interpretation of the determinants and directions of technical change', *Research Policy*, **11**, 147–62.
Dunleavy, Patrick (1991), *Democracy, Bureaucracy and Public Choice.*
Ebbinghaus, Bernhard (2005) 'Can path dependence explain institutional change? Two approaches applied to welfare state reform', *Max Planck Institute for the Study of Societies Discussion Paper 05/2.*
Eckardt, Martina (2001), *Technischer Rechtswandel und Rechtsevolution. Ein Beitrag zur ökonomischen Theorie der Rechtsentwicklung am Beispiel des deutschen Unfallschadensrechts im 19. Jahrhundert*, Tübingen.
Eckardt, Martina (2004), 'The evolution of the German tort law in the 19th century – An economic analysis of the evolution of law', in Oliver Volckart (ed.), *Institutional Analysis of History*, Homo Oeconomicus, Special Issue, München, 83–116.
Eggertsson, Thráinn (1990), *Economic Behaviour and Institutions*, New York.
Eichenberger, Reiner and Angel Serna (1996) 'Random errors, dirty information, and politics', *Public Choice*, **86**, 137–56.
Fon, Vincy and Francesco Parisi (2003) 'Litigation and the evolution of legal remedies: A dynamic model', *Public Choice*, **116**, 419–33.
Fon, Vincy, Francesco Parisi, and Ben Depoorter (2005), 'Litigation, judicial path-dependence, and legal change', *European Journal of Law and Economics*, **20**, 43–56.
Frey, Bruno S. and Reiner Eichenberger (1991), 'Anomalies in political economy', *Public Choice*, **68**, 71–89.
Furubotn, Eirik G. and Rudolf Richter (1998), *Institutions and Economic Theory. The Contribution of the New Institutional Economics.*
Hackney, James R. (2003), 'Law and neoclassical economics theory: A critical history of the distribution/efficiency debate', *Journal of Socio-Economics*, **32**, 361–90.
Hathaway, Oona A. (2001), 'Path dependence in the law: The course and pattern of legal change in a common law system', *Iowa Law Review*, **86**, 601–661.
Hayden, Grant M. and Stephen E. Ellis (2007) 'Law and economics after behavioral economics', *Kansas Law Review*, **55**, 629–75.
Hayek, Friedrich A. (1948a), 'Economics and knowledge', in Friedrich A. Hayek (ed.), *Individualism and Economic Order*, Chicago: University of Chicago Press, pp. 33–56.
Hayek, Friedrich A. (1948b), 'The use of knowledge in society' in Friedrich A. Hayek (ed.), *Individualism and Economic Order*, Chicago: University of Chicago Press, pp. 77–91.
Hayek, Friedrich A. (1948c), 'The meaning of competition', in Friedrich A. Hayek (ed.), *Individualism and Economic Order*, Chicago: University of Chicago Press, 92–106.
Hayek, Friedrich A. (1967), 'The results of human action but not of human design', in Friedrich A. Hayek (ed.), *Studies in Philosophy, Politics, and Economics*, London: Henley, pp. 95–105.
Hayek, Friedrich A. (1968/2002), 'Competition as a discovery procedure', *The Quarterly Journal of Austrian Economics*, **5**, 9–23.
Hayek, Friedrich A. (1969) 'Rechtsordnung und Handelnsordnung', in Hayek, Friedrich A. (ed.), *Freiburger Studien. Gesammelte Aufsätze*, Tübingen, pp. 161–98.
Hayek, Friedrich A. (1973), *Law, Legislation and Liberty, Vol.I, Rules and Order*, London: Henley.
Hayek, Friedrich A. (1979), *Law, Legislation and Liberty, Vol.III, The Political Order of a Free Society*, London: Henley.
Hayek, Friedrich A. (1988), *The Fatal Conceit – The Errors of Socialism*, London: Routledge & Kegan Paul.
Heine, Klaus (2003), *Regulierungswettbewerb im Gesellschaftsrecht. Zur Funktionsfähigkeit eines Wettbewerbs der Rechtsordnungen im europäischen Gesellschaftsrecht.*
Herrmann-Pillath, Carsten (2002), *Grundriß der Evolutionsökonomik*, München: Wilhelm Fink.
Hodgson, Geoffrey M. (1993), *Economics and Evolution. Bringing Life Back into Economics.*
Hutter, Michael (1986), 'Transaction cost and communication. A theory of institutional change, applied to the case of patent law', in Göran Skogh and Johann-Matthias Graf von der Schulenburg (eds), *Law and Economics and the Economics of Regulation*, North-Holland, pp. 113–132.
Jolls, Christine, Cass R. Sunstein and Richard Thaler (2001), 'A behavioral approach to law and economics', *Stanford Law Review*, **50**, 1471–1550.

Kerber, Wolfgang (1996), 'Recht als Selektionsumgebung für evolutorische Wettbewerbsprozesse', in Birger P. Priddat and Gerhard Wegner (eds), *Zwischen Evolution und Institution. Neue Ansätze in der ökonomischen Theorie*, pp. 297–326.

Kerber, Wolfgang (2008), 'Institutional change in globalization – Transnational commercial law from an evolutionary economics perspective', *German Law Journal*, **9**, 411–436.

Kerber, Wolfgang and Klaus Heine (2003), 'Institutional evolution, regulatory competition and path dependence', in Pavel Pelikan and Gerhard Wegner (eds), *The Evolutionary Analysis of Economic Policy*, pp. 191–222.

Kerber, Wolfgang and Oliver Budzinski (2003), 'Towards a differentiated analysis of competition of competition laws', *Zeitschrift für Wettbewerbsrecht*, **1**, 411–448.

Kirchgässner, Gebhard and Werner W. Pommerehne (1993), 'Low-cost decisions as a challenge to public choice', *Public Choice*, **77**, 107–115.

Kiwit, Daniel (1995), 'Path-dependence in technological and institutional change – Some criticisms and suggestions,' Max-Planck-Institut zur Erforschung von Wirtschaftssystemen, *Diskussionsbeitrag 10-95*, Jena.

Klepper, Steven (1996), 'Entry, exit, growth, and innovation over the product life cycle', *American Economic Review*, **86**, 562–83.

Klepper, Steven and Elisabeth Graddy (1990), 'The evolution of new industries and the determinants of market structure', *Rand Journal of Economics*, **21**, 27–44.

Knight, Jack (1992), *Institutions and Social Conflict*, Cambridge, MA.

Kuhn, Thomas (1970), *The Structure of Scientific Revolutions*, 2nd ed., Chicago.

Landes, William M. and Richard A. Posner (1979), 'Adjudication as a private good', *Journal of Legal Studies*, **8**, 235–84.

Liebowitz, S.J. and Stephen E. Margolis (1995), 'Path dependence, lock-in and history', *Journal of Law, Economics, and Organization*, **11**, 205–226.

Lindenberg, Siegwart (1998), 'The cognitive turn in institutional analysis: Beyond NIE and NIS?', *Journal of Institutional and Theoretical Economics*, **154**, 716–727.

Meier, Alfred and Susanne Haury (1990) 'A cognitive-evolutionary theory of economic policy', in Kurt Dopfer and Karl F. Raible (eds), *The Evolution of Economic Systems. Essays in Honour of Ota Sik*, p. 77.

Meier, Alfred and Tilman Slembeck (1998), *Wirtschaftspolitik: kognitiv-evolutionärer Ansatz.*

Mercuro, Nicholas and Steven G. Medema (1997), *Economics and the Law. From Posner to Post-Modernism.*

Metcalfe, Stanley J. (1998), *Evolutionary Economics and Creative Destruction.*

Mialon, Hugo M., Paul H. Rubin and Joel L. Schrag (2007), 'Judicial hierarchies and the rule-individual tradeoff,' *Supreme Court Economic Review*, **15**, 3–20.

Mueller, Dennis C. (2003), *Public Choice III*, 3rd ed., Cambridge, MA.

Mueller, Dennis C. (ed.) (1997), *Perspectives on Public Choice: A Handbook*, Cambridge, MA.

Nelson, Richard (1995), 'Recent theorizing about economic change', *Journal of Economic Literature*, **33**, 48–90.

Nelson, Richard and Sidney G. Winter (1982), *An Evolutionary Theory of Economic Change*, Cambridge.

Nelson, Richard and Sidney G. Winter (2002), 'Evolutionary theorizing in economics', *The Journal of Economic Perspectives*, **16**, 23–46.

Niskanen, William (1971), *Bureaucracy and Representative Government*, Hawthorne.

North, Douglass C. (1990a) *Institutions, Institutional Change and Economic Performance*, Cambridge.

North, Douglass C. (1990b), 'A transaction cost theory of politics', *Journal of Theoretical Politics*, **2**, 355–67.

Ogus, Anthony (1999), 'Competition between national legal systems: A contribution of economic analysis to comparative law', *International and Comparative Law Quarterly*, **48**, 405–418.

Ogus, Anthony (2002), 'The economic basis of legal culture: Networks and monopolization', *Oxford Journal of Legal Studies*, **22**, 419–434.

Okruch, Stefan (1999), *Innovation und Diffusion von Normen: Grundlagen und Elemente einer evolutorischen Theorie des Institutionenwandels.*

Olson, Mancur (1965), *The Logic of Collective Action.*
Olson, Mancur (1982), *The Rise and Decline of Nations: Economic Growth, Stagflation and Social Rigidities.*
Parisi, Francesco (2001), 'Sources of law and the institutional design of lawmaking', *Journal of Public Finance and Public Choice*, **19**, 95–122.
Parisi, Francesco (2002), 'Rent-seeking through litigation: Adversarial and inquisitorial systems compared', *International Review of Law and Economics*, **22**, 193–216.
Parisi, Francesco and Jonathan Klick (2004), 'Functional law and economics: The search for value-neutral principles of lawmaking', *Chicago-Kent Law Review*, **79**, 431–50.
Popper, Karl R. (1972), *Objective Knowledge – An Evolutionary Approach*, Oxford: Clarendon Press.
Posner, Eric (1996), 'Law, economics, and inefficient norms', *University of Pennsylvania Law Review*, **144**, 1697–1706.
Posner, Richard A. (1998), *Economic Analysis of Law.*
Posner, Richard A. (2007), *Economic Analysis of Law.*
Priest, George L. (1977), The common law process and the selection of efficient rules'. *Journal of Legal Studies*, **6**, 65–82.
Priest, George L. and Benjamin Klein (1984), 'The selection of disputes for litigation', *Journal of Legal Studies*, **13**, 1–55.
Rowley, Charles K. (1989), 'Public choice and the economic analysis of law' in N. Mercuro (ed.), *Law and Economics*, Boston/Dordrecht/London, 123–173.
Rowley, Charles K., Robert D. Tollison, and Gordon Tullock (eds) (1988), *The Political Economy of Rent Seeking.*
Rubin, Paul H. (1977), 'Why is the common law efficient?', *Journal of Legal Studies*, **6**, 51–63.
Rubin, Paul H., Christopher Curran, and John F. Curran (1999), 'Litigation versus legislation: Forum shopping by rent seekers', *Independent Institute Working Paper #8*, http://www.independent.org/tii/WorkingPapers/LitigationVsLeg.pdf, 11.11.2003, accessed on 27 March 2008.
Saviotti, Paolo P. (1996), *Technological Evolution, Variety and the Economy.*
Schumpeter, J. (1934), *Theory of Economic Development.*
Schumpeter, Joseph A. (1950), *Capitalism, Socialism, and Democracy.*
Slembeck, Tilman (1997), 'The formation of economic policy: A cognitive-evolutionary approach to policy-making', *Constitutional Political Economy*, **8**, 225–54.
Slembeck, Tilman (2003), 'Ideologies, beliefs, and economic advice – A cognitive-evolutionary view on economic policy-making', in Pavel Pelikan and Gerhard Wegner (eds), *The Evolutionary Analysis of Economic Policy*, Cheltenham: Edward Elgar, pp. 128–61.
Tullock, Gordon (1998), *On Voting. A Public Choice Approach.*
Vanberg, Viktor (1994), *Rules and Choice in Economics.*
Wangenheim, Georg von (1993), 'The evolution of judge-made law', *International Review of Law and Economics*, **13**, 381–411.
Wangenheim, Georg von (1995), *Die Evolution von Recht. Ursachen und Wirkungen häufigkeitsabhängigen Verhaltens in der Rechtsfortbildung.*
Witt, Ulrich (2003), *The Evolving Economy: Essays on the Evolutionary Approach to Economics.*
Wittman, Donald (1989), 'Why democracies produce efficient results', *Journal of Political Economy*, **97**, 1395–1424.
Wittman, Donald (1995), *The Myth of Democratic Failure: Why Political Institutions are Efficient.*
Woerdman, Eric (2004), 'Legal inertia and path dependence: An economic exploration of analogies and definitions', in Aloys Prinz, Albert E Steenge and Jörg Schmidt (eds), *Institutions in Legal and Economic Analysis*, Münster: LIT Verlag, pp. 23–45.
Wohlgemuth, Michael (2002a), 'Evolutionary approaches to politics', *Kyklos*, **55**, Fasc.2, 223–246.
Wohlgemuth, Michael (2002b), 'Democracy and opinion falsification: Towards a new Austrian political economy', *Constitutional Political Economy*, **12**, 223–46.

10. The genesis of law: on the paradox of law's origin and its *supplément*

Marc Amstutz

How did law originate? Was it by distinguishing itself from that which was not lawful? But then, which came first, lawfulness or unlawfulness? Or is there another possibility? *Ex facto ius oritur*? As so often the case, it is Luhmann who takes the most radical stance: law has no beginning, it starts from the middle. 'Legal practice,' he writes, 'always operates in situations where the law is an historical given, since otherwise the idea that it is distinguishable as legal practice would never even occur to it. Thus, from an historical point of view, law does not have any beginning; there are only situations in which it is sufficiently plausible to assume that the practice of observing legal norms also existed prior to that time.'[1] Law begins, in other words, with an act of differentiation, perhaps no more than the creation of a before and an after, a construct that, like all such distinctions, is possible only in hindsight.

In systems theory, every social system requires a primary distinction on the basis of which it operates. The political system distinguishes between power and the lack thereof; the economy between what represents value and what does not; art between what fits certain aesthetic criteria and what fails to do so. For the legal system, the primary distinction upon which it operates is that between the lawful and the unlawful. A side product of this logic of distinctions, however, is that it obscures all beginnings. This is its inevitable consequence, as it were. The logic of distinctions thus makes it impossible to provide an origin to law 'by referring to a supreme norm.'[2] Every legal system is founded, rather, on a paradox: on the impossibility of applying its primary distinction to itself. The fact that law is incapable of providing an answer as to whether the distinction between the lawful and the unlawful is, in itself, lawful or unlawful, devolves from the very purpose of drawing distinctions in the first place. That purpose is to create two distinct sides, and to oblige an observing system to choose one of them as its observation point – while keeping the other side in reserve, in case it decides to change places. The line that divides them lies neither on one side nor on the other: 'If observation is an act of differentiation, the point of differentiation itself still remains unobservable.'[3] This is the blind spot intrinsic to all systems.[4]

It follows that all systems (including legal systems) originate in a paradox. It is this very paradox – in the form of blind spot – that actually makes the act of observation possible.

1 Luhmann 2004: 91.
2 Luhmann 2004: 103.
3 Luhmann 2002: 64.
4 Von Foerster 1984: 289.

The logical consequence of this is that any attempt to provide legal systems with a foundation must necessarily be dogmatic in character. There can be no 'first cause' (such as God, the king, reason or, the most recent candidate, efficiency). Law rests upon itself or, more precisely, upon its own operations. The question this raises is, of course, whether the paradox of its origin leads to a paralysis of the legal system. This does not seem to be the case, for the system has developed well-proved instruments for rendering the paradox invisible: in real life, the founding paradox tends either to be obscured, by a self-invented myth, or to be externalized[5] (by being relegated to the realm of politics, for example, under the pretext of what is termed political sovereignty).[6]

A legal system's observation operations are, as a rule, fully capable of dealing with law's foundational paradox as long as the system (like life itself) remains a *long fleuve tranquille*,[7] that is, as long as it is taken as an 'historical given' operating on a 'social continuum.' The question arises, however, as to whether this also applies to legal systems operating in a situation of social *anomie*,[8] that is, in situations where the social discourse faces a crisis, becomes unstable, is disrupted or destroyed. An example of legal systems that must operate on such shaky ground are those of 'transitional justice.'[9] This is the term currently in use to describe a flourishing branch of interdisciplinary research dealing with the processes by which totalitarian or dictatorial regimes are transformed into democratic ones.[10] As concerns the development of law during such processes, researchers address the issue of the contribution law can make in efforts to come to terms with prior injustice. What, in other words, is the function of law as a function of transition? I will refer to such law as 'transitional law.' The results of *transitional justice scholarship* on this subject have remained – in striking contrast to the effort that has been expended – surprisingly uncertain, vague and obscure. What scholars are trying to do is to tame a legal monster: the gorgon of retroactivity, which has been turning jurists to stone for quite some generations now.[11] The reason for their mortification is that retroactivity is seen as an affliction, caused by a fundamental perversion of the concept of justice. Subjecting an unjust regime to legal norms that came into force only after the fall of that regime, to which, in other words, the members of the fallen regime had no possibility of adjusting their conduct, it is argued, leads only to a multiplication of injustice – or more accurately, to its dissemination.[12]

This, as can easily be seen, is mere dogma. It serves only to obscure, or to externalize, the paradox that inheres both in the old and in the new legal system. What are the

---

5 This strategy (and its limitations where there is an unfortunate choice of antonyms) is recognizable, for example, in Koschorke 1999: 57, who tries to avoid the problem by introducing the term 'technical genesis' – with only limited success.

6 See Luhmann 1988: 153–7; Clam 2004: 136–8.

7 This in the sense of the ambivalence in the film by Chatiliez 1988.

8 Durkheim 1998: 360–1.

9 Roht-Arriaza 2006: 1–2.

10 See the overview in Teitel 2000.

11 See Ehard 1949; there is, of course, a certain distinction that must be drawn here: the concept of retroactivity differs in continental European usage not insignificantly from that prevailing in Anglo-Saxon legal circles; on this, see the detailed treatment in Burchard 2006: 827–8. No further elaboration on this distinction is required here.

12 Meltzer 1947: 456.

arguments put forth to render the dogma more plausible? In the period immediately following the Second World War, when the subject of transitional justice first began to attract scholarly interest,[13] there were basically two main lines of reasoning that developed.[14]

The first seems to treat the mystery of *transitional justice* as if it were the Rosetta stone, attempting to decipher it by constructing a seemingly endless series of communication loops between the various social systems in society. Hart's positivism is the representative example of this type of argument.[15] Hart saw the retroactive abrogation of the corrupt laws of a fallen regime as a dangerous precedent. Violation of the principle of non-retroactivity involved, in his view, the sacrifice of 'a very precious principle of morality endorsed by most legal systems,' and he advised against superimposing new laws on the old *ex post facto*.[16] New laws, so the argument goes, should be applied only to future events; for past events the laws in force at the time must be allowed to stand.[17] The problem with this standpoint, of course, is that the Lyotardian collision between the origin paradox of the abrogated legal system and that of the transitional laws is further exacerbated by another, no less paradoxical question: was it lawful or unlawful to institute a new legal system in the place of the one that had been demolished. By what right does this legal demolition take place, if not by brute force? If we accept the right of force, however, we shift the paradox of law to an entirely different realm, namely that of politics. Like Hart, with his construct of overlapping cross-references between morality, justice, law and politics, we find ourselves caught up in a never-ending chain of discordant systemic resonances.[18]

The inadequacy of positivism for dealing with transitional periods led to the development of a second line of argument. This was an attempt to resolve the paradox of transitional justice by engaging in a kind of 'bidding war' between law and morality,[19] or, perhaps more accurately, by hedging them against each other:

> [T]he dilemma . . . [is] that of meeting the demands of order [viz. the internal morality of law] on the one hand, and those of good order [viz. the external morality of law], on the other. Of course no pat formula can be derived from this phrasing of the problem. But, unlike legal positivism, it does not present us with opposing demands that have no living contact with one another, that simply shout their contradictions across a void.[20]

Law and morality, in other words, are invited to sit down at the social negotiating table as equal partners![21] Fuller, the leading proponent of this view (and not all that much at

---

[13] See e.g. Teitel 2005: 839.
[14] Meltzer 1947: 455–6.
[15] For a further example, see Teitel 2005: 847–9.
[16] Hart 1958: 619.
[17] Ehard 1949: 234–6.
[18] Finch 1947: 34, discloses superbly this type of paradox in his analysis of the motives of the Nuremberg decision; see also Dubber 1993: 1807–9.
[19] Fuller 1958: 657; see also Dubber 1993: 1826; for the differentiation between *internal* and *external morality of law,* see Fuller 1964.
[20] Fuller 1958: 657; see also Dubber 1993: 1826.
[21] See also Burchard 2006: 827.

variance with the position famously taken by Radbruch)[22] begins with the observation that the law of the regime that has been overthrown has in most cases become so far removed from (external) morality that it ceases to be law. In such cases, he argues, the enactment of a retroactive statute would be preferable: 'I would see such a statute as a way of symbolizing a sharp break with the past.'[23] The difficulty with this line of reasoning is that the social relevance of the retroactive laws remains necessarily uncertain: are they law or non-law? A living system or *lettre morte*, socially speaking, with neither function nor effect? In this sense, Fuller's theory falls apart precisely at the point where it comes to answering the central question of transitional law. Despite this failure, however, it is rich in insight: in speaking of a '*sharp break with the past*,' it admits that even retroactive law depends on social embeddedness. *Ex post facto* law represents, after all, only a break with past law, not with the social discourse. It is, however, only able to perform its function, can only stabilize normative expectations in society, where such expectations exist for it to work with, that is, where such expectations – in the form of social practices, conventions, customs, usages, standards, deep-rooted convictions, and so forth – are actually present in the transitional society. Unless such expectations are there, no law can emerge, the enactment of statutes becomes simply window dressing and the courts no longer serve any real purpose. But do normative expectations exist in periods of transition? This is a question that it might have been useful to investigate further.

Unfortunately, it is precisely this insight that was left by the wayside in the follow-up to the exchange between Hart and Fuller.[24] Discouraged by the apparently insuperable difficulties of transitional law, vexed by the seeming impossibility of reconciling the demands of legal, moral and political fairness, transitional justice scholarship gradually reached a consensus that the paradoxical dilemmas of transitional law that plagued the discipline's founding generation were nothing but an unnecessary encumbrance, a heuristic obstacle to be discarded as thoroughly as possible.[25] Today one reads:

> [T]he dominant view in the academic literature is that transitional justice is counterproductive because it interferes with the development of democratic institutions and market economies. The interference takes many forms – overburdening courts, undermining property rights, depriving the government of experienced personnel, draining the treasury, burdening officials with complex technical problems, and confronting the judicial system with insoluble moral dilemmas.[26]

It is thus not surprising that an interdisciplinary, holistic approach to the subject has emerged in recent years, which seeks to develop a methodology for weighing and accommodating historical, political, cultural, social welfare, economic, societal and technological considerations – and manifests the characteristic lack of analytical precision found in all trade-off models.[27] What this means, quite simply, is that the function of transitional

---

22 Radbruch 1946: 105–6.

23 Fuller 1958: 661; see also Ehard 1949: 223 (with references to materials from the Nuremberg trial).

24 Dubber 1993: 1807–8.

25 Roht-Arriaza 2006: 7; Huyse 1995: 51–2; Elster 2004.

26 Posner and Vermeule 2004: 825.

27 Sriram 2005: 101–3; Lutz 2006: 328, 336–8.

law has been sacrificed at the altar of pragmatism – and this without having first determined whether a question of existential social importance is involved. What remains is an uneasy feeling: can we just leave it at that, that transitional law rests on a game of judicial roulette, that it is nothing but a matter of institutional chance?

Legal theory has, of course, not been idle while all this was going on. In response to the *non liquet* of transitional justice scholarship, jurists have developed a new, counter-intuitive theory: transitional law, they posit, is, in fact, ordinary law and, in its operations, entirely indistinguishable from 'historically given' law.[28] This is not to deny the existence of retroactivity in periods of transitional justice. Rather, it is argued that, in order to remain functional, every legal system, whether transitional or ordinary, must avail itself of certain techniques for the *post hoc* adaptation of rights and obligations.[29] How is this to be understood, however, from the perspective of the logic of distinctions? Must we interpret the theory of *transitional justice as ordinary justice* in the sense that transitional law also starts from the middle? Does Luhmann's dictum concerning ordinary law also hold for transitional law? Can transitional law operate only in situations where 'it is sufficiently plausible to assume that the practice of observing legal norms also existed prior to that time'?[30] What does 'prior to that time' mean in this context? Which legal norms was it ostensibly the practice to observe? How does it occur to transitional law that it is distinguishable as a form of legal practice when it has not yet practiced any law?

If transitional law is understood (as it is here) in the narrower sense of retroactive law,[31] that is, in the sense of law that is in the process of emerging, it follows that the only thing such law can see, in observing itself, is the distinction between the lawful and the unlawful. The legal system, however, has not yet begun to communicate along the lines of this primary distinction. This being the case, it is clear that there can be no simple yes or no answers to the questions just posed. The brief recapitulation of current theories of transitional justice, as described above, is sufficient to allow us to surmise the reasons that our understanding of these matters is still so confused. On the one hand, the legal scholarship does not seem to have any existing theory at its disposal on which transitional law can plausibly be founded. At the same time, transitional justice scholarship has failed to draw a sharp enough distinction between sociological observation, which is external to law, and theoretical analysis, based on the internal logic of law, to allow an adequate treatment of the phenomenon. In the following I would like to demonstrate that the development of sound theories of transitional law will be possible only if we can devise sufficiently viable methods of observation to permit a fuller socio-legal understanding of transitional justice. What this means is that if we are to overcome the paralysis of orthodox legal

---

28 Posner and Vermeule 2004: 761–2; Meltzer 1947: 456.

29 As examples of such techniques, Posner and Vermeule (2004: 793–6) name: (1) the appeal to higher law (up to and including natural law), (2) the application of nominal law (that is, of legal norms that were not taken seriously under a former regime, such as the administration of an outgoing President in the US, and were thus not enforced), (3) the enactment of interpretative statutes (in order to give new meaning to the laws of the ousted regime), and (4) the extension of statutes of limitations (in order to prosecute violators of the old law even after the regime has changed).

30 See above p. 226.

31 See above pp. 228–9.

theory in the face of transitional law, it will be necessary to arrive at an understanding of the origin of law that is sophisticated enough to match the complexity of the problem. In more concrete terms, my thesis is as follows:

(1) Observation based on the logic of distinctions is not capable of providing a basis for differentiating between transitional law and 'historically given' law, and is, thus, unable to determine the extent to which transitional law is, in fact, law. This is due to the circumstance that the blind spot of legal systems is precisely that: blind. As a result, the point at which each of the two categories of law takes its respective beginning is imperceptible. In order to get past this obstacle, it is necessary to adopt a mode of observation based on function, which provides a different approach to the problem, namely this: in contrast to ordinary law, transitional law does not act to stabilize any manifest expectations. In a transitional society, the kinds of expectations that are suitable for use as the foundation of a transitional legal system have not yet emerged – at least not fully enough to be tangible. This leads then to the question: is law, in order to be characterized as law, contingent upon expectations?

(2) To this my response would be: expectations are law's *supplément*, the hidden but essential element that fills in something that is missing from a *logos* – in the present case, from law – the lack of which severely compromises the consistency of the *logos*. But how, precisely, is this to be understood? It is clear that expectations are not the 'source' from which law springs. This follows not only from the logic of distinctions, but also from the autopoietic nature of law, that is, from the fact that it is the law itself that generates the elements out of which it is constructed. In order to fully comprehend the concept of expectations as law's supplement, a far less simplistic theory of law's origin must be developed. This can be achieved, I would argue, by extending Girard's fundamental anthropology and, in particular, of his theory of the scapegoat, in a direction that has not yet been investigated. By doing so, it becomes possible to demonstrate that expectations – in Derridan *différance* to law (and vice versa) – do indeed provide the matrix of distinctions that is required for the practice of law. In a further step, we are able to arrive at a concept of the genesis of law that is not based on origins, and is thus freed from metaphysical argument, which serves only as an impediment. This, however, gives rise to another question: does transitional law also have a supplement, a functional equivalent to expectations, which is able to provide an equally effective matrix of distinctions for the practice of transitional law?

(3) My suggestion here would be to make use of the concept of latency. It has been known for some time now that it is possible for structures to exist within a system, of which the system itself is not aware and cannot make operative use, but which may nevertheless, as 'contingencies,' be retrieved by the system when it needs them. The question then is whether the latent expectations of a society are also capable of giving rise to the range of distinctions that the operations of law require for achieving social relevance. Obviously, from a metaphysical point of view, this process will be unobservable, since no synchronous loops between the legal order and that of the latent social expectations will be visible. On the other hand, if we shift our conception of origin from one based on creation to one based on *différance* – as will be attempted in what follows – the situation takes on a different aspect. It then makes perfect sense to seek the connections between transitional law and the latent expectations that lie dormant in the society. By identifying certain distinctions, which were previously obscured, we arrive at a basis from which we

can observe transitional law, and thus provide ourselves with the firm footing we need to unravel the conundrum of transitional justice.

The great contribution of Luhmann's *Rechtssoziologie*[32] lies in its having succeeded in formulating the normative 'ought' in empirical terms. The hypothesis it presents is that 'law solves a problem in relation to time. This problem always occurs when one communicates in society and when the ongoing communication is not sufficient in itself . . . but is guided by expectations in a temporal extension of its meaning and expresses those expectations.'[33] Expectations are thus seen not as an element of individual psychology, but as a temporal aspect to the significance of discourse. This leads further to a definition of the function of law: the stabilization of expectations over time. Because law must build on expectations to stabilize relationships over time, it must accept the fact that, in certain cases, expectations do not correspond with reality and are, in consequence, disappointed. It is for this reason that law is obliged to decide the outcome of conflicts in advance, to demonstrate 'social partiality,' in other words. It is obliged to discriminate, without being seen to do so, and must therefore resort to camouflage. It does this by using symbols. Accordingly, legal norms appear as a weave of *symbolically* generalized expectations: 'In this way, not only are generalized instructions issued which are independent of given situations, but also symbols always represent something which is invisible and cannot become visible – here that something is the future. Using symbolization society produces specific stabilities and specific sensibilities . . . One relies on the symbol precisely because one cannot see what the meaning of the symbol refers to.'[34] The function of legal norms, accordingly, lies within society's attempt to use expectations as a means of coming to terms with an uncertain future. They provide a sense of security.

In discussing the sociological function of law, Luhmann argues that the legal system as a whole is anchored in the expectations that themselves arise out of other expectations.[35] This suggests that expectations must be seen as a 'precondition' to law. Law without expectations has no function – and not having any function it leads the existence of a barren planet (which creates a conceptual problem for transitional law, to be discussed in detail, below[36]). This makes it necessary to ask what the nature of the relationship is between expectations and the operations of the legal system. It is clear that this cannot be a generative/causative relationship, if for no other reason than that law's differentiation is founded on the reflexivity of its own operations. Luhmann has a somewhat fatalistic take on the question. On the one hand, he notes, law serves to restrain and control the unbridled proliferation of untold expectations in society, thus making it possible to determine what is officially lawful or unlawful. At the same time, however, in modern society it is virtually impossible for law to make co-expectation, that is, the development of normative expectations out of normative expectations, a binding condition upon which decisions are premised. It remains completely indifferent thereto.[37] Luhmann here adopts

32 Luhmann 1987: 27–8.
33 Luhmann 2004: 142.
34 Luhmann 2004: 146.
35 Luhmann 2004: 159.
36 See below pp. 241–4.
37 Luhmann 2004: 160–1.

– and surprisingly so, as it seems to me – the prevailing attitude in legal theory, largely descended from positivistic arguments: 'Law puts itself at the disposal of the individual users in this way, abstracting from the social context of their motives, from the pressures to which they are exposed or, conversely, from their separate motivations.'[38] This he sees as the price that modern society pays for 'cutting the legal system loose from its social moorings.'[39] What this means, however – and this alone is what matters here – is that the relationship between expectations and law has been set off into blind flight, left to the toss of a coin.

There are today good reasons for undertaking a reassessment of the grounds for Luhmann's fatalism. Fully in line with the legal realist school of thought, which took law as being 'erected upon an edifice of social practice,'[40] more recent approaches to legal theory assume that the interconnections between the orders of social expectations and the operations of legal systems are more densely looped than Luhmann suspected even as late as 1993. This, in any case, is the sense in which modern theories of legal argumentation must be understood. These estimate the degree to which judicial and administrative decisions are free from internal systemic constraints as markedly higher than is taken to be the case in traditional theories of statutory interpretation.[41] Proponents of these more recent theories have set themselves the goal of getting closer to the bottom of the seemingly unfathomable but nevertheless unmistakably vibrant relationship between law's operations and society's expectations.[42] A similar proposition today also moves the theory of conventions,[43] which begins by identifying a range of social normativities, which are constantly in motion, acting to stimulate, encourage and strengthen each other. Law, it is then posited, joins in this ongoing process, cooperating as a means of reinforcing its own normativity.[44] The gradually emerging discipline of juridical grammatology also points in this direction, arguing that written laws consist in a differentiation of signs, the meaning of which undergoes constant transformation through the 'iterability' of writing. Seen in this way, they can be said to work within their context as a source of mutual irritation between society (social expectations) and the law (legal norms), practically forcing and accelerating an exchange between them.[45]

But how is the fact of a relationship between expectations and the law to be provided with a theoretical basis? The metaphysical concept of a beginning, or an origin, as we have seen,[46] does not bring us any further. Luhmann once remarked – and his remark will serve as the point of departure for the discussion that follows – that the strict demarcation of decision-making structures within the legal system can have an erosive effect on the system's own foundations, insofar as those foundations rest on social expectations. A legal system that takes its own decisions, without regard for expectations can, in the end,

---

38 Luhmann 2004: 161–2.
39 Luhmann 2004: 162.
40 Patterson 1992: 956; Cohen 1935; Llewellin 1930.
41 Larenz 1991; Bydlinski 1991.
42 Ladeur and Augsberg 2005; Müller and Christensen 2004; Goebel 2001.
43 Vesting 2007: 124–5.
44 Ladeur 2000: 110–11, 153; 2004: 31–4; 2006: 43–7.
45 Amstutz 2007.
46 See above p. 231.

only survive if it is 'supported by politics.'[47] As this is not normally the case, it would seem that expectations are a peculiar kind of imperative condition for law, impalpable though they may be. I would like to take this theory even one step further and postulate that there is a 'logic of the supplement' that forms the link between expectations and the law:[48] expectations are law's supplement, which, as we shall see, provides us with a sufficiently nuanced response to the paradox of origin to come to terms with its complexity.[49]

Derrida's concept of the *supplément*,[50] like so much of what has productively unsettled contemporary philosophy, was introduced in the second part of his *Grammatology*. There, in a reading of Rousseau's *Essay on the Origin of Languages* – a reading that is expressly meant to tantalize, that is, in Derrida's own words, a reading that is both seductive and dangerous – he deconstructs the logocentrism of traditional Western thought.[51] Derrida argues determinedly against the idea that writing is something secondary to speech, to '*la parole*.' In fact, it is a supplement to the *logos*,[52] that is, there inheres in it a strange ambiguity, 'a fatal necessity . . . that the substitute [viz., writing] make one forget the vicariousness of its own function and make itself pass for the plenitude of a speech whose deficiency and infirmity it nevertheless only *supplements*.'[53] Accordingly, the notion of the supplement is to be understood in two different, but strangely and, at the same time, necessarily interwoven senses. On the one hand, the supplement adds something to the *logos* that fills a gap, a deficiency that had gone unnoticed because of the apparent perfection of the *logos*. At the same time, however, the supplement also has a second meaning,

---

47 Luhmann 2004: 160; a great deal of caution must be used when speaking of legal systems as being supported 'politically,' as the term easily lends itself to misunderstanding. What is meant here is not the political process of lawmaking. This process produces statutes that disrupt the existing legal system and thus goad it into action, without in any way having a manipulative effect on the conditions that allow for the autopoiesis of the legal system (see Amstutz 2003). The idea behind the term 'politically supported legal systems' is something entirely different: what is intended here is not the legislative process, but situations in which political forces use their power to intervene in the workings of society in order to keep the legal system alive 'artificially.' This 'artificial' legal system is (at least in its most extreme forms) no longer an autopoietic system, but an *opérateur politique*. It serves merely as an alibi for politically motivated judicial proceedings which, in reality (due to the fact that no real legal system exists) are not judicial proceedings at all but merely an operation of the political system. It is this phenomenon that is referred to in the present text when speaking of 'politically supported legal systems' or of 'political law.'

48 Dupuy and Varela 1992: 2.

49 Naturally, Luhmann (2004: 461) also recognized the potential of this construct, but then, in a curious logical somersault, turned the notion of the supplement on its head: 'Of course, one can – on detecting the secret of such arbitrariness – "deconstruct" this solution [viz., the hierarchization of the relationship between the *logos* and its supplement, as widely accepted in the literature]. However, one can then also deconstruct the deconstruction itself, by demonstrating that this step only leads to the paradox of the beginning or the paradox of the origin, which every system has dealt with in its past.' There is, of course, no logical or other mistake in Luhmann's attempt to reduce deconstruction *ad absurdum*. The question nevertheless arises as to the usefulness of inviting metaphysics back into the argument, by deconstructing deconstruction, after it has been just been deconstructed out.

50 Derrida 1997: 144–5.

51 See as a general introduction to the concept of the *supplément* Dooley and Kavanagh 2007: 24; see also the finely nuanced remarks on the concept of deconstruction in Courtine 2007: 21–2.

52 Nancy 2007: 121–2.

53 Derrida 1997: 144.

namely that of a substitute, of a representative: '[T]he supplement supplements. It adds only to replace. It intervenes or insinuates itself *in-the-place-of* . . . Somewhere, something can be filled up *of itself*, can accomplish itself, only by allowing itself to be filled through sign and proxy. The sign is always the supplement of the thing itself.'[54] What both of these senses of the supplement have in common is their 'exteriority':[55] regardless of whether the supplement serves as an addition or as a substitute, it is always something foreign to the *logos*, external, peripheral. But it is also not a particular occurrence, but only a trace, an *archi-trace*, an originary absence in the sense of an *absence of origin*. What this indicates is that the supplement is, in fact, a means of understanding origins. In order to demonstrate this, it will be necessary first to take a step back.

The supplement functions in such a manner that its encounter with the *logos*, which behaves as if it were autonomous, and sees itself as sufficient unto itself, inevitably sets in motion a 'vicious circle . . ., which undermines . . . [the *logos*'] pretension to autonomy from within.'[56] This occurs because the supplement is entwined with the *logos* in a strangely reciprocal relationship: although the *logos* appears to be whole and pure, it would lose all of its consistency without the supplement.[57] The supplement is both superfluous and indispensable at the same time. 'Since the ideal of philosophy is to reach the truth without mediation it must therefore deny the only means it has of expressing itself: writing. Bluntly put, philosophy writes W: 'W: "this is not writing."'[58]

How precisely does the logic of the supplement bring us here any further? On closer inspection, one sees that it serves to transform the relationship between *logos* and supplement into one of circular causality – or to use the language of systems theory: it brings the relationship to operative closure. The question of origin shifts from a stagnant debate over 'first causes' to the far more compelling proposition of *différance* – and one sees immediately what Derrida was thinking, when he made the apposition: '. . . supplement, another name for *différance*.'[59] By equating these two notions, Derrida brings into play a dimension of supplement theory that he describes as '*constitutive, productive, and originary causality*.'[60] *Différance* draws attention to a 'generative motion' intrinsic to the function of the supplement, but which is contained neither in the additive nor in the substitutive sense of the term,[61] and is brought to light by Derrida's now famous 'gross spelling mistake':[62] 'We must consider that in the usage of our language the ending *-ance* remains undecided *between* the active and passive.'[63] *Différance* is thus, by nature, neither active nor passive, but lies somewhere in-between[64] – a notion that, as we shall see, is of crucial importance in the relationship between expectations and law. Derrida's

---

54 Derrida 1997: 145.
55 Levinas 1961.
56 Dupuy and Varela 1992: 2.
57 Sallis 2007: 43.
58 Dupuy and Varela 1992: 3.
59 Derrida 1997: 150.
60 Derrida 1982: 9.
61 On these two senses of the term *supplément*, see above p. 234–5.
62 Derrida 1982: 3.
63 Derrida 1982: 9.
64 Bass 2007: 417, 419–20.

ideas concerning *différance*, which is '*neither a concept nor a word among others*,'[65] were worked out, like those concerning the supplement, within the context of linguistic theory. Here, Derrida takes as his point of departure Saussure's theory of signs,[66] according to which the identity of a sign is constituted by its delimiting itself from all other signs at the moment it is expressed.[67] A sign acquires its precise contours by being that which the others are not.[68] The semantic meaning of signs is thus defined by Saussure not positively, by their content, but negatively, by their difference to other signs ('difference with an "*e*"'[69]). Their meaning, in consequence, is a function of an open system, constantly engaged in further differentiation. 'This interweaving results in each "element" – phoneme or grapheme – being constituted on the basis of the trace within it of the other elements of the chain or system.'[70]

Against this backdrop, it becomes possible to grasp the idea that *différance* (which – again – is neither a 'concept' nor a 'word') carries with it. In Derrida's words:

> What is written as *différance*, then, will be the playing movement that 'produces' – by means of something that is not simply an activity – these differences, these effects of difference. This does not mean that the *différance* that produces differences is somehow before them, in a simple and unmodified – in-different – present. *Différance* is the non-full, non-simple, structured and differentiating origin of differences. Thus, the name 'origin' no longer suits it.[71]

Seen in this light, the supplement (once again: 'another name for *différance*') begins to show a new, dynamic facet to its nature. The supplement functions not only as a substitutive addition, or as an additive substitute within the *logos*, but also enters into a generative relationship with it. The supplement brings about the differences within the *logos* that create its sense – since what is implied by the *logos* is not a content with a positive sense or meaning, but a negative delimitation, an interplay ('*jeu*'), the interplay of differences, which create sense by forming an interwoven aggregate: '[O]n the one hand, these differences *play* . . . On the other hand, these differences are themselves *effects*. They have not fallen from the sky fully formed . . . . [They proceed from] the movement according to which language, or any code, any system of referral in general, is constituted "historically"as a weave of differences.'[72] 'Interplay' and 'effect,' 'tissue of differences': Derrida's choice of words alone illustrates the nature of the supplement (and of *différance*) as something hovering between the active and the passive – and which, in consequence, makes the concept of origin something infinitely more complex than it is in theories of direct causality as found in traditional metaphysical thought.

The question now is: how does the logic of the supplement get us any further in our attempts to gain a more precise understanding of the interplay between social expectations and legal system than has thus far been possible with Luhmann's sociology of law?

---

65 Derrida 1982: 11.
66 Derrida 1997: 30–44.
67 de Saussure 2005: 158–9.
68 Derrida 1981: 25–6.
69 Derrida 1982: 4.
70 Derrida 1981: 26.
71 Derrida 1982: 11; on this conception of origin, see also Caputo 2007: 40–1.
72 Derrida 1982: 11–12.

The thesis that expectations are the supplement of law (which itself then takes on the role of the *logos*), would appear to imply that the relationship between these two factors is 'undecidably' both passive and active: expectations would no longer serve only to passively take up the space left by law's 'hidden deficiency,' but would, at the same time, actively fill the gap with something of import, something operative. In order to argue this thesis, it is necessary to descend from the level of high abstraction at which Luhmann and Derrida construct their theories, and return to that of more concrete theories of social reality. Unfortunately, this also leads us into considerable difficulties, for the simple reason that the current state of legal sociology and legal theory do not offer any conceptual models on which to build such an argument. In other words, the various existing theories of legal order move in a realm that is beyond that of the supplement and *différance* (being, as they are, nearly always of a metaphysical nature). This makes it necessary to cross the bounds of legal theory and look elsewhere – where we find that there do exist, for example (and above all), in anthropological theory, approaches that take into account the categories of thought that derive from the notion of the supplement. Specifically intended here is Girard's fundamental anthropology,[73] to which the parallels in Derrida's conceptual thought have been impressively demonstrated by McKenna.[74]

In order to substantiate my thesis, I will adopt Girard's approach in a very specific manner: I will be using it *parasitically*. What this means, is that because it is not Girard's intent to produce either a sociology of law or a legal theory, his findings cannot simply be assimilated here just as they are. Indeed, they say nothing at all about what it means to consider social expectations as a supplement to law. Their importance bears upon an entirely different field of investigation, which attempts to articulate the role of the sacred in the emergence of the social order. What then, is the purpose of introducing Girard here? The reason is that Girard's theory is structured in a very specific manner, which, I would suggest, can serve as a blueprint for a sociology of law, provide a structure for legal theory. In other words, it can provide a skeleton for the drafting of theories, whereby the original content is replaced with new references, new matter, new resonances. It represents, in the truest sense of the term, a paradigm, according to which thoughts may be structured, not only with regard to the genesis of the sacred and of the cultural (as in Girard's case), but also in connection with other schemes for ordering society. This being the case, in outlining here – in all due brevity – Girard's thought, my intent is not to gain new insights into the theory of social expectations as a supplement to law. What I am attempting, rather, is to identify a design for the theory, a design that is capable of enveloping the various arguments that substantiate this theory into a coherent whole. In a word: the point of the following discussion is to analyse the architectural plan Girard employs in constructing his theory, not the theory itself – in order then to appropriate, parasitically, his infra- or substructures.

Girard's hypotheses on the origin of culture is founded on the theory of mimesis, on the one hand, and that of *méconnaissance*, on the other. The former asserts that we never want anything – have no other 'object' of desire – but that which is desired by others.[75]

---

[73] Girard 1979; 1985; 1986; 1987.

[74] McKenna 1992.

[75] See for the concept of mimetic rivalry, Webb 2002: 2–3.

The mimetic rivalry this gives rise to is seen by Girard as a 'machine,' which stores up conflictual energy and disrupts society by sowing violence in all directions. Mimesis – in contrast to imitation – is not conscious and, in that sense, can be said to take place on a communicative (as opposed to a psychological) level.[76] It detaches itself from the 'object,' on which the mimesis originally focused, and metamorphoses into an explosively violent form of antagonism. As the mimetic attraction of the rival grows, the object of the conflict slowly tends to disappear: it is ripped apart, torn to shreds, destroyed in the clash between all the rivals. In order for mimesis to transform itself into pure antagonism, the object *must* disappear. When that happens, the mimetic crisis spreads and intensifies, ever increasingly.[77] At that point, the society is ruled by naked violence. In reaction to this, archaic and ancient societies invented the scapegoat. The arbitrary choice of a victim and its subsequent sacrifice, which also serves to sanctify it, focuses the violence sown throughout the entire society on a single point, on the victim, and so resolves the mimetic crisis.[78] This engenders ritual, gives birth to the sacred, which, through repetition becomes institutionalized. And it is through such institutions, in Girard's view, that culture emerges.[79]

This final point is, for our present purposes, of no further interest. Of greater importance, in this context, is the fact that, as Girard sees it, such institutions do not function without preconditions. This is where his second theory comes in, that of *méconnaissance.*[80] The mechanism of the sanctified victim only works if the injustice that accompanies it is ignored: the victim – this is its whole significance – is chosen arbitrarily. It is innocent. There is no need for any connection between the victim and the mimetic crisis or the violence it provokes. In order for cohesion to be restored to society, the victim's innocence must remain concealed. Otherwise it would be completely impossible for the victim to fulfill its role as the outsider who, in his guilt, draws the full violence of legitimate rage upon himself. Institutions rest on *méconnaissance* – that is Girard's central thesis.

Girard's theoretical construct is able to hold only because it does not rely on the concept of origins, beginnings, sources, a 'zero hour.'[81] As McKenna[82] explains, Girard replaces the concept of origin with mimetic striving – or, more abstractly, with *différance.* All metaphysical notions of origins, sources, or beginnings are eliminated. This gives Girard's theory a very particular structure, which is in consonance with the concept of the supplement:[83] because it is impossible to trace cultural institutions back to the 'object' on which mimetic desire is focused – that is, because they are, properly speaking, 'without foundation' – they appear, at first glance, as a self-sufficient, autonomous, self-contained *logos.* This, however, is merely a façade, which will not stand up to decon-

---

[76] Girard 2004: 66.
[77] Girard 2004: 76.
[78] Girard 1992: 29–31.
[79] Dumouchel 1992: 80.
[80] Girard 2004: 85–7.
[81] See McKenna 1992: 50–5.
[82] McKenna 1992: 50.
[83] Dumouchel 1992: 77–8.

structive analysis:[84] the existence of Girard's institutions is contingent, indispensably, on the condemnation of the victim to *méconnaissance*. This is ever-present. It is what allows deferral – the deferral of violence through violence. The scapegoat is the supplement to cultural institutions.[85]

If I now prey parasitically on Girard's thesis, in order to substantiate my own with regard to expectations as the supplement to law, what is required is a substitution of the symbiotic pair around which Girard's theoretical structure is built: mimesis and the scapegoat. But how? The first question to be asked relates to how the idea of an imitative rivalry, which, in ancient societies, gives rise to the dissemination of violence, can be translated to a modern context. The truest image, in this context, can be found by shifting the focus – as Dumouchel has most clearly seen – from the aspect of violence to that of complexity: because Girard's anthropology is basically a morphogenetic hypothesis, that is, a theory for explaining the emergence of new forms, it can correspondingly be assumed that in modern societies mimetic antagonisms give rise to ever-increasing complexity.[86] In the following, in a more modern context, I will replace the term 'mimetic antagonisms' with that of 'polemogenetic conflicts.'[87] My point of departure will thus be as follows: polemogenetic, conflictual striving disseminates systemic complexity throughout the society.[88] This then brings us back, once again, to Luhmann's sociology of law, according to which, conflict leads to an immense increase in the complexity of the system.[89] Seen from this perspective, it is clear that, in contrast to the ancient societies Girard deals with, the image of the scapegoat is not of great use for the purpose of 'suspending' complexity – which leads to the question: what, in the modern society, takes the place of the victim Girard postulates? In seeking the answer, it must be kept in mind that conflict, contrary to a view that one finds creeping into even contemporary sociology of law scholarship, is not necessarily a negative phenomenon. Its influence can, on occasion, be quite positive, creative and productive. Society actually has a need for conflicts, which serve as a means of creating, transforming and generalizing expectations.[90] Without conflict it would not be possible to design the main mechanisms used by systems to deal with complexity. The consequence of this for the architecture of my hypothesis is that the role played by the scapegoat in Girard's theoretical edifice is occupied, in the theory here under construction, by social expectations.

Social expectations are what 'defer' social complexity, in that they institutionalize the respective behavioral pattern, which makes them the modern functional equivalent of the victims, who in Girard's model paradoxically 'suspend' violence through violence. Thus, just as the use of scapegoats becomes ritual, giving rise to the sacred, expectations arise out of polemogenetic movements and put themselves on offer for selection by the legal

[84] Note, however: 'La déconstruction ne tue pas les choses: elle les engage dans un entrejeu spectral, hantologique' (Caputo 2007: 142).
[85] Dupuy and Varela 1992: 7.
[86] Dumouchel 1992: 77–9; see also Dupuy and Varela 1992: 8: 'The mimetic mechanism can produce new complexifications, the simple can give birth to the complex.'
[87] Freund 1974: 47; 1983.
[88] Luhmann 1981: 101.
[89] Luhmann 1981: 102.
[90] Luhmann 1981: 105.

system. But this is not all. A further consequence results from this parasitic exploitation of Girard's theoretical structures: *méconnaissance* also plays an essential role with regard to expectations, parallel to that of the innocence of the scapegoat. For the mechanism to function, there must also be a concrete *méconnaissance* of expectations – both by and in the law. Expectations are the legal system's hidden actants, that is, the connective intermediaries that, working in secret, unnoticed and unseen, 'translate' popular jargon, society's slang, into the language of legal operations. They are the multilingual 'interpreters,' as it were, that make it possible for society and the legal system to communicate with each other. Luhmann saw the fact that law fails to take expectations consciously into account as connected with the limitations inherent in the decision-making processes of legal systems: 'The decision-making system cannot transform normative co-expectation into a binding condition upon which decisions are premised. While it is fully capable of providing individuals with individually allocated rights and obligations, it can provide no guarantee for the co-expectations of all other individuals . . . It cannot see the requirement for mutual confirmation inherent in normative expectations . . . and cannot treat it as being a legally material fact. It remains indifferent towards this institutionalization of normative expectations. It is legally irrelevant. Nobody can put forth the strength (or lack) of other people's insistence on maintaining normative expectations as an argument, much less sue for it. The limits of the decision-making system do not let such information through; they filter it out. As a result, this aspect is absent in the official presentation of "valid law."'[91]

To this last comment, one should add: 'official' law does not know any expectations. But this is not the end of the story. On the contrary: just like Girard's victim, which in its hidden conceptuality conveys something of which the community of its persecutors is unaware, namely innocence (for the victim has done no wrong), so also are expectations etched into law's hidden recesses. They are, as is the scapegoat in relation to the sacred, the supplement to law – Luhmann might call them 'inofficial' law, Ehrlich[92] possibly 'living' law, and finally Cover[93] would perhaps use the term '*texts of resistance*.' In this sense, expectations are a Derridian token of *différance*: they order the manner in which society deals with complexity. One might say, they 'defer' complexity through complexity. This can occur, however, only within a generative context, which brings to light the productive aspect of the supplement: social expectations function as a productive gesture in law, as the forerunner to legal operations. Seen from this perspective, the relationship between expectations and law is transcendental, in the sense that, in a 'generative movement,' it produces the matrix within which the interplay of distinctions in law develops. In one sentence: expectations are (in the non-causal, non-originary sense already described) the 'force' within the system that initiates the perpetual series of new distinctions that first provides law with the reservoir of meanings it requires in order to ensure that legal operations have a social significance. Without the supplement of expectations, these operations would be empty, with no relation to society and, at the same time, monadic in nature (which is precisely what Luhmann is thinking of when he refers to the possibility that a highly differentiated legal system may run the risk of eroding its own foundations,

---

91 Luhmann 2004: 161.
92 Ehrlich 2001.
93 Cover 1983.

so that its continued existence comes to depend solely on the support of the political powers that be).[94]

Now that we have a theoretical framework for analysing the relationship between expectations and law, where does it get us? There are two points of central consequence for the next stage in our investigation. First, as the preceding discussion has shown, by utilizing the notion of the supplement, it is possible to construct a non-causal, non-originary theory of the genesis of law, unencumbered by any metaphysical trappings. At the same time, the discussion has also helped to decipher the functional interrelationship between law and social expectations. This has crucial implications for any sociological concept of law: for unless law maintains some form of connection with social expectations, it has no real function. It may serve political, educational or possibly even entertainment purposes, but it is not law in the functional sense. Keeping these two central points in mind then, we can now ask: what does the preceding discussion tell us about the social function of transitional law?

I would like to attempt an answer to this question not *in abstracto*, but by taking a concrete example: the fourth charge of the indictment submitted in the Nuremberg Trial of the Major War Criminals, that is, the accusation of Crimes against Humanity, as set forth in art. 6 (c) of the London Charter of the International Military Tribunal (IMT), of 8 August 1945.[95] A full discussion of the myriad legal questions posed by this charge would go far beyond the scope of the present considerations. The question that interests me here is much narrower in scope: can the application of article 6 (c) of the London Charter be seen as the point at which legal norm took its beginning? Does it provide an example of transitional law actually functioning as law? Among jurists there is a controversy as to whether article 6 (c) of the IMT Charter can be considered as having been legally binding at the time the offenses were committed – and thus, as to whether or not it must be characterized as *ex post facto* law.[96] The crux of the problem lies, above all, in the troubling historical background to the provision.

Borgwardt has demonstrated that even future research will never be able to fully refute the contention the fourth charge in the Nuremberg indictment, that of Crimes against Humanity, did, in fact, constitute the application of *ex post facto* law.[97] It is true that the so-called Martens Clause of the 1907 Hague Convention with Respect to the Laws and Customs of War on Land bears a certain similarity to article 6 (c) of the London Charter,[98] and could thus be taken as a precedent. Unfortunately, however, the Convention also contained a *si omnes* clause, that is, a provision foreseeing that the Convention would cease to be binding from the time when a non-contracting country became involved in the conflict. And with that, the genie is out of the bottle: there were a number of the countries involved in the Second World War that were not signatories to the Hague Convention. In consequence, the Martens Clause was not applicable. That being the case, the situation at the time of the Nuremberg trial was that at no time in

---

94 See above pp. 233–4 and also supra note 47.

95 Online at <http://en.wikisource.org/wiki/London_Charter_of_the_International_Military_Tribunal>.

96 Sussman 2007: 691.

97 Borgwardt 2005: 437–9.

98 Bassiouni 2002: 262–5, 286–7.

history had the prohibition contained in article 6 (c) of the London Charter ever been invoked in circumstances to which the *si omnes* clause was applicable. In that sense, the application of article 6 (c) of the London Charter at the Nuremberg Tribunal would have to be seen as an irrefutable instance of a law being applied retroactively.

Whether this view must necessarily be accepted, is not a question that needs to be decided here and now. For the purposes of the present considerations, it is sufficient to adopt, as a working hypothesis that, at the time of the judgment, article 6 (c) of the IMT Charter was in the nature of an *ex post facto* law. What then, we may then ask, are the socio-legal consequences of this hypothesis? In order to answer that, it is necessary first to determine whether, at the time of the IMT judgment, expectations had already taken shape in National Socialist German society, on which article 6 (c) of the London Charter, by the mechanism of *difference*, could have a stabilizing influence. As far as manifest expectations are concerned, this was almost certainly not the case. As will be seen, the Nazi propaganda in Germany had created an atmosphere in which there was a permanent 'lack of certain subjects for the enabling and guiding of communication.'[99] But does the absence of manifest expectations necessarily imply that article 6 (c) of the London Charter was entirely wanting in the supplement needed by law in order to properly fulfill its function?

What must be determined is whether synchronicity between law and manifest expectations is absolutely indispensable in order for legal operations to perform their function. Here, one must take Derrida quite literally, when he states that the motion of *différance* that gives rise to differences does not take place 'in a simple and unmodified – in-different – present.'[100] In other words, the expectations that can serve as a force driving law's functionality need not always be synchronously manifest. They can also be present in a latent state. But how is the system's theoretical concept of latency to be understood? Central to the concept is the idea that a system may possess structures or functions to which the system itself has no access. This is evident, for example, when one system (such as science) observes another from an incongruent perspective: 'In its analysis, science uses conceptual abstractions that do not do justice to the observed system's concrete knowledge of its milieu or to its ongoing self-experience.'[101] How does this bring us further? Among other things, it expresses the notion that science is able to shed light on latent structures and functions that are invisible to the system that is itself under observation. Regardless of the cause of their invisibility, these latent components of the system are at all time present, as a contingency, providing the means for a 'possible formation of expectation structures, a possible rearrangement of a system's meaning references, which for historical reasons is not yet visible or, for structural reasons, is blocked'.[102]

Understood in this way, it becomes clear that latent expectations, where they indeed exist, possess the potential for developing the productive gesture needed for the interplay of internal distinctions in the rearranged, retroactively instituted legal system – that is, they have the potential of performing the gesture that distinguishes the role of the

---

99 Luhmann 1995: 458.
100 Derrida 1982: 12.
101 Luhmann 1995: 88.
102 Luhmann 1995: 399.

supplement. In order for this to occur, however, there must be an 'evolutionary jump' in the legal system. The new law must '[be able to mirror] the demands of structural selection,'[103] that is, it must lie within selective range offered by those latent expectations. Where the new law meets this condition, the latent expectations 'defer' *ipso facto* one complexity through another – and this without any regard for the fact that other interconnections between law and expectations may be developing synchronously along the same time axis. This *mouvement générateur*, through which latent expectations give rise to the distinctions that are, as we have seen, essential for the existence of functional law, may yet be of a very tentative nature – but this does not alter the fact that these expectations function in the manner of a supplement. The consequences of this proposition for our understanding of transitional law are highly significant. It introduces a distinction between transitional law that is possessed of a supplement and that which is not so possessed. Where a society that has undergone destruction still maintains, in that state of anomie, latent expectations that are able to serve as a supplement to retroactive law, such law is able to assume its social function. Where that is not the case, the opposite holds true: *ex post facto* law is no law at all.

To return to our case study: did there still exist in the ruins of the Germany that collapsed on 8 May 1945, any latent expectations that were capable of serving as a supplement to article 6 (c) of the IMT Charter? It is a difficult question to answer. In contemporary scholarship on the issue there is just barely in agreement on the fact that any analysis of the weave of expectations that existed in German society under National Socialism is rendered immensely more difficult by the relentlessness of the propaganda used by the state to support its use of terror.[104] Nevertheless, the prodigious inventory of historical material available does furnish a sufficient evidence to render not implausible the hypothesis that such latent expectations did in fact exist. For reasons of space, I will confine myself here to a few, brief examples.

To begin, there is Kershaw's general observation that Nazi attempts to conceal knowledge of the 'Final Solution' from the general populace is one of the most convincing indications of the fact that the regime was, in this instance, not acting on the basis of a popular mandate.[105] As concerns measures of public opinion under National Socialism, particularly noteworthy is a study by Longerich, who attempts to discern the attitude of the population towards the 'Jewish Question' through an analysis of official reports by Nazi security forces.[106] Longerich suggests that the intensive propaganda efforts undertaken by the regime should be interpreted as a reaction to what was perceived as the absence of a 'broad, radically anti-Semitic consensus' among the people.[107] Longerich speaks even of a reluctance on the part of the population towards accepting the anti-Jewish statutes enacted by the regime. Moreover, he argues, this reluctance increased as the persecution grew more and more intense.[108] Further such case studies abound.

Here again, it is not necessary that we arrive at a definitive conclusion on the question.

---

103 Luhmann 1995: 460.
104 Longerich 2006: 10–21.
105 Kershaw 1979.
106 Longerich 2006.
107 Longerich 2006: 320–3.
108 Longerich 2006: 321.

Once more, we are proceeding on a hypothesis, according to which the extremely limited, meagre and sketchy evidence just cited is nevertheless sufficient to furnish a sign that a corresponding reservoir of latent structures did exist in German society even under Hitler. To the extent that this is accepted as providing the required supplement, it can thus be maintained that article 6 (c) of the IMT Charter does, in fact, for the reasons stated, perform the social function of law. In that sense, the controversy over this provision can be considered as resolved. In reflecting the latent expectations of the population, the transitional legal norm on crimes against humanity can be said to have functioned as law already at the time of the Nuremberg trial. It was, in fact, 'law,' and not something else. And what does all this teach us? I would like to concentrate on just one specific point and, with that – in the guise of a concluding remark – return full circle to the subject of the genesis of law.

Neither 'historically given,' nor transitional law is amenable to a metaphysical approach based on origins. Such an approach leads only to 'tangled hierarchies,' contradictions, a breakdown of meaning, the ogre of the Lyotardian *différend*. By postulating the paradox of origin, Luhmann placed the problem on a higher, more productive plane of observation. Theoretically, one could leave all of the questions surrounding the genesis of law right there, and stop worrying about them altogether – were it not for the troubling reverberations still emanating from the direction of *transitional justice*: what happens when the legal system finds itself in a situation of social *anomie*. That such a question can be raised is symptomatic of the fact that the systems theoretical paradox of origin is still in need of further investigation, that it must still be supplemented. And 'supplement' is precisely the right word here: it is only with the help of the Derridian notion of the *supplément* that it becomes possible to arrive at a thorough understanding of the reciprocal relationship between law and society. The supplement of law, as we have seen, takes the form of social expectations, which in a generative movement give rise to the distinctions that provide law with its social relevance. Out of this interplay between distinctions, law *arises*. And in this, non-originary, non-metaphysical sense, we find confirmation for that so wonderfully oracular pronouncement: *ex facto ius oritur*.

BIBLIOGRAPHY

Amstutz, Marc (2003), 'Das Gesetz' in P. Gauch and P. Pichonnaz (eds), *Figures juridiques/ Rechtsfiguren: Mélanges dissociés pour Pierre Tercier/K(l)eine Festschrift für Pierre Tercier*, Zürich: Schulthess, pp. 155–65.

Amstutz, Marc (2007), 'Der Text des Gesetzes: Genealogie und Evolution von Art. 1 ZGB', *Zeitschrift für Schweizerisches Recht*, **126**, 237–86.

Bass, Alan (2007), 'Répétition dans la zone' in R. Major (ed.), *Derrida pour les temps à venir*, Paris: Stock, pp. 408–422.

Bassiouni, Cherif (2002), 'World War I: "The War to End All Wars" and the birth of handicapped international criminal justice system', *Denver Journal of International Law and Policy*, **30**, 244–91.

Bauman, Zygmunt (1989), *Modernity and the Holocaust*, Cambridge/Maldon, MA: Polity.

Borgwardt, Elizabeth (2005), 'Re-examining Nuremberg as a new deal institution: Politics, culture and the limits of law in generating human rights norms', *Journal of International Law*, **23**, 401–62.

Burchard, Christoph (2006), 'The Nuremberg trial and its impact on Germany', *Journal of International Criminal Justice*, **4**, 800–829.

Bush, Jonathan A. (2002), '"The Supreme . . . Crime" and its origins: The lost legislative history of the crime of aggressive war', *Columbia Law Review*, **102**, 2324–424.
Bydlinski, Franz (1991), *Juristische Methodenlehre und Rechtsbegriff*.
Caputo, John D. (2007), 'Avant la création: Le souvenir de Dieu de Derrida', in R. Major (ed.), *Derrida pour les temps à venir*, Paris: Stock, pp. 140–58.
Chatiliez, Etienne (1988), *La vie est un long fleuve tranquille*, Paris: TF1 Vidéo.
Clam, Jean (2004), *Kontingenz, Paradox, Nur-Vollzug: Grundprobleme einer Theorie der Gesellschaft*, Konstanz: UVK.
Cohen, Felix S. (1935), 'Transcendental nonsense and the functional approach', *Columbia Law Review*, **35**, 809–849.
Courtine, Jean-François (2007), 'Un sombre problème de traduction', *Revue de métaphysique et de morale*, **114**, 33–45.
Cover, Robert M. (1983), 'The Supreme Court 1982 term foreword: Nomos and narrative', *Harvard Law Review*, **97**, 4–68.
De Saussure, Ferdinand (2005), *Cours de linguistique générale*, Paris: Payot.
Derrida, Jacques (1981), *Positions*, Chicago, IL: The University of Chicago Press.
Derrida, Jacques (1982), *Margins of Philosophy*, Chicago, IL: The University of Chicago Press.
Derrida, Jacques (1997), *Of Grammatology*, Baltimore, MD and London: The Johns Hopkins University Press.
Dooley, Mark and Liam Kavanagh (2007), *The Philosophy of Derrida*, Montreal: McGill-Queen's University Press.
Dubber, Markus Dirk (1993), 'Judicial Positivism and Hitler's Injustice: Book Review: Hitler's Justice: The Courts of the Third Reich. By Ingo Muller. Translated from the German by Deborah Lucas Schneider. Cambridge: Harvard University Press, 1991', *Columbia Law Review*, **93**, 1807–32.
Dumouchel, Paul (1992), 'A morphogenetic hypothesis on the closure of post-structuralism', in F.J. Varela and J.-P. Dupuy (eds), *Understanding Origins: Contemporary Views on the Origin of Life, Mind and Society*, Dordrecht: Kluwer, pp. 14–27.
Dupuy, Jean-Pierre and Francisco J. Varela (1992), 'Understanding origins: An introduction', in F.J. Varela and J.-P. Dupuy (eds), *Understanding Origins: Contemporary Views on the Origin of Life, Mind and Society*, Dordrecht: Kluwer, pp. 1–25.
Durkheim, Emile (1998), *De la division du travail social*, Paris: Quadrige/PUF.
Ehard, Hans (1949), 'The Nuremberg trial against the major war criminals and international law', *American Journal of International Law*, **43**, 223–45.
Ehrlich, Eugene (2001), *Fundamental Principles of the Sociology of Law*, Piscataway, NJ: Transaction Publishers.
Elster, Jon (2004), *Closing The Books: Transitional Justice in Historical Perspective*, Cambridge: Cambridge University Press.
Finch, George A. (1947), 'The Nuremberg trial and international law', *American Journal of International Law*, **41**, 456–8.
Freund, Julien (1974), 'Le droit comme motif et solution de conflits', in L. Legaz y Lacambra (ed.), *Die Funktionen des Rechts: Vorträge des Weltkongresses für Rechts- und Sozialphilosophie, Madrid, 7.IX.–12.IX.1973*, Wiesbaden: Franz Steiner, pp. 47–62.
Freund, Julien (1983), *Sociologie du conflit*, Paris: PUF.
Fuller, Lon L. (1958), 'Positivism and fidelity to law – A reply to Professor Hart', *Harvard Law Review*, **71**, 630–72.
Fuller, Lon L. (1964), *The Morality of Law*, New Haven/London: Yale University Press.
Girard, René (1979), *Violence and the Sacred*, Baltimore: The Johns Hopkins University Press.
Girard, René (1985), *La route antique des hommes pervers*, Paris: Grasset.
Girard, René (1986), *The Scapegoat*, Baltimore: The Johns Hopkins University Press.
Girard, René (1987), *Things Hidden Since the Foundation of the World*, Stanford, CA: Stanford University Press.
Girard, René (1992), 'Origins: A view from the literature', in: F.J. Varela and J.-P. Dupuy (eds), *Understanding Origins: Contemporary Views on the Origin of Life, Mind and Society*, Dordrecht: Kluwer, pp. 27–42.

Girard, René (2004), *Les origines de la culture*, Paris: Hachette.
Goebel, Joachim (2001), *Rechtsgespräch und kreativer Dissens: zugleich ein Beitrag zur Bedeutung der Sprache in der interpretativen Praxis des Zivilprozesses*, Berlin: Duncker & Humblot.
Hart, H.L.A. (1958), 'Positivism and the separation of law and morals', *Harvard Law Review*, **71**, 593–629.
Huyse, Luc (1995), 'Justice after transition: On the choices successor elites make in dealing with the past', *Law & Social Inquiry*, **20**, 51–78.
Kershaw, Ian (1979), 'Antisemitismus und Volksmeinung: Reaktionen auf die Judenverfolgung', in M. Broszat et al. (eds), *Bayern in der NS-Zeit, Band 2: Herrschaft und Gesellschaft im Konflikt*, München: Oldenbourg, pp. 281–348.
Koschorke, Albrecht (1999), 'Die Grenzen des Systems und die Rhetorik der Systemtheorie', in A. Koschorke and C. Vismann (eds), *Widerstände der Systemtheorie: Kulturtheoretische Analysen zum Werk von Niklas Luhmann*, Berlin: Akademie, pp. 49–60.
Ladeur, Karl-Heinz (2000), *Negative Freiheitsrechte und gesellschaftliche Organisation: Die Erzeugung von Sozialkapital durch Institutionen*, Tübingen: Mohr Siebeck.
Ladeur, Karl-Heinz (2004), *Kritik der Abwägung in der Grundrechtsdogmatik: Plädoyer für eine Erneuerung der liberalen Grundrechtstheorie*, Tübingen: Mohr Siebeck.
Ladeur, Karl-Heinz (2006), *Der Staat gegen die Gesellschaft: Zur Verteidigung der Rationalität der 'Privatrechtsgesellschaft'*, Tübingen: Mohr Siebeck.
Ladeur, Karl-Heinz and Ino Augsberg (2005), 'Auslegungsparadoxien: Zu Theorie und Praxis juristischer Interpretation', *Rechtstheorie*, **36**, 143–84.
Larenz, Karl (1991), *Methodenlehre der Rechtswissenschaft*, 6th edn, Berlin: Springer.
Levinas, Emmanuel (1961), *Totalité et infini: Essai sur l'extériorité*, The Hague: Nijhoff.
Llewellin, Karl (1930), 'A realistic jurisprudence: The next step', *Columbia Law Review*, **30**, 431–65.
Longerich, Peter (2006), *Davon haben wir nichts gewusst!: Die Deutschen und die Judenverfolgun 1933–1945*, München: Siedler.
Luhmann, Niklas (1981), *Ausdifferenzierung des Rechts: Beiträge zur Rechtssoziologie und Rechtstheorie*, Frankfurt: Suhrkamp.
Luhmann, Niklas (1987), *Rechtssoziologie*, 3rd edition, Opladen: Westdeutscher Verlag.
Luhmann, Niklas (1988), 'The third question: the creative use of paradoxes in law and legal history', *Journal of Law and Society*, **15**, 153–65.
Luhmann, Niklas (1995), *Social Systems*, Stanford, CA: Stanford University Press.
Luhmann, Niklas (2002), ‚Wie lassen sich latente Strukturen beobachten?', in P. Krieg and P. Watzlawick (eds), *Das Auge des Betrachters: Beiträge zum Konstruktionismus, Festschrift für Heinz von Foerster*, Heidelberg: Carl-Auer-Systeme, pp. 61–74.
Luhmann, Niklas (2004), *Law as a Social System*, Oxford: Oxford University Press.
Lutz, Ellen (2006), 'Transitional justice: Lessons learned and the road ahead', in N. Roht-Arriaza and J. Mariezcurrena (eds), *Transitional Justice in the Twenty-First Century: Beyond Truth versus Justice*, Cambridge: Cambridge University Press, pp. 325–41.
McKenna, Andrew J. (1992), 'Supplement to apocalypse: Girard and Derrida', in F.J. Varela and J.-P. Dupuy (eds), *Understanding Origins: Contemporary Views on the Origin of Life, Mind and Society*, Dordrecht: Kluwer, 45–76.
Meltzer, Bernard D. (1947), 'A note on some aspects of the Nuremberg debate', *University of Chicago Law Review*, **14**, pp. 455–69.
Müller, Friedrich and Ralph Christensen (2004), *Juristische Methodik, Band 1: Grundlagen, Öffentliches Recht*, 9th edition, Berlin: Duncker & Humblot.
Nancy, Jean-Luc (2007), 'Ipso facto cogitans et demens', in R. Major (ed.), *Derrida pour les temps à venir*, Paris: Stock, pp. 118–39.
Patterson, Dennis M. (1992), 'Law's pragmatism: Law as practice and narrative', *Virginia Law Review*, **76**, 937–96.
Posner Eric A. and Adrian Vermeule (2004), 'Transitional justice as ordinary justice', *Harvard Law Review*, **117**, 761–825.
Radbruch, Gustav (1946), 'Gesetzliches Unrecht und übergesetzliches Recht', *Süddeutsche Juristenzeitung*, **5**, 105–108.

Roht-Arriaza, Naomi (2006), 'The new landscape of transitional justice', in N. Roht-Arriaza and J. Mariezcurrena (eds), *Transitional Justice in the Twenty-First Century: Beyond Truth versus Justice*, Cambridge: Cambridge University Press, 1–16.
Sallis, John (2007), 'Derniers mots: générosité et réserve', *Revue de métaphysique et de morale*, **114**, 47–59.
Sriram, Chandra Lekha (2005), 'Transitional justice comes of age: Enduring lessons and challenges', *Berkeley Journal of International Law*, **23**, 101–118.
Sussman, Alan (2007), 'Introduction: Guantánamo, history, and responsibility', *Seton Hall Law Review*, **37**, 691–98.
Teitel, Ruti G. (2000), *Transitional Justice*, Oxford: Oxford University Press.
Teitel, Ruti G. (2005), 'The law and politics of contemporary transitional justice', *Cornell International Law Journal*, **38**, 837–62.
Vesting, Thomas (2007), *Rechtstheorie: Ein Studienbuch*, München: Beck.
Von Foerster, Heinz (1984), *Observing Systems*, Seaside, CA: Intersystems.
Webb, Eugen (2002), 'Girard, sacrifice, and religious symbolism, psychomedia,' *Journal of European Psychoanalysis*, **14**, available at http://www.psychomedia.it/jep/number14/webb.htm.

11. Gene-culture co-evolutionary theory and the evolution of legal behavior and institutions

Bart Du Laing*

1. INTRODUCTION

Some of the chapters in this edited volume are likely to have at least two things in common. First, they aim to contribute to a research project on 'legal certainty for globalized exchange processes' and to the latter's attempts to explain the observed transformation 'towards the transnationalization of commercial law, which is understood as a combination of the internationalization and privatization of the responsibility of the state for the production of the normative good of legal certainty for global commerce'. Secondly, they aim to fulfill this task by making use of 'evolutionary theory' or, as it was again expressed in the original conference announcement giving rise to earlier drafts of this chapter, by dealing with 'a theoretical perspective that gives some substance to the meaning of the term "evolution" with regard to law, social organization, and the state'. Since, as I will try to explain shortly, my own particular take on this – it would appear – relatively small set of commonalities involves more specifically the use of contemporary evolutionary approaches to human behavior, I must admit to having been surprised that no one else seemed to have much use for these approaches in their respective takes on the problems that united us in the conference from which this chapter stems. After all, what better use to make of a theory originating from biology than to elucidate the biological underpinnings of our behavior and its underlying psychological mechanisms as they relate to law and legally relevant phenomena? Perhaps some of the reasons for these at first sight striking differences in opinion on which 'evolutionary theory' to make use of, or what meaning to impinge upon the term 'evolution' will become clearer in the pages that follow, offering ways in which eventually to combine them. Or perhaps the two things

* A provisional draft of this article was presented at 'Law, the State, and Evolutionary Theory', Joint Conference Sfb 597 – Project A4: Transformations of Commercial Law, and The German Law Journal – Annual Conference, University of Bremen, 5 October 2007. I would like to take the opportunity to thank the organizers for inviting me to a very stimulating gathering. I also want to thank the participants for their critical questions and remarks. The usual disclaimer applies. An earlier version appeared as 'Dual Inheritance Theory, Contract Law, and Institutional Change – Towards the Co-evolution of Behavior and Institutions' in 9 *German Law Journal* 491 (2008). The title of this revised version makes obvious reference to Boyd and Richerson (2008), and is meant as a tribute to these authors whose work will be central throughout this article.

we had in common when we started out will turn out to be all there is left to look at in the end.

Whatever its outcome may be, this chapter is structured as follows: Section 2 aims to provide a summary overview of the different contemporary evolutionary approaches to human behavior, including, but not limited to, the approach known as gene-culture co-evolutionary theory or dual inheritance theory.[1] In section 3, this particular approach is further elaborated upon in order to show how evolutionary analysis in law could benefit from incorporating it into its theoretical framework. This is further illustrated using examples of the field of contract law. After a digression into evolutionary economics and systems theory, and their respective possible relationships with gene-culture co-evolutionary theory, I investigate in section 4 what the latter, qua evolutionary theory, has to offer to the study of the transformations of commercial law and its institutions that are of central concern to the research project giving rise to this edited volume. In guise of conclusion, I offer two take home messages to consider when attempting to make evolutionary theory fruitful for the study of law and legally relevant phenomena.

2. EVOLUTIONARY APPROACHES TO HUMAN BEHAVIOR AND GENE-CULTURE CO-EVOLUTIONARY THEORY

As will readily become apparent when going through the various contributions to this volume, 'evolutionary theory' can mean many things, both on its own and in its relation to law and legal phenomena. This renders it necessary to pin down somewhat more precisely what I have in mind when using the words 'evolutionary theory' in conjunction to the word 'law'.

For me, using the words 'evolutionary theory' in conjunction to the word 'law', or conducting what has been called evolutionary analysis in law,[2] means trying to find out what, if anything, contemporary evolutionary approaches to human *behavior* (and its underlying psychological mechanisms) could teach us with regard to law and legally relevant phenomena. In doing so, my approach could be regarded as inscribing itself, at least to some extent, in a tradition which, in recent times, can be traced back to Margaret Gruter's pioneering efforts to incorporate sociobiological thinking into legal analysis.[3] However, it needs to be emphasized at the onset that sociobiological thinking itself has,

---

[1] A brief note on the use of terms like 'gene-culture co-evolutionary theory', 'dual inheritance theory' or 'cultural evolutionary theory' is perhaps in order here. Indeed, some authors seem to reserve the first term for cases where cultural practices actually affect gene frequencies (such as dairy farming and lactose tolerance), whereas 'dual inheritance theory' would refer to more indirect connections between genes and culture, and 'cultural evolutionary theory' to the separate study of, unsurprisingly, the evolution of cultures themselves. Other authors, however, appear to use these terms more or less interchangeably in order to designate, again more or less, the same fields of research. Hence, I chose to use 'gene-culture co-evolutionary theory' throughout this article, because this term, in my view, expresses best to a legal audience this approach's insistence on combining different ways and levels of evolution.

[2] See Jones (1997).

[3] On which see, e.g., Gruter Morhenn and Gruter (2001). See also Gruter (1976); Gruter (1980).

say, 'evolved' into a much broader framework of different approaches than was the case for the 'narrower' classical sociobiology of the late seventies and eighties of the previous century, on which these and similar pioneering efforts were indeed primarily based.

Of course, adding the adjective 'evolutionary' to 'legal analysis' can be used to confer other meanings as well. Indeed, not unlike what appears to be the case for the majority of the quite varied approaches to economics sometimes collectively referred to as 'evolutionary economics', legal scholars perhaps more often than not look to evolutionary theory and related fields of enquiry in order to address the ways in which legal rules or even legal systems themselves change and evolve. I will come back to this later.

For now, let me start by briefly presenting the three major contemporary evolutionary approaches to human behavior, thereby aiming at providing what has been called a 'guide for the perplexed'[4] to the existing diversity of often competing theoretical frameworks. In a fairly recent and rather fair review of the field, Eric Alden Smith distinguishes between three major styles of evolutionary approaches to human behavior, namely evolutionary psychology, human behavioral ecology and dual inheritance theory or gene-culture co-evolutionary theory.[5] One could think of other, somewhat more detailed, classifications of the field under consideration,[6] but for my introductory purposes here Smith's threefold division will do just fine.

The first major style, also currently perhaps the most popular or at least the most readily visible one, evolutionary psychology,[7] holds that evolutionary explanations of human behavior need to refer to genetically evolved psychological mechanisms which can be traced back to features of our ancestral environment, the so-called 'environment of evolutionary adaptedness'. These highly specialized psychological mechanisms or 'modules' are regarded as adaptations resulting from evolution by way of natural selection in the distant past. Given that our psychological mechanisms are adapted to this long bygone past, human behavior is expected to be subject to a considerable adaptive lag, frequently leading to maladaptive outcomes in our current environments. Moreover, more general mechanisms, involving 'learning', 'culture' or 'rational choice', are deemed insufficiently domain-specific and modular to serve as plausible outcomes of the process of selection. Thus, evolutionary psychologists are highly skeptical towards what they call the 'Standard Social Science Model', which allegedly entails a blank slate view of the human brain, allowing for a nearly infinite malleability of the behavior to which it gives rise. These views are reflected in the model of culture developed by two leading evolutionary psychologists, John Tooby and Leda Cosmides. They make a distinction between 'metaculture', 'evoked culture', and 'epidemiological (or transmitted) culture'. Whereas the latter refers to what most people intuitively would associate with the notion of culture, this is contrasted to, first, cross-cultural universalities ('metaculture') and, secondly, differences triggered by the environment ('evoked culture') in order to highlight their asserted neglect in the 'Standard Social Science Model'.[8]

---

4 Smith *et al.* (2001).

5 Smith (2000).

6 See, e.g., Laland and Brown (2002); Janicki and Krebs (1998). See also Borgerhoff Mulder *et al.* (1997).

7 See, e.g., Barkow *et al.* (eds.) (1992); Buss (ed.) (2005).

8 For more extensive characterizations, see Tooby and Cosmides (1992).

According to the second approach, human behavioral ecology,[9] humans are capable of rapid and adaptive phenotypic changes. Put differently, human behavior is characterized by a considerable degree of flexibility. Hence, according to human behavioral ecologists, it is likely that we are overall well adapted to our current environments.[10] Existing diversity in human behavior would then largely be the result of different contemporary socio-ecological conditions eliciting different conditional behavioral strategies (framed in the form of 'if context X, then perform A; if context Y, then perform B'). In order to study these behavioral strategies, human behavioral ecologists then for instance construct optimality models and analyse the trade-offs an individual faces in (consciously or unconsciously) deciding upon which strategy to use in a given situation.

The third and final approach concerns the proponents of gene-culture co-evolutionary theory or dual inheritance theory who,[11] like Robert Boyd and Peter Richerson, consider culture to be a whole of ideas, values, knowledge, and the like that is learned and socially transmitted between individuals. Since cultural information exhibits the characteristics required for evolution by way of natural selection – namely variation, retention and selection, they argue that Darwinian *methods* can in principle be used to analyse cultural evolution, important differences between biological evolution and cultural evolution notwithstanding. According to Linnda Caporael, 'Boyd and Richerson propose a theory of forces to describe the Darwinian evolution of cultural creatures. Some of the forces are random, analogs of genetic drift and mutation; others are the outcome of individual decision making and choice, and finally, there is natural selection of cultural variation.'[12] Which cultural variants an individual adopts is sometimes, but by no means always, a function of genetically evolved psychological mechanisms. Indeed, Boyd and Richerson and their collaborators have spent a lot of time modeling the evolution of so-called decision-making forces in cultural evolution. They plausibly argue that learning biases are an important force in cultural evolution, including, for instance, a frequency-based conformity bias ('do what the majority of the population is doing') and a model-based prestige bias ('do what successful individuals in the population are doing'). Besides investigating the ways in which genetic evolution could give rise to cultural capacities and how these cultural capacities affect cultural evolution, gene-culture co-evolutionary theorists also address the interactions between the cultural and the genetic system of inheritance. This aspect of their theoretical framework aims at elucidating the complex feedback relationships between these two inheritance systems. Since gene-culture co-evolutionary theory will be in the center of attention throughout the remainder of this chapter, I think it is useful to complete my sketch of some of its important features with another rendering by two former students of Boyd and Richerson whose work has been very helpful to me in trying to connect this particular evolutionary theoretical framework to the study of law and legally relevant phenomena. According to Joseph Henrich and Richard McElreath:

> Culture, cultural learning and cultural evolution arise from genetically evolved psychological adaptations for acquiring ideas, beliefs, values, practices, mental models, and strategies

---

[9] See, e.g., Winterhalder and Smith (2000); Cronk *et al.* (eds.) (2000).

[10] See also, e.g., Laland and Brown (2006).

[11] See, e.g., Richerson and Boyd (2005); Henrich and McElreath (2007), and Durham (2002).

[12] Caporael (2001), 615.

> from other individuals by observation and inference. Thus, the first step is to use the logic of natural selection to theorize about the evolution and operation of our cultural learning capacities.
>
> (. . .) Our cultural learning mechanisms give rise to a robust second system of inheritance (cultural evolution) that operates by different transmission rules than genetic inheritance, and can thus produce phenomena not observed in other, less cultural, species. Theorizing about this process requires taking what we know about human cultural learning and human cognition, embedding these into evolutionary models that included social interaction, and studying the emergent properties of these models. This approach allows researchers to cobble up from psychology and individual decision-making to sociology and population-level phenomena.[13]

(I will assume for now that these last two sentences should spark at the very least some interest with those interested in the topic central to this volume, but will further discuss their relevance in section 4 of this chapter.)

It goes without saying that there are many different ways in which to contrast and compare these three different approaches, and I will not attempt to provide a full overview here, if only for the very simple reason that I obviously have not been able to treat all of them as fully as they doubtlessly would deserve in their own right. I just want to draw attention to three possible ways of distinguishing between them.[14] One way would be to distinguish between them on the basis of the importance they attach to (individual and/or social) learning.[15] Evolutionary psychologists would then most likely argue that people are predisposed to learn what once was adapted, human behavioral ecologists would preferably contend that humans preferentially learn what currently is adaptive, whereas gene-culture co-evolutionary theorists in most cases would envisage a much larger role for a quite varied array of social learning mechanisms with regard to cultural information, capable of leading to adaptive as well as maladaptive outcomes. Another way would be to try to map these approaches onto the evolutionary psychologists' threefold division of the concept of culture. Gene-culture co-evolutionary theorists could then be regarded as focusing their study on 'epidemiological (or transmitted) culture', human behavioral ecologists as (mainly) investigating 'evoked culture', and evolutionary psychologists themselves as (primarily) addressing 'metaculture'. Finally, the timescales of interest would seem to differ between the three approaches. Human behavioral ecology could be seen as focusing on short-term (behavioral) change and evolutionary psychology on long-term (genetic) change, which would leave gene-culture co-evolutionary theory – perhaps not very surprisingly – as occupying an intermediate timescale.[16] Notwithstanding these (and other) important differences, it should be emphasized that most commentators within the field at the same time acknowledge the existence of not only points of agreement, but also important complementarities, and have not given up the hope that these diverse approaches will somehow be able to converge in the not too distant future,[17]

---

13 Henrich and McElreath, *supra* note 11, 556.

14 See generally Laland and Brown, *supra* note 6, 287–318; Smith, *supra* note 5, 33–9.

15 See also Flinn (1997).

16 Interesting parallels can be drawn with Hejl (2001), especially 21, 30-31 and 49. Compare also, e.g., Arnhart (2007).

17 See most recently Sear *et al.* (2007).

culminating perhaps in what has been called 'evolutionary psychology in the round',[18] as opposed to the 'narrower' brand of evolutionary psychology discussed earlier.[19]

Nevertheless, when we ask ourselves the question as to how these different contemporary evolutionary approaches to human behavior have managed to make their appearance in evolutionary analysis in law in the sense given above, I think it is fair to say that the latter approach has been marked by a rather clear preference for the more 'narrow' kind of evolutionary psychological reasoning and for the relatively 'classical' sociobiology on which the latter is often based.[20] This will readily become clear when we take a closer look at the work of Owen Jones, one of the main proponents of evolutionary analysis in law,[21] bearing in mind, however, that the following observations merely represent my own way of connecting some, but by no means all of the key elements of this author's approach to evolutionary analysis in law with their evolutionary psychological counterparts we have encountered earlier. For instance, according to Jones, 'the legal features of any legal system will reflect not only the sifting and sorting of social and economic processes that lead to legal change, but will also reflect specific features of evolved, species-typical, human brain design'.[22] This assertion can indeed be interpreted as reflecting 'narrow' evolutionary psychology's preponderance towards finding a 'metacultural' universal human nature. Similarly, evolutionary psychology's reverting to the 'environment of evolutionary adaptedness' and the related adaptive lag hypothesis are present and accounted for in the treatment of behavioral law and economics' (seemingly) irrational behavior, as well as in the discussion of ways to assess the effectiveness of legal interventions.[23]

As has been pointed out by others,[24] the problem with these views is not that they are necessarily incorrect, but that they are as incomplete, be it in a different way, as the views they are seeking to amend. Hence, in the next section, using the example of contracts and their regulation – legal or otherwise, I will try to show why evolutionary analysis in law would do well to enlarge its perspective by consistently incorporating gene-culture co-evolutionary theory into its theoretical framework, thereby most likely considerably strengthening and broadening its explanatory scope.

3. GENE-CULTURE CO-EVOLUTIONARY THEORY AND (CONTRACT) LAW

In previous work on evolutionary analysis in law,[25] I argued that, in order to make contemporary evolutionary approaches to human behavior fruitful for legal analysis,

---

[18] See Dunbar and Barrett (2007).

[19] For the use of the term 'narrow', see, e.g., Wilson (2003), 57–60; Mameli (2007), 25–7.

[20] See more extensively Du Laing (2007), 329–43.

[21] See, e.g., Jones (2005); Jones (2004); Jones and Goldsmith (2005). Compare also Cosmides and Tooby (2006).

[22] Jones (2001a), 858.

[23] See Jones (2001b).

[24] See, e.g., Wilson (1999); Gintis (2007).

[25] See Du Laing (2009). For a more extensive discussion of the issues treated in this section, the reader is referred to this article.

it would be necessary to be able to fulfill at least two requirements. First, we have to be able to give a plausible evolutionary account for *both* the behavior that is supposed to be regulated *and* what could be referred to as the regulating behavior itself. Secondly, rather than focusing exclusively on the – indeed not all that unlikely – universal aspects of the regulated behavior, this universality has to be connected more explicitly with the – cultural – diversity encountered in the world's legal systems. I will deal with these two requirements successively and show how they are intimately connected *not only* to each other, *but also* to the larger evolutionary framework of gene-culture co-evolutionary theory. In each case, I will clarify my position by referring to examples from the legal field of contract law – which, incidentally, will also lead us a few steps closer to the research on transnational commercial law and institutional change in globalization that is central to this volume.

3.1 Regulated Behavior and Regulating Behavior

First, evolutionary analysis in law has to take into account the regulating behavior itself. After all, law not only *affects* human behavior, it also, in a way, *is* human behavior. What does this have to do with gene-culture co-evolutionary theory? Well, one way of approaching legal systems or systems of rules in general – but perhaps a very different way than the ones preferred by other 'evolutionary' approaches to law – is to regard them as manifestations of large-scale cooperative behavior involving the production of a public good.

An important part of Boyd and Richerson's work that I failed to mention earlier concerns finding an evolutionary explanation for the human propensity to cooperate in large groups of unrelated individuals.[26] Indeed, from the mathematical models associated with gene-culture co-evolutionary theory, it appears that (traditional) reciprocity-based solutions to cooperative dilemmas cannot easily be extended beyond rather small groups of individuals. Perhaps more importantly, it is also shown that culture, understood as shared information on values, beliefs, practices and their likes, can greatly enhance the scope of cooperation. More specifically, a combination of the biased cultural transmission mechanisms we have encountered earlier with what is called moralistic punishment can lead to the adoption of a wide variety of possibly individually costly social norms in a population.[27,28] According to Joseph and Natalie Henrich:

> When both adherence to a norm and a willingness to punish norm violations are influenced by cultural learning, the mechanisms of prestige-biased and conformist transmission can lead to

[26] See generally Richerson and Boyd, *supra* note 11; Boyd and Richerson (2006); Richerson *et al.* (2003); Henrich and Henrich (2007).

[27] On the element of 'moralistic punishment' see (and compare) also, from various angles, Sripada (2005); Smirnov (2007); Sigmund (2007).

[28] It should be noted, however, that this particular evolutionary path to within-group similarity (and cooperation) has recently been subjected to important criticism and is at any rate unlikely to be the only possible one. For a discussion of these issues, I would recommend Eriksson *et al.* (2007). Moreover, recent work on evolving social contracts by members of the same research group promises to be a more than worthy alternative to the specific approach treated more extensively in this chapter. See also, *infra*, section 4.

> stable situations in which most people acquire and follow the rules, prescriptions and punishments associated with a social norm. This applies to any norm, be it adaptive, neutral or maladaptive, and includes norms for costly cooperation.[29]

So from this point of view one could say that culture appears more as a part of the solution than as a part of the problem. I strongly believe that this emphasis on a plausible evolutionary theory of social norms and institutions is of particular relevance for an evolutionary analysis in law aiming at incorporating regulating behavior in its analyses.

For instance, when relating evolutionary theory to contracts and contract law, I think it can be very useful to distinguish the behavior supposed to be regulated – contracts – from the behavior *by which* it is regulated – contract law. Contracting behavior itself can be seen – at least in its archetypical case – as an instance of small-scale dyadic cooperative behavior. A lot about contracts thus is likely to be adequately explained from an evolutionary point of view on the basis of reciprocal altruism and the mechanisms that are known to sustain it in dyadic interactions.[30] For example, this could be the case for so-called 'relational contracts' and the fact that they are largely self-regulating. Here evolutionary theory could be seen as helping to determinate the relative importance of law, a suggestion that was also made by Thomas Ulen in a reaction to the article by Owen Jones from which I have quoted previously.[31] The different norms regulating contracts, however, often bear more resemblance to large-scale n-person forms of cooperative behavior. To account for these norms themselves, as well as for their variety, I think we will need an evolutionary approach to human behavior that fully incorporates human cultural capacities.

3.2 Universality and (Cultural) Diversity

Secondly, gene-culture co-evolutionary theory also provides a suitable evolutionary point of entry to the problem of reconciling legal universality and legal diversity. Indeed, I am convinced that evolutionary analysis in law, as it stands, has a lot to gain from explicitly taking into account cultural diversity.

We have seen that moralistic punishment combined with biased cultural transmission can sustain an arbitrarily wide variety of social norms in a population.[32] Hence, we face what is known as an equilibrium selection problem. Cultural group selection offers one mechanism capable of selecting among various costly social norms that can lead to different pro-social or cooperative social norms. Again in the Henrichs' formulation:

> While neutral and somewhat maladaptive norms could be maintained *within* any particular group, group beneficial norms can spread by competition and selection *across* social groups that

---

[29] Henrich and Henrich (2006), 239.

[30] On this reciprocal altruism see, e.g., Trivers (2006).

[31] See Ulen (2001), 941–3.

[32] Arguably, this combination also appears to leave ample room for what could be called a measure of 'violent arbitrariness' in normative systems, and has elsewhere, if I understood the argument correctly, been referred to as the 'arbitrariness, inconsistencies, antinomies, paradoxes and even violence' that 'lie at the bottom of the most refined constructs in economic and legal action' and of which 'rational choice, games theory and decision theory' apparently would be unable to account. See namely Teubner (2001), 29–30. See also, *infra*, section 4.

> have different culturally evolved norms that vary in their group-beneficial properties – a process termed *cultural group selection*.[33]

This approach clearly has the potential of providing additional insights into how similar problems are solved differently in various legal systems or systems of rules, with, for instance, varying degrees of cooperativeness as a result.

To illustrate this further, I would like to take a closer look at the issue of equality or substantive fairness in exchange transactions. In his survey of legal anthropological literature on exchange in pre-commercial societies, James Gordley made the general observation that:

> The rules or standards that govern personalized transactions are shaped by the fact that every party is a repeat player in a series of transactions. One consequence is that these standards need not ensure that every single transaction is fair; they may ensure that the series of transactions is fair.[34]

Again, this phenomenon could be related quite easily to reciprocal altruism – which is central to classical sociobiological and 'narrow' evolutionary psychological explanations for the phenomenon of cooperation. Modern Western contract theory, however, manifests a considerable tendency to expect mutual performances in isolated exchanges to be more or less equal, or substantively fair. This large-scale pro-social fairness norm, as it is expressed in the law regarding contracts, appears to be explained better by gene-culture co-evolutionary theory. Furthermore, it seems to resonate quite well with the cross-cultural data obtained from conducting economic experiments, even though I am aware of the controversies surrounding these findings and their interpretation. Indeed, some behaviorally inclined economists, like Herbert Gintis and Ernst Fehr, use the concept of 'strong reciprocity' to refer to 'a predisposition to cooperate with others and to punish those who violate the norms of cooperation, at personal cost, even when it is implausible to expect that these costs will be repaid by others or at a later date'.[35] This other-regarding type of predisposition appears difficult to explain without making appeal to a gene-culture co-evolutionary theoretical framework, resulting in something like Boyd and Richerson's so-called 'tribal social instincts'.[36] Moreover, as predicted by the gene-culture co-evolutionary theoretical framework within which at least some of this research is explicitly situated, cross-cultural differences in 'strong reciprocity' appear largely correlated with group-level differences, rather than with individual-level differences.[37]

Let me offer an intermediary conclusion for this section. I believe that 'narrow' evolutionary psychology is not at all unlikely to provide us with valuable insights regarding universal aspects of individual human behavior, which may very well be useful in legal analysis. Put differently, just as one needs a plausible theory of universals to address diversity,[38] gaining knowledge of what elements of human psychology are likely to remain

---

33 Henrich and Henrich, *supra* note 29, 239.
34 Gordley (1997), 4.
35 Gintis *et al.* (2003), 154. See also Fehr and Fischbacher (2005).
36 On which see Richerson and Boyd (2001).
37 See Henrich *et al.* (2005) (and the discussion following the main article).
38 See also Barkow (2001).

constant on relatively short timescales could affect our understanding of institutions and institutional change on these relatively short timescales. Gene-culture co-evolutionary theory, however, is especially likely to provide us with indispensable additional evolutionary theoretical building blocks to relate individual behavior and group-level phenomena like norms and institutions with one another.

Interestingly enough, quite a few of the topics associated with the problems of fairness and legal certainty as they manifest themselves when taking into account what has been called the transnationalization of commercial law, could quite easily be related, at least to a certain extent, to the problem of cooperation that was central to this section. This brings us then, finally, to the issues that were actually at hand in the conference from which most of the chapters in this volume originate. I will start by offering some perhaps rather tentative points of comparison between, on the one hand, gene-culture co-evolutionary theory as one of the currently prevailing evolutionary approaches to human behavior and, on the other hand, the perhaps equally diverse fields of evolutionary economics and systems theory. I will then focus on what gene-culture co-evolutionary theory more specifically has to offer to the study of the transnationalization of commercial law.

4. INSTITUTIONAL CHANGE: TOWARDS THE CO-EVOLUTION OF BEHAVIOR AND INSTITUTIONS

4.1 Tentative Digressions into Evolutionary Economics and Systems Theory

In order to assess to what extent contemporary evolutionary approaches to human behavior in general, and gene-culture co-evolutionary theory in particular, could further our understanding of the phenomenon of transnationalization of commercial law, or certain parts pertaining to it, it might prove useful to start by offering some points of comparison between them and other theoretical frameworks sailing under the relatively broad 'evolutionary' banner. This brings us right back to the beginning of this chapter, where I noted that there are many ways in which to use the words 'evolutionary theory' in conjunction to the word 'law', and consequently promised to return to the tendency of quite a few legal scholars to look to evolutionary theory and related fields of enquiry in order to address the ways in which legal rules or even legal systems themselves change and evolve. At the same time, this will allow me to discuss in a more general fashion how gene-culture co-evolutionary theory and related evolutionary frameworks can inform studies of institutional change, like the one the contributors to this volume were asked to comment on from their respective evolutionary perspectives.

4.1.1 Evolutionary Economics

Let us start with evolutionary economics. As is the case for legal scholars drawing upon evolutionary theory, evolutionary economists differ greatly in their respective views on the 'proper' use of evolution in economic theorizing. A very interesting way to look at these and similar issues – in economics that is, but much the same could apply for law, if only the possible analog legal discussion had already reached the same level of advancement – is provided by the philosopher Jack Vromen. In order to lay bare the bones of contention separating different approaches to evolutionary economics from one another,

Vromen distinguishes between three clusters of related but distinct issues,[39] namely (1) the issue of universal (or generalized) Darwinism – often associated with, e.g., the work of Geoffrey Hodgson and Thorbjørn Knudsen,[40] (2) the issue of continuity between genetic and socio-cultural evolution – often associated with, e.g., the work of Ulrich Witt and Christian Cordes,[41] and (3) the issue of (the relationships between different) levels of organization – on which various authors have commented from a variety of angles.[42]

I find it useful to present Vromen's own characterizations of these issues in full, bearing in mind however that we will likely want to replace 'economic' with 'legal' where applicable:

> I. *The 'biological metaphor' and Universal Darwinism* – There are processes of economic evolution going on that exhibit the same essential abstract features as Darwinian evolutionary processes in biology.[43]
>
> II. *The Continuity Thesis* – Prior non-economic evolutionary processes made ongoing economic evolutionary processes possible. Furthermore, outcomes of prior non-economic evolutionary processes and concurrently ongoing non-economic evolutionary processes still affect ongoing economic evolutionary processes.[44]
>
> III. *A Layered Ontology* – There are several related levels of organization in the economic realm that in turn are realized in lower levels of organization (studied by psychology, biology, chemistry and physics), and at which evolutionary processes may be going on concurrently.[45]

Interestingly, teasing apart these three clusters of issues at the same time allows Vromen, in offering some speculations on how to make 'credible combinations' between his clusters, to mention the work of some authors who otherwise – for reasons I still fail to fully understand – appear to be only rarely discussed in the literature on 'evolutionary economics'. Perhaps unsurprisingly, these include the (among other things behavioral) economists influenced by gene-culture co-evolutionary theory I already mentioned, Gintis and Fehr, as well as other economists who sometimes would seem to prefer to stick more closely to the 'narrower' evolutionary psychological style of theorizing.[46] Still according to Vromen:

> The belief that there are evolutionary processes going on in the economic realm need not be accompanied by the acceptance of the continuity thesis or of a layered ontology (. . .). Conversely, acceptance of the continuity thesis or of a layered ontology may be accompanied

---

[39] See Vromen (2004), 222–33. See also more recently Vromen (2008).

[40] See, e.g., Hodgson and Knudsen (2006).

[41] See, e.g., Witt (2004); Cordes (2006).

[42] It should also be mentioned here that Hodgson recently proposed a taxonomy of the relationship between biology and economics, involving a basic distinction between '(1) *Theories of interaction – theories addressing the nature and extent of causal interaction between biological and social phenomena*' and '(2) *Theories of commonality – theories proposing common laws or principles that apply to both biological and social phenomena*'. See Hodgson (2007), 171–2. Whereas his 'theories of commonality' seem to map onto Vromen's first cluster, the 'theories of interaction' appear more related to the 'continuity thesis' of the second cluster in Vromen's terminology.

[43] Vromen, *supra* note 39, 222.

[44] *Id.*, 226.

[45] *Id.*, 229.

[46] Such as Robson (2001); Ben-Ner and Putterman (2000); Hoffman *et al.* (1998).

> by an implicit or explicit denial that there are evolutionary processes going on in the economic realm.[47]

Of course, this does not have to mean that these analytically separable clusters of contentious issues are somehow inherently incapable of being effectively combined, as, for that matter, Vromen himself clearly acknowledges.

Quite to the contrary, I believe that the work of Boyd and Richerson and other gene-culture co-evolutionary theorists shows that a flexibly conceived 'generalized Darwinism' – focusing on population thinking rather than on natural selection *per se* – can go hand in hand with an acceptance of (some version of) the 'continuity thesis'. Rendered in the language of gene-culture co-evolutionary theory, the latter manages to address *both* cultural evolution *and* the evolution of culture and human cultural capacities within one and the same evolutionary theoretical framework. Furthermore, this approach appears capable of accommodating, at least in principle, Vromen's third cluster of related issues, namely the question of a layered ontology, involving multiple levels of organization and the upward and downward causal relationships between them. Let me quote again from McElreath and Henrich's work:

> In evolutionary models, this classical conflict between explanations at the level of the society (think Durkheimian social facts) and explanations at the level of individuals (think microeconomics) simply disappears. Population models allow explanation and real causation at both levels (and more than two levels) to exist seamlessly and meaningfully in one theory. We don't have to choose between atomistic and group-level explanations. Instead, one can build models about how individuals can create population-level effects which then change individuals in powerful ways.[48]

Boyd and Richerson themselves put it very succinctly, but accurately like this: 'Darwinian tools were *invented* to integrate levels'.[49] While recognizing two levels of organization – the genetic one and the cultural one – is likely to turn out to be insufficient,[50] it would nonetheless seem to be a good starting point. So what we have here are at the very least some promising ways in which to address micro–macro type problems that could be of interest to the study of legal institutional change.[51]

In this respect, however, mention should at least be made of three other, related, current strands of research. The first regards David Sloan Wilson's widely discussed continuing quest to (re-)introduce multi-level evolutionary approaches into the human behavioral sciences.[52] The second concerns Kevin Laland, John Odling-Smee and Marcus Feldman's proposal on niche construction.[53] Niche construction can indeed be said to add a third, intermediary level to the levels mentioned earlier, allowing for what has been called 'ecological inheritance' and an increasingly active role of (human) organisms in molding

---

47 Vromen, *supra* note 39, 234.
48 McElreath and Henrich (2007), 571.
49 Richerson and Boyd, *supra* note 11, 247.
50 See already, e.g., in evolutionary economics: Hodgson and Knudsen (2007).
51 Similar views are expressed for economics in van den Bergh and Stagl (2003), to which the title of this chapter obviously also makes reference. See also van den Bergh and Gowdy (2003).
52 See Wilson (2007); Wilson (2004). See also Wilson's analyses of religions in Wilson (2002).
53 See Laland *et al.* (2001); Laland *et al.* (2000). See also, e.g., Plotkin (2002), 213–46.

their own (cultural) environments. Commenting on this niche construction theoretical framework, Samuel Bowles for that matter already argued that economic institutions could usefully be conceptualized as exactly such ecological niches.[54] Perhaps a similar type of reasoning could apply for legal institutions. Finally, I would like to draw attention here to the work of Kimmo Eriksson, Magnus Enquist and their various collaborators on cultural evolutionary theory, learning mechanisms and social contracts.[55] Especially their ongoing research on evolving collective regulations and their relation to behavioral types, plausibly entailing markedly different types of institutional arrangements, provides a promising alternative evolutionary route to cooperation in social dilemmas than the one I have been focusing on throughout this chapter.

Even though the exact relations between all of these relatively recent approaches remain debated, there are clear common points of reference between them. Indeed, what these approaches share is a multi-level and multi-process perspective on evolution, leading to a hierarchical evolutionary theory, and thereby allowing for more 'complexity' to enter into the picture.

4.1.2 Systems Theory

This brings me to an even briefer and even more tentative digression into systems theory – or at least sociological systems theory in the sense developed by Niklas Luhmann and further developed by other authors, in law most notably Gunther Teubner.[56] As to the latter, I can only assume that he is not a great supporter, to say the very least, of 'socio-biological' approaches to human society and culture. Indeed, in an attempt to replace '(t)he straightforward idea of law's evolution towards efficiency'[57] – an attempt with which I have as such absolutely no problem whatsoever, given that there most likely is no straightforward relation between efficiency and evolutionary theory – Teubner states, among other things, the following:

> The evolving unit is neither a text nor is it a group but a self-organizing social system. (. . .) This excludes from the outset sociobiology, which reduces social phenomena (behavior, rules, laws) to their function of maintaining biological units, whether individuals, species, groups, or genes.[58]

But does it really? Are the legal and other social subsystems as autonomous and supra-organic as Teubner and likeminded theorists would have it?[59] Although I would not want to claim to have an answer to the last question – far from it actually – I do find it

---

[54] Bowles (2000).

[55] See Eriksson *et al., supra* note 28; Enquist *et al.* (2007); Eriksson and Strimling (2008).

[56] A thorough comparison of Luhmann's theoretical framework with gene-culture co-evolutionary theory and other multi-level evolutionary approaches would in any case be well beyond the scope of this altogether short contribution. Some aspects of such a comparison can perhaps be gleaned from the German reactions to Richerson and Boyd (2000). See also Luhmann (1975/1991), 193.

[57] Teubner (2002), 167.

[58] *Id.*, 164. See also Teubner (1993), 52–53.

[59] See also, e.g., the exchange between Marc Amstutz and Manfred Aschke in, respectively, Amstutz (2003) and Aschke (2003).

necessary to point out that at least some of the approaches developed – and developing – in the wake of sociobiology are quite prepared to take into account the possibility of emergent properties at higher levels of organization, to introduce non-linear dynamics or feedbacks between different levels into their models or to incorporate non-genetic systems of inheritance, in short, to expand the received view of the neo-Darwinian modern synthesis in various ways. However, they are equally likely to provide a different view on the relationships between different levels of organization than the ones espoused by some proponents of self-organization and systems theory. More specifically, they offer a promising starting point to more rigorously address, so to speak, the 'structural couplings' between *different types* of systems (biological, psychic, social).

Moreover, regardless of the usefulness of Luhmann's specific sociological systems theoretical framework in describing societal subsystems like the legal system, their development and their connections, it is rather questionable whether the most appropriate way to view the relationship between systems theory and evolutionary theory more generally really is to regard them as if this relationship is one of mutual exclusion or – to use David Sloan Wilson's apt phrasing – as if more self-organization necessarily means less natural selection and vice versa.[60] This having been said, it does warrant repetition that most of the theorists on whose work I have drawn so far in this and the previous section of this chapter appear quite open to the prospect of combining their evolutionary framework with insights and methods associated with systems theoretical approaches. To reconcile both theoretical frameworks will likely require movement from both sides,[61] and, given my own point of departure, I am simply more inclined to be interested in the movement that is being made from what could be called the 'evolutionary side', which, obviously, does not imply any *a priori* negative assessment of any movement concurrently being made from the 'opposite' direction.

4.2 Transnationalization of Commercial Law and Gene-culture Co-evolutionary Theory

Apart from, in my view at least, the general advantage of gene-culture co-evolutionary theory of being able to cut across Vromen's clusters of troubling issues apparently continuing to divide the field of evolutionary economics – and, by way of analogy, most likely, even if so far largely implicitly, also the various evolutionary approaches to law presented in this edited volume – there are, I believe, a few more concrete linking pins between gene-culture co-evolutionary theory, or research informed by gene-culture co-evolutionary theory, and the project on transformations of commercial law on which we were invited to comment. I would like to loosely structure these more specific linking pins around two basic notions arising from Gralf-Peter Calliess' writings on the subject, even though they

---

[60] Wilson (2005), 152. ('This view of evolution and complexity suffers from being – well, too simple'). For an in some respects similar argument in evolutionary economics, see Hodgson (2002), 264–6; Hodgson and Knudsen, *supra* note 40, 6–10.

[61] In other words, not that much appears to have changed since Luhmann wrote that 'das Problem (. . .) verlagert sich heute mehr und mehr in die Frage des Verhältnisses von Evolutionstheorie und Systemtheorie, oder genauer: des Verhältnisses von Variation/Selektion und System/Umwelt als verschiedener, abstimmungsbedürftiger Formwahlen einer Theorie' (Luhmann (1993/1995), 241).

may not (yet) map exactly onto his conceptualizations. One concerns the privatization of civil law and the problem of legal certainty, the other the civilization of private law and the problem of fairness.[62]

4.2.1 Privatization of civil law and legal certainty

The emergence of private ordering mechanisms in globalized exchange actually fits quite nicely with gene-culture co-evolutionary theorists' attempts to provide an evolutionary explanation for larger-scale cooperation in groups of unrelated individuals. At least an important part of an evolutionary approach to private ordering mechanisms like the ones that appear to have caught the attention of people working on globalized exchange processes, would indeed seem to involve an answer to the question of how they, or perhaps better some of them, can work in the first place. And it has been pointed out repeatedly that such an answer excludes reference being made to already existing and (more or less) functioning institutions like states.[63]

Now if we follow Calliess and his co-authors in their claim that 'generally the bundling of a plurality of trilateral governance mechanisms such as private norms, arbitration and social sanctions into effective private governance regimes (. . .) or private legal systems (. . .) is essential in order to get anywhere in terms of production of legal certainty',[64] more information on the origins and characteristics of the mechanisms underlying such 'trilateral governance mechanisms' may prove to come in handy. A few cursory examples from the, in my view, very relevant evolutionary literature should be able to clarify this further.

For instance, in formulating her theory of – privately ordered – ethnically homogeneous middleman groups and explaining their success, Janet Landa not only draws on both New Institutional Economics and Boyd and Richerson's work,[65] but also receives enthusiastic endorsement from David Sloan Wilson, who sees certain aspects of his ideas on multi-level selection theory and group selection confirmed by her work.[66] Similarly, in their contribution to a recent book entitled 'Moral Sentiments and Material Interests: The Foundations of Cooperation in Economic Life', Samuel Bowles and Herbert Gintis investigate, within their framework of strong reciprocity and other-regarding preferences, the role of what they call community governance, arguing that 'communities work well relative to markets and states where the tasks are qualitative and hard to capture in explicit contracts, and the conflicts of interest among the members are limited'.[67] Richerson and Boyd for their part reach the conclusion that 'social innovations that make larger-scale society possible, but at the same time effectively simulate life in a tribal-scale society, will tend to spread'.[68]

Again, insofar as Calliess and his co-authors quite plausibly stress that 'the competitive

---

62 See Calliess (2002). See also Calliess (2005).
63 See, e.g., Fehr and Fischbacher (2004); Henrich *et al.* (2001), 350–352.
64 Calliess et al. (2007), 100.
65 See Landa (1999).
66 See Wilson (2000). See also more recently Landa (2008) (target paper in a theme issue on Group Selection: Theory and Evidence).
67 Bowles and Gintis (2005), 395. See also Kahan (2005).
68 Richerson and Boyd, *supra* note 11, 230.

capacity of private and public governance mechanisms is decisive for the evolution of the institutional mix',[69] evolutionarily informed research projects like the ones I mentioned could be vital in filling in parts of the 'competitive capacity' aspect of their hypothesis with regard to certain types of what could be referred to as 'internationalized communities'. It is exactly here that for instance recent work by Kimmo Eriksson and Pontus Strimling on social contracts could profitably enter into the legal theoretical picture. As mentioned earlier, these authors have started investigating through mathematical modeling and experimental studies how social groups arrive at workable norms of behavior in social dilemmas and which elements help explain the differences between collective regulations arrived at by differently composed groups.[70]

4.2.2 Civilization of private law and fairness

Related to the foregoing – and presumably already given away by the use of the words 'moral sentiments' there – is the fact that adopting an evolutionary approach to human behavior like gene-culture co-evolutionary theory need not imply that values are left out of sight. So, when looked at from an evolutionary behavioral perspective, the privatization of civil law does by no means necessarily have to lead to a de-civilization of private law.

To briefly illustrate this in what little space I have left, I would first like to mention a recently completed research endeavor that, in taking similar issues to heart, makes use of gene-culture co-evolutionary theory, among other theoretical frameworks. I am referring to the Gruter Institute for Law and Behavioral Research's project entitled 'Free enterprise: Values in action'.[71] In this project, a multi-disciplinary group of scholars, including the apparently nearly omni-present Boyd and Richerson,[72] make a strong case for the existence of a variety of mechanisms able to sustain values in market environments, even increasingly globalized ones. The upshot of the project thus far seems to be that values are indeed forgotten ingredients in what makes markets work, 'they are ubiquitous behavioral realities that play a critical role in facilitating the trustworthiness, fairness, and honesty that promote cooperation between individuals, firms, and institutions, and within society as a whole'.[73]

Moreover, often evolutionarily informed research on the dynamics between formal contract law and values like fairness and trust can provide us with valuable insights regarding the differences between various 'institutional mixes' as to their respective capacities of sustaining these values. While as yet perhaps inconclusive, several experimental analyses indeed at the very least suggest that such values are by no means necessarily supported most or best by formal contract law.[74] Finally, and similarly, gene-culture co-evolutionary theory would seem to provide a useful encompassing framework for research aimed at relating 'micro-level' (behavioral) variables with 'macro-level' (institutional) variables, possibly including features of the legal systems under consideration, and thereby at least in principle capable of contributing to our understanding of the factors influencing

---

[69] Calliess *et al.*, *supra* note 64, 102.
[70] See Eriksson and Strimling, *supra* note 55.
[71] The results have recently been published (Zak, ed. (2008)).
[72] See Richerson and Boyd (2008).
[73] See Goodenough and Gruter Cheney (2008), xxiii.
[74] See, e.g., Simpson and Eriksson (2009); Bohnet *et al.* (2001).

the success, or lack thereof, of often quite diverse 'private' and 'non-private' ordering mechanisms.[75]

5. CONCLUDING REMARKS

In the previous sections, I hope to have shown that gene-culture co-evolutionary theory – while at first sight perhaps less useful to illuminate our understanding of (relatively) short-term institutional change than are other 'evolutionary' approaches to law, which to a greater or lesser extent emphasize or imply the discontinuity between biological and socio-cultural evolution – nonetheless is likely to be able to provide us with some of the indispensable building blocks needed to study the co-evolution of behavior and institutions. Hence, I would like to conclude this chapter with two perhaps somewhat provocative take home messages.

First, perhaps the time has come for evolutionary minded legal scholars to replenish from the original source, being *biological* evolutionary theory, as currently applied in a variety of ways to our own species. To quote once more from Vromen's work, just as 'evolutionary economists who forego the opportunity to be informed about what is happening in evolutionary theorizing elsewhere do this to their own detriment',[76] evolutionary minded legal scholars in my view should try to resist the temptation to stray too far from what is currently happening within the actually quite broad field of evolutionary approaches to human behavior – by now clearly including human socio-cultural behavior. This is not to say that there cannot be anything specific about evolutionary processes, if any, in the legal realm. It just means that this specificity should not always be presumed. Leaving aside premature presumptions about the specificity of evolutionary processes, again if any, in the legal realm, is likely to pay the additional dividend of being able to reconnect with other social scientific disciplines devoted to the study of human behavior and institutions from an evolutionary perspective.

Secondly, this article could also be seen as a plea for not leaving out of sight 'lower' levels of organization when discussing change at 'higher' levels of organization. Indeed, especially when addressing issues like the globalization or transnationalization of commercial activities and their regulation, one easily runs the risk of losing sight of what is happening at 'lower' levels of organization, like the behavioral one. Multi-level evolutionary theories like gene-culture co-evolutionary theory then offer one possible and promising way of thinking about the complex relationships between these different levels of organization.

---

75 See, e.g., Efferson *et al.* (2007); Herrmann *et al.* (2008).

76 Vromen, *supra* note 39, 234.

BIBLIOGRAPHY

Amstutz, Marc (2003), 'Widerstreitende Götter: Zu Manfred Aschkes Rekonstruktion der systemsoziologischen Evolutionstheorie und ihrer rechtstheoretischen Bedeutung', *Rechtsgeschichte: Zeitschrift des Max-Planck-Instituts für europäische Rechtsgeschichte*, **2**, 14.

Arnhart, Larry (2007), 'The behavioral sciences are historical sciences of emergent complexity', *Behavioral and Brain Sciences*, **30**, 18.

Aschke, Manfred (2003), 'Evolutionstheorie für das Recht der Marktgesellschaft: Zu Marc Amstutz, Evolutorisches Wirtschaftsrecht. Vorstudien zum Recht und seiner Methode in den Diskurskollisionen der Marktgesellschaft', *Rechtsgeschichte: Zeitschrift des Max-Planck-Instituts für europäische Rechtsgeschichte*, **2**, 25.

Barkow, Jerome H. (2001), 'Universalien und evolutionäre Psychologie', in Peter M. Hejl (ed.), *Universalien und Konstruktivismus*, Frankfurt: Suhrkamp, p. 126.

Barkow, Jerome H., Leda Cosmides and John Tooby (eds) (1992), *The Adapted Mind: Evolutionary Psychology and the Generation of Culture*, Oxford: Oxford University Press.

Ben-Ner, Avner and Louis Putterman (2000), 'On some implications of evolutionary psychology for the study of preferences and institutions', *Journal of Economic Behavior & Organization*, **43**, 91.

Bohnet, Iris, Bruno S. Frey and Steffen Huck (2001), 'More Order with Less Law: On Contract Enforcement, Trust, and Crowding', *American Political Science Review*, **95**, 131.

Borgerhoff Mulder, Monique, Peter J. Richerson, Nancy W. Thornhill and Eckart Voland (1997), 'The place of behavioral ecological anthropology in evolutionary social science' in Peter Weingart, Sandra D. Mitchell, Peter J. Richerson and Sabine Maasen (eds), *Human By Nature: Between Biology and the Social Sciences*, Mahwah, NJ: Lawrence Erlbaum, p. 253.

Bowles, Samuel (2000), 'Economic institutions as ecological niches', *Behavioral and Brain Sciences*, **23**, 148.

Bowles, Samuel and Herbert Gintis (2005), 'Social capital, moral sentiments, and community governance' in Herbert Gintis, Samuel Bowles, Robert Boyd and Ernst Fehr (eds), *Moral Sentiments and Material Interests: The Foundations of Cooperation in Economic Life*, Cambridge, MA: MIT Press, p. 379.

Boyd, Robert and Peter J. Richerson (2006), 'Solving the puzzle of human cooperation' in Stephen C. Levinson and Pierre Jaisson (eds), *Evolution and Culture*, Cambridge, MA: MIT Press, p. 105.

Boyd, Robert and Peter J. Richerson (2008), 'Gene-culture coevolution and the evolution of social institutions' in Christoph Engel and Wolf Singer (eds), *Better Than Conscious?: Decision Making, the Human Mind, and Implications For Institutions*, Cambridge, MA: MIT Press, p. 305.

Buss, David M. (ed.) (2005), *The Handbook of Evolutionary Psychology*, Hoboken, NJ: Wiley.

Calliess, Gralf-Peter (2002), 'Reflexive transnational law: The privatisation of civil law and the civilisation of private law', *Zeitschrift für Rechtssoziologie*, **23**, 185.

Calliess, Gralf-Peter (2005), 'Billigkeit und effektiver Rechtsschutz: Zu Innovation und Evolution des (Zivil-)Rechts in der Globalisierung', *Zeitschrift für Rechtssoziologie*, **26**, 35.

Calliess, Gralf-Peter, Thomas Dietz, Wioletta Konradi, Holger Nieswandt and Fabian Sosa (2007), 'Transformations of commercial law: new forms of legal certainty for globalized exchange processes?' in Achim Hurrelmann, Stephan Leibfried, Kerstin Martens and Peter Mayer (eds), *Transforming the Golden-Age Nation State*, Basingstoke: Palgrave Macmillan, p. 83.

Caporael, Linnda R. (2001), 'Evolutionary psychology: Toward a unifying theory and a hybrid science', *Annual Review of Psychology*, **52**, 607.

Cordes, Christian (2006), 'Darwinism in economics: from analogy to continuity', *Journal of Evolutionary Economics*, **16**, 529.

Cosmides, Leda and John Tooby (2006), 'Evolutionary psychology, moral heuristics, and the law' in Gerd Gigerenzer and Christoph Engel (eds), *Heuristics and the Law*, Cambridge, MA: MIT Press, p. 175.

Cronk, Lee, Napoleon Chagnon and William Irons (eds) (2000), *Adaptation and Human Behavior: An Anthropological Perspective*, Hawthorne, CA: Aldine de Gruyter.

Du Laing, Bart (2007), 'Evolutionary analysis in law and the theory and practice of legislation', *Legisprudence: International Journal for the Study of Legislation*, **1**, 327.

Du Laing, Bart (2009), 'Equality in exchange revisited: from an evolutionary (genetic and cultural) point of view' in Michael Freeman and Oliver R. Goodenough (eds), *Law, Mind and Brain*, Aldershot: Ashgate, p. 267.
Dunbar, Robin and Louise Barrett (2007), 'Evolutionary psychology in the round' in R.I.M. Dunbar and Louise Barrett (eds), *Oxford Handbook of Evolutionary Psychology*, Oxford: Oxford University Press, p. 3.
Durham, William H. (2002), 'Cultural variation in time and space: The case for a populational theory of culture' in Richard G. Fox and Barbara J. King (eds), *Anthropology Beyond Culture*, Oxford: Berg, p. 193.
Efferson, Charles, Masanori Takezawa and Richard McElreath (2007), 'New methods in quantitative ethnography: Economic experiments and variation in the price of equality', *Current Anthropology*, **48**, 912.
Enquist, Magnus, Kimmo Eriksson and Stefano Ghirlanda (2007), 'Critical social learning: A solution to Rogers's paradox of nonadaptive culture', *American Anthropologist*, **109**, 727.
Eriksson, Kimmo and Pontus Strimling (2008), 'Cooperation through evolution of social contracts', Working paper presented at European Human Behaviour & Evolution Conference 2008 (Montpellier, 2–4). April).
Eriksson, Kimmo, Magnus Enquist and Stefano Ghirlanda (2007), 'Critical points in current theory of conformist social learning', *Journal of Evolutionary Psychology*, **5**, 67.
Fehr, Ernst and Urs Fischbacher (2004), 'Social norms and human cooperation', *Trends in Cognitive Sciences*, **8**, 185.
Fehr, Ernst and Urs Fischbacher (2005), 'Human altruism – proximate patterns and evolutionary origins', *Analyse & Kritik*, **27**, 6.
Flinn, Mark V. (1997), 'Culture and the evolution of social learning', *Evolution and Human Behavior*, **18**, 23.
Gintis, Herbert (2007), 'Book Review: David J. Buller, Adapting Minds: Evolutionary Psychology and the Persistent Quest for Human Nature', *Journal of Bioeconomics*, **9**, 191.
Gintis, Herbert, Samuel Bowles, Robert Boyd and Ernst Fehr (2003), 'Explaining altruistic behavior in humans', *Evolution and Human Behavior*, **24**, 153.
Goodenough, Oliver R. and Monika Gruter Cheney (2008), 'Preface: Is free enterprise values in action?' in Paul J. Zak (ed.), *Moral Markets: The Critical Role of Values in the Economy*, Princeton, NJ: Princeton University Press, p.xxiii.
Gordley, James (1997), *Contract in Pre-Commercial Societies and in Western History (International Encyclopedia of Comparative Law, VII/2, Contracts in general*, Tübingen: Mohr Siebeck.
Gruter, Margaret (1976), *Die Bedeutung der Verhaltensforschung für die Rechtswissenschaft (Schriftenreihe zur Rechtssoziologie und Rechtstatsachenforschung 36)*, Berlin: Duncker & Humblot.
Gruter, Margaret (1980), 'Soziobiologische Grundlagen der Effektivität des Rechts', *Rechtstheorie*, **11**, 96.
Gruter Morhenn, Monika and Margaret Gruter (2001), 'The evolution of law and biology' in Steven A. Peterson & Albert Somit (eds), *Evolutionary Approaches in the Behavioral Sciences: Toward a Better Understanding of Human Nature (Research in Biopolitics 8)*, New York: JAI Press, p. 119.
Hejl, Peter M. (2001), 'Konstruktivismus und Universalien – eine Verbindung contre nature?' in Peter M. Hejl (ed.), *Universalien und Konstruktivismus*, Frankfurt: Suhrkamp, p. 7.
Henrich, Joseph and Natalie Henrich (2006), 'Culture, evolution and the puzzle of human cooperation', *Cognitive Systems Research*, **7**, 220.
Henrich, Joseph and Richard McElreath (2007), 'Dual-inheritance theory: The evolution of human cultural capacities and cultural evolution' in R.I.M. Dunbar and Louise Barrett (eds), *Oxford Handbook of Evolutionary Psychology*, Oxford: Oxford University Press, p. 555.
Henrich, Joseph, Wulf Albers, Robert Boyd, Gerd Gigerenzer, Kevin A. McCabe, Axel Ockenfels and H. Peyton Young (2001), 'Group report: What is the role of culture in bounded rationality?' in Gerd Gigerenzer & Reinhard Selten (eds), *Bounded Rationality: The Adaptive Toolbox*, Cambridge: MIT Press, p. 343.
Henrich, Joseph, Robert Boyd, Samuel Bowles, Colin Camerer, Ernst Fehr, Herbert Gintis, Richard

McElreath, Michael Alvard, Abigail Barr, Jean Ensminger, Natalie Smith Henrich, Kim Hill, Francisco Gil-White, Michael Gurven, Frank W. Marlowe, John Q. Patton and David Tracer (2005), '"Economic Man" in cross-cultural perspective: Behavioral experiments in 15 small-scale societies', *Behavioral and Brain Sciences*, **28**, 795.

Henrich, Natalie and Joseph Henrich (2007), *Why Humans Cooperate: A Cultural and Evolutionary Explanation*, Oxford: Oxford University Press.

Herrmann, Benedikt, Christian Thöni and Simon Gächter (2008), 'Antisocial punishment across societies', *Science*, **319**, 1362.

Hodgson, Geoffrey M. (2002), 'Darwinism in economics: From analogy to ontology', *Journal of Evolutionary Economics*, **12**, 259.

Hodgson, Geoffrey M. (2007), 'Taxonomizing the relationship between biology and economics: A very long engagement', *Journal of Bioeconomics*, **9**, 169.

Hodgson, Geoffrey M. and Thorbjørn Knudsen (2006), 'Why we need a generalized Darwinism, and why generalized Darwinism is not enough', *Journal of Economic Behavior & Organization*, **61**, 1.

Hodgson, Geoffrey M. and Thorbjørn Knudsen (2007), 'From group selection to organizational interactors', MPI Jena Papers on Economics and Evolution 0716.

Hoffman, Elizabeth, Kevin A. McCabe and Vernon L. Smith (1998), 'Behavioral foundations of reciprocity: Experimental economics and evolutionary psychology', *Economic Inquiry*, **36**, 335.

Janicki, Maria G. and Dennis L. Krebs (1998), 'Evolutionary approaches to culture' in Charles Crawford and Dennis L. Krebs (eds), *Handbook of Evolutionary Psychology: Ideas, Issues, and Applications*, Mahwah, NJ: Lawrence Erlbaum, p. 163.

Jones, Owen D. (1997), 'Evolutionary analysis in law: An introduction and application to child abuse', *North Carolina Law Review*, **75**, 1117.

Jones, Owen D. (2001a), 'Proprioception, non-law, and biolegal history', *Florida Law Review*, **53**, 831.

Jones, Owen D. (2001b), 'Time-shifted rationality and the law of law's leverage: Behavioral economics meets behavioral biology', *Northwestern University Law Review*, **95**, 1141.

Jones, Owen D. (2004), 'Law, evolution and the brain: applications and open questions', *Philosophical Transactions of the Royal Society of London B Biological Sciences*, **359**, 1697.

Jones, Owen D. (2005), 'Evolutionary psychology and the law' in David M. Buss (ed.), *The Handbook of Evolutionary Psychology*, Hoboken, NJ: Wiley, p. 953.

Jones, Owen D. and Timothy H. Goldsmith (2005), 'Law and behavioral biology', *Columbia Law Review*, **105**, 405.

Kahan, Dan M. (2005), 'The logic of reciprocity: Trust, collective action, and law' in Herbert Gintis, Samuel Bowles, Robert Boyd & Ernst Fehr (eds), *Moral Sentiments and Material Interests: The Foundations of Cooperation in Economic Life*, Cambridge, MA: MIT Press, p. 339.

Laland, Kevin N. and Gillian R. Brown (2002), *Sense and Nonsense: Evolutionary Perspectives on Human Behaviour*, Oxford: Oxford University Press.

Laland, Kevin N. and Gillian R. Brown (2006), 'Niche construction, human behavior, and the adaptive-lag hypothesis', *Evolutionary Anthropology*, **15**, 95.

Laland, Kevin N., John Odling-Smee and Marcus W. Feldman (2000), 'Niche construction, biological evolution, and cultural change', *Behavioral and Brain Sciences*, **23**, 131.

Laland, Kevin N., F. John Odling-Smee and Marcus W. Feldman (2001), 'Niche construction, ecological inheritance, and cycles of contingency in evolution' in Susan Oyama, Paul E. Griffiths and Russell D. Gray (eds), *Cycles of Contingency: Developmental Systems and Evolution*, Cambridge, MA: MIT Press, p. 117.

Landa, Janet T. (1999), 'The law and bioeconomics of ethnic cooperation and conflict in plural societies of southeast Asia: A theory of Chinese merchant success', *Journal of Bioeconomics*, **1**, 269.

Landa, Janet T. (2008), 'The bioeconomics of homogeneous middleman groups as adaptive units: Theory and empirical evidence viewed from a group selection framework', *Journal of Bioeconomics*, **10**, 259.

Luhmann, Niklas (1975/1991), 'Systemtheorie, Evolutionstheorie und Kommunikationstheorie' in *Soziologische Aufklärung 2: Aufsätze zur Theorie der Gesellschaft*, Opladen: Westdeutscher Verlag, p. 193.

Luhmann, Niklas (1993/1995), *Das Recht der Gesellschaft (suhrkamp taschenbuch wissenschaft 1183)*, Frankfurt: Suhrkamp.
Mameli, Matteo (2007), 'Evolution and psychology in philosophical perspective' in R.I.M. Dunbar and Louise Barrett (eds), *Oxford Handbook of Evolutionary Psychology*, Oxford: Oxford University Press, p. 21.
McElreath, Richard and Joseph Henrich (2007), 'Modelling cultural evolution' in R.I.M. Dunbar and Louise Barrett (eds), *Oxford Handbook of Evolutionary Psychology*, Oxford: Oxford University Press, p. 57.
Plotkin, Henry (2002), *The Imagined World Made Real: Towards a Natural Science of Culture*, London: Penguin.
Richerson, Peter J. and Robert Boyd (2000), 'Evolution: The Darwinian theory of social change – An homage to Donald T. Campbell' in Waltraud Schelkle, Wolf-Hagen Krauth, Martin Kohli and Georg Elwert (eds), *Paradigms of Social Change: Modernization, Development, Transformation, Evolution*, Frankfurt: Campus Verlag, p. 257.
Richerson, Peter J. and Robert Boyd (2001), 'The evolution of subjective commitment to groups: A tribal instincts hypothesis' in Randolph M. Nesse (ed.), *Evolution and the Capacity for Commitment*, New York: Russell Sage Foundation, p. 186.
Richerson, Peter J. and Robert Boyd (2005), *Not by Genes Alone: How Culture Transformed Human Evolution*, Chicago: University of Chicago Press.
Richerson, Peter J. and Robert Boyd (2008), 'The evolution of free enterprise values' in Paul J. Zak (ed.), *Moral Markets: The Critical Role of Values in the Economy*, Princeton: Princeton University Press, p. 107.
Richerson, Peter J., Robert T. Boyd and Joseph Henrich (2003), 'Cultural evolution of human cooperation' in Peter Hammerstein (ed.), *Genetic and Cultural Evolution of Cooperation*, Cambridge, MA: MIT Press, p. 357.
Robson, Arthur J. (2001), 'The biological basis of economic behavior', *Journal of Economic Literature*, **39**, 11.
Sear, Rebecca, David W. Lawson and Thomas E. Dickins (2007), 'Synthesis in the human evolutionary behavioural sciences', *Journal of Evolutionary Psychology*, **5**, 3.
Sigmund, Karl (2007), 'Punish or perish? Retaliation and collaboration among humans', *Trends in Ecology and Evolution*, **22**, 593.
Simpson, Brent and Kimmo Eriksson (2009), 'The dynamics of contracts and generalized trustworthiness', *Rationality and Society* **21**, 59.
Smirnov, Oleg (2007), 'Altruistic punishment in politics and life sciences: Climbing the same mountain in theory and practice', *Perspectives on Politics*, **5**, 489.
Smith, Eric Alden (2000), 'Three styles in the evolutionary analysis of human behavior' in Lee Cronk, Napoleon Chagnon and William Irons (eds), *Adaptation and Human Behavior: An Anthropological Perspective*, Hawthorne: Aldine de Gruyter, p. 27.
Smith, Eric A., Monique Borgerhoff Mulder and Kim Hill (2001), 'Controversies in the evolutionary social sciences: A guide for the perplexed', *Trends in Ecology and Evolution*, **16**, 128.
Sripada, Chandra Sekhar (2005), 'Punishment and the strategic structure of moral systems', *Biology and Philosophy*, **20**, 767.
Teubner, Gunther (1993), *Law as an Autopoietic System*, Oxford: Blackwell.
Teubner, Gunther (2001), 'Economics of gift – Positivity of justice: The mutual paranoia of Jacques Derrida and Niklas Luhmann', *Theory, Culture & Society*, **18**, 29.
Teubner, Gunther (2002), 'Idiosyncratic production regimes: Co-evolution of economic and legal institutions in the varieties of capitalism' in Michael Wheeler, John Ziman and Margaret A. Boden (eds), *The Evolution of Cultural Entities (Proceedings of the British Academy 112)*, Oxford: Oxford University Press, p. 161.
Tooby, John and Leda Cosmides (1992), 'The psychological foundations of culture' in Jerome H. Barkow, Leda Cosmides and John Tooby (eds), *The Adapted Mind: Evolutionary Psychology and the Generation of Culture*, Oxford: Oxford University Press, p. 19.
Trivers, Robert (2006), 'Reciprocal altruism: 30 years later' in Peter M. Kappeler and Carel P. van Schaik (eds), *Cooperation in Primates and Humans: Mechanisms and Evolution*, Berlin: Springer, p. 67.

Ulen, Thomas S. (2001), 'Evolution, human behavior, and law: A response to Owen Jones's Dunwody Lecture', *Florida Law Review*, **53**, 931.

van den Bergh, Jeroen C.J.M. and John M. Gowdy (2003), 'The microfoundations of macroeconomics: an evolutionary perspective', *Cambridge Journal of Economics*, **27**, 65.

van den Bergh, Jeroen C.J.M. and Sigrid Stagl (2003), 'Coevolution of economic behaviour and institutions: Towards a theory of institutional change', *Journal of Evolutionary Economics*, **13**, 289.

Vromen, Jack (2004), 'Conjectural revisionary economic ontology: Outline of an ambitious research agenda for evolutionary economics', *Journal of Economic Methodology*, **11**, 213.

Vromen, Jack (2008), 'Ontological issues in evolutionary economics: The debate between generalized Darwinism and the continuity hypothesis', MPI Jena Papers on Economics and Evolution 0805.

Wilson, David Sloan (1999), 'Tasty slice – But where is the rest of the pie? (Book Review David M. Buss, *Evolutionary Psychology: The New Science of the Mind*)', *Evolution and Human Behavior*, **20**, 279.

Wilson, David Sloan (2000), 'Religious groups and homogeneous merchant groups as adaptive units: A multilevel evolutionary perspective', *Journal of Bioeconomics*, **2**, 271.

Wilson, David Sloan (2002), *Darwin's cathedral: Evolution, religion, and the nature of society*, Chicago: University of Chicago Press.

Wilson, David Sloan (2003), 'Evolution, morality and human potential' in Steven J. Scher and Frederick Rauscher (eds), *Evolutionary Psychology: Alternative Approaches*, Boston: Kluwer Academic Publishers, p. 55.

Wilson, David Sloan (2004), 'The new fable of the bees: Multilevel selection, adaptive societies, and the concept of self interest' in Roger Koppl (ed.), *Evolutionary Psychology and Economic Theory (Advances in Austrian Economics 7)*, Amsterdam: Elsevier, p. 201.

Wilson, David Sloan (2005), 'Natural selection and complex systems: a complex interaction' in Charlotte K. Hemelrijk (ed.), *Self-Organisation and Evolution of Complex Systems*, Cambridge: Cambridge University Press, p. 151.

Wilson, David Sloan (2007), 'Group-level evolutionary processes' in R.I.M. Dunbar and Louise Barrett (eds), *Oxford Handbook of Evolutionary Psychology*, Oxford: Oxford University Press, p. 49.

Winterhalder, Bruce and Eric Alden Smith (2000), 'Analyzing adaptive strategies: Human behavioral ecology at twenty-five', *Evolutionary Anthropology*, **9**, 51.

Witt, Ulrich (2004), 'On the proper interpretation of "evolution" in economics and its implications for production theory', *Journal of Economic Methodology*, **11**, 125.

Zak, Paul J. (ed.) (2008), *Moral Markets: The Critical Role of Values in the Economy*, Princeton, Princeton University Press.

12. Making evolutionary theory useful for legal actors

Mauro Zamboni*

As pointed out by many scholars, there is a general skeptical attitude of a large sector of the legal scholarship towards the evolutionary approach.[1] The main objective of this chapter is to make the first step in the direction of making evolutionary theory more useful for and therefore sympathetic to lawyers and legal actors in general. This step consists in elevating evolutionary theory from the status of external investigation of the legal phenomenon to being a fundamental contributor to the legal discourse also in its normative parts. The focus in particular is to understand why, though the evolutionary theory approach to law has been around quite a while in the legal scholar's discussion, the legal world has left it at the front step of the legal house.[2] Based on this analysis, the task is also to evaluate whether it is possible, after certain adjustments, to invite evolutionary theory into the larger family of legal thinking, in particular as part of the legal theories of law-making.

As stressed by many critiques, it is possible to detect in most of the evolutionary approaches to the law some hidden normative components.[3] For example, when using statements such as 'legal uniformity . . . *should* to a large extent come about in an organic way,' evolutionary scholars implicitly assume a normative proposal (i.e. that 'the organic way ought to be pursued') while, at the same time, they hide the criteria according to which this proposal is preferable to another (if the 'organic way' is to be chosen, is it because it is more economically efficient or because it is more just?).[4] The task of this work is to cut these critiques at their very roots by somehow convincing the legal evolutionary scholars to bring such components to the surface of their legal discussion in form of explicit guidelines for future law-making and law-applying.

Before proceeding to the analysis, it is necessary to clarify at least two of the fundamental concepts used throughout this work, namely 'legal theory' and 'law-making.' Following Herbert L.A. Hart's definition, the concept of *legal theory* is used here in order to indicate that part of the legal discipline (or legal scholarship) aimed at generally

* I would like to deeply thank Gralf-Peter Calliess, Laura Carlson, and Jakob Heidbrink for their many and invaluable comments on earlier drafts.

1 See Sinclair (1993), 56. See also Holmes (1899), 447. See, e.g., Leiter and Weisberg (2006), 48; or Jones (1994), 265. But see Elliott (1985), 38; or Hutchinson (2005a), 10.

2 See Stein (1980), 69–98.

3 See, e.g., Blankenburg (1984), 279, 281, 284–285. But see Teubner (1984), 294.

4 Smits (2002), 81. As other examples of hidden normative proposals, see Teubner (1983), 273; or Teubner (note 3), 300.

seeking (i.e. not being bound to any particular legal order or legal culture) 'to give an explanatory and clarifying account of law as a complex of social and political institutions' from the perspective of the legal actors or, as expressed by Hart, the 'internal point of view of a legal system'.[5] Legal theory as used in this work is then that part of the jurisprudential studies which focuses on and questions, from the standpoint of rationality typical of Western legal cultures, the 'prevailing patterns of argumentation and interpretation' both in law-making and law-applying.[6]

As to that which legal theory aims to explain and clarify, traditionally it has to be pointed out that legal theory can always be categorized as either *descriptive* (or *positive*) legal theory, when explaining what the law is (and the reasons and effects of this definition), or *normative* legal theory, in case it has as its main target what the law ought to be.[7] However, this separation has progressively disappeared in recent decades; nowadays, most legal theories comprise a descriptive and normative component. Due in particular to the critiques of the idea of 'description' as developed by critical legal theories and Ronald Dworkin, at least all the major legal schools incorporate in their theoretical frameworks both a description of what law is (*descriptive component*) and a prescription of what law ought to be (*normative component*).[8] Contemporary legal theory varies considerably of course as to what kinds of ideal-models the law ought aim to (e.g. economic efficiency, consistency, justice); moreover, differences remain as to the goal of legal theory being the description of the 'normative' proposals legal actors ought to follow (as for the modern versions of legal positivism) or the prescription of those proposals (as for Critical Legal Studies).[9] In any case, normative proposals in general are a necessary component of every legal theory, either in the form of identifying or sponsoring them, since its object of observation (the law) 'is normative in that it *serves* [descriptive component], and it *means to serve* [normative component], as a guide for human behavior.'[10]

As to the concept of law-making, this encompasses the mechanisms and procedures having legal recognition and directed to the production and enforcement of the law. This

---

5 Hart (1994), 239. See also Hart (1983), 103–105; and MacCormick (1981), 37–40. But see, concerning this general and descriptive idea of legal theory, the criticism in Dworkin (1997), 32. See also Hart's defense by Raz (2001), 27–36; and by Endicott (2001), 41–7.

6 Tuori (2002), 320. In this sense, legal theory is part of a broader (legal) culture; see Plotkin (2000), 74.

7 See Wacks (2005), 7–8; Rodriguez-Blanco (2006), 26–7; and, as a concrete example of the necessity to keep in mind this distinction, Schauer (1996), 343–5. As to the historical roots of this distinction, see Austin (1954 [1832], 184–5); and Bentham (1970[1789]), Ch. XVII, § 2, part XXI. See also Holmes (1897), 457–60. But see Deakin (2002), 36 as to the different meaning attached to the term 'normative' by the evolutionary theory's scholars, i.e. as purely descriptive of the binding character of the law for its being inserted in a hierarchical system of norms.

8 See Tuori (note 6), 300–304, showing the necessity for each legal-theoretical approach to (explicitly or implicitly) begin with the acceptance of a certain evaluative social theory. See also Pound (1997 [1942]), 118 and Raz (1994), 219–221. As to the criticisms of the distinction, see, e.g., Dworkin (note 5), 13–14; and Unger (1996), 122–3.

9 See Radin and Michelman (1991), 1020, 1023–4. See, e.g., Raz (1990), 153 and Schlag (1991), 811. See also Cotterrell (2003), 3; and Pavlakos (2005), 101–102 But see Rodriguez-Blanco (note 7), 27.

10 Raz (1980), 3 [*italics added*]. See also Gavison (1991), 731. But see Marmor (2006), 688–9; Waluchow (1994), 15–30; and Postema (1987), 85.

also includes the institutional actors (hereinafter 'actors') participating in such production and enforcement. In other words, law-making refers to the operational aspects of the legal phenomenon, the mechanisms that make certain moral propositions or political declarations directly relevant, either in legislative or judicial forms, for the legal world and its actors.[11]

1. EVOLUTIONARY THEORY AND LAW: READJUSTING THE LEGAL THEORETICAL PERSPECTIVE

Mentioning 'evolutionary theory' in a legal environment or to a legal audience always creates the same kind of general reaction: Most people will raise their eyebrows in skeptical disbelief. The skeptical disbelief is based on the presumption of some sort of association of this legal theoretical approach to the idea of a natural selection as a basic mechanism for explaining and understanding the modern legal world.[12] In other words, evolutionary theory is not popular among lawyers and legal thinkers because it is conceived as an attempt to introduce into the legal world a sort of Social Darwinism ideology, just slightly modified on the surface in order to satisfy specific formal features of the legal phenomena.[13] This erroneous perception is mostly due to a deep terminological confusion and vague depiction shared by the legal audience, and therefore it is necessary to provide certain readjustments as to what an 'evolutionary approach to the law' is, especially when viewing it from the legal actors' perspective in relation to legal theory.[14]

The first readjustment a legal theoretical audience needs to consider making is that it is necessary to distinguish between a *theory of legal evolution* and *evolutionary theory and law*.[15] Inside legal scholarship, a theory of legal evolution is a general label attached to all legal thinking aiming at discovering and explaining general patterns of continuity and change in the law. In this sense, the works of Henry James Sumner Maine, Oliver Wendell Holmes, or more recently of the economic approach, Peter Stein and Alan Watson can be considered, for example, as presenting a theory of legal evolution.[16] Among the different theories of legal evolution, one can find an approach defined as 'evolutionary theory and

[11] See, e.g., Raz (note 10), 156–66; and the Hartian idea of legal system as interpreted by MacCormick (note 5), 20–24.

[12] See, e.g., Ruse (1999), 198. But see Hovenkamp (1985), 646.

[13] See Beckstrom (1989), 34. See, e.g., Palmer (1945), 571; or Dudziak (1986), 835–6. See also Duxbury (1997), 34–5, 41–6. But see the critique moved by Holmes himself to the evolutionary approach as intended by the US Supreme Court in the famous decision *Lochner v. New York*, 198 US 75 (1905). See also a list of possible Social Darwinist evolutionary legal thinkers as in Hovenkamp (note 12), 664–71.

[14] See Luhmann (2004), 230. As to the other applications of the evolutionary approach (in particular in economics and social sciences), these will not be here considered in this work. See, e.g., Haferkamp and Smelser (1992), 4–6; and Nelson (1995), 48–90.

[15] See Sinclair (note 1), 32; and Elliott (note 1), 90–91. As an example of this confusion, see Hutchinson (2005b), 254–7.

[16] See, e.g., Maine (2005 [1861]), Ch. 2; Holmes (1963 [1881]), 1–2; Clark (1981), 1250–4, 1257–8; generally Rubin (1977), 51; Watson (1985), 98–114; and Stein (note 2), 122. See also Deakin (note 7), 3.

law' to whose scrutiny this work is limited. The approach of evolutionary theory and law under whose roof several schools can be grouped, is characterized in general not only by its attention to points of change and stability in the law through the centuries and among various legal systems.[17] Evolutionary theory and law distinguishes itself also for evaluating these aspects of the legal phenomenon from the point of view that Hart would define as typical of theories external to the law and its system: Luhmann's sociological theory on law (as in Europe) and biological evolutionary theory as metaphor or analogy for explaining the evolution of the law (as in the United States).[18]

A second aspect legal scholars should also take into account, is namely that evolutionary theory and law is an evolutionary approach, in the sense of explaining changes in the law and legal system, but not necessarily also an 'evolutionist' way of investigating the legal phenomenon.[19] From an evolutionist perspective, which for instance can be attributed to Marxist legal theory or a majority of Law and Economics scholars, the central point of investigating changes in law are both the mechanisms of legal evolution and the directions to which the law or some of its parts (e.g. torts law) are bound.[20] The evolutionary theory and law focuses its attention instead exclusively on the explanation of the mechanisms underlying the changes and continuities of a certain legal system (or part of it); this approach does not also explicitly designate the points of arrival to which such a system (or its parts) is obliged to aim.[21]

Finally there is a third aspect as to the idea of an evolutionary approach to the law, to which the legal discipline should pay particular attention. This aspect has to do with the very object of the investigation in this approach, namely the evolution of the components of the legal phenomenon which is under scrutiny. At least if seen from a legal perspective, evolutionary theory applies neither to a single statute, nor to a single judicial decision nor, more generally, to a single legal rule.[22] Those under the spotlight of an evolutionary approach actually are in general more 'legal concepts'. Law-making cannot be identified by one single process leading to one single legal decision. It is more a question of several and usually chronologically asymmetrical processes leading to the production, often

---

[17] See Strahlendorf (1993), 23–5 though the author uses the concept of 'evolutionary jurisprudence' instead of 'evolutionary theory and law.' See also Hutchinson and Archer (2001), 31; and Hovenkamp (note 12), 646: 'not every theory of jurisprudence that includes a theory of legal change qualifies as "evolutionary"'. However, as pointed out by Michael S. Fried, 'the enormous change in sophistication over time suggests that the literature on evolution and the law may itself be as susceptible to an evolutionary analysis as its subject'. Fried (1999), 303–304.

[18] See Sinclair (1987), 451. See also Teubner (note 4), 241, and Hart (1961), 90. But see Deakin and Wilkinson (2005), 28. In this sense, in this work 'evolutionary approaches to the law' coincide with Elliot's 'doctrinal' theories of legal evolution (note 1), 50–62.

[19] See MacCormack (1985), 252–253. See also Fried (note 17), 313–15 (as an example of 'evolutionary' approach); Ruhl (1996), 857 (as an example of 'evolutionist' approach); and Blankenburg (note 3), 273, purposely mixing the terms 'evolutionary' and 'evolutionist.'

[20] See Gordon (1984), 103. See, e.g., Marx (1977 [1848]), 234; or Priest (1977), 65; or Posner (1992), 534–6. See also Stein (note 2), 46–50, 67–8; and Horowitz (1994), 244–247. But see, e.g., Roe (1996), 654–658.

[21] See Teubner (1993), 48–49, 54. As to a similar line of defense for Holmes' evolutionary approach, see Wiener (1949), Ch. 8.

[22] See, e.g., Luhmann (note 14), 250 (focusing on 'property' and 'contract'); or Deakin (2001), 29–33.

through several statutes and/or judicial law-making decisions, to a legal concept. The latter can be defined as a group (often scattered) of rules and normative regulations that aim, through their coordination and combination, at building an interaction responding to the criteria required by the rationality of the law.[23] Depending on several factors (legal system under consideration, theoretical assumptions of the observer and so on), the legal rationality can demand the various rules in order to be called as legal concept, to be grouped either according to formal criteria, e.g. with the idea of consistency or coherence, or according to substantial criteria, e.g. economic efficiency or justice.[24] This product of the evolution process, namely the rationalized interaction of rules (legal concept), forms a theoretical matrix with the primary classificatory and normative functions of helping primarily legal actors (but often also all actors dealing with the law) in diagnosing and systematizing legal problems occurring both in the creation and interpretation of the law.[25]

As can be seen from this brief and necessarily rough sketch of the main claims by evolutionary theory and law (at least as perceived from a legal theoretical perspective), the skepticism that this approach encounters in legal theory is largely unfounded, or at least, is based on the wrong ideas. To immediately connect evolutionary theory to a social Darwinism explanation of the law and its making, i.e. an explanation justifying the dominant legal cultures and their paradigms (or principles) as being *per se* the best in a sort of deterministic way, paradoxically neglects the very evolution that the evolutionary theories have gone through.[26] If one considers the basic ideas behind the modern evolutionary approaches to the legal phenomenon in particular, there are only two things they have in common with Darwin's original evolution theory and its subsequent distortions as a social theory. They both aim at finding some general explanatory model to clarify how complex phenomena such as an animal species or a legal system change.[27] Moreover, both Darwin and contemporary evolutionary approaches to law aim at pointing out that such changes always occur in multiple phases; the law and its parts, like the animal species and its parts, have continuous relations both with the surrounding environments and with their internal structures, relations which in the end determine the shape of the law as it does for the animal species.[28]

The basic feature characterizing the evolutionary approach to the law as 'Darwinian'

---

[23] See Samuel (2003), 220–222 as to the definition of legal concept. See, e.g., Bell (1983), 40–43, 68–77; or MacCormick (1997), 259.

[24] See, e.g., Kelsen (1970), 89–91; Finnis (1980), 276; or Posner (1998), 182.

[25] See Hart (1983), 93; and Weber (1978), 656–7. See also Hohfeld (1917), 712–13. Legal concepts and categories play both a classificatory and a normative function as pointed out by Tuori (note 6), 218. Compare Pound (1958), 84; and Samuel (note 24), 139–140 as to the distinction between normative and descriptive legal concepts. See, e.g., Kurki-Suonio (2000), 187–99 (as to the legal concept known as joint custody).

[26] See, e.g., Sward (2004), 391.

[27] See Gould (1991), 455.

[28] See, e.g., Sinclair (note 18), 471. But see Luhmann (note 14), 233, where the author distances himself (and in general the modern evolutionary approach to law) from the historical antecedents (e.g. Friedrich von Savigny) pointing out that '[e]volution is not a gradual, continuous, seamless increase in complexity but a model . . . compatible with radical erratic changes . . . and with long periods of stagnation.' See also Deakin (note 7), 39.

eventually is the same as that characterizing each legal theoretical approach to the law-making process: the attempt to explain the processes of law-making by taking into consideration not only the internal structures and different parts of a legal system, but also how these internal aspects relate and somehow 'survive' the confrontation with the external realities in which the results of the evolution (e.g. a new law) are to exist.[29] As pointed out by Herbert Hovenkamp:

> Jurisprudence was also 'evolutionary' long before Darwin, and it continues to be evolutionary. Like most other intellectual disciplines, jurisprudence needs a theory of change. . . . Today every theory of jurisprudence worth contemplating incorporates a theory of change.[30]

Having this common point with the theory of law-making, it is then worth investigating whether and, if so, what benefits can be derived in using the evolutionary approach to construct a theory of the law-making processes.

2. WHAT EVOLUTIONARY THEORY CAN('T) DO FOR THE LEGAL ACTORS

The distinguishing feature of evolutionary theories, when applied to the legal phenomenon, is their focus on the various stages of the law-making process, namely variation, selection and retention.[31] As pointed out by several scholars, the focus of evolutionary theory is on legal change.[32] From the perspective of a legal actor, legal change is always identified with law-making, as long as the latter is intended in the broad meaning of the process of creation and implementation of certain legal concepts in legislative or judicial forms.[33]

For most of legal actors in modern times, the very essence of the law and its normative nature can be traced in it being considered as binding by its addressees (or the community at large) regardless of the 'empirical' surrounding, i.e. in it being perceived as an 'Ought' regardless of the surrounding 'Being.'[34] As a consequence, changes of legal systems and categories can only be achieved by producing other (alternative) legal systems and categories, i.e. only by making new and different laws. The sources of legal changes of course can be different, going from a changing economic reality pressuring for a better Ought to purely doctrinal developments of the legal system. Moreover, law-making (as legal

---

[29] See Deakin and Wilkinson (note 18), 30.

[30] Hovenkamp (note 12), 645–6 [footnotes omitted]. See also Stein (note 2), ix; Stone (1966), 36; and Deakin (note 7), 41–2, talking in particular of 'a very tenuous link' between Darwinian thought and established evolutionary approaches to the law.

[31] See Luhmann (note 14), 230–31; Holmes (note 1), 448–50; and Clark (note 16), 1241. See also Sinclair (note 1), 36; and Campbell (1965), 27–9.

[32] See Teubner (1988), 7–9; and Clark (note 16), 1239. See also Hovenkamp (note 12), 647; and Elliott (note 1), 41, 46, 49 as to the historical roots of this connection between 'legal evolution' and 'legal change.'

[33] See Smits (note 4), 81: and Beckstrom (1985), 3–5. See also Jabbari (1992), 529.

[34] See, e.g., MacCormick (note 24), 236–8; Hart (note 18), 86–8, 181–2; Posner (2001), 158; Kelsen (1996 [1934]), 15–16; Holmes (note 7), 461; and Ross (1957), 818–22. But see Note (1982), 1678.

change) can produce different and sometimes opposite outcomes to the ones planned. In any case, all legal actors agree that to change the law, one always eventually needs a new law or, as stated by Teubner, '[l]aw itself defines the preconditions of a legal act and thus the preconditions of every change in the law.'[35]

This being one of the central axioms of contemporary legal culture, and one of the major contributions of evolutionary theory, the explanation of how the legal system arrived to produce the new law, the insertion of the evolutionary approach (in its current version) in the world of legal thinking is very much desirable, both as a theory of law-applying and as a theory of law-making. As to the first, evolutionary theory still retains in both its European and American versions one of the fundamental aspects of the evolutionary theory as formulated by Darwin: Evolutionary theory is a theory directed at explaining the present by looking at its past or, in other words, directed to answer the question of how we became what we are.[36] The basic goal for each evolutionary theory is then to provide legal scholars, law-makers and, last but not least, judges with clearer knowledge as to the background of legal concepts in force in a certain legal system.[37]

As to the second possible contribution to legal theory, the major focus of the evolutionary theory is on changes in the law; therefore it seems pretty natural that this approach should be directed to the theory of law-making, i.e. that part of legal thinking that more than the others investigates the mechanisms and results of shifting from one legal regulation to the other.[38] In other words, the contribution that evolutionary theory can offer to a theory of law-making becomes fundamental since, by its attention to the process of creation, selection and stabilization of a new legal concept, it shows how a certain change has taken place in the legal system.

Despite its contributions to legal theory, the evolutionary theory cannot provide as a theoretical tool for the legal actors – from judges to law-drafters – because it lacks the necessary criteria to face future challenges.[39]

In its present form, the evolutionary approach to the law tends to be not so useful for legal actors because it does not take into consideration one of the basic points for law-making in modern capitalistic society (at least according to Max Weber): its instrumental rationality (*Zweckrationalität*), both in its substantive and more formal meaning.[40] According to Weber, instrumental rationality can be defined as the criteria leading to get

---

35 Teubner (note 21), 59. See also Raz (1994), 192; and Raz (note 8), 201.

36 See, e.g., Deakin (note 7), 35; or Jabbari (note 36), 530. See also Hutchinson and Archer (note 17), 24.

37 See, e.g., Jones (1997), 1157–8. See also Teubner (note 21), 49, where the author, however, limits the possible contribution of evolutionary approach to legal theory to a (rather obscure) idea of 'discouraging' the faith in a possible 'legal progress.' But see the critiques in Hutchinson (note 1), 8–9.

38 See, e.g., Shapo (1974), 1369–86 as to the usefulness for the future law-making of understanding the process of creation of legal concepts such as 'consumer protection' and 'products liability.'

39 See, e.g., Elliott (note 1), 92–93; Smits (note 4), 93; or Teubner (note 21), 49. See also Roe (note 20), 667. But see Strahlendorf (note 17), 723–35 attempting to sketch a framework of normative component for an evolutionary approach to the law.

40 See Weber (note 26), 654–8, 866. See also Rheinstein (1954), xlii. But see, e.g., Trubek (1972), 746–7; or Hunt (1978), 122–8. Compare Weber's defense in Ewing (1987), 494–7.

the aimed-at result by using the best means available, i.e. relative to the circumstances in a certain time and space.[41] It is often the very changes in the circumstances (internal or external to the legal system) in which the law operates that force legal, political and social actors to activate the law-making.[42] An evolutionary approach to law-making, therefore, in order to be taken to work by the legal actors or, in other words, in order to become a 'legal' evolutionary approach, needs not only to explain the past but also to be directed into the future, in particular by elaborating a normative theory capable of helping law-making actors create, select and stabilize future legal concepts adapted to changed circumstances.[43]

To summarize, by explaining the change in law, evolutionary theory can be useful for lawyers, judges and scholars. However, this use by legal actors is heavily restricted by the fact that this approach tends to limit its attention to what has happened. At the very moment a lawyer working for a drafting committee would need a general theory for some guidelines, i.e. in order to face a legal dilemma caused either by change of the surrounding environment or by internal development to the legal world, evolutionary theory as a possible legal theoretical first-aid kit fails, being focused on explaining what and why the change has happened instead of how to 'remedy' to it.[44] A major adjustment is therefore required in order to transform the evolutionary approach to law into a possible legal theory for law-making.[45]

3. EVOLUTIONARY THEORY AND LAW: RE-ADJUSTING THE EVOLUTIONARY PERSPECTIVE

The adjustment of evolutionary theory in order to become a legal evolutionary theory of the law in general and law-making in particular, is necessitated by the fact that evolutionary theory was born in order to explain phenomena different from the law, or at least to explain the legal phenomenon from a non-legal perspective.[46] The evolutionary approach was born as a metaphorical or analogical reproduction of the results reached in the natural sciences and biology (as to some American versions of evolutionary theory) or as a (more or less) direct transposition into legal analysis of methodologies created for

---

[41] See Weber (note 26), 636–7. But see the different meanings of 'rationality' traceable in Weber's works as in Kronman (1983), 73–5; and the criticisms in Habermas (1984), 262.

[42] See, e.g., Weber (note 26), 669. But see Gordon (note 20), 36.

[43] See Beckstrom (note 13), 28–41, where the author develops the same kind of criticisms, though limited to the socio-biological version of the evolutionary approach to the law. See also Elliott (1984), 114.

[44] See, e.g., Beckstrom (note 36), 58–9, not giving any reason why law-making actors should opt for a conservative line instead of a more liberal orientation on the issue of succession law; or Luhmann (note 14), 265, where the author points out the birth and development of a certain legal concept (self defense), while not offering to future law-making or law-applying actors possible criteria on where to draw the line where the legal/illegal border ought to be drawn. See also Gordon (note 20), 68, 71 as to the 'hidden' political agenda behind this lack of indication for the future law-making by evolutionary approach to the law.

[45] See Holmes (note 7), 474.

[46] See, e.g., Strahlendorf (note 17), 26–7, 574. See also the critique in Sinclair (1992), 81.

social and economic sciences (as for the European side of the story).[47] As a consequence, evolutionary theory tends to disregard, when applied to the legal phenomenon, both the specific nature of its object of investigation (the law), and especially the fundamental role played in the very formation of this object by the (internal) perspective adopted by the legal players, among which legal scholars should be included.[48]

One feature of the role of legal discipline in the legal phenomenon in particular, as pointed out by Alf Ross among the others, is its capability of changing the very object of observation.[49] In contrast to most natural sciences, and to a more direct and higher degree than for most of the social and economic sciences, legal scholars can actually directly influence the choice of patterns of future development of the law.

> Legal categories such as 'contract', 'tort' and 'crime' have all, for example, been the objects of intense theoretical writing and this theoretical literature has in turn had important influences in shaping directly or indirectly the functioning of the legal reasoning within each category.[50]

In other words, one can also state that legal theory is not only a 'theory of explaining and predicting' but also a 'theory for design and action.'[51] For example, law professors, by claiming the existence of a certain legal principle of efficiency inside tort law as an established 'fact,' can actually force future generations of law-makers and law-applying actors to introduce this principle, even if the original claim was false.[52] Using an epistemological vocabulary, it can be said that Karl Popper's criteria of falsification, at least when applied to legal theories, can (and often tends to) leave room for Robert K. Merton's idea of theory as capable of being a self-fulfilling (or a self-destroying) prophecy.[53]

This quality of the legal discipline in its turn has to do with the specific nature of the

---

[47] See Teubner (note 21), 52–3. As to the American version of evolutionary approach to the law, see, e.g., Elliott (note 1), 38–9; or Hutchinson (note 15), 262–5. See also Duxbury (note 13), 25–32. But see, as representative of a direct application (i.e. not metaphorical) of biology and behaviorist sciences in the understanding of the evolution of the law, O'Hara (2004), 1055; or Jones (2001), 207. As to the European version of evolutionary approach, see, e.g., Teubner (note 21), 49. See also Smits (note 4), 83–8, as a bridge between the two different evolutionary traditions.

[48] See Teubner (note 3), 300. But see Teubner (1991), 29. Compare Robin (1996), 562–3. See also the accusation of 'reductionism' as addressed to the evolutionary approach to the law in Blankenburg (note 3), 381. Another reason behind such lack of normative component can possibly be traced in the fact that evolutionary theory scholars want to clearly mark their distance from Social Darwinism and its 'normative hypostasizations.' See Teubner (note 21), 51.

[49] See Ross (1959), 47. See also Ulen (2002), 894–5. But see Luhmann (note 14), 252. See also *id.*, 270. See, e.g., Deakin (note 7), 26–9.

[50] Samuel (note 24), 222. See also Sinclair (1986), 384–6; and Ross (note 53), 50. See, e.g., Vogenauer (2006), 630–637.

[51] Gregor (2002), 16–20. See also Posner (1979), 285. pointing out the inevitability of the normative component in (law and economics) legal theory due to the normative nature of the very object to be theorized.

[52] As to a similar example in family issues, see Laquer Estin (1996), 9.

[53] See Merton (1948); and Ross (note 53), 47 n. 5. Compare Popper (1961), 40–41. See also Weinreb (2005), 2–3; and Hovenkamp (note 12), 648. But see, as an example of the current trend of evaluating evolutionary works mainly according to Popper's criteria of falsifiability, Clark (note 16), 1258–9; or Sinclair (note 18), 471–4.

law: Law is a human product aiming at regulating the relations of human beings with each other and with the surrounding environment.[54] As many legal scholars have pointed out, legal reasoning most of the time is a type of common sense reasoning, i.e. it often incorporates and uses moral, political, economic, or other kinds of values as criteria for regulating human behaviors.[55] However, legal reasoning has special requirements, due specifically to its normative and conflict resolution roles.[56] The regulation of human behaviors then is not based for instance on statements directed at convincing or persuading the addressees (as in politics). Legal reasoning is based instead on the use of specific language which, once it has transformed certain religious, cultural, moral, or economic values into legal concepts, indicates to the addressees (legal actors and/or the community at large) not models of behaviors they will 'probably' embrace, but model of behaviors that the addressees 'ought' to embrace.[57]

As seen already above, if one considers legal theory as that part of the legal discipline directed at explaining the law and the functioning of a legal system, legal theory necessarily carries with it a normative component. This is formed by a complex of statements made by the legal theoretician in which the latter indicates the direction in which legal actors 'ought' to proceed in order to fulfill certain goals that 'ought to be' in the legal system.[58] The indication of the 'ought-to-be' goals can then be made by using a descriptive terminology, i.e. 'by looking at the situation X, the addressee ought to behave as Y' (as for some modern legal positivists), or in prescriptive terms, i.e. 'value X is good, and therefore the addressee ought always to behave as Y' (as for some critical legal theories).[59] In both cases, due to the very normative nature of the law, legal theory is always expected not only to contribute through its descriptive component to a better understanding of the past and present law. Modern legal theory is expected to always offer a normative component, i.e. a part in which the directions to be used for future law and law-making not only are indicated, but are also 'justified' as to be the one that ought-to-be taken, for instance because they save the consistency and therefore the legitimacy of the legal system or because by following it, welfare will be maximized or gender discrimination will be eliminated.[60]

Some followers of the evolutionary theory at this point could reply that the evolutionary

---

[54] See Friedman (1985), 42. See, e.g., Fuller (1969).

[55] See, e.g., MacCormick (2005), 114–20; Sunstein (1996), 14–17; and Alexy (2002), 77. But see Friedman (1988), 253.

[56] See Bell (1986), 55–64. See also Gordon (1988), 112–120.

[57] See Kelsen (note 25), 4. As for the meaning of legal reasoning as used in this work, this is the process of deployment of legal argument, i.e. of 'argument in favor of or against a particular resolution of a gap, conflict, or ambiguity in the system of legal rules.' Kennedy (1991), 75.

[58] See Coleman (2003), 178, 199–201. See also Coleman (2001), 108 n. 22; and Rubin (1997), 543.

[59] As an example of 'descriptive terminology' of normative components, see Coleman (note 62), 179–86; Kelsen (1949); or Kelsen (1960). See also the criticisms in Hart (1998), 70–76. As an example of 'prescriptive terminology' of a normative component, see Tushnet (1992). See also Gordon (1990), 414–417.

[60] See Summers (1991), 1304–1305. See also Cicchino (2000). Compare the shifting of Law and Economics from a hard line descriptive legal theory, such as in Posner (1986), 14–15 to a mixture more of descriptive and normative components, such as in Posner (1990), 353–74.

approach, based on the investigations of how the law became what it is, actually devotes a relevant part of its analysis to future law and law-making. One fundamental component of evolutionary theory is its 'predictivist' component, where evolutionary theory, by explaining how a certain legal concept has been created, chosen and 'stabilized' in a certain legal system, aims to be able to also predict possible alternative patterns of creations of other legal concepts.[61] In other words, by explaining how a certain legal concept has established itself, evolutionary theory can predict how the latter will probably evolve and/or how it will be substituted.[62] For example, by looking at the history of financial leasing, evolutionary theory can predict that, in the future, the economic factors (namely the efficiency of a certain legal construction) in similar cases in the end will play a more important role than the legal formal factors (namely the lack of space inside a certain legal system for new types of legal concepts).

However, 'predictions' are not 'normative propositions,' or at least not explicitly.[63] The directions each legal theory is to offer to legal actors are not predictions (at least not directly) of what will happen; they are 'normative' directions, i.e. patterns that lawyers, judges and law-makers ought to take because they are (morally, politically, culturally, legally and so on) 'the right thing' to do, often regardless of the surrounding legal, political, social, or economic environment.[64] Moreover, normative propositions can have a direct performative force.[65] By taking the suggested normative patterns and due to the very nature of the law as human creation, legal actors in the end are able to shape the law in a certain direction, regardless of all the possible predictions made by the legal scholarship.[66] A classical example is the concept of 'separation based on race as inherently unequal.' This was unconsidered as a legal concept by legal actors throughout most of American legal history when it suddenly exploded as a legally relevant concept for interpreting the constitutional principle of the prohibition against discrimination (Equal

---

61 See Hutchinson and Archer (note 17), 30. 'A theory of legal evolution will be able to explain or *even predict* general structures of the law.' Teubner (note 21), 49 [*italics added*]. Though in a much more cautious way, see also Nonet and Selznick (1978), 17. But see Luhmann (note 14), 273: 'The concept of evolution itself prohibits . . . prognoses.' As to the meaning of 'predictivist' as used in this work, 'predictivist' identifies the feature of a theory of deducing from the theory itself some events that are not known yet or has not yet taken place. See Brush (1994), 135.

62 See, e.g., Jones (2001), 1194–5. But see Ruhl (note 19), 853.

63 See Dewey (1939), 51–2. But see, as to the relative nature of this distinction, Carnap (1971), 5, 7–9. where one of the axioms of a predictivist perspective, namely probability, is in the end treated as a normative claim. Cf. Dworkin (note 5), 154–5.

64 See Hart (note 18), 132–7. See, e.g., Summers (1982), 123, where the author points out the often clashing relations between predictivist vision and normative nature when dealing with the concept of 'valid law.' But see Abramowicz (2006), 70–73.

65 For instance, '[t]he modern legal discourse of civil rights is as much a cause as an effect of civil rights thinking within liberal ideology at large.' Kennedy (1998), 152. See also Cotterrell (1995), 250–252; Sunstein (note 59), 191; and Luhmann (1989), 140. But see Luhmann (note 14), 252. See also *id.*, 270. See, e.g., Deakin (note 7), 26–9.

66 See Ackerman (1999), 2287 and his 'ten-year test' in order to reclassify what is reconstructed *ex post* 'normal evolutionary development' as an actual 'juridical revolution.' See also Blankenburg (note 3), 278–80 as to the historical reasons behind the European evolutionary theories' distance from the actual developments in legal practice.

Protection Clause) due to the legal landslide provoked by the Supreme Court's decision in *Brown v. Board of Education*.[67]

In other words, being predictivist in the legal world, i.e. the idea of being able to 'objectively' determine possible evolutions of the law, can be quite a risky business: Law and its evolution (especially in its decisive moments) takes into serious consideration that which legal actors 'subjectively' consider what the law ought to be from economic, political or purely systematic criteria.[68]

For example, the conditions as to the issue of discrimination of the surrounding environments and of the legal system were roughly (and relatively) the same under *Brown v. Board of Education* as they were more than 50 years prior under *Plessy v. Ferguson*, where the principle of 'separate but equal' was sanctioned.[69] Nevertheless, the majority of the justices sitting in the Supreme Courts subjectively considered that the same text (Equal Protection Clause) meant the very opposite of that stated in *Plessy v. Ferguson*.[70] As consequence, their normative accounts as to American constitutional law (it ought to prohibit separation) not only were quite 'unpredictable' (i.e. it was an uncertain outcome in light of the previous decisions and the factual situation).[71] Though fairly unpredicted, the Justices' normative statements also became legal reality (constitutional law actually prohibits separation), setting the agenda for predictions as to future law-making on the legal concept of discrimination based on race.[72]

As pointed out by Hutchinson, 'law will always be a relatively open ended and stylized form of politics in which "anything might go".'[73] For this reason, and almost paradoxically, the evolutionary theory, in order to become as predictivist as possible, i.e. to foresee which directions the law *will* take, should itself explicitly provide legal actors with some normative criteria, i.e. to offer directions that the law *ought to* take. As pointed out by Popper, '[t]heories are nets cast to catch what we call "the world"; to rationalize, explain and to *master* it.'[74]

This actually is one of the major goals of each legal theory and, in the end, the

---

67 See *Plessy v. Ferguson*, 163 US 548–552 (1896) and *Brown v. Board of Education*, 347 US 483 (1954). See also Bell (2004), 136. But see, e.g., Strauss (2007), 862–8; or Konvitz (1961), 70–72.

68 See Summers (note 68), 134–5. See also Brown (1920), 398; and Cohen (1933). But see Deakin (note 7), 32, 34 as to the limitation of the subjective element due to the constraint of the legal discourse.

69 See Goldberg (2006), 1977–8, pointing as key factor the 're-construction' by the Court of '"new" facts to justify new conclusions about previously settled matters while avoiding mention of an underlying norm shift.' See, e.g., Justice Holmes' refusal of the concept of 'equal protection' in *Buck v. Bell*, 274 US 200, 208 (1927). But see Cottrol *et al.* (2003), 78; and Klarman (2004), 364–6, 377, 468.

70 As recently pointed out, 'the great Brown decision derives from a courageous Court acting alone.' Lipkin (2006), 1085.

71 See Wechsler (1959), 32–3. But see Klarman (1994), 10. Cf. the reply in Tushnet (1994), 175–7.

72 See Schwartz (1993), 286; and Friedman (2002), 502. See also Ford (2004), 1333: '*Brown*'s relevance is less to our history than to our future' [italics in the text]. As to the 're-constructivist' attitude of evolutionary approach literature when dealing with the unpredictable nature of these type of 'revolutions' in legal (and social) history, see Deakin (note 7), 14.

73 Hutchinson (note 15), 265.

74 Popper (note 57), 59 [*italics added*].

measurement of its success or failure as such: the capacity to provide law-makers (when facing new realities) and law-appliers (when facing 'hard cases') not only with a better picture of the present, but also to present normative criteria or somehow general analytical tools to face and master the future.[75]

4. THE 'OUGHT-TO-BE' IN THE STAGES OF THE LEGAL EVOLUTION

The results and methodologies used by evolutionary theory as discussed above will then benefit greatly from being considered by legal actors as a legal theory instead of a simple theoretical approach to the law.[76] Evolutionary theory will then in particular start to actually influence legal actors in their decisive role in law-making, and in this way render evolutionary theory's predictions more reliable. However, there is a step that needs to be taken: the integration of a normative component into evolutionary theory.

It is necessary to point out how this combination of evolutionary theory with normative proposals, making this approach useful also for legal reasoning, is not going to totally revolutionize this theoretical approach to the law.[77] The evolutionary approach to the law, despite its descriptive claims as to the present and future law, already has some passages where the normative proposals play a crucial role. In other words, the need of a clear and explicit normative component for a 'legal' evolutionary theory is stressed by the fact that legal actors and their idea of what law 'Ought to be' participate in decisive (though not monopolistic) ways in all three stages through which, according to the evolutionary approach, the law of a certain legal system evolves.[78]

Starting with the Variation Phase, i.e. the moment of creation of several possible legal concepts, this stage of the legal evolution is often commenced by factors external to the legal world, e.g. needs or changes occurring in the economic and political environments.[79] However, legal actors and the legal ideologies in which they are educated can still play a crucial role.[80] A classical example in this direction is Weber's analysis of the birth and growth in Western nations of the part played in capitalistic economic systems by the legal concept of corporation. Weber's investigation shows how the legal world can sometimes itself create the various possible legal concepts, based primarily on internal needs of systematic character of the legal world (i.e. the 'Ought-to-be-done' proposals aiming at maintaining the coherence inside the legal system).[81] Moreover, even if this is a variation

---

[75] See D'Amato (1984), 50–51; and MacCormick (note 59), 14–15.

[76] See, e.g., Corwin (1950), 186.

[77] See, e.g., Sward (note 28), 489–90.

[78] See Teubner (note 21), 56–9, where Teubner implicitly stresses the central role played by the legal actors' normative ideology in order to explain the evolution of the law in all the three stages. See, e.g., Teubner (note 4), 280.

[79] See Luhmann (note 14), 252; or Elliott (note 1), 38: 'Law is a scavenger. It grows by feeding on ideas from outside, not by inventing new ones of its own.'

[80] See, e.g., the history of the French law of torts in the nineteenth and early twentieth centuries as in Tunc (1989), 56, 71–2; and Tomlinson (1988), 1357–60.

[81] See Weber (note 26), 720–725, 855. See also Trubek (note 44), 751. As to other examples of purely legal construction, see Luhmann (note 14), 251–2.

induced by the external environment, it is almost always legal actors, due to the complexity of modern law, who create the new legal concept to be tested on the legal market.[82]

It should be noted that the idea of a certain degree of autonomy of the legal evolution, in particular if one takes a more European (and especially Teubner's) stand on the issue, is strongly underlined by the very evolutionary theory.[83] This being the basic idea, one can draw the conclusion that evolutionary theory also tends to attribute to legal thinking a decisive role not only in better understanding the legal evolution, since it explains the ideas according to which legal actors tend to reasons. Evolutionary theory must also recognize that a legal theory, as a fundamental part in shaping legal culture, can decisively contribute to the development of the law into one direction instead of the other, in particular in its normative component. As recently stressed by Sinclair, '[t]hat the variation or selection mechanisms in a developing system involve rational agency does not preclude an evolutionary explanation; however, it may diminish the value of such explanation.'[84]

Second, as far as concerns the Selection Phase of the law-making, even here the ideological apparatus of legal actors have a decisive role, at least in contemporary Western or 'Westernized' national, transnational, and international legal systems. As also stressed by the followers of evolutionary theory approach to the law, a fundamental function in determining what the law is, i.e. in selecting the 'winning' legal concepts among the various proposals, is played by the basic ideas as to the issue of 'what is law' and 'what is not-law' of legal actors such as legal staff working for law-makers or judges of international courts of arbitration or international lawyers of multinational corporations.[85] As clearly pointed out by Teubner, '[t]he main criteria for selection are whether the innovation fits in with the existing normative structures.'[86]

These normative structures or ideas have the fundamental task of legitimizing certain solutions (instead of others) to legal problems as 'legal' and therefore binding the addressees or at least the parties.[87] Therefore, the recognition of this crucial role of legal culture should also encourage evolutionary theory to take a step further and provide lawyers, judges and legal scholars with normative patterns, i.e. with directions as to what road to take and explanations why the proposed directions ought to be taken.[88]

As evolutionary theory's studies constantly point out, lawyers and judges are certainly not the only actors participating in the process of selection. For instance, non-legal actors also play a fundamental role by using a certain concept such as 'corporate interest' regardless of whether it is formally sanctioned as legal, simply because it helps to protect 'the public interest in profitability of the enterprise.'[89] However, the very

---

82 See Stone (note 33), 56–62. See also Teubner (note 4), 249–50; Malloy (2003), 83; and Deakin and Wilkinson (note 18), 32. But see Kirzner (1985), 141–4 as to the inefficiency (at least from an economic perspective) of the legally-based process of 'discovery' or variation.

83 See, e.g., Teubner (note 21), 59. See also Teubner (note 4), 248; and Deakin and Wilkinson (note 18), 28–9.

84 Sinclair (note 1), 39.

85 See Teubner (1996), 165. See also Hutchinson (note 15), 260.

86 Teubner (note 21), 59. See also Jacobson (1989), 1662.

87 See Kennedy (note 69), 1; and Unger (1983), 582. See, e.g., Olsen (1983), 1498–9.

88 See Friedman (note 58), 148. But see Macaulay *et al.* (1995), 7.

89 Teubner (1994), 50. As another example of the central role played by economic actors in the selection phase, see Skeel (1998), 1356.

construction of the idea of relevant legal concepts is based on their acceptance as part of the valid law and valid legal system, which, in their turn, are based on two fundamental elements. In case of conflict, i.e. when the legal system is facing the selection of the surviving legal concept, one institutional actor (e.g. the court of arbitrators or the law-making authority) is chosen to decide what concept is part of valid law (and therefore binding) and what is not. In other words, one actor is assigned with the specific task of selecting which legal proposal, among those promoted by the conflicting parties or group interests, has to be considered valid law (or according to the valid law). The performance of this task also brings with it the (implicit or explicit) consequence of quashing all the non-compatible solution as 'not legally valid' and therefore as non-binding for the addressees.[90]

Moreover, at least in Western or Westernized legal systems, the individuals comprising this institutional actor in charge of the selection usually are educated at law faculties and (most of the time) have a certain experience of working either as lawyers or judges.[91] As a consequence and paralleling the selection taking place in the surrounding environments, there still is a need for the non-legal actors to 'win' the crucial selection taking place in the legal arena so that, for example, their economic efficient concept can always be used with binding force against all the parties. This victory can be obtained only by selling their winning products in terms of the culture in which legal actors have been educated for their jobs, either as judges, lawyers or legal staff working for the law-makers.[92] For instance, the selection taking place in the economic surrounding can certainly choose financial leasing as the most economically efficient tool for both parties. However, in order to become law, the parties need to sell to the legal institutional actors the tool of financial leasing as a legally possible variation (e.g. based the legal criterion of *ex analogia legis*) of the already legally legitimized concept of loan.

Finally, as to the Stabilization (or Retention) Phase of the evolution of the law, here too the normative legal culture, i.e. the culture of legal actors as to what ought to be the law, plays an important role, though more hidden than during the other two phases. At first blush, in the stage of retention of a newly formed legal concept, the legal ideology as to what is law is not the dominating factor in order to explain how and why a certain selected legal concept becomes a stable part of the body of national, transnational, or international law. Decisive at this stage are the practices taking place mostly in the surroundings of the legal arena. For example, these can be the appraisal of a certain type of contract as being 'efficient' for the financial market in the economic arena; or a certain idea of human rights as including private property, helps to promote the political liberal ideology in the political arena.

However, though these non-legal assessments are important in order to stabilize certain legal concepts, they still all tend to be always paralleled or supported by the legal reasoning. The latter's use by non-legal actors aims above all at strengthening the non-legal arguments by also pointing out the validity, i.e. the very existence as binding law of

---

[90] See, e.g., Teubner (1989), 745. See also Watson (1991), 109.

[91] See Cotterrell (1992), 84, 203–204; and Bourdieu (1987), 831–2, 834–9. See also Summers (1997), 1204–1207; and, as to the over-representation of legal profession in the legislative 'selecting' agencies (i.e. National Assembly), Vago (2003), 115–116.

[92] See Valverde (2003), 5–6. See also Friedman and Macaulay (1977).

a certain type of contract or a certain idea of human right. After all, as pointed out by Luhmann,

> [t]he specification of the way in which arguments refer to legal materials in the legal system [i.e. the legal reasoning] is the true carrier of the evolution of the legal system and the breakthrough to an autonomous culture.[93]

In particular in case of an uncertain situation, i.e. circumstances where conflicting non-legal values are at stake, the legal arguments are used as decisive factors in promoting the stabilization of value A instead of B as not only for being economically efficient but also for being incorporated in the valid law.[94]

This importance of the legal culture at all three stages of the production of new legal concepts is due to one of the features of modern legal systems (even at the transnational level), especially in their relations to the surrounding environments: the specialization of law.[95] As a result of the increasingly detailed 'marking out of what counts as legal knowledge, legal reasoning and legal issues,' one can detect the progressive marginalization of all other discourses from the mechanisms of law-making, as well as their substitution by the specific knowledge and discourses provided by specific actors, the legal actors.[96]

For example, the relations between law and politics are nowadays heavily influenced by one typical feature of the welfare state, namely the increasing use of secondary legislation (or administrative rule-making).[97] This supremacy of delegated law-making, in its turn, tends to distance the legal discourse from the political control exercised by political actors such as national or local assemblies and, instead, promotes the role of ('undemocratic') actors such as legal experts working for administrative agencies.[98] Similarly, the growth at the transnational level of new types of laws (e.g. international labor law or the law of commercial transactions) is characterized by the very domination, in both its law-creation and law-implementation, of legal actors such as international courts of arbitration panels or multinational corporate attorneys.[99]

It is possible to state in general, as put forward by Luhmann, that nowadays a force influences the relations between law and its surrounding environments in such a way that the role of non-legal actors operating in legislative bodies (e.g. political representatives) almost appears no longer to be one of creating law but simply choosing among the bulk of legal concepts already available and produced by legal expertise through the centuries.[100]

Legal reasoning and its normative nature then is not only an important part in all three stages of the legal evolution as presented by evolutionary theory, it is also a reality of

---

93 Luhmann (note 14), 248. See also Teubner (note 21), 59. See, e.g., Deakin (2003), 109–110.
94 See Tuori (1997), 16. See, e.g., Cotterrell (note 94), 203–204; and Bell (note 24), 60–67.
95 See Bourdieu (note 94), 835–6; Hunt (1997), 82–3; and Luhmann (1988), 346.
96 Cotterrell (note 69), 12. See also Summers (2000), 49; and Weber (note 26), 895.
97 See Evan (1990), 89–96; and Cotterrell (note 94), 177.
98 See, e.g., Luhmann (note 14), 366, 411–412; and Habermas (1996), 430. See also Zumbansen (2003), 144–7.
99 See Shams (2001), 1602–1603. See also Watson (1977), 91–113; and Teubner (1997), 770.
100 See Luhmann (1985), 159–60.

contemporary law and law-making.[101] As pointed out by Dworkin, '[w]e live in and by the law. It makes us what we are: citizens and employees and doctors and spouses and people who own things.'[102]

As every theory ultimately aims to be the one considered as depicting the 'real' reality, it then appears natural that evolutionary theory becomes a 'legal' evolutionary theory, that is a theory which is able to understand and explain the work of legal actors to the actors themselves from the internal normative perspective or, in Stanley Fish's words, from the perspective of the same 'interpretative community.'[103] In order to do so, evolutionary theory should then integrate its predictivist component with Ought-statements or normative proposals, i.e. the essential element of legal reasoning.[104]

As legal actors are so central for modern law and law is a human product, evolutionary theory in the end increases the probabilities of producing *ex post* correct predictions by convincing the crucial legal actors that the predictions are normatively the 'right things to do.'[105] In short, evolutionary theory will have more success in being the correct theory if it shifts from pure predictivist statement such as 'if legal concept *x* is created, then *y* is most likely to happen in the legal system,' to predictivist statements integrated with normative proposals, such as 'if legal concept *x* is created, then *y* is most likely to happen in the legal system and *y* ought to happen because, in this way, the criterion *C* is fulfilled.'

Each theory claiming to be legal not only aims at explaining the legal phenomenon but also seeks to help legal actors to work 'better' by offering some evaluative cornerstones (*criterion C*) according to which lawyers, law-makers and judges can consider solution *y* as 'legal' and solution *z* as 'non-legal.'[106] The incorporation of a normative component then is a necessary step in order to transform the evolutionary approach to the law into a *legal* evolutionary approach.[107] This integration means that evolutionary scholars must explicitly offer to legal actors the evaluative cornerstone to be chosen as an axiomatic term in the normative reasoning; as in the previous example, a legal evolutionary theory needs to explicitly state whether and why the criterion *C* separating law from non-law, for instance, is the one of justice, or the one of economic efficiency, or the one of formal consistency within the legal system.[108]

---

[101] See Weber (note 26), 687. See also *id.*, 655. For a more recent literature on the issue, see Teubner (note 3), 297; Deakin (note 7), 31; and Kennedy (note 69), 152.

[102] Dworkin (note 5), vii.

[103] See Fish (1980), 14. See also Hart (note 18), 81.

[104] See, e.g., Teubner (1996), 1; or Njoya (2004), 239–40.

[105] See Sinclair (note 53), 385. See, e.g., Dworkin (note 5), 225.

[106] See Eng (2003), 312–26.

[107] In the end, as highlighted also by MacCormick, there is always a normative component in the very act of choosing to describe the law from a legal actors' perspective, i.e. in what in this work has been defined as the perspective of legal theory. See MacCormick (note 24), 63–4, 139–40 (1997). See also Perry (2001), 322; and Dworkin (2004), 2. But see Rodriguez-Blanco (note 7), 29–44.

[108] See Waldron (1993), 153. See also Feteris, (1997), 355.

5. CONCLUSION

The main purpose of this chapter has been to attempt to make the evolutionary approach to the law a helpful methodological device in order to better understand law-making in modern times. After having in Section One presented the evolutionary approach from a legal theoretical perspective, Section Two pointed out, however, the main obstacle for a complete acceptance of the evolutionary approach to law as a tool for legal actors: the lack of an explicit normative side, where lawyers, law-makers and judges can retrieve 'Ought' criteria to be used for deciding in which directions future law-making should proceed. In Section Three, the necessity of normative proposals has been especially underlined for a theoretical approach like the evolutionary one, that aims not only in explaining the past and present of the law, but in also making predictions for its future development. Finally, Section Four has highlighted that this integration of normative proposals will not revolutionize the evolutionary approach, having the 'Ought-to-be' culture of the legal actors already a central role in all the fundamental mechanisms behind legal change as described by this approach.

To conclude, since law is a human product and human beings do not always act in predictable ways, the goal is simply to make the evolutionary theory into a theory more appealing to legal actors. In this way, it can be used to understand not only the actual legal reality but also its potential developments by channeling them in more predictable patterns. Regardless which choice of normative components can be considered best, e.g. own-production or borrowed from more established legal theory such as legal positivism, two elements have to be considered for further discussion. First, the passage from a simple 'evolutionary approach to the law' to a more 'legally articulated' evolutionary theory is essential, due in particular to the fact that by applying a certain theory to the creation of new laws, legal actors can immediately mould the evolution of the legal phenomenon. Second, a necessary step in order to make this transbordering into legal theory is certainly equipping the evolutionary approach with a normative side, since in the end legal actors search in legal theory not only for a clearer description of their reality but also for a clearer guidance in face of difficult decisions.[109]

BIBLIOGRAPHY

Abramowicz, Michael (2006), 'Predictive decisionmaking', *Virginia Law Review*, **92**, 69–122.

Ackerman, Bruce (1999), 'Revolution on a human scale', *Yale Law Journal*, **108**, 2279–2349.

Alexy, Robert (2002), *The Argument from Injustice. A Reply to Legal Positivism*, Oxford: Oxford University Press.

Austin, John (1954 [1832]), *The Province of Jurisprudence Determined and the Uses of the Study of Jurisprudence*, London: Weidenfeld and Nicolson.

Beckstrom, John H. (1985), *Sociobiology and the Law*, Urbana: University of Illinois Press.

Beckstrom, John H. (1989), *Evolutionary Jurisprudence: Prospects and Limitations on the Use of Modern Darwinism throughout the Legal Process*, Urbana: University of Illinois Press.

Bell, Derrick (2004), *Silent Covenants: Brown v. Board of Education and the Unfulfilled Hopes for Racial Reform*, Oxford: Oxford University Press.

---

109 See Dworkin (note 5), 110; and Singer (1984), 57–9.

Bell, John (1983), *Policy Arguments in Judicial Decisions*, Oxford: Clarendon Press.
Bell, John (1986), 'The acceptability of legal arguments', in N. MacCormick and P. Birks (eds), *The Legal Mind: Essays for Tony Honoré*, Oxford: Clarendon Press, pp. 45–65.
Bentham, Jeremy (1970 [1781–1789]), *An Introduction to the Principles of Morals and Legislation*, in J.H. Burns and H.L.A. Hart (eds.), London: The Athlone Press–University of London.
Blankenburg, Erhard (1984), 'The poverty of evolutionism: A critique of Teubner's case for "reflexive law"', *Law and Society Review*, **18**, 273–89.
Bourdieu, Pierre (1987), 'The force of law: Toward a sociology of the juridical field', *Hastings Law Journal*, **38**, 814–53.
Brown, Jethro W. (1920), 'Law and evolution', *Yale Law Journal*, **29**, 394–400.
Brush, Stephen G. (1994), 'Dynamics of theory change: The role of predictions', in D. Hull, M. Forbes, and R. M. Burian (eds), *PSA 1994: Proceedings of the 1994 biennial meeting of the Philosophy of Science Association*, Vol. 2, East Lansing, MI: Philosophy of Science Association, pp. 133–45.
Campbell, Donald T. (1965), 'Variation and selective retention in socio-cultural evolution', in H. Barringer, G.I. Blanksten and R.W. Mack (eds), *Social Change in Developing Areas: A Reinterpretation of Evolutionary Theory*, Cambridge, MA: Schenkman, pp. 19–49.
Carnap, Rudolf (1971), 'Inductive logic and rational decisions', in R. Carnap and R.C. Jeffrey (eds), *Studies in Inductive Logic and Probability*, Berkeley, CA: California University Press, pp. 5–31.
Cicchino, Peter M. (2000), 'Building on foundational myths: Feminism and the recovery of human nature: A response to Martha Fineman', *American University Journal of Gender, Social Policy and the Law*, **8**, 73–75.
Clark, Robert C. (1981), 'The interdisciplinary study of legal evolution', *Yale Law Journal*, **90**, 1238–74.
Cohen, Morris R. (1967 [1933]), *Law and Social Order: Essays in Legal Philosophy*, Hamden, CT: Archon Books.
Coleman, Jules L. (2001), 'Incorporationism, conventionality, and the practical difference thesis', in *Hart's Postscript. Essays on the Postscript to the Concept of Law*, J. Coleman (ed.), Oxford, New York: Oxford University Press, pp. 99–147.
Coleman, Jules L. (2003), *The Practice of Principle. In Defence of a Pragmatist Approach to Legal Theory*, Oxford, New York: Oxford University Press.
Corwin, Edward S. (1950), 'The impact of the idea of evolution on the American political and constitutional tradition', in S. Persons, *Evolutionary Thought in America*, New Haven: Yale University Press, pp. 182–201.
Cotterrell, Roger (1992), *The Sociology of Law: An Introduction*, 2nd ed., London, Dublin, Edinburgh: Butterworths.
Cotterrell, Roger (1995), *Law's Community. Legal Theory in Sociological Perspective*, Oxford: Clarendon Press.
Cotterrell, Roger (2003), *The Politics of Jurisprudence. A Critical Introduction To Legal Philosophy*, 2nd ed., London, Dublin, Edinburgh: Butterworths.
Cottrol, Robert J., Raymond T. Diamond, and Leland B. Ware (2003), *Brown v. Board of Education: Caste, Culture, and the Constitution*, Lawrence: University Press of Kansas.
D'Amato, Anthony (1984), *Jurisprudence: A Descriptive and Normative Analysis of Law*, Dordrecht: Martinus Nijhoff Publishers.
Deakin, Simon (2001), 'The contract of employment: A study in legal evolution', *Historical Studies in Industrial Relations*, **11**, 1–36.
Deakin, Simon (2002), 'Evolution for our time: A theory of legal memetics', *Current Legal Problems*, **55**, 1–42.
Deakin, Simon (2003), '"Enterprise-Risk": The juridical nature of the firm revisited', *Industrial Law Journal*, **32**, 97–113.
Deakin, Simon and Frank Wilkinson (2005), *The law of the labour market: industrialization, employment and legal evolution*, Oxford: Oxford University Press.
Dewey, John (1939), *Theory of Valuation*, Chicago: University of Chicago Press.
Dudziak, Mary L. (1986), 'Oliver Wendell Holmes as a eugenic reformer: Rhetoric in the writing of constitutional law', *Iowa Law Review*, **71**, 833–67.

Duxbury, Neil (1995), *Patterns of American Jurisprudence*, Oxford: Clarendon Press.

Dworkin, M. Ronald (1997), *Law's Empire*, Cambridge, MA: Harvard University Press.

Dworkin, M. Ronald (2004), 'Hart's postscript and the character of political philosophy', *Oxford Journal of Legal Studies*, **24**, 1–37.

Elliott, Donald E. (1984), 'Holmes and evolution: Legal process as artificial intelligence', *Journal of Legal Studies*, **13**, 113–46.

Elliott, Donald E. (1985), 'The evolutionary tradition in jurisprudence', *Columbia Law Review*, **85**, 38–94.

Endicott, Timothy A.O. (2001), 'Herbert Hart and the semantic sting', in J. Coleman (ed.), *Hart's Postscript. Essays on the Postscript to the Concept of Law*, Oxford, New York: Oxford University Press, pp. 39–58.

Eng, Svein (2003), *Analysis of Dis/agreement – With Particular Reference to Law and Legal Theory*, Dordrecht: Kluwer Academic Publishers.

Evan, William M. (1990), *Social Structure and Law. Theoretical and Empirical Perspectives*, London: Sage Publications.

Ewing, Sally (1987), 'Formal justice and the spirit of capitalism: Max Weber's sociology of law', *Law and Society Review*, **21**, 487–512.

Feteris, Eveline T. (1997), 'A survey of 25 years of research on legal argumentation', *Argumentation*, **11**, 355–76.

Finnis, John (1980), *Natural Law and Natural Rights*, Oxford: Clarendon Press.

Fish, Stanley (1980), *Is There a Text in This Class? The Authority of Interpretive Communities*, Cambridge, MA: Harvard University Press.

Ford, Richard Thompson (2004), 'Brown's ghost', *Harvard Law Review*, **117**, 1305–1333.

Fried, Michael S. (1999), 'The evolution of legal concepts: The memetic perspective', *Jurimetrics Journal*, **39**, 291–316.

Friedman, Lawrence M. (1985), *Total Justice*, New York: Russell Sage Foundation.

Friedman, Lawrence M. (1988), 'On the interpretation of laws', *Ratio Juris*, **3**, 252–62.

Friedman, Lawrence M. (2002), *American Law in the 20th Century*, New Haven: Yale University Press.

Friedman, Lawrence M. and Stewart Macaulay (1977), *Law and the Behavioral Sciences*, 2nd ed., Indianapolis, IN: Bobbs-Merrill.

Fuller, Lon L. (1969), *The Morality of Law*, Revised Edition, London: Yale University Press.

Gavison, Ruth (1991), 'Legal theory and the role of rules', *Harvard Journal of Law and Public Policy*, **14**, 727–70.

Goldberg, Suzanne B. (2006), 'Constitutional tipping points: civil rights, social change, and fact-based adjudication', *Columbia Law Review*, **106**, 1955–2022.

Gordon, Robert W. (1984), 'Critical legal histories', *Stanford Law Review*, **36**, 57–125.

Gordon, Robert W. (1990), 'New developments in legal theory', in D. Kairys (ed.), *The Politics of Law. A Progressive Critique*, 2nd ed., New York: Pantheon Books, pp. 413–25.

Gordon, Thomas F. (1988), 'The importance of nonmonotonicity for legal reasoning. in H. Fiedler, F. Haft, and R. Traunmüller (eds), *Expert Systems in Law: Impacts on Legal Theory and Computer Law*, Tübingen: Attempto, pp. 111–126.

Gould, Stephen Jay (1991), *Bully for Brontosaurus: Reflections in Natural History*, New York: W.W. Norton & Company.

Gregor, Shirley (2002), 'Design theory in information systems', *Australasian Journal of Information Systems*, **10**, 14–22.

Habermas, Jürgen (1984), *The Theory of Communicative Action. Volume One: Reason and the Rationalization of Society*, Boston, MA: Beacon Press.

Habermas, Jürgen (1996), *Between Facts And Norms: Contributions to a Discourse Theory of Law and Democracy*, Cambridge, MA: The MIT Press.

Haferkamp, Hans and Neil J. Smelser (1992), 'Introduction', in H. Haferkamp and N.J. Smelser (eds), *Social Change and Modernity*, Berkeley: University of California Press, pp. 1–33.

Hart, Herbert L.A. (1961), *The Concept of Law*, Oxford: Clarendon Press.

Hart, Herbert L.A. (1983), 'Problems of the philosophy of law', in H.L.A. Hart, *Essays in Jurisprudence and Philosophy*, Oxford: Clarendon Press, pp. 88–119.

Hart, Herbert L.A. (1994), 'Postscript', in H.L.A. Hart, *The Concept Of Law*, 2nd ed., P.A. Bulloch and J. Raz (eds.), Oxford: Clarendon Press, pp. 238–76.
Hart, Herbert L.A. (1998), 'Kelsen visited', in S.L. Paulson and B. Litschewski Paulson (eds), *Normativity and Norms. Critical Perspectives on Kelsenian Themes*, Oxford: Clarendon Press, pp. 69–87.
Hohfeld, Wesley N. (1917), 'Fundamental legal conceptions as applied in judicial reasoning', *Yale Law Journal*, **26**(8), 710–770.
Holmes, Oliver W., Jr. (1897), 'The path of the law', *Harvard Law Review*, **10**, 457–78.
Holmes, Oliver W., Jr. (1899), 'Law in science and science in law', *Harvard Law Review*, **12**, 443–463.
Holmes, Oliver W., Jr. (1963 [1881]), *The Common Law*, Cambridge, MA: Harvard University Press.
Horowitz, Donald L. (1994), 'The Qur'an and the common law: Islamic reform and the theory of legal change', *American Journal of Comparative Law*, **42**, 236–92.
Hovenkamp, Herbert (1985), 'Evolutionary models in jurisprudence', *Texas Law Review*, **64**, 645–85.
Hunt, Alan (1978), *The Sociological Movement in Law*, London: Palgrave Macmillan.
Hunt, Alan (1997), 'The politics of law and the law of politics', in *Law and Power. Critical and Socio-Legal Essays*, K. Tuori, Z. Bankowski and J. Uusitali (eds), Liverpool: Deborah Charles Publications, pp. 51–83.
Hutchinson, Allan C. (2005a), *Evolution and the Common Law*, Cambridge: Cambridge University Press.
Hutchinson, Allan C. (2005b), 'Work-in-progress: Evolution and common law', *Texas Wesleyan Law Review*, **11**, 253–66.
Hutchinson, Allan C. and Simon Archer (2001), 'Of bulldogs and soapy Sams: The common law and evolutionary theory', *Current Legal Problems*, **54**, 19–59.
Jabbari, David (1992), 'From criticism to construction in modern critical legal theory', *Oxford Journal of Legal Studies*, **12**, 507–542.
Jacobson, Arthur J. (1989), 'Autopoietic Law: The New Science of Niklas Luhmann (Book Review)', *Michigan Law Review*, **87**, 1647–89.
Jones, Owen D. (1994), 'Law and evolutionary biology: Obstacles and opportunities', *Journal of Contemporary Health Law and Policy*, **10**, 265–83.
Jones, Owen D. (1997), 'Evolutionary analysis in law: An introduction and application to child abuse', *North Carolina Law Review*, **75**, 1117–1242.
Jones, Owen D. (2001a), 'Evolutionary analysis in law: Some objections considered', *Brooklyn Law Review*, **67**, 207–232.
Jones, Owen D. (2001b), 'Time-shifted rationality and the law of law's leverage: Behavioral economics meets behavioral biology', *Northwestern University Law Review*, **95**, 1141–1205.
Kelsen, Hans (1949), *General Theory Of Law and State*, Cambridge, MA: Harvard University Press.
Kelsen, Hans (1960), 'What is the pure theory of law?', *Tulane Law Review*, **34**, 769–76.
Kelsen, Hans (1970), *The Pure Theory of Law*, Berkeley, Los Angeles, London: University of California Press.
Kelsen, Hans (1996 [1934]), *Introduction to the Problems of Legal Theory*, Oxford: Clarendon Press.
Kennedy, Duncan (1991), 'A semiotics of legal argument', *Syracuse Law Review*, **42**, 75–116.
Kennedy, Duncan (1998), *A Critique of Adjudication (fin de siècle)*, Cambridge, MA: Harvard University Press.
Kirzner, Israel M. (1985), *Discovery and the Capitalist Process*, Chicago: University of Chicago Press.
Klarman, Michael J. (1994), 'Brown, racial change and civil rights movement', *Virginia Law Review*, **80**, 7–150.
Klarman, Michael J. (2004), *From Jim Crow to Civil Rights: The Supreme Court and the Struggle for Racial Equality*, Oxford: Oxford University Press.
Konvitz, Milton R. (1961), *A Century of Civil Rights*, New York: Columbia University Press.
Kronman, Anthony T. (1983), *Max Weber*, Stanford: Stanford University Press.
Kurki-Suonio, Kirsti (2000), 'Joint custody as an interpretation of the best interests of the child

in critical and comparative perspective', *International Journal of Law, Policy and the Family*, **14**, 183–205.
Laquer Estin, Ann (1996), 'Can families be efficient? A feminist appraisal', *Michigan Journal of Gender and Law*, **4**, 1–33.
Leiter, Brian and Michael Weisberg (2006), 'Why evolutionary biology is (so far) irrelevant to law', The University of Texas School of Law – Public Law and Legal Theory Research Paper 89, 1–49.
Lipkin, Robert Justin (2006), 'Which constitution? Who decides? The problem of judicial Supremacy and the interbranch solution', *Cardozo Law Review*, **28**, 1055–1132.
Luhmann, Niklas (1985), *A Sociological Theory of Law*, London: Routledge & Kegan Paul.
Luhmann, Niklas (1988), 'Closure and openness: On reality in the world of law', in G. Teubner (ed.), *Autopoietic Law: A New Approach to Law and Society*, Berlin, New York: Walter de Gruyter, pp. 335–48.
Luhmann, Niklas (1989), 'Law as a social system', *Northwestern University Law Review*, **83**, 136–50.
Luhmann, Niklas (2004), *Law as a Social System*, Oxford: Oxford University Press.
Macaulay, Stewart, Lawrence M. Friedman and John Stookey (1995), *The Law and Society: Readings on the Social Study of Law*, New York: W.W. Norton & Co.
MacCormack, Geoffrey (1985), 'Historical jurisprudence', *Legal Studies*, **5**, 251–60.
MacCormick, Neil D. (1981), *H.L.A. Hart*, Stanford, CA: Stanford University Press.
MacCormick, Neil D. (1997), *Legal Reasoning and Legal Theory*, Oxford: Clarendon Press.
MacCormick, Neil D. (2005), *Rhetoric and the Rule of Law: A Theory of Legal Reasoning*, Oxford: Oxford University Press.
Maine, Henry James Sumner (2005 [1861]), *Ancient Law: Its Connection With the Early History of Society, and Its Relation to Modern Ideas*, Ann Arbor, MI: Scholarly Publishing Office, University of Michigan Library.
Malloy, Robin Paul (2003), 'Framing the market: Representations of meaning and value in law, markets, and culture', *Buffalo Law Review*, **51**, 1–126.
Marmor, Andrei (2006), 'Legal positivism: Still descriptive and morally neutral', *Oxford Journal of Legal Studies*, **26**, 683–704.
Marx, Karl (1977 [1848]), 'Communist manifesto', in D. McLellan (ed.), *Karl Marx: Selected Writings*, Oxford: Oxford University Press, pp. 219–44.
Merton, Robert K. (1948), 'The self-fulfilling prophecy', *Antioch Review*, **8**, 193–210.
Nelson, Robert (1995), 'Recent evolutionary theorizing about economic change', *Journal of Economic Literature*, **33**, 48–90.
Njoya, Wanjiru (2004), 'Employee ownership and efficiency: An evolutionary perspective', *Industrial Law Journal*, **33**, 211–41.
Nonet, Philippe and Philip Selznick (1978), *Law and Society in Transition: Toward Responsive Law*, New York: Harper and Row.
Note (1982), '"Round and round the bramble bush": from legal realism to critical legal scholarship', *Harvard Law Review*, **95**, 1669–90.
O'Hara, Erin Ann (2004), 'Apology and thick trust: What spouse abusers and negligent doctors might have in common', *Chicago-Kent Law Review*, **79**, 1055–89.
Olsen, Frances E. (1983), 'The family and the market: A study of ideology and legal reform', *Harvard Law Review*, **96**, 1497–1578.
Palmer, Ben W. (1945), 'Hobbes, Holmes and Hitler', *American Bar Association Journal*, **31**, 569–73.
Pavlakos, George (2005), 'Normative knowledge and the nature of law', in S. Coyle and G. Pavlakos (eds), *Jurisprudence or Legal Science? A Debate about the Nature of Legal Theory*, Oxford: Hart Publishing, pp. 101–145.
Perry, Stephen R. (2001), 'Hart's methodological positivism', in J. Coleman (ed.), *Hart's Postscript. Essays on the Postscript to the Concept of Law*, Oxford: Oxford University Press, pp. 312–54.
Plotkin, Henry (2000), 'Culture and psychological mechanisms', in R. Aunger (ed.), *Darwinizing Culture: The Status of Memetics as a Science*, Oxford: Oxford University Press, pp. 69–82.
Popper, Karl (1961), *The Logic of Scientific Discovery*, New York: Science Editions.
Posner, Richard A. (1979), 'Some uses and abuses of economics in law', *University of Chicago Law Review*, **46**, 281–306.
Posner, Richard A. (1986), *Economic Analysis of Law*, 3rd edn, Boston: Little, Brown & Company.

Posner, Richard A. (1990), *The Problems of Jurisprudence*, Cambridge, MA: Harvard University Press.
Posner, Richard A. (1992), *Economic Analysis of Law*, 4th edn, Boston: Little, Brown & Company.
Posner, Richard A. (1998), *Economic Analysis of Law*, 5th edn., Boston: Little, Brown & Company.
Posner, Richard A. (2001), *Frontiers of Legal Theory*, Cambridge, MA: Harvard University Press.
Postema, Gerald (1987), 'The normativity of law', in R. Gavison (ed.), *Issues in Contemporary Legal Philosophy: The Influence of H.L.A. Hart*, Oxford: Clarendon Press, pp. 81–104.
Pound, Roscoe (1958), *The Ideal Element in Law*, Calcutta: Calcutta University Press.
Pound, Roscoe (1997 [1942]), *Social Control Through Law*, New Brunswick, NJ: Transaction Publishers.
Priest, George L. (1977), 'The common law process and the selection of efficient rules', *Journal of Legal Studies*, **6**, 65–82.
Radin, Margaret Jane and Frank Michelman (1991), 'Pragmatist and poststructuralist critical legal practice', *University of Pennsylvania Law Review*, **139**, 1019–1058.
Raz, Joseph (1980), *The Concept of A Legal System. An Introduction to the Theory of Legal System*, 2nd edn, Oxford: Clarendon Press.
Raz, Joseph (1990), *Practical Reason and Norms*, Oxford: Oxford University Press.
Raz, Joseph (1994), 'Authority, law and morality', in J. Raz (ed.), *Ethics in The Public Domain. Essays in the Morality of Law and Politics*, Oxford: Clarendon Press, pp. 194–221.
Raz, Joseph (1994), 'The problem about the nature of law', in J. Raz (ed.), *Ethics in The Public Domain. Essays in the Morality of Law and Politics*, Oxford: Clarendon Press, pp. 179–93.
Raz, Joseph (2001), 'Two views of the nature of the theory of law. A partial comparison', in J. Coleman (ed.), *Hart's Postscript. Essays on the Postscript to the Concept of Law*, Oxford: Oxford University Press, pp. 1–37.
Rheinstein, Max (1954), 'Preface', in M. Rheinstein (ed.), *Max Weber on Law in Economy and Society*, Cambridge, MA: Harvard University Press, pp. xxv–lxxii.
Rodriguez-Blanco, Veronica (2006), 'The methodological problem in legal theory: Normative and descriptive jurisprudence revisited', *Ratio Juris*, **19**, 26–54.
Roe, Mark J. (1996), 'Chaos and evolution in law and economics', *Harvard Law Review*, **109**, 641–68.
Ross, Alf (1957), 'Tû-tû', *Harvard Law Review*, **70**, 812–25.
Ross, Alf (1959), *On Law and Justice*, London: Stevens & Sons.
Rubin, Edward L. (1996), 'Legal scholarship', in D. Patterson (ed.), *A Companion to Philosophy of Law and Legal Theory*, Oxford: Blackwell Publishing, pp. 562–72.
Rubin, Edward L. (1997), 'Law and the methodology of law', *Wisconsin Law Review*, **1997**, 521–65.
Rubin, Paul H. (1977), 'Why is common law efficient?', *Journal of Legal Studies*, **VI**, 51–63.
Ruhl, B.J. (1996), 'Complexity theory as a paradigm for the dynamical law-and-society system: A wake-up call for legal reductionism and the modern administrative state', *Duke Law Journal*, **45**, 849–928.
Ruse, Michael (1999), 'Evolutionary ethics in the twentieth century: Julian Sorell Huxley and George Gaylord Simpson', in J. Maienschein and M. Ruse (eds), *Biology and the Foundations of Ethics*, Cambridge: Cambridge University Press, pp. 198–224.
Samuel, Geoffrey (2003), *Epistemology and Method in Law*, Aldershot: Ashgate Publishing Ltd.
Schauer, Frederick (1996), 'Defining originalism', *Harvard Journal of Law and Public Policy*, **19**, 343–6.
Schlag, Pierre (1991), 'Normativity and the politics of form', *University of Pennsylvania Law Review*, **139**, 801–932.
Schwartz, Bernard (1993), *A History of the Supreme Court*, Oxford: Oxford University Press.
Shams, Heba (2001), 'Law in the context of globalisation: A framework of analysis', *International Lawyer*, **35**, 1589–1626.
Shapo, Marshall S. (1974), 'A representational theory of consumer protection: Doctrine function and legal liability for product disappointment', *Virginia Law Review*, **60**, 1109–1388.
Sinclair, Michael B.W. (1986), 'The semantics of common law predicates', *Indiana Law Journal*, **61**, 373–99.

Sinclair, Michael B.W. (1987), 'The use of evolution theory in law', *University of Detroit Law Review*, **64**, 451–77.

Sinclair, Michael B.W. (1992), 'Autopoiesis: Who needs it?', *Legal Studies Forum*, **16**, 81–102.

Sinclair, Michael B.W. (1993), 'Evolution in law: Second thoughts', *University of Detroit Mercy Law Review*, **71**, 31–58.

Singer, Joseph William (1984), 'The player and the cards: Nihilism and legal theory', *Yale Law Journal*, **94**, 1–70.

Skeel, David A., Jr. (1998), 'An evolutionary theory of corporate law and corporate bankruptcy', *Virginia Law Review*, **51**, 1325–98.

Smits, Jan M. (2002), 'The harmonisation of private law in Europe: Some insights from evolutionary theory', *Georgia Journal of International and Comparative Law*, **31**, 79–99.

Stein, Peter (1980), *Legal Evolution: The Story of an Idea*, Cambridge: Cambridge University Press.

Stone, Julius (1966), *Social Dimensions of Law and Justice*, London: Stevens & Sons.

Strahlendorf, Peter W. (1993), 'Evolutionary jurisprudence: Darwinian theory of juridical science', Mimeographed copy.

Strauss, David A. (2007), 'The common law genius of the Warren Court', *William and Mary Law Review*, **49**, 845–79.

Summers, Robert S. (1982), *Instrumentalism and American Legal Theory*, Ithaca, NY: Cornell University Press.

Summers, Robert S. (1991), 'Judge Richard Posner's jurisprudence', *Michigan Law Review*, **89**, 1302–1333.

Summers, Robert S. (1997), 'How law is formal and why it matters', *Cornell Law Review*, **82**, 1165–1229.

Summers, Robert S. (2000), 'Law as a type of "machine" technology', in R.S. Summers ed., *Essays in Legal Theory*, Dordrecht, Boston, London: Kluwer Academic Publishers, pp. 43–54.

Sunstein, Cass R. (1996), *Legal Reasoning and Political Conflict*, Oxford: Oxford University Press.

Sward, Ellen E. (2004), 'Justification and doctrinal evolution', *Connecticut Law Review*, **37**, 389–493.

Teubner, Gunther (1983), 'Substantive and reflexive elements in modern law', *Law and Society Review*, **17**(2), 239–85.

Teubner, Gunther (1984), 'Autopoiesis in law and society: A rejoinder to Blankenburg', *Law and Society Review*, **18**, 201–301.

Teubner, Gunther (1988), 'Introduction to autopoietic law', in G. Teubner (ed.), *Autopoietic Law: A New Approach to Law and Society*, Berlin, New York: Walter de Gruyter, pp.1–11.

Teubner, Gunther (1989), 'How the law thinks: Toward a constructivist epistemology of law', *Law and Society Review*, **23**, 727–57.

Teubner, Gunther (1991), '"And God Laughed . . .": Indeterminacy, self-reference and paradox in law', in J.-P. Dupuy and G. Teubner (eds), *Paradoxes of Self-Reference in the Humanities, Law and the Social Science*, Stanford: Anma Libri, pp. 15–51.

Teubner, Gunther (1993), *Law as an Autopoietic System*, Z. Bankowski (ed), Oxford: Blackwell.

Teubner, Gunther (1994), 'Company Interest: The Public Interest of the Enterprise 'In Itself', in R. Rogowski and T. Withagen (eds), *Reflexive Labour Law*, Boston: Kluwer, pp. 21–52.

Teubner, Gunther (1996a), 'Altera pars audiatur: Law in the collision of discourses', in R. Rawlings (ed.), *Law, Society and Economy. Centenary Essays for the London School of Economics and Political Science 1895–1995*, Oxford: Clarendon Press, pp. 149–76.

Teubner, Gunther (1996b), 'Global Bukowina: Legal pluralism in the world society', in G. Teubner, *Global Law Without a State*, London: Dartmouth, pp. 3–28.

Teubner, Gunther (1997), 'The King's many bodies: The self-deconstruction of law's hierarchy', *Law and Society Review*, **1**, 763–87.

Tomlinson, Edward A. (1988), 'The tort liability in France for the act of things: A study of judicial lawmaking', *Louisiana Law Review*, **48**, 1299–1367.

Trubek, M. David (1972), 'Max Weber on law and the rise of capitalism', *Wisconsin Law Review*, **1972**, 720–753.

Tunc, André (1989), *La responsabilité civile*, 2nd edn, Paris: Economica.

Tuori, Kaarlo (1997), 'Law, power and critique', in *Law and Power. Critical and Socio-Legal Essays*,

K. Tuori, Z. Bankowski, and J. Uusitali (eds), Liverpool: Deborah Charles Publications, pp. 7–29.
Tuori, Kaarlo (2002), *Critical Legal Positivism*, Aldershot: Ashgate Publishing.
Tushnet, Mark (1992), 'Constitutional interpretation, character, and experience', *Boston University Law Review*, **72**, 747–63.
Tushnet, Mark (1994), 'The significance of Brown v. Board of Education', *Virginia Law Review*, **80**, 173–184.
Ulen, Thomas S. (2002), 'A Nobel Prize in legal science: Theory, empirical work, and the scientific method in the study of law', *University of Illinois Law Review*, **2002**, 875–920.
Unger, Roberto Mangabeira (1983), 'The critical legal studies movement', *Harvard Law Review*, **96**, 561–675.
Unger, Roberto Mangabeira (1996), *What Should Legal Analysis Become?* London: Verso.
Vago, Steven (2003), *Law and Society*, 7th edn, Upper Saddle River, NJ: Prentice Hall.
Valverde, Mariana (2003), *Law's Dream of a Common Knowledge*, Princeton, NJ: Princeton University Press.
Vogenauer, Stefan (2006), 'An empire of light? II: Learning and lawmaking in Germany today', *Oxford Journal of Legal Studies*, **26**, 627–63.
Wacks, Raymond (2005), *Understanding Jurisprudence: An Introduction to Legal Theory*, Oxford: Oxford University Press.
Waldron, Jeremy (1993), 'Legislation and moral neutrality', in J. Waldron, *Liberal Rights. Collected Papers 1981–1991*, Cambridge: Cambridge University Press, pp. 143–67.
Waluchow, J. Wilfrid (1994), *Inclusive Legal Positivism*, Oxford: Clarendon Press.
Watson, Alan (1977), *The Nature of Law*, New York: Columbia University Press.
Watson, Alan (1985), *The Evolution of Law*, Baltimore, MD: The Johns Hopkins University Press.
Watson, Alan (1991), *Roman Law & Comparative Law*, London: The University of Georgia Press.
Weber, Max (1978), *Economy and Society: An Outline of Interpretative Sociology*, G. Roth and C. Wittich (eds), Berkeley, CA: University of California Press.
Wechsler, Herbert (1959), 'Toward neutral principles of constitutional law', *Harvard Law Review*, **73.**
Weinreb, Lloyd L. (2005), *Legal Reason: The Use of Analogy in Legal Argument*, Cambridge: Cambridge University Press.
Wiener, Philip P. (1949), *Evolution and the Founders of Pragmatism*, Cambridge, MA: Harvard University Press.
Zumbansen, Peer (2003), 'Quod omnes tangit: Globalization, welfare regimes and entitlements', in G. Nolte and E. Benvenisti (eds), *The Welfare State in an Era of Globalization*, Berlin: Springer, pp. 135–73.

PART III

Transnational law and evolutionary governance

13. Transnational commercial law, multi-level legal systems, and evolutionary economics

Wolfgang Kerber

1. INTRODUCTION

Markets need a complex set of institutions in order to work properly. Within a state, the national legal order with its legal rules, courts, and enforcement agencies have the task of fulfilling this role. Besides safeguarding property rights, the national legal order encompasses (1) the facilitating of market transactions by offering enabling (facilitative) law (as legal standard solutions) and helping private parties to enforce contracts within the domain of freedom of contract, and (2) the regulation of market transactions for solving or mitigating market failures problems and achieving other policy objectives. A comparable consistent legal system is missing on the international level for ensuring the working of global markets and the governance of cross-border transactions. However, the dynamic process of globalization has brought about the development of a number of new institutional solutions for solving these problems. The most prominent issue is the regulation of international markets ('global governance'). This chapter, however, will focus on the evolution of institutions for the enforcement of contracts for cross-border transactions between firms. Although there have always been institutional solutions for the governance of cross-border contracts (*lex mercatoria*), in recent years, a number of new governance solutions for the enforcement of cross-border transactions have emerged ('transnational commercial law').[1] The increasing use of choice of law, private governance instead of private law (provided by states), and private arbitration instead of public courts are the most important characteristics of this development. This also includes hybrids as new combinations between private and public solutions for the governance of cross-border contracts. Therefore, the process of globalization is accompanied and enabled by a complex process of institutional evolution.

The aim of this article is to demonstrate how evolutionary economics might contribute to the explanation of this institutional evolution on the international and global level. Although New Institutional Economics (NIE) has developed a number of helpful theories for explaining institutions as devices for reducing transaction costs or limiting agency problems, it has not been very successful in explaining the evolution of institutions. The main reason is that NIE is primarily based upon static neoclassical equilibrium models that do not allow the analysis of dynamic, evolutionary processes

[1] Calliess *et al.* (2007); Calliess *et al.* (2008); with a greater focus on the EU see also Cafaggi (2006).

of economic, technological, and institutional change. Evolutionary economics, based upon ideas of Schumpeter and Hayek, and closely linked with modern innovation economics, might be able to provide a better approach for explaining institutional change. From this perspective institutional evolution can be analysed as the result of innovation and imitation of institutions, of their variation and selection, and as the result of path dependencies.

The analysis of how evolutionary economics can be used for explaining the evolution of the governance of cross-border transactions will be carried out within the following theoretical frameworks:

(1) There are both private and public governance solutions for negotiating and enforcing contracts for transactions, which partly can substitute each other but which also can be complements (hybrids). Therefore, the evolution of governance solutions for the enforcement of cross-border transactions can be seen as the result of an evolution along this dimension of private and/or public governance.

(2) The process of globalization has led to a very complex multi-level legal structure, in which a large number of jurisdictions offer legal services as, e.g., facilitative legal rules, court services and enforcement assistance. Due to choice of law for cross-border transactions, private parties can choose between different public governance solutions. We will see that the ensuing processes of horizontal and vertical competition between legal rules and public courts can be a powerful driving force for the evolution of governance solutions.

The paper is structured as follows. Section 2 presents a general introduction into evolutionary economics. Particular emphasis is given to the evolutionary concept of competition as innovation-imitation process as well as to an overview about approaches for explaining institutional change from the perspective of evolutionary economics. The main section (Section 3) will demonstrate that both the evolution of public/private governance solutions as well as horizontal and vertical processes of regulatory competition within a multi-level legal system can contribute to the explanation of the evolution of 'transnational commercial law'. It will also emphasize the importance of conflict/choice of laws rules for this evolution. The final section (Section 4) will conclude that the transnational governance solutions are the outcome of complex and interrelated evolutionary competition processes between private and public solutions on one hand and between public solutions of different jurisdictions on the other hand.

2. EVOLUTIONARY ECONOMICS AND INSTITUTIONAL CHANGE

2.1 Evolutionary Economics

Evolutionary economics encompasses a broad array of different approaches which emphasize the dynamic character of economic processes. Beyond all their differences, they share the conviction that mainstream neoclassical economics with its basic tenets of optimization and static equilibrium models is not capable to grasp properly the dynamic dimension of economic development, especially innovations and technological progress as the main determinant for long-term economic growth.[2] Therefore it is not surprising that the broad interdisciplinary field of innovation research is closely connected with evolutionary economics. From the perspective of the history of economic thought, particularly Schumpeter and Hayek can be seen as the most influential figures who contributed to the basic tenets of evolutionary economics. In his seminal book 'Theory of Economic Development' Schumpeter introduced the theoretical concepts entrepreneur, innovation, and economic development into economic theory. He claimed that economic development cannot be explained by general equilibrium theory but needs a fundamentally different theoretical approach.[3] Building upon Schumpeter's basic ideas, dynamic (and evolutionary) concepts of competition as an innovation-imitation process have been developed.[4] This is also true for modern innovation economics. Nelson and Winter with their evolutionary simulation models for technological progress and economic growth have integrated the biological notion of evolution as processes of variation, selection, and retention into this Schumpeterian tradition of innovation economics.[5] Another important strand of evolutionary thought in economics is Hayek with his idea of cultural evolution as a process of variation and selection of behavioral rules and his concept of competition as a discovery procedure, which views market competition as a trial and error process.[6] Other approaches of evolutionary economics encompass, for example, 'old institutionalists' (Veblen), evolutionary game theory, and new biological approaches to evolutionary economics.[7]

What are important tenets of evolutionary economics?

(1) The dynamic advantages through innovation and technological progress are viewed much more important for the long-term increase of wealth than solving the problem of static inefficiencies as in neoclassical welfare economics. Therefore evolutionary economists emphasize the eminent importance of dynamic efficiency (innovations) in comparison to static efficiency (efficient allocation).

(2) Evolutionary economics is very critical to the model of purely rational human actors (*homo oeconomicus*) and prefers the taking into account of additional dimensions as, e.g., bounded rationality, subjectivism, learning and cognitive processes (mental models and creativity), and the insights of behavioral economics.

(3) Evolutionary economists are skeptics. They do not believe that the best solutions are already known. In particular, Hayek asserted vehemently that both the economic agents and policy makers suffer from severe knowledge problems. How to deal with these knowledge problems is one of the crucial questions from an evolutionary economics perspective. This is linked to the notion of structural uncertainty and the ontological openness of the future, caused by the non-predictability of innovations and of economic and social change.

---

2 For broad overviews see Dosi (1988); Hodgson (1993); Nelson (1995); Saviotti (1996); Metcalfe, (1998); Nelson and Winter (2002); Herrmann-Pillath (2002); Witt, (2003); Dopfer, ed. (2005).

3 Schumpeter (1934).

4 Clark (1961); Heuss (1965); Ellig, ed. (2002).

5 Nelson and Winter (1982).

6 Hayek (1978a); Hayek (1973).

7 Hodgson, *supra* note 2; see article by du Laing (2008).

(4) Therefore, the generation and diffusion of innovations as new solutions for old and new problems is crucial (innovative problem-solving behavior). Market competition, understood as a process of parallel experimentation and mutual learning, is seen as a device for searching for innovations and dealing with these knowledge problems.

(5) An important method for analysing evolutionary economic processes is the use of the variation-selection framework, which views developments as processes of (random) variation and (systematic) selection of products (or technologies, institutions etc.). From that perspective, the (often observed) heterogeneity of firms is a productive resource and need not indicate market failure (as in neoclassical economics).

(6) History matters. Evolutionary economists have always emphasized the path-dependence of economic development. Dynamic economies of scale, network effects, technological paradigms and mental models can cause path dependencies – with potentially serious 'lock in'-effects of inefficient technologies or institutions.

Since in this chapter regulatory competition will be considered as one of the major drivers for institutional change, the evolutionary dimension of competition should be elaborated more clearly.[8] In contrast to neoclassical microeconomics and the model of perfect competition, in which the best products and technologies are usually assumed as known by the firms, the evolutionary concept of competition starts from Hayek's assumption that the firms do not have perfect knowledge about the preferences of the consumers and how to fulfill them best. Rather, this knowledge about superior products and production technologies is generated through the competition process. Therefore, competition is viewed as a trial and error process, in which firms create and test hypotheses about superior products (or services) and cheaper ways to produce them. These hypotheses can be seen as fallible hypotheses in the Popperian sense, which are tested in the market. The positive or negative feedback from the market (through profits and losses) reveals which of the hypotheses of the firms are superior to others. This allows for a learning process, which also includes the imitation of the superior hypotheses by other competing firms. This can be seen as a process of parallel experimentation with mutual learning. From that evolutionary perspective competition of firms in markets can also be analysed as a variation and selection process. The innovation of new products can be interpreted as variation, whereas the market test represents the systematic selection process, which ensures that only those products survive in the market that correspond best to the preferences of the consumers. Consequently, competition on markets can be viewed as a process of variation and selection of products and production technologies, which lead to a gradual process of knowledge accumulation. From that perspective, the diversity of tested products and technologies is crucial for the knowledge-generating effect of competition.[9] This concept of competition as a test of hypotheses is based upon Hayek's idea of competition as a discovery procedure but is also compatible with the Schumpeterian concept of competition as a dynamic process of innovation and imitation as well as the general evolutionary approach of Popper about 'growth of knowledge'.[10]

---

[8] See in much more detail Hayek (1978b); Kerber (1997); Kerber and Saam (2001).

[9] For a thorough recent analysis of the potential positive effects of (maintaining) diversity in market competition see Linge (2008).

[10] Popper (1972); Harper (1996).

Such an evolutionary concept of market competition can also be applied to competition among institutions or regulatory competition.[11]

2.2 Evolutionary Theories of Institutional Change: An Overview

Since the main focus of evolutionary economics has been on the explanation of the process of the innovation and diffusion of new products and technologies, the issue of institutional change has been discussed mainly only in recent years. However, this must be qualified in several respects. One of the most stimulating evolutionary approaches was Hayek's theory of cultural evolution. His basic idea is that the rules of behavior that are used in a society are the outcome of a very long process of variation and selection of rules, in which the superior rules survive and less suitable rules are sifted out. Since these rules are learnt by each new generation, this notion implies that these rules encompass knowledge about the solution of problems, which we often do not know explicitly. From a Hayekian perspective this process of cultural evolution can be seen as a spontaneous order which emerge from human actions, but which is not the result of human design (closely linked to 'invisible hand' explanations).[12] The details of Hayek's theory of cultural evolution have been criticized to a large degree, but the basic idea that rules of behavior are the outcome of an unintended process of variation and selection has been very influential and is compatible with the basic tenets of evolutionary economics. The second qualification refers to the insight that some approaches to institutional and legal change have used an implicit evolutionary approach, e.g. Posner's theory of the efficient common law process. Thirdly, a number of theoretical arguments that have been developed for explaining technological change can also be applied to institutional change, i.e. they can be used for analysing processes of innovation and imitation in the legal realm. The next paragraphs will give a very brief overview about approaches to institutional change from an evolutionary economics perspective.[13]

Legal change is driven both by legislation and by the jurisprudence of courts. Especially the legal evolution that emerges through the ongoing decisions of courts has been the focus of ex- or implicit evolutionary approaches. Hayek had previously posited that judge-made law was the result of an evolutionary process of trial and error.[14] When new situations turn up, judges try out new legal solutions (legal innovations). Since they are not able to predict all the consequences of these new legal rules, a kind of experimental process ensues. Such an approach can also be found much more elaborated in the Law and Economics literature about the evolution of common law, which seems to be driven much more by jurisprudence than by legislation. The evolution of the common law is explained as the result of an ongoing sequence of cases that are decided by courts and which also include precedents and step-by-step refinements of the law. An implicit evolutionary process emerges through the kind of cases that are brought by the litigants, through the legal innovations of the judges (including unintended mistakes), and the

---

11 For a direct comparison of market competition and institutional (or regulatory) competition from an evolutionary economics perspective, see Vanberg and Kerber (1994).

12 Hayek, *supra* note 6; Hayek (1967).

13 For a much more detailed overview see Eckardt (2008); Eckardt (2001).

14 Hayek, *supra* note 6.

hierarchical judicial system, which works as a selection device. Posner's hypothesis that this process leads to an ever larger proportion of efficient legal rules, because primarily the inefficient ones are challenged by litigants (efficient common law process thesis), has been criticized convincingly, e.g., because litigants will not only attack legal rules due to their inefficiency but also because of distributional effects.[15] However, the basic approach to interpret the evolution of judge-made law as an ongoing process of trial and error or variation and selection of legal rules offers promising perspectives for an economic analysis of legal change by scrutinizing the specific mechanisms of the judicial system in regard to their impact on the innovation, diffusion, and selection of legal solutions.

Although there are more economic theories about political decision-making (as it is relevant for legislation and therefore for statutory legal change) than about judge-made legal change, evolutionary approaches have played a much smaller role in the theories of political economy (public choice). Through the rigorous analysis of rent seeking activities of interest groups on political decision-making, the (re)distributional dimension of legislation has been an important issue. Despite the arguments of Hayek about the 'pretence of knowledge' of policy makers, public choice theory has not sufficiently taken into account the severe knowledge problems of legislators or the theoretical implications of Schumpeterian political entrepreneurs.[16] However, several recent approaches can be mentioned which try to take into account some aspects of evolutionary thinking. The later writings of North are especially important in this respect.[17] Although initially firmly rooted in Public Choice and New Institutional Economics, he acknowledges the importance of bounded rationality, subjective theories and beliefs, ideologies and mental models for explaining institutional change and therefore opens up the perspective for an evolutionary approach, based also on cognitive science. An elaborated cognitive-evolutionary approach to policy-making was presented by Meier and Slembeck.[18] They depict a multi-level variation-selection approach to statutory legal change, in which problems of perception and knowledge, creative cognition and legal innovations, opinion formation and selection mechanisms are taken into account.

Both Hayek and North have emphasized path dependency as a very important aspect of institutional and legal evolution. Path dependence means that the future development of the law is dependent on the previous states of the law. This historical dimension of evolution has always been stressed by evolutionary economics. In evolutionary innovation economics, a number of theoretically well-founded arguments about reasons for path dependencies in regard to technological developments have been developed. Path dependencies can lead to 'lock in' problems, i.e. that an industry might get stuck with an inefficient technology, because path dependence effects impede the ousting of this old technology through a superior new one. A well-known example is the (in the meantime) inefficient QWERTY keyboard on computers, which has not been replaced by a more efficient one because tens of millions of people have acquired the complementary

---

15 Priest (1977); Cooter and Kornhauser (1980); De Alessi and Staaf (1991); Posner (1998); Cooter and Ulen (2007).

16 See, for example, the textbook of Mueller (2003); for an overview about evolutionary approaches to public choice see Wohlgemuth (2002).

17 North (1990); Denzau and North (1994).

18 Meier and Haury (1990); Slembeck (1997).

capability of typewriting with this old keyboard. The switching costs would be too high. Important causes for path dependence effects are dynamic economies of scale, sunk costs, complementary (human) capital, network effects, but also uncertainty and mental models.[19] All of these economic arguments can also be applied to legal evolution.[20] For example, the well-known fact that the quality of a law increases with the number of decisions by courts which clarify the precise content of the law can be interpreted as the consequence of dynamic economies of scale from an economic perspective. This can lead to the typical path dependency problem that an older law with already much case law is superior to a potentially more efficient new law which still lacks sufficient jurisprudence.[21] A particularly important cause for path dependencies in legal evolution can be complementarities between legal rules, i.e. that the effectiveness of particular legal rules depend on the context of other legal rules.[22] It is also possible to apply the concept of 'technological paradigms' and 'technological trajectories', which was developed in innovations economics by Dosi using Thomas Kuhn's concept of 'scientific paradigms',[23] to legal evolution (legal paradigms and legal trajectories) for explaining different legal developments in legal systems as the consequence of path dependencies.[24] North particularly emphasized (based upon historical examples) that path dependencies can lead to the danger that societies can get stuck permanently with inefficient institutional structures leading to economic decline instead of economic growth.[25]

The recent discussion on globalization with its emphasis on the importance of competition among states (interjurisdictional competition) for attracting production factors and regulatory competition has also led to a new approach for explaining institutional change. If skilled labor, capital, and firms are mobile between jurisdictions, then the jurisdictions have incentives to improve their institutions for increasing their attractiveness as a location for these mobile production factors. The services of a legal order might then be one part of the bundle of taxes and public services that jurisdictions offer on such a market for locations. From that perspective, the innovation and diffusion of new legal rules or other services of a legal order (quality and rapidity of court decisions and enforcement measures) might be explained as a consequence of evolutionary competition between jurisdictions. In contrast to the other above-mentioned approaches here legal evolution is driven more by competition with other jurisdictions instead of being determined by intrajurisdictional developments. The discussion about interjurisdictional competition is closely linked to the question of the advantages of centralization and decentralization, because interjurisdictional or regulatory competition can only flourish in fairly decentralized systems.[26] Due to the potential advantages of competition as a process of parallel

---

19 Arthur (1988); David (1985); Dosi , *supra* note 2.

20 North, *supra* note 17; Hathaway (2001); Eckardt (2001); Kerber and Heine (2003).

21 Kahan and Klausner (1996).

22 Kerber and Heine, *supra* note 20, 211.

23 Dosi (1982).

24 Kerber and Heine, *supra* note 20, 200–213.

25 North, *supra* note 17.

26 Tiebout (1956); Vanberg and Kerber, *supra* note 11; Sun and Pelkmans (1995); Bratton and McCahery (1997); Oates (1999); Ogus (1999); Van den Bergh (2000); Esty and Gerardin, eds. (2001); Marciano and Josselin, eds. (2003); Kerber (2008).

experimentation, a number of scholars have emphasized the advantages of decentralized systems and competitive federalism for the innovation and diffusion of superior legal rules and institutions.[27] However, the thesis about a 'race to the top' through regulatory competition is hotly disputed by other scholars who demonstrate convincingly that also 'race to the bottom' processes might be possible.[28] Although this discussion about the advantages and problems of regulatory competition is mainly driven by policy questions, the arguments can also be used for the explanation of legal evolution. This regulatory competition approach will be used primarily in the following sections for the explanation of the emergence and evolution of transnational commercial law.

3. EVOLUTION OF TRANSNATIONAL COMMERCIAL LAW IN MULTI-LEVEL LEGAL SYSTEMS

3.1 Research Questions from an Evolutionary Economics Perspective

The most important developments about the governance of cross-border transactions can be summarized as follows:[29] The globalization process has led to the development of international and often global markets with the implication of a huge expansion of cross-border transactions with an increasing demand for effective governance of these contracts. So far, the nation states have not succeeded (or even seriously attempted) in establishing a legal order for cross-border transactions that will lead to similar legal certainty as for domestic transactions. The soaring demand for governance of cross-border contracts has been increasingly satisfied by a number of new modes of private governance (e.g., private arbitration). In addition, there are often new combinations of private governance modes with public solutions of the nation states. These 'recombinant governance' modes refer both to the combination of private and public governance solutions as well as to the combination with public solutions from different jurisdictions (through choice of law). In any case, the relevance of the public governance solutions of the nation states is considerably reduced in comparison to domestic transactions. Therefore, the evolution of this 'transnational commercial law' is also characterized by the generation and diffusion of new forms of governance (legal innovations).

What research questions can be asked about this development from an evolutionary economics perspective?

(1) Why do we have this development to more cross-border transactions? This is the question for the causes of the globalization process itself, which we will not pursue in this

---

[27] See, for example, Behrens (1986); Easterbrook (1994); Van den Bergh (1998); particularly from an evolutionary economics perspective see Kerber (2005); Saam and Kerber (2008).

[28] For this discussion see Oates and Schwab (1988); Hauser and Hösli (1991); Revesz (1992); Sun and Pelkmans, *supra* note 26; Vogel (1995); Bratton and McCahery, *supra* note 26; Sinn (1997); Garcimartín (1999); Trachtman (2000); Van den Bergh, *supra* note 26; Esty and Gerardin, *supra* note 26; Kieninger (2002); Heine and Kerber (2002); Marciano and Josselin, *supra* note 26; Kerber, *supra* note 26.

[29] See Calliess *et al.* (2007), *supra* note 1.

chapter. From an evolutionary economics perspective, this is, on one hand, the consequence of decreasing costs for transportation and communication caused by technological progress in the course of normal economic development. Harder to explain (not only for evolutionary economics) is the second cause for globalization, i.e. the tremendous policy shifts to liberalization and deregulation in many countries all over the world since the 1990s.

(2) In this article, we will focus on the research question of how evolutionary economics might be applied to explain the emergence and diffusion of these new modes of governance for alleviating cross-border transactions. As a first step, the evolution of the relation between private and public solutions for the governance of contracts generally will be discussed (Section 3.2). Secondly, the complexity of horizontal and vertical processes of regulatory competition in a multi-level legal system from an evolutionary economics perspective will be analysed (Sections 3.3 and 3.4). The thesis is that the evolution of these new governance modes are the overall result of a number of complex evolutionary processes of regulatory competition, innovation of private governance modes and choice of law rules.

(3) Evolutionary economics can also contribute to policy questions[30] about the best way to improve legal certainty for cross-border transactions. Should the nation states try to close the gap by establishing a global harmonized contract law? Or should they strengthen their efforts for enacting international rules for a mutual recognition of the decisions of public courts in order to ensure a better enforcement for cross-border contracts? Since regulatory issues are also important in that respect, this research question aims at addressing the general problem how a global institutional framework for such a multi-level legal system should look. This includes both the question of the extent of convergence and harmonization as well as of the appropriate conflict and choice of laws rules. This research question cannot be dealt with here. However, in Section 3.4, some policy conclusions to ensure the long-term possibility of innovation and learning processes for improving public and private governance mechanisms are suggested.

3.2 Private vs. Public Solutions for Governance: Evolution Between Competition and Cooperation

Within nation states, the legal order provides legal services for helping private parties in the governance of their transactions. These public governance solutions encompass the provision of standard contracts (as default solutions which save bargaining costs for the private parties within their freedom of contract) as well as the support for enforcing contracts. The latter entails both the services of public civil courts for settling disputes and the help of the state to enforce claims and court decisions. From an economic perspective, these public governance solutions for facilitating transactions have the task of reducing transaction costs (facilitative or enabling law). The quality of these public governance solutions can be very different, leading to different levels of transaction costs by using domestic contract law and civil courts. Most of the services of these public governance

---

30 For a discussion about the specific problems for policy recommendations from an evolutionary economics perspective see Wegner (1997).

solutions can also be provided by private agencies. Transaction cost-saving legal standard solutions for certain types of contracts can also be written and offered by private law firms. The settling of disputes about the precise content of a contract or the correct performance of the parties can also be carried out by private arbitrators, to whom the parties agree *ex ante*. More difficult is the ultimate enforcement of claims of the contract or of arbitration. However, economic theory has demonstrated that there are a number of possibilities for self-enforcing contracts, i.e. that the parties have an incentive for performing, even in the absence of powerful enforcement agencies. Well-known examples are long-term relationships with repeated transactions (repeated games), reputation mechanisms or the exchange of 'hostages'. All of these solutions can be called private governance solutions for enforcing transactions.[31] Currently, within a national legal order, these public and private governance solutions act as substitutes due to a certain degree of 'functional equivalence'.[32] Private parties will choose between these private and public governance solutions according to their relative transaction costs. However, private and public solutions need not always be substitutes but can also complement each other, e.g., if parties agree on private arbitration for their contracts but rely on the public enforcement of the decisions of the private arbitrator. Those hybrid solutions may require the public provision of interfaces between private and public solutions, as, e.g., the recognition of the decision of a private arbitrator by the public legal order.

Also, within a national legal order the relation between these private and public governance solutions will evolve. Since the firms as users of these governance solutions compete with each other, they have large incentives in searching for new and better solutions that reduce their transaction costs or allow for more sophisticated transactions that increase the gains from their cooperation. From an evolutionary economics perspective, it can be expected that the firms will search for and experiment with new private governance solutions. If these experiments are successful, then their competitors (and also firms in other markets) will imitate them, leading to a competition-driven diffusion of these new private governance solutions. Lawyers, as specialists in 'legal engineering', will help them or even be the entrepreneurs themselves by creating new governance solutions and offering them to the firms.[33] This evolutionary process of experimentation with new governance solutions encompasses also the search for new, sophisticated combinations of private and public governance solutions (new hybrids). Much more difficult is the question of whether there will be an evolution of public governance solutions. Most important is that the national legal order is traditionally a monopolistic institution funded by the taxpayer. Therefore, there are no comparable clear-cut incentives for improving the public governance solutions provided by the national legal order and the judicial system. This does not preclude a slow evolutionary process of step-by-step improvement, analysed by evolutionary theories of judge-made law or political economy; but this process can also fail. A particularly large problem can be path dependencies in the evolution of

[31] For the many forms of private governance see Williamson (1985); Ellickson (1991); Hadfield (2001); Dixit (2004); Furubotn and Richter (2005); Eggertsson (2005); Williamson (2005); Greif (2006); Cafaggi (2006).

[32] Calliess *et al.* (2007), *supra* note 1.

[33] Therefore the Schumpeterian entrepreneur can also be applied to legal innovations; see, for example, McBarnet (1994); Gardner (2003).

the public governance solutions with the possibility of 'lock in' situations. If the public governance solutions for facilitating domestic transactions are ineffective (as is the case within a number of countries), then a more or less capable system of private governance solutions will emerge in order to compensate for the failing of the legal order provided by the state. In general, we can expect that market competition will lead to the evolution of private governance solutions for transactions, which also encompass new combinations with presumably slowly evolving public governance solutions.

This evolution also depends on the extent of freedom of contract in comparison to mandatory regulations and on the number and quality of interfaces between private and public governance solutions. Both are very important for the extent of competition and cooperation between private and public governance. If we take into account the possibility of cross-border transactions on international markets, then two considerations are important. First, due to the lack of effective public governance solutions on international markets, private governance has to fulfill a much larger role than within a nation state. In addition to that, through international mobility and choice of law, the 'legal engineers', who try to improve private governance, can now also use the public governance solutions of different countries for their search of optimal combinations in order to reduce transaction costs. This, secondly, can lead to regulatory competition between the public governance solutions and can change the conditions for their evolution considerably. Therefore, the problem of competition and cooperation between private and public governance solutions is closely intertwined with the horizontal and vertical processes of regulatory competition, which are analysed in the next two sections.

3.3 Institutional Evolution as a Result of Horizontal Regulatory Competition Between Legal Systems

Horizontal regulatory competition can take place on any level of a multi-level legal system. For example, the famous competition among corporate laws in the US is a competition between several US federal states for the incorporation of large firms.[34] In accordance with the literature, we will use the term regulatory competition very broadly. It can refer to all types of legal rules as well as to the services of the judicial system of the state (courts, enforcement agencies). In the following analysis, we need not focus on the much more difficult problem of competition of mandatory regulations but can limit ourselves to competition among facilitative law. We will see that some hotly disputed problems of regulatory competition are of minor importance, if the legal rules have no other regulatory aims than helping the private parties to reduce their transaction costs. The evolution of legal rules through regulatory competition can also work very differently due to different transmission mechanisms; this leads to different types of regulatory competition. In the next paragraph, we will see that, in terms of facilitative law, we can mostly limit ourselves to one type of regulatory competition, which emerges through choice of law. Another particular focus will be the evolutionary dimension of regulatory competition, i.e. the aspect of variation and selection of new public governance solutions (legal innovations).

---

[34] Romano (1985).

The specific incentives and competitive pressures that ensue from regulatory competition depend very much on the extent of mobility of firms, capital, goods, or the legal rules and services themselves. Therefore different types of regulatory competition can be distinguished:[35]

- Indirect regulatory competition through yardstick competition: In this case, only mobility of information between different jurisdictions is necessary. In different jurisdictions different public governance solutions for transaction problems are used, which might have a different quality. Here no direct competition between the firms or the jurisdictions themselves are assumed, however, the governments, citizens, and/or academic scholars (e.g., comparative lawyers) can compare the performance of these different solutions, and the jurisdictions with inferior solutions can learn from those with better solutions by imitating them. The history of legal evolution provides many examples in which legal orders have learnt from other systems of law, either by directly copying them or by using their experience for the development of their own law. From an evolutionary perspective, this can be interpreted as a process of parallel experimentation and mutual learning, in which different legal orders make experiences with different new solutions (variation) and an ensuing process of selection through imitation of the best solutions ('yardstick'). However, here only intrajurisdictional incentives for the innovation and imitation of better public governance solutions are assumed, as, e.g., intrajurisdictional competition of political parties for the majority of votes.[36]
- Indirect regulatory competition through international trade: More outside pressures for improving facilitative law emerges if domestic firms compete with foreign firms on international markets. More efficient public governance solutions for transactions reduce the production costs of domestic firms and increase their international competitiveness. The decisive difference in comparison to the former type of regulatory competition is that the jurisdictions have considerably more incentives for improving their facilitative law, because the ensuing competitive advantages on export markets lead to an increase of domestic welfare.
- Direct regulatory competition through interjurisdictional competition: If we take additionally into account that firms and production factors (especially capital) is mobile between jurisdictions, then the transmission mechanism of interjurisdictional (or locational) competition emerges. In contrast to the indirect competition between facilitative law in the last paragraph, here the users of public governance solutions have the possibility to choose directly between the legal systems through their interjurisdictional mobility. The quality of a public legal system is part of the bundle of public services and taxes, which are offered by a jurisdiction for attracting mobile firms and production factors. From that perspective, a superior quality of public governance solutions (e.g., high legal certainty and a well-educated

---

[35] For this distinction see Kerber and Budzinski (2003); Heine (2003).

[36] In public choice theory the term 'yardstick competition' is used for the specific intrajurisdictional mechanism that the voters, who decide on the re-election of their government, compare the performance of their government with the performance of the governments of other countries. See Besley and Case (1995); the basic idea can be found in Salmon (1987).

judiciary) is an advantage in interjurisdictional competition. Therefore, jurisdictions have an incentive for improving their facilitative law and their judicial system. However, the quality of the public governance solutions is only a (perhaps small) part of the whole bundle of public services offered by jurisdictions; thus its relevance both for mobile firms and for governments who want to increase the attractiveness of their jurisdictions might be limited.

- Direct regulatory competition through free choice of law: This changes dramatically, if the firms have the right to choose between the facilitative law of different legal orders without having to migrate to another jurisdiction.[37] Free choice of law and free choice of forum might lead to a very intensive competition between public governance solutions, because the users have much lower switching costs and they can choose specific governance solutions from different legal orders. Since the right to choose between the facilitative law of different countries was always the dominant conflict of law rule for cross-border transactions, it is this type of regulatory competition which might be most relevant for contributing to the explanation of the evolution of governance solutions. Whereas the facilitative law of a legal order is under competition for cross-border transactions, this is not true for the much larger number of domestic transactions, where the private parties usually have no right to choose foreign law. Therefore, especially in large countries, where the proportion between cross-border and domestic transactions might be small, the facilitative law of the legal order might not be under much competitive pressure due to its monopolistic position in regard to domestic transactions. This has implications for the incentives of a legal order to react to the losing of market shares on the market for public governance solutions for cross-border transactions. This demonstrates the crucial importance of the extent of choice of law: if private parties would also have the possibility to choose foreign law for their purely domestic transactions, then it would also be possible that an inefficient facilitative law might disappear completely.

The results of the general discussion about the advantages and problems of regulatory competition (race to the top vs. race to the bottom) can be summarized as follows:[38] the initially strong contrast between those who think that regulatory competition leads to an improvement of the law, and their opponents, who denounce regulatory competition as a process of deterioration, has been replaced by a much more differentiated view. Regulatory competition can have a number of advantages and problems and it depends on the specific legal rules, the type of regulatory competition as well as on the size of the positive and negative effects, whether regulatory competition is on balance beneficial or harmful. There is a broad consensus as to what the most important potential advantages and problems are. Important advantages of regulatory competition are a higher efficiency of legal rules in regard to the fulfillment of preferences (or solving the problems of the users of law), less rent-seeking through lobbyism of interest groups (through the exit options of those who do not benefit from the distributive effects of legal rules), and more

---

37 For a brief economic analysis of choice of law in general, see Parisi and Ribstein (1998).

38 For overviews and contributions to this discussion, see the references in note 28.

innovation and adaptability of legal rules in regard to changing problems. Deemed as important problems are the danger of race to the bottom processes (because jurisdictions might lower their standards in order to attract more users of their law), the problem of circumventing regulations, higher information and transaction costs (through the existence of several facilitative laws instead of one), the possible lack of incentives for politicians to improve the legal rules, and the problem of combining the legal rules of different legal orders (legal transplant problem). Another more recent discussion refers less to the question of whether the law will improve or deteriorate through regulatory competition, but asks whether free choice of law might be insufficient for triggering a dynamic process of regulatory competition at all. In the following, the relevance of some of these arguments in regard to the evolution of facilitative law will be discussed.

In contrast to the field of mandatory regulations, which have the task of solving market failure problems or of protecting third parties, there need not be much concern in regard to race to the bottom problems. Since the legal rules have only the task of reducing the transaction costs of the parties, there are no incentives for jurisdictions to lower their quality in order to induce more private parties using them. Also no serious circumvention problems can emerge. At first sight, it might be a problem that regulatory competition can lead to higher information and transaction costs, because the firms have to spend resources in order to get acquainted with foreign law. However, the firms can decide themselves whether they want to bear these information costs and use the advantages of a better governance solution from another legal order or not. Law firms can reduce these costs by fulfilling the role of information intermediaries, who specialize on the collection and processing of this information. The problem that the use of the legal solution of one legal order might lead to different effects within the context of another legal order due to complementarities between different legal rules (implying institutional path dependencies) might be important. This is one of the reasons for the famous 'legal transplant' problem.[39] Complementarities between legal rules within a legal order can limit considerably the scope for combining the public governance solutions of different legal orders, and therefore also the extent of regulatory competition.[40] Another important problem for regulatory competition in regard to facilitative law might be the incentive problem, at least in the long run. What are the incentives for jurisdictions to improve their facilitative law and for public courts to attract additional litigation by providing good and fast decisions? In the example of competition among US corporate laws, the federal states have incentives through franchise taxes.[41]

The advantage of regulatory competition to limit rent-seeking problems is less relevant, because interest groups do not have large incentives to influence facilitative law. A much more important advantage is that choice of law leads to the possibility that the private parties can select the best public governance solutions from a much broader set of alternative solutions. Since the private parties might have very different transaction problems, choosing from a larger set of different solutions increases the efficiency of the

---

[39] See for the legal transplant problem Legrand (1997); Berkowitz *et al.* (2003).

[40] For an analysis of this effect in regard to competition among corporate laws see Heine and Kerber, *supra* note 28.

[41] It should be noted that this problem increases with the extent of choice of law, because choice of law also reduces the incentives for domestic interest groups to lobby for a better facilitative law.

governance of cross-border transactions. Choice of law not only implies a better matching between the transactions and their governance but also leads to a selection effect, i.e. the market shares of the facilitative laws from different legal orders changes over time. Inferior public governance solutions are replaced by better ones, leading to an increase of the average efficiency of the applied governance solutions. Therefore even without a direct dynamic reaction of the legal order with the inferior solutions, such a systematic selection process with the consequence of sifting out inefficient legal solutions leads to an evolution of the governance of cross-border transactions.[42] The situation changes, if, in addition to that, the jurisdictions also react to their falling market shares by improving their facilitative law, either by imitating others or by searching for innovative solutions. Another possibility would be a differentiation strategy, i.e. that legal orders try to defend their market shares by specializing upon certain kinds of transaction problems and types of contract.[43]

Most interesting from an evolutionary economics perspective is the innovation dimension of regulatory competition.[44] Even if a dynamic (action-reaction like) process of competition between jurisdictions in regard to public governance solutions for cross-border transactions might not work well due to incentive problems and institutional rigidities, at least a process of parallel experimentation with different new governance solutions and a certain degree of mutual learning between legal orders might take place. Since in a rapidly changing world a lot of new transaction and governance problems emerge regularly, to which at least the jurisprudence must react in their decisions about facilitative law cases, a certain amount of different new responses to these problems (legal innovations) can be expected. The evolutionary theories of judge-made law can be used in that respect. The resulting diversity of legal solutions feeds the evolutionary selection mechanism of regulatory competition, driven by choice of law through private parties. Consequently, an evolutionary process of variation and selection ensues which can lead to a cumulative process of improvements of public governance solutions, if there are no serious problems of market failure. Particularly important is that such a process can also encompass the finding of new forms of combinations of private and public governance solutions (hybrids), e.g. through the innovation of better interfaces between both. For example, a jurisdiction can get a competitive advantage in this regulatory competition, if its legal order provides better possibilities of how its public governance solutions can be used for making the internationally vital private governance solutions more effective.

---

42 For an evolutionary model of technological progress, which is only based upon a pure selection effect, see Metcalfe, *supra* note 2.

43 For a comprehensive analysis of variation-selection models in regard to their impact on innovation see generally Linge, *supra* note 9.

44 The famous empirical article of Romano, *supra* note 34, about competition of US corporate laws emphasized particularly this dimension of innovation and imitation of new corporate law innovations. For explicit evolutionary approaches to regulatory competition see Vanberg and Kerber, *supra* note 11 and Kerber, *supra* note 27.

3.4 The Vertical Dimension of Multi-level Legal Systems: Its Impact on Institutional Evolution

In order to explain the evolution of transnational commercial law in the governance of transaction, the vertical dimension in a multi-level legal system is also important. Facilitative law can be supplied on all jurisdictional levels of such a system, and free choice of law can imply that private parties might additionally choose between the public governance solutions of different levels. From that perspective, an evolutionary process of vertical competition as a driving-force for institutional evolution can also ensue. Let us take as example the project of the introduction of an optional European contract law. In the EU, there are very well-established contract laws in all Member States. When concerning cross-border transactions, the private parties have the right to choose between these national contract laws. Since the European Commission deemed the existence of different national contract laws as an impediment to the internal market due to the ensuing transaction costs, the project of a common European contract law emerged. Mainly for political reasons, it is conceived as an optional instrument, i.e. that it is offered in addition to the national contract laws (and does not replace them).[45] This project will not be discussed here in detail. However, as far as the EU offers an additional facilitative law, which the private parties can choose for their cross-border transactions, the national contract laws and the future European contract law would compete with each other. It would be a good example for vertical regulatory competition.[46]

This example can also be used for demonstrating some of the problems of vertical regulatory competition, which can have considerable impact on the legal evolution.[47] One of the biggest problems for the introduction of an optional European contract law is that it might fail entirely, if a sufficient number of private parties do not use it for their cross-border transactions. Since we know that the quality of a law increases with the extent of its applications (and therefore the emerging case law), a 'critical mass' of users is necessary for achieving a similar high quality as the well-established national contract laws. From an evolutionary economics perspective, this is the consequence of dynamic economies of scale, which lead to path dependencies and potential 'lock ins'. If this threshold of a minimum application of the European contract law is not achieved, then it might not survive, even if it is more efficient than the national contract laws. However, a European contract law could have the competitive advantage as firms can use the European law for all cross-border transactions within the EU, which would imply economies of scale effects, especially for large firms. Therefore, in the long run, one possible result of such a vertical competition could also be the monopoly of the European contract law. Very important for the outcome of this evolution is the specific design of the choice of law rules about the optionality (opt in or opt out rule?). It can be expected that the European contract law would have better chances, if in the case of cross-border transactions European contract law is automatically applied (as a default rule) except the private parties choose to opt out, than in the reverse case that the private parties must explicitly decide to opt into the

45 See for the optional European contract law Grundmann (2004); Röttinger (2006).
46 For another very complex example of vertical competition see Röpke and Heine (2005).
47 See for the following argumentation Kerber and Grundmann (2006), 215, 227–230.

European contract law. This demonstrates that the specific conflict of law and choice of law rules can be very important for the evolution of the law. Although the ultimate result of this vertical regulatory competition process is uncertain, it can be argued from an economic perspective that it might be beneficial for the evolution of contract law in the EU, if facilitative law is also supplied on the European level in addition to the national public governance solutions for (cross-border) transactions.[48]

Another important development in multi-level legal systems is the often-observed tendency towards harmonization and centralization, i.e. the gradual shifting of the competencies for providing legal rules to higher levels of the system. Although there are attempts to explain problematic centralization processes by using political economy theories, economic theory cannot offer much in this regard. This is also true for evolutionary economics, which – in addition to the above-mentioned mechanism of vertical regulatory competition through choice of law – so far cannot contribute to the explanation of the tendency to harmonization and centralization in the evolution of law. The decisive question is: Does this process only respond to the requirements of a more globalized economy or is it the result of some deficient process of institutional evolution? Both in regard to the EU and the global level, there is a widespread debate whether the observed tendency to convergence and centralization might not go too far, at least in some fields of the law. Based upon economic theories of federalism and regulatory competition, a number of economic criteria can be developed, which can be used for assessing whether the competence for enacting legal rules should be centralized or remain with lower-level jurisdictions, whether (and what type of) regulatory competition should be recommended, and what the most appropriate conflict of law rules would be.[49] Similar to the assessment of regulatory competition, the question of the optimal vertical allocation of the competencies for enacting legal rules can also only be answered by balancing the often manifold advantages and disadvantages of centralization and decentralization.

The long-term effects of a specific institutional solution within a multi-level legal system, however, can be very complex and are often hard to predict. An interesting example is the introduction of the principle of mutual recognition of regulations as a specific conflict of laws rule within the EU. Both in the literature on economic integration and trade policy, the principle of mutual recognition is praised as a very successful institutional innovation, which is capable of integrating markets through the removal of barriers to trade without embarking on a pathway to harmonization and centralization.[50] Within the EU, the principle of mutual recognition was introduced both by the Cassis de Dijon judgment of the European Court of Justice (judicial mutual recognition) and by the European Commission in its internal market strategy (regulatory mutual recognition). In the meantime, its application has been expanded to all fundamental economic freedoms of the EU, and even to the area of security. Also at the level of global trade, the introduction of the principle of mutual recognition is seriously discussed as a promising means for removing the manifold obstacles for a deeper integration of world-wide

---

[48] Kerber and Grundmann, *supra* note 47, 227.

[49] For sets of economic criteria see Van den Bergh (1996); Kerber and Heine (2002); Kerber and Grundmann, *supra* note 46; Kerber, *supra* note 26.

[50] See, for example, Weiler (2005); Pelkmans (2005); Pelkmans (2007); Nicolaidis and Shaffer (2005); Trachtman (2006).

markets. So far, mutual recognition is not an established principle within the World Trade Organization (WTO) system, although first attempts for developing a doctrine of 'equivalent regulations' exist as well as a number of bilateral 'Mutual Recognition Agreements' that have been concluded between states. From a law and economics perspective, the principle of mutual recognition is a specific conflicts of law rule, which stipulates that the importing (host) country has to accept the regulations of the exporting (home) country, i.e., it cannot require the fulfillment of its own specific regulations.

Both in the legal and in the economic discussion there has been a nearly unanimous consensus that the introduction of mutual recognition would both reduce mobility barriers and create the institutional preconditions for a horizontal regulatory competition between the states and prevent centralization and harmonization. However, recent research about the impact of the introduction of the principle of mutual recognition demonstrates that this view is grossly misleading. Although it is true that mutual recognition has contributed considerably to the removal of obstacles to trade and cross-border mobility, Kerber and Van den Bergh argue that it leads to a number of serious problems and inconsistencies, which call for a much more critical assessment.[51] Neither does mutual recognition defend the regulatory autonomy of the states nor can it be seen as an appropriate meta-rule for regulatory competition. In the case of consumer regulations, the application of mutual recognition leads either to a process of de facto harmonization (for avoiding race to the bottom problems) or to potentially very problematic industrial policy strategies, because the states are left with only the authority of regulating their domestic industries (instead of domestic markets). The rule of mutual recognition does not seem to be a long-term stable conflicts of law rule, rather either (de facto) harmonization or the transition to a rule of free choice of law (free choice of regulations) appears superior. Instead, the introduction of the rule of mutual recognition should be reinterpreted as initiating a dynamic process of reallocation or regulatory authorities within a two-level system of regulations (as in the EU). Its introduction can be seen as a test, whether the traditional national regulatory sovereignty is still the most appropriate, or whether another allocation of regulatory authority (as centralization/harmonization or free choice of law with the consequence of a competitive system of regulations) is the superior solution. The experiences in the EU clearly have shown that the introduction of the principle of mutual recognition has led to a long-term process of centralization and harmonization. Therefore, it seems to be more another pathway to harmonization instead of a rule that preserves competences on a decentralized level. For our analysis, the decisive conclusion is that the introduction of a (on first sight, horizontal) conflict of laws rule as mutual recognition can lead to a long-term evolution of changing the vertical allocation of regulatory competences within a multi-level legal system. Such a potential harmonization and centralization effect should also be considered, if the principle of mutual recognition should play a larger role at the level of global trade.

These policy questions will not be pursued further. However, the following implication of centralization and harmonization for institutional evolution should be emphasized. The positive effects of regulatory competition on the innovation of new legal rules and

---

[51] For the following, see in more detail Kerber and Van den Bergh (2008); Kerber and Van den Bergh (2011).

their adaptations to new circumstances have already been mentioned. In the economic theory of federalism as well as in the discussion about legal federalism the advantages of a decentralized legal order as a field of experimentation with the possibility of mutual learning have been stressed. In his survey article on fiscal federalism in the *Journal of Economic Literature*, Oates (as the leading economist in the field of federalism) developed the perspective of federalism as 'laboratory federalism': 'In a setting of imperfect information with learning-by-doing there are potential gains from experimentation with a variety of policies for addressing social and economic problems. Additionally, a federal system may offer some real opportunities for encouraging such experimentation and thereby promoting "technical progress" in public policy.'[52] Oates views these advantages as very important, although he is not able to integrate them consistently in his otherwise static welfare-theoretic approach to federalism. These advantages can be much better explained by an evolutionary approach to federalism, which analyses the effects of decentralized experimentation and mutual learning (variation-selection process) in a multi-level legal system.[53] A crucial consequence for our problem is that all processes of harmonization and centralization reduce the capability of a multi-level legal system to generate knowledge through decentralized experimentation and learning from the experiences of other jurisdictions. Therefore, from an evolutionary economics perspective harmonization and centralization processes are dangerous due to its effect of eliminating regulatory competition and decentralized experimentation. If we are convinced that the best public governance solutions for transactions have already been found, and furthermore, if adaptations to new transaction problems are of minor importance in the future, then harmonization and centralization need not be a big problem. However, if we are skeptical about that, then harmonization and centralization processes can seriously impede the long-term capability of the evolution of public governance solutions. Harmonization and centralization might also be a problem for the evolution of private governance solutions, because the possibilities for recombinations between private and public governance solutions might be shrinking considerably.

4. THE EVOLUTION OF TRANSNATIONAL COMMERCIAL LAW: THE RESULT OF COMPLEX AND INTERTWINED EVOLUTIONARY PROCESSES

In this chapter it is not possible to include more examples and analyse the results of empirical studies about these new modes of governance. Therefore I have described this development of transnational commercial law only in a stylized form at the beginning of Section 3 and focused instead on some theories from evolutionary economics that might help to explain this evolution. In a first step, we have seen that the development of private governance solutions for transactions is not specific for cross-border transactions but a general possibility to solve governance problems in the absence of effective

---

52 Oates, *supra* note 26, 1132; for a simulation model that analyses advantages of both centralization and decentralization see Kollman *et al.* (2000).

53 Kerber, *supra* note 27; Saam and Kerber, *supra* note 27.

public governance solutions. Even if workable public solutions exist, private governance solutions will always play an important role, either as alternative to more costly or slower public governance solutions (private arbitration) or as a complement to public governance solutions. For cross-border transactions, both the relative importance of private and public governance solutions as well as their modes of combination are very different from those observed within a national legal order. From an evolutionary economics perspective, however, both the private governance solutions and (although to a lesser extent) the public governance solutions will evolve over time as a consequence of the permanent search for new and better solutions for the governance of transactions.

Nevertheless, in regard to governance solutions for cross-border transactions, this search takes place within the context of a wide set of different public governance solutions, from which the private parties (or law firms as 'legal engineers') are able to choose. Besides the mobility of capital (implying interjurisdictional competition), it is mainly this right to free choice of law in the case of cross-border transactions which leads to various processes of horizontal and vertical regulatory competition between public governance solutions within a multi-level legal system. These processes of regulatory competition can work very differently. They may only consist of selection processes (increasing the market share of superior solutions without inducing changes of the solutions themselves), but they often can also entail the innovation of public governance solutions and their imitation through other jurisdictions. Due to the large uncertainty of how the best governance solutions will look like under the conditions of rapid technological and economic change in a globalized world, the search of firms and jurisdictions for better governance solutions appears as a manifold process of experimentation, in which different solutions are in competition with each other. Crucial for the complexity of this process is that several horizontal and vertical evolutionary processes of regulatory competition take place simultaneously, and are also intertwined with each other. They are also linked to and mutually influenced by the evolutionary search of firms and law firms for new sophisticated combinations of private and public governances. From an evolutionary economics perspective, it can be suggested that the evolution of this new 'transnational commercial law' can be studied by an analysis of these different evolutionary processes of experimentation and their relation with each other. Such an analysis can be complemented by using additional evolutionary theories as, e.g., evolutionary theories of judge-made law as well as path dependency.

The evolution of transnational commercial law is here seen as the common result of the simultaneous existence of a number of different evolutionary processes of competition and parallel experimentation and mutual learning. Conflict of law and choice of law rules play a decisive role for the enabling and channeling but also restricting or even eliminating these evolutionary processes of regulatory competition. Changing these rules and therefore the extent to which firms can choose between (or recombine) public governance solutions of different legal orders will lead to a change of the extent or the direction of these evolutionary processes and therefore to a different development of governance solutions for cross-border transactions. Closely connected to these rules are the rules which determine the vertical allocation of regulatory competencies. Harmonization and centralization can eliminate entirely certain evolutionary processes of parallel experimentation and mutual learning, whereas devolution enables additional variation and selection processes of legal solutions. Another important type of rules are the institutional interfaces between private and public governance solutions on one hand and between the public governance solutions of different legal orders on the other hand. The first refers to the possibilities that the legal order accepts and helps to enforce private governance solutions (as, e.g., private arbitration). The second one asks, for example, for the possibilities that public governance solutions of one state are recognized by other states (as, e.g., in the case of court decisions). In that respect, international treaties, which allow for the mutual recognition and enforcement of court decisions, such as the Hague Convention on Choice of Court Agreements, might be very important as institutional interfaces between different legal orders. They might enable extraterritorial litigation and therefore also a global market for judicial services with the perspective of competition between public courts of different countries.[54] As a consequence, all of these rules, which can be interpreted as part of the institutional framework for the multi-level legal system, are important suitable policy instruments for the improvement of the process of the evolution of transnational commercial law, in order to facilitate the governance of cross-border transactions.[55]

BIBLIOGRAPHY

Arthur, W. Brian (1988), 'Self-reinforcing mechanisms in economics', in Philip W. Anderson, Kenneth Arrow and David Pines (eds), *The Economy as an Evolving Complex System*, Reading, MA: Addison-Wesley, pp. 9–32.

Behrens, Peter (1986), 'Voraussetzungen und Grenzen der Rechtsfortbildung durch Rechtsvereinheitlichung', *RabelsZ*, **50**, 19–33.

Berkowitz, Daniel, Katharina Pistor and Jean-Francois Richard (2003), 'The transplant effect', *American Journal of Comparative Law*, **51**, 163–204.

Besley, Timothy and Anne Case (1995), 'Incumbent behavior, tax-setting, and yardstick competition', *American Economic Review*, **85**, 25–45.

Bratton, William W. and Joseph A. McCahery (1997), 'The new economics of jurisdictional competition: Devolutionary federalism in a second-best world', *The Georgetown Law Journal*, **86**, 201–278.

Cafaggi, Fabrizio (2006), 'Rethinking private regulation in the European regulatory space', in Fabrizio Cafaggi (ed.), *Reframing Self-regulation in European Private Law*, Alphen aan den Rijn: Kluwer Law International, pp. 3–75.

Calliess, Gralf-Peter, Thomas Dietz, Wioletta Konradi, Holger Nieswandt and Fabian Sosa (2007), 'Transformations of commercial law', in Achim Hurrelmann, Stephan Leibfried, Kerstin Martens and Peter Mayer (eds.), *Transforming the Golden Age Nation State*, Basingstoke Palgrave Macmillan, pp. 83–108.

Calliess, Gralf-Peter, Jörg Freiling and Moritz Renner (2008), 'Law, the state, and private ordering: Evolutionary explanations of institutional change', *German Law Journal*, **9**, 397–410.

Clark, John M. (1961), *Competition as a Dynamic Process*, Washington, DC: Brookings Institution.

Cooter, Robert D. and Lewis Kornhauser (1980), 'Can litigation improve the law without the help of the judges?', *Journal of Legal Studies*, **9**, 139–63.

Cooter, Robert D. and Thomas Ulen (2007), *Law and Economics*, 5th edn, Reading, MA: Addison-Wesley.

Dammann, Jens and Henry Hansmann (2007), 'A global market for judicial services', Yale Law & Economics Research Paper No. 347.

---

54 Dammann and Hansmann (2007).

55 For the regulatory function of the conflict of laws rules see Muir Watt (2003).

David, Paul (1985), 'Clio and the economics of QWERTY', *American Economic Review*, **75**, 332–7.
De Alessi, Louis and Robert J. Staaf (1991), 'The common law process: Efficiency or order?', *Constitutional Political Economy*, **2**, 107–126.
Denzau, Arthur T. and Douglass C. North (1994), 'Shared mental models: Ideologies and institutions', *Kyklos*, **47**, 3–13.
Dixit, Avinash K. (2004), *Lawlessness and Economics: Alternatives Modes of Governance*, Princeton, NJ: Princeton University Press.
Dopfer, Kurt (ed.) (2005), *The Evolutionary Foundations of Economics*, Cambridge: Cambridge University Press.
Dosi, Giovanni (1982), 'Technological paradigms and technological trajectories: A suggested reinterpretation of the determinants and directions of technical change', *Research Policy*, **11**, 147–162.
Dosi, Giovanni (1988), 'Sources, procedures, and microeconomic effects of innovation', *Journal of Economic Literature*, **26**, 1120–71.
du Laing, Bart (2008), 'Dual inheritance theory, contract law, and institutional change – Towards the co-evolution of behaviour and institutions', *German Law Journal*, **9**, 491–514.
Easterbrook, Frank H. (1994), 'Federalism and European business law', *International Review of Law and Economics*, **14**, 125–32.
Eckardt, Martina (2001), *Technischer Rechtswandel und Rechtsevolution. Ein Beitrag zur ökonomischen Theorie der Rechtsentwicklung am Beispiel des deutschen Unfallschadensrechts*, Tübingen: Mohr Siebert.
Eckardt, Martina (2008) 'Explaining legal change from an evolutionary economics perspective', *German Law Journal*, **9**, 437–64.
Eggertsson, Thráinn (2005), *Imperfect Institutions: Possibilities and Limits of Reform*, Ann Arbor, MI: University of Michigan Press.
Ellickson, Robert C. (1991), *Order Without Law: How Neighbours Settle Disputes*, Cambridge, MA: Harvard University Press.
Ellig, Jerry (ed.) (2002), *Dynamic Competition and Public Policy: Technology, Innovation, and Antitrust Issues*, Cambridge: Cambridge University Press.
Esty, Daniel C. and Damien Gerardin (eds) (2001), *Regulatory Competition and Economic Integration. Comparative Perspectives*, Oxford: Oxford University Press.
Furubotn, Eirik and Rudolf Richter (2005), *Institutions and Economic Theory: The Contribution of the New Institutional Economics*, 2nd edn, Ann Arbor, MI.: University of Michigan Press.
Garcimartín, Francisco (1999), 'Regulatory competition: A private international law approach', *European Journal of Law and Economics*, **8**, 251–70.
Gardner, Peter (2003), 'A role of the business attorney in the twenty-first century: Adding value to the client's enterprise in the knowledge economy', *Marquette Intellectual Property Law Review*, **7**, 17–73.
Greif, Avner (2006), *Institutions and the Path to the Modern Economy: Lessons from Medieval Trade*, Cambridge: Cambridge University Press.
Grundmann, Stefan (2004), 'The optional European code on the basis of the acquis communautaire – Starting point and trends', *European Law Journal*, **10**, 698–711.
Hadfield, Gillian K. (2001), 'Privatizing commercial law', *Regulation*, **24**, 40–45.
Harper, David A. (1996), *Entrepreneurship and the Market Process: An Enquiry into the Growth of Knowledge*, London: Routledge.
Hathaway, Oona A. (2001), 'Path dependence in the law: The course and pattern of legal change in a common law system', *Iowa Law Review*, **86**, 601–663.
Hauser, Heinz and Madeleine Hösli (1991), 'Harmonization or regulatory competition in the EC (and the EEA)?', *Aussenwirtschaft*, **46**, 497–512.
Hayek Friedrich A. von (1967), 'The results of human action but not of human design', in Friedrich A. von Hayek (ed.), *Studies in Philosophy, Politics, and Economics*, Chicago: University of Chicago Press, pp. 96–105.
Hayek Friedrich A. von (1973), *Law, Legislation and Liberty, Vol.1: Rules and Order*, Chicago and London: University of Chicago Press.
Hayek Friedrich A. von (1978a), 'Notes on the evolution of systems of rules of conduct', in

Friedrich A. von Hayek (ed.), *New Studies in Philosophy, Politics, Economics, and the History of Ideas*, Chicago: University of Chicago Press, pp. 66–81.
Hayek, Friedrich A. von (1978b), 'Competition as a discovery procedure', in Friedrich A. von Hayek (ed.), *New Studies in Philosophy, Politics, Economics, and the History of Ideas*, Chicago: University of Chicago Press, pp. 179–90.
Heine, Klaus (2003), *Regulierungswettbewerb im Gesellschaftsrecht. Zur Funktionsfähigkeit eines Wettbewerbs der Rechtsordnungen im europäischen Gesellschaftsrecht*, Berlin: Duncker & Humblot.
Heine, Klaus and Wolfgang Kerber (2002), 'European corporate laws, regulatory competition and path dependence', *European Journal of Law and Economics*, **13**, 43–71.
Herrmann-Pillath, Carsten (2002), *Grundriß der Evolutionsökonomik*, München: Fink.
Heuss, Ernst (1965), *Allgemeine Markttheorie*, Tübingen: J.C.B. Mohr (Paul Siebeck).
Hodgson, Geoffrey M. (1993), *Economics and Evolution. Bringing Life Back into Economics*, Cambridge: Polity Press.
Kahan, Marcel and Michael Klausner (1996), 'Path dependence in corporate contracting: Increasing returns, herd behavior and cognitive biases', *Washington Law Quarterly*, **74,** 347–364.
Kerber, Wolfgang (1997), 'Wettbewerb als Hypothesentest: Eine evolutorische Konzeption wissenschaffenden Wettbewerbs', in Karl von Delhaes and Ulrich Fehl (eds.), *Dimensionen des Wettbewerbs: Seine Rolle in der Entstehung und Ausgestaltung von Wirtschaftsordnungen*, Stuttgart: Lucius & Lucius, pp. 29–78.
Kerber, Wolfgang (2005), 'Applying evolutionary economics to economic policy: The example of competitive federalism', in Kurt Dopfer (ed.), *Economics, Evolution and the State: The Governance of Complexity*, Cheltenham, UK, and Northampton, MA, US: Edward Elgar, pp. 296–324.
Kerber Wolfgang (2008), 'European system of private laws: An economic perspective', in Fabrizio Cafaggi and Horatia Muir Watt (eds.), *The Making of European Private Law*, Cheltenham, UK and Northampton, MA, US: Edgar Elgar, pp. 64–97.
Kerber, Wolfgang and Oliver Budzinski (2003), 'Towards a differentiated analysis of competition of competition laws', *Journal of Competition Law (ZWeR)*, **1**, 411–448.
Kerber Wolfgang and Stefan Grundmann (2006), 'An optional European contract law code: Advantages and disadvantages', *European Journal of Law and Economics*, **21**, 215–236.
Kerber, Wolfgang and Klaus Heine (2002), 'Zur Gestaltung von Mehr-Ebenen-Rechtssystemen aus ökonomischer Sicht', in Claus Ott and Hans-Bernd Schäfer (eds.), *Vereinheitlichung und Diversität des Zivilrechts in transnationalen Wirtschaftsräumen*, Tübingen: Mohr Siebeck, pp. 167–94.
Kerber, Wolfgang and Klaus Heine (2003), 'Institutional Evolution, Regulatory Competition and Path Dependence', in Pavel Pelikan and Gerhard Wegner (eds.), *Evolutionary Analysis of Economic Policy*, Cheltenham, UK and Northampton, MA, US: Edward Elgar, pp. 191–222.
Kerber, Wolfgang and Nicole J. Saam (2001), 'Competition as a test of hypotheses: Simulation of knowledge-generating market processes', *Journal of Artificial Societies and Social Simulation (JASSS)*, Vol. 4, No. 3, http://www.soc.surrey.ac.uk/JASSS/4/3/2.html, last accessed 27 March 2008.
Kerber, Wolfgang and Roger van den Bergh (2008), 'Mutual recognition revisited: Misunderstandings, inconsistencies, and a suggested reinterpretation', *Kyklos*, **61**, 447–465.
Kerber, Wolfgang and Roger van den Bergh (2011), 'Mutual recognition in the global trade regime: lessons from the EU Experience', in Ioannis Lianos and Okeoghane Odudu (eds), *Regulating Trade in Services in the EU and the WTO: Trust, Distrust and Economic Integration*, Cambridge: Cambridge University Press (forthcoming).
Kieninger, Eva M. (2002), *Wettbewerb der Privatrechtsordnungen im Europäischen Binnenmarkt*, Tübingen: Mohr Siebeck.
Kollman Ken, John H. Miller and Scott E. Page (2000), 'Decentralization and the search for policy solutions', *The Journal of Law, Economics, & Organization*, **16**, 102–28.
Legrand, Paul (1997), 'The impossibility of legal transplants', *Maastricht Journal of European and Comparative Law*, **4**, 111–24.
Linge, Gisela (2008), *Competition Policy, Innovation, and Diversity*, Marburg: Tectum.

Marciano, Alain and Jean M. Josselin (eds) (2003), *From Economic to Legal Competition. New Perspectives on Law and Institutions in Europe*, Cheltenham, UK, and Northampton, MA, US: Edward Elgar.
McBarnet, Doreen (1994), 'Legal creativity: Law, capital and legal avoidance', in Maureen Cain and Christine Harrington (eds), *Lawyers in a Postmodern World: Translation and Transgression*, New York: New York University Press, pp. 73–84.
Meier, Alfred and Susanne Haury (1990), 'A cognitive-evolutionary theory of economic policy', in Kurt Dopfer and Karl-F. Raible (eds), *The Evolution of Economic Systems. Essays in Honour of Ota Sik*, London: Palgrave Macmillan, pp. 77–787.
Metcalfe, Stan J. (1998), *Evolutionary Economics and Creative Destruction*, London, New York: Routledge.
Mueller, Dennis C. (2003), *Public Choice III*, 3rd edn, Cambridge: Cambridge University Press.
Muir Watt, Horatia (2003), 'Choice of law in integrated and interconnected markets: A matter of political economy', *The Columbia Journal of European Law*, **9**, 383–409.
Nelson, Richard (1995), 'Recent theorizing about economic change', *Journal of Economic Literature*, **33**, 48–90.
Nelson, Richard and Sidney G. Winter (1982), *An Evolutionary Theory of Economic Change*, Cambridge, MA: Belknap Press of Harvard University Press.
Nelson, Richard and Sidney G. Winter (2002), 'Evolutionary theorizing in economics', *Journal of Economic Perspectives*, **16**, 23–46.
Nicolaidis, Kalypso and Gregory Shaffer (2005), 'Transnational mutual recognition regimes: Governance without global government', *Law and Contemporary Problems*, **68**, 263–318.
North, Douglass C. (1990), *Institutions, Institutional Change and Economic Performance*, Cambridge: Cambridge University Press.
Oates, Wallace E. (1999), 'An essay on fiscal federalism', *Journal of Economic Literature*, **37**, 1120–49.
Oates, Wallace E. and Robert M. Schwab (1988), 'Economic competition among jurisdictions: Efficiency enhancing or distortion inducing?', *Journal of Public Economics*, **35**, 333–54.
Ogus, Anthony (1999), 'Competition between national legal systems: A contribution of economic analysis to comparative law', *International and Comparative Law Quarterly*, **48**, 405–18.
Parisi, Francesco and Larry E. Ribstein (1998), 'Choice of law', in Peter Newman (ed.), *The New Palgrave Dictionary of Economics and the Law*, Vol. 1, London: Macmillan, pp. 236–41.
Pelkmans, Jacques (2005), 'Mutual recognition in goods and services: An economic perspective', in Fiorella K.P. Schioppa (ed.), *The Principle of Mutual Recognition in the European Integration Process*, New York: Palgrave Macmillan, pp. 85–128.
Pelkmans, Jacques (2007), 'Mutual recognition in goods. On promises and disillusions', *Journal of European Public Policy*, **14**, 699–713.
Popper, Karl R. (1972), *Objective Knowledge. An Evolutionary Approach*, Oxford: The Clarendon Press.
Posner, Richard A. (1998), *Economic Analysis of Law*, 5th edn, New York: Aspen Law & Business.
Priest, George L. (1977), 'The common law process and the selection of efficient rules', *Journal of Legal Studies*, **6**, 65–82.
Revesz, Richard L. (1992), 'Rehabilitating interstate competition: Rethinking the "race to the bottom" rationale for federal environmental regulation', *New York University Law Review*, **67**, 1210–54.
Romano, Roberta (1985), 'Law as a product: Some pieces of the incorporation puzzle', *Journal of Law, Economics, and Organization*, **1**, 225–83.
Röpke, Katarina and Klaus Heine (2005), 'Vertikaler Regulierungswettbewerb und europäischer Binnenmarkt – die Europäische Aktiengesellschaft als supranationales Rechtsangebot', *ORDO*, **56**, 157–85.
Röttinger, Moritz (2006), 'Towards a European Code Napoleon/ABGB/BGB? Recent EC activities for a European contract law', *European Law Journal*, **12**, 807–27.
Saam, Nicole and Wolfgang Kerber (2008), 'Policy innovation, decentralised experimentation, and laboratory federalism', available at SSRN: http://ssrn.com/abstract=1301502.

Salmon, Pierre (1987), 'Decentralisation as an incentive scheme', *Oxford Review of Economic Policy*, **3**, 24–42.
Saviotti, Paolo P. (1996), *Technological Evolution, Variety and the Economy*, Cheltenham, UK, and Brookfield, VT, US: Edward Elgar.
Schumpeter, Joseph A. (1934), *Theory of Economic Development*, 2nd edn (1st edn, 1911), Cambridge, MA: Harvard University Press.
Sinn, Hans-Werner (1997), 'The selection principle and market failure in systems competition', *Journal of Public Economics*, **88**, 247–74.
Slembeck, Tilman (1997), 'The formation of economic policy: A cognitive-evolutionary approach to policy-making', *Constitutional Political Economy*, **8**, 225–54.
Sun, Jeanne-Mey and Jacques Pelkmans (1995), 'Regulatory competition in the single market', *Journal of Common Market Studies*, **33**, 67–89.
Tiebout, Charles M. (1956), 'A pure theory of local expenditures', *Journal of Political Economy*, **64**, 416–24.
Trachtman, Joel P. (2000), 'Regulatory competition and regulatory jurisdiction', *Journal of International Economic Law*, **3**, 331–48.
Trachtman, Joel P. (2006), 'Embedding mutual recognition at the WTO', available at SSRN: http://ssrn.com/abstract=923903.
Van den Bergh, Roger (1996), 'Economic criteria for applying the subsidiarity principle in the European Community: The case of competition policy', *International Review of Law and Economics*, **16**, 363–83.
Van den Bergh, Roger (1998), 'Subsidiarity as an economic demarcation principle and the emergence of European private law', *Maastricht Journal of European and Comparative Law*, **5**, 129–52.
Van den Bergh, Roger J. (2000), 'Towards an institutional legal framework for regulatory competition in Europe', *Kyklos*, **53**, 435–66.
Vanberg, Viktor and Wolfgang Kerber (1994), 'Institutional competition among jurisdictions: An evolutionary approach', *Constitutional Political Economy*, **5**, 193–219.
Vogel, David (1995), *Trading Up: Consumer and Environmental Regulation in the Global Economy*, Cambridge, MA: Harvard University Press.
Wegner, Gerhard (1997), 'Economic policy from an evolutionary perspective', *Journal of Institutional and Theoretical Economics*, **153**, 485–509.
Weiler, Josef H.H. (2005), 'Mutual recognition, functional equivalence and harmonization in the evolution of the European Common Market and the WTO', in Fiorella K.P. Schioppa (ed.), *The Principle of Mutual Recognition in the European Integration Process*, New York: Palgrave Macmillan, pp. 25–84.
Williamson, Oliver E. (1985), *The Economic Institutions of Capitalism: Firms, Markets, Relational Contracting*, New York: Free Press.
Williamson, Oliver E. (2005), 'The economics of governance', *American Economic Review*, **95**, 1–18.
Witt, Ulrich (2003), *The Evolving Economy: Essays on the Evolutionary Approach to Economics*, Cheltenham, UK, and Northampton, MA, US: Edward Elgar.
Wohlgemuth, Michael (2002), 'Evolutionary approaches to politics', *Kyklos*, **55**, 223–46.

14. Darwin at work: how to explain legal change in transnational and European private law

Jan M. Smits*

1. INTRODUCTION

This contribution aims to apply some insights from evolutionary theory to transnational private law and in particular to the harmonisation of private law in the European Union.[1] By doing so, it hopes to provide a fresh perspective to the theoretical underpinning of the development of both transnational commercial law and European private law. For transnational commercial law, it has already been well explained that the transformation of the role of the State led to new forms of governance.[2] If there was previously a State monopoly on providing legal certainty and enforcement mechanisms, today the goods of legal certainty and enforcement are often provided by others rather than the State institutions, in particular in cross-border transactions. In European private law, an organic development – in which the role of the national States is also rather limited – is the most likely way to create a successful unified law.[3] Both developments raise many questions. This contribution only aims at providing a framework to deal with one of these questions: how to explain the evolution of law beyond the State (of which transnational commercial law and European private law are important examples)?[4] If legal development can no longer be explained by positivist or natural law thinking, can evolutionary theory fill the gap?

As there are many varieties of evolutionary theory, it seems first necessary to sketch the specific evolutionary framework on which this chapter is built. Section 2 therefore sets out the analytical presuppositions underlying the application of evolutionary ideas to the development of private law. This framework is a relatively simple one, building on the core of Darwin's idea of natural selection. Section 3 subsequently goes on to apply the general framework to understand legal change (looking at law as an organism), while Section 4 takes the argument one step further by applying some evolutionary lessons to transnational commercial law and European private law. Section 4 raises the important

* This paper is based on the lecture given at the conference *Law, The State, And Evolutionary Theory*, University of Bremen, 5 October 2007.

1 It builds on two previous articles: Smits (2002b) and Smits (2002).

2 See e.g. Calliess (2008) and Zumbansen (2006).

3 See further Smits (2002a).

4 See now Michaels and Jansen (2006).

question of what we can learn from evolutionary analysis of law, if anything. Section 5 draws some conclusions.

2. THE THEORETICAL MODEL: A DARWINIAN EVOLUTIONARY FRAMEWORK

Despite the many variations in evolutionary thinking,[5] the core of the theory of evolution as developed in Charles Darwin's *On the Origin of Species*[6] is clear enough. It is that change in organisms takes place through natural selection. The individual members of a species organise their lives as to produce the most surviving offspring and in doing so, they necessarily adapt themselves to changing circumstances.[7] The descent of one or more trees of life thus leads to a diversity of species through speciation, extinction and the evolving of new characteristics within these species. In Darwinism, this process of evolution by natural selection presupposes three requirements.[8] First, there must be variation in species (otherwise some species could not better survive than others); second, the variation must concern variation in fitness (understood as the ability to survive and reproduce, some species being more able to adapt themselves to changing circumstances than others); third, the characteristics constituent for the fitness of the species must be inherited, meaning they must be able to move from one generation to the next. This means that the heritable *favourable* traits become more common in future generations, while the *non-favourable* traits become *less* common, allowing adaptation of the species as such. Only with these three constituents, a 'struggle for life' in the Darwinian sense can originate.[9]

This idea of development being driven by natural (spontaneous) selection is an extremely successful one. Daniel C. Dennett characterizes Darwin's view as the 'single best idea anyone has ever had',[10] claiming that evolutionary theory offers the only explanation for structural change, regardless of the discipline involved. The idea was indeed applied to many other disciplines outside of biology, including political theory,[11] ethics,[12] economics[13] and psychology.[14] Like in case of 'real' organisms, also social systems and the human brain are then considered to be developing in a spontaneous way. Consequently, their development is made dependent on two different factors. On the one hand, there is the external environment in which the organism has to survive, while on the other hand there are the internal qualities of the organism itself. The latter decide to what extent

---

5 The wide variety of approaches in this book is evidence of this. Also see Kitcher (2005).
6 Darwin (1859).
7 See Rodgers (1998) and Sober (1984).
8 Sober (1993).
9 *Id.*, 9 and Kitcher (note 5), 821.
10 Dennett (1995), 21. Also see Wilson (1998), declaring biology to be the mother of all science.
11 Hayek (1973–1979).
12 By e.g. Wilson (1975) and Alexander (1987).
13 See e.g. Hodgson (1993a) and (1993b).
14 See e.g. Plotkin (1979).

adaptation to a changing environment is really possible. Put otherwise: evolution is dependent on both nature (in organisms: the genes) and nurture (the environment).

One can argue about the extent to which either nature or nurture is decisive for the development of an organism. Thus, several years ago the debate about the most important determinant of human behaviour seemed to have been won by the nurture factor. It was in line with the mainstream cultural climate of the 1960s and 1970s that human behaviour would not primarily be dependent on human genes as this would go against the idea of society being 'made' by human intervention and equal opportunities for everyone. It was more of Jean-Jacques Rousseau's idea of a human being as a *tabula rasa*: man is born noble and subsequently spoiled by its environment. Today, however, nature is recognized to be just as important as nurture in explaining human behaviour.[15] Thus, Steven Pinker explains how the 'blank slaters' based their idea of equal opportunities for everyone on the wrong assumption that all people have the same genes.[16] This is not the place to delve deeply into this debate; it suffices to say that if law is looked at as an organism being steered by spontaneous selection of rules, both the factor of nature (the intrinsic characteristic of the law) and the factor of nurture (the socio-economic and cultural environment in which the law operates) need to be taken into account.

3. UNDERSTANDING LEGAL CHANGE: LAW AS AN ORGANISM

If natural selection is indeed the main factor steering the development of organisms, the question is whether the development of law can also be seen as guided by this evolutionary process. On first sight, this view may seem mistaken as law is usually seen as either given by some authority (like a legislator or a court) or as derived from some transcendental nature (like in natural law thinking). But this argument is mistaken: what the evolutionary perspective has to offer is an *external* account of how law develops. It does not inform us about the contents of law, but only explains why the law develops as it does. This evolutionary perspective was already applied in the 19th century by, *inter alia*, Friedrich Von Savigny[17] and Henry Sumner Maine[18] but it gradually disappeared behind a horizon of more positivist and transcendental accounts of legal development.[19] However, as Section 4 demonstrates, looking at law as a spontaneous order of which the development is dependent on both external and internal factors can sometimes be surprisingly insightful.

This section looks at the theoretical hurdles to overcome when applying an evolutionary framework to legal change. The three requirements for natural selection (identified in Section 2) therefore need to be transplanted to the legal domain. Can we do so?

The first requirement for natural selection is variation in species. The equivalent of

---

[15] See further Wilson (1975).
[16] Pinker (2002).
[17] Savigny (1814) and (1840).
[18] Sumner Maine (1861).
[19] Leaving aside the relevance of their work today, Cf. Elliott (1985), 43: 'by modern standards Savigny's work seems hopelessly metaphorical and unscientific'. Also see Clark (1981).

this requirement in law is the existence of diverse *national* (and sometimes European) legal rules to solve identical problems. In private law, we have various rules on, e.g., the bindingness of an offer, on tort liability and on transfer of property. These rules mainly evolved in national (socio-economic and cultural) environments. They sometimes relate to essential differences between jurisdictions that reflect differing views of society (such as differing levels of solidarity, of duties to help others, levels of social security, etc.).

Second, these rules are also likely to vary in fitness. Many of the present day rules in the various European countries are the result of a long evolution during which these rules were adapted to the environment they had to operate in. According to evolutionary theory, other rules that once existed in these countries must have been eliminated in this process of natural selection and any change of the environment in the future would – again – lead to adaptation of the present rules. Some rules may become extinct while others become more important. Legal history shows telling examples of this process. Thus, the rule on *laesio enormis* and the *numerus clausus* of contracts in Roman law had to go because they no longer fit the economic environment after the Middle Ages. Rules on animal trials were abolished because of new societal insights. And also the rule that only men could vote for Parliament had to be replaced because of a changing societal and political environment.

The third requirement for natural selection (the characteristics constituent for the fitness of the species must be inherited) is more problematic in the context of law. This is because of the simple fact that descendants taking over the genes of their predecessors do not exist. Rules do not procreate in the literal sense of the word. But one can think of an analogy with genes. In evolutionary economics, Nelson and Winter have used *routines* as playing the same role in firms as genes do in organisms.[20] The routines of a firm establish a *stable identity* of the firm that endures over time and – just like genes – programme its behaviour. As long as the routine is profitable, firms stick to it. The same analogy can be used in law. Rules are not just rules: they are *learnt* by students and *applied* in practice. Normally, agents (in our case: the legal actors) will not deviate from these rules because of considerations of legal certainty and equality. In this sense, the practice of application is being transferred from one generation to another. And just like genes in biological organisms, these rules may gradually change under influence of a changing environment (society).

The possibility to apply these general requirements for evolution to the law allows us to see legal change as a process dependent on both the nature (the inherent characteristics) and the nurture (the environment) of the law. The next question is what this means exactly for the development of transnational commercial law and European private law. Can we indeed apply general evolutionary lessons to these areas?

4. EVOLUTIONARY LESSONS FOR TRANSNATIONAL AND EUROPEAN PRIVATE LAW?

The present debate about the development of transnational commercial law and European private law is to a large extent determined by its *normative* character: it usually

---

20 Vromen (1997).

takes as a starting point that present national rules are not always suited to deal with transnational commercial relationships or with transactions on the European internal market. Subsequently, one goes on to define the desired *substantive* rules that would better reflect the needs of an international market. This is very clear in the present debate about European private law, in which the question about the *need* for a common European law seems to be less important than efforts to draft actual rules.[21] In this view, as in other opinions of how a more uniform European private law should be achieved, diversity of law is often looked at as a coincidence or historical accident. In this respect, these views focus on what is at the normative level a *desired* development. But evolutionary theory has the potential to inform us whether establishing uniform law is also *likely* to happen in this way. The present view falls short of how likely it is that unification efforts, both at the European and at the global level, will succeed and, if so, how this unification is likely to take place. In the following, three different evolutionary insights are tested on their usefulness for this harmonization debate.

4.1 The Importance of 'Nature': Path Dependence and Legal Change

The first possible insight is about the importance of nature.[22] The development of any organism is to a large extent governed by its own characteristics and not so much by its environment. This means that organisms are shaped by transformations in the past that are now irreversible. Human beings will never be able to run the hundred metres in three seconds because their legs and lungs were formed in an environment in which it was apparently not so important to be able to run that fast in order to survive. These characteristics are now constraints upon adaptive change[23] or, put otherwise, the future development is affected by the *path* it has traced out in the past. In biology, it was Stephen J. Gould who pointed out that evolution often depends on 'accidents', leading to a so-called eccentric path.[24] In economics, it is well known that the most efficient organizations may not come out on top because of irreversible decisions made in the past.[25]

The importance of path dependence was also recognized for law.[26] Sometimes rules have become extinct in their past environment even though they could still serve a useful purpose today. A good example of this phenomenon is the elimination of mechanisms that decide which promises are binding and which are not. *Causa* and *laesio enormis* served this particular purpose in continental Europe before the great codifications.[27] However, these concepts lost their main function in the nineteenth century because of their uselessness in a system that put more emphasis on the intention to create legal relationships and on the absolute bindingness of contracts. It would have been fruitful to have these concepts available at a later stage, when contract law had to find new ways to decide which contracts were binding upon the parties and which were not. But in most

---

21 See now the draft Common Frame of Reference: Bar *et al.* (eds) (2008).
22 This section is based on my account of path dependence in Smits (note 1), 79.
23 Hirshleifer (1993).
24 Gould (1989).
25 Hodgson, *supra* note 13, 204.
26 See e.g. Roe (1996).
27 On this, see Gordley (1991) and Gordley and Von Mehren (2006), 461.

European legal systems, courts were not able to refer to these concepts anymore: they now had to use other legal concepts like good faith and the reliance principle to reach desired results in concrete cases.

It seems useful to look at path dependence in somewhat more detail if we want to establish how it influences transnational private law. Mark J. Roe[28] makes an interesting distinction between weak and strong path dependence. Weak path dependence only explains what has survived; it does not entail that the survivor is better than another: 'a society chose between two institutions and the choice became embedded, but the chosen institution functions as well as the one discarded would have'.[29] A road may be built at either the left bank or the right bank of the river, but the left bank is not in itself any 'better' than the right bank.

In case of this weak-form path dependence, there are no obstacles for harmonization. The types of rules one would think of as touched by this form are those related to more technical aspects of law. Whether prescription periods or other time-related devices in law are two years, five years or ten years is usually arbitrary. On the other hand, an evolution toward some 'best' rule is not really feasible here either. Courts are usually not willing to reconsider these types of legal norms once they are put into place by the legislator. In this case, harmonization is therefore only possible through the imposition of a rule in a centralist way.

This makes it important to identify these more 'technical' rules from other types of rules. Alan Watson seems to attribute a large role to such arbitrary rules: 'The truth of the matter seems to be that many legal rules make little impact on individuals, and that very often it is important that there be a rule; but what rule actually is adopted is of restricted significance for general human happiness.'[30] As far as the substantive parts of contract law, tort law and the law of property are concerned, I would rather not qualify these as examples of weak-form path dependence. I do not endorse the view that it is indifferent which rule to adopt and that any evolution towards 'better' rules (i.e. better suited for their environment than others) is impossible.

This is not to say that path dependence does *not* play a role in the traditional private law disciplines. To the contrary: forms other than weak path dependence[31] are certainly present. If we assume that the Europeanization of private law presents a crisis in the evolutionary sense, the path already taken may thus prevent the best possible rules for the new European environment from evolving. Evolution leading to a great amount of uniformity is the least probable where it is only possible to change the present rules at the expense of high cost. This is the least the case with rules that many people rely upon; on the other hand, the amount of uniformity to be attained should theoretically be the most in the case of rules that are only of use for parties that set these rules themselves. Gambaro states the following about the law of real property:

> When one considers the nature of various property rights (obligations between neighbours, riparian rights, condominium law, rights of superficies, servitudes, and the like), it becomes

---

[28] Roe, *supra* note 26, 646.
[29] *Id.*, 647.
[30] Watson (1974).
[31] See further Roe (note 26), 648.

> rather clear that much property law is deeply rooted in locally developed legal traditions. And, for this reason it is better left to those local legal traditions which for hundreds of years have addressed these issues in the manner most adapted to the locality.[32]

Gambaro is certainly right, but the reason why these rules are looked at as most adapted to the 'locality', has, in my view, more to do with the investments already made in the path of property law and from which it is too costly to deviate, than with 'the nature' of property rights. To change national law in the areas mentioned by Gambaro would mean that third parties' interests have to be reconsidered on a very large scale. The reliance of the parties involved on the existence of 'absolute' rights that have effect *erga omnes* would be violated if the applicable rules on, for example, the establishment of limited real rights and the registration of these rights would be eliminated or even changed. The taking into account of so many different interests has led to delicate static systems of property law with – most of the time – a *numerus clausus* of limited real rights. Moreover, to get to know the ins and outs of property law in a specific system is far more difficult than to get to know a country's law of contract: the information costs of the former are higher.[33] In this sense, property law is indeed stuck in a 'local equilibrium'. In most parts of property law this does not pose a true problem: any need to have uniform law is virtually absent. It is a problem, however, where there *is* a need, namely in the field of security interests: here, the *desire* to create uniform law and the present *practice* as it has evolved in the past (adapted as it is to a national system of law) diverge.

This is all different in case of the law of contract. The parties to a contract would not be truly hampered by a change of the law because of their ability to set the rules for their relationship themselves. The law of contract's dynamic character guarantees the elimination and survival of rules that are respectively the least and the most suited for their new environment. Rubin says: 'if conditions change (. . .) and two individuals decide that, for their purposes, behaviour that was attractive in the past has ceased to be useful, they can voluntarily devise a new contract stipulating any behaviour that they wish'.[34] Evidence from both economic analysis of law and comparative law support this evolutionary thesis. Economic analysis of law shows the need for a distinction between default and mandatory rules. This type of analysis makes clear that rules should be mandatory when any other rule that the parties would adopt would be violating third parties interests. Mattei and Cafaggi rightly point out that the amount of mandatory rules should decrease in a system where alternative means of protection for third parties are available. They mention, for example, there would be fewer mandatory rules in contract law if the tort system protected third parties.[35] It is obvious that property law is much more related to these mandatory rules than contract law. The economic reason for property law having more mandatory rules runs parallel to the evolutionary idea of property law being less able to change when confronted with a changing environment.

---

32 Gambaro (1997).

33 See further, Dreher (1999), 109: 'Da Wissen und Kosten eng miteinander verbunden sind, stellt Unwissenheit zumindest vor Informationskosten und begrenzt so auch die Faktormobilität ganz entscheidend.'

34 Quoted by Benson (1998).

35 Mattei and Cafaggi (1998), 348.

Comparative law also provides us with evidence on the evolutionary thesis. Legal transplants in the field of contract law are far greater than in the field of property law. This may be partly due to private international law's *lex rei sitae* (accordingly there is no need to incorporate foreign property rights into one's own legal system), but it is certainly also due to the high costs of transplanting from another system in the case of property law and the much lower costs in the case of contract and tort law. In the latter, legal transplants have been vigorous; the relative uniformity already existent in the field of European contract law is undoubtedly caused by these transplants. In particular, English law was to a great extent influenced by the civil law of the nineteenth century,[36] as continental European law is influenced in the late twentieth century by the law of financial transactions on, for example, swaps, lease and franchising, coming from the common law world.

The general lesson is that evolution of legal norms may not under all circumstances lead to an optimal outcome. Whether a national rule will be replaced by a new European or transnational one also depends on whether lawyers and other legal actors are willing to deviate from existing practices.

4.2 How Law Develops: A Race to the Bottom?

The second evolutionary insight useful to explain legal change is about the way in which evolution takes place. This is usually not through the complete extinction of a species, but through adaptation of it. Evolutionists would say the external identity of an organism remains identical while its contents changes. This phenomenon is well known in legal development as well. Legal concepts tend to change as to contents while remaining the same in terminology and outlook. Contract and property today have a completely different content compared to contract and property in Roman times or in the nineteenth century. This 'Funktionswandel' of a rule takes place more frequently than the clear-cut elimination of a rule.

Evolutionary theory also tells us that the direction in which adaptation takes place is usually toward simplicity, in particular when homogenization of the environment reduces the number of distinct niches available. The movement is toward complexity when there are only a few species that proliferate within a new environment with many unfilled niches.[37] The more homogeneous an environment is, the more homogeneous the organisms are. In the desert, organisms are less complex than in the rainforest. The interesting question is what this means in the context of legal harmonization. If the direction of adaptation is indeed towards simplicity in case of homogenization of the environment, this is an indication of the direction private law would take in uniform economies (such as the one of the European Union). It seems likely that the more homogeneous the economy is, the more uniform the applicable private law will be. This fits in remarkably well with the criticism usually expressed against allowing a spontaneous selection of the proper rules on the market. Critics of jurisdictional competition emphasize this may lead to a 'race to the bottom'.[38] If private actors are free to choose the law applicable to their

---

36 See Reimann, ed. (1993).
37 Hirshleifer, *supra* note 23, 205.
38 See further, Kraus (1997) and Barnard (2000).

relationships with others, it is likely they will choose for the law of the jurisdiction with the lowest standards (like in the case of American company law the state of Delaware would be such a jurisdiction). The 'home country control principle' subsequently guarantees this low standard to be exported to other jurisdictions. This race to the bottom may thus be said to arise when 'in a deregulated internal market, a state unilaterally lowers its social standards in an attempt to attract business from other states'.[39]

The concerns usually expressed about this 'race to the bottom' are mostly normative: the possible lowering of standards is usually seen as a negative thing without too much evidence of this actually happening in practice. Evolutionary theory approaches the problem from a different angle: it shows us to what extent a race to the bottom will indeed take place in a changing economic environment. Barnard shows there is little evidence so far of this phenomenon in Europe.[40] She identifies six conditions that have to be met if a race to the bottom is to emerge. Among these conditions are a wide choice of different jurisdictions (like more than 50 legal systems in the United States) and full knowledge of each jurisdiction's characteristics. These requirements are not met in Europe, where – until recently – there were only 15 jurisdictions and where it is often difficult to obtain the necessary information about the various legal systems.

However, from the evolutionary perspective a race to the bottom is likely to emerge if these two requirements are met in the future. As to the first requirement, the recent enlargement of the European Union with 12 new member-states implies that the differences between the various systems could very well increase. A migration of companies toward jurisdictions with lower standards is then likely to occur. In order to meet the condition of full knowledge of all the European jurisdictions, there is a need for more comparative law study. The only barrier for a true race to the bottom would be constituted by the minimum standards of law, set by the European Union's directives and regulations. However, the fact that these standards are a barrier to evolution can also be explained by evolutionary theory: the path that has been traced out in the past has – in Europe – been one of not giving economic considerations the upper hand. A social policy was always part of the European venture. In this sense, the investments already made in this policy would be too costly (perhaps not only in a social or cultural sense, but also in a financial sense in that it would entail large costs of changing the present legal position of workers, unemployed, and so on) to deviate from.

But not all of the present social guarantees in the European legal systems (namely those guaranteeing more than the European minimum standard) will be kept intact. Hayek is right when he stresses that legal rules may have come into being through historical accident, but that natural selection decides which rules are to survive. The natural selection process then chooses between competing groups of humans, letting survive those groups whose cultural norms and rules are more suited to efficiently coordinate social interactions.[41] The European venture of creating a common market then implies it is the group of those who are best able to operate on that market whose rules will eventually survive.

---

39 Barnard (note 38) 57.

40 *Id.*, 70.

41 Hayek (1967); see further the critical assessment by Vanberg (1993).

4.3 Extinction or Living Together?

The third point is about the results of the evolutionary process. Does evolution lead to the survival of one organism only (with extinction of other organisms) or to different organisms living together at the same time? Biology clearly shows that more fit organisms compete with less fit organisms in a constant struggle for survival.[42] This is even the core of biodiversity. If considered from the viewpoint of efficiency or some other external goal, there would be no need for such diversity but this way of reasoning misses the point entirely. To consider biodiversity from a functional perspective would be absurd. The mere fact of some organisms being more successful than others is not relevant in this context: each organism has its proper place in the environment of which it is part. Also from the economic viewpoint, Cooter and Kornhauser have shown that evolution does not necessarily lead to only one surviving efficient rule, but always to some equilibrium of better and worse rules.[43]

Is this evolutionary insight also of importance to understand legal change? I think it is: it can provide a theoretical explanation and justification for legal diversity. The normative arguments in favour of legal diversity are well known.[44] On the one hand, there is the argument of Tiebout[45] that competition of legal systems leads to more preferences being satisfied. If legal actors can leave the jurisdiction they dislike (they can 'vote with their feet'), national governments are stimulated to make their jurisdiction as attractive as possible. The introduction of uniform law would reduce this exit-opportunity and lead to fewer preferences being satisfied. On the other hand, it is often claimed legal diversity enhances innovation of existing law: it allows jurisdictions to serve as 'experimenting laboratories'.[46]

These two normative arguments for legal diversity can be supplemented with the evolutionary insight that fit and less fit solutions often co-exist at the same time. This insight may not only be used to explain present-day legal diversity, but also to *justify* the existence of different rules to deal with similar problems. In the latter meaning, biodiversity sets an example for the legal domain: it warns us for attempts to eliminate legal diversity in a centralist way. Instead of a European legislator identifying one 'best rule', the selection process should be left to practice. The result of this process may be that not one uniform rule emerges in the end, but this is nothing to worry about. It is the logical result of a spontaneous legal order created by natural selection.

---

42 Elliott, *supra* note 19, 70.
43 Cooter and Kornhauser (1980).
44 See further, e.g. Smits (2006).
45 Tiebout (1956). Also see Ogus (1999).
46 L. Brandeis, in: *New State Ice Co. v. Liebmann*, 285 U.S. 262: 'It is one of the happy incidents of the federal system that a single courageous State may, if its citizens choose, serve as a laboratory; and try novel social and economic experiments without risk to the rest of the country.'

5. CONCLUSIONS

The aim of this contribution was to establish whether evolutionary theory can help to explain the development of transnational commercial law and European private law. Increasing Europeanization and globalization lead away from traditional explanations for legal change founded in positivist and natural law thinking. The above shows that some evolutionary insights can indeed be applied. The necessary prerequisite for this is to consider law as an evolutionary organism and to apply the three requirements for natural selection to legal change. Once this hurdle is taken, three lessons from evolutionary theory can be applied to law.

The first lesson is about the importance of path dependence: just as organisms are shaped by now irreversible transformations in the past, the law is also affected by the path traced out in its previous development. Legal rules are therefore never completely shaped by the needs of their environment, but also dependent on their own characteristics. This works out in different ways in different areas of law. It is likely that transnational commercial law and European contract law are the least affected by the factor nature and therefore the most susceptible for change.

Second, evolutionary insights are useful to explain how legal change takes place. It is usually not through the complete extinction of a species, but through adaptation that change happens. This adaptation is usually towards more simple species if the environment becomes more homogeneous. This insight can be applied to law: legal diversity is likely to decrease in those areas where the environment becomes more uniform. There is little doubt this is the case in transnational commercial law and European private law. It remains uncertain whether this uniformity will manifest itself as a 'race to the bottom'.

The third lesson is that evolution often leaves diversity in place: several organisms exist at the same time. This insight can be used to explain why different rules exist to deal with similar problems. This is also true at the European or global level: evolutionary theory can explain why competition of legal rules is to be preferred over centralist unification of law. This does not mean that natural selection of rules will always produce optimal outcomes, but this is because evolutionary theory does not say anything about desired law: it only provides a framework for explanation.

BIBLIOGRAPHY

Alexander, R. (1987), *The biology of moral systems.*

Barnard, C. (2000), 'Social dumping and the race to the bottom: Some lessons for the European Union from Delaware', *European Law Review*, **25**, 57–78.

Bar, Chr. Von, E. Clive and H. Schulte-Nölke (eds) (2008), *Principles, Definitions and Model Rules of European Private Law: Draft Common Frame of Reference, Interim Outline Edition.*

Benson, Bruce L. (1998), 'Evolution of commercial law', in Peter Newman (ed.) *The New Palgrave Dictionary of Economics and The Law*, Vol. I, p.90.

Calliess, Gralf-Peter (2008), 'Transnational civil regimes: Economic globalization and the evolution of commercial law', in Volkmar Gessner (ed.), *Legal Certainty Beyond The State: Empirical Studies and Theories of Change.*

Clark, R.C. (1981) 'The interdisciplinary study of legal evolution', *Yale Law Journal*, **90** 1238.

Cooter R. and R. Kornhauser (1980), 'Can litigation improve the law without the help of judges?', *Journal of Legal Studies*, **9**, 139.

Darwin, C. (1859), *On The Origin of Species by Means of Natural Selection.*

Dennett, Daniel C. (1995), *Darwin's Dangerous Idea.*

Dreher, Meinrad (1999), 'Wettbewerb oder Vereinheitlichung der Rechtsordnungen in Europa?', *Juristenzeitung*, **54**, 105.

Elliott, E. Donald (1985), 'The evolutionary tradition in jurisprudence', *Columbia Law Review*, **85**, 38.

Gambaro, Antonio (1997), 'Perspectives on the codification of the law of property: An overview', *European Review of Private Law*, **5**, 497.

Gordley, James (1991), *The Philosophical Foundations of Modern Contract Doctrine.*

Gordley, J. and Arthur Taylor von Mehren (2006), *An Introduction to the Comparative Study of Private Law.*

Gould, Stephen J. (1989), *Wonderful Life.*

Hayele, Friedrich A. (1973–79), *Law, Legislation and Liberty.*

Hayek, F.A. (1967), 'Notes on the evolution of systems of rules of conduct', in *Studies In Philosophy and Economics*, p. 66.

Hirshleifer, Jack (1993), 'Evolutionary models in economics and law', in Ulrich Witt (ed.) *Evolutionary Economics*, p. 205.

Hodgson, G.M. (1993a), *Economics and Evolution.*

Hodgson, G.M. (1993b), *Evolutionary Economics.*

Kitcher, Philip (2005), 'Philosophy of biology', in Frank Jackson and Michael Smith (eds), *The Oxford Handbook of Contemporary Philosophy*, p. 819.

Kraus, Jody S. (1997), 'Legal design and the evolution of commercial norms', *Journal of Legal Studies*, **26**, 377.

Mattei, Ugo and Fabrizio Cafaggi (1998), 'Comparative law and economics', in Peter Newman (ed.), *The New Palgrave Dictionary of Economics and the Law*, Vol. I, p. 346.

Michaels, R. and Nils Jansen (2006), 'Private law beyond the state? Europeanization, globalization, privatization', *American Journal of Comparative Law*, **54**, 843.

Ogus, A. (1999), 'Competition between national legal systems: A contribution of economic analysis to comparative law', *International and Comparative Law Quarterly*, **48**, 405.

Pinker, Steven (2002), *The Blank Slate: The Modern Denial of Human Nature.*

Plotkin , Henry (1979), *Evolution in Mind: An Introduction to Evolutionary Psychology.*

Reimann, Matthias (ed.) (1993), *The Reception of Continental Ideas in the Common Law World* 1820–1920.

Rodgers, William H. (1998), 'Law and biology', in Peter Newman (ed.), The New Palgrave Dictionary of Economics and the Law, Vol. II, p. 451.

Roe, Mark J. (1996), 'Chaos and evolution in law and economics', *Harvard Law Review*, **109**, 643, 667.

Savigny, F.C. von (1814), reprint 1967, *Vom Beruf Unsrer Zeit Für Gesetzgebung Und Rechtswissenschaft.*

Savigny, F.C. von (1840), *System Des Heutigen Römischen Rechts*, Vol. I, p. 290.

Smits, Jan M. (2002a), *The Making of European Private Law.*

Smits, Jan M. (2002b), 'The harmonisation of private law in Europe: Some insights from evolutionary theory', *Georgia Journal of International and Comparative Law*, **31**, 79.

Smits, Jan M. (2002c), 'How to predict the differences in uniformity between different areas of a future European private law? An evolutionary approach', in Alain Marciano and Jean-Michel Josselin (eds) (2002), *The Economics of Harmonizing European Law*, p. 50.

Smits, Jan M. (2006), 'European private law: A plea for a spontaneous legal order', in Deirdre M. Curtin et al. (eds), *European Integration and Law*, p. 55.

Sober, E. (1984), *The Nature of Selection.*

Sober, E. (1993), *Philosophy of Biology*, p. 9.

Sumner Maine, H.J. (1861), *Ancient Law.*

Tiebout C. (1956), 'A pure theory of local expenditures', *Journal of Political Economy*, **64**, 416.

Vanberg, Viktor (1993), 'Spontaneous market order and social rules', in Ulrich Witt (ed.), *Evolutionary Economics*, p. 482.

Vromen, Jack J. (1997), 'Evolutionary economics: Precursors, paradigmatic propositions, puzzles and prospects', in Jan Reijnders (ed.), *Economics and Evolution*, p. 52.

Watson, Alan (1974), *Legal Transplants*, p. 96.
Wilson, Edward O. (1975), *Sociobiology: The New Synthesis.*
Wilson, Edward O. (1998), *Consilience.*
Zumbansen, Peer (2006), 'Transnational law', in Jan Smits (ed.), *Elgar Encyclopedia of Comparative Law*, p. 738.

15. Linking extra-legal codes to law: the role of international standards and other off-the-rack regimes*

Erich Schanze

1. INTRODUCTION

In the famous article on the basic design of legal rules Calabresi and Melamed refer to Monet's cycle of paintings of the Cathedral of Rouen.[1] The circumspection of a monumental object in the turn of the sunlight displays the whole cosmos of forms and colors. For the equally famous eighteen haystacks Monet is quoted to have intended 'to fix a genuine impression of a certain aspect of nature'. The 'nature' of the relation of law and the associated extra-legal norms such as standards or 'codified' 'off-the-rack' practices is rather vague. An exploration by circumspection may be an adequate approach in this matter.

Let us first inspect a number of views concerning the relevance of extra-legal norms for law. Then we will explore a variety of 'linkage mechanisms' between law and extra-legal norms, notably national and international standards, which can be found in a number of technical contexts of law – so-called 'reference norms'.[2] All reference norms are styled from a legal centrist perspective, that of a judge who has to determine whether and to what extent a specific extra-legal norm can be 'included' in the legal considerations for reaching an equitable result in a given conflict. This legal centrist perspective starts from the premise that extra-legal norms are relevant only to the extent that a *legal* norm permits their 'application'. It looks at a specific rule or mechanism that provides for them to be 'included' into the legal system. This perspective is essentially a backward-looking one, taking both legal and extra-legal norms for granted and using legal norms to determine their reciprocal relevance.

Planning of business transactions requires a different approach. I will argue that we might gain new insights into the relation of law and extra-legal norms by looking at it from a drafting perspective.[3] In what light do draftspersons develop and use extra-legal

---

* This is a revised version of an earlier paper on 'International Standards – Functions and Links to Law', first published in Peter Nobel (ed.), *International Standards and the Law* (2005), 83; reprinted in: Christian Brütsch & Dirk Lehmkuhl (ed.), *Law and Legalization in Transnational Relations* (2007), 166–84. For this new version I am grateful to Peer Zumbansen for valuable comments and suggestions.

[1] Calabresi and Melamed (1972).

[2] German term: '*Verweisungsnorm*'.

[3] See Gilson (1984).

norms such as standards, guidelines or codes of practice? What are the working tools and building blocks? Where and to what extent do they consider limitations of their production? This perspective swaps the backward-looking view for a forward-looking perspective, largely uncommon to Continental European legal systems.[4] To be sure, the legal centrist view and the drafting view do not exclude each other. They are complementary perspectives of a complex relationship in the present system of economic governance which both merit attention in the legal process.

2. SOME CURRENT VIEWS ON THE RELATIONSHIP BETWEEN LAW AND STANDARDS

The analysis of the relation between standards and law is perplexing because there is little consensus about the province of both modalities of ordering.[5] I will list three views, and then turn to a fourth perspective of a draftsperson who is concerned with regime design of international transactions. To illustrate the choices I will look at 'neighboring' governance structures – hoping that the affinity will produce some insights into why and how standards are 'produced' and 'used', and how conflicts with the legal order (in a narrower sense) are aligned there.

Lawyers usually assume that they operate with clear-cut definitions of law. However, once they reach the area of complex economic regulation (what Europeans term 'economic law') they realize a need for surprising extensions of a legal centrist position.

2.1 The 'Realist' Economic Law Perspective: Mertens, Kirchner and Schanze

Obviously, a textbook on 'economic law' needs a definition of its subject matter. Looking at the conventional sources of law making including parliamentary legislation, constitutionally delegated law making by government authorities on various levels etc. did not capture what 'courts do in fact'[6] in the area of economic regulation. Therefore, the textbook of Mertens *et al.* (1982) turned the issue from the 'sources of law' aspect to a 'law-in-action' analysis.[7] Therein we tried to capture all rules relevant for decision making in the regulatory process. What would a judge or a regulator consider to be relevant for decisions in individual cases? In the decision making context, she or he would not only look at those rules which are 'official sources of law' but also to the extra-legal norms which structure the relevant transactions. Thus we arrived at a 'pragmatic' extension of classical law including, *inter alia*, the 'relevant' practices, guidelines and technical standards.

---

[4] See for a comparison of the 'logic of antecedents' with the 'logic of consequences' Posner (2003); for a broadening of the fact set in a 'constructive jurisprudence' see Ackerman (1984), 72; Schanze (1993); Mnookin *et al.* (2000).

[5] See Schreiber listing the main definition of 'standard' (2005).

[6] Holmes (1897).

[7] Mertens *et al.* (1982), 125: '. . . *die Rechtsordnung [kann] als Inbegriff von Normen, als Inbegriff aller rechtlichen Entscheidungen und als Inbegriff aller entscheidungsleitenden Gesichtspunkte verstanden werden*' [the legal order may be understood as an epitome of legal norms, as an epitome of legal decisions, and as an epitome of all legally relevant decision making criteria].

Hence, we considered 'standards' as a part of 'economic law'.[8] Relevance alone, however, may lead into a full circle. Obviously, an *inclusion or 'linking' mechanism* has to be named that 'legitimizes' the reference.

2.2 The International Governance Perspective: Abbott and Snidal

Whereas our definition starts from the centrist ('constitutional') national law view by stretching it to include the 'relevant' aspects of social ordering, the influential analysis of Abbott and Snidal[9] starts, in a distinct variant of 'realism', from the other end by defining standards broadly as 'guides for behavior or for judging behavior'. Naturally, they have no problem including the important instance of standard setting. This would be trivial where a standard is 'incorporated' by legislation or other forms of legitimate recognition in the classical concept of law, be it national law or public international law.

Abbott and Snidal share, in part, Ellickson's basic notion that 'law' is largely inoperative, if it is separated from – what Ellickson calls – the 'social norms'.[10] A related concept may be found in Eric Posner's 'Law and Social Norms', where he broadly refers to social norms as behavioral regularities which actors observe in order to show that they are desirable partners of cooperative endeavors.[11] In a world of transacting, 'compliance' with 'standards' signals that these conditions are met. However, it is noteworthy that 'standards' or 'social norms' are of relevance in this concept not because of their very substance, but because of the credibility players gain by incurring the costs of observing these norms. Later, I will also return to the issue of 'compliance' as a general norm of legitimizing extra-legal norms, and will put it in the center of my analysis.

Obviously, an approach starting from the 'social norm' side is less interested in a clear-cut definition of law and extra-legal norms, nor does it provide a satisfying answer why decision-makers resort to extra-legal norms. The emphasis is, as Abbott and Snidal state, on the general problem of internalizing externalities by appropriate governance structures, be they technically 'legal' or 'non-legal'.

2.3 The New Institutional Economics Perspective: Furubotn and Richter

The aforementioned international transaction perspective is related to the analysis of the function of institutions by the neo-institutional school of economics. In their standard text Richter and Furubotn[12] stress that markets do not work as abstractions but that they operate in a complex setting of 'elementary operational rules and prescriptions'. In this view, opposing the neo-classical perspective, a set of institutions is not only a 'second-best' surrogate for the price mechanism of the market, but the very foundation of it. These preconditions of transacting in an economy based on property rights do not only include the stipulation of the property rights themselves for the transaction partners but also a long list of further preconditions, including, for example, language and writing,

---

8 Mertens *et al.* (1982), 140.
9 Abbott and Snidal (2001).
10 Ellickson (1991).
11 Posner (2002), 18–27.
12 Richter and Furubotn (2003), 316.

ethical values, the numerical system, measures and weights, time and its units, money, means of communication and transport, legal norms plus the mini-rules of technical market order concerning the variety of goods and services at the various locations. In the list, a number of preconditions may qualify as 'standards', although their origin and relevance may not fully comply with the procedural elements stressed by Abbott and Snidal. The institutional economics perspective is concerned with all facilitating and restraining factors (and their 'economics'). They are eligible or unavoidable 'frames' for real market choices influencing the outcomes significantly ('institutions matter'). In essence, this spectrum of market framing norms deals, in a normative sense, with the general problem of internalizing externalities. The Neo-Institutionalists stress that all relevant institutional settings serve as devices reducing the pervasive presence of uncertainty.[13]

2.4 A Drafting Perspective

The three mentioned views on the relationship of law and standards are guided by different motivations. As our original 'economic law' perspective tried to capture the relevant rules for legal decision making in the economic sphere, the Abbott and Snidal view is oriented towards the functioning of standards in relation to other guides of behavior in the international system.[14] The neo-institutional economics view tries to remedy the myopia of the neo-classical economic explanation of the functioning of markets.

Without denying the usefulness and relevance of these approaches, I will advance, for purposes of a deeper analysis, a different perspective, which I call a 'drafting perspective'. My questions are: Under what circumstances will a professional draftsperson refer to 'law' and when will she refer to extra-legal norms such as standards? How do standards, practices, off-the rack clauses and guidelines operate in the drafting process?

No doubt, this is primarily an issue of the individual task or case. However, I expect some general observations which may shed additional light on the governance structures of international business transactions. Let us turn to the process of institutional choice, particularly to the 'mix' of 'law' and 'extra-legal norms' found in practice. I view the legislature, standard setters and draftspersons as 'regime producers'. Draftspersons can create value by 'facilitating' transactions. They are primarily interested in the *functioning* of the 'regime product' which they are designing, be it a contract, a hybrid arrangement or a corporate charter with its by-laws.

In all instances there is the basic objective of designing a *valid* transactional vehicle. Moreover, the regime has to be workable. Therefore it should be immune against charges of lawlessness. Draftspersons care for the 'legitimacy' of the used regimes. 'Legitimacy' is, indeed, one of the preconditions of the success of private ordering. Neglecting the rare and costly case of self-enforcing arrangements, or the abstraction of a complete incentive-compatible arrangement, a draftsperson will typically resort to those legally enforceable solutions, which are not only provided by the law but which will also include lawful references to extra-legal norms and procedures. 'Law' in this perspective is a modification of Holmes' 'realistic' definition ('what courts will do in fact'). From the viewpoint

---

13 Callon (1998), 244, 250; see generally Dawes (1988).
14 Abbott and Snidal (2001).

of the drafting profession, 'law' is what professional consultants cautiously assume courts and regulators 'will do in fact' (and enforce).

The legitimacy of a transactional design is frequently discovered in a trial-and-error process of the drafting practice.[15] One of the most successful strategies here is the use of 'off-the-rack' solutions. Legal consultants will make use of standardized clauses and routines that have been tried in earlier transactions. They are partly contained in 'cook books', partly in proprietary files. The structure and/or language might not account for all idiosyncratic features of the transaction to be handled, but may save high transaction costs associated with fully 'tailored' solutions. In a way, the written and judge-made facilitating law (what is called 'dispositive law' on the European Continent, or 'defaults' in the US) is 'off-the-rack' by definition.[16] It is a standardized system of ordering between the parties in a legitimate context. The interesting part is that 'dispositive' law may be found in both the acclaimed legal text and in the 'legitimate' private practice. Nevertheless, the choice of a facilitating regime is complex. The real choices are sometimes difficult to explain.

Take the example of the choice of an incorporation jurisdiction in the United States. New York/Metropolitan lawyers mainly select Delaware law. Some attribute this to Delaware allegedly offering the least demanding preconditions, Delaware being the winner of a 'race to the bottom' of the preconditions for corporate chartering. Today, the original claim by Cary is reduced to laxness toward managers.[17] The present mainstream literature points out that New York lawyers select Delaware because it is a specialist jurisdiction which offers particularly useful and predictable regimes. They claim that Delaware has won the 'race to the top'.[18]

From the perspective of this paper which is interested in the role of routines and associated transaction cost economies it seems plain that Delaware is, indeed, a specialist jurisdiction, but that the choice of the professional draftspersons is essentially related to the fact that Delaware offers, by and large, the most *standardized* routines and services in this field. The incorporation business and the corporate litigation in Delaware are more 'convenient', because the interplay between the profession and this jurisdiction is best known. It is the 'standard', and its usefulness and legitimacy has been tried in a multitude of cases – notwithstanding the existence of 'superior' possible choices. In this sense, Delaware comes closest to the ideal of being a jurisdiction which is completely 'off-the-rack'. Successful standards, practices and guidelines have almost the same properties: they can typically also be taken 'off-the-rack'.

3. LINKING SOCIAL NORMS, ESPECIALLY STANDARDS TO LAW: THE NEED FOR REFERENCE NORMS

If the task were a pure description of social practice, the borderline between 'social norms' and 'legal norms' is irrelevant. If non-legal norms, however, become relevant as

---

15 Schanze (1996); Schanze (1995); Schanze (1993).

16 See for a general discussion Ayres and Gertner (1989).

17 Bebchuk and Ferrell (2001) with references.

18 Romano (2002); but see Roe (2003).

'guiding criteria' for legal decisions, we need 'linkage mechanisms' which 'authorize' the 'inclusion' of relevant norms in the 'official' rules. This need for and the use of reference norms is well-known in a number of technical settings of all legal orders. I will browse through some conventional situations where the existing law is extended or changed by the 'application' of 'foreign' law or 'external' norms.

3.1 Conflict-of-laws-methodology

The most elaborate system of 'inclusion', of 'linking' external 'rules' with the internal legitimate order is private international law. The 'foreign rule' is included if an internal conflicts rule contains an authorization for its application. The debate about the underlying reasons why courts 'include' 'foreign laws' in their deliberations of a case has become less urgent with the comprehensive positive statutory or judge-made regulation of this complex set of rules. The Continental approach to 'private international law' has, indeed, turned this area into a separate legal field: It contains technical rules and policies which are understood as distinct from the policies of the relevant substantial laws. However, for understanding the general mechanism of 'choice-of-law' we should note that two relevant basic arguments have been advanced. They should be also of interest for a theory of 'inclusion of social norms'. The first is the classical argument of 'comity'.[19] It says, in essence, that the courts will recognize a foreign rule in cases with a foreign element because the 'friendly relations' between the nations require reciprocity of recognition of rules. This view bases, by and large, on the notion that the foreign legal norm is, albeit 'foreign', a *legal* one and therefore generally well-suited for inclusion by the domestic *legal* system. The more rigid, even unfriendly, argument was advanced by Brainerd Currie. He denies, in essence, the viability of 'friendly recognition' of a foreign rule if the state has expressed its regulatory interest in a legal subject matter. The court is bound by the policies of its own laws. Only an issue in which the state is 'disinterested' could then be decided with reference to a 'foreign' rule.[20]

If we transfer both conceptions to the recognition of standards: Do we recognize them for reasons of 'friendliness' or because we are 'disinterested'? Currie may be closer to reality. I will show that 'disinterest of the state' is frequently a central rationale for the increasing use of standards.

3.2 Private Autonomy as a Link

The next, even more significant 'inclusion rule' for non-legal norms in structures of private governance is the constitutional principle of private autonomy.[21] It comprises both freedom of contracting (i.e. stipulating freely terms in contracts and organizational charters) and the choice of the applicable law for contracts. This authorization for designing private transactions is an important avenue of 'including' extra legal standards, because the parties are authorized by the principle to refer to 'outside' norms as part

---

19 Kegel and Schurig (2004), 6.
20 Currie (1963); on this Joerges (2004).
21 Mertens *et al.* (1982), 133.

of their 'legitimate' binding private arrangement. Indeed, many contracts and charters contain explicit or implicit references to standards. Size and quality aspects are typically backed up by such reference.

The most elaborate scheme of 'including' private norms is the system of control developed for 'adhesion contracts' or 'standard terms'.[22] In essence, it is a negative system of 'avoiding' illegal components of private legislation. It is hidden in the theory that generally standard terms are considered part of the private agreement between the parties. On closer inspection, this is a fairly far-fetched concept, because it neglects the very fact that 'standard terms' used in a multitude of transactions resemble much more abstract norms than concrete private arrangements, but it operates nicely within its limits. It is based on a hypothetical bargain which is used as a method of comparing the boiler plate clause to a 'fair' hypothetical agreement. In essence a deviation from reasonable expectations of the parties puts the private legislation under the pressure of justification.

3.3 Standards as Trade Usages

A third relevant mechanism for the inclusion of extra-legal standards is the reference to 'trade usages' (cf. Section 346 German Commercial Code). There are many standards that could be classed as parts of trade usages.

The concept of trade usages is theoretically interesting in that it contains an explicit set of legitimizing criteria for 'inclusion':[23]

(1) factual exercise of the practice,
(2) certain duration of the practice,
(3) 'consent' of the participating business community,
(4) definiteness of the practice as a matter of fact.

Looking at examples, one usually refers to the highly standardized INCO-terms which are, so to speak, 'frozen trade usages'. However, in this case, many commentators (adhering to the prevalent view of 'standard terms') assume that they are not incorporated by the methodology of inclusion under Art. 346 German Commercial Code, but are rather short-hand stipulations under the inclusion rule of private autonomy.

3.4 Customary International Law as a Standard?

For completeness sake, reference should be made to the inclusion mechanism used in public international law referring to customary international law. It resembles the inclusion technique used for the trade usages. It is, so-to-speak, a reference to a pervasive use of the relevant norm in a number of relevant jurisdictions. The names of both controversial basic concepts used for explaining the binding nature of customary international law are telling: 'state practice' and '*opinio iuris*'.[24]

---

22 On contract regulation see Collins (1999), 256; Trebilcock (1993), 250.
23 See for a full account of the German doctrine: Schmidt (1999), 23.
24 See Kokott (2005); Roberts (2001); Stephan (1999); Koh (1997).

3.5 Structural Lessons

What can we learn from the various patterns linking extra-legal norms to law? First of all, we understand that local law is obviously interested in a number of situations to 'apply' extra-legal norms. The second point is that law is concerned about the 'inclusion' and establishes some limitations. This does not contradict the sociological/neo-institutional observation that legal norms do not operate in a vacuum, but that they relate to established social practices, and that, under some circumstances, law is rather an expression of the bright lines dividing it from patent illegality than reflecting a comprehensive set of norms of behavior of a given societal order.

In terms of the structure of all discussed mechanisms which link law to certain extra-legal norms, it is apparent that they are defined from a viewpoint of the judge. For the decision-maker there is no problem if the 'extra-legal' norms do not challenge the validity and scope of application of the local legal order. The most telling example is private international law. Brainerd Currie makes the convincing point that – from a democratic constitutional perspective – foreign law should only be applied if a state is disinterested. The remaining puzzling question is, however, to define – in a legally predictable fashion – under what circumstances the judge can declare the state being disinterested. Driven to the extreme, a state court would have no jurisdiction in this case. In most cases some 'concerns' can be established. The same may be true for the problem of regulating a context by standards or guidelines.

If we start from the conventional Western assumption of a comprehensive legal order and a system of remedies monopolized by the state, we can hardly claim, in important matters of regulation, a disinterest of the legal system or lack of concern for these norms. There is no 'principle of subsidiarity' between law and extra-legal rules. Is there a general system of testing extra-legal norms from a legal centrist perspective? Could we conceive, for example, of a committee of the parliament or a regulatory agency which would 'screen' all extra-legal norms in a procedure and declare them eventually 'applicable'?[25]

If we look at the available mechanisms, by and large, we find a system of traditional screening on a case-by-case basis, resembling the system of determining the validity of standard term contracts. It is interesting that for standard terms all leading legal systems have developed complex testing schemes which guide decision making. For the European Union consumer contracts the scheme has even entered a 'harmonized' state by using directives which have been transformed into the various national laws.[26] As has been mentioned earlier, the basic concept of reference here is the 'fair' hypothetical bargain. From a legal centrist perspective this is probably the most viable approach for 'admitting' extra-legal rules.[27]

A current puzzle in German law is the nature and the quality of the new 'corporate governance codex', which is attached to section 161 of the Aktiengesetz.[28] Naturally, it would be very hard to say what a 'fair hypothetical bargain' would mean in this context

---

[25] See for the 'constitutional' dimension of standard setting in the area of accounting: Kirchner and Schmidt (2005); and for the associated 'political' and 'technical' deadlocks: Wüstemann (2002).

[26] See Schulze and Schulte-Nölke (1999).

[27] Mertens *et al.* (1982), 134.

[28] See Ulmer (2002); Kley (2003); generally Gilson (2001).

of an institutional arrangement (the corporation), which at least from a neo-institutional perspective seems to evade the picture of a 'fair' contractual transaction. Here, the legislator declares explicitly that the rules of the codex are not binding legal norms but rules describing the desirable practice. The problem may have to do with the hybrid nature of this sort of 'codification'. The draftspersons may have felt that codification of textbook aspirations for good management might eventually lead to legal entropy.

If we cannot establish fairness of the use of extra-legal norms by reference to a fair hypothetical bargain, we might be inclined to be more modest from the outset. If we ought to formulate minimal rules, we would probably be able to define at least a bright-line from a legal centrist perspective which would be consistent with the following two basic rules for 'inclusion'.[29]

(1) Extra-legal norms should not contradict the legal rules in 'relevant' legal orders (a rule which is largely identical with a control criterion developed for contracts under the rule of private autonomy). In the case of 'off-the-rack' solutions (like 'standard terms') this includes not only compatibility with the non-fungible norms (*ius cogens*) but also adherence to those default rules, which belong to the 'core' of the balancing of interests envisioned by the legislator (see e.g. Sec. 307 of the German Civil Code).

(2) Extra-legal norms should be 'incentive compatible' in that they encourage actors to operate in a cost-effective, friction-avoiding way, which would also involve the absence of material externalities associated with the transaction at stake.

4. PRODUCING AND USING STANDARDIZED REGIMES

4.1 Reasons

Let us now turn to a perspective of 'regime production' and 'regime use' of standardized non-legal regimes. I will first discuss reasons why private actors who are interested in the functioning of transactions produce and use these regimes. There are three reasons which relate to the limits of legislation and the legislative process.

4.1.1 Lack of generality

One of the central features of law is general applicability. A legal rule is – by definition – applicable to a large set of cases including the characteristic of equal application. We observe that general laws, which would comply with these conditions, become increasingly dysfunctional in view of the increasing specificity. In Continental European private law, this process typically ends in delegations to judges, especially by using general clauses or broad formulations. Courts then develop a closely-knit case law for dealing with the specifics of the situations. A good example is the law on unfair trade practices where case law uses the legal norms in the statute mainly as a reference system. The same is true for tort law where few general norms cover a huge field of highly specified legal practice.

---

[29] Schanze (1999), 195.

4.1.2 Political deadlocks

The second problem relates to the increasing inability of legislators to settle issues in the legislative process. Political deadlocks lead to escape strategies. A well-known example is either leaving the issue for settlement in a High Court, particularly the Constitutional Court, or to refer it to the *comitology* process in European law. However, an important escape strategy is also to 'privatize' the issue and to refer it to a non-legal rule-making body. Thus, there is a – at first glance – somewhat odd interaction between the legal system and private activity: in fields traditionally considered to be a domain of private action, i.e. the price mechanism of the market, there is increasing state intervention (as in the case of consumer contracts), while the making of general rules is, at least in the field of economic law, no longer a prerogative of the state, but also open to private institutions.

4.1.3 Mobility of the issue

A third reason for escaping the system of constitutionally constrained law making is the inherent mobility of the issue. If goods or services or other factors are fungible, a national regulation may simply lead to avoidance of this jurisdiction. A comprehensive transnational regulation is frequently unavailable. Hence, legislators try to stimulate 'private' or 'quasi-public' norm-producing bodies in the hope that they can influence this process indirectly by measures which they are able to control locally. The banking regulation in the Basel I and II processes may be partly explained in the shortcomings of a possible national legislation.[30] Another example for a 'mobile' issue was the case of currency adjustments at the introduction of the Euro. It was obvious that this problem could not be settled by the governments in technical and consistent legal rules. Here the major banks of Europe agreed on certain practices which they codified privately. Finally, the President of the European Monetary Institute declared that he approved of the practice suggested.[31] The states remained silent.

4.1.4 Cost of legislation

There are cases in which rule-making in the legislative process is too costly, particularly if information costs would be fully included. This especially happens in the grey area between legislation and standard terms formulated by the industry. Take industry-specific rules for insurance, banking, or most recently, the internet.[32] An interesting aspect in developing fields such as the internet is the sequential nature of private rule-making. What first seems to be a rather negligible area, developed and used by a few academics, may establish itself incrementally, developing and stabilizing the necessary rule sets, which are then tolerated or even expressly acclaimed by the constitutionally legitimized

---

[30] Nobel (2005); Simmons (2001); see also for the massive extension of competences of regulatory agencies: Zaring (1998); Choi and Pritchard (2003).

[31] European Monetary Institute (1997): 'The EMI welcomes and supports the initiative taken by the associations of the banking and financial industry. It notes that there is broad consensus among market participants on common conventions for the Euro financial markets. Implementation of those conventions will enhance integration of, and ensure more transparency in, the Euro financial markets.'

[32] von Bernstorff (2004).

bodies. In these new areas general legislation may then operate more as a repair shop than an independent legitimate source of rules.[33]

4.1.5 Private entrepreneurship for extra-legal norm-making

Standards and privately codified practices are sometimes developed by persons or organizations who detect a market for private norms. Not only technological necessity, as in the case of the original industrial standards, may be a motivation for this kind of entrepreneurship. Once a rudimentary system is established, the standardizing organization discovers new potential markets for standardization services. The current extensions of the ISO-process can be explained in these terms.[34] The success of standardization in the old industrial fields led to extensions to numerous new service areas. In lucrative areas, the classical standardizing agencies compete with market entrants. Sometimes new organizations promoting standards are developed by a clientele that is dissatisfied with the traditional set-up. The competition between industrial standards (e.g. TV, media standards, and computer systems) are fascinating examples for fights between leading groups in the industries in a competitive international market.[35] Entrepreneurship and lobbying activities may then convince the legislators to include formally a standard or codified practice in the current law. Moreover, a tacit consensus between the legislator and the business circles about the desirability of private law-making in specific cases may justify the absence of formal law-making.

4.2 Functions of Standardized Non-legal Regimes in Contract Drafting

From the perspective of drafting a transaction, standards serve three main 'facilitating' functions: They are 'definers', 'monitors' and 'ex-post-references' of a given transaction.

In many cases contracts cannot be understood without a reference to a standard. Standards are, in this sense, shorthand descriptions of a performance schedule. A simple example would be the order and delivery of a widget with a reference to a DIN- or ISO-standard. Increasingly we also see services being marketed with a reference to a standard, not only to emphasize quality aspects, but also the 'content' of the service.[36]

The references to standards may control the transaction throughout its duration from the pre-contractual to the post-contractual stage. Standards may serve as patterns of information. They have an orientation function in the contracting phase.[37] They may enter in the contract as part of the definition of performances. Hence, they serve a stipulation function. In the devolution phase of a contract, performances deviating from existing standards may be considered as inadequate or defective. Hence, standards also serve as references for a better understanding of the performance modalities if the stipulation of the term is unclear. This may be called an interpretation function or even a gap-filling function of standards. During the performance process standards may be used for monitoring by specifying quality aspects of goods and services including disclosure

---

33 See Herwig (2004).
34 See the homepage of ISO: http://www.iso.org/iso/en/ISOonline.frontpage.
35 For media standards see: Lemley (2002); Teece and Sherry (2003).
36 See ISO 9000.
37 See Deakin and Mitchie (1997).

and liability issues. Finally, if the contract fails, remedies may be specified by reference to standards. For example, the monetary damage resulting from the non-delivery of a certain good at a certain time may be determined by reference to generally accepted private data sheets about customary leasing rates for that good.

4.3 Standards as Indicators of a Shift from Personal to Professional Transaction Practices

The increasing and pervasive 'production' and use of standards and private codes signal a secular phenomenon of 'code shifting'. Apart from law, the former classical transactional code referred to vocationally trained business networks. In this system characterized by stylized individuals, such as 'the merchant', 'the entrepreneur', 'the banker', business practices and ethical codes were internalized as behavioral codes specific for the membership in the individual trade or craft. These codes were acquired by personal in-house training in apprenticeship procedures.

The massive arrival of standards signals a form of abstraction and specialization. The new, written standards and codes are taught in general teaching systems such as universities; they are exercised by a class of professionals outside the old trading patterns. In this system, the use of standards reflects both a standardization and abstraction of personal modes of trading with implicit business codes. Today, business codes are made explicit and defined, exercised and enforced by specialists.[38]

The shift from vocational networks to the recruitment of professionals is, on the other hand, associated with a breakdown of the traditional unwritten codes of business ethics. The informal codes are thus substituted by an array of written codes which are administered and interpreted by 'norm specialists'. Thus, the rise of professional standards is part of the incremental transformation of business relations from close-knit groups with personal elements to anonymous transactions in which the 'terms of the trade' are the only tie between the parties.[39]

An interesting extension of this phenomenon of code shifting and specialization is the arrival of administrative specialists for standardized practices. Large law firms, for example, have created 'knowledge management' systems, which collect computerized knowledge and constantly upgrade the documentation of deals.[40] This used to be a matter of personal knowledge of specialist partners of law firms who would 'remember' their experience from earlier transactions. Standardized written codes of practice instead of conventional vocational knowledge are especially visible in the area of corporate governance, accounting, credit rating and related areas.

A vital problem of this shift from vocational training to systems of knowledge management should be mentioned: documentation of routines and routine enforcement of these new abstract codes may eventually lead to a petrification of practices and standards.

---

[38] A most visible example is the financial market: Choi and Guzman (1997); Nobel (2005); Nobel (2000); Simmons (2001).

[39] See Maine (1894), chapter 5.

[40] Schulz and Klugmann (2006).

4.4 Professional Demand for Off-the-rack Regimes

4.4.1 Tailored solutions as modifications of ready-made solutions

Let us now review the production technology of draftspersons. Typically, an individual contract or charter is a modification of an earlier draft relating to a similar or comparable problem set. Resembling the production in fashion design, legal draftspersons 'customize' regimes. They develop a fitting solution by variation of a standardized arrangement. Most standardized regimes have ready-made properties, which may fit in tailored solutions.

In the architecture of complex contracting we find mixes of standardized clauses with largely unchanged headings and language, and incremental variations of specific arrangements.[41]

There are a number of ways how new institutional design is developed for business transactions. Copying is the main exercise. In a contracting world there is a vivid exchange of contractual documentation, simply driven by the fact that parties and their legal agents exchange not only goods and services, but also contracts. In some cases workable arrangements are transported by the draftspersons from one industry to another. There are cases where the house lawyers address external collaborators in a transaction for getting access to an innovative institutional design. Moreover, there is a constant proliferation of institutional design patterns through fluctuations on the job market for professionals. For the improvement of the international drafting practices it is fortunate that contract design is typically a free intellectual good which cannot be protected by the copyright system. Of course, the relevant consulting firms with specialties have ways and means to protect valuable 'shelved' regime products.

4.4.2 The relation of shelved regime products and standards

Draftspersons will gain reputation by referring to the proven workability of a drafted arrangement over time. Workability establishes itself mainly in trial-and-error procedures. Error can be avoided by using a tried ready-made regime that has worked well in earlier comparable contexts. Standardization organizations as institutionalist specialists offer on the market for regimes those off-the-rack arrangements, which are consented and used by the relevant industries. This leads to an important trait of standard setting as part of the regime production process. Standard setting organizations do not only care for the workability of design and the consent of the parties affected by the contract. They rather look for a broader consensus of the potentially relevant users.[42] Thus we find, in increasing scale and scope, forms of involvement of the relevant business circles in a quasi-democratic process.[43] Some observers assume that this 'democratization process' is a necessary item for the viability of standards.[44]

---

41 For investment agreements see Schanze (1986); for project finance see Sester (2004).

42 Axelrod *et al.* (1997).

43 For the standard setting process Abbott and Snidal (2005); also Austin and Milner (2001); Besen and Farrell (1994).

44 Steffek (2004); Morais (2002); but see Abbott and Snidal (2005).

5. RECONSIDERING 'LINKS TO LAW' FROM A DRAFTING PERSPECTIVE

5.1 Conflict Avoidance as a Legitimating Strategy

From a legal centrist perspective the application of extra-legal norms needs a positive legal rule for 'legitimizing' the inclusion, for linking standards to law. Viewed from a drafting perspective a negative strategy may be sufficient. A draftsperson may simply follow the policy of avoiding potential conflicts between law and extra-legal norms. As mentioned, a draftsperson will see that an extra-legal component of a transaction regime will not contradict the positive legal orders affected by the transaction. This process of clearing the 'legal compliance' is typically the most time consuming and most highly priced exercise of legal consultants.

5.2 The Exceptional Case of Circumvention

In a limited set of cases consultants will be ready to recommend non-compliance. They will advise their clients to try a 'circumvention' of the given rule set of the affected positive law. This, however, will typically be associated with other strong equities. The risk of living with a possibly void transaction – a situation which may amount to a Knightean uncertainty, and thus requires the assessment of worst case outcomes – has to be evaluated in the light of the overall efficiency of the transaction. I have shown elsewhere that judges and regulators will ratify such circumventions if strong attributes of a new Pareto superior regime can be demonstrated.[45]

5.3 The Circle of Transactional Hermeneutics

Most salient international transactional regimes are composed of legal and extra-legal components. Think, for example, of international franchise regimes, systems of exclusive dealerships, of production networks, umbrella agreements, international finance consortia, money clearing schemes, international joint ventures, or mergers and acquisitions of firms. Even if – in relatively rare cases – the basic agreements in these instances are distanced from local court intervention, e.g. by agreeing on a-national dispute settlement under a-national law,[46] they still would have to comply with a massive remaining set of 'local' legal prerequisites.

For making the transaction viable, draftspersons regularly enter in a screening process of substantive and formal elements, which are interrelated, and which I propose to analyse as follows.

The current transactional practice is reflected in three theoretical elements, which are contained in a 'circle of transactional hermeneutics':

---

45 Schanze (1995).

46 Mertens (1996), 857; Dasser (2001).

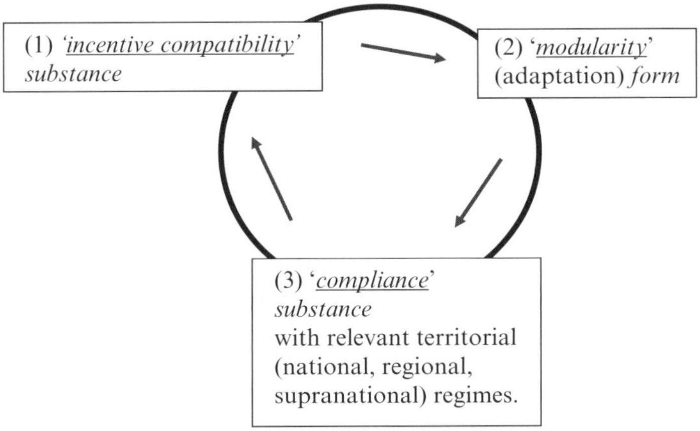

Figure 15.1 Circle of transactional hermeneutics

5.3.1 Incentive compatibility

Draftspersons will, first, ensure that the regime is incentive compatible. In legal usage this is frequently expressed as accommodating the 'interests' of the parties. However, 'interest accommodation' includes overarching elements such as functioning of the arrangement during its life span, from the negotiation stage to the post-contractual phase. Thus, compatibility also includes aspects of accommodating externalities, because visible externalities endanger the execution of the transaction. Third parties might rightfully intervene, backed by the local courts. A highly relevant example for cautionary externality control by the draftspersons is the screening of antitrust concerns of arrangements.

5.3.2 Modularity

Draftspersons will, secondly, verify that the regime contains viable, 'tried' regime components, which operate like 'modules' put into mainframes of electronic systems. Hence, I term them institutional modules. Modules are standardized regimes which can be 'plugged' in the draft with the assurance that they 'function' whenever the contingency arises. In this sense draftspersons must be interested in a high content of modularity in every regime. Some commentators allude to this phenomenon by using the unfortunate term of 'lex mercatoria'. Modules are neither 'leges' nor are they used by 'merchants'.

5.3.3 Compliance

Draftspersons will, thirdly, screen the regime for compliance with regard to the relevant 'territorial' i.e. national, regional and international 'lawful' regimes.

If all three interrelated tests are met, draftspersons will endorse the regime. Professional care in the screening process will not only be enforced by professional liability, but mainly by considerable reputation sanctions. These sanctions insure a 'fair use' of extra legal norms, and full compliance with the relevant legal orders in the vast majority of business transactions.

6. CONCLUSION: REMEDIES FOR ABUSE?

Parallel to a secular increase of norm production falling within the scope of the constitutional law making process and the other recognized sources of law there is an exponentially growing production of 'codified' extra-legal norms, formalized as standards, off-the-rack clauses and routines, administered by professionals. From a legal centrist perspective, these norms, which may have a large degree of regulatory substance and impact, are typically 'legitimized' by technical rules of inclusion, linkage mechanisms. Here, the key issue is 'legality'. From a drafting perspective, however, the main scrutiny is placed on 'incentive compatibility', 'modularity', and 'compliance', i.e. on the design of facilitative regimes that are mitigating transaction costs and evidently comply with the relevant legal orders. In view of the fact that consulting lawyers and economic consultants organized in professional consulting and law firms do not and cannot write share-cropping agreements with their clients for exploiting the mutual benefits of illegal transactions, professional incentives point to a pervasive 'legality' in the practical production and use of extra-legal norms.

A short final look at the 'remedial' side. I tried to show that the danger of abuse of standards and other off-the-rack regimes is overstated in the standard literature concerned with the 'constitutional basis' of these extra-legal norm sets. However, abuses by fraudulent schemes and arrangements with latent or overt damaging effects to third parties, externalities, cannot be ruled out. In thc discussion of thc 'links to law' I pointed at the available avenues of court intervention, especially in the field of standard terms, or in other areas in which private legislation is 'incorporated'. Given the increasing relevance of international extra-legal 'coding' it might be wise to consider – either on the national or World Trade Organization (WTO) level – the creation of small advisory bodies, with a secretariat that would regularly screen new forms of private regulation especially relating to the externalities of these regimes. These 'standard screening panels', which could eventually be attached to the existing national antitrust authorities, would have a watchdog function. They would issue statements and recommendations which could be used by courts, governments and relevant regulatory agencies. Given the effectiveness of 'naming and shaming' as a regulatory tool, the mere existence of such panels would deter some of the abusive practices.

BIBLIOGRAPHY

Abbott, K.W. and D. Snidal (2001), 'International "standards" and international governance', *Journal of European Public Policy*, **8**, 345–70.

Abbott, K.W. and D. Snidal (2005), 'The international standards process: Setting and applying global business norms', in P. Nobel (ed.), *International Standards and the Law*, Bern: Staempfli Publishers, pp. 105–142.

Ackerman, B.A. (1984), *Reconstructing American Law*, Cambridge, MA: Harvard University Press.

Austin, M. and H. Milner (2001), 'Strategies of European standardization', *Journal of European Public Policy*, **8**, 411–31.

Axelrod, R. et al. (1997), 'Setting standards, coalition formation in standard setting alliances', in R. Axelrod (ed.), *The Complexity of Cooperation*, Princeton, NJ: Princeton University Press, pp. 96–120.

Ayres, I. and R. Gertner (1989), 'Filling gaps in incomplete contracts: An economic theory of default rules', *Yale Law Journal*, **99**, 87.

Bebchuk, L. and A. Ferrell (2001), 'A new approach to regulatory competition in takeover law', *Virginia Law Review*, **87**, 111–164.
Besen, S. and J. Farrell (1994), 'Choosing how to compete: Strategies and tactics in standardization', *Journal of Economic Perspectives*, 117–131.
Calabresi, G. and A.D. Melamed (1972), 'Property rules, liability rules, and inalienability: One view of the cathedral', *Harvard Law Review*, 1089–1128.
Callon, M. (1998), 'An essay on framing and overflowing: Economic externalities revisited by sociology', in M. Callon (ed.), *The Laws of the Markets*, Oxford: Blackwell, pp. 244–69.
Choi, S. and A. Guzman (1997), 'National laws, international money: Regulation in a global capital market', *Fordham Law Review*, **65**, 1855.
Choi, S. and A. Pritchard (2003), 'Behavioral economics and the SEC', *Stanford Law Review*, **56**, 1–73.
Collins, H. (1999), *Regulating Contracts*, Oxford: Oxford University Press.
Currie, B. (1963), *Selected Essays on the Conflict of Laws*, Durham, NC: Duke University Press.
Dasser, F. (2001), 'Lex mercatoria – Critical comments on a tricky topic', in R.P. Appelbaum, W.L.F. Felstiner and V. Gessner (eds), *Rules and Networks. The Legal Culture of Global Business Transactions*, Oxford: Hart Publishing, p. 186.
Dawes, R. (1988), *Rational Choice in an Uncertain World*, Thousand Oaks, London, New Delhi: SAGE Publications.
Deakin, S. and J. Mitchie (1997), 'The theory and practice of contracting', in S. Deakin and J. Mitchie (eds), *Contracts, Co-operation, and Competition*, Oxford: Oxford University Press, pp. 1–39.
Ellickson, R.C. (1991), *Order Without Law*, Cambridge: Harvard University Press.
European Monetary Institute (1997), *Joint statement on market conventions for the Euro*, 16 July.
Gilson, R. (1984), 'Value creation by business lawyers: Legal skills and asset pricing', *Yale Law Journal*, **94**, 239–313.
Gilson, R. (2001), 'Globalizing corporate governance: Convergence of form or function', *American Journal of Comparative Law*, **49**, 329–429.
Herwig, A. (2004), 'Transnational governance regimes for foods derived from biotechnology and their legitimacy', in C. Joerges, I.-J. Sand and G. Teubner (eds), *Transnational Governance and Constitutionalism*, Oxford: Hart Publishing, pp. 199–223.
Holmes, O.W. (1897), 'The Path of the Law', *Harvard Law Review*, **10**, 457–469.
ISO: http://www.iso.org/iso/enlISOonline.frontpage.
Joerges, C. (2004), 'Constitutionalism and transnational governance: Exploring a magic triangle', in Ch. Joerges, I.-J. Sand and G. Teubner (eds), *Transnational Governance and Constitutionalism*, Oxford: Hart Publishing, pp. 339–77.
Kegel, G. and K. Schurig (2004), *Internationales Privatrecht*, Munich: Beck.
Kirchner, C. and M. Schmidt (2005), 'Private law-making; IFRS–Problems of hybrid standard setting', in P. Nobel (ed.), *International Standards and the Law*, Bern: Staempfli Publishers, pp. 67–82.
Kley, K. (2003), 'Neue Corporate Governance Regeln in den USA und Europa – Mehr Probleme als Uisungen', *Der Konzern in Recht und Wirtschaft*, 264–8.
Koh, H. (1997), 'Review essay: Why do nations obey international law?', *Yale Law Journal*, **106**, 2599.
Kokott, J. (2005), 'Soft law standards under public international law', in P. Nobel (ed.), *International Standards and the Law*, Bern: Staempfli Publishers, pp. 15–41.
Lemley, M. (2002), 'Intellectual property rights and standard-setting organizations', *California Law Review*, **90**, 1889.
Maine, H.S. (1894), *Ancient Law*.
Mertens, H.-J. (1996), 'Das lex mercatoria-Problem', in R. Bottcher, G. Hueck and B. Jahnke (eds), *Festschriftöfur Walter Odersky zum 65. Geburtstag*, Berlin: de Gruyter.
Mertens, H.-J., C. Kirchner and E. Schanze (1982), *Wirtschaftsrecht*, Opladen: Westdeutscher Verlag.
Mnookin, R., S. Peppet and A. Tulumello (2000), *Beyond Winning*, Cambridge, MA: Harvard University Press.

Morais, H. (2002), 'The quest for international standards: Global governance vs. sovereignty', *Kansas Law Review*, **50**, 779–821.
Nobel, P. (2000), 'The concept of disclosure within European financial institutions', *Fordham International Law Journal*, **23**, 41–44.
Nobel, P. (2005), 'Globalization and international standards with an emphasis on finance law', in: P. Nobel (ed.), *International Standards and the Law*, Bern: Staempfli Publishers, pp. 43–66.
Posner, E. (2002), *Law and Social Norms*, Cambridge, MA: Harvard University Press.
Posner, R.A. (2003), *Law, Pragmatism, and Democracy*, Cambridge, MA: Harvard University Press.
Richter, R. and E.G. Furubotn (2003), *Neue Institutionenökonomik*, Tübingen: Mohr Siebeck.
Roberts, A.E. (2001), 'Traditional and modern approaches to customary international law', *American Journal of International Law*, **95**, 757–91.
Roe, M. (2003), 'Delaware's competition', *Harvard Law Review*, 588–646.
Romano, R. (2002), *The Advantage of Competitive Federalism for Securities Regulation*, Washington, DC: AEI Press.
Schanze, E. (1986), *Investitionsverträge im internationalen Wirtschaftsrecht*, Frankfurt am Main: Metzner.
Schanze, E. (1993), 'Legalism, economism, and professional attitudes toward institutional design', *Journal of Institutional and Theoretical Economics*, **149**, 122–40.
Schanze, E. (1995), 'Hare and hedgehog revisited: The regulation of markets that have escaped regulated markets', *Journal of Institutional and Theoretical Economics*, **151**, 162–76.
Schanze, E. (1996), 'New directions in contract research', in B. Dahl and R. Nielsen (eds), *New Directions in Business Law*, Copenhagen: Gradjuraj Verlag, pp. 61–72.
Schanze, E. (1999), 'Die Entwicklung von Institutionen', in Ch.J. Meier-Schatz (ed.), *Forschungsgespräch der Rechtswissenschaftlichen Abteilung anlässlich des 100-Jahr-Jubiläums der Universität St. Gallen im Juni 1998*, Basel, Genf, München: Bibliothek zur Zeitschrift für Schweizerisches Recht, Beiheft, vol. 28.
Schmidt, K. (1999), *Handelsrecht*, Köln: Heymann.
Schreiber, V. (2005), 'What are international standards?', in: P. Nobel (ed.), *International Standards and the Law*, Bern: Staempfli Publishers, pp. 1–13.
Schulz, M. and M. Klugmann (2006), *Wissensmanagement für Anwälte*, Köln: Heymann, pp. 195–206.
Schulze, R. and H. Schulte-Nölke (1999), *Europäische Rechtsangleichung und nationale Privatrechte*, Baden-Baden: Nomos.
Sester, P. (2004), *Projektfinanzierungvereinbarungen als Gestaltungs- und Regulierungsaufgabe*, Köln: Schmidt.
Simmons, B. (2001), 'The international politics of harmonization: The case of capital market regulation', *International Organization*, **55**, 589–620.
Steffek, J. (2004), 'Sources of legitimacy beyond the state: A view from international relations', in Ch. Joerges, I.-J. Sand and G. Teubner (eds), *Transnational Governance and Constitutionalism*, Oxford: Hart Publishing, pp. 81–103.
Stephan, P.B. (1999), 'The new international law – Legitimacy, accountability, authority, and freedom in the new global order', *University of Colorado Law Review*, **70**, 1555.
Teece, D. and E. Sherry (2003), 'The interface between intellectual property law and antitrust law: Standard setting and antitrust', *Minnesota Law Review*, **87**, 1913–94.
Trebilcock, M. (1993), *The Limits of Freedom of Contract*, Cambridge, MA: Harvard University Press.
Ulmer, P. (2002), 'Der Deutsche Corporate Governance Kodex – ein neues Regulierungsinstrument für börsennotierte Aktiengesellschaften', *ZHR*, **166**, 150–66.
von Bernstorff, J. (2004), 'ICANN as a global governance network: The rise and fall of a governance experiment', in Ch. Joerges, I.-J. Sand and G. Teubner (eds), *Transnational Governance and Constitutionalism*, Oxford: Hart Publishing, pp. 257–83.
Wüstemann, J. (2002), 'Transnational legalization of accounting and disclosure', in *CIS Workshop on Hard Law, Soft Law and Private Legalities: The Legalization of International Relations*.
Zaring, D. (1998), 'International law by other means: The twilight existence of international financial regulatory organizations', *Texas International Law Journal*, **33**, 281–330.

16. Transnational governance and evolutionary theory

Gralf-Peter Calliess, Jörg Freiling and Moritz Renner

1. CROSS-BORDER COMMERCE AND TRANSNATIONAL INSTITUTIONS

In spite of all efforts to harmonize private law and to facilitate judicial cooperation,[1] the nation-state and its legal system still appear largely unable to effectively regulate global commerce. Depending on the specifics of the involved jurisdictions, cross-border transactions face varying degrees of uncertainty. In sum, international trade operates under circumstances which are appropriately described by the eye-catching term of 'lawlessness'.[2] At the same time, a host of private governance mechanisms is available to international commerce. Such private legal services might be bundled into effective private governance regimes or private legal systems, stepping in the place of national regulatory structures.[3] Empirical research, conducted as part of an interdisciplinary research project in Bremen,[4] has revealed an increasing *transnationalization* as a basic pattern in the governance of cross-border transactions.[5] Triggered by the globalization of commerce, economic governance, understood as the provision of 'good order and workable arrangements'[6] for business purposes, is at the same time *internationalized* and *privatized*.

In international trade, private governance mechanisms thus provide for what used to be thought of as a genuinely sovereign affair: legal certainty. In this regard, our studies on off-shoring in the software industry,[7] the international timber trade,[8] and the role of international law firms,[9] have shown that economic agents in cross-border settings increasingly tend to rely on transaction-type or industry-specific governance regimes, recombined from different public and private mechanisms of control, when it comes to the enforcement of their mutual obligations.[10] Instead of exclusively or at least predominantly relying on the state legal system, these regimes build on relational contracting,[11] reputation-based

1 For the failed Hague Judgments Convention see e.g. Calliess (2004).
2 See further, Dixit (2004).
3 See e.g. Bernstein (1992); Teubner (2000).
4 For the research programme see www.sfb597.uni-bremen.de.
5 See Calliess *et al.* (2007).
6 Williamson (2005).
7 Dietz and Nieswandt (2009).
8 Konradi (2009).
9 Sosa (2009).
10 Calliess *et al.*, *supra* note 5.
11 See further, Macaulay (1963); MacNeil (1980).

social sanctions,[12] alternative dispute resolution[13] and other kinds of private governance mechanisms,[14] while public institutions like contract law, courts, or legal sanctions are of rather peripheral importance. Thus, 'institutions (. . .) to create order and reduce uncertainty in exchange'[15] gradually emerge outside the state legal system. These institutions, however, are not the product of political will or of any legislative process, but the mere result of the trial-and-error interaction of market participants.

How can such processes be explained? The question tackles an issue that lies in the focus of a growing interdisciplinary research agenda. Business, Economics (in particular institutional theories) and Economic Sociology are currently struggling to elaborate an adequate theory for analysing the change of social structures. At the same time, different theoretical traditions increasingly agree that markets are constituted by their 'embeddedness'[16] into a distinct institutional framework. There are, however, considerable differences between those theories as to the factors that determine the emergence of social structures. Is it a competition for transaction-cost efficiency as Williamson suggests,[17] or history and culture, as North tends to argue[18] – or even mere power in a Foucauldian sense?[19]

The current turn towards evolutionary theories takes up many of those ideas and tries to mold them into a consistent conceptual framework. In the following paragraphs we will try to outline some necessary elements of this framework with a view to the specific field of transnational commerce. First, we give a short overview of the basic elements of evolutionary models in the social sciences before hinting at two distinct perspectives that seem especially promising for a theory of institutional change in transnational commerce: a theory of institutional competition on the one hand and a systems theory approach on the other. We will then conclude our brief inquiry with a tentative outlook on the possibilities and the problems of integrating evolutionary theory into a social science analysis of institutional change.

2. EVOLUTIONARY PERSPECTIVES

The basic tenet of evolutionary theory can be put quite simply as 'history matters'.[20] And if it holds true that 'history (. . .) is largely a story of institutional evolution',[21] then it is only logical that the concept of evolution itself has moved into the focus of the social sciences. What evolutionary theory, generally speaking, seeks to explain is the mechanisms of change in structures over time. Evolution as a descriptive concept is used in a variety

---

12 Most prominently Posner (2000).

13 See generally Redfern and Hunter (2004), paras. 1–69 et seq.

14 See e.g. for the general role of trust and commitment: Woolthuis *et al.* (2005).

15 North (1991); see also Commons (1934).

16 For an extensive interpretation of the concept, understood as a critique of the rational-actor model, see Beckert (2003). For a more general discussion on the concept of embeddedness see Granovetter (1985), 481–510.

17 Williamson, *supra* note 6.

18 North (1990).

19 Foucault (2004).

20 For example, Teece *et al.* (1997).

21 North, *supra* note 18.

of disciplines. Historically, building upon the analysis of species evolution as a biological phenomenon by Lamarck[22] and in the seminal work of Darwin,[23] the concept has very soon crossed disciplinary boundaries and spread to fields as diverse as theology, cosmology, stellar astronomy, and – in the realm of the social sciences – sociology, political science, law, business and economics.[24] This development has mainly been triggered by the emergence of scientific empirical methods in the nineteenth century that has fundamentally transformed the style of argumentation and the production of knowledge in all academic disciplines.[25] However, it can be very difficult to recognize to what extent the terminology of evolutionary theory is used in a merely metaphorical way and to what extent it is actually employed as an analytical framework for research.[26]

2.1 Elements of a Theory of Change

In the terminology of Burrell and Morgan,[27] most evolutionary theories can be described as following an 'interpretive paradigm', which means that they focus on gradual, as opposed to revolutionary, change and predominantly rely on subjectivist explanation models. This implies the use of 'ideographic' research methods, i.e. an orientation towards qualitative rather than quantitative research.

The basic theoretical conceptions of evolutionary theory center around three mechanisms: Evolutionary theory argues that the starting point of each kind of change is the *variation* of the structural elements in question. Whether and to what extent variations have a sustaining impact on evolution depends on processes of *selection*. Selection mechanisms differentiate between fitting and non-fitting variations with regard to the relevant environment. Variations which pass the fitness test are then preserved in a phase of *retention* or *stabilization*. This simplified account of evolutionary mechanisms raises three important questions. First, what is the relevant unit of description, i.e. what are the elements that are varied, selected, and stabilized? Second, what is the criterion for selection? And, third, what is the relationship of the aforementioned mechanisms, i.e. are these processes connected by any causal logic? All three questions, however, are answered rather differently and sometimes even inconsistently in different strands of evolutionary theory.

2.2 Evolution of Legal Institutions and Economic Transactions

Valuable insights for the analysis of institutional change in international commerce can be found in both New Institutional Economics (NIE) and Evolutionary Economics.[28]

---

22 Lamarck (1809).

23 Darwin (1859).

24 For example, Bateson (1972); Boulding (1978); Keller (1919); von Hayek (1983).

25 For the impact on jurisprudence see Kiesow (1997), especially chapter IV.

26 See Luhmann (2004), 230 who deplores that most contemporary approaches lack 'theoretical precision' and a 'clear structure'.

27 Burrell and Morgan (1979).

28 See especially Williamson (2005) on the one hand and Nelson and Winter (1982) on the other; on the substantial overlaps – and differences – between both strands of theory see e.g. Eckardt (2004).

Both theories, starting from a principally agent-based approach, address the behavior of single economic decision-makers as well as the resulting emergence of transactions and transaction types, institutions, and markets. Private agents on the one hand and public agents, i.e. the state or supra-/international organizations, on the other are defined as the starting points of any evolutionary process. Their respective choices directly influence the emergence and development of the institutions that govern commercial relations. The unit of analysis is thus defined as institutional designs or norms, understood broadly as patterns of behavioral expectations,[29] which are subject to the mechanisms of variation, selection and retention.

2.2.1 Institutional competition

The issue at stake for private actors of international commerce is the resolution of cooperation problems.[30] In order to enter into exchange relationships, these actors must overcome their respective opportunism, as (boundedly rational) economic actors tend to '[destroy] part of the cooperation surplus to secure a larger share of it'.[31] The possibility of opportunistic behavior, such as defection, leads to uncertainty of expectations, which is typically aggravated by the cross-border nature of the transaction.[32] The function of private governance mechanisms in international commerce is to eliminate opportunistic behavior (or at least to make it unlikely) and thus to enable and/or facilitate economic exchange. New Institutional Economics assume that among different possible modes of governance (such as the market, the firm or hybrid forms of governance) private agents will design and choose those mechanisms that are most efficient in terms of transaction costs by perfectly matching the criteria constituting the transaction environment. Depending on the attributes of a specific transaction (asset specificity, uncertainty, frequency) certain governance mechanisms will prove more efficient than others and therefore be preferred. The criterion of selection, then, is transaction-cost efficiency.

Among the public agents of international commerce, the nation-state is particularly relevant. Even in the ambit of globalization, the nation-state is still responsible for the provision of legal institutions, although it has long lost its monopoly in this respect. As Kerber rightly points out, it is still primarily up to the nation-state to develop 'regulatory law' in contrast to mere 'facilitative law'.[33] While regulatory law denotes the – mostly mandatory – norms laying down the 'rules of the (market) game', facilitative law refers to all rules increasing the market's 'capability to facilitate exchange or, more generally, voluntary cooperation'.[34] Facilitative law can thus be effectively replaced by the norm-generating governance mechanisms employed by private regimes.[35] With regard to regulatory legislation, however, nation-states are forced into a regulatory competition as private agents make their investment decisions and choose their place of business according to

---

29 For details see Okruch (1999), 47–51.
30 Williamson, *supra* note 6; Okruch, *supra* note 29, 102–127.
31 Cooter (1996), 141–145, Williamson (1985), 47 defines opportunism as 'self-interest seeking with guile'.
32 Backhaus *et al.* (2001); Freiling (2009).
33 See Wolfgang Kerber's contribution to this volume.
34 Kerber and Vanberg (2001).
35 See generally Teubner (1997).

the respective attractiveness of different regulatory environments. Inter- or supranational agents that might eliminate or at least ease this regulatory competition are hardly to be found on a global level.

An agent-centered explanation of institutional change in international commerce thus focuses on *choice* and *competition*. From the perspective of private actors, the variation, selection and retention of institutions take place in the following constellations:

- *Trilateral Private Governance*: The case (and history) of the law merchant (*lex mercatoria*) shows that norms might develop in a wider social context (e.g. an industry). Codes of conduct and the application of general principles of law by arbitral tribunals can effectively reduce legal uncertainty without or with only little state intervention. The threat of reputation-losses in markets that are 'value-sensitive' makes defective behavior unlikely. In addition, the common acknowledgement of arbitration panels facilitates the workability of such governance designs. Moreover, mega law firms in particular act as 'legal entrepreneurs'[36] in international business, while the practice of institutional arbitration can also contribute to the emergence of a body of 'transnational law'.[37]
- *Bilateral Private Governance*: Private agents use, modify, and develop governance designs in 'repeated games', e.g. supplier and customer interact and resolve cooperation problems without external pressure. Especially in long-term relationships where trust and commitment play a decisive role, typically no third party participates in the coordination process. Relational norms, i.e. bilateral behavioral expectations, routines, trust, and commitment, dominate the governance structure and the mix of institutional elements, which is very often complemented by (facilitative) state law.
- *Unilateral Private Governance*: According to Williamson's transaction-cost approach,[38] uncertainty and specificity issues of transactions might require 'hard modes' of governance to stabilize economic coordination by means of vertical integration. As for international commerce, Buckley and Casson as well as Rugman[39] have argued similarly, introducing an internalization theory based on transaction-cost reasoning. Dunning[40] has further developed this approach assuming that foreign direct investments which constitute multinational or transnational firms[41] are efficient in case of simultaneous advantages of ownership, internalization, *and* location ('OLI paradigm'). In this case inter-firm coordination provides for 'hard' governance modes (e.g. command and control) that replace the 'softer' ones we know from bilateral coordination. Other theories (with an evolutionary background) suggest that coordination of multi- or transnational firms rests to a

---

[36] Sosa (2007).
[37] Zumbansen (2006); Calliess and Renner (2009).
[38] See Williamson, supra note 31.
[39] See Buckley and Casson (1991) and Rugman (1986).
[40] See among others: Dunning (1980), 9–31.
[41] For an overview of a taxonomy of firms in international business and a definition of terms see Bartlett and Ghoshal (2002).

large extent on informal mechanisms (e.g. routines, capabilities).[42] Keeping in mind that corporate governance systems steer internal processes of firms acting globally, unilateral governance is particularly suitable for organizing cross-border transactions without (direct) reliance on the state legal system.

2.2.2 Path dependence

That the above-mentioned governance mechanisms emerge and develop according to their competitiveness in terms of transaction costs, however, is only part of the story. Evolutionary Economics argue that the institutions of international commerce are, to a certain extent, idiosyncratic. These idiosyncrasies might be the result of agent-caused variation, selection, and retention processes. But not only are the entities under scrutiny idiosyncratic, they also evolve in specific ways. They are embedded into specific environments that none of them faces in the same way. These environmental conditions might to some extent constrain the evolutionary path of the respective entity.

In management theory, this has been discussed in connection with path dependence and institutional trajectories under the catchphrase of 'increasing returns'. Increasing returns refer to the phenomenon of self-reinforcing developments based on certain triggers.[43] Whereas technological evolution shows us many examples of evolutionary lock-in based on network effects (e.g. the final adoption of the so-called QWERTY keyboard which proved to be ergonomically and economically inefficient), similar trends are possible in the institutional evolution of international business as well. However, the question as to the underlying factors of increasing returns is open. In this regard we can identify at least four driving forces:[44]

- *Coordination*: In international business, the transaction partners interact so that bilateral adaptations take place. These adaptations facilitate interorganizational coordination by the development of proven common rules and routines. Both effectiveness and efficiency gains are the result.
- *Investments*: Sometimes closely connected with coordination considerations, the agents participating in the governance of international transactions make investments in certain governance modes. These – often specific – investments create commitment since a shift to another mode would generate sunk costs. In trying to avoid these losses, actors stick to the initial solution and might trigger others to adopt it.
- *Power*: Powerful agents might exert certain pressures on other parties and make them follow the chosen path. This implies the adoption of governance modes preferred by powerful actors by others.
- *Learning effects*: The more agents get used to a certain governance design, the more knowledge develops which fosters effectiveness and efficiency gains as well.

As a consequence, increasing returns step by step create a certain trajectory of institutional development. Although this is certainly not a one-way path, lock-in effects of more

---

[42] See e.g. Penrose (1968) and Lierow (2005).
[43] Arthur (1989).
[44] Cf. Freiling, *supra* note 32.

and more agents might occur, which makes self-reinforcing effects even more likely. The result is a strong retention of certain governance modes in international business.

This effect is reinforced by the fact that the institutional selection process is not only driven by demand, but also by the supply side. The individual partners to cross-border transactions buy private ordering services from a variety of providers, among them industry-specific self-regulatory bodies, international law firms, and arbitration institutions. These organizations invest in the development of certain governance-designs and hence have an interest in promoting their third-party control mechanisms on the market for private ordering. The members of these organizations often do act as advisors to businesses at the same time and, thus, may channel the demand towards the established and lucrative governance mechanisms such as international commercial arbitration.[45]

The concept of increasing returns thus helps us to understand that it is not necessarily the most efficient or effective solutions that will survive in competition. Instead, we have to analyze historical developments in connection with rigidities (e.g. by collective decision-making in institutions such as the state) and power relations. This debate has given rise to the impression voiced by Nelson and Winter that economic and social change is primarily a matter of establishing new or modified norms and rules because this way all the agents involved have at least some incremental discretion to provide the development with a certain sense of direction.[46]

2.2.3 Empirical evidence

In the light of path dependence, what are the reasons for selection processes that favor predominantly private instead of public governance modes? Our empirical research suggests that the reasoning differs depending on the industry. However, the results reveal many commonalities.

As for the case of timber trade, 30 expert interviews in connection with the review of accompanying relevant data were conducted between 2005 and 2006 in Germany[47] with the finding that trilateral and bilateral governance designs dominate. In particular, the so-called new law merchant ('lex mercatoria')[48] plays a pivotal role in timber trade. Lex mercatoria has developed over centuries and thus furnishes a lot of information and experience of the market participants on how to manage transnational transactions. Therefore, many formal and informal norms, customs, and habits have developed and become taken for granted in market processes due to learning processes, specific investments of the economic agents, and, finally, coordination issues. Merchants have developed a set of both formal and informal norms that is respected by the majority of the market participants. As for formal norms, complex standard contracts have developed over time that can be used by the market participants to govern transactions. Moreover, international arbitral tribunals ensure the execution of these norms. Relying on this set of norms, it is easily possible for customers and suppliers to manage transactions bilaterally so that relational agreements (both formally and informally) accompany those

---

[45] A description of the networks of lawyers and arbitrators can be found in the case study of Sosa, *supra* note 9.

[46] Nelson and Winter (1982).

[47] See Konradi (2009), 49–86.

[48] See especially Schmitthoff (1961); Goldman (1964).

industry-specific norms. In other words, the availability and reliability of lex mercatoria rules allows for an effective and efficient use of the means of relational exchange, resting to a large extent on means like trust and commitment. The interview partners report that the two different private governance modes combined sufficiently reduce transactional uncertainty.

The non-availability of workable domestic law institutions is one particular reason for the market participants to look for institutional alternatives, as one interview partner describes:

> You can only be successful in this industry if you are able to build business relationships that have a strong personal character. The term 'business friendship' really means friendship: the connections to most of our suppliers and clients are intense friendships which we strive to maintain. A friendship is a value you do not easily deceive whereas it is easy to break up a business relationship if there are no personal bonds. (. . .) Hence, we try to build personal relations to create an atmosphere which guarantees that problems in everyday situations can be solved in a way that both parties feel comfortable with. This is vital to make sure the business relationship does not break up. Buy once and never again: this is not our practice (. . .).

Contracts are not particularly relevant in this regard, as another interviewee notes:

> You may in principle avoid a lot of eventualities and hide behind regulations specified by the contract, but in real life the business turns out to be incompatible with strict regulations: a contract – this is not much more than a piece of paper, when it comes to practice. In practice a lot of things are handled completely differently.

The case studies reveal the significance of increasing returns in many regards. Obviously, coordination, investment, and learning issues are decisive. Customers and suppliers have simply got used to governance mechanisms and found them workable and/or convenient. Domestic law does not play a considerable role in cross-border transactions. In some situations, however, transaction partners do seek recourse to domestic courts as an *ultima ratio* solution. Moreover, letters of credit are issued that rest on the domestic legal system. Nevertheless, large parts of the markets are organized through private governance mechanisms that provide market participants with very reliable and efficient solutions of uncertainty reduction.

In contrast to timber trade, the product concerned in the case of outsourcing software development is quite different. Whereas timber products are more or less commodities, software solutions belong to the specialties. At first glance and adopting transaction cost reasoning, one might therefore expect completely different governance modes. Instead, our studies based on 20 expert interviews in Germany and India between 2005 and 2006 reveal no fundamental differences.[49] Software development projects are typically recorded in a detailed, formalized, and contract-based way. A general agreement is used to specify contract issues whereas a catalogue of functional specifications contains technical details. The extraordinary role of bilateral means of governance seems to be the result of the young history of this industry, where industry-wide customs and habits have not had sufficient time to develop. Moreover, relational governance provides the parties with

---

[49] See Dietz and Nieswandt (2009), 87–105.

more flexibility to cope with rather specific sources of uncertainty. As for the concrete means of governance, adaptation is mainly achieved through detailed and formalized procedural institutions, e.g. steering committees allow for the setting of common goals and mitigate potential conflicts in relational contexts. Besides legal rules, which usually stem from the jurisdiction of the client company, technical standards serve as important guidelines for the interaction in software development, e.g. the ISO 9001 standard and capability maturity models (CMM). Intensive customer/supplier interaction surrounds bilateral governance in a rather informal fashion, fosters bilateral adaptations and avoids manifest conflicts by giving 'voice' options (Hirschman[50]). Moreover, conflict mitigation takes place by escalation procedures involving higher management layers in the issues at stake, as one Indian interview partner states:

> I think that (. . .) most of the things seem to be more easily handled by an escalation procedure. We say that 'alright, the source of the conflict is that you are saying "I should have delivered this", but I am saying "this is not a part of scope"'. It is very easy for the senior management team of both sides, or the delivery managers of both sides to sit across a table and come to a mutual agreement. It is not that difficult, it happens all the time. And then you agree on that and then you move forward. Life moves forward. If I take the same thing and I say that neither the project manager, nor the program managers, nor the senior management team, nor the boards of both the organizations (. . .) – there are so many levels (. . .) it is practically impossible that all of them will choose to disagree. It is very unlikely.

So far, it seems that bilateral governance modes matter. However, similarly to timber trade, trilateral governance matters as well. In particular, the support of third parties is useful in case of accessing external advice, mediation, or arbitration to solve disputes. The expertise of third parties is often of indispensable value – be it in mitigating conflicts or for enforcement purposes.

It is quite obvious that facing the peculiarities of an outsourcing project the two parties involved in a cross-border transaction have to find a way to cooperate. To this end, they may rely to some extent on proven coordination structures established in the industry. However, the individual circumstances require more adaptations between customer and supplier so that relational coordination modes are the result. The same holds true for the necessity of relation-specific investments. The involvement in offshore software development requires a significant amount of specific investment from both sides. For an offshore software development project to be successful, both parties have to invest time and money to build up the necessary working environment. The investments made by the supplier can only be profitable if the business relation lasts for a longer time. For the client, too, it becomes increasingly difficult and expensive to replace the supplier once the cooperation works. The supplier has gathered much cooperation-specific knowledge and he becomes the only one who can guarantee a punctual delivery of the software which often is vital to the client. Besides investments of the partners, power issues matter as well. In particular in case of power asymmetries the more powerful partner sets the relationship standard. A major issue in this regard is the dependence of the customer on the supplier for all the issues of maintenance and support. Finally, the importance

---

50 See Hirschman (1970).

of learning processes should not be underestimated since the partners get used to the relationship due to learning how to cooperate with a particular partner.

From an Evolutionary Economics perspective, institutional change is thus structured by the 'twin ideas of spontaneous order and evolution' (Hayek).[51] Actors in international commercial transactions develop institutional solutions in response to coordination problems. These governance designs are varied, selected and stabilized depending on their competitiveness in terms of transaction-cost efficiency. This competition, however, is limited by path-dependencies that ultimately cannot be controlled by commercial agents.

2.3 The Evolution of Law

But what do these economic analyses tell us about the importance of legal rules for cross-border transactions? The empirical evidence presented here strongly suggests that domestic law, being unable to provide a uniform legal framework for transnational commerce, is increasingly replaced by non-legal means of contract enforcement. The very idea of the Alternative Dispute Resolution mechanisms relied upon by commercial actors is the settlement of disputes without recourse to the legal system. It seems premature, however, to equate these developments with a general demise of the law. Driven by the forces of economic globalization, the concept of law is itself undergoing fundamental changes. This becomes apparent when we look at processes of 'juridification'[52] in the institutional design of cross-border commerce. Most notably in international commercial arbitration, it can be observed that an increasingly autonomous legal discourse is emerging beyond the reach of the nation-state.[53] Global governance mechanisms thus often oscillate between legal and non-legal modes of regulating individual behavior; private ordering, thus, is an issue not only for economics but for jurisprudence as well.[54]

This oscillation can be analyzed by drawing upon Luhmann's distinction between the performance and the function of law, i.e. the services a legal system provides to other functional subsystems of society like the economy, politics, etc. on the one hand, and its relation to society as a whole on the other.[55] The concept of performance ties in with the competition-oriented approaches outlined above. When legal institutions are analyzed as providing dispute resolution services and a certain level of behavioral control to the economic system, a host of functional equivalents to law comes into mind. Law therefore stands in a performance competition to non-legal governance mechanisms.[56] Its ability to attract potential claimants is a decisive factor in the development of any institutional design. In many cases, non-legal methods of dispute resolution are chosen by the parties for their superiority over state legal systems in terms of accessibility (standing), speed (rules of procedure), affordability, and – most importantly – attractiveness of remedies.[57]

---

51 This expression is used by von Hayek throughout his work, see e.g. (1967), 66, 77.
52 See Teubner (1987), 3, 9; for a political science approach see Abbott *et al.* (2000).
53 On the conceptual background of such developments see Michaels and Jansen (2006).
54 Calliess and Renner, *supra* note 38.
55 Luhmann (1998), 757–8.
56 Calliess (2005), 35, 41.
57 *Id.*

The concept of function, in contrast, takes us back to the path dependence of institutional evolution. Systems theory offers an outstanding conceptual framework for explaining path dependence. Thereto, we must shift our analytical focus from the level of actors to the level of communication. In systems theory terminology, law is a communicative system that consists of all communications marked by the binary code 'legal/illegal'. As such, it is a functional subsystem of society, which in turn is defined as the totality of all communications. In relation to society as a whole, law fulfills a unique function: 'the stabilization of normative expectations', i.e. the creation of social expectations with general validity that are upheld even in cases of disappointment.[58] This function is what, on the one hand, distinguishes law from every other social system and, on the other hand, determines the way in which legal communications are processed. Because '[i]f law has the function of stabilizing normative expectations in the face of an unorganized growth of normative expectations (. . .), this can be achieved only by a selection of those expectations that are worth protecting'.[59]

The selection and stabilization of normative expectations, however, is not necessarily bound to a state legal system. There is a growing literature debating the existence of a genuinely transnational law[60] emerging in the ambit of private governance.[61] At the point where, in the context of private governance regimes e.g. in the fora of international arbitration, conflicts are verbalized and processed with the help of an institutionalized memory,[62] we can observe an 'evolutionary shift' from a state of institutional competition in terms of economic efficiency to a state of autopoietic[63] legal evolution. The concept of autopoiesis implies an understanding of law that is based on the idea of recursivity: law both produces and is a product of legal communications. The stability of normative expectations is thus guaranteed by the 'operative closure' of law in a network of legal communications perpetually referencing other legal communications.[64]

In the context of the global economy, it is especially the customs of international trade as well as arbitral practice that contribute to the emergence of transnational legal norms and institutions by establishing a 'logic of remembering and forgetting' which guarantees that certain behavioral expectations are 'condensed and confirmed', while others fall into oblivion.[65] At this point the development of institutional structures is no longer determined by a mere competition between governance mechanisms but begins to follow its own recursive logic – the logic of establishing the adequate complexity of a communicative system in relation to its social environment: 'it is not economic efficiency but complexity that is the intervening variable that translates evolutionary structural changes to adjustments within the system'.[66] This insight responds to growing doubts

---

58 Luhmann, *supra* note 27, 148.
59 *Id.*, 152.
60 See Zumbansen, *supra* note 38.
61 Most notably Teubner, *supra* note 36.
62 For details see Calliess and Renner, *supra* note 38.
63 Luhmann, *supra* note 27, 81.
64 *Id.*, 106 et seq.
65 Calliess (2002), 185, 196.
66 Luhmann, *supra* note 27, 271.

in economic theory with regard to analysing legal institutions solely under standards of efficiency.[67]

When it comes to explaining the particulars of this recursive change of systemic structures over time, systems theory employs evolutionary concepts in order to explain 'the conditions for possible unplanned changes of structure', 'diversification' and the 'increase in complexity' within social systems.[68] In this context, the mechanisms of variation, selection and stabilization are refined by putting them in relation to communicative systems. Variation is accordingly defined as referring to autopoietic elements, i.e., in the case of law, communications based on the binary code 'legal/illegal'. It is triggered by concrete disputes brought before judicial bodies. Selection, in contrast, is understood as referring to legal structures, i.e. norms.[69] Selection is the act that is performed by the judge/arbitrator when deciding a particular case according to a specific legal consideration (*ratio decidendi*). The overall decisive evolutionary mechanism, however, is the maintenance of stability, the unity of the system. Stability in this regard is understood as 'dynamic stability, that is, continuation of the autopoietic, structurally determined reproduction in the changed form'.[70] Put more simply: The judge/arbitrator will effectively select those norms that fit into a consistent pattern of decision-making, as evidenced e.g. by a long-standing line of precedents.

These processes of legal evolution can be observed in a number of increasingly autonomous private regimes[71] regulating various aspects of international commerce and thus contributing to the evolution of the above-mentioned lex mercatoria. A striking example for such regimes is provided by the emerging 'lex maritima' that is currently being researched in Bremen.[72] Lex maritima denotes a growing network of norms from different sources including domestic law, international law, standardized contracts and private standard-setting that regulates the specific issue-area of maritime trade. Whereas state courts are hardly ever involved in the resolution of maritime disputes, private arbitration courts such as the tribunals set up by the London Maritime Arbitrators Association (LMAA) or the Society of Maritime Arbitrators (SMA) contribute to the formation of a 'creeping codification'[73] of transnational law. Legal institutions in the field of maritime trade are thus increasingly de-coupled from state-based processes of law-making and adjudication. Instead, arbitral tribunals relying on their own as well as on domestic precedents[74] form part of autopoietic processes of norm-generation that transcend the classical doctrine of legal sources.

At the same time, the evolution of particular legal institutions within these regimes is no longer only a question of their respective efficiency but rather determined by the

---

67 See e.g. Cooter and Ulen (1988), 496.

68 It is crucial to note, however, that the concept of norms/structures is not a static one, but structures merely represent a temporary state in the flux of legal communication. *Cf.* Luhmann, *supra* note 27, at 231.

69 *Id.*, 84–5.

70 *Id.*, 232.

71 On the concept of legal regimes see Teubner (2004); Fischer-Lescano and Teubner (2004).

72 For an outline see Beckers and Maurer (2009).

73 See Berger (1999).

74 See especially Berger (1992); Kaufmann-Kohler (2007).

internal consistency requirements of legal discourse. This is evidenced by one of our current studies that analyzes the use of the concept of public policy in international arbitration.[75] The legal concept of public policy refers to those legal norms that are deemed mandatory within a particular legal system, i.e. that cannot be abrogated by the parties to a transaction. Those norms include rules on the protection of third parties, human rights standards, competition and anti-corruption laws etc. International arbitral tribunals, in spite of being merely based on private agreements, generally respect such public policy provisions.[76] To this end, they both rely on domestic legal traditions and re-interpret those traditions ('legal transplants'[77]) by developing their own concept of a 'transnational public policy'.[78] Domestic courts can stimulate these processes as far as they are involved in the recognition and enforcement of arbitral awards under the pertinent international agreements.[79] The concrete form of this transnational concept of public policy, however, is largely determined by the selection mechanisms intrinsic to legal discourse, especially the reliance on arbitral precedents. This is especially apparent with regard to dispute-resolution mechanisms that enjoy almost complete autonomy from domestic law, such as arbitration under the Convention on the Settlement of Investment Disputes Between States and Nationals of Other States (ICSID Convention).

3. OUTLOOK AND PERSPECTIVES FOR RESEARCH

These considerations have two distinct implications on our initial problem, the emergence and change of governance structures that provide legal certainty in international commercial transactions. As a first step, it seems necessary to combine the complementary evolutionary perspectives of actor-based explanation models on the one hand and a theory of communicative systems on the other. By doing so, the valuable insights of NIE can be taken as a basis for modeling the competition-induced 'spontaneous' emergence of different governance designs. The explanatory gaps left open by this approach can be addressed by a theory of communicative systems that is based on recursive structural change. This theory can then be fruitfully employed to explain both economic aspects of institutional competition and the law-specific processes of norm evolution.

As a second step, the evolution of private economic governance as well as transnational legal regimes must be analyzed as posing major challenges to regulatory policy. As far as domestic legal institutions are competing with alternative modes of governance for cross-border transactions, enhancing the attractiveness of laws and court proceedings necessarily becomes an issue to national legislators.[80] Furthermore, the relation of public regulation and private self-governance needs to be re-conceptualized. The extent to which domestic legislation should either enable or interfere with the emergence of

---

75 For first results see Renner (2009).

76 See e.g. Voser (1996).

77 Watson (1974); cf. also the critical perspective in Teubner (1998).

78 Lalive (1987).

79 Most notably the 1958 New York Convention on the Recognition and Enforcement of Foreign Arbitral Awards.

80 See Calliess and Hoffmann (2009).

private regimes and transnational law must be determined with a view to both empirical evidence and a normative assessment of these processes. Evolutionary theories can provide a powerful conceptual framework for empirical analysis. The – unanswered – politico-normative question arising from this analysis regards the design of an appropriate regulatory 'framework for competition' laying down the rules for an institutional competition between different forms of private and public governance mechanisms.[81]

BIBLIOGRAPHY

Abbott, Kenneth, Andrew Moravcsik, Anne-Marie Slaughter and Duncan Snidal (2000), 'The Concept of Legalization, International Organization', **54**, 401.

Arthur, Brian W. (1989), 'Competing Technologies, Increasing Returns, and Lock-in by Historical Events', *Economic Journal*, **99**, 116.

Backhaus, Klaus, Joachim Büschken and Markus Voeth (2001), *Internationales Marketing*, Stuttgart.

Bartlett, Christopher A. and Sumantra Ghoshal. (2005), *Managing Across Borders: The Transnational Solution*, 2nd ed., Boston.

Bateson, Gregory (1972), *Steps to an Ecology of Mind. Collected Essays in Anthropology, Psychiatry, Evolution, and Epistemology*, San Francisco.

Beckers, Anna and Andreas Maurer (2009), 'Lex maritima', in G.-P. Calliess, A. Fischer-Lescano, D. Wielsch and P. Zumbansen (eds), *Soziologische Jurisprudenz. Festschrift für Gunther Teubner*.

Beckert, Jens (2003), 'Economic sociology and embeddedness: How shall we conceptualize economic action?', *Journal of Economic Issues*, **37**, 769.

Berger, Klaus-Peter (1992), 'The international arbitrators' application of precedent', *Journal of International Arbitration*, **9**, 5.

Berger, Klaus-Peter (1999), *The Creeping Codification of the Lex Mercatoria*.

Bernstein, Lisa (1992), 'Opting out of the legal system: Extralegal contractual relations in the diamond industry', *Journal of Legal Studies*, **21**, 138.

Boulding, Kenneth E. (1978), *Ecodynamics. A New Theory of Societal Evolution*.

Buckley, Peter J. and Mark Casson (1991), *The Future of the Multinational Enterprise*.

Burrell, Gibson and Gareth Morgan (1979), *Sociological Paradigms and Organisational Analysis: Elements of the Sociology of Corporate Life*.

Calliess, Gralf-Peter (2002), 'Reflexive transnational law. The privatisation of civil law and the civilisation of private law', *Zeitschrift für Rechtssoziologie*, **23**, 185.

Calliess, Gralf-Peter (2004), 'Value-added norms, local litigation, and global enforcement: Why the Brussels-philosophy failed in The Hague', *German Law Journal*, **5**, 1489.

Calliess, Gralf-Peter (2005), 'Billigkeit und effektiver Rechtsschutz. Zu Innovation und Evolution des (Zivil-) Rechts in der Globalisierung', *Zeitschrift für Rechtssoziologie*, **26**, 35.

Calliess, Gralf-Peter, Thomas Dietz, Wioletta Konradi, Holger Nieswandt and Fabian Sosa (2007), 'Transformations of Commercial Law', in Achim Hurrelmann, Stephan Leibfried, Kerstin Martins and Peter Mayer (eds), *Transforming the Golden Age Nation State*, p. 83.

Calliess, Gralf-Peter and Moritz Renner (2009), 'Between law and social norms: The evolution of global governance', *Ratio Juris*, **22**, 260.

Calliess, Gralf-Peter and Hermann Hoffmann (2009), 'Judicial services for global commerce – Made in Germany?', *German Law Journal*, **10**, 115.

Commons, John R. (1934), *Institutional Economics. Its Place in Political Economy*.

Cooter, Robert D. (1996), 'The theory of market modernization of law', *International Review of Law and Economics*, **16**, 141.

Cooter, Robert D. and Thomas Ulen (1988), *Law and Economics*.

81 Vanberg and Kerber (1994).

Darwin, Charles (1859), *On the Origin of Species by Means of Natural Selection or: The Preservation of Favoured Races in the Struggle for Life*.
Dietz, Thomas and Holger Nieswandt. (2009), 'The emergence of transnational cooperation in the software industry', in *Contractual Certainty in International Trade*, Oxford: Volkmar Gessner, p. 87.
Dixit, Avinash K. (2004), *Lawlessness and Economics: Alternative Modes of Governance*.
Dunning, John H. (1980), 'Toward an eclectic theory of international production: Some empirical tests', *Journal of International Business Studies*, **11**, 9.
Eckardt, Martina (2004), 'Institutionen- und evolutionsökonomische Erklärungen des Rechtswandels', in W. Kerber (ed.), *IX Studien zur Evolutorischen Ökonomik*, p. 165.
Fischer-Lescano, Andreas and Gunther Teubner (2004), 'Regime-collisions: The vain search for legal unity in the fragmentation of global law', *Michigan Journal of International Law*, **25**, 999.
Foucault, Michel (2004), *Sécurité, territoire, population*.
Freiling, Jörg (2009), 'Institutional designs in international transactions – An evolutionary economics perspective', in Volkmar Gessner (ed.), *Contractual Certainty in International Trade*, p. 257.
Goldman, Berthold (1964), 'Frontières du droit et "lex mercatoria"', *Archives de philosophie du droit*, **9**, 177.
Granovetter, Mark (1985), 'Economic action and social structure: The problem of embeddedness', *American Journal of Sociology*, **91**, 481.
Hirschman, Alfred O. (1970), *Exit, Voice, and Loyalty. Responses to Decline in Firms, Organizations, and States*.
Kaufmann-Kohler, Gabrielle (2007), 'Arbitral precedent: Dream, necessity or excuse?', *Arbitration International*, **23**, 357.
Keller, Albert G. (1919), 'Law in evolution', *Yale Law Journal*, **28**, 769.
Kerber, Wolfgang and Viktor Vanberg (2001), 'Constitutional aspects of party autonomy and its limits – The perspective of constitutional economics', in Stefan Grundmann, Wolfgang Kerber and Stephen Weatherill (eds), *Party Autonomy and the Role of Information in the Internal Market*.
Kiesow, Rainer Maria (1997), *Das Naturgesetz des Rechts*.
Klein Woolthuis, Rosalinde, Bas Hillebrand and Bart Nooteboom (2005), 'Trust, contract and relationship development', *Organization Studies*, **26**, 813.
Konradi, Wioletta (2009), 'The role of lex mercatoria in supporting globalised transactions: An empirical insight into the governance structure of the timber industry', in Volkmar Gessner (ed.), *Contractual Certainty in International Trade*, p. 49.
Lalive, Pierre (1987), 'Transnational (or truly international) public policy in international arbitration', in *Comparative Arbitration Practice and Public Policy in Arbitration*, ICCA Congress Series No. 3, P. Sanders ed., Deventer, 257.
Lamarck, Jean-Baptiste (1809), *Philosophie Zoologique*.
Lierow, Michael A. (2005), *Competence-Building und Internationalisierungserfolg*.
Luhmann, Niklas (1998), *Die Gesellschaft der Gesellschaft*.
Luhmann, Niklas (2004), *Law as a Social System*, Fatima Kastner, Richard Nobles, David Schiff and Rosamund Ziegert (eds).
Macaulay, Stewart (1963), 'Non-contractual relations in business: A preliminary study', *American Sociological Review*, **55**, 86.
MacNeil, Ian R. (1980), *The New Social Contract: An Inquiry Into Modern Contractual Relations*.
Michaels, Ralf and Nils Jansen (2006), 'Private law beyond the state? Europeanization, globalization, privatization', *American Journal of Comparative Law*, **54**, 843.
Nelson, Richard E. and Sydney G. Winter (1982), *An Evolutionary Theory of Economic Change*.
North, Douglass C. (1990), *Institutions, Institutional Change, and Economic Performance*.
North, Douglass C. (1991), 'Institutions', *Journal of Economic Perspectives*, **5**, 97.
Okruch, Stefan (1999), *Innovation und Diffusion von Normen. Grundlagen und Elemente einer evolutorischen Theorie des Institutionenwandels*.
Penrose, Edith T. (1968), *The Large International Firm in Developing Countries*.
Posner, Eric A. (2000), *Law and Social Norms*.

Redfern, Alan and Martin Hunter (2004), *Law and Practice of International Commercial Arbitration.*
Renner, Moritz (2009), 'Towards a hierarchy of norms in transnational law', *Journal of International Arbitration*, **26**, 533.
Rugman, Alan M. (1986), New theories of the multinational enterprise. An assessment of internalization theory', *Bulletin of Economic Research*, **38**, 101.
Schmitthoff, Clive M. (1961), 'International business law: A new law merchant', *Current Law and Social Problems*, **2**, 129.
Sosa, Fabian (2007), *Vertrag und Geschäftsbeziehung im grenzüberschreitenden Wirtschaftsverkehr.*
Sosa, Fabian (2009), 'Cross-border dispute resolution from the perspective of mid-sized law firms: The example of international commercial arbitration', in Volkmar Gessner (ed.), *Contractual Certainty in International Trade*, p. 107.
Teece, David, Gary Pisano and Amy Shuen (1997), 'Dynamic capabilities and strategic management', *Dynamic Capabilities and Strategic Management*, **18**, 509.
Teubner, Gunther (1987), 'Juridification – concepts, aspects, limits, solutions', in Gunther Teubner (ed.), *Juridification of Social Spheres*, pp. 3, 9.
Teubner, Gunther (1988), 'Legal irritants: Good faith in British law or how unifying law ends up in new differences', *Modern Law Review*, **61**, 11.
Teubner, Gunther (1997), '"Global bukowina": Legal pluralism in the world society', in Gunther Teubner (ed.), *Global Law without a State*, p. 3.
Teubner, Gunther (2000), 'Contracting worlds: The many autonomies of private law', *Social and Legal Studies*, **9**, 399.
Teubner, Gunther (2004), 'Global private regimes: Neo-spontaneous law and dual constitution of autonomous sectors in world society', in G. Teubner and K.-H. Laer (eds), *Globalization and Public Governance*, p. 71.
Vanberg, Viktor and Wolfgang Kerber (1994), 'Instititutional competition among jurisdictions: An evolutionary approach, *Constitutional Political Economy*, **5**, 193.
von Hayek, Friedrich August (1967), 'Notes on the evolution of systems of rules of conduct', in von Hayek (ed.), *Studies in Philosophy, Politics, and Economics*, p. 66.
von Hayek, Friedrich August (1983), *Knowledge, Evolution and Society.*
Voser, Nathalie (1996), 'Mandatory rules of law as a limitation on the law applicable in international commercial arbitration', *American Review of International Arbitration*, **7**, 319.
Watson, Alan (1974), *Legal Transplants. An Approach to Comparative Law.*
Williamson, Oliver E. (1985), *The Economic Institutions of Capitalism.*
Williamson, Oliver E. (2005), 'The economics of governance', *American Economic Review*, **95**, 1.
Zumbansen, Peer (2006), 'Transnational law', in J. Smits (ed.), *Encyclopedia of Comparative Law*, p. 738.

Index